Intellectual Property and the Design of Nature

Intellectual Property and the Design of Nature

Edited by

JOSE BELLIDO
AND
BRAD SHERMAN

OXFORD
UNIVERSITY PRESS

OXFORD
UNIVERSITY PRESS

Great Clarendon Street, Oxford, OX2 6DP,
United Kingdom

Oxford University Press is a department of the University of Oxford.
It furthers the University's objective of excellence in research, scholarship,
and education by publishing worldwide. Oxford is a registered trade mark of
Oxford University Press in the UK and in certain other countries

First Edition published in 2023

Published in the United States of America by Oxford University Press
198 Madison Avenue, New York, NY 10016, United States of America

British Library Cataloguing in Publication Data

Data available

Library of Congress Control Number: 2023912284

ISBN 978–0–19–286440–6

DOI: 10.1093/oso/9780192864406.001.0001

Printed and bound by
CPI Group (UK) Ltd, Croydon, CR0 4YY

Acknowledgements

We are grateful to the authors of the essays in this volume for their contributions. Thanks also to Bob Beebe, Stephen Spence, Pamela Anderson, Dennis Conrow, Deborah Yuill, Cara Levey, John Maher, and Ross Carder for archival and editorial assistance. The book was supported with funding from the ARC Australian Laureate Fellowships *Harnessing Intellectual Property to Build Food Security*, the ARC Centre for Plant Success, the ARC Centre for Synthetic Biology, and the University of Kent.

Contents

List of Figures

List of Abbreviations

ABG	Archives, Bartram's Garden, Kingsessing, PA
AHL	Anderson Horticultural Library
APHA	Animal and Plant Health Authority
ANABORAPI	National Association of Breeders of the Piemontese Bovine Breed
APS Proc	American Pomological Society Proceedings
ASSINSEL	International Association of Plant Breeders for the Protection of Plant Varieties
BBF	BioBricks Foundation
CCMHSD	Catalogue Collection, Massachusetts Horticultural Society Depository
CCPs	composite cross populations
CIOPORA	International Community of Breeders of Asexually Reproduced Horticultural Plant Varieties
COALVI	Consortium for the Protection of the Piemontese Breed
CPC	cooperative patent classification
CSIRO	Commonwealth Scientific and Industrial Research Organisation
Defra	Department for Environment, Food and Rural Affairs, UK
DNA	deoxyribonucleic acid
DUS	distinct, uniform, and stable
EB	Ellwanger & Barry Catalogues in CCMHSD
EBA	Enlarged Board of Appeal, European Patent Office
EBNR	Ellwanger and Barry Nursery Records, Special Collections, Rush Rhees Library, University of Rochester, Nursery Company Correspondence
EPC	European Patent Convention
EPO	European Patent Office
EU	European Union
FAO	Food and Agriculture Organization of the United Nations, Rome
FIS	International Seed Federation
GM	genetic modification
GMOs	genetically modified organisms
GNA	Gambia National Archives
IA	Iowa State University
IRCCs	internationally recognized certificates of compliance
ITPGRFA	International Treaty on Plant Genetic Resources for Food and Agriculture
JCPPL	Japan Campaign for the Promotion of a Plant Patent Law
JIC	John Innes Centre, Norwich
JPO	Japanese Patent Office
KA	Kew Archives
MAF	Ministry of Agriculture and Forestry, Japan

MAFF	Ministry of Agriculture, Forestry, and Fisheries, Japan
MIT	Massachusetts Institute of Technology
MTA	material transfer agreement
NARA	National Archives and Record Administration, United States
NBA	National Biodiversity Authority
OECD	Organisation for Economic Co-operation and Development
ORC	Organic Research Centre, Cirencester
PBI	Plant Breeding Institute, Cambridge
PBR	Plant Breeders' Rights
PCT	Patent Cooperation Treaty
PDOs	protected denominations of origin
PGI	protected geographical indication
PPA	US Plant Patent Act 1930
PRO HK	Public Records Office, Hong Kong
PVP	plant variety protection
RRI	responsible research and innovation
SOAS	School of Oriental and African Studies, London
STS	Science and Technology Studies
TNA	The National Archives, United Kingdom
TRIPs	Agreement on Trade-Related Aspects of Intellectual Property Rights
UDEL	Special Collections, Manuscripts and Archives Department, University of Delaware Library
UGA	Hargrett Rare Book and Manuscript Library, University of Georgia, Athens
UPOV	International Union for the Protection of New Varieties of Plants
USDC NY	United States District Court for the Southern District of New York
USPTO	United States Patent and Trademark Office
WIPO	World Intellectual Property Organization

List of Contributors

Isabella Alexander is a professor in the Faculty of Law at the University of Technology Sydney.

Jose Bellido is a reader in law at the University of Kent.

Dominic J Berry is a research fellow at the London School of Economics and Political Science.

Mario Biagioli is a distinguished professor of law and communication at UCLA.

Veit Braun is a research associate in the Institute of Sociology at Goethe-University Frankfurt.

Susannah Chapman is a research fellow at the University of Queensland.

Annalisa Colombino is a researcher at the Department of Economics, Ca' Foscari, University of Venice.

Kjell David Ericson is an assistant professor at Kyoto University.

Allison Fish is a senior research fellow at the University of Queensland.

Marie-Angèle Hermitte is honorary director of studies at the École des hautes études en sciences sociales (EHESS) and honorary research director at the Centre national de la recherche scientifique (CNRS) in Paris.

Daniel J Kevles is professor emeritus of history at Yale University and visiting Interdisciplinary Fellow, NYU Law School.

Brendan Matz is a historian of science and technology at NYU Gallatin School of Individualized Study.

Paolo Palladino is an independent researcher, formerly professor of history and theory at Lancaster University.

Daniel Schneider is emeritus professor of urban and regional planning at the University of Illinois Urbana-Champaign.

Brad Sherman is an ARC laureate fellow and professor at the University of Queensland.

The Place of Nature in Intellectual Property

Jose Bellido and Brad Sherman

Nature casts a long shadow over intellectual property law. As well as being a resource, a limit, and a metaphor, different conceptions of nature have been used to delineate and define the intangible, to set its boundaries, and to shape its relations. Nature is also a powerful and elusive force to be stabilized, a case to appeal, a matter to be authored or invented, and a subject to be dominated, excluded, or isolated.[1] Intellectual property law has constantly been challenged in its interactions with a modified nature.[2] The repeated development of new reproductive and experimental technologies that intervene in nature has forced intellectual property law to draw and redraw distinctions between the artificial and the natural, the synthetic and the real.[3] Recently, in interacting with molecular level interventions the law has been confronted with a series of ontological and existential questions that go to the heart of intellectual property.[4] As a result of these interactions, the law has been forced to rethink fundamental ideas such as how to define invention and how to protect volatile subject matter which is replicated at a distance.[5] In grappling with modified nature, intellectual property recognized a secondary nature; one that was already artificial and which contributed to the development of commodity and information networks, performance ideals, and systems of evaluation for properties to be exchanged, monitored, and transacted. Triggered by the unstable divide between nature and society upon which intellectual property emerged and whose boundaries are constantly being renegotiated, the links that connect intellectual property and nature are numerous. One starting point for exploring these links is to consider the ways in which nature was industrialized, explored, transported, and transformed, and the role that intellectual property law played in these processes. Another starting point is to recognize that as the meanings of nature and

[1] Brad Sherman, 'What Does It Mean to Invent Nature?' (2015) 5 *University of California Irvine Law Review* 1193.

[2] Bernard Edelman, 'The Law's Eye: Nature and Copyright' in Brad Sherman and Alain Strowel (eds), *Of Authors and Origins: Essays on Copyright Law* (Clarendon Press 1994) 79–91.

[3] *Cancer Voices Australia v Myriad Genetics Inc* [2013] FCA 65 [102].

[4] As Jane Calvert observes: 'In forcing biology into the mould of engineering, by developing discrete and substitutable parts, synthetic biology is simultaneously making biology better fit intellectual property regimes.' See Jane Calvert, 'The Commodification of Emergence: Systems Biology, Synthetic Biology and Intellectual Property' (2008) 3 *BioSocieties* 383, 392.

[5] On this see generally Alain Pottage and Brad Sherman, 'Organisms and Manufactures: On the History of Plant Inventions' (2007) 31(2) *Melbourne University Law Review* 539.

culture are not fixed, the study of intellectual property and the design of nature require a consideration of the relationship between the mechanical and the organic, and hence the corresponding trajectories between nature, art, science, and technology.[6]

Given the important place that nature occupies in intellectual property law, it is surprising that there has not yet been a sustained attempt to the trace the role that nature has played in shaping the law or the ways in which the law has been influenced by nature. Only in limited areas such as the law of geographical indications have intellectual property scholars regularly engaged with and given a voice to nature. When this occurs, however, this has often only been as an attempt to demonstrate the sui generis character of the law in relation to other areas of intellectual property.[7] By contrast, our view is that nature occupies a central position across the whole discipline, not only in the way it has been imagined, legislated, and adjudicated, but also in the ways it has been historicized. One of the aims of this volume is to show that the ways in which intellectual property law has engaged with and understood nature is part of a long history and that many of the problems we face today require a more profound understanding of this interaction. To this end, the volume brings together scholars from different disciplines to reflect on such historical intersections. In doing so, the contributions show how the boundaries between nature and intellectual property law are often more complex, permeable, and porous than is commonly recognized.

The volume is organized around four overlapping themes. The first concerns the rhetorical and pragmatic appeal of nature in intellectual property law. The opening chapter, Mario Biagioli's 'Vegetable Genius: Organic Figures of Originality' shows the role that plants, vegetable production, and natural ecologies have played in the conceptualization of copyright law. Instead of viewing nature as something that was ignored in the emergence of copyright, Biagioli shows how the establishment of literary property was underpinned by nature or more specifically by the idea of natural organic growth. Interestingly, similar ideas reappeared centuries later not in terms of authorial originality but as part of the way that the commons and the public domain are thought about.[8] The second contribution, by Daniel Schneider, 'Denaturing Bacteria: The Sewage Patent Controversy and Biotechnology', considers the contested ways in which bacteria have been defined in science and law. Reflecting upon the patent history of biological sewage treatment, Schneider looks at the ways in which the 'natural' became incorporated into the industrial

[6] Marilyn Strathern, *Reproducing the Future: Anthropology, Kingship and the New Reproductive Technologies* (Manchester University Press 1992) 19.

[7] Dev Gangjee, *Relocating the Law of Geographical Indications* (Cambridge University Press 2012) 77–126.

[8] See also Mario Biagioli, 'Nature and the Commons: The Vegetable Roots of Intellectual Property' in Jean-Paul Gaudillière, Daniel J Kevles, and Hans-Jörg Rheinberger (eds), *Living Properties: Making Knowledge and Controlling Ownership in the History of Biology* (Max-Planck-Institut für Wissenschaftsgeschichte 2009) 241–50.

ecosystem, as well as how the industrial moved into the wild. In other words, he looks at the ways in which genetic material from activated plants became incorporated into wild species.[9] Instead of looking at nature as a legal metaphor or as an unknown territory to discover or modify, here nature has become part of the way science frames patent law. The third contribution from this section, Veit Braun's 'The Essence of Biology: Tomatoes, Broccoli, and European Patents on Native Plant Traits', examines recent litigation over the patenting of modified broccoli and tomatoes at the European Patent Office. Braun shows that in considering how biology fits into the framework of patent law, the European Patent Office saw life as something that was beyond the reach of intellectual property rights.[10]

The volume's second theme explores the role intellectual property law plays in the circulation of nature. More specifically, it considers the ways in which intellectual property juridically links creators with their nature-based outputs as they circulate beyond their physical or contractual control. In so doing, it discusses how creators manage the way those outputs are used by third parties at a distance. For example, in 'Intellectual Property's Antecedent: Seednut Storage Laws and the Regulation of Living Materials from a Distance in British Colonial Gambia', Susannah Chapman looks at the emergence of distinct legal devices that allow nature to circulate. Focusing on seed laws in colonial Gambia, the argument here is that intellectual property has a prehistory of unconventional or premodern laws that played an important role in the eventual assimilation of biological subject matter into mainstream intellectual property law.[11] Her views about experimentation and intellectual property law in colonial settings directly touch on the historical assumptions that have served to define and establish the discipline. In 'Some Outlandish Legal Tales: The Debate over Plant Propagation', Marie-Angèle Hermitte raises similar questions to Chapman, but in the context of the emergence of plant intellectual property law in twentieth-century France. Specifically, Hermitte examines the problems French law-makers had in ensuring that biological innovations were able to circulate as forms of intellectual property. Hermitte focuses on the problems plant breeders faced in translating into suitable legal form the notion that their trade combines human creativity with the interplay of natural forces.[12] The next chapter, by Daniel J Kevles, 'Novelties, Frauds, and Protections: The Seed and Nursery Business in Nineteenth-century America' looks at the ways in which natural products were sold by nineteenth-century American nurseries as a way to discuss the rise of branding practices in US trade mark law.

[9] A more extensive development of this argument is found in Daniel Schneider, *Hybrid Nature. Sewage Treatment and the Contradictions of the Industrial Ecosystem* (The MIT Press 2011).

[10] See also Veit Braun, 'Holding on to and Letting Go of Seed: Quasi-commodities and the Passage of Property' (2021) 14(3) *Journal of Cultural Economy* 306.

[11] Susannah Chapman and Brad Sherman, 'Finding a Place for Agriculture in Intellectual Property' (2018) 49 *International Review of Intellectual Property and Competition Law* 759.

[12] More generally see Marie-Angèle Hermitte, *L'emprise des droits intellectuels sur le monde vivant* (Éditions Quae 2016).

More specifically, Kevles examines the different marketing practices that nurseries used to strengthen their trustworthiness. In so doing, Kevles shows how trademark law became emblematic of a desire to use intellectual property to protect material objects of the living world.[13] The contribution by Annalisa Colombino and Paolo Palladino, entitled 'Brands Matter: Nature, Economy, and the Gift', looks at protected denominations of origin (PDOs) for meat in Europe. By shifting the focus of attention from the processes of production to the act of consumption, Colombino and Palladino challenge the focus on exchange and exploitation that dominates within intellectual property scholarship. In doing so, they open up new ways of thinking about the relationship between intellectual property and biological resources.[14] Similarly, the final contribution to this section, Isabella Alexander's 'Copyright, Nature, and Travel Narratives: Publishing Cook's Voyages', looks at the image of nature central to the colonial enterprise and the role copyright law played in its circulation. Alexander explores how print technology and copyright conferred authority upon the travel account that ordered and unified nature within an imperial context. These contributions remind us how intellectual property law reorganizes practices of production and distribution; how its activation at one point in a supply chain can lead to juridification at other points; and how the law interacts with and is transformed by the social, economic, biological, and technological relations that constitute supply chains and networks.

The volume's third theme takes as its point of departure the unstable distinction between the 'natural' and the 'artificial', and how the law manages that distinction in dealing with nature-based creations. The contributions to this theme highlight how rather than struggling to meet the injunction to draw a distinction between the 'natural' and the 'artificial', the law has been continually creative in identifying diverse ways of accommodating this distinction. The first contribution, Jose Bellido and Brad Sherman's 'Artificial Flowers: Plastic Nature, Synthetic Biology', explores the role that life plays in the way intellectual property law interacts with nature and how this changes when dealing with artificial or synthetic biology.[15] Bellido and Sherman regard intellectual property law's treatment of artificial flowers, which are at once artificial and at the same time extrinsically intertwined with nature, as an overlooked but paradigmatic example of the resourceful ways in which

[13] See also Daniel J Kevles, *Heirloom Fruits of America: Selections from the USDA Watercolor Pomological Collection* (Heyday Books 2020).

[14] Palladino has also explored how branding devices sometimes break the link with the animal of flesh and bone and become disconnected from the places in which they originate (or graze); see Paolo Palladino, 'What's in a Name? On Affect, Value and the Bio-economy' (2020) 15(1) *BioSocieties* 70. Colombino has also looked at the commercialization of Piedmontese beef to conclude that it is not a reflection of the animal's genetic characteristics but as 'the result of the complicated negotiations amongst veterinaries, livestock technicians, farmers and butchers, which have taken place from the second half of the 19th century to the present day'; see Annalisa Colombino and Paolo Giaccaria, 'Breed contra beef: The making of Piedmontese cattle' in Jody Emel and Harvey Neo (eds), *Political Ecologies of Meat* (Routledge 2015) 161.

[15] See also Brad Sherman, 'Taxonomic Property' (2008) 67(3) *Cambridge Law Journal* 560.

legal techniques have been used to construct intangible properties and how life figures in that process. The second contribution, Kjell D Ericson's 'Modified Pearl Oysters and Repeatable Peaches: Cultivation, Invention, and the Laws of Nature in Twentieth-Century Japan', looks at Japanese pearl cultivation to consider how intellectual property law facilitated a system for separating 'cultured' from 'natural' pearls in the first decades of the twentieth century. Ericson recognizes the ways in which the law was reinterpreted to accommodate the application of human artifice to the 'laws of nature', a logic that would resurface in attempts to justify intellectual property in the realms of agriculture and fisheries.[16] The third contribution in this section, Dominic Berry's 'Scientific Activism and Intellectual Property: How Agroecologists and Plant Synthetic Biologists Have Attempted to Challenge the Status Quo', sharpens our understanding of the ways in which different actors have managed to develop practices that enable broader sharing and use of biological materials. By looking at the making of the Open Material Transfer Agreement, Berry examines how the logic of appropriation embedded in intellectual property was reformed from within. The argument here is that the 'natural' and the 'artificial' are both being imagined and co-constructed.

The volume's fourth theme addresses a challenge that intellectual property law has consistently faced in dealing with nature-based subject matter, namely ensuring that nature is legible to a legal audience. The contribution by Brendan Matz, 'Selling Science: Creating New Values in Animals in the Era of Mendel's Rediscovery', considers the rise of breeders' associations and the shift to a performance ideal, paying close attention to the relationship between intellectual property and the market for purebred livestock. Matz's contribution highlights the important role that social practices play in constructing cattle breeds.[17] Matz also shows the role that stud books and portraiture played in ensuring that breeding innovations were recorded in a form that was visible and thus amenable to intellectual property protection. Allison Fish takes up a similar theme in 'Conceptualizing Nature as Information: Rendering South Asian Genetic Resources and Associated Knowledge Searchable and Legible'. The chapter focuses on the development of the Traditional Knowledge Digital Library, which was established by the Indian state to deal with the problem of biopiracy and subsequent information technology-related innovations. Fish explores the problems that arise when nature is neither visible nor legible to the law. She also shows some of the unexpected consequences

[16] Kjell D Ericson, 'The Life and Times of Patent No. 2,670: Industrial Property and Public Knowledge in Early Twentieth Century Japan' in Graeme Gooday and Steven Wilf (eds), *Patent Cultures: Diversity and Harmonization in Historical Perspective* (Cambridge University Press 2020) 319–40 and Kjell D Ericson, 'Judging the Perle Japonaise: The Techno-Legal Separation of Culture from Nature in 1920s Paris' (2021) 62(4) *Technology and Culture* 1032.

[17] Brendan Matz, 'Crossing, Grading and Keeping Pure: Animal Breeding and Exchange around 1860' (2011) 35(1) *Endeavour* 7.

that arise when in responding to these problems the law sets out to render nature visible. In many ways, the contributors to this volume share a similar concern, highlighting the role that nature plays in intellectual property law. In doing so, they not only shed light on issues that are at the heart of contemporary law, they also begin to sketch a history that has largely been overlooked.

1
Vegetable Genius
Organic Figures of Originality

Mario Biagioli

An original may be said to be of a vegetable nature;
it rises spontaneously from the vital root of genius;
it grows, it is not made.[1]

Introduction

The creation and protection of value in selectively bred or genetically modified organisms have occupied farmers, breeders, policy-makers, and scholars for centuries.[2] Like them, this chapter examines the connection between property and living things, but approaches it from the other end: rather than considering how organisms have become objects of property, it focuses on the positive role that figures of plants, vegetable growth, and natural ecologies have played in the conceptualization of copyright law and, subsequently, in modelling the consequences of those protections. This chapter looks at early discussions of the foundations of copyright law that mobilized organic growth and differentiation as models of authorial creation—the irreducible phenotypical singularity of living beings cast as the paradigmatic exemplar of originality. No two plants of the same variety can ever be completely alike. Accordingly, original compositions are not laboriously crafted but grow naturally the way plants and flowers do: more fruits of authorship than works of authorship. Promoted primarily in eighteenth-century literary circles, the image of vegetable growth and singularity supported and reverberated with the conceptualization of the author as genius.

[1] Edward Young, *Conjectures on Original Composition* (Millar 1759) 12.

[2] Glenn Bugos and Daniel J Kevles, 'Plants as Intellectual Property' (1992) 7 *Osiris* 74; Daniel Kevles, 'New Blood, New Fruits: Protections for Breeders and Originators, 1789–1930' in Mario Biagioli, Peter Jaszi, and Martha Woodansee (eds), *Making and Unmaking Intellectual Property* (University of Chicago Press 2011) 253–68; Christine MacLeod and Gregory Radick (eds), *Owning and Disowning Invention: Intellectual Property and Identity in the Technosciences in Britain, 1870–1930* (2013) 2(2) *Studies in History and Philosophy of Science* 44.

Mario Biagioli, *Vegetable Genius* In: *Intellectual Property and the Design of Nature*. Edited by: Jose Bellido and Brad Sherman, Oxford University Press. © Mario Biagioli 2023. DOI: 10.1093/oso/9780192864406.003.0001

This chapter is meant as a contribution to the study of figures that frame the thinking and articulation of intellectual property (IP). Pottage and Sherman have shown that machines were not just the most common object of nineteenth-century technology but that, as a figure, the machine provided patent law with the paradigm of the very concept of invention—a paradigm that is now beginning to be eclipsed by another figure, that of information.[3] It is proposed here that their argument about the role of the machine in nineteenth-century patent law may be paralleled by one about the role of the plant in early copyright law. The machine encapsulated the concept of invention, the plant that of originality.[4]

After emerging in the second half of the eighteenth century, vegetable, and organic figures of growth faded into the background only to reappear more than two centuries later, in the early 2000s, through the efforts of self-styled cultural environmentalists. This time, however, images of organic growth were not mobilized as emblems of authorial originality, but as figures of the commons and the public domain that, formerly lush green pastures, were now depleted by the excessive production and protection of patents and copyrighted works.[5] Vegetable and natural imagery thus captured key elements of both ends of copyright's historical trajectory. Cast as a process of natural organic growth and differentiation, original authorial creation supported the establishment of literary property, but eventually that growth became stifled by excessive IP production that depleted the nutritious ecology from within, like overgrowing oxygen-consuming algae that push rivers and lakes to the verge of biological death. The goal here is to neither resurrect nor criticize such figurations, but to understand what their emergence, eclipse, and re-emergence can tell us about the difficulty of capturing and visualizing the processes through which intellectual property is established.

[3] Alain Pottage and Brad Sherman, *Figures of Invention* (Oxford University Press 2010); Alain Pottage, 'Law Machines: Scale models, forensic materiality and the making of modern patent law' (2011) 41 *Social Studies of Science* 621. For the shift to information see Mario Biagioli and Alain Pottage, 'Patenting Personalized Medicine: Molecules, Information, and the Body' (2021) 36 *Osiris* 221, esp 229–35.

[4] The focus here is exclusively on figures of originality, but Jose Bellido has discussed a different mobilization of the image of the plant in the debates surrounding the introduction of copyright law in nineteenth-century Spain; see Jose Bellido, 'Codified Anxieties: Literary Copyright in Mid-nineteenth Century Spain' in Isabella Alexander and H Tomás Gómez-Arostegui (eds), *Research Handbook on the History of Copyright Law* (Edward Elgar Publishing 2016) 423–43, 431. In a speech to the Senate on 10 March 1847, Roca de Togores, one of the promoters of the bill, justified granting copyright protection to authors because: 'This work is like a plant whose fruits are harvested by the entire society from its creation. However, such is the benefit dispensed by the first to plant that society must reward him and recognize a kind of extensive property' in *Legislación de la Propiedad Literaria en España* (Jose Bellido tr Librería de Moya y Plaza 1864) 23.

[5] James Boyle, 'The Second Enclosure Movement and the Construction of the Public Domain' (2003) 66 *Law and Contemporary Problems* 33: 'It may be that intellectual property rights slow down innovation, by putting multiple roadblocks, multiple necessary licenses, in the way of subsequent innovation' (at 44).

In the Beginning Was the Vegetable

Searching for conceptual and rhetorical tools to justify the introduction of a new kind of property, some of the proponents of copyright in eighteenth-century England (and other European countries) analogized written texts to cultivated land—the exemplar for the kind of stable property they strove to establish for literary compositions.[6] What has received less attention, however, is that several copyright advocates saw land not just as the exemplar of real property but as a site of creative production. Unique things grew from it. As the concept of literary property became eventually tied to the originality of the work, it no longer sufficed to claim that, like homesteads, novels were legitimate objects of property because they resulted from human labour.[7] Conceiving and writing novels did require labour, but that would not account for their specificity—what made them identifiable and different from others.[8]

But as a clear definition of authorial creativity proved elusive, the focus shifted from originality per se to the relationship between originality and imitation—an attempt to save originality's emergent role in literary property while acknowledging its roots in (or at least close coexistence with) imitation. Agricultural imagery helped to articulate that kind of narrative. Arthur Murphy, an English lawyer involved in the landmark 1774 *Donaldson v Beckett* copyright case, framed the difference between originality and imitation by comparing it to that between owning and renting a farm:

> The ancient patriarchs of Poetry are generous, as they are rich: a great part of their possessions is let on lease to the moderns. *Dryden*, besides his own hereditary estate, had taken a large scope of ground from *Virgil*, Mr. *Pope* held *by copy* near half of *Homer's* rent roll.[9]

[6] Mark Rose, 'Copyright and Its Metaphors' (2002) 50 *UCLA Law Review* 1; Mark Rose, *Authors and Owners* (Harvard University Press 1993) esp 114–20; and Brad Sherman and Lionel Bently, *The Making of Modern Intellectual Property Law: The British Experience* (Cambridge University Press 1999) 9–59. The connection between intellectual property, land, and cultivation reemerges also in early nineteenth-century Spanish copyright discourse: 'The cultivation of dramatic literary property paralleled the agricultural processes to be controlled by private landholders'; see Lisa Surwillo, *The Stages of Property: Copyrighting Theatre in Spain* (University of Toronto Press 2007) 47. See also 39: 'Quite simply, a cultivation of literary property was analogous to the appropriation and cultivation of land.'

[7] Sherman and Bently (n 6) 15–28.

[8] The 'sweat of the brow' doctrine found rejected in case law and modern registration practices: 'When examining a work for original authorship, the U.S. Copyright Office will focus on the appearance or sound of the work that the author created but will not consider the amount of time, effort, or expense required to create the work. These issues have no bearing on whether a work possesses the minimum creative spark required by the Copyright Act and the Constitution' US Copyright Office, *The Compendium of U.S. Copyright Office Practices* (3rd edn USCO 2021) 310.7 https://www.copyright.gov/comp3/docs/compendium.pdf (accessed 10 September 2022).

[9] Arthur Murphy, *The Gray's-Inn Journal*, No 4 (11 November 1752) (emphases in the original) in *The Works of Arthur Murphy*, vol 5 (Cadell 1786) 34–35. Murphy served as counsel in two landmark cases: *Millar v Taylor* (1769) and *Donaldson v Becket* (1774). 'Mental harvest' is also mentioned in Catherine Macaulay, *A Modest Plea for the Property of Copyright* (Cruttwell 1774) 15.

Authors can be original even when appearing otherwise. Murphy suggests, for example, that modern authors do not copy the compositions of the ancients but rather borrow from them the 'farmland' that nourished those compositions. Accordingly, Dryden did not copy Virgil's work but simply leased some of his vast estate, which Dryden then cultivated to grow his own original work from it. (The difference between Virgil's books and what Murphy refers to as Virgil's 'ground' was, however, never described; nor were the arrangements through which Dryden could have leased an estate from the long-departed Virgil.) Similarly, Murphy refers to Dryden's 'hereditary estate', perhaps to recast imitation as a form of legitimate property transfer, not appropriation. Dryden lawfully inherited it (although what exactly he inherited, or from whom, he does not say). Made possible by analogies between writing and agriculture, literary property, and real property, these discursive moves were deployed less to protect the reputation of famous early modern authors who had borrowed from the ancients than to expand the meaning of originality by blurring or displacing copying with 'leasing' or 'inheriting'. The vast chronological distance between lessors and lessees created ample space for staging these imaginary arrangements.[10] The goal was to show (or rather gesture) that originality existed and could be relied upon to justify literary property despite the fact that originality did not appear to be independent of imitation or other forms of transfer from one author to another.

Agricultural images also helped to negotiate the relationship between originality and imitation through simple quantitative considerations: 'The Field of Knowledge is large enough for all the World to find Ground in it to plant and improve.'[11] Referencing Locke's narrative of the establishment of private property from the communal state of nature, this author suggested that if there is a large amount of unclaimed land available, one does not need to lease or take any of it from other authors.[12] Many different writers can pursue literary homesteading, claiming their

[10] It is distinctive of these debates that the discussion of originality and imitation seemed to be framed as a *querelle* between the original ancients and the typically imitative moderns, rather than about moderns imitating (or not) other moderns. The vast temporal distance between the ancients and the moderns seems necessary to some of the specific defenses of originality articulated in these debates. For instance, without an epochal separation between ancients and moderns it would have been difficult or impossible to mobilize tropes of inheritance and intergenerational leasing of landed estates, leaving imitation to look very much like unreconstructed imitation. In addition, it was crucial that the ancients could not be present to dispute these narratives. Are we really sure the ancients wished to lease their estates or leave them in inheritance to the moderns? Like nature, the ancients were presented as nonchalantly generous—they had plenty of land to share and leave behind to the moderns. But was their generosity overstated or just made up by modern commentators? Thankfully, the ancients were too dead to object.

[11] Anonymous, *Letter from an Author to a Member of Parliament occasioned by a late letter concerning the BILL now depending in the House of Commons, For the Encouragement of Learning*, &c. (London 1735) 2.

[12] John Locke, *Two Treaties of Government* (Cambridge University Press 1967) 305–306: '[E]very Man has a Property in his own Person. This no Body has any Right to but himself. The Labour of his Body, and the Work of his Hands, we may say, are properly his. Whatsoever then he removes from the State that Nature hath provided, and left it in, he hath mixed his Labour with, and joined to it something that is his own, and thereby makes it his Property.'

own share of land on which to grow and improve their own unique varieties. They can all be original. We are not told, however, how the busy 'Field of Knowledge' of eighteenth-century London could still look like an endless expanse of empty plots ready for the taking.

Other commentators articulated agricultural imagery in different directions, drawing a direct analogy between the land and the mind, placing originality not in the author's farming skills but in the qualities of their creative intellect—their very personal mental farm. Literary production thus became a 'mental harvest,'[13] an image that could also suggest both the naturalness of literary originality and the different forms it took among different authors: 'the mind of a man of Genius is a fertile and pleasant field' or, as a different author put it: 'His Brain, which was his Estate, had as regular and different Produce as other Men's Land.'[14] A contemporaneous pamphlet expands on this theme, while also pointing to the analogies underneath the differences between real and literary property:

> In this various world, different men are born to different fortunes. One inherits a portion of land; he cultivates it with care, it produces him corn and fruits and wool: another possesses a fruitful mind, teeming with ideas of every kind; he bestows his labor in cultivating that: the produce is reason, sentiment, philosophy.[15]

Finally, instead of focusing on the diversity of mental terroirs, one could consider the layout and appearance of different fields and gardens to appreciate that genius is bound to come in different shapes and forms. Wild or polished, it is always different, always natural:

> The Genius of both these Classes of Authors may be equally great, but shews itself after a different Manner. In the first it is like a rich Soil in a happy Climate, that produces a whole Wilderness of noble Plants rising in a thousand beautiful landskips without any certain Order or Regularity. In the other it is the same rich Soil under the same happy Climate, that has been laid out in Walks and Parterres, and cut into Shape and Beauty by the Skill of the Gardener.[16]

Or, in *Donaldson v Beckett:*

[13] Macaulay (n 9) 14.

[14] Young (n 1) 9; Anon, *Tatler*, no 101, (November 29–1 December 1709) 1. The author is identified as Joseph Addison in Mark Rose, *Authors and Owners* (Harvard University Press 1993) 40, where the figure of the gentleman farmer is discussed.

[15] The quote is included, without attribution, in William Enfield, *Observations on Literary Property* (Johnston 1774) 21–22.

[16] Anon, *Spectator*, no 161 (Monday 3 September 1711) 2. The author is identified as Joseph Addison in Mark Rose, *Authors and Owners* (Harvard University Press 1993) 41.

> [Shakespeare's] possessions were very near as extensive as *Homer's*, but in some places had not received sufficient culture. But even there spontaneous flowers shot up, and in the *unweeded garden, which grows to seed*, you might cull lavender, myrtle, and wild thyme.[17]

Drawn from court arguments and pamphlets published around the British cases through which modern copyright law was slowly fleshed out in the late eighteenth century, these quotes give us a taste of how pervasive and diverse the agricultural discourse of authorship could be. The relation between genius and vegetable originality, however, was most systematically articulated in Edward Young's 1759 *Conjectures on Original Composition*.

Some of the terroir-inflected views on the growth of literary production sampled above tended to focus on the qualities of the soil and its location—'rich Soil under … happy Climate'—while others likened the author to a breeder who 'improves' their crops, a farmer who can extract the best from the land he 'cultivates with care', or a gardener who knows how to make their gardens look elegant, but could as easily decide to let them go wild. Young bypassed most of that, concentrating instead on the plant and its singularity:[18]

> An original [work] may be said to be of a vegetable nature; it rises spontaneously from the vital root of genius; it grows, it is not made. Imitations are often a sort of manufacture wrought up by those mechanics, art, and labor, out of pre-existent materials not their own.[19]

Soil quality mattered to Young (as did other 'externals' like rain, air, and sun, whose nurturing function he analogized to literary patronage), but did not account for the production of specifically original compositions.[20] Nor did originality stem from the author's labour or skills:[21] 'A *Genius* differs from a *good Understanding*, as a Magician from a good Architect; *That* raises his structure by means invisible, *This* by the skilful use of common tools.'[22] Originality comes only from genius, and genius is in the plant itself, not in the breeder or in the terroir.[23]

[17] Murphy (n 9) (original emphasis).

[18] This theme can be found in other texts from the literary property debates such as, Anon (n 16) 2.

[19] Young (n 1) 12.

[20] ibid 46–47: 'An Evocation of vegetable fruits depends on rain, air, and sun; an Evocation of the fruits of Genius no less depends on Externals. What marvellous crop bore it in *Greece*, and *Rome*? … What encouragement from the nature of their governments, and the spirit of their people?'

[21] ibid 12.

[22] ibid 26.

[23] Genius seems able to conjure its own growing environment into existence: 'The pen of an original writer, like Armida's wand, out of a barren waste calls a blooming spring'; see ibid 10. The reference to Armida's wand also confirms genius' kinship with magic.

Strange Genius, Simple Plant

Since Martha Woodmansee's 'The Genius and the Copyright', historians have focused on the emergence of the author's original personal expression as the centrepiece of modern copyright jurisprudence and its relation to late eighteenth-century discussions of the figure of genius, especially romantic genius.[24] The details and full chronology of that trajectory remain complicated[25] but scholars agree that literary property underwent a radical reconceptualization during the long eighteenth century, becoming eventually tied to authorial expression, as it presently remains. In particular, Woodmansee has suggested that Young's celebration of the author as genius gained wide circulation in Germany, especially within Romantic circles,[26] as part of what M H Abrams has termed the development of 'theories of vegetable genius' in philosophy, literature, and art criticism.[27] There, Young's work informed Fichte's 1793 'Proof of the Illegality of Reprinting', whose framing of authorship found its way into early German copyright laws.[28] Comparable discursive developments have been seen in England where, according to Mark Rose, 'the production of the discourse of original genius coincided with that of authorial property'.[29]

[24] Martha Woodmansee, 'The Genius and the Copyright: Economic and Legal Conditions of the Emergence of the Author' (1984) 17 *Eighteenth-Century Studies* 425. Within the substantial literature on the history of theories and perceptions of genius see Penelope Murray (ed), *Genius: The History of an Idea* (Wiley-Blackwell 1989); Edgar Zilsel, *Le genie* (Minuit 1999); Darrin M MacMahon, *Divine Fury: A History of Genius* (Basic Books 2013).

[25] On Young in Britain and the conceptual overlap between British and German debates see Rose (n 6) 117–22, 130–32. John Luis Kind, *Edward Young in Germany* (Columbia University Press 1906); Martin William Steinke, *Edward Young's "Conjectures on Original Composition* (FC Stechert 1917).

[26] Woodmansee (n 24) 430; MH Abrams, *The Mirror and the Lamp* (Oxford University Press 1953) 201–205, 210. On Young in the context of eighteenth-century British discussions of genius see Andrew Elfenbein, *Romantic Genius: The Prehistory of a Homosexual Role* (Columbia University Press 1999) 27 38. Darrin MacMahon argues that, more than just Young's work, 'British theorists of genius were widely admired and read' in Germany; see MacMahon (n 24) 84.

[27] Abrams (n 26) 201. An example is Johann Georg Sulzer's 1771 claim that: 'It is a remarkable thing, belonging among the mysteries of psychology, that at times certain thoughts will not develop or let themselves be clearly grasped … yet long afterwards will present themselves in the greatest clarity of their own accord … like a plant, and now suddenly stood before us in their full development and bloom. Many a conception ripens gradually within us and then, freeing itself as though of its own accord from the mass of obscure ideas, emerges suddenly into the light'. Abrams discusses Herder's different use of 'the plant as the prototype for the development of an art form' (204–205). A similar motif is found in Diderot's 'Eloge de Richardson': 'Dans ce livre immortel, comme dans la nature au printemps, on ne trouve point deux feuilles qui soient d'un même vert.' See *Oeuvres de Denis Diderot*, vol 1 (Belin 1818) 607. A similar reference is at 454. Thanks to Jose Bellido for this reference.

[28] Woodmansee (n 24) 445. The 1837 Prussian Copyright Act did not refer to Fichte by name but clearly adopted his conceptualization: 'The buyer of a book gets by the purchase the physical property in his copy and the right to use and to process the expressed thoughts in his particular manner. What inviolably remains the author's and can be identified as the real intellectual property, is the particular form, in which he has expressed his thoughts. These principles are not new, they already have been laid down in the 90s of the last century by learned men,' quoted in Martin Kretschmer and Friedemann Kawohl, 'History and Philosophy of Copyright' in Simon Frith and Lee Marshall (eds), *Music and Copyright* (University of Edinburgh Press 2004) 21–53.

[29] Rose (n 6) 115.

In hindsight, it is not surprising to see the originality of genius morph from a trope of literary originality into the foundational concept of copyright. It helped to cast a composition (independently of its genre and content) as a unique artefact that emerged in the author's mind, free from external influences and borrowings (whose existence it made possible to both acknowledge and dismiss as needed). It also made it seem largely irrelevant that, if a book arrived in the reader's hands, it was because of the labour and different contributions of many other people who were not its author.[30] The authorship of the original composition trumped all other contributions in importance, channelling virtually all rights and rewards towards the author because it was the author that supplied originality.

But while the flash of genius is a poor description of the process of literary production, it is not a myth of origin either if, by that expression, one means an artefactual narrative meant to cover up or distort actual genealogies. It could be better seen, instead, as a sort of legal fiction that grounded early copyright law; a productive fiction that filled a foundational gap but did not displace or hide what authorship 'really is'—a question that, it would seem, has never been answered by either copyright law or literary scholars.[31] Rather than critiquing or embracing one side of the dichotomy between the flash of genius and the sweat of the brain, or between the opaque roots of creativity and the documentable long and diverse chain of material agency through which books are produced, it is more productive to question those dichotomies altogether. Young's text lends itself to that kind of reading.

As he articulates agricultural images of originality and literary property, Young ends up presenting the emergence of an original work as a process of vegetable growth rather than the result of human imagination, skill, or labour. That does not, however, amount to a definition of originality, which he explicitly bypasses: 'I shall not enter into the curious enquiry or what is, or what is not, strictly speaking, *Original*, content that all must allow, that some Compositions are more so than others.'[32] Despite writing a book in praise of literary originality, Young could conjure it only by leveraging imitation or, more precisely, by introducing a crucial distinction between two kinds of imitation. (Other pamphlets followed the same strategy with different agricultural imagery).[33] Rather than positing originality as

[30] See eg the entry for 'book' in the *Allgemeines Oeconomisches Lexicon* (1753) cited in Woodmansee (n 24) 425.

[31] Far from providing a unitary definition of 'author', historians and literary scholars have mapped the many different shapes and metamorphoses it has gone through at different times and in different disciplines. (Foucault's 'What is An Author?' is the best example of that approach). Copyright law, instead, simply assumes the author to be the source of the 'original works of authorship'. In one case we have a list, in the other a tautology, but never a definition. It is safe to assume we will never have one.

[32] Young (n 1) 9–10.

[33] Young's distinction between imitating the author and imitating the work resonates with Arthur Murphy's quote (see n 9), where he describes a difference between copying the ancients and renting their creative land to grow original works on it. In both cases, a distinction is made between imitative practices to make some look relatively more 'original', but while in Murphy's case it seems that the 'lessee' could grow an original work on borrowed land by applying their specific skills and labour, Young

presence and imitation as its poor copy, Young acknowledges that all literature is imitative. What matters is not the presence of imitation but its type: 'Imitations are of two kinds; one of Nature, one of Authors. The first we call *Originals* and confine the term *Imitation* to the second.'[34] More precisely:

> He that imitates the divine *Iliad*, does not imitate *Homer*, but he who takes the same method, which *Homer* took, for arriving at a capacity of accomplishing a work so great. Tread in his steps to the sole fountain of immortality; drink where he drank, at the true *Helicon*, that is, at the breast of nature: Imitate; but imitate not the *Composition*, but the *Man*. For may not this paradox pass into a maxim? *Viz*. 'The less we copy the renowned antients, we shall resemble them the more'.[35]

We see a telltale slippage here between Young's first claim that the imitation of authors produces imitative compositions[36] and his subsequent exhortation that authors who wish to produce original compositions should imitate 'not the *Composition*, but the *Man*'. This apparent contradiction—'author' having two meanings tied to two opposite outcomes—suggests that in the first quote Young uses 'author' as a synonym for an author's *oeuvre* while in the second he refers to the author as a person. These two meanings, however, should not have been confused. Young's argument rests precisely on the assumption that, like cause and effect, genius and the work of genius must be essentially distinct.

If you copy the *Iliad* (effect), the outcome will be an imitation, but if you instead imitate Homer (cause) as he imitates nature—drinking with him at the 'breast of nature', etc.—your composition will be original because you would have become an author as original as Homer. Young turns this scenario into a catchy paradox about the counterintuitive effects of different types of imitation: the less you imitate the works of the ancients, the more you will resemble them as an author. Less imitation of one kind is more imitation of a different kind which, Young tells us, produces originality. It is meaningful, therefore, that Young slips between Homer-as-*oeuvre* and Homer-as-author precisely when he should hold firm his fundamental distinction between cause and effect—between genius and works of genius. His punchline that 'the less we copy the renowned antients, we shall resemble them the more' is catchy precisely because it involves an unavoidable contradiction that he tries to diffuse by turning it into a witticism.

(n 1) suggests that one can freely imitate and be original at the same time, provided s/he imitates nature (the other author's genius) rather than his/her work.

34 ibid 9.

35 ibid 21.

36 ibid 9: 'Imitations are of two kinds; one of Nature, one of Authors. The first we call *Originals* and confine the term *Imitation* to the second.'

This slippage (and there are others)[37] indicates that dichotomies like those between originality and imitation, 'good' imitation and 'bad' copy, or between nature and artefact are inherently unstable. Young can never define or hold stable the positive element of his dichotomies (originality, nature, genius, etc.) All he can do is to conjure them as the opposite of the other half of his framing dichotomy—the half he construes as negative. Good originality is the opposite of bad imitation, good nature is the opposite of bad artefact, and so on. In fact, only the negative half of the dichotomy can be substantiated empirically. It is possible to tell whether a composition has been copied (by comparing two texts and recognizing that they contain the same words in the same sequence), but it cannot conclusively be known that a composition is original, because it could have been copied from other compositions that may exist out there, beyond reach. While imitation is empirically ascertainable, the judgment of originality is never final and always deferred.[38] But it means that, being empirically unprovable, originality can be conjured into existence only in opposition to imitation—the only half of Young's dichotomy that is empirically ascertainable. A bad presence is mobilized to supplement a good absence.

Trying to tie genius and originality to nature does not solve the problem but simply replicates it. Young states that we were all 'born Originals', but his text keeps showing otherwise.[39] Cast as 'the true *Helicon*' or the 'breast of nature', nature is presented both as nature itself and as a source or spring of naturalness, including the naturalness of genius. That suggests that even Homer was not born fully natural but became a genius by imitating nature, by drinking from it, by engaging in a rite of passage that involved partaking (in a seemingly eucharistic fashion) of the naturalness of nature. But because Young states that genius cannot use 'preexistent materials not their own', that implies that whatever Homer drank at the sacred springs of the 'true *Helicon*' must have been his already. To be an original genius, Homer could not have drunk something that did not already belong to him, which in turn suggests that nature must have gifted it to him before he drank it. (In this sense, genius must always be a gift because otherwise it would be an imitator, even if it copied nature.) Homer can drink what nature gifts him, but nature cannot teach him how to be natural because genius cannot be taught. Only the form of the

[37] Young slips when he says that 'he who takes the same method which Homer took' (21) remains an original author. His use of the term 'method'—the epitome of rules, steps, and training—to make a case for its opposite—originality—shows that he cannot keep his discursive ship watertight. The paradoxical relationship he sees between originality and imitation cannot be turned into a maxim because it is, in fact, an aporia. A comparable slippage is contained in his statement that 'Originals' are in fact the result of a certain kind of imitation (9).

[38] This refers to the late eighteenth-century notion of copying, that is, verbatim copying, not the modern test of substantial similarity, which involves a more complex inquiry.

[39] Young (n 1) 42.

gift can cast Homer as taking-without-taking, representing something going from nature to Homer without tainting his genius status.[40]

However, that means that Homer was (and could only be) one step removed from nature, always imitating it.[41] He could only drink nature, accessing it from the outside, accepting its gift.[42] Similarly, modern authors can become natural geniuses by copying Homer, but they can never become Homer. Young's claim that 'the less we copy the renowned antients, we shall resemble them the more' acknowledges that there can be no end to imitation. Caught in a Zeno paradox, it is impossible for us to truly reach originality: although resembling them *more*, they never become *identical* to them.[43] The very moment that Young celebrates originality, he also shows that it can only be an endless chain of imitations: geniuses imitating nature, moderns imitating ancient geniuses imitating nature, and so on. Imitation is thus always already inside genius, sustaining rather than tainting it. Young says that genius is not made, that it grows naturally, but he also shows that it grows through imitation.

Finally, if one wished to take Young at his word and try to imitate Homer rather than his works, how would that look, exactly? Setting aside questions about Homer's identity, that person (if indeed Homer was a person) is long gone. He might have drunk plenty from the 'sole fountain of immortality', but the only kind of immortality Homer has achieved is as the name attached to famous works. The

[40] Young's unstated assumption is that nature, in its copiousness, is willing or happy to feed authors with naturalness. Because he and other contemporaneous authors presented the ancients as generous owners of vast literary estates, Young seems to have envisaged nature as a scaled-up version of that. Obviously not an empirical claim, nature's (or the ancients') putative generosity seems mobilized to make appropriation look like a gift. The nature of the gift is essentially different—gift of works in the first case and gift of genius in the latter—but the gift form is the same. This suggests a supplemental function of the gift. No matter whether they concern Homer or John Doe, narratives of originality as an essential natural feature of the author have to contend with the 'original sin' problem, that is, that the author (ancient or modern) is never quite born an original genius. Even Homer needed a cleansing drink. It is suggested here that, because there is no clearly conceivable way to redeem oneself from the sin of unoriginality (and Young admits that authors actually tend to get more imitative with time), unoriginality (either original or acquired) can be 'cleansed away' only by the forgiveness of those from whom one has copied. Forgiveness takes the form of the gift—a gift that cannot be witnessed or documented, but only cast as the natural outcome of the generosity of the ancients or of nature. This is a gift that does not require a counter-gift: a one-way gift signals that it is an act of forgiveness, not a challenge. The theological framings of early conceptualizations of the author have been widely discussed. But while the focus there has tended to be on narratives about the provenance of original inspiration (*donum dei*, author as creator, etc.), it may be worth looking also at mentions of rites of passage, pilgrimages to and ritual cleansings at sacred springs and rivers, as well as divine forgiveness—actions and rituals concerning the 'purification' of the author from imitation on their way to genius and originality.

[41] The notion of inspiration is mobilized for the same reason, to acknowledge that while one received something, it did not amount to copying. In some cases that can also be done by presenting this borrowing as a gift. But while casting it as a gift would neutralize charges of appropriation, it would not solve the fact that there would still be borrowing involved—a borrowing that reduces originality even when the borrowing is consented to or even presented as an offering.

[42] It does not matter whether this was meant as a cleansing ritual involving the sacred water from Helicon (for Homer to attain full natural genius status), or to nourish the genius he already had. Either way, Homer is represented as receiving something he needed but did not have already.

[43] Young (n 1) 21.

works are all that remain, and yet Young states that any author seeking originality should not imitate them but rather strive to imitate an unknown and no longer existing genius, following in the imaginary footsteps of originality's Garden of Eden. Homer is not a person, but an image mobilized to give a body to a non-present originality—an originality that Young can claim to exist only by keeping it natural (if not divine) and undefinable.[44] Homer is as unreachable as originality itself.

The genius-as-plant could not save Young's discourse of originality from its fundamental tensions and lacunae. What it could do, however, was to reduce sharply the visibility of the problems by relocating his argument on a different stage, with a much smaller cast of characters acting in a much simpler and shorter play. Homer, the *Iliad*, Helicon, thousands of years of literary history, and three centuries of book printing were replaced by the image of one single generic slow-growing brainless vegetable—a vegetable that never wrote a word. The plant growing by absorbing natural nutrients through its roots conveys the same narrative as the one Young tried to articulate through the image of Homer gaining inspiration for the *Iliad* by drinking from the 'breast of nature', but it did so through a simple image with just a few clearly distinguishable parts: leaves, stem, and roots. The plant did not provide Young with a proper stable exemplar of literary originality but rather with a 'living model' through which one could at least *imagine* genius in *slow motion*.

As Young did not pursue a definition of originality as a list of specific attributes but described it as a process of differential imitation, an essentially still image would not have helped him. By contrast, his argument was better supported by a figure that conveyed change, a figure that could capture not a fixed feature, thing, or concept but a process or narrative. When Young says, 'an original [work] may be said to be of a vegetable nature; it rises spontaneously from the vital root of genius; it grows, it is not made', the picture formed is a living plant, not a still life painting of one. Young's reader envisages a plant *in the process of growing*, which allows them to imagine natural originality in action as an organic process of diversification.

At the same time, that action can only be imagined. The plant grows so slowly that the process of its organic differentiation is not perceivable by the human eye. One can *think* of originality as a vegetable process but cannot in fact *see* it. In this sense, the plant functions as an instrument of radical deferral, providing a reasonable-sounding excuse that although originality cannot be seen in action right now, that does not mean that originality does not exist. Its unfolding is presently undetectable, but it will become clear at a later time, slowly but surely. The belief that originality exists rests on the fact that plants always grow.

44 ibid 27: 'Hence Genius has ever been supposed to partake of something Divine.'

Plants Versus Copies

As a living organism, the plant also provided an understandable image for Young's slippery but crucial distinction between imitating and copying, growing, and making. It did so by translating imitation into biological reproduction. Unlike coins identically struck from the same dice, a sexually reproduced plant is a necessarily unique organism that simultaneously 'imitates' its parent plants but cannot be a literal copy of any of them.[45] The figure of genius-as-plant could thus visualize the difference between imitation and copy, while also exemplifying how originality could be born from a certain kind of 'imitation'. This specific role of the plant resurfaces behind Young's claims about the unconsciousness of genius:[46]

> Nor are we only ignorant of the dimensions of the human mind in general, but even of our own. That a man may be scarce less ignorant of his own powers, than an oyster of its pearl, or a rock of its diamond; that he may possess dormant, unsuspected abilities, till awakened by loud calls . . . not more to the world's great surprise, than their own. Few authors of distinction but have experienced something of this nature, at the first beamings of a yet unsuspected genius on their hitherto dark Composition: The writer starts at it, as at a lucid meteor in the night; it is much surprised; can scarce believe it true. During this happy confusion, it may be said to him, as to Eve at the lake, *What there you seest, fair creature, is thyself.*[47]

Because, like a brainless plant, genius grows without any consciousness of itself, its workings remain hidden from and incontrollable by its human host. (It is not the author that has genius, but genius that 'has' the author.)[48] That means that genius can hold other authors' works somewhere within itself and still be perfectly unaware of those works.[49] Genius can 'absorb' other works through the vegetable roots Young says it has, but such absorption does not imply copying or, worse, plagiarism. (From the point of view of a plant's roots, everything is in the public domain, free for the absorbing.) Whatever is drawn in by genius is absorbed as a natural substance, not cultural content; nutritive juices, not somebody's texts.[50]

[45] Even if it were an asexually reproduced clone—a grafted plant—it would not be, properly speaking, a copy but a part of the original plant itself.

[46] Young (n 1) 49–51.

[47] ibid 49–50. The last line in the quote is from Milton's *Paradise Lost*.

[48] Roberta Rosenthal Kwall, *The Soul of Creativity* (Stanford Law Books 2009).

[49] While modern copyright law does not treat unconscious copying as a defense, it construes 'unconscious copying' in opposition to conscious copying—an opposition that is absent in Young's genius. Genius essentially operates outside of consciousness and is thus paradoxically original even if it happened to imitate. Genius does not strive to be either original or imitative because it does not know what is doing. Its originality is rooted in the absence of creative decisions. In that sense, genius is *not* an author.

[50] Young (n 1) 75.

This motif re-emerges in other British literature on creativity, such as Alexander Gerard's 1774 *An Essay on Genius*:

> This faculty [of genius] bears a greater resemblance to nature in its operations than to the less perfect operations of art. When a vegetable draws in moisture from the earth, nature, by the same action by which it draws it in, and at the same time, converts it into the nourishment of the plant: it at once circulates through its vessels, and is assimilated to its several parts. In like manner, genius arranges its ideas in the same operation, and almost at the same time, that it collects them.[51]

The slow absorption of nutrients through the roots of genius looks nothing like the flash of genius but plays the same role. In strikingly different ways—one excruciatingly slow, the other instantaneously fast—both make it look like the author is organically drawing from the unowned public domain, or not copying anything at all.[52]

Slipping into nature

From Justinian to Puffendorff and Locke, it is only when humans modify or control resources drawn from the public domain (or the 'state of nature') that property is produced. But, as mobilized by Young, the genius-as-plant explicitly breaks the distinction between nature and artefact, public domain, and private property. It provides an image of how an original work comes into being but does so by linking originality to non-human natural agency.[53] The notion of 'natural author', however, is an oxymoron that lands Young's argument in a strange place.

[51] Alexander Gerard, *An Essay on Genius* (Strahan 1774), 63–64. (I wish to thank Jose Bellido for bringing Gerard's text to my attention). In addition to Gerard, Martha Woodmansee has commented on how Herder, in 1778, was fascinated by 'the "marvelous diligence" with which living organisms take in and process alien matter, transforming it in such a way as to make it part of themselves', citing his *Vom Erkennen un Empfinden der menschlinchen Seele*: 'The herb draws in water and earth and refines them into its own elements; the animal makes the lower herbs into the nobler animal sap; man transforms herbs into organic elements of his life, converts them to the operation of higher, finer stimuli'. See Woodmansee (n 24) 446–47.

[52] The spring is an additional metaphorical figure that Young deploys to naturalize borrowing. The spring seems to offer its water without telling us where it comes from, providing the drinker with an alibi.

[53] In a private conversation, Simon Stern has argued that Locke's narrative of property-making contains this same tension, which does not, however, undermine it. Humans produce private property by adding their labour to unclaimed materials drawn from the state of nature, and yet the body of the property-maker is a natural body—as natural as the genius that Young attributes to original authors. However, the natural body of the Lockean property-maker (a body that, Stern correctly argues, the property-maker owns despite having done nothing to own it) produces property for its owner by engaging in transformative activities driven by the human owner's decisions (tilling, fencing, picking, etc.). It is a natural body and yet it produces property by enacting the human owner's inventive agency. But that is not the case with Young's genius that, while being as natural as the body of the property-producing person, it just 'does its thing'. It is utterly undirected and uncontrolled by its human host—a host that, rather than possessing and controlling genius, is possessed by it. Locke's narrative includes

In his quest to find and uphold originality, Young ends up presenting the author as two entities folded into one. There is a human person with a name, a history, and a cultural background but in fact, despite inhabiting or sharing that body, the genius authoring the original work is not human but natural, or perhaps even supernatural. This human-natural hybrid, however, is at odds with the legal definition of author—the author whose work may become property.

As the US Copyright Office reminds us, they will register a work only if it 'was created by a human being'[54] and that, conversely, will deny registration to 'works produced by nature, animals, or plants', including 'a work purportedly created by divine or supernatural beings'.[55] The paradoxical implication of Young's argument is that literary compositions can become property because they can be truly original but, by the same token, the naturalness (or perhaps preternaturalness) of that originality would undermine their property status. Vegetable genius is simultaneously cure and poison for literary property.[56]

This fundamental slippage from artefact to nature resurfaces in other descriptions of the production of intellectual property. In 1813, Jefferson wrote about the inventive process as 'a fugitive fermentation of an individual brain'.[57] A fermenting brain is not a growing plant and yet, like the plant, it describes a natural process: not the purposeful sweat of a human inventor's hard-working brain but a natural and 'fugitive' fermentation of their mind. The fermenting brain, the growing plant, and the flashing genius tell different creation stories, but the plot is the same, and always natural.

The naturalization of human authorship is equally central and problematic to Fichte's 1793 'Proof of the Illegality of Reprinting'—the text that most explicitly grounded literary property in the unique form that each author uses to express themselves: 'Each individual has his own thought processes, his own way of forming concepts and connecting them … Hence, each writer must give his thoughts a certain form, and he can give them no other form than his own because he has no other.'[58] The form that Fichte claims each person has does not result from

human agency (in the direction of the body's labour), but Young's narrative represents a purely natural production of private property.

[54] US Copyright Office (n 8) 306.

[55] Like, for instance, '[a]n application for a song naming the Holy Spirit as the author of the work'. See US Copyright Office (n 8) 313.2. On some exceptions to this rule see Andrew Ventimiglia, *Copyrighting God* (Cambridge University Press 2018).

[56] Here and elsewhere, the borrowings from Derrida should be obvious.

[57] Thomas Jefferson to Isaac McPherson (13 August 1813): 'It would be curious then, if an idea, the fugitive fermentation of an individual brain, could, of natural right, be claimed in exclusive and stable property' cited in Merrill D Peterson (ed), *The Portable Thomas Jefferson* (Penguin 1977) 529.

[58] Johann Gottlieb Fichte, 'Proof of the Unlawfulness of Reprinting: A Rationale and a Parable' *Berlinische Monatschrift* (1793) 443, 450–51. See also Martha Woodmansee, 'Fichte: Proof of the Unlawfulness of Reprinting' in L Bently and M Kretschmer (eds), *Primary Sources on Copyright 1450-1900* (Arts & Humanities Research Council 2008) www.copyrighthistory.org. On Fichte's text see Martin Kretschmer and Friedemann Kawohl, 'Johann Gottlieb Fichte, and the Trap of *Inhalt* (Content) and *Form*' (2009) 12(2) *Information, Communication & Society* 41; Maurizio Borghi, 'Owning Form,

education or cultivated taste. The author was born with it and can express himself only with that form because 'he has no other'. It is a necessity, but necessity is the opposite of choice—the distinctive feature of creativity. The author's innate form does produce difference that sets one work apart from others (what Young calls the 'mark of separation'), but that difference or originality is produced through a 'hardwired' natural process—as hardwired and choice-free as the process that makes a plant grow.[59] This tension is explicit in Fichte's key statement about literary property, which is simultaneously powerful and paradoxical: 'What ... can absolutely never be appropriated by anyone else, because this is physically impossible, is the form of the ideas, the combination in which, and the signs through which [the ideas] are presented.'[60] He directly connects literary property with the author's unique form through which s/he thinks, reads, and writes, seemingly anticipating modern copyright law's definition of the original work of authorship. At the same time, his argument flies in the face of received notions of property.[61] One of property's defining features is that it can be alienated, but Fichte states the very opposite: the author owns their expression because it is so unique and internal to the person that it cannot be separated from it (any more than genius can be separated from its human host). This form 'thus remains forever his exclusive property'.[62] It is the author's property not because s/he can alienate it but because s/he *cannot*. One *is* one's form.[63] This is a replay of Young's paradox: a person's expressive form is her property because it is not property, the same way the author is a plant because it is only by being a plant that it can be truly original. (Except that a plant, being not human, cannot produce or hold property.)

Bare difference

Young's discussion of originality explicitly referenced literary property, but mostly treated it as an aesthetic-moral value authors ought to pursue.[64] Fichte's analysis of authorial form and expression provided a conceptual foundation for literary

Sharing Content: Natural-Right Copyright and Digital Environment' in Fiona MacMillan (ed), *New Directions in Copyright Law*, vol 5 (Edward Elgar Publishing 2007) 197–222; Mario Biagioli, 'Genius Against Copyright: Revisiting Fichte's Proof of the Illegality of Reprinting' (2011) 86 *Notre Dame Law Review* 1847.

59 Young (n 1) 42.

60 Fichte (n 58) 450.

61 Thanks to Alain Pottage for pointing out the paradoxical nature of Fichte's statement. Interestingly, Fichte did not use this definition of property in his later work on the subject (see Jean-Christoph Merle, 'Fichte's Political Economy and His Theory of Property' in David James and Gunter Zoller (eds), *The Cambridge Companion to Fichte* (Cambridge University Press 2016) 199–221).

62 Fichte (n 58) 451.

63 Straddling the line between possessing a unique expressive form and being possessed by one's own genius.

64 Young (n 1) 20, 54.

property, but it was only the first episode of his life-long philosophical engagement with the nature of subjectivity.[65] These concerns were not commonly found in the trenches of eighteenth-century copyright disputes, where the operational definition of originality was not connected to philosophical or aesthetic discussions of human creativity but to a simple forensic test: a composition was original if its words and the order of those words were different from that of other compositions.[66] What mattered were visible character sequences, not the opaque workings of the human mind. And in any case originality seemed to be more the exception than the rule in book publishing.[67] Even Young had to admit that 'it is a medly, a mass; and a hundred books, at bottom, are but One'.[68]

Does this mean that Young's and Fichte's philosophical-aesthetic discussions were less central to the development of copyright than they have been made out to be? After all, modern copyright doctrine hinges on the author's personal expression but not on the aesthetic qualities of the work produced by such expression. Taken at face value, Young's obsessive celebration of literary originality would seem to diverge from legal questions of copyrightability, but while the praise of famous 'originals' took up much of his book, his figure of genius as plant captured, in fact, the production of bare difference, not of aesthetic quality.[69] Young was not interested in vegetable growth because plants are beautiful but because they all grow differently from all other specimens of their same variety. Products of genius may be aesthetically pleasing but genius was not an aesthetic concept itself.

Similarly, Fichte's essay is often taken to exemplify the Romantic concept of genius, but that overlooks the fact that Fichte does not discuss the uniqueness of expressive form as a mark of literary quality.[70] His claim encompasses human

[65] Fichte started to lecture and circulate drafts of what became the *Wissenschaftslehre* at Jena in 1794, one year after publishing 'Proof of the Unlawfulness of Reprinting'. The centrality of the unique cognitive and expressive form seems to dovetail with his later discussion of the creatively representational nature of knowledge, which 'is not in things, and does not stream out of them. It streams out of [us], insofar as it exists, and it exists out of our own being', quoted in Robert Richards, *The Romantic Conception of Life* (University of Chicago Press 2002) 73.

[66] Simon Stern, 'Copyright, Originality, and the Public Domain in Eighteenth Century England' in Reginald McGinnis (ed), *Originality and Intellectual Property in the French and English Enlightenment* (Routledge 2008) 69, 79.

[67] That is one of the central claims of Stern (n 66).

[68] Young (n 1) 43.

[69] Young drew a surprisingly simple connection between originality and aesthetics: people appreciate original compositions more than imitative ones because they are surprised by them: 'Our spirits rouze at an *Original*; that is a perfect stranger, and all throng to learn what news from a foreign land' (12).He actually exoticized original compositions by comparing them to a prince from the New World: 'And tho' it comes, like an *Indian* Prince, adorned with feathers only, having little of weight, yet of our attention it will rob the more Solid, if not equally New' (12). The value of originality, therefore, is essentially psychological: surprise. Originality is also valuable to the author, who receives credit for their whole new work rather than partial credit for a new elaboration of a pre-existing work (11).

[70] Commenting on a painting by Correggio, Fichte does, however, connect a viewer's attraction to a painting to the artist's unique form: '[E]very painter can put colors on a canvas, paint light and shadow, a child and a young woman. But that it not what interests us; what interests us is rather the indescribable yet perceptible form of the presentation.' See Fichte (n 58) 468. His short and isolated comment,

cognition in general: each and every human can think and write only through their unique form, which is irreducible to others. Everybody is a genius, which means that nobody is one. (It is also completely irrelevant to Fichte's argument what one may be thinking or writing about).

Despite their substantially different goals, audiences, and styles, Young, Fichte, and those deep in the trenches of eighteenth-century copyright *querelles* all agreed that an original literary composition (that is, one that had not been copied from another) was bound to look *visibly* different from that of any another author. As Fichte put it, an author's proprietary form amounts to 'the phrasing and wording in which [her ideas] are presented'.[71] Conversely, according to Blackstone, if two texts displayed the same character sequence, one was a copy: 'the same composition, cloathed in the same words, must necessarily be the same composition'.[72] While they could not reach an agreement on where originality came from, or on its aesthetic and philosophical significance, they all shared the same operative *forensic* view of originality: different words in a different sequence. That was a literary composition's birthmark or, as some argued, its 'face'.

According to Young, 'No two faces, no two minds are just alike; but all bear nature's evident mark of separation on them'.[73] Two decades later, in a text that Francis Hargrave had planned to deliver in *Donaldson v Beckett*, he argued that a 'literary work [that is] *really* original, like the human face, will always have some singularities, some lines, some features, to characterize it, and to fix and establish its identity'.[74]

The two arguments—one by a poet and literary critic and one by a lawyer—are virtually identical. They also indicate the functional equivalence between the face and the plant. Young was concerned with 'nature's mark of separation' or 'mental individuality'—that which makes original authors 'singulars'.[75] Similarly, Hargrave looked at the unavoidable lines in one's face to establish identity, that is, its *perceivable* marks of originality. However small the differences between two faces (or two plants) may be, there will be differences. And no matter its cause, that kind of irreducible difference is a visible fact, not a matter of complex judgment. A face is a fingerprint writ large, not a signature one learns how to inscribe (and possibly forge).

The face is explicitly presented as human—a simultaneous affirmation of the uniqueness of the work and of its human author—and yet Young's and Hargrave's argument does not depend on its humanness at all. The face's identifying function

however, does not elaborate on 'what interests us', leaving it unspecified whether that 'interest' in Correggio lies in his style and composition or just in the uniqueness of his style—its difference.

[71] ibid 447.

[72] William Blackstone, *Commentaries on the Laws of England*, vol 2 (Oxford 1766) 406.

[73] Young (n 1) 42.

[74] Francis Hargrave, *An Argument in Defence of Literary Property. The Second Edition: To Which Is Added*... (Otridge 1774) 6.

[75] Young (n 1) 42.

results from the lines it carries—lines that, like the unique look of a plant, have been produced by nature, time, and accidents not by the creativity of the human whose body the face is part of. As an image of irreducible difference, the face and its unique lines are equivalent to the irreducible singularity of the plant. Unlike the plant, however, the figure of the face and its lines can migrate across the human/animal divide.

In the wake of *Naruto v Slater*,[76] the US Copyright Office denies registration to works of animals like monkey selfies (which have attracted much attention precisely because of the human-like expression of Naruto, a photogenic crested macaque). But it has also denied registration to works resulting from 'the appearance of actual animal skin'[77] like, for instance, prints of okapi rumps—'like okapi, each imprint is unique and one-of-a-kind'—or those that rhinoceros produce by pressing their face on paper.[78] What would Young and Hargrave say about these unique animal faces?[79] Do they still exemplify originality?

There is no clear evidence that some people thought of animals as 'authors' in the late eighteenth century, although similar possibilities are present today, owing to the questions arising around non-human authorship by AI systems.[80] That is not, of course, a direct consequence of Hargrave's or Young's early mobilization of the face as an image or originality. All the figures of the plant and the face did was to help to bypass unsuccessful attempts to define human originality, recasting it instead as the natural production of bare difference unconnected to aesthetic quality, canons, or genres. That did not amount to a critique of the assumption that authorship could only be human. However, once originality is thought of as bare difference produced by natural causes and exemplified by plants or faces, it no longer seems strange to entertain the possibility that the work of authorship could be also the product of animals or machines. And while the reduction of originality to bare

[76] 888 F 3d 418 (9th Cir 2018).

[77] US Copyright Office (n 8) 313.2: 'To qualify as a work of "authorship" a work must be created by a human being', and gives these examples as uncopyrightable works produced by animals or natural processes: 'A photograph taken by a monkey', 'A mural painted by an elephant', 'A claim based on the appearance of actual animal skin', 'A claim based on driftwood that has been shaped and smoothed by the ocean', 'A claim based on cut marks, defects, and other qualities found in natural stone' https://www.copyright.gov/comp3/docs/compendium.pdf (accessed 1 September 2022).

[78] See eg the 'Savage' exhibits at the Bakehouse Art Complex, Miami, FL (1 June 2013) https://www.youtube.com/watch?v=Jk5xBnE6maQ. The rhino facial imprints are at 00:58. Various other skin imprints (lizards, snakes, iguanas) can be seen throughout the exhibit. But see also prints of okapi rumps: 'Striking white imprint on black canvas … Like okapi, each imprint is unique and one-of-a-kind and is available from the Cincinnati Zoo on 12"x16" canvas and numbered card of authenticity' https://support.cincinnatizoo.org/site/Donation2;jsessionid=00000000.app30112a?idb=1653399013&DONATION_LEVEL_ID_SELECTED=1&df_id=1562&mfc_pref=T&1562.donation=form1&NONCE_TOKEN=1FE1C8BDD61DD5B119B64DD14A4BFA7C&idb=0.

[79] https://support.cincinnatizoo.org/site/Donation2;jsessionid=00000000.app30112a?idb=1653399013&DONATION_LEVEL_ID_SELECTED=1&df_id=1562&mfc_pref=T&1562.donation=form1&NONCE_TOKEN=1FE1C8BDD61DD5B119B64DD14A4BFA7C&idb=0.

[80] Annemarie Bridy, 'Coding Creativity: Copyright and the Artificially Intelligent Author' (2012) 25 *Stanford Technology Law Review* 5.

difference may now undermine the humanness of copyright, it was a conceptualization that, over two centuries ago, seemed fundamental to giving foundations to copyright law.

Single plant to complex ecologies

Today's cultural environmentalists have refocused attention on the romantic genius' importance in copyright law and policy, but paint it in distinctly negative terms.[81] No longer an image of radical innovation, it now stands accused of enabling an ideology of maximal authorial rights that stifles innovation by privatizing and depleting the public domain.[82] However, as they try to reverse what they see as the deleterious effects of the ideology of the romantic author, the cultural environmentalists do so with yet more images of organic growth: pastures, forests, and wetlands.[83]

That figuration started to emerge in the early 1980s, with David Lange arguing that:

> In certain useful respects, the public domain in the field of intellectual property today can be compared to the public grazing lands on the Western plains of a century ago ... If it is fair, as we seem to have decided in this century it is, to require the users of public lands to prepare impact statements as a condition of their use, then perhaps it is also fair to require similar assurances before we permit the outright appropriation of the territory of the creative subconscious.[84]

While early copyright supporters converged on the figure of the *individual* author or genius and their originality (figured as one individual plant), today's critics focus on the public domain (figured as a naturally thriving but increasingly threatened ecology of *many interconnected* entities).[85] Accordingly, while the workings of genius were inherently mysterious, Lange's opaque reference to

[81] James Boyle and Lawrence Lessig have been the main promoters of cultural environmentalism and the knowledge commons. See the articles in James Boyle (ed), 'Public Domain' (2003) 66 *Law and Contemporary Problems* 1–2, 1 ff and the anniversary issue on cultural environmentalism in the same journal: James Boyle and Lawrence Lessig (eds), 'Cultural Environmentalism @ 10' (2007) 70 *Law and Contemporary Problems* 2, 1 ff.

[82] This is the central claim of James Boyle's *Software, Shamans, and Spleens* (Harvard University Press 1995).

[83] This reflects an important positive recasting of the public domain. Until very recently, it was seen as something between a quarry and a cemetery, providing the raw materials for the production of property, as well as a resting place for expired patents and copyrighted works. Exceptions were David Lange, 'Recognizing the Public Domain' (1981) 44 *Law and Contemporary Problems* 147; Jessica Litmann, 'The Public Domain' (1990) 39 *Emory Law Journal* 965.

[84] Lange (n 83) 175–76. He then concluded: 'The field of intellectual property law at large sometimes seems to be beyond the possibility of exhaustion. But then, that was the view taken by the public toward the buffalo as they were being hunted one hundred years ago. And where are the buffalo now?' (178).

[85] James Boyle, 'The Opposite of Property?' (2003) 66 *Law and Contemporary Problems* 1.

the public domain as 'the territory of the creative subconscious' signals a similar difficulty in describing the relationship between the public domain and the production of the new. The same way genius was unintelligible to the author's human consciousness, Lange paints creativity as a feature of an ecology whose complexity makes it opaque to understanding, rendering it 'unconscious'.

Once the public domain becomes conceptually and visually analogized to the environment (and, somewhat confusingly, to both the early modern commons and the 'commons of the mind'),[86] a series of discursive moves become not only possible but almost natural (pun intended). Cultural production and IP are assumed to somehow grow from the public domain. A healthy public domain can then sustain the production of IP that, at the expiration of patent or copyright protection, goes back into the public domain, refertilizing it.[87]

In an age when it has become natural to talk about complex and often collaborative multi-factoral processes of cultural production as ecologies, Boyle's articulation of Lange's image of the public domain into a full-fledge framework for cultural environmentalism and commons-based, collaborative knowledge production was rather apt and, twenty years later, even commonplace. Except that a cursory glance at science and technology studies shows that when scholars and policymakers refer to knowledge commons or collaborative innovation ecologies, they do not have in mind wetlands, forests, and village pastures but highly techno-legal infrastructural arrangements—platforms, not prairies.[88]

One could argue that the contradiction is only apparent, that the parallel between the public domain and the knowledge commons (or the 'commons of the mind') was meant only as a catchy analogy. The public domain, the environment, or the 'commons of the mind' are materially distinct and Boyle never literally identifies collaborative knowledge production with organic growth in the public domain *qua* environment. What connects them is a functional analogy: they are all threatened by 'enclosure' through privatization, which causes either ecological harm (in the environment) or the depletion of creative capacities (in the case of the public domain and the knowledge commons). However, far from marginal or

[86] On the blurry edges of the public domain and its overlap with information commonly or functionally described as being in the commons see Pamela Samuelson, 'Mapping the Digital Public Domain' (2003) 66 *Law and Contemporary Problems* 147. The title of James Boyle's book on the topic—*The Public Domain: Enclosing the Commons of the Mind* (Yale University Press 2008)—indicates an embrace of the conceptual merger, despite the essential difference between the two concepts.

[87] The conceptualization of IP production in environmental terms is also found in Peter Jaszi and Martha Woodmansee, 'Beyond Authorship: Refiguring Rights in Traditional Culture and Bioknowledge' in Mario Biagioli and Peter Galison (eds), *Scientific Authorship* (Routledge 2003) 165–223. It resurfaces, as we will see, in the discourse of *terroir* at the foundation of geographical indicators.

[88] Brett Frischmann, *Infrastructure: The Social Value of Shared Resources* (Oxford University Press 2012); Brett Frischmann, Michael Madison, and Katherine Strandburg (eds), *Governing Knowledge Commons* (Oxford University Press 2014).

accidental, these functional and structural analogies frame and animate the entire cultural environmentalist discourse.

Despite their material differences, Boyle closely relates the public domain, the early modern agricultural commons, and the knowledge commons because of the perceived dematerialization of contemporary knowledge-making processes, making them ecological in form. The modern knowledge commons do not involve rivalrous excludable things and resources but very many bits of information distributed across the ecology:

> [I]nformation products are often made up of fragments of other information products; your information output is someone else's information input. These inputs may be snippets of code, discoveries, prior research, images, genres of work, cultural references, or databases of single nucleotide polymorphisms— each is raw material for future innovation.[89]

It does not matter to knowledge-making whether these information bits relate to music or polymorphisms because, according to Boyle, knowledge and cultural products are no longer produced from things or the elaboration of material evidence but emerge from information gathering, sampling, and recombining. In this new informational terroir, knowledge means producing information from other information, mashup-style.

It crucially follows from this assumption that if one manages to keep all that information freely accessible to many differently skilled and variously incentivized networked collaborators, more information will be produced somehow. (No individual genius required.) Such newly produced information will then become the input for the development of more information down the line, and so on. The ecology will keep going, fed by and feeding 'distributed creativity'.[90] This is key to Boyle's ecological model. In response to the question of 'whether a global network actually transforms our assumptions about creativity and innovation', he proposes:

> Assume a random distribution of incentive structures in different people, a global network: transmission, information sharing and copying costs that approach zero, and a modular creation process. With these assumptions, it just does not matter why they do it. *In lots of cases, they will do it.* One person works for love of the species, another in the hope of a better job, a third for the joy of solving puzzles, and so on. Each person has his own reserve price, the point at which he says, 'Now I will turn off Survivor and go and create something'. But on a global network, *there are a lot of people, and with numbers that big and information*

[89] James Boyle, 'Second Enclosure Movement and the Construction of the Public Domain' (2003) 66 *Law and Contemporary Problems* 33, 41.

[90] ibid 44.

> *overhead that small, even relatively hard projects will attract motivated and skilled people* ... Under these conditions ... we will get distributed production without having to rely on the proprietary/exclusion model. The whole enterprise will be much, much, much greater than the sum of the parts.[91]

This scenario looks diametrically opposite to the workings of the individual romantic genius, but the picture turns out to be comparably natural. The production of new information does not require an individual flash of genius or driving inspiration from the springs of Helicon. It results instead from the work of millions of intelligent but not unique authors relentlessly gathering, sorting, and collaboratively processing information following standardized modular protocols—the opposite of how genius was said to operate. However, out of sheer number, some of them (irrespective of their specific personal motivations) are bound to produce new relevant knowledge, provided the information is there—plenty and accessible. The opacity of the instantaneous performance of the individual romantic genius is now replaced—as already suggested by Lange—by the comparable opacity of the complex interactions of multiple actors, actants, and data spread across a knowledge ecology. In both cases, cultural production somehow 'grows'—as a plant in the first instance and as network effects and spillovers in the second: 'The whole enterprise will be much, much, much greater than the sum of the parts'.

Ecological figures of cultural production convey a powerful large-scale image of both the production of intellectual property and the problems stemming from its overuse, but they do so by formally naturalizing the production of knowledge and intellectual property—a scaled-up and de-individualized replay of Young's and Fichte's naturalization of authorial originality. Genius theorists naturalized individual creativity, but Boyle naturalized distributed creativity by rendering individual motivations irrelevant and replacing 'inspiration' with the dispersed presence of massive amount of accessible information, thus transferring to the ecology the capacity to produce the new. Reframing the public domain as an ecology has supported a very effective critique of the ideology of the romantic author, directing us to rethink the author in terms of distributed agency and creativity. However, free from human motivations and incentives and opaque in its complexity, this distributed agency looks like a new kind of genius called emergence.[92]

[91] ibid 46 (author's emphases).

[92] It is suggested here that the mushroom, not the plant, may be its figure. See Anna Lowenhaupt Tsing, *The Mushroom at the End of the World: On the Possibility of Life in Capitalist Ruins* (Princeton University Press 2015).

Conclusion

If the seemingly unavoidable categorical slippages between originality and imitation, nature and culture, or between the public domain and private property can be found in different sophisticated works from different countries and periods (works that try either to establish the figure of the creative and property-making author or oppose the effect of that role and figure), then it may be worth considering that the problem starts with the dichotomy, not with the slippages.

Like real property, IP has been conceptualized as the result of a transformation brought about by either the author or the inventor—a transformation that takes something from the unowned public domain (which includes nature) and turns it into property (a social artefact). Dichotomies between nature and society, discovery and invention, originality and imitation are inherently unstable, but are there other ways to conceive and justify the protection of intellectual products that would neither reify these dichotomies nor endlessly slip between one side and the other? That question can only take us to a hypothetical and virtually unchartered territory, but there are a few developments in IP law that could be used as starting points.

In both the US Plant Patent Act (PPA) of 1930 (about asexually reproduced plants) and the International Convention for the Protection of New Varieties of Plants (UPOV) of 1961, 1972, 1978, and 1991 (also concerning sexually reproducible plants), the breeder is not required to disclose the ways in which she has produced the plant variety she wishes to protect. What replaces that traditional requirement is a detailed description and illustration (typically a photograph) of the plant itself. To obtain a patent or 'breeder's rights', the applicant also needs to show that such a variety is new, distinct, and stable, and that the breeder can reproduce it.[93] This radical departure from patent law's fundamental emphasis on the inventive step and its specification means that, in these cases, the crucial distinction between invention and discovery, nature and artefact, has been effectively bypassed.

In turn, this means that the inventive step is not expected to be the result of human agency alone. If what creates the patentable innovation or the breeder's right is the distinctiveness of the variety rather than how its distinctiveness came to be, then it does not matter how the credit for the production of that variety ought to be parsed between nature's random mutations and the breeder's selective interventions. For instance, UPOV bypasses discussions of the nature of the inventive step altogether, limiting itself to defining 'breeder' as 'a person who bred, or *discovered and developed* a variety'.[94] Similarly, the PPA states that: 'Whoever *invents or*

[93] Bugos and Kevles (n 2); Alain Pottage and Brad Sherman, 'Organisms and Manufactures: on the History of Plant Inventions' (2007) 31 *Melbourne University Law Review* 539; UPOV, art 1 http://www.upov.int/en/publications/conventions/1991/act1991.htm.

[94] UPOV, art 1 (n 93) (author's emphasis).

discovers and asexually reproduces any distinct and new variety of plant, including cultivated sports, mutants, hybrids, and newly found seedlings ... may obtain a patent therefor.'[95] The PPA even allows that a new plant variety may have two kinds of coinventors—one who discovered it and one who successfully reproduced it.[96]

The distinction between discovery, reproduction, and development or breeding is thus treated as utterly irrelevant to patentability. Obviously the breeder has to be human in order to apply for breeder's rights, but there is no pretence that what s/he may gain protection for was ever the exclusive product of human inventiveness. The varieties protected by UPOV and PPA are not Young's vegetable geniuses, but they still end up destabilizing notions of authorship and inventorship conceived in strictly human terms.[97]

The doctrine of geographical indicators (GIs) provides another case in which intellectual property law seems to forget or dismiss the nature/society divide that provides its conceptual and political foundations. Increasingly important, for different reasons, in both developed and developing countries, GIs are conceptually related to trademarks and protect place-specific denominations like 'parmesan cheese', 'tequila', or 'champagne'.[98] In this case, much more so than in the UPOV and the PPA, there is an explicit acknowledgment that the distinctiveness of a certain product—a cheese, a wine, a kind of rice, a traditional artefact—derives from a mix of human agency, technique, and natural environment or *terroir*. A geographical indicator 'serves to designate a product originating therein, the quality/characteristics of which are due exclusively or essentially to the geographical environment, including *natural and human factors*'.[99]

Even more intriguing is that GIs do away with the traditional assumption that authors and inventors should be individually identified. The individuals who contributed to the development of a certain food product or cultural artefact[100] now

[95] US Plant Patent Act, amended 3 September 1954, 68 Stat 1190 http://www.uspto.gov/web/offices/pac/plant/index.html#3 (author's emphasis).

[96] 'Inventorship' http://www.uspto.gov/web/offices/pac/plant/index.html#3. It should be borne in mind that, in this case, 'reproduction' is even less authorial than it already sounds. It means, literally, cloning—as in the physical transfer of part of a plant onto another plant stub through grafting.

[97] There is a further analogy between the two cases. Like Young's ineffable genius that produces novelty without knowing or being able to describe how, at the time that PPA and UPOV were first introduced, it seemed unreasonable or even impossible to ask the breeders to describe the genetic changes that had rendered their varieties new and distinct. There might, therefore, be a relation between the implicit partial crediting of the inventive step to nature (that is, the blurring of discovery and invention), and the fact that, in those cases, the inventive step could not be fully described.

[98] See Madhavi Sunder, 'The Invention of Traditional Knowledge' (2007) 70 *Law and Contemporary Problems* 97, who offers a sympathetic reading of the possibilities provided by GIs for the protection of so-called traditional knowledge. A more critical take is Rosemary Coombe, 'Legal Claims to Culture in and Against the Market' (2005) 1 *Law, Culture and the Humanities* 32. A more comprehensive discussion of GIs and their history is in Dev Ganjee, *Relocating the Law of Geographical Indications* (Cambridge University Press 2012).

[99] 'Lisbon Agreement for the Protection of Appellations of Origin and their International Registration', art 2(1) (author's emphasis) http://www.wipo.int/lisbon/en/legal_texts/lisbon_agreement.htm#P2 2_1099.

[100] See eg several Indian sarees https://web.archive.org/web/20150427132918/http://textilescommittee.nic.in/services/geographical-indications#pochamp (accessed 16 September 2022).

protected by GIs are not treated as individual authors, nor do they hold individual rights in the knowledge involved in producing those products. They are instead seen as 'human factors'—elements of an ecology. They need to be local, but their individual identity is irrelevant as is, to some extent, the point in time at which they made their contributions to the development of that product. Humans are almost cast as assistants to either a *terroir* or a cultural ecology—the more stable and enduring agential entity.

These are only a few examples, but hopefully sufficient to show that the nature/society dichotomy, the definition of author and inventor, and the distinction between discovery and invention involve seemingly intractable conceptual tensions[101]—tensions that, however, do not seem to prevent the articulation of new forms of intellectual property, some of them concerning plants. Does that suggest that the conceptual foundations of IP are perhaps less foundational than has been assumed? Or does it mean that it is necessary to reform those foundations to better align them with the actual processes through which innovation is produced, even though that might yield something rather different from intellectual property as it has always been known?

The figure of the plant and of organic growth have not solved the conceptual conundrums discussed in this chapter but have been able to capture them, for both supporters and critics, from the eighteenth-century to the present. Like the canary in the coalmine, the plant has kept alerting us to some of difficult problems developing in the tunnels of intellectual property but, unlike other sentinel species, it has not signalled to get out. Or maybe we were not paying attention.

[101] For another example of how the discovery/invention distinction may be becoming essentially blurred see Biagioli and Pottage (n 3) 236–40.

2
Denaturing Bacteria
The Sewage Patent Controversy and Biotechnology

Daniel Schneider

Introduction

In 1914, sanitary engineers in the United States formed an organization with the unlikely name 'National Septic Process Protective League'. Eventually representing over 200 municipalities, the league was established to battle the Cameron Septic Tank Company of Chicago, which had sued the cities for infringing their patented sewage treatment process. After a 'long and stubborn contest in which many engineers and municipalities ... cooperated to resist' the patents, Cameron and the league reached an agreement in 1919. Relieved that the controversy might finally be over, the *Engineering News Record* praised 'this remarkable league of states, cities, companies and individual engineers who have stood united in the long fight'.[1] The Cameron Septic Tank case was just one of several sewage patent cases in the early part of the century in which public health officials, sanitary workers, and municipal and state engineers organized against the commercialization of science and engineering. They formed groups opposed to the patents, published detailed critiques, testified in court, and encouraged municipalities to resist the demands of patent syndicates.

The conflict over patents centred on issues of public over private interests in sewage treatment, municipal infrastructure, and science and engineering more broadly. By 'public' is meant public in multiple senses, all of which contributed to the opposition to patents. Biological sewage treatment was established on research performed by public bodies in the public interest. The research was funded by the public itself, typically through municipal governments and local taxation. The research was also made public—disclosed to the broader scientific community—in journal articles, in scientific meetings, and through the movement of scientists and engineers nationally and internationally. Finally, and perhaps most fundamentally, scientists and engineers considered the bacterial action responsible for treating the sewage to be essentially a natural biological process. These engineers believed that,

[1] 'Septic Tank Patent Settlement in Sight' (1919) 82 (22) *Engineering News Record* 1041.

Daniel Schneider, *Denaturing Bacteria* In: *Intellectual Property and the Design of Nature*. Edited by: Jose Bellido and Brad Sherman, Oxford University Press. DOI: 10.1093/oso/9780192864406.003.0002

as 'Nature's means or methods',[2] sewage treatment processes should belong to the public at large. Because the controversy implicated the idea of natural processes as common property, whether a sewage process could be privatized by the grant of a patent led to a questioning of whether the process was considered natural or artificial. As a result, many engineers charged that inventors and courts distorted nature itself.

Much of this early twentieth-century opposition to patents resonates with current controversies over the patenting of software, business practices, pharmaceuticals, or research performed by public institutions. Scholars have typically dated these concerns to the late twentieth century, when developments in biotechnology and related public policy led to an increased emphasis on patents. A constellation of factors in the 1980s led to the establishment of the so-called triple helix of industry, government, and university involvement in technological innovation and intellectual property. During this period, the key techniques for producing recombinant DNA were developed and patented, the Supreme Court case *Diamond v Chakrabarty* permitted the patenting of life forms, and the US government passed the Bayh–Dole Act and other legislation that encouraged researchers to file for patents on work funded by the government. As a result, governments and academia made patenting an important part of their research, and licensing and joint undertakings with industry increased substantially.[3]

However, as Angela Creager points out, much of the recent history of biotechnology has focused on the manipulation of DNA as a novel characteristic in the structure of the new industry rather than on the altered relations between laboratory and market exemplified by patenting.[4] The sewage patent controversies

[2] *Cameron Septic Tank Company v Village of Saratoga Springs and Others* 151 F 242 (1907) 261.

[3] RS Eisenberg, 'Public Research and Private Development: Patents and Technology Transfer in Government-Sponsored Research' (1996) 82 *Virginia Law Review* 1663; Henry Etzkowitz and Loet Leydesdorff, *Universities and the Global Knowledge Economy: A Triple Helix of University–Industry–Government Relations* (Pinter 1997). Sally Smith Hughes, 'Making Dollars Out of DNA: The First Major Patent in Biotechnology and the Commercialization of Molecular Biology, 1974–1980' (2001) 92 *Isis* 541; Daniel J Kevles, '*Diamond v Chakrabarty* and Beyond: The Political Economy of Patenting Life' in Arnold Thackrey (ed), *Private Science: Biotechnology and the Rise of the Molecular Sciences* (University of Pennsylvania Press 1998) 65–79; Daniel L Kleinman, *Impure Cultures: University Biology and the World of Commerce* (University of Wisconsin Press 2003); Harold Varmus, 'Perspectives from Different Sectors: Government' in National Research Council, *Intellectual Property Rights and Research Tools in Molecular Biology: Summary of a Workshop Held at the National Academy of Sciences, 15–16 February 1996* [1997]; Andrew Webster and Kathryn Packer, 'When Worlds Collide: Patents in Public-Sector Research' in Henry Etzkowitz and Loet Leydesdorff, *Universities and the Global Knowledge Economy: A Triple Helix of University–Industry–Government Relations* (Pinter 1997) 48–59.

[4] Creager and a number of other researchers have examined the much earlier controversies over the patenting of scientific research supported by universities and the government. Angela NH Creager, 'Biotechnology and Blood: Edwin Cohn's Plasma Fractionation Project, 1940–1953' in Arnold Thackrey (ed), *Private Science: Biotechnology and the Rise of the Molecular Sciences* (University of Pennsylvania Press 1998) 39–62; Rima D Apple, 'Patenting University Research: Harry Steenbock and the Wisconsin Alumni Research Foundation' (1989) 80 *Isis* 375; C Weiner, 'Patenting and Academic Research: Historical Case Studies' in Vivian Weil and John W Snapper (eds), *Owning Scientific and Technical Information: Values and Ethical Issues* (Rutgers University Press 1989) 87–109; John W Servos,

highlighted those relations. These patent conflicts called into question the proper role of the scientist and engineer in society. Sewage treatment patents generated such opposition because of the important relationship between sanitary science and engineering and public interest. A significant group of engineers worked in local and state government, on sanitation, roads, and public utilities. These municipal engineers—working for public agencies rather than corporations—were instrumental in the development of modern sewage treatment. The contrast between the public character of sanitary engineering practice and the privatization inherent in patenting produced a profound unease from the engineers. They reserved particular opprobrium for municipal engineers who, despite the public nature of their work, patented the processes they developed while working for cities. This history complicates histories of engineering by David Noble and others, who emphasize its instrumental role in the rise of corporate capitalism as engineers mobilized the powers of science and technology.[5] In the sewage treatment patent controversies, however, engineers were central in critiquing the patenting and privatization of research and the reach of corporate interests.

Patent law and policy have not been static. In Britain, patents were originally a grant from the British crown for a monopoly to produce a given product, but were eventually restricted to new inventions only. They were still granted on an ad hoc basis and no formal administrative structure for patenting existed. In the United States, the 1789 Constitution specifically empowered Congress to provide for patents and copyright. The first US patent law was enacted in 1790 and specified that a patent could be granted to 'any useful art, manufacture, engine, machine, or device, or any improvement therein not before known or used'. Through a variety of legislation and legal interpretation, a modern, bureaucratized patent system began to emerge in the mid-1800s out of the 'pre-modern' assemblage of common law and traditional practice that had existed previously.[6]

'Engineers, Businessmen, and the Academy: The Beginnings of Sponsored Research at the University of Michigan' (1996) 37(4) *Technology and Culture* 721.

[5] Debate in the literature on the engineering profession, its accommodation to capital, and attempts at reform largely ignore the role of publicly employed, municipal engineers. With interests very different from those of privately employed engineers, they strongly promoted the public interest and were the ones involved in the patent controversies. David F Noble, *America by Design: Science, Technology and the Rise of Corporate Capitalism* (Oxford University Press 1979) 84–109; see also Peter Meiksins, 'The "Revolt of the Engineers" Reconsidered' (1988) 29(2) *Technology and Culture* 219 for a re-examination of Noble's argument.

[6] Brad Sherman and Lionel Bently, *The Making of Modern Intellectual Property Law: The British Experience, 1760–1911* (Cambridge University Press 1999). This transition was by no means smooth. Adrian Johns describes the powerful mid-century attacks on patents by important industrialists in Great Britain that was almost successful in repealing the whole patent system. Nonetheless, despite the developing critique, the patent system emerged even stronger and, by the end of the nineteenth century, intellectual property rights systems were further reinforced through national laws and international conventions. See Adrian Johns, *Piracy: The Intellectual Property Wars from Gutenberg to Gates* (University of Chicago Press 2009) 258–89.

Despite the legal systematization of patenting and the modernization and bureaucratization of the process, sanitary engineers remained deeply opposed to certain classes of intellectual property. In the nineteenth century, courts in the United States and England began expanding on what class of invention qualified for the term 'manufacture', and began to treat the process, or the method of making a product or performing a task, as a manufacture itself. The courts expanded what was considered a patentable invention to include these less tangible manufactures. The sewage patent controversy called these long-standing decisions in the US and English courts into question. Despite the opposition, however, US courts ruled that the sewage patents were valid. For the courts, the key determination was not whether sewage processes should be public or private, but whether they were natural or artificial; the term 'useful Arts'—enshrined in the US Constitution as the subject matter for patents—is, after all, related to 'artifice' and 'artificial'. In ruling sewage processes to be fundamentally artificial, they became valid subject matter for patents and were subsequently privatized.

The debates concerning sewage were instrumental in establishing patents in industrial microbiology in general. In these cases, scientists, engineers, patent officials, and the courts fought out fundamental questions on the patentability of bacterial processes, as well as of the micro-organisms themselves. The failure of this opposition movement to curtail the patenting of sewage treatment processes had direct implications for the modern expansion of patenting, leading to the classification of living organisms themselves as intellectual property.

The Septic Tank Syndicate

In 1896, Donald Cameron, surveyor for the English city of Exeter, received a British patent on his design for a tank that he had built to treat the city's sewage. Many previous sewage treatment techniques had prevented the putrefaction of sewage and its resultant odours by killing the resident micro-organisms. In contrast, Cameron's tank relied on the action of anaerobic bacteria to digest—or liquify—sewage solids. The septic tank's preliminary treatment allowed the sewage to be more easily treated by other chemical or bacteriological means. Cameron, coining the term 'septic tank' to contrast his tank with the *anti*septic nature of previous processes, promoted his invention in the engineering press and to the British Royal Commission on Sewage Disposal. He received a British patent for the septic tank in 1896 and was issued with a US patent in 1899. The Cameron Septic Tank Company was established soon afterwards to receive royalties for the invention's use in the United States.[7]

[7] Donald Cameron and Frederick James Commin, 'Improvements in the Treatment of Sewage, and in Apparatus therefor' (1896) 21 *British Patent* 142; Donald Cameron, 'The Septic Tank System of Sewage Treatment' (1897) 74 *The Builder* 27; 'The Exeter Septic Tank System' (1899) 39 *Engineering*

The Exeter treatment plant attracted the great interest of sanitary engineers around the world. Cameron even erected an observation chamber in the tank to enable visiting engineers to climb down through a manhole and see the septic process in action from behind a viewing window. Engineers in the United States saw great promise in the system and began designing their own treatment plants. However, instead of modelling their tanks on the Exeter design, engineers applied the concept of septic action in general to tanks of a wide variety of shapes and configurations. The Cameron Septic Tank Company notified the cities that had installed any tank using anaerobic action that they were in violation of the patent. Indeed, the US patent differed from the British in one key respect. When Cameron filed for a US patent, he claimed to have invented not only a tank of a specific design in which the septic process took place, but also to have invented the septic process itself. The company demanded 5 per cent of the construction cost of the plant as a licence fee, as well as an additional 3 per cent for each year the plant had been operating without a licence.[8]

Leonard Metcalf, a consulting engineer from Boston, was surprised to receive a letter from the Cameron Septic Tank Company claiming infringement from a tank he had designed and installed. He initiated the broader opposition to the patent by presenting a paper to the American Society of Civil Engineers that criticized Cameron and encouraged his 'brother engineers' to resist the patents. Cameron's tank, he argued, was anticipated by the long history of sewage treatment tanks going back to 1852.[9] Other engineers soon joined Metcalf and, on the basis of their arguments, many cities refused to pay royalties. Few engineers expected that the Cameron patents would be upheld. F Herbert Snow, a consulting engineer, city engineer for Brockton, Massachusetts, and later chief engineer of the Pennsylvania State Department of Health, did 'not think for a moment that proprietary rights in the septic system need be a subject for serious apprehension'.[10] Another engineer, busy designing a sewage plant for an Illinois town, assured its mayor: 'I am paying no attention to the claims of the Cameron Company.'[11]

Record 379; 'Testimony of Mr Donald Cameron' (18–19 October 1898) *Royal Commission on Sewage Disposal, vol II, Evidence* (London 1902) [Cd 686]; Donald Cameron, Frederick J Commin, and Arthur J Martin, 'Process of and Apparatus for Treating Sewage' US Patent 634, 423 (3 October 1899).

[8] Anson Marston, 'Septic Tank Patents' (1908) 35 *Municipal Engineering* 288.

[9] Leonard Metcalf, 'The Antecedents of the Septic Tank' (1901) 27 *Proceedings of the American Society of Civil Engineers* 506; see also 'Review of the History of the Septic Tank' (1906) 5 *Engineering News* 56, 111–12.

[10] Frank Herbert Snow, 'Discussion: Antecedents of the Septic Tank' (1901) 46 *Transactions, American Society of Civil Engineers* 472, 472.

[11] Testimony of John W Alvord in *Cameron Septic Tank Company v Village of Saratoga Springs and Others* 1100 US 276 *Record*, vol II (1908) 852–55, 852, US Court of Appeals, 2nd Cir National Archives and Records Administration, Northeast Region, New York, NY (Transcript of *Cameron Septic Tank Company v Village of Saratoga Springs and Others*).

Some towns and cities succumbed to Cameron's demand for royalties. Plainfield, New Jersey, confronted by the company, sought the assistance of New Jersey's Sewage Commission, but the Attorney General determined that the state did not have funds to hire special counsel to defend the city. The Sewage Commission encouraged Plainfield to contest the suit, but the city settled with the company as a cheaper alternative to going to court.[12] In contrast, Saratoga Springs, New York, faced with an infringement suit, joined with other cities to defend in court its use of the septic process. The trial and subsequent appeals were followed closely by the engineering profession. The most prominent sanitary engineers of the period testified for the cities; each development in the case was reported in the chief newspaper for the civil engineering profession. Engineers could follow the course of the legal proceedings, and the texts of the trial and appeals court decisions were reprinted in full.

In 1907, the trial judge agreed with the municipal engineers on the validity of the septic patents, stating: 'There is no new … function performed by the tank. It receives and holds sewage as it always has.' Nor had Cameron invented a new process, the judge declared; rather, he had simply relied on a 'process of nature'. 'As a closed tank, pure and simple', the judge ruled that:

> [i]t holds the sewage placed therein … and enables one of the processes of nature to go on therein. Such always has been and such always will be the function of such a tank. That the process described goes on therein may have been a new discovery, but the process of nature is not caused by the tank.[13]

Cameron appealed the decision. While the Appeals Court agreed with the trial court on the apparatus claims—that is, there was nothing novel about the design of the tank itself—it sustained all of the process claims. The septic process itself—the liquefaction of sewage solids using anaerobic bacteria—was found to be patentable.[14]

The engineering community reacted with shock: 'This is the reverse of all former decisions in lower courts, both state and United States and of the opinions of engineers generally', reported *Municipal Engineering*.[15] In response, engineers organized more broadly. 'Without some organization, all municipalities having sewage tanks would practically be at the mercy of a strong company', wrote Anson Marston, an engineering professor at Iowa State University who had designed a

[12] 'Patent Claims. Plainfield's Case' Report of the State Sewerage Commission of the Legislature, Session of 1905, 13–15.

[13] *Cameron Septic Tank Company v Village of Saratoga Springs and Others* (n 2) 248–49. The decision was also reprinted in the engineering press: 'Decision in the Cameron Septic Tank Suit against Saratoga Springs, NY' (1907) 57 *Engineering News* 347.

[14] *Cameron Septic Tank Company v Village of Saratoga Springs and Others* 159 F 453 (1908) 458,

[15] 'Septic Tank Patents Sustained' (1908) 34(2) *Municipal Engineering* 94.

number of septic tanks. In response to the threat from Cameron, Marston became chair of an organization representing mostly small Iowa towns.[16] Two months after the Appeals Court decision, engineers representing over twenty municipalities and state boards of health formed the larger 'Association for the Defense of Septic Process Suits'[17] to take an appeal to the US Supreme Court. Although the appeal failed, the engineers were not deterred. On studying the Appeals Court decision, their argument was that there could be many ways of constructing and operating a septic tank that would not infringe the patent—for instance, by simply cleaning the tanks every few months. The association thus advised its members not to pay any damages to Cameron until their specific plant had been determined to infringe patent laws.[18] The League of California Municipalities also organized a group to defend its member cities against the Cameron patent claims, with the state and the Association for the Defense of Septic Process Suits both providing legal assistance.[19] As a result of this nationwide organizing, the Appeals Court decision was widely ignored. The *Engineering News Record* later reported that: 'Numerous cities, counties, states, the United States itself, have ignored the patents. So have public institutions, private corporations and individuals. And so have unnumbered engineers.'[20]

When Cameron initiated additional suits even after the presumed expiration of their patent, the League of Iowa Municipalities called for another organization to defend infringement suits and formed the National Septic Process Protective League. Within five months, over seventy municipalities had joined this organization.[21] In 1919, their resources finally exhausted by the endless litigation, Cameron offered to settle all remaining claims by the league for a nominal sum of US$5,000. The *Engineering News Record* noted this final disposition of the case with its testimony to the 'remarkable league of states, cities, companies and individual engineers'.[22]

[16] Marston (n 8) 294.

[17] 'Statement of the Association for the Defense of Septic Process Suits' (1908) 60(7) *Engineering News* 181.

[18] Marston (n 8); 'The Association for the Defense of Septic Process Suits' (1909) 61(1) *Engineering News* 26, at 26. The Appeals Court noted that the septic tank differed from previous tanks in that there was no accumulation of sludge, so the tank never needed cleaning. Engineers argued that by cleaning tanks periodically, they would no longer infringe on the patent. A Marston to EW Stanton (27 May 1909), Anson Marston Papers, University Archives, Iowa State University, Ames, IA.

[19] 'The Septic Tank in California' (1910) 28 *Municipal Journal and Engineer* 119.

[20] 'End of Septic Tank Patent' (1916) 74(14) *Engineering News* 663.

[21] 'League of Iowa Municipalities Calls Conference to Contest Claims for Payment of Royalty for Use of Septic Process of Sewage Treatment' (1916) 45 *Engineering and Contracting* 216; 'National Septic Process Protective League' (1916) 75(12) *Engineering News* 578; 'The National Septic Process Protective League' (1916) 76(3) *Engineering News* 141; 'A Septic Tank Infringement Suit' (1916) 76(18) *Engineering News* 866.

[22] 'Septic Tank Patent Settlement in Sight' (1919) 82(22) *Engineering News Record* 1041.

Monopolizing Natural Processes

The most fundamental critique of the sewage patents centred on the contested position of the bacterial processes involved in treating sewage. Proponents of bacterial processes considered biological sewage treatment to rest on natural processes. As such, both critics of patents and inventors themselves thought of the septic process as 'natural'. Metcalf, for instance, described the septic process as 'essentially a natural one, a process of Nature'.[23] The Merchants Association of New York declared Saratoga Springs' septic plant an illustration of 'the employment of Nature's forces'.[24] But it was not only opponents of the patents who viewed the process as natural. The patent examiner for the septic tank had initially denied the patent on such grounds, arguing that the process occurred by itself in ordinary sewers and stagnant ponds, and was not patentable.[25] Even Cameron, before he patented the septic tank, considered the process to be natural in a fundamental sense: 'In this system . . . there is no "treatment" of the sewage in the ordinary sense of the term; its purification being accomplished entirely by natural agencies.'[26]

However, as a natural process, biological treatment had another fundamental property. It could not be patented, privatized, or monopolized because it belonged to the public at large. As expressed by the trial judge in the septic tank case: 'This development of bacteria is a fundamental truth in nature. In patent law it is a principle. It is a process of nature, but a principle, and not patentable.' As 'nature's means and methods', he continued, these bacterial processes are 'common property, and cannot be appropriated and monopolized by anyone'.[27]

Processes had occupied a complicated position in patent law since Watt's eighteenth-century steam engine patents. In early patent law, patents were to be granted for a 'manufacture', considered to be a tangible thing. It was clear that an apparatus, like a steam engine, might fall into that category, but what about a 'method of lessening the consumption of steam in steam engines' to make them more efficient? When Watt developed such an invention, his patent was challenged on the grounds that it was not 'a manufacture' and thus not a valid subject matter for a patent, resulting in the landmark case of *Boulton v Bull*. The court debated whether Watt's invention was a method, a principle, or a machine. Was a method a manufacture if it did not produce a new substance? Or could a method 'detached

[23] Metcalf (n 9).

[24] The Merchants' Association of New York, *The Battle of the Microbes: Nature's Fight for Pure Water* (1908) 6.

[25] United States Patent and Trademark Office (USPTO), Patent No 634, 423.

[26] Cameron (n 7) 27. Nevertheless, when Cameron applied for his patent in the United States, he emphasized in his specification that he had invented an 'artificial method . . . for the purification of sewage' (USPTO, US Patent 634, 423).

[27] *Cameron Septic Tank Company v Village of Saratoga Springs and Others* (n 2) 261.

from all physical existence whatever' be patented? The judges of the court were initially split on this question, and Watt's patent was not found to be valid.[28]

Over the next fifty years, perhaps paying heed to Chief Justice Eyre's warning in *Boulton v Bull*, courts began defining processes in such a way that they increasingly came under patent protection. Eyre noted that 'two-thirds, I believe I might say three-fourths, of all patents granted ... are for methods of operating and of manufacturing' and cautioned that 'we should well consider what we do in this case, that we may not shake the foundation upon which these patents stand'. At first, patents on processes were allowed because the courts judged that the patents were in fact not on a method, but on an altered machine that would implement that method. Thus, Watt's patent on a 'method for lessening steam consumption' was considered to be, in fact, a patent for the critical modification he made to engine design, in this case that of a separate condenser. Patents on chemical processes were not on the processes themselves, but rather on the saleable product of the chemical process—the medicine or dye or other chemicals produced. By the mid-nineteenth century, however, processes themselves, independent of their products or implementing machinery, began to be fixed in law as patentable in both the United States and England. Eyre's opinion in the Watt patent case had begun to establish this distinction:

> The word 'manufacture', in the statute ... applied not only to things made, but to the *practice of making*, to principles carried into practice in a new manner ... Under the *practice of making*, we may class all new artificial manners of operating with the hand, or with instruments in common use, new processes in any art producing effects useful to the public ... I think these *methods* may be said to be *new manufactures*.[29]

It was not until 1842, however, that the courts firmly established methods as proper subject matter for patents in the United Kingdom.[30] These decisions in England influenced patent law in the United States. In 1877, a process was defined by the US Supreme Court as:

> [a] mode of treatment of certain materials to produce a given result. It is an act or a series of acts, performed upon the subject matter, to be transformed and reduced to a different state or thing. If new and useful, it is just as patentable as a piece of machinery.

[28] With the judges split, the case was not decided either way. See *Boulton v Bull*, 2 H Bl 463, 494 (1795). The patent was affirmed unanimously in a later case, *Hornblower v Boulton* 8 T R 95 (1799).

[29] *Boulton v Bull* (n 28) 492, 494.

[30] Sherman and Bently (n 6) 108.

This decision severed the connection of a process with any particular device: 'The process requires that certain things should be done with certain substances, and in a certain order; but the tools to be used in doing this may be of secondary consequence.'[31] Processes were thus legally distinct from apparatus, and each category of invention was patentable.

Distinguishing either a process or a machine from a principle was perhaps more difficult for the courts. Patents were to be granted for invention, not discovery. The discovery of a natural principle could not come under protection of a patent. Around the middle of the nineteenth century, courts in England and the United States, in a series of related cases, began to grapple with these distinctions. According to the US Supreme Court ruling in 1853: 'A principle is a fundamental truth.' 'A principle is not patentable', the Court declared.[32] A treatise on patents from this period reiterated one of the justices' remarks from *Boulton v Bull*: while a 'mere principle' could not be considered a 'manufacture', 'a principle so far embodied and connected with corporeal substances, as to be in a condition to act and to produce effects in any art . . . becomes the practical manner of doing a particular thing. It is no longer a principle but a process'.[33] As the Supreme Court ruled, invention lay not in the discovery of the principle, but in the development of 'the processes used to extract, modify, and concentrate natural agencies'.[34] Altering nature thus became a prerequisite for finding an invention. As intellectual property scholars Brad Sherman and Lionel Bently concluded, the mid-nineteenth century marked the period when 'it was clear that in law it was the artificial or created nature of the final product, its distance from Nature, which ensured that an object became an invention rather than a mere discovery'.[35]

Processes, then, were differentiated from machines on the one hand, and principles on the other. They were a distinct kind of invention and became valid material for patents. By the time of the sewage battles, legal scholars considered the law settled on this matter.[36] Yet while the courts and legal scholars may have delineated the philosophical and legal outlines of processes, principles, and machines, the distinctions were still highly problematic in the scientific and engineering community, and there was no consensus. Patentees, patent examiners, and the scientific community at large were commonly confused by these distinctions and, despite the rulings of the courts, engineers resisted the notion that processes themselves

[31] *Cochrane v Deener* 94 US 780 (1877) 788.

[32] *Le Roy v Tatham* 55 US 156 (1853) 175.

[33] George Tickner Curtis, *A Treatise on the Law of Patents for Useful Inventions in the United States of America* (Charles C Little and James Brown 1849); see also *O'Reilly v Morse* 56 US 62 (1854).

[34] *Le Roy v Tatham* 55 US 156 (1853) 175.

[35] Sherman and Bently (n 6) 46.

[36] For the United States see William C Robinson, *The Law of Patents for Useful Inventions*, vol 1 (Little, Brown 1890) 230–59; for Great Britain see Robert James, *The Grant and Validity of British Patents for Inventions* (John Murray 1903).

could be patented and monopolized, with one engineering commentator noting that there persisted a marked 'prejudice against process patents'.[37]

Sanitary engineers drew a fundamental distinction between the ethics of patenting apparatus and patenting processes in sewage treatment. Much of the apparatus used in a sewage plant—pumps, distributers, diffusers—was patented, and there were no engineer protests over these patents. Rather, it was patents on processes themselves that created the most controversy. As F Herbert Snow wrote: 'The validity of patents issued for appliances to facilitate the [septic] action is not questioned.' However, he added that 'the exclusive right to the natural process may well be'.[38]

This distinction between apparatus and process on the part of the engineers can be seen in the different reception of Cameron's septic tank patent and another patent for a sewage digestion tank. Because of Cameron's royalty demands, many cities turned to other means of treating sewage, most notably the so-called Imhoff tank, designed by German sanitary scientist Karl Imhoff. Even though this tank too was patented, it did not provoke the same outcry as Cameron's patent. Imhoff's patent was on the design of the tank itself—on apparatus—rather than on the process. In contrast to the many tanks that had been used to digest sewage, including the septic tank, the Imhoff tank was a two-storey tank that separated the physical settling process from anaerobic digestion. Engineers recognized the novelty of the design and were willing to accept its patenting. Further, Imhoff's royalty demands were seen as modest, reflecting a commitment to the public interest in sewage treatment rather than a desire for profit.[39] As a result, many cities converted their septic tanks to Imhoff tanks and these tanks became the standard treatment technique prior to activated sludge.[40]

In the *Cameron* case, the distinction between process and apparatus led to nonsensical results that helped reinforce the widespread prejudice from sanitary engineers towards process patents. The Appeals Court denied the apparatus claims for the septic tank, ruling that the design of the tank was anticipated and thus not novel. The process claim, however, was left intact, leaving builders of septic tanks in

[37] For confusion of patent examiners over sewage process patents see USPTO, Patent No 770,490. The quotation is from ED Sewall, 'The Status of Process Inventions' (1910) 17 *Machinery* 10.

[38] Snow (n 10) 474.

[39] Karl Imhoff, 'Sewage Treatment Apparatus' US Patent 924, 664 (15 June 1909); Leonard P Kinnicutt, CEA Winslow, and R Winthrop Pratt, *Sewage Disposal* (Wiley 1919) 174–75; 'Cameron Septic Process and the Imhoff Tank' (1912) 66 *Engineering Record* 504; WT Waters, 'Sewage Disposal Plans of Atlanta, Ga' (1911) 40 *Municipal Engineering* 1. For a town with a population of 100, the licence on an Imhoff tank was US$10. For a city of 100,000, the fee was US$2,550. 'War Status of Imhoff and Other German Patents' (1917) 78 *Engineering News Record* 565. The primary opposition to Imhoff's tank came from other inventors. Imhoff was (unsuccessfully) sued in Germany for infringement on Travis' patent for the hydrolytic tank, and Cameron considered Imhoff's tank to infringe on the septic process and threatened suit, but these suits never materialized.

[40] 'Remodeling of Septic Tanks into Imhoff Tanks Eliminates Odors from Land Irrigation' (1915) 71 *Engineering News Record* 747.

a very confused situation. 'The decision of the Court of Appeals permits the public to build without infringement tanks in strict accordance with Cameron's apparatus claims', explained the Association for the Defense of Septic Process Suits in disparaging the opinion. The association continued:

> While the public may do this much without infringement the one thing the public must *not* do is to permit natural agencies to become operative, for then, the Court decides, Cameron's process patent claims are infringed. Nature must be circumvented in some way (the Court does not say how), or legal difficulties will follow.[41]

By patenting a process of nature, Cameron had twisted reason, logic, and nature itself.

The distinction between principle and process was made more complex by the actions of the sanitary profession itself. Bacterial treatment processes had not always been viewed as natural. When these were first introduced, many sanitary scientists considered the septic tank, bacteria bed, and biological filter to be artificial processes, compared with the natural process of treating sewage by distributing it on soil. Researchers on bacterial treatment undertook an explicit programme to naturalize these 'artificial' processes by emphasizing their reliance on natural bacteria. Thus, Cameron emphasized how his septic tank was based on 'natural agencies'. At the same time, however, engineers also denatured these biological processes through a continual concentration, intensification, and control of the bacterial activity. These simultaneous processes of naturalization and denaturing were fundamental in creating the industrial ecosystem of the sewage treatment plant, but also allowed researchers, lawyers, and judges to emphasize distinct aspects of the system. Opponents of patenting saw the ecosystems as fundamentally natural and thus not open to appropriation. The courts, however, negated that view by declaring the denatured biological processes artificial, one of the 'useful arts' that might be patented under the US Constitution.[42]

The Cameron Septic Tank Company denied that it was trying to patent the natural process of anaerobic action itself. As one spokesman argued: 'The patent … makes no pretense that Cameron was the inventor of putrefaction, and of course, such a pretense would be absolutely absurd.'[43] Instead, Cameron claimed his invention was to separate the anaerobic action from the aerobic, in a way that was not present in nature, making the septic process an 'artificial method'. The trial judge had concluded that the septic process was natural. Does 'nature's method and means of doing a thing become an "artificial method" of doing the same thing', he

[41] 'Statement of the Association for the Defense of Septic Process Suits' (n 17) 181.

[42] US Constitution, art 1 s 8.

[43] 'Testimony of William Main' *Record*, vol I, 272, Transcript of *Cameron Septic Tank Company v Village of Saratoga Springs and Others* (n 11).

asked, simply by providing 'an artificial place … like a tank, constructed by human hands, in which nature by its own instrumentalities is to perform its own process?' 'No', the judge concluded. The bacteria 'develop, as they always had done, and always will do, under certain conditions, and when developed they liquefy certain materials, as they always had done, and as they always will do if not prevented'.[44] Unlike the trial judge, however, the Appeals Court accepted the argument that the septic process was indeed an artificial method. To Saratoga Springs' argument that septic action 'is a process of nature and one which cannot be covered by any one', the Appeals Court ruled that the septic process was not natural, but rather artificial. It emphasized the industrial nature of the process as the feature that distinguished the microbial activity in the septic tank from a natural one, ruling that 'the distinctively novel feature is the … separate workshop for the microbes'.[45] Cameron had separated the processes of aerobic oxidation and anaerobic putrefaction, making his septic tank an artificial, rather than a natural process.

'The Chaos of Pure Science and Natural Processes'

Controversy over the patentability of natural processes permeated other industrial ecosystems as well. 'Micro-organisms appear to have gone into business', declared patent lawyer J Howard Flint in 1930. 'Imperceptibly their myriads have crept into industry, where they are nourished and pampered for the work they do.' While extolling the potential of the innovations coming from industrial microbiology, he wondered: 'Will patent law protect investments in this new factor in industry?' Flint saw the critical impediment to patent protection to be how the courts interpreted the kinds of problems that the engineering and scientific communities had been exposing in the sewage patents, asking: 'Can any good patent at all come out of the chaos of pure science and natural processes involved?'[46] The decisions in the septic tank case helped firmly establish the patentability of bacterial processes in general.

Two key cases in industrial bacteriology addressed these issues, and both cases relied heavily on the findings of the court in the *Cameron* septic tank case. These cases centred on the patenting of bacterial cultures and process for the production of acetone and butyl alcohol. Chaim Weizmann, future president of Israel, was appointed in the chemistry department at Manchester University in 1904, and worked on industrial fermentations. At Manchester, Weizmann isolated a bacterium that fermented starch to produce acetone and butyl alcohol. By the

[44] *Cameron Septic Tank Company v Village of Saratoga Springs and Others* (n 2) 259–60.

[45] *Cameron Septic Tank Company v Village of Saratoga Springs and Others* (n 14) 462.

[46] J Howard Flint, 'The Relation of Patent Law to Biological Processes' in Henry Field Smyth and Walter Lord Obold (eds), *Industrial Microbiology: The Utilization of Bacteria, Yeasts and Molds in Industrial Processes* (Williams and Wilkins Co 1930) 285.

beginning of the First World War, acetone had become essential to the British war effort in the production of smokeless cordite. With its supplies cut off from the Continent, England was desperate to find replacements. Weizmann's bacteria were able to accomplish the efficient conversion of corn-starch to acetone, with butyl alcohol as a by-product. Weizmann was at first reluctant to file a patent, but at the urging of the head of research for Nobel's Explosives Company, he applied in 1915.[47] The process was implemented on an industrial scale, first in Canada and then in Peoria, Illinois, and Terre Haute, Indiana, closer to the sources of corn-starch.[48] Following the war, it was found that butyl alcohol could be used in the manufacture of quick-drying lacquers used for automobile finishes. With this potentially large commercial market, the production of the alcohol became the primary goal, with acetone as a by-product. Weizmann licensed his process to the Commercial Solvents Corporation, which began commercial production. A competitor, the Union Solvents Corporation, soon began producing butyl alcohol using the same bacterial process, and perhaps the same bacteria.

In 1931, Commercial Solvents sued Union Solvents for patent infringement. In its defence, Union Solvents claimed the invention unpatentable, as a patent on 'the life process of a living organism'.[49] The court case focused on whether the production of butyl alcohol and acetone was simply a 'natural function' of the bacteria and thus not a patentable invention.[50] To demonstrate that the process was natural, Union Solvents presented the court with evidence of the natural soil environment of the bacteria and attempted to show that the same processes that occurred in the fermentation vessels also occurred in the natural soil habitat of the bacteria:

> The bacteria ... by their life processes during their growth and multiplication, produce, as a kind of by-product butyl alcohol, ethyl alcohol, acetone and gases ... This is the natural function of these bacteria. There is not the slightest proof in the record that they can go through their life processes ... without necessarily producing the products named above.[51]

Union Solvents' expert was the by-then renowned bacteriologist Edwin O Jordan, who had first studied sewage bacteria at the Lawrence Experiment Station. Jordan

[47] Jehuda Reinharz, *Chaim Weizmann: The Making of a Statesman* (Brandeis University Press 1985) 45–46.

[48] See Reinharz (n 47) for the most detailed account of the development of this fermentation process.

[49] The decision is in *Guaranty Trust Company of New York and Others v Union Solvents Corporation* 54 F 2d 400 (1931); *Union Solvents Corporation v Guaranty Trust Company of New York, The Butacet Corporation, and Commercial Solvents Corporation* Brief for Appellant, 74, National Archives and Records Administration (NARA), vol 1725, NARA-Mid Atlantic, RG 276, US Court of Appeals, 3rd Cir, Case 4866.

[50] Comment of Court, 53; Opening for Defendant, 63; 'Testimony of Clark' 53, *Record*, vol I, *Union Solvents v Guaranty Trust*, Equity 802, District Court, Delaware, NARA-Mid Atlantic RG 21, Box 272.

[51] Brief for Appellant, 74–75, NARA, vol 1725, NARA-Mid Atlantic, RG 276, US Court of Appeals, 3rd Cir, Case 4866.

applied the ecological perspective that he had shown in his studies at Lawrence and argued that the butyl-alcohol bacteria were producing these products 'in the soil feeding upon the substances found there'.[52] Commercial Solvents' response to this argument reveals the contradictory nature of the industrial organism. Commercial Solvents engaged the services of a bacteriologist at the University of Wisconsin, Dr Elizabeth McCoy, a leading expert on the particular class of bacteria used in the process. Asked if she considered the industrial use of the bacteria as 'carrying out the natural functions of those organisms', McCoy replied: 'They are, of course, natural functions in the sense that the organisms are doing this process.' However, she continued, that 'they are not natural functions in the sense that they occur in nature necessarily'.[53] By providing the right conditions in an artificial environment, people had turned a *natural* process into an *artificial* one.

The courts of the time were willing to consider patents on processes *using* bacteria, but they were unwilling to grant patents on living things themselves. Union Solvents accused Weizmann of trying to patent the bacteria themselves. This was the same argument that had been used in the *Cameron* case, where the court had ruled that the septic patent was valid as it was on a process, not the bacteria. Union Solvents tried to use the *Cameron* decision to argue that no such process was claimed by Weizmann, only the bacteria themselves: 'If the Weizmann patent is a patent on anything at all, it is a patent upon this alleged Weizmann bacteria as such, and that only.'[54] To Commercial Solvents' reply that 'we have not attempted in the patent to patent the organism itself', the Court replied: 'You hardly could.' Commercial Solvents' lawyer agreed: 'Of course, you could not do it.' Instead, Commercial Solvents argued that bacteria were simply an 'agency of nature, the use of which for practical purposes can be patented', in the same way that 'chemicals, minerals, or anything else' could be patented.[55] The court agreed with Commercial Solvents, citing *Cameron* as precedent for its decision.

Another important contemporary patent case in industrial microbiology also rested on the decisions in *Cameron* as well as *Guaranty Trust*. The US Patent Office saw this case as an opportunity to rule definitively against microbial patents. In the end, however, with the help of the decision in *Cameron*, the Patent Office was overruled, and microbial process patents continued. In the 1920s, Samuel C Prescott and Kisaku Morikawa studied the bacterial flora of the ferment used to produce rice wine, in search of undescribed bacteria that 'may have technical significance and

[52] 'Testimony of Edwin O Jordan' *Record*, vol II, 1317–18, *Union Solvents v Guaranty Trust*, Equity 802, District Court, Delaware, NARA-Mid Atlantic RG 21, Box 272. On Jordan see Carolyn G Shapiro-Shapin, '"A Really Excellent Scientific Contribution": Scientific Creativity, Scientific Professionalism, and the Chicago Drainage Case, 1900–1906' (1997) 71(3) *Bulletin of the History of Medicine* 385.

[53] *Union Solvents v Guaranty Trust*, Equity 802, District Court, Delaware. *Record*, vol II, 1524–25, NARA-Mid Atlantic RG 21, Box 272.

[54] Arguments on Final Hearing, 195. *Union Solvents v Guaranty Trust*, Equity 802, District Court, Delaware, NARA-Mid Atlantic RG 21, Box 272.

[55] ibid 131.

find use in industry'. They isolated a bacterium that fermented the sugar in rice to isopropyl and butyl alcohols when grown in pure culture. Their name for this new species emphasized the industrial character of their research: *Bacillus technicus*.[56] They sought a patent on the culture of *Bacillus technicus* as well as on the process of using the culture to produce the higher alcohols. The Prescott patent came out of an environment of sewage and industrial bacteriology at the Massachusetts Institute of Technology (MIT) similar to that of Weizmann at Manchester. Prescott was a student of William Sedgwick, who had conducted the first studies on the bacteria of sewage filters. His first job after graduating from MIT was as a chemist and bacteriologist at the Worcester sewage treatment plant, and he was the author of the primary text in the early 1900s on the bacteriology of water and sewage. Along with MIT graduates and professors Earle Phelps, William Sedgwick, and Lawrence Experiment Station biologist Stephen DeM Gage, he formed a loose association of industrial and sanitary bacteriologists named the 'Bug Club' that would discuss advances in sanitary and industrial microbiology. He later succeeded Sedgwick as head of the Department of Biology and Public Health at MIT, but he shifted the focus of the department from sanitation towards industrial microbiology.[57]

In their patent application, Prescott and Morikawa claimed a 'ferment consisting of a culture of the hereinbefore described *Bacillus technicus*'. The patent examiner rejected the claim of the 'ferment' 'as being for essentially a living organism'. 'Living organisms are not patentable', he declared.[58] The inventors replied by arguing that bacteria were fundamentally different from other organisms: 'Of course the statement that a living organism is unpatentable sounds plausible because when we think of living organisms we think of a man or a dog or a bear or something which has a separate and known existence and is old.' Rather, they were claiming 'a culture of the bacillus ... free of admixture with other organisms'.[59] Following this reply, all official responses to the patent application were drafted by the Principal Examiner in the division, Vernon I Richard. For several years, Richard had been faced with numerous claims on both bacterial processes and the bacteria themselves and was unwilling to approve patents for what he considered to be 'principles of nature'.[60] Richard tried to use the Prescott and Morikawa patent to establish a standard in the Patent Office of denying claims on bacteria and many bacterial processes. Richard

56 K Morikawa, 'A New Butyl and Isopropyl Alcohols Fermentation' (1927) 3 *Bulletin of the Agricultural Chemical Society of Japan* 28.

57 Samuel A Goldblith, *Pioneers in Food Science Volume I. Samuel Cate Prescott: M.I.T. Dean and Pioneer Food Technologist* (Food & Nutrition Press 1993); SC Prescott, 'A Brief Sketch of the History of the 'Bug Club' (Boston Bacteriological Club),' Appendix E in Goldblith ibid.

58 'Specification', 13; 'Paper No. 2' 2; USPTO, Patent No 1,933,683.

59 'Paper No 3a, 16 March 1928'; USPTO, Patent No 1,908,361.

60 See eg the patent application of Alexander Izsak and Forest J Funk for a process of producing butyl alcohol, acetone, and isopropyl alcohol using *Clostridium saccharobutylicum-gamma*. The claims 'are for no more than the inherent activity of the organism named, or, in other words, for a principle of nature', stated Richard. USPTO, Patent No 1,908,361.

stated that his decision in rejecting the Prescott and Morikawa application was to act as a precedent in the Patent Office for all similar future claims.[61]

Richard provided the inventors with an analogy to support his contention that claiming the 'ferment' was the same as claiming the bacteria. As Sedgwick had naturalized bacterial action by invoking natural selection and ecology, Richard's analogy served to naturalize the *Bacillus technicus* in the face of attempts to industrialize it:

> A 'culture' of bacteria consists of a substance, which contains the bacteria, and maintains it in living conditions, and is analogous to a mass of water containing gold-fish. The gold-fish are grown, that is, 'cultured' in water ... and almost identical words will describe the culture, handling, and maintaining of bacteria. It frequently occurs that a previously unknown or unidentified organism is found in a pond of stagnant water, but its discoverer never for a moment believes he made or invented it ... The 'ferment' of [the] applicant cannot be an article of manufacture. Nor is it a composition of matter, any more than water containing a gold-fish is such a composition.[62]

For Richard, the inventors could claim a process for isolating the bacillus, a new process for culturing it, or a new process 'in which it might be used to produce either a new or old substance'. Yet, the inventors could not claim the bacterium itself. Neither, argued Richard, could they receive a patent for the process they had described, for the bacterial fermentation was simply an inherent character of the bacteria. 'The function of all bacteria is fermentation', he stated. '*B. Technicus* fermentation produces butyl- and isopropyl alcohols. That is their natural function and these claims recite nothing more ... It is a "principle of nature" that these bacteria produce those alcohols.'[63] The inventors gave up on trying to convince the Patent Office to approve the claim on the bacteria itself and withdrew the claim on the ferment. However, they insisted on the patentability of their 'process of producing mainly butyl- and isopropyl alcohols ... with a substantially pure culture of the herein described *Bacillus technicus*'. Once again, the examiner denied the claims: 'These claims are for a law of nature.' The Patent Office's response demonstrates that, despite rulings such as that in *Cameron*, there was no consensus on the status of process patents.

Prescott and Morikawa appealed the denial to the Patent Board of Appeals. Richard saw the opportunity to establish a precedent and provided a detailed Examiner's Statement that first presented the biology of single-celled organisms,

[61] 'Amended Feb 26, 1931' (30 July 1931); USPTO, Patent No 1,933,683.

[62] 'In response to amendment filed Mar 15, 1928' (4 January 1929); USPTO, Patent No 1,933,683.

[63] 'Responsive to amendment of June 26 and letter of July 11 1929' (1 February 1930); USPTO, Patent No 1,933,683.

their habitat, their food, their biochemical processes, and, finally, the relation between their biology and their use in industrial processes. By focusing on the biology of the bacteria, Richard sought to naturalize them. He forcefully stated his opposition to the patentability of living processes: 'Bacteria grow. Man has never made one, and, so far as known, cannot make one. Their function is fixed without human agency; why then should a man receive a patent which is for no more than that function?' He added that Prescott and Morikawa's patent 'is not a claim for a process in which the power of the bacteria to ferment material is made use of ... but a claim for the power, the fermentation itself'.[64]

In the appeal, both sides grappled with the decision in the *Cameron* case. The inventors emphasized the similarities between the industrial production of alcohol using bacteria and the septic tank stating that: 'The Cameron case was a bacteriological case. The patentability of bacteriological processes such as is here under discussion has long been recognized.' The brief placed the process using *Bacillus technicus* in the context of the septic tank: 'In the words of the Court in Cameron v. Saratoga Springs, [Prescott and Morikawa] put the force of nature into a certain specified condition.'[65] By doing so, they had invented a new process, eligible for patenting. Richard, for his part, made a point of distinguishing this case from *Cameron* by emphasizing the specific steps 'each caused by an act of man' by which the sewage was 'subjected to the action of anaerobic bacteria'. In contrast, he argued, Prescott and Morikawa were claiming only the fermentation itself, with no separate steps caused by human action.

The inventors also emphasized the similarity of their process to other chemical processes. 'It is merely confusing the issue to talk about living organisms', they stated, continuing that:

> The question why we call bacteria things of life, yeast a plant and a crystal growing in a solution an inorganic compound and devoid of life is interesting philosophically but not important from the point of view of the Patent Office. The organism in question is a chemical agent ... In a sense it is comparable to a synthetic dyestuff first made in a laboratory. This reagent when placed in a certain chemical environment, that is, a sterile fermentable sugar mash, operates in some specifically unknown way to effect a chemical reaction which is new and which produces a new result of high importance in the arts.[66]

Even the name, *Bacillus technicus*, seemed to imply that the bacteria were more chemical than living organisms.

[64] 'Examiner's Statement' (20 April 1932) 14; USPTO, Patent No 1,933,683.
[65] 'Brief for Applicants' Paper 16, 5, 8; USPTO, Patent No 1,933,683.
[66] ibid 13.

During the six years that the Prescott patent was being examined and adjudicated in the Patent Office, the *Guaranty Trust* case was decided in the Appeals Court. The Patent Board of Appeals relied on this decision, which was itself decided on the basis of *Cameron*, and rejected the argument of the examiner. Quoting *Guaranty Trust*, that Weizmann 'obtained his patent not for the bacteria per se, but for a process which consists in the employment of certain bacteria', the Board of Appeals argued that the *Prescott* case was even stronger. The board accepted the analogy between the bacteria and a chemical reagent. The appellant has 'discovered a new reagent, the *bacillus technicus*', it declared.[67]

The failure of the engineers' movement to keep sewage treatment processes in the public domain was thus extended, with *Guaranty Trust* and *Prescott*, to other industrial ecosystems, culminating in the 1980 Supreme Court case *Diamond v Chakrabarty*. In this landmark case, the US Supreme Court ruled for the first time that 'a live, human-made micro-organism is patentable'.[68] *Diamond v Chakrabarty* enabled the growth of the biotechnology industry and established a new arena of privatization. Ananda Chakrabarty, working for General Electric, had created a strain of bacteria that could use crude oil as a growth substrate and could thus help clean up oil spills. He sought to patent not only the process of making his organisms but the organism itself.[69] The patent examiner, repeating the argument first articulated by Vernon Richard in the 1930s in the *Prescott* case, denied the patent. Chakrabarty appealed, but the Patent Office Review Board affirmed the examiner's decision. However, it was reversed by the Court of Customs and Patent Appeals, a reversal later affirmed by the Supreme Court. Sewage treatment and the sewage patent cases were instrumental in this decision as the sewage cases provided important legal precedent for this landmark case. Furthermore, the cultural work of biological sewage treatment in denaturing natural processes was critical as well.

Conclusion

Daniel J Kevles looks to the history of plant patents as the precursors to *Chakrabarty*, with the first patent protection for living organisms granted in the 1930 Plant Patent Act. The direct ancestors of the *Chakrabarty* patent, however, were not plant patents but rather the microbial process patents granted in *Cameron*. In a line of decisions over the twentieth century, precedents initially established in the sewage

[67] Despite the repudiation of his arguments in this case, Richard was not a rogue examiner. He was a leading member of the Patent Office Society, principal examiner in the Chemical Division of the Patent Office and was later appointed examiner-in-chief of the Patent Office and member of the Patent Board of Appeals by President Roosevelt. 'New Members of the Board of Appeals' (1942) 24 *Journal of the Patent Office Society* 736.

[68] *Diamond v Chakrabarty* 447 US 303 (1980).

[69] Ananda Chakrabarty, 'Micro-organisms Having Multiple Compatible Degradative Energy-generating Plasmids and the Preparation Thereof' US Patent No 4,259,444 (31 March 1981).

patent cases were applied to the patenting of first, industrial bacterial processes, such as the production of butyl alcohol and acetone by *Clostridium*, patented by Weizmann, and by *Bacillus technicus*, patented by Prescott and Morikawa. All of these cases, resting ultimately on *Cameron*, were then mobilized to support the ruling in *Diamond v Chakrabarty* that not only the microbial processes but the bacteria themselves were subject to patenting and privatization.

Furthermore, the nature of DNA was not critical in this finding. Kevles argues that the Supreme Court justices came to see bacteria as simply DNA: 'What enabled the patenting of Chakrabarty's bacterium was the finding of molecular biology that genes are DNA.'[70] Instead, the justices came to see bacteria not as DNA but as industrial products. Viewing bacteria as an industrial product rather than as a living organism was critical. It was the denaturing accomplished by industrial microbiology that allowed the courts to uphold the septic tank and activated sludge patents, and it was this same denaturing that allowed the courts in *Chakrabarty* to see bacterial activity as a chemical rather than a vital process. At the beginning of the nineteenth century, when the engineering opposition failed to convince the courts that the bacterial processes in sewage treatment were natural and thus public, the stage was set for finding bacteria themselves to be the result of artifice.

Although they were critical to the reasoning in the case, *Cameron* and *Activated Sludge* do not appear in the Supreme Court's opinion in *Chakrabarty*. Rather, their influence is clear in the lower court decisions that were affirmed by *Chakrabarty*. Chakrabarty's lawyers cited *Cameron* and *Activated Sludge* as well as *Guaranty Trust*, but the reasoning goes deeper.[71] The court's arguments in the *Chakrabarty* case were first developed in reference to another patent application, that of Malcolm Bergy and colleagues.[72] Bergy had isolated a pure culture of a fungus that produced the antibiotic lincomycin. They sought patents not only on the process of producing the antibiotic, but, like Prescott's patent application, on the microbial culture itself. This was the precise claim successfully rejected by the Patent Office in the *Prescott* case, and it denied it for Bergy as well. Following the rulings in the early sewage cases, the Patent Office granted Bergy's process patents but denied the patent on the culture itself, reasoning that living organisms could not be patented.[73] Bergy appealed to the Court of Customs and Patent Appeals, which overturned the decision of the Patent Office and allowed the claim for the pure culture. When *Chakrabarty* later came before the same court, the court simply applied *Bergy* as ruling precedent without any additional analysis.[74] The commissioner of patents

[70] Daniel J Kevles, 'Patents, Protections, and Privileges: The Establishment of Intellectual Property in Animals and Plants' (2007) 98 *Isis* 323, 324; Glen Bugos and Daniel J Kevles, 'Plants as Intellectual Property: American Law, Policy, and Practice in World Context' (1992) *Osiris* 119.

[71] Brief for the Respondent, *Diamond v Chakrabarty*, 1979 US Briefs 136; Brief for the Petitioner, 1979 US Briefs 136.

[72] *In the Matter of the Application of Malcolm E Bergy, John H Coats, and Vedpal S Malik*, 563 F 2d 1031 (1977); 596 F 2nd 952 (1979).

[73] 563 F 2d 1031 (1977), 1033.

[74] *In the Matter of the Application of Ananda M Chakrabarty* 571 F 2d 40 (1978).

appealed both rulings. As *Bergy* and *Chakrabarty* moved up to the Supreme Court, the two cases were formally linked. Fearing that his part of the case was weaker and hoping for a successful test case of the Patent Office's procedures, Bergy withdrew, leaving only *Chakrabarty* to be decided. But the wording of the decision had been almost completely framed for *Bergy*.[75] To understand the court's reasoning in *Chakrabarty*, then, it is necessary to examine *Bergy*.

Relying on the decisions in *Cameron*, *Guaranty Trust*, and *Prescott* that found bacterial processes to be patentable, the Court of Customs and Patent Appeals ruled in *Bergy* that in addition to processes, bacterial cultures were also patentable, 'notwithstanding the employment therein of living organisms and their life processes'. The court found it 'illogical' to deny patent protection to a bacterial culture yet allow protection for the 'functioning' of that culture, and it extended the patentability of a process to the organism itself.[76] In *Bergy*, the court equated the production of lincomycin using *Streptomyces vellosus* to any commonly understood industrial manufacturing process and declared that 'what we have before us is an industrial product used in an industrial process'. The industrial product the judge referred to was not lincomycin, the product of the microbial fermentation, but rather the organism *Streptomyces* itself. How had a natural, living organism become an industrial product? The court's justification was based on an understanding of bacterial processes as chemical processes, 'the essential similarity of what we normally think of as "chemical reactions" and the complex procedures wrought by the life processes of micro-organisms'.[77] This was the argument made in *Guaranty Trust* and *Prescott*. In *Guaranty Trust*, the court ruled that the bacterial process relied on an 'agency of nature, the use of which for practical purposes can be patented', in the same way that 'chemicals, minerals, or anything else' could be.[78] In *Prescott*, the court further equated the life process of bacteria with a 'chemical process', calling the discovery of the bacteria, *Bacillus technicus*, simply 'a new reagent'.[79]

The industrialization and denaturing of bacterial sewage treatment had helped courts at the beginning of the century overcome the opposition to the patenting of bacterial processes. It was the denaturing inherent in the use of bacteria for sewage treatment that allowed the courts to uphold the septic tank patent. Moreover, it was this same denaturing that allowed the courts in *Chakrabarty* to see bacterial

[75] The Patent Office appealed *Bergy* to the Supreme Court, where it was vacated and remanded. *Parker v Bergy* 438 US 932 (1978). It was combined with *Chakrabarty* and ruled on again by the US Court of Customs and Patent Appeals, in 596 F 2nd 952 (1979), which repeats much of 563 F 2d 1031 quoted previously, but applied to both *Chakrabarty* and *Bergy*. The Patent Office appealed to the US Supreme Court. On Bergy's decision to withdraw see Linda Greenhouse, 'Commerce Cases Taken by Justices' *The New York Times* (15 January 1980).

[76] 596 F 2d 952 (1979), 977.

[77] 563 F 2d 1031 (1977), 1037–38.

[78] Arguments on Final Hearing, 131. *Union Solvents v Guaranty Trust*, Equity 802, District Court, Delaware, NARA-Mid Atlantic RG 21, Box 272.

[79] 19 USPQ 178 (1932).

activity as a chemical rather than a vital process. This, in turn, initiated the transformation of patent law that allowed the patenting of living organisms themselves. Sanitary engineers themselves were complicit in this industrialization of the bacterial processes. Engineers and scientists had thoroughly industrialized the biological processes of purification, making bacterial treatment appear more and more like a chemical manufacturing process and less like a biological one. The continuous nature of the process, the application of process control techniques, and the biological simplification all denatured the fundamental living character of the system. Thus, it should have come as no surprise that the courts began to treat the bacterial processes more like chemical manufacturing processes than 'nature's methods'.

Emphasizing the view of bacterial processes as simply another example of an industrial, chemical process, the judge in the *Bergy* case stated that: 'The nature and commercial uses of biologically pure cultures of micro-organisms . . . are much more akin to inanimate chemical compositions such as reactants, reagents, and catalysts than they are to horses and honeybees or raspberries and roses.'[80] Because the Patent Appeals Court's reasoning relied heavily on the industrial nature of bacterial processes and the professed similarity between bacterial and chemical processes, the judges in the *Bergy* case viewed their decision as limited to bacteria and other lower forms of life. They dismissed warnings that their decision could lead to the patenting of animals as 'far-fetched'.[81]

The Supreme Court, in a narrow five to four decision, affirmed the reasoning in *Bergy* (but now applied only to *Chakrabarty*) and allowed the first patent on a living organism itself—the bacteria created by Chakrabarty. The decision has had far-reaching implications. Although the lower court decision was crafted for particularly chemical-like bacteria, the Supreme Court opinion applied to any life-form modified or created by people, 'anything under the sun that is made by man'. Once one form of life was patented, there was no logical obstacle to patenting others. In 1988, the cancer-susceptible mouse, 'onco-mouse', was successfully patented by Harvard University.[82] Since that first animal patent, there have been well over 1,000 patents granted in the United States on animals themselves, including fish, pigs, birds, sheep, and cows.[83]

[80] 563 F 2d 1031 (1977), 1038.

[81] 563 F 2d 1031 (1977), 1038 and 596 F 2d 952 (1979), 997.

[82] Philip Leder and Timothy A Stewart, 'Transgenic Non-human Mammals' US Patent No 4,736,866 (12 April 1988).

[83] 447 US 303 (1980) 309. Estimated from a total of 2,355 patents until 17 August 2010, listed within US Patent and Trademark Office classification codes 800/8–20 (Multicellular Living Organisms, Non-human Animals). Some patents are listed in multiple sub-classes and some do not claim the animal itself. There were 689 unique mouse patents alone.

3

The Essence of Biology

Tomatoes, Broccoli, and European Patents on Native Plant Traits

*Veit Braun**

Introduction

With the surge of patents on cells, genes, organisms, and other living subject matter from the 1980s onwards, two dominant critiques developed in popular discourse and in scholarly analysis to address the issues that surround this form of intellectual property: one speaking of patents on 'life'; the other about the appropriation of 'nature'.[1] The first, largely of an ethical nature, seeks to problematize biopatents as a form of category error in which living subjects are wrongly turned into property objects. Why, it asks, do living beings have to be systematically disregarded as subjects in order to make the property fiction work—and what problems follow from that?[2] The second, situated in a political–economic tradition, criticizes biopatents as an instrument of privatizing nature or, in Rousseau's words, for forgetting that 'the fruits of the earth belong to all'.[3] Highlighting how living nature is far from self-reproducing, overabundant, or indeed invented by those who claim it, it focuses on biopatents as a means for redistributing wealth in unequal ways.[4]

* I would like to thank David Lahav for answering my questions about the Volcani Center, as well as Brad Sherman and Jose Bellido for their instructive and helpful editorial feedback on this text. Arthur Schaffer kindly provided a photo for this text.

[1] For the first tradition see eg Alain Pottage, 'The Inscription of Life in Law: Genes, Patents, and Bio-Politics' (1998) 61 *The Modern Law Review* 740; Melinda Cooper, *Life as Surplus: Biotechnology and Capitalism in the Neoliberal Era* (University of Washington Press 2008); Shobita Parthasarathy, *Patent Politics: Life Forms, Markets, and the Public Interest in the United States and Europe* (University of Chicago Press 2017); for the second one see Cori Hayden, *When Nature Goes Public: The Making and Unmaking of Bioprospecting in Mexico* (Princeton University Press 2003); Jack Ralph Kloppenburg, *First the Seed: The Political Economy of Plant Biotechnology* (University of Wisconsin Press 2004). Stefan Helmreich provides a useful taxonomy for the overlaps and divergences between prominent concepts from both traditions: Stefan Helmreich, 'Species of Biocapital' (2008) 17 *Science as Culture* 463.

[2] Some commentators have criticized this approach for reifying life and mystifying the origin of value in the organic; see David Tyfield, 'A Surplus of "Surplus"?' (2009) 18 *Science as Culture* 497; Kean Birch and David Tyfield, 'Theorizing the Bioeconomy: Biovalue, Biocapital, Bioeconomics or ... What?' (2012) 38 *Science, Technology & Human Values* 299.

[3] Jean-Jacques Rousseau, *Discourse on the Origin and Foundations of Inequality among Men* (first published 1755, Bedford/St Martins 2011) 70.

[4] For a problematization of this latter critique see Mario Biagioli, 'Vegetable Genius: Organic Figures of Originality' (ch 1 in this volume); Veit Braun, 'Tools of Extraction or Means of Speculation? Making

Veit Braun, *The Essence of Biology* In: *Intellectual Property and the Design of Nature*. Edited by: Jose Bellido and Brad Sherman, Oxford University Press. © Veit Braun 2023. DOI: 10.1093/oso/9780192864406.003.0003

Both critiques have their merits, insofar as they bring to the fore important issues and questions that are all too quickly obscured by a mainstream discourse celebrating innovation and intellectual property. Yet despite their differences, they all too often rely on a juxtaposition of intellectual property with its alleged others which, at the same time, they seek to question and deconstruct. However, the life forms, things, and entities grouped together under the umbrellas of 'life' and 'nature' are not unified, and neither is the stance of patent laws (in the plural) towards them.[5] What 'nature' and 'life' thus do is to problematize certain notions and aspects of patent law, but at the price of coming heavily loaded with normative assumptions as to what these problems are and how they should be resolved.

The difficulty here is that both 'life' and 'nature' are terms very much ingrained in patent law. Practitioners speak of 'products of nature', 'living matter', or 'organisms' when discussing the intricacies of applying intellectual property to things that are, have been, or could be alive. 'Nature' and 'life' are thus not simply part of a scholarly vocabulary that is freely chosen. Rather, concepts from legal discourse, among both scholars and practitioners, reconnect to other established notions such as the dignity of life, the antecedence of nature, or the enclosure of open spaces. To avoid the established divisions and juxtapositions raised by these terms, how else could patented organisms, genes, cells, or organic substances be spoken of?

In this chapter, it is argued that 'biology' allows us to highlight a number of issues often overlooked when referring to 'life' or 'nature'. This argument is not entirely new: deviating from the common critiques of the latter two, intellectual property (IP) scholars have found themselves drawn towards 'biology' time and again.[6] What is less often discussed, however, is the significance of 'biology' in

Sense of Patents in the Bioeconomy' in Maria Backhouse and others (eds), *Bioeconomy and Global Inequalities: Socio-Ecological Perspectives on Biomass, Sourcing and Production* (Palgrave Macmillan 2021) 65–84.

[5] Brad Sherman, 'What Does It Mean to Invent Nature?' (2015) 5 *UC Irvine Law Review* 1193.

[6] Johanna Gibson (ed), *Patenting Lives: Life Patents, Culture and Development* (Ashgate Publishing 2008) is a case in point here: despite its title, the contributions overwhelmingly address 'technical' questions of biology rather than 'fundamental' ones of nature or life. Other examples include Daniel J Kevles, 'Ananda Chakrabarty Wins a Patent: Biotechnology, Law, and Society, 1972–1980' (1994) 25 *Historical Studies in the Physical and Biological Sciences* 111; Alain Pottage (n 1) 740; Jane Calvert, 'Patenting Genomic Objects: Genes, Genomes, Function and Information' (2007) 16 *Science as Culture* 207; Brad Sherman, 'Taxonomic Property' (2008) 67 *The Cambridge Law Journal* 560; Jane Calvert and Pierre-Benoît Joly, 'How Did the Gene Become a Chemical Compound? The Ontology of the Gene and the Patenting of DNA' (2011) 50 *Social Science Information* 157; Alain Pottage and Brad Sherman, 'Organisms and Manufactures: On the History of Plant Inventions' (2007) 31 *Melbourne University Law Review* 539; Alain Pottage and Brad Sherman, *Figures of Invention: A History of Modern Patent Law* (Oxford University Press 2010); Alain Pottage and Brad Sherman, 'Kinds, Clones, and Manufactures' in Mario Biagioli, Peter Jaszi, and Martha Woodmansee (eds), *Making and Unmaking Intellectual Property* (University of Chicago Press 2011); Jean-Paul Gaudillière, Daniel J Kevles, and Hans-Jörg Rheinberger (eds), *Living Properties: Making Knowledge and Controlling Ownership in the History of Biology* (Max Planck Institute for the History of Science 2009); Sherman (n 5).

discussions among practitioners and in legal texts. To shine a light on these aspects, two patent disputes dealing with biological subject matter are reconstructed:[7] *Broccoli/Tomatoes I* and *II*. From the filing of both patents in the early 2000s to the (so far) last word on the matter in 2020, the legal dispute dragged on for almost two decades. Upon the initial grants by the European Patent Office (EPO) in 2002 (*Broccoli*) and 2003 (*Tomatoes*), opposition was filed by Limagrain, Syngenta, and Unilever.

The EPO's Technical Board of Appeal examined the cases and relayed them to the Enlarged Board of Appeal to clarify the meaning and significance of 'essentially biological processes', as defined in the European Patent Convention. The EPO rejected the process claims of the applications in 2010 (*Broccoli/Tomatoes I*), but in 2015 upheld the patents as far as the plants resulting from the same breeding processes were concerned (*Broccoli/Tomatoes II*). After this decision, the case and the issue briefly left the closed walls of the EPO's headquarters in Munich and its boards of appeal in nearby Haar. Breeders' associations issued press releases, newspapers reported on the case, and national and European members of parliament set out to fix in legislation what apparently had gone wrong in the judiciary. In the aftermath, first the president of the EPO and then eventually the Enlarged Board of Appeal changed their minds and declared that plants resulting from 'essentially biological' processes were not patentable.

The case not only highlights the particularity of certain forms of life—conventionally bred plants—but also their relations to economic and political questions, as well as the geographically fragmented nature of an allegedly 'global' regime of biopatents. In its decisions, the EPO had to navigate the exemptions of Article 53 of the European Patent Convention (EPC), which were originally intended to function as a bulwark against the intrusion of patent law into the domain of plant breeding. Whereas the debate on patentability of genes and genetically modified organisms (GMOs) in 1980s and 1990s North America focused on the question of whether DNA or organisms were *products of nature*, *Tomato/Broccoli* and its aftermath had to answer a slightly different question: namely how *biology* fits into the framework of patent law. When compared with older controversies over genetically modified food and biotechnology patents, as well as patents on embryos and animals, there was very little critical public involvement in this case.

While informed by past battles over 'life' and 'nature' in European plant-breeding and patent law,[8] the question of 'essentially biological processes' and

[7] This text is a result of ethnographic research, expert interviews, and document analysis the author conducted for his PhD thesis from 2015 to 2018 and that he has followed up since.

[8] Sheila Jasanoff, *Designs on Nature: Science and Democracy in Europe and the United States* (Princeton University Press 2007) 94; Parthasarathy (n 1).

their implications for the patentability of plants had little resonance with these older debates. Although 'biology' might appear more or less synonymous with (animate) nature and is often treated as such in the literature, it has taken on a specific meaning in European patent law, referring not so much to ethical or political considerations, but rather to the pragmatics of distinguishing between different types and qualities of intervening in vital processes. What is of interest here, therefore, is who and what is mobilized by 'biology', rather than by 'nature' or 'life', and what may be learned from *Tomatoes/Broccoli* beyond the geographical confines of Europe. What the case and the term offer, it is suggested here, is a way of rethinking the relationship between technology and life, as well as the role of economics and politics when naming living subject matter.

Public Plant Science and Patenting

In the early 2000s, in the midst of fierce debates and controversies over genetically modified plants—their potential benefits to agriculture, their effects on the seed industry, and their possible hazards for health and the environment—two inconspicuous patent applications reached the EPO's examining division. Neither gained public interest at the time. Although they both related to plants, more precisely vegetables, the applications referred to traditional breeding methods rather than to the techniques of genetic transformation that were at the centre of the debate over biotech plants. It was food and plant multinationals, not non-governmental organizations, who would oppose the patents, and while the EPO's Enlarged Board of Appeal was to arrive at a decision contested across the board, from seed activists to industry leaders, it was difficult to explain what exactly the controversy was about.

Indeed, the applications titled 'Method for selective increase of the anticarcinogenic glucosinolates in Brassica species' (EP1069819) and 'Method for breeding tomatoes having reduced water content and product of the method' (EP1211926), or the *Broccoli* and the *Tomatoes* patents, as they would respectively come to be known, were unlikely to strike their intended reader as containing ground-breaking inventions. The *Broccoli* patent in its initial form claimed a process for breeding plants of the genus *Brassica* that are high in glucosinolates, a group of compounds characteristic of the Brassicaceae family and responsible for the bitter, pungent aroma of brussels sprouts, mustard, rape, and horseradish, among others. Similarly, the *Tomatoes* application claimed a method for cross-breeding tomatoes (*Solanum esculentum*) with a wild relative (*S. hirsutum*) and subsequently selecting the offspring to obtain fruits that will shrivel and dry while still attached to the plant. While both vegetables are somewhat curious, they are far from the biotechnological marvels of herbicide-tolerant and insect-resistant plants that excited the seed industry during the 1990s and 2000s and caused so much resistance among concerned activists and consumers in Europe. It would not be derogatory to characterize them as fairly ordinary vegetables, like hundreds of others that are planted in greenhouses and polytunnels every year. Yet it is precisely the fact that what was described and claimed in the applications was so conventional that led to their opposition.

Although the history recounted in this chapter is a European one, it did not start as such. Neither application was written with a particularly European focus in mind. Instead, both were filed via the World Intellectual Property Office (WIPO) and entered their regional phase in Europe after the WIPO relegated them to the EPO for examination.[9] Filing through the WIPO is standard procedure in many industries and saves applicants the trouble of sending applications to various patent offices around the world.[10] Other than Europe (ie the signatory countries to the European Patent Convention (EPC)), both *Tomatoes* and *Broccoli* were filed in the United States, Japan, Australia, and Canada. However, it was only at the EPO that they were opposed, ruled upon by two boards of appeal, and attained status as a landmark case with profound implications for plant IP law and the seed sector. While the applications were not (in a strict sense) biotechnological in nature or specifically aimed at the European seed market, their legal career cannot be understood without reference to the GM wars of the 1990s or the particular history of plant IP law in Europe.

The *Tomatoes* and *Broccoli* patents are part of a cohort of patent applications that started to reach the EPO from the early 1980s onwards. Initially only a trickle, their numbers increased over the 1990s to an average of ten every year until 2000, and twenty-three applications a year between 2001 and 2010.[11] While these figures may appear unimpressive, they are roughly equal to those of biotechnology plant applications over the same period of time. Graphs for both rise more or less in unison over the 1990s and 2000s.[12] Just as with the early biotech patents of the 1990s, many of the conventional applications of the time pertained to agricultural crops such as maize, rapeseed, and sunflowers. However, towards the turn of the millennium,

[9] 'About This File: EP1211926' European Patent Register (20 February 2022) https://register.epo.org/application?number=EP00940724&lng=en&tab=main (accessed 21 February 2022); 'About This File: EP1069819' European Patent Register (20 February 2022) https://register.epo.org/application?number=EP99915886&lng=en&tab=main (accessed 21 February 2022).

[10] Lionel Bently and others, *Intellectual Property Law* (5th edn, Oxford University Press 2018) 416.

[11] 'PATSTAT 2018 Spring edition', years 1991–2000 (PATSTAT 2018) https://data.epo.org/expert-services/index.html (accessed 2 October 2018). All patents in category A01H and subcategories whose cooperative patent classification (CPC) does not include biotechnology (C12N and subcategories), symbiosis with bacteria (A01H 3), or tissue culture (A01H 4) were searched for. To specify the search further, algae (A01H 13) and fungi (A01H 15) were excluded. Patents referring to processed plant materials instead of germplasm (F and subcategories) were excluded, as were patents for processes and products involving marker-assisted breeding (C12Q). Duplicates and false positives were removed from the results based on their abstracts and claims.

[12] PATSTAT 2018 (n 11), classification C12N and subcategories.

when the *Broccoli* and *Tomatoes* patents were filed, vegetable applications gained in prominence. And while the 'usual suspects'—leading biotech multinationals such as Monsanto, Pioneer, and Sandoz (later Novartis)—account for roughly a third of conventional plant patent applications at the EPO at that time, two other types of actors emerged towards the 2000s: traditional Dutch vegetable-breeding companies such as Rijk Zwaan, Enza Zaden, and Bejo, and national (non-university) public research institutions, such as the French INRA, the Spanish CSIC, and the Australian CSIRO.[13]

Attempts to understand the story behind *Tomatoes* and *Broccoli*—including the author's own—have largely focused on the antagonism between the former two groups: multinational public companies with a history in biotechnology and chemistry versus family-owned, conventional plant-breeding firms.[14] Indeed, there are good reasons to do so. Much of the political debate before and after the 2015 ruling by the EPO's Enlarged Board of Appeal in the case was driven by these actors. It is usually assumed that patents on native traits represent an extension of the business model behind genetically engineered traits such as herbicide tolerance or insect resistance.[15] In turn, both the European seed industry lobby and critical observers of the case emphasized that patents on native traits are at odds with the legal regime of plant variety protection and the business models of conventional breeders who rely on it (and have nonetheless participated in the native patent rush).[16] However, what has been neglected in this framing, it is argued here, is the third group, which is driven by quite different motives and incentives.

Notably, neither *Broccoli* nor *Tomatoes* were filed by seed companies in the strict sense. The former's applicant is Plant Bioscience (or PBL Technology), a technology-transfer joint venture of the John Innes Centre in Norwich, the Sainsbury Laboratory in Cambridge, and the UK Biotechnology and Biological Sciences Research Council, each being public, semi-public, or formerly public institutions.[17] The research behind the application was largely carried out by

[13] ibid classification A01H and subcategories excluding C12N, A01H 3, A01H 4, A01H 13, and A01H 15.

[14] Ivan Mammana, 'Concentration of Market Power in the EU Seed Market: Study Commissioned by the Greens/EFA Group in the European Parliament' (The Greens/EFA in the European Parliament 2014); Fabien Girard and Christine Noiville, 'Propriété industrielle et biotechnologies végétales: la Nova Atlantis: À propos de la recommandation du Haut Conseil des Biotechnologies' (2014) 28 *Revue internationale de droit économique* 59; Fabien Girard, '"Though the Treasure of Nature's Germens Tumble All Together": The EPO and Patents on Native Traits or the Bewitching Powers of Ideologies' (2015) 33 *Prometheus* 43; Veit Braun, 'Holding on to and letting go of seed: Quasi-commodities and the passage of property' (2021) 14 *Journal of Cultural Economy* 306; Braun (n 4); Christine Noiville and Fabien Girard, 'Gènes des plantes: International Licensing platform' in Marie Cornu, Fabienne Orsi, and Judith Rochfeld (eds), *Dictionnaire des biens communs* (Presses universitaires de France 2021) 632.

[15] Girard (n 14) 46.

[16] Braun (n 4).

[17] 'About Us' (2022) PBL Technology https://www.pbltechnology.com/about-us; 'A Short History of the John Innes Centre' John Innes Centre (8 June 2009) http://web.archive.org/web/20131207040

Kathy Faulkner (first a PhD student and later postdoctoral researcher at the John Innes Centre), Ruth MacCormack (who led the Brassica Department at the John Innes Centre, Gary Williamson (leader of a phytochemicals research group of the Institute of Food Research in Norwich), and Richard Mithen, who supervised Faulkner's PhD. The group had specialized in commercial *Brassica* species and their wild relatives and had made a series of experimental crosses between commercial broccoli (*B. oleracea* var. *italica*) and two endemic and threatened Sicilian species of cabbage (*B. villosa* and *B. drepanensis*) to increase the low glucosinolate content of the former.[18] The *Tomatoes* application was an outcome of research carried out by Arthur Schaffer's research group at the Volcani Center, Israel's national institution for agricultural sciences, and a subsidiary of the Israeli Ministry for Agriculture.[19] It resulted from experimental breeding with commercial tomatoes (*Solanum esculentum*) and a Peruvian relative (*S. habrochaites*), which was aimed at introducing a fruit cuticle (or peel) that would allow water to evaporate from the intact fruit, thus letting tomatoes dry while still attached to the plant (Fig 3.1).[20]

Although Plant Bioscience and the Volcani Center are very different institutions and with different histories, they share roots in the public sector as well as the pressure to monetize potentially useful outcomes of their research—something they also have in common with other public and semi-public research institutes after the advent of 'academic capitalism'.[21] Starting with the 1980 US Bayh–Dole Act,[22] public

745; http://www.jic.ac.uk/corporate/about/history.htm (accessed 28 July 2022); for the recent history of British plant-breeding see Andrew J Webster, 'Privatisation of Public Sector Research: The Case of a Plant Breeding Institute' (1989) 16(4) *Science and Public Policy* 224 https://doi.org/10.1093/spp/16.4.224 (accessed 28 July 2022); Katrina Stengel and others, 'Plant Sciences and the Public Good' (2009) 34 *Science, Technology & Human Values* 289; Viktoriya Galushko and Richard Gray, 'Privatization of Crop Breeding in the UK: Lessons for Other Countries' Paper prepared for presentation at the 87th Annual Conference of the Agricultural Economics Society, University of Warwick (8–10 April 2013).

[18] Richard Mithen, K Faulkner, and G Williamson, 'Method for the selective increase of the anticarcinogenic glucosinolates in *Brassica* sp.'; Sally Hines, 'From Lab to Classroom: an Alumni Career' John Innes Centre (9 September 2020) https://www.jic.ac.uk/blog/lab-to-classroom-alumni-career (accessed 21 February 2022); Richard Mithen, 'Richard Mithen' (2022) OMICS International https://biography.omicsonline.org/united-kingdom/quadram-institute/richard-mithen-874840 (accessed 21 February 2022).

[19] Arthur Schaffer, 'Method for breeding tomatoes having reduced water content and product of the method'. For a short history of the Volcani Center and its role in Israel's agricultural and research policies see Danielle Abraham and others, *How Israel Became a World Leader in Agriculture and Water: Insights for today's developing countries* (2019) Tony Blair Institute for Global Change.

[20] Schaffer (n 19). The application refers to *Lycopersicon esculentum*, a common taxonomic synonym for *Solanum esculentum*, and *L. hirsutum* (a synonym for *S. habrochaites*).

[21] Rebecca S Eisenberg, 'Biotech Patents: Looking Backward While Moving Forward' (2006) 24 *Nature Biotechnology* 317; Sheila Slaughter and Larry L Leslie, *Academic Capitalism: Politics, Policies, and the Entrepreneurial University* (Johns Hopkins University Press 1997); Sheila Slaughter and Gary Rhoades, *Academic Capitalism and the New Economy: Markets, State, and Higher Education* (Johns Hopkins University Press 2004).

[22] Bayh–Dole Act 1980 (US).

research institutions around the world were first allowed and then increasingly obliged to patent findings that had a potential industrial application. The philosophy behind this push for public patenting is to use patents as an interface for public–private partnerships to facilitate technology transfer and reclaim some of the profits the private sector makes with tax-funded, public knowledge. Today, this obligation to deliver a 'return on investment' to the taxpayer and transfer technology by filing for patents and licensing them to interested parties is one of the main drivers behind public research bodies' attempts to patent conventionally bred plants.[23]

For public research institutes operating under the 'imperative of valorisation',[24] patents thus represent an indispensable instrument for transferring technology and receiving royalties across the globe. Through the Paris Convention, the World Intellectual Property Organisation (WIPO) Convention, the Patent Cooperation Treaty (PCT) and the Agreement on Trade-Related Aspects of Intellectual Property Rights (TRIPs), patents have become ever-more globalized, allowing national entities to license their IP worldwide and to attract licensing offers from companies around the globe. This is especially important with vegetables, since greenhouses, polytunnels, and irrigation technologies have largely detached them from local or regional agricultural regimes such as climate, topography, or seasonality, which still govern field crops to a large extent.[25] 'Shotgun' filing of patents through the WIPO without knowing in advance which licensees or markets would be interested in a patented plant is characteristic of this business model for technology transfer, and stands in contrast to the strategies of patent hoarding, defensive patenting, and rigorous financial valuation of patents that corporate patent holders often pursue.[26] Public plant-breeding institutes usually follow a liberal, non-exclusive licensing strategy, as they do not use their patents themselves.[27] Nevertheless, although such patents are biologically independent of their place of origin and should ideally operate everywhere in a legally homogenized world, *Broccoli/Tomatoes I* and *II* (as well as the later *Pepper* case) had to deal with the question of whether a particular regional history of plant IP and innovation would disrupt this globalized logic in the complicated and contradictory legal space all too often conflated in the term 'Europe'.

[23] Although few plants and technologies successfully make it from a research finding to a commercial product, there are exceptions to the rule, such as the French INRA's Ogura rapeseed, a cytoplasmic male sterile hybrid, which was successfully licensed to a number of plant-breeding companies. See Steward Redqueen, *Who Benefits from IP Rights for Agricultural Innovation? The Case of Ogura Oilseed Rape in France* (2015) Croplife International and EuropaBio).

[24] Florence Bellivier, 'Biobanque' in Marie Cornu, Fabienne Orsi, and Judith Rochfeld (eds), *Dictionnaire des biens communs* (Presses universitaires de France 2021) 143.

[25] Annabel Ipsen, 'Manufacturing a Natural Advantage: Capturing Place-based Technology Rents in the genetically modified corn seed industry' (2016) 2 *Environmental Sociology* 41; Barbara Brandl, *Wissenschaft, Technologieentwicklung und die Spielarten des Kapitalismus: Analyse der Entwicklung von Saatgut in USA und Deutschland* (Springer VS 2018) 17.

[26] Holger Ernst, 'Intellectual Property as a Management Discipline' (2017) 19 *Technology & Innovation* 481; Braun (n 4).

[27] This is somewhat in contrast to (especially US) universities, which in some fields of technology pursue exclusive partnerships for technology transfer: Bhaven N Sampat, 'Patenting and US Academic Research in the 20th Century: The World before and after Bayh–Dole' (2006) 35 *Research Policy* 772.

Figure 3.1 The Volcani Center's self-drying tomatoes on the vine, 2002.
Courtesy of Ari Schaffer. Reproduced here with permission.

From Field to Paper: Disclosing Organisms

In retrospect, it is unclear why the *Broccoli* and *Tomatoes* patents, of all the applications for conventionally bred vegetables, would become the landmark cases they are. They were opposed by Syngenta and Limagrain, as well as by Unilever, respectively; companies that each had stakes in the vegetable business in Europe.[28] While there were concerns over monopolization and that competitors would be locked out from central technologies, there is little in the patents that justify such concerns.

[28] Limagrain, a former French cooperative, is one of the biggest plant-breeding companies in Europe, as is Syngenta, a spin-off from the biotech multinational Novartis and today a subsidiary of ChemChina. Unilever has dabbled in the seed business in the past, briefly owning the Plant Breeding Institute, which was later merged with the John Innes Centre.

Both the *Tomatoes* and *Broccoli* patents describe and claim a fairly straightforward (if generic) process of introgression and back-breeding, ie transferring desired traits from one species or variety of plant to another, as well as a plant that results from this process: self-desiccating tomatoes in the former, a glucoraphanin-rich broccoli in the latter. In fact, the process as described in the *Broccoli* patent reads as if it could have been taken straight from an introductory plant-breeding textbook:

I.) Crossing wild species with broccoli double haploid breeding lines;
II.) Analyzing F1 hybrids, selecting the hybrids with the highest level of 4-methylsulfinylbutyl and/or 3-methylsulfinylpropyl glucosinolates and back-crossing to broccoli breeding lines;
III.) Analysis of glucosinolates in individual plants of the B1 (Backcross 1) generation;
IV.) One or two further rounds of backcrossing (B2, B3) with selection of plants with the highest level of 4-methylsulfinylbutyl and/or 3-methylsulfinylpropyl glucosinolates, anticarcinogenesis screening of selected individuals by induction of phase II enzymes;
V.) Analysis of B3 (Backcross 3) population with selection of plants with the highest level of 4-methylsulfinylbutyl and/or 3-methylsulfinylpropyl glucosinolates, anticarcinogenesis screening of selected individuals by induction of phase II enzymes;
VI.) Selection of a broccoli line with elevated levels of 4-methylsulfinylbutyl and/or 3-methylsulfinylpropyl glucosinolates which carries the anticarcinogenic trait capable of causing a strong induction of phase II enzymes.[29]

In a similarly straightforward fashion, *Tomatoes* claims:

1. A method for breeding tomato plants that produce tomatoes with reduced fruit water content comprising the steps of:
   - crossing at least one *Lycopersicon esculentum* plant with a *Lycopersicon* spp. to produce hybrid seed;
   - collecting the first generation of hybrid seeds;
   - growing plants from the first generation of hybrid seeds;
   - pollinating the plants of the most recent hybrid generation;
   - collecting the seeds produced by the most recent hybrid generation;
   - growing plants from the seeds of the most recent hybrid generation;
   - allowing plants to remain on the vine past the point of normal ripening; and
   - screening for reduced fruit water content as indicated by extended preservation of the ripe fruit and wrinkling of the fruit skin.
2. The method according to claim 1 wherein the steps of pollinating, collecting the seeds, and growing plants are repeated at least once.

[29] Mithen, Faulkner, and Williamson (n 18) 17.

3. The method according to claim 1 wherein the step of pollinating includes self-pollination.[30]

Both plants failed to make a considerable commercial impact: the self-drying tomatoes were licensed to a company but never turned into a product,[31] while the anticarcinogenic broccoli enjoyed some modest spotlight on Marks & Spencer and Asda supermarket shelves in the UK.[32] Even so, there was much to take issue with, in the eyes of the industry. On 22 April 2004, Syngenta filed a formal notice of opposition to the *Broccoli* patent at the EPO. Its grounds included lack of novelty, a false date of priority, lack of inventive step, and insufficient disclosure either for selected claims or the patent in total.[33] Two days later, Limagrain followed, citing the same reasons.[34] Unilever's notice of opposition to the *Tomatoes* patent arrived on 12 August in the same year, similarly citing insufficient disclosure, lack of novelty, and a lack of inventive step.[35]

The two patents had a number of flaws in common. The plants claimed relied on a random recombination of alleles during the breeding process and the patents did not, in the eyes of the opposition, provide enough information as to how to arrive at the final plant from the initial cross or, in the case of *Broccoli*, define the attribute 'elevated' in relation to the plant[36] or consistently stick to one definition of *Brassica oleracea*[37] (insufficient disclosure). The EPO opposition claimed that neither plant was in fact new, seeing as there had been publications predating the applications that mentioned broccolis 'with elevated levels of [glucosinolates]',[38] and Arthur Schaffer had described the same tomato-breeding process in a previous patent[39] (lack of novelty). Furthermore, all three notices of opposition claimed that introgression of traits using wild relatives and back-breeding was an entirely obvious procedure for anyone reading plant science publications.[40] The *Broccoli* application had further been amended compared with its US priority application to claim 'A

30 Schaffer (n 19) 10.

31 Interview with IP lawyer (November 2017).

32 Plant Biosciences Ltd teamed up with the Dutch seed company Seminis (acquired by Monsanto shortly after) to develop a commercial variety marketed under the name 'Beneforté' from 2011 onwards: 'The Story behind Super Broccoli' https://nutraceuticalbusinessreview.com/news/article_page/The_story_behind_super_broccoli/97820 (accessed 28 December 2021). At the time of writing, it is not available in either Asda's or M&S Ocado partner's online stores.

33 W Smolders 'Opposition to European Patent No EP-1 069 819-B1 (Appl No 99915885.8)' (22 April 2003) 2.

34 Carol Almond-Martin, Notice of opposition, 'Opposition against European Patent No. EP-B-1 069 819 Granted on 24 July 2002 in the Name of Plant Bioscience Limited' (24 April 2003) 3.

35 G Tjon Tiel Ril, Annex 1 to the Notice of Opposition against EP-B-1 211 926 (Appl No 0094 0724.8) (State of Israel—Ministry of Agriculture)—Facts and Arguments' (12 August 2004) 4.

36 Smolders (n 33) 2.

37 Almond-Martin (n 34) 16.

38 Smolders (n 33) 4; Almond-Martin (n 34) 9.

39 Tjon Tiel Ril (n 35) 8.

40 Smolders (n 33) 4; Almond-Martin (n 34) 12; Tjon Tiel Ril (n 35) 12.

Brassica plant cell' rather than 'plant cell extracts' (incorrect priority date).[41] More important than all these concerns was one that encompassed and yet transcended them and thus takes a prominent place in all three notices of opposition:[42] the issue of whether the two applications sought to claim essentially biological processes and their products.

The applications were badly drafted, perhaps owing to the fact that public research institutes often lack the capacities for writing patent applications effectively and strategically. They also demonstrate a more fundamental problem that goes beyond the flaws of the two applications, namely how to discern and document human contributions to the evolution of a particular plant, and how to make the documentation comply with the genre of the patent. The question of how to disclose and recreate properly has a long history, going back to the early twentieth century, when plant breeders on both sides of the Atlantic first sought patent protection for their plants.[43] Patent offices had difficulty processing plant applications, which described plant phenotypes through words and drawings, but failed to provide a theory on how exactly a particular plant phenotype came about—and more importantly, how another breeder could recreate that phenotype from scratch. Unlike mechanical, electrical, or chemical inventions, which could be disclosed in technical drawings and recipes, the process of producing new plants was too random to be considered repeatable. Furthermore, in the absence of a doctrine that would enable another person to make a patented plant themselves (as in *Tomatoes* and *Broccoli*), it was even doubtful whether breeders were actually the creators, rather than the plants themselves.[44]

Early twentieth-century breeders seeking patent protection were faced with the difficulty of stating how their new traits, sports, and mutants had come about; or, perhaps more importantly, how others could imitate what they sought to disclose in their patent applications. Although they enclosed detailed drawings of new petal colours or unheard-of leaf shapes, neither these graphical depictions nor a minute account of the steps taken to arrive at the plant to be patented were sufficient to reproduce it. Even if the same breeder were to repeat one and the same cross-pollination between two parental plants, the possibility that a plant identical to the one described in the patent application would emerge from them was minuscule. Patent offices thus began to reject such applications not so much for metaphysical

[41] Smolders (n 33) 2.
[42] ibid 4; Almond-Martin (n 34) 2; Tjon Tiel Ril (n 35) 2.
[43] Pottage and Sherman (n 6) 153; Daniel J Kevles, 'New Blood, New Fruits: Protections for Breeders and Originators, 1789–1930' in Mario Biagioli, Peter Jaszi, and Martha Woodmansee (eds), *Making and Unmaking Intellectual Property* (University of Chicago Press 2011) 253–68; Pottage and Sherman, 'Kinds, Clones, and Manufactures' (n 6); Braun (n 14).
[44] Kevles (n 43) 262.

reasons (because they had in fact been found in nature rather than created through human ingenuity) or political–economic reasons (because they would deprive others of what had already been 'published' by nature) as for simple technical difficulties. In other words, breeders could not fulfil their part of the patent bargain by enabling others to use the knowledge behind the invention. Therefore, plant breeders were imperfect inventors, relying on the (largely undefined) biology of their plants to produce and reproduce new traits and varieties.[45] They could provide suitable conditions for such innovations to occur (for example, by increasing the number of crosses between two parental plants), but eventually relied on the plants' own knowledge for bringing these about. At a loss when asked about the principle behind their invention, they could only point to the organism itself as the source.

Politics in the US and Europe, caught between the desire to stimulate the plant-breeding industry and breeders' inability to comply with the basics of patent law, came up with two similar yet diverging answers to the problem. The US Plant Patent Act of 1930 provided reduced protection (compared to full patent protection) for breeders working towards new plant traits. The question of whether a breeder invented or simply discovered a particular plant feature—one of the tests for telling technology from nature—did not play a role for plant patents, unlike the ability to reproduce that feature true to form.[46] As a result, the US Plant Patent Act only grants protection for those plants that can be reliably reproduced, that is clonally reproduced plants (excluding tubers).[47] The Act targeted the horticultural sector (ie fruit trees), which relies heavily on grafting and is characterized by extremely long generational times.[48] While every new act of sexual reproduction involves new mixing and therefore unforeseeable results, clonal propagation promises to recreate a filial plant identical to its parent.[49]

Whereas 'nature' was one of the biggest roadblocks for the expansion of US patent law into the realm of life, the situation in Europe was somewhat different. The dualism in Europe, as became apparent once more in *Tomatoes/Broccoli*, was not between 'nature' and 'technology' or 'invention', but between 'biology' and

[45] Jay Sanderson, *Plants, People and Practices: The Nature and History of the UPOV Convention* (Cambridge University Press 2017) 81.

[46] 'Whoever invents or discovers and asexually reproduces any distinct and new variety of plant, including cultivated sports, mutants, hybrids, and newly found seedlings, other than a tuber propagated plant or a plant found in an uncultivated state, may obtain a patent therefor, subject to the conditions and requirements of this title.' Plant Patent Act 1930 (US).

[47] ibid.

[48] Cary Fowler, 'The Plant Patent Act of 1930: A Sociological History of Its Creation' (2000) 82 *Journal of the Patent & Trademark Office Society* 621.

[49] In practice, asexual reproduction, too, is of course subject to variation: George Acquaah, *Principles of Plant Genetics and Breeding* (2nd edn, Wiley 2012) 152. Compared to sexual reproduction, however, reproduction true to kind is much more likely with asexual than with sexual reproduction.

'technicity', a seemingly trivial yet crucial difference.[50] European plant variety protection (PVP) laws, first established in the 1940s and harmonized in 1961 in the International Union for the Protection of New Varieties of Plants (UPOV) Convention, took a different approach from the US Plant Patent Act by protecting asexually as well as sexually reproducing plants. PVP, modelled on field crops rather than horticulturals as in the US plant patents, was more optimistic when it came to the ability of sexually reproducing plants to yield identical offspring, but also relied on thorough inbreeding of varieties to achieve genetic homogeneity.[51] At the time, breeders freely crossed existing varieties, selected the offspring, and selfed it to achieve genetically homogenous plants. PVP limited protection to varieties, excluding other forms of plant innovations such as traits, individual mutants, or sports because they did not comply with an idea of breeding that saw breeders as producers and farmers as consumers of commodified farm input.[52] Importantly, PVP also explicitly allowed third parties to use protected varieties for cross-breeding (the so-called 'breeder's exemption') precisely because the random nature of sexual reproduction would produce new varieties rather than reproducing existing ones. In this regard, PVP reflects the nature of commercial plant breeding in the twentieth century as well as its epistemic and ontological underpinnings whereby breeders invested money, time, and labour into developing new plants, not inventive ideas. What they needed protection for was a marketable, standardized product, not for a speculative and more or less abstract idea that was still in search of a commercial embodiment.[53]

The Essence of Biology

When European countries sought in the 1960s and 1970s to establish a common legal space for patents with the EPC, one aim was to keep PVP and patent law separate.[54] Far-reaching prohibitive powers of patent holders were not to interfere with the liberties granted by PVP legislation, while the breeder's exemption should not undermine the economic principles of patent protection. This resulted in Article 53(b) of the 1973 EPC, wherein plant varieties and 'essentially biological processes

[50] Kelvin W Willoughby, 'How Much Does Technology Really Matter in Patent Law? A Comparative Analysis of Doctrines of Appropriate Patentable Subject Matter in American and European Patent Law' (2009) 18 *Federal Circuit Bar Journal* 63. The European doctrine of technicity bears resemblance with the considerations raised in the early US legal discourse on plant patents, and in fact it is tempting to contemplate how *Chakrabarty* would have turned out if technicity and biology, not nature and technology, had been at the heart of it. See Sherman (n 6); Pottage and Sherman, *Figures of Invention* (n 6); Pottage and Sherman, 'Kinds, Clones, and Manufactures' (n 6).

[51] Sanderson (n 45) 116.

[52] Braun (n 14).

[53] ibid. For the epistemics of plant breeding see Martin Timmermann, *Der Züchterblick: Erfahrung, Wissen und Entscheidung in der Getreidezüchtung* (Shaker 2009).

[54] For the history of the EPC see Parthasarathy (n 1); Sanderson (n 45) 126.

for the production of plants and animals' are explicitly exempt from patentability.[55] The clause is clearly related to the preceding Article 52, which precludes non-technical innovations from patenting, in turn also (implicitly) requiring patented inventions to be of technical character.[56] However, the biological is not always simply the technological's other, as the German Federal Court's *Rote Taube* ruling of 1969, a landmark case for European patent law, clarifies. While the judges found animal breeds to lack reproducibility and therefore patent eligibility, they explicitly noted that the relationship between technical and biological was ambiguous and non-technicality alone did not preclude inventions from patentability.[57] As far as plant varieties are concerned, the motives behind Article 53(b) of the EPC can be read economically, as an attempt at protecting an established industry and its existing IP instruments from disruption. With PVP, there was already an IP specifically for plant varieties, while breeders should not be excluded from using the most basic of plant-breeding techniques, ie crossing, selecting, and back-breeding. However, a legal–technical reading is also possible, whereby plant varieties are not patentable because their biological character does not lend itself to the same forms of explication as chemical compounds, machines, or electronic devices. For the same reasons, the same clause exempts 'essentially biological processes' as they can be described in minute detail, but the relationship between this description and the results produced by following it is loosely defined at best.

The frequent mixture of biological and technical elements in plant—and animal breeding has remained a contentious issue at the EPO for the last three decades. With the end of patent barriers to conventional as well as biotech organisms in the US, Europe, also, saw a rise in non-transgenic plant patent applications between 1990 and 2010, with a total of 438 applications for non-transgenic plants filed at the EPO.[58] Against this background, the EPO found itself prompted to take a clear stance on the matter in *State of Israel/Tomatoes* and *Plant Biosciences/Broccoli*.[59] Two main questions arose with regard to Article 53(2). First, what was the meaning and extent of 'essential' in 'essentially biological'? Secondly, what about the non-variety products of essentially biological processes? The former was raised with regard to breeding techniques that were more or less conventional; that is, they were based on cross-fertilization and subsequent selection of progeny, but involving one or more elements that were clearly non-biological or in their totality qualifying as non-biological. In both *Hybrid Plants/Lubrizol*[60] and *Transgenic Plant/*

[55] EPC 1973, art 53(b). The article was carried over into the 2000 revision of the EPC without changes to the numbering or wording: EPC 2000, art 53(b).

[56] Bently and others (n 10) 478.

[57] BGH X ZB 15/67, 8.

[58] PATSTAT 2018 (n 11). During the same period, the EPO received 7,859 applications for patents on biotech plants.

[59] Rumour within the patent lawyer community has it that there were forces in the EPO specifically pushing for the two applications to be granted to bring about a landmark decision that would clear up open questions in plant patent law.

[60] T 032087 (EPO 1988).

Novartis,[61] the EPO's Technical and Enlarged Board of Appeal (EBA), found that either overall composition of the process or the presence of key non-biological elements could qualify breeding processes for patentability but did not set a general position for the EPO to adopt in this regard. In *Transgenic Plant/Novartis*, the EBA also ruled that genetic material could be patented as long as such 'material' was either more (ie included in several varieties) or less than a variety (ie included in one plant or cell line only, which did not amount to a variety in the UPOV sense).[62] It thus gave clear guidance with respect to the variety provisions in Article 53(2) of the EPC.

In their response to the opposition, the Volcani Center's lawyers pointed out that the last step of the breeding process claimed in the patent, 'screening for fruit water content', went beyond mere selection as performed by breeders and amounted to a technical step, in turn qualifying the entire process for patentability. They argued that since the trait could be applied to more than one variety of plants, the variety clause of Article 53(2) of the EPC did not apply either.[63] The same stance was taken by Plant Bioscience, whose lawyers claimed that the preparation of cell extracts went beyond 'essentially biological' and therefore rendered the entire process 'essentially technical'.[64] Oral proceedings were held by the EPA's Opposition Division in June 2004 (*Broccoli*) and March 2006 (*Tomatoes*), where Richard Mithen and Arthur Schaffer testified as inventors and technical experts. In both cases, the Opposition Division rejected the opposing parties' demands to reject the patents but instead granted them in amended form after both patent proprietors dropped the methods claims from their applications.[65] As was to be expected, the opposing parties appealed these decisions, taking the cases to the Technical Board of Appeal, which in turn relegated both patents to the Enlarged Board of Appeal in 2006 and 2007, respectively, asking for clarification on the nature of a process that contained an additional non-biological step and, in case the Enlarged Board of Appeal deemed it essentially biological, on the patentability of its products.[66]

The Enlarged Board of Appeal gave interested observers time to file a total of 233 *amici curiae* to comment on the matter and consolidated both cases into one in July 2010 before handing down its ruling in December of the same year.[67] Therein,

[61] G1/98 (EPO 1999).

[62] Sanderson (n 45) 130.

[63] R Perry, Reply of the patent proprietor to the notice of opposition, 'Proprietor's Observation on the Opposition' (8 April 2005) 1.

[64] A Maschio, Reply of the patent proprietor to the notices of opposition, 'Opposition to European Patent No EP-1 069 819-B1 (formerly Appl No 99915885.8) Plant Bioscience Limited' (21 November 2003) 8.

[65] T Kania, 'Minutes of the Oral Proceedings before the Opposition Division' (17 April 2004); J Puonti-Kaerlas, 'Minutes of the Oral Proceedings before the Opposition Division' (3 April 2006).

[66] ibid.

[67] European Patent Office, 'All Documents: EP1069819' European Patent Register https://register.epo.org/application?number=EP99915886&lng=en&tab=doclist (accessed 21 February 2022) (43 *amicus* briefs); European Patent Office, 'All Documents: EP1211926' European Patent Register) https://

the EBA focused on the meaning and implications of Article 53(2) EPC and of rule 26(5) of the EPC, which defines the terms of the EPC and states that 'A process for the production of plants or animals is essentially biological if it consists entirely of natural phenomena such as crossing or selection'[68] but remains silent on whether an additional technical step would in turn confer a technical nature on the same process. The patent holders and some *amicus* writers argued that what the EPC authors had in mind was to exclude only plant varieties and their production from patent protection, rather than plants and plant breeding in general. They pointed to the drafting history of the EPC, in which the first exemptions referred to 'plant varieties' rather than 'plants', and claimed that this showed the authors only intended to carve out a narrow exemption. Given the lack of historical evidence for such an intention, the EBA rejected this view, interpreting the article as applying to all plant-breeding processes.[69]

The main challenge faced by the EBA was to situate the 'essentially biological' between the poles of 'all or nothing'; that is, the idea that any technical step in a process automatically rendered the whole process technical or, conversely, that even a single biological step within a process exempted it from patentability altogether.[70] In this decision, the EBA argued that there are technical elements that in the spirit of the EPC should be considered accidental to the breeding process or the plant that results from it (such as greenhouses, scissors for cutting branches, or molecular markers), whereas other technical elements and steps are central to it because their effects could not occur in nature, without human intervention.[71] The EBA concluded that it was the plants, their genomes, and the process of meiosis in sexual reproduction that determined the outcomes of an essentially biological process and not human ingenuity and control.[72] The EBA argued that the opposite was the case where human intervention did not occur before or after but during reproduction.[73]

register.epo.org/application?number=EP00940724&lng=en&tab=doclist (accessed 21 February 2022) (180 *amicus* briefs).

[68] EPC 2000, r 26(5).

[69] G 2/7 (EPO 2010) 52.

[70] ibid 55, 60. The 'technical' character of an invention is of special importance to the EPC, especially because of the German version of EPC 2000, art 52(1). Although German has 'Technologie' as a cognate to English 'technology', German patent law prefers *Technik* when referring to the realm of patentable subject matter. The doctrine that inventions refer to 'technical teachings' (*technische Lehren*) was first put forward by the German Federal Court in *Rote Taube*: see n 57.

[71] The board refers to the early drafts of the EPC from 1961 here, in which 'purely' was changed to 'essentially', and argues that it was knowledge of such auxiliary breeding technologies that prompted the authors of the convention to do so. See G 2/7 (EPO 2010) 64.

[72] ibid 66.

[73] The Enlarged Board of Appeal justified this stance with the existence of EPC 2000, R 27(c), which explicitly mentions technical or microbiological steps as qualifying elements for patent eligibility of biotechnological inventions. See G 2/7 (EPO 2010) 68.

The 'biological', as construed here, can neither be fully subsumed under nature nor under human intervention. Although, as the EBA noted, recombination and selection are natural processes, the exclusion of biology in the case of plant breeding cannot be reduced to crossing and selection in the wild without human intervention, as it would render the provisions of the EPC irrelevant because such processes would never qualify for patent protection in the first place. To the contrary, the judges noted that recombination and selection in the nursery always take place under a regime of human intervention.[74] At the same time, as they pointed out, the results of the breeding process cannot fully be attributed to human intervention, as the mixing of whole genomes is unpredictable and can only be sorted out through subsequent reiterative selection. The 'biological' in the EBA's reasoning is best understood as a third instance, neither simply 'out there' nor invented, but instead creative in its own right. Curiously, however, the EBA remained silent on the status of plants resulting from essentially biological processes. If the latter were unpatentable, did that also extend to the former?

Of Products and Processes: Delimiting an Exemption

After the first ruling by the Enlarged Board of Appeal, both patents were amended and all process claims dropped by the applicants. As it was still unclear whether Article 53(b) of the EPC only had implications for processes, or conversely, if patent protection for conventionally bred plants rendered the process exemption meaningless, the cases were again referred to the Enlarged Board of Appeal for clarification in May 2012 (*Tomatoes II*) and July 2013 (*Broccoli II*).[75] The Technical Board put forward four questions with regard to the patents, asking whether the exclusion of breeding processes could have a negative effect on the patentability of conventionally bred plants and whether such plants were patentable as product-by-process—even if the process as a whole or in part was biological and it was the only way to obtain such a plant.[76] Benoît Batistelli, then president of the EPO, was asked by the Enlarged Board to give his opinion on these questions and strongly affirmed that conventionally bred plants should indeed be considered patentable.[77] Interestingly, he was joined in this opinion not only by the patent proprietors

[74] G 2/7 (EPO 2010) 39.

[75] Although the Technical Board of Appeal, following *Transgenic Plant/Novartis*, considered plants and plant parts patentable in general (hence not touching upon the 'variety' provision of art 53(2)), the key difference here rested on the fact that the tomatoes and the broccoli had been obtained only by conventional, non-biotechnological reproductive techniques. See G 2/7 (EPO 2010) 9–10.

[76] The first referral (*Tomatoes*) included three questions, which the Technical Board expanded to four in its referral of *Broccoli* a year later. See G 2/13 (EPO 2015) 3, 12.

[77] B Batistelli, 'Case G 2/12: Invitation to Comment under Article 9 of the Rules of Procedure' (28 November 2012); B Batistelli, 'Case G 2/13: Invitation to Comment under Article 9 of the Rules of Procedure' (21 November 2013).

and dozens of *amicus* authors, but also by the opponents to the *Broccoli* patent, Syngenta and Limagrain.[78]

After joining both cases into *Broccoli/Tomatoes II*, the Enlarged Board of Appeal eventually sided with the proponents of patent protection for conventionally bred plants. The EBA concluded that there was nothing in the EPC (or elsewhere) that would preclude the EPO from issuing such patents. It thus read the exclusion for essentially biological processes narrowly and drew a clear line between processes on the one hand and products on the other, despite considerable criticism and demands to the contrary from outside the court.[79] While the EBA acknowledged the existence of 'various ethical, social and economic aspects in the general debate',[80] it refrained from engaging with them, pointing out that 'considering such general arguments in the present referrals did not fall under the judicial decision-making powers of the enlarged board'.[81] Instead, it focused on the letter of the applicable law, an approach that led Axel Metzger, pre-eminent commentator on plant IP law in Germany, to speak of '[l]egal [p]ositivists at [w]ork'.[82] Beyond the court chamber, it was indeed difficult to explain why breeding processes should be exempt, yet the plants produced by such processes to be perfectly patentable.

However, this was not entirely the Enlarged Board's decision. During the drafting of the EPC, there was, as the EBA pointed out in its 2010 decision, a strong intention to keep patent law and PVP separate. At the time, varieties were the only manifestation of plants that had a legal status in Europe and, seven years before *Diamond v Chakrabarty*, the patenting of organisms was not on anyone's mind. Hence, it was only breeding processes that were explicitly exempt from patent eligibility, and so there was in practice no interference between patent and PVP law. When in the 1980s the European Community (later Union) sought to stimulate research and development in biotechnology and create a domestic industry in that field, there was a clear interest in granting patent protection for transgenic plants, a technology then expected to revolutionize agriculture. Although the legislative process started in 1988, it would take ten years to pass the final Biotechnology Directive 98/44/EC.

78 G 2/13 (EPO 2015) 23. Limagrain, however, added that a breeders' exemption similar to UPOV would be desirable for patents on native traits. Unilever had at that point withdrawn its appeal. For the possible motives of plant biotech and conventional breeding companies to endorse and pursue patents see Braun (n 4).

79 Some European legislators, such as the Dutch and the German parliaments, had already moved towards excluding conventionally bred plants from patent eligibility in their national patent laws. See Timo Minssen and Ana Nordberg, 'The Impact of "Broccoli II" and "Tomatoes II" on European Patents in Conventional Breeding, GMOs, and Synthetic Biology: The Grand Finale of a Juicy Patents Tale?' (2015) 34 *Biotechnology Law Report* 81; Parthasarathy (n 1) 183.

80 G 2/13 (EPO 2015) 63.

81 ibid 64.

82 Axel Metzger, 'Patents on Tomatoes and Broccoli: Legal Positivists at Work' (2016) 47 *IIC—International Review of Intellectual Property and Competition Law* 515.

Many of the issues that slowed down the drafting and adoption of the directive were ethical concerns over the patenting of life forms, especially in 'red' (ie medical) biotechnology.[83] However, in the field of plant breeding, the foreseeable clash between the exclusions afforded by patent protection and the liberal breeders' exemption, which allowed companies to use any commercial variety for breeding, prompted economic rather than ethical concerns among the plant-breeding industry. Since the right to exclude competitors in patent law is limited by the breeders' exemption, the existence of a commercial variety with a transgenic trait such as herbicide tolerance would have rendered either one or the other meaningless. The Biotechnology Directive sought to remedy this by limiting patent protection to traits that were not restricted to one variety and by offering the possibility of compulsory licences if inventors or breeders found that they could not practise their business without infringing on others' variety titles or patents.[84] In practice, however, the requirements for a compulsory licence are high and they are costly and uncertain to obtain.[85]

Thus, what stopped patent and PVP law and new and old plant-breeding companies from clashing was not so much the legal provisions of European patent law, but the political death of agricultural biotechnology on the continent. From the early 2000s onwards, first consumers, then supermarkets, farmers, and politicians turned their backs on genetic engineering. With skyrocketing regulatory costs and no market for biotechnological traits, they could no longer interfere with the free cross-breeding of varieties as practised by breeders.[86] Yet the architecture of European plant patent law remained in place, disproportionately favouring patents on traits over titles on plant varieties. What *Tomatoes/Broccoli* did was to lay bare the latent conflict between the two forms of IP. The exemption of PVP from the patent framework carved out in the 1990s was very limited. It froze the status quo of PVP law and laid the groundwork for a further extension of patent law to new subject matters.[87] What the Enlarged Board of Appeal did in *Tomatoes/Broccoli II* was to read the spirit of the 1990s into the matter, concluding that wherever legislators had failed to put a clear stop to the expansion of patent law, they had at least implicitly approved of it. By seeking to refrain from practising politics, the board had simply reproduced the politics baked into the 1998 directive.

[83] Parthasarathy (n 1).

[84] Directive 98/44/EC of the European Parliament and of the Council of 6 July 1998 on the legal protection of biotechnological inventions [1998] OJ L 213/13, art 12(1–3).

[85] A breeder or inventor needs to apply for a regular licence first and, after failing, has to demonstrate that 'the plant variety or the invention constitutes significant technical progress of considerable economic interest compared with the invention claimed in the patent or the protected plant variety'. See Directive 98/44/EC (n 84) art 12(3). As variety breeders are much more dependent on a licence than inventors, the directive puts the former at a disadvantage. See Girard (n 14).

[86] Sanderson (n 45) 81; Braun (n 14).

[87] See Eisenberg (n 21) for a discussion of patent law and its transformation from an IP right for specific industries into a general regime expanding into ever-new fields of technology.

In doing so, however, the board had misread that things had changed since the 1990s. The European public and politicians had become suspicious of plant patents, viewing them as instruments for the business interests of powerful biotech multinationals.[88] Conventional breeders, once excited about the possibilities of new molecular tools, now faced the threat of increasing transaction costs for obtaining licences and entering into patenting themselves, without the prospect of benefiting from a new technology.[89] Although technically the last word on the matter, the Enlarged Board of Appeal's ruling became more and more untenable in the aftermath of the decision. Plant breeders' associations and members of the EU Parliament pushed for exemptions for conventional plants in national and European patent law. The EU Commission was called upon to clarify that no one had originally intended to grant patents for conventionally bred plants. In 2017, the president of the EPO, abandoning his earlier stance on the matter, took the Commission's clarification as cause for introducing a new rule to the implementing regulations of the patent convention, stating that no patents should henceforth be granted for plants obtained by essentially biological processes.[90]

This step would prove problematic for several reasons. First, there was now a divide within the EPO, with the president on one side and the boards of appeal on the other. Secondly, while the EPO's president is in charge of executive matters and implementing regulations, the Enlarged Board of Appeal is its highest juridical authority in interpreting the EPC. Lastly, the 'change of mind' had come about through political rather than legislative means. The Commission had given (unsolicited) legal advice to a non-EU entity (the EPO) on a directive created by the Council and the Parliament some twenty years earlier. Unsurprisingly, the case entered another round, this time under the title *Pepper*. Syngenta filed an appeal to the Technical Board of Appeal, this time demanding that one of its applications on a bell-pepper plant rejected under the new rule be re-examined. Citing the Enlarged Board's decision in *Tomato/Broccoli II*, the Technical Board of Appeal sided with Syngenta in late 2018 and ruled that the former's interpretation of the European Patent Convention trumped the presidential office's implementing regulations.[91] The new president of the EPO, António Campinos, again requested an authoritative interpretation from the Enlarged Board of Appeal, which seized the opportunity to declare the new rule valid in May 2020.[92] After more than two decades, the question raised by two inconspicuous vegetable patent applications was finally answered—for now.

[88] See Daniel Charles, *Lords of the Harvest: Biotech, Big Money, and the Future of Food* (Perseus Books Group 2001); Bernhard Gill, *Streitfall Natur: Weltbilder in Technik—und Umweltkonflikten* (Westdeutscher Verlag 2003); Jasanoff (n 8).
[89] Braun (n 14).
[90] EPC 2000, r 28(2).
[91] T 1063/18 (EPO 2018).
[92] G 3/19 (EPO 2020).

Conclusion: Biology and After

At first sight, little remains of *Tomatoes/Broccoli*, other than the status quo and 'common sense' with respect to conventionally bred plants being reinstated. Yet two things are worth noting about the series of cases and decisions that came in its wake. First, the question of what was 'essentially biological' was opened by the EPO in order to answer questions it had inherited from the biotech revolution of the 1990s, but subsequently took on a life of its own. Just as patent law had redefined life in the 1980s and 1990s, biotechnology redefined the boundaries between old and new plant-breeding industries and their practices. In addition, the 'old' plant-breeding industry had changed too, with traits gaining in importance compared with varieties.[93] The attempts by the Enlarged Board to discern the meaning of 'essentially biological' at the end of the 1990s or calls by plant-breeding associations to return to the legal status quo before *Tomatoes/Broccoli* were thus understandable but ultimately futile. Even if the EPO, much to the dismay of some constitutional scholars, patent lawyers, and plant-breeding institutes dependent on patent royalties, eventually relented following pressure from politics, the economic and political consensus of 1961, 1973, or 1998 could not be revived.

This leads to my second point. In *Tomatoes/Broccoli I*, the Enlarged Board of Appeal went to great lengths to arrive at an understanding of biology that was compatible with patent law. At the same time, it showed a deep sense of the historical shifts that plant breeding had undergone over the past half century, from glasshouses to molecular markers. What if, instead of seeking simply to re-enact the status quo of the late twentieth century, the board had pursued the same sensibility in *Tomatoes/Broccoli II*? While the Enlarged Board's wish to limit itself to legal questions is understandable, staying out of politics, ethics, and economics is not the same as staying out of biology, as its earlier ruling had demonstrated. What the board risked in sticking to the letter of the law was not only an eventual loss of face at having to bow to political pressure; it also risked losing sight of the conflicts and contradictions resulting from a biology infused with law and economics. Legally, the reaffirmation of 'biology' in *Tomatoes/Broccoli II* thus enshrines a form of post-war plant breeding whose practices, tools, and plants have changed considerably over the past decades.[94]

The blame would be misplaced if laid solely on the Enlarged Board of Appeal. The focus on 'biology', rather than 'nature' or 'life' made it difficult for activists and groups critical of life science patents to intervene, as their usual critiques

[93] Veit Braun, 'Die Neuerfindung Des Rades? Zur Rolle Der Innovation in Der Bioökonomie' in Lukas Fehr and Reinhard Johler (eds), *Bioökonomie(n). Ethnografische Forschungszugänge und Felder* (TVV-Verlag 2021).

[94] Sanderson (n 45) 81; Braun (n 14).

and arguments hardly resonated with the matters discussed in court.[95] Actors with much more political space for manoeuvre, such as the breeders' associations and legislators, did little more than press for a return to the status quo during the twenty years of *Tomatoes/Broccoli*. Proposals that acknowledged the shifting realities of plant breeding, calling for a harmonization rather than separation of patent and PVP law, were few and far between.[96] There is a general pessimism within the European plant-breeding industry that plant patent law can be reformed. Plant-breeding associations fear that any attempt to facilitate access to patented traits and to waive the right to exclude for native trait patents would be read as attempts to undermine biopatents as a whole. They would be met with considerable resistance by more powerful industries. As such, the sector pursued the path of least resistance and the reaffirmation of the consensus reached in the Biotechnology Directive.[97]

This attitude is understandable. But is it tenable? With the advent of new molecular tools for plant breeding, the demarcation line between the biological and technical is once again up for debate. Plant-breeding companies are eager to use molecular techniques such as gene editing to breed plants faster and cheaper, yet there is no clear idea as to how this desire can be squared with the idea of a separation of PVP and patent law. In order to maintain the status quo so acrimoniously defended in *Tomatoes/Broccoli I* and *II*, the European plant-breeding industry would have to stay 'clean', or rather 'essentially biological'. Already, European plant breeders' wish to do business as usual is being undermined by their hope of transcending the limits of traditional breeding techniques and the proliferation of gene-edited seeds elsewhere in the world.[98] This is reminiscent of the late 1990s, when the sector endorsed genetic engineering despite the negative consequences that

[95] Viola Prifti, 'Die Rolle Des Öffentlichen Interesses an Pflanzenpatenten: Eine Europäische Perspektive' in Barbara Brandl and Stephan Schleissing (eds), *Biopatente* (Nomos 2016); Parthsarathy (n 1) 182.

[96] The greatest exception here is certainly the ILP Vegetable, a clearinghouse initiated by Michael Kock, then head of IP at Syngenta and the company's representative in the *Broccoli* appeal. The initiative seeks to remedy the shortcomings of European patent law through contract law and elaborate arbitration mechanisms and is regarded as a model for similar platforms in field crops. See Michael A Kock and Floris ten Have, 'The "International Licensing Platform—Vegetables": A Prototype of a Patent Clearing House in the Life Science Industry' (2016) 11 *Journal of Intellectual Property Law & Practice* 496; Geertrui Van Overwalle, 'Patent Pools and Clearinghouses in the Life Sciences: Back to the Future' in Duncan Matthews and Herbert Zech (eds), *Research Handbook on Intellectual Property and the Life Sciences* (Edward Elgar Publishing 2017). Limagrain's endorsement of conventional plant patents, combined with its simultaneous calls for a facilitated compulsory licence system in *Tomatoes/Broccoli II*, can be read along the same lines. Girard (n 14) provides a critical perspective on the ILP.

[97] Braun (n 4). The *Tomatoes/Broccoli II* ruling has since been followed by Mexico's national IP office, which issued a similar regulation regarding conventionally bred plants: Corina Silva, 'Mexico: New Hurdles for Plant Rights Owners' *Life Sciences Intellectual Property Review* (23 September 2021) https://www.lifesciencesipreview.com/contributed-article/mexico-new-hurdles-for-plant-rights-owners (accessed 28 July 2022).

[98] Michael A Kock, 'Open Intellectual Property Models for Plant Innovations in the Context of New Breeding Technologies' (2021) 11 *Agronomy* 1218.

patent law had had on the North American seed market.[99] Back then, the European sector was 'saved' by the political failure of agricultural biotechnology and consumers' disavowal, which rendered the collision of PVP and patents a purely theoretical scenario. Whether molecular technologies will sail under the radar of public scepticism or trigger it once more is difficult to tell at this point. But what is already clear is that the issues and contradictions debated in *Tomatoes/Broccoli I* and *II* are bound to resurface once gene editing and other molecular technologies are adopted by plant breeders.

Disregarding political and economic considerations about the effects of patent protection on the legal side, only to push them through in a haphazard, semi-legislative, semi-judicial process is unlikely to make these two forms match. Whereas 'nature' almost automatically conjures—albeit in an often crude juxtaposition between the few and the many— matters of distribution, access, and political economy, 'biology' does not come with the same ability. What is at stake instead is a rather technical question of which types of forces and elements contribute to an organism and whether it can be reproduced without relying on that organism itself. Similarly, where 'life' brings into question the applicability and legitimacy of patents on organisms as such, 'biology' can at best modify the universal claim of patent law to all practices and objects of innovation. European patent legislators did not exempt conventionally bred plants from patent protection because they considered IP's idea of ownership as being at odds with the dignity of life, but because patent law historically had difficulty applying some of its assumptions to them and because the plant-breeding industry could rely on other ways of claiming IP in living beings.

And yet, although 'biology' has, as argued here, become problematic again, *Tomatoes/Broccoli I* and *II* also demonstrate its usefulness. Unlike 'nature', which mostly denotes an abstract realm predating human interference, 'biology' can in fact be meaningfully employed and upheld as a concept in the vicinity of technicity and invention, as the Enlarged Board of Appeal demonstrated in its 2010 ruling. In delimiting the boundaries of 'biology', it also pointed to the limits of 'technology', two concepts that in the field of plant breeding should best be understood as going hand-in-hand, not separately. In this regard, 'biology' seems to be more productive than the battles over 'nature' and 'life' that haunted public debate over biopatents in the 1990s and 2000s. As Hannah Landecker so aptly remarks, there is not only a history of biology (a genealogy and trajectory science), but also a biology of history (a material force entering into the politics of its time).[100] At the heart of *Tomatoes/Broccoli I* and *II* is not a shifting understanding of biology but rather a shifting

[99] Piet Schenkelaars, Huib de Vriend, and Nicholas Kalatzaidonakes, 'Drivers of Consolidation in the Seed Industry and Its Consequences for Innovation' (COGEM 2011).

[100] Hannah Landecker, *Culturing Life: How Cells Became Technologies* (Harvard University Press 2007).

biology, which undermines established notions of what is biological and technical, bred and invented in the wake of new biotechnologies, changing ways of breeding plants, and novel techniques that enter into the relationship of humans and plants. If there is anything to learn from these two cases, it is that 'biology' is not a fixed realm to look to in search for ethical, political, or legal clarity, but a standing call to critically re-examine our relationship with our organic others, time and again.

4

Intellectual Property's Antecedent

Seed Law and the Regulation of Biological Materials in British Colonial Gambia

*Susannah Chapman**

Introduction

It is sometimes argued that one of the defining features of modern agribusiness is its capacity to monopolize life itself.[1] The extension of intellectual property protection to plants—whether in the form of plant patents, plant variety protection, or utility patents—has enabled a control over biological life that appears to be novel, not only in how it regulates the reproduction, form, and circulation of living materials, but also in the way it shifts the locus of capital accumulation in agricultural production.[2] Whereas colonial and early industrial agriculture were based upon the coercion of labour, the monopolization of trade, or the transformation of peasant economies, contemporary agribusiness is seen to rest upon control of living materials and the capture of life's productivity.[3]

This chapter explores programmes to control the reproduction, form, and circulation of biological materials within colonial agricultural schemes of the early twentieth century. Specifically, it follows the design and implementation of a series of colonial projects that focused on the regulation of groundnut seed in British Gambia during the interwar period. In following this history, I am interested in how attention to colonial regulatory projects that focused on the control of living

* Many people have helped bring this chapter into being. I thank Tad Brown and Xan Chacko for their comments on multiple drafts of this chapter, and Jose Bellido and Brad Sherman for their support and feedback from abstract to final draft. My thinking on the laws I explore here has evolved in conversation with members of the ARC Laureate Group on Intellectual Property and Food Security at The University of Queensland. In particular, conversations with Brad Sherman and Kencho Peldon have pushed my thinking on these legal schemes. None of this research would have been possible without the assistance of archivists at the Gambia National Archives, the National Archives in the UK, the Bristol Archives, and the Kew Archives. My readings of archival materials are always in conversation with the accounts of seed management practices offered by farmers in Jarra West, The Gambia. As always, all mistakes and shortcomings are my own.

1 Vandana Shiva, *Stolen Harvest: The Hijacking of the Global Food Supply* (South End Press 2000).

2 Raj Patel, 'The Long Green Revolution' (2013) 40 *The Journal of Peasant Studies* 1.

3 David Nally, 'The Biopolitics of Food Provisioning' (2011) 36 *Transactions of the Institute of British Geographers* 37; Melanie Cooper, *Life as Surplus: Biotechnology and Capitalism in the Neoliberal Era* (University of Washington Press 2008).

Susannah Chapman, *Intellectual Property's Antecedent* In: *Intellectual Property and the Design of Nature*. Edited by: Jose Bellido and Brad Sherman, Oxford University Press.
DOI: 10.1093/oso/9780192864406.003.0004

materials provides insight into the diverse genealogies of power that shape the various forms of plant intellectual property law today; that is, I am interested in tracking the legal regulation of biological life into times and places where the primary focus of regulatory schemes seemed to be engaged elsewhere, whether on labour or markets or standards, to consider how 'older elements of knowledge and understanding remain available and selectively applicable' within in new regulatory terrains.[4]

In tracing the rise and fall of colonial seed law, this chapter shows how programmes to regulate the reproduction and circulation of living materials possess a long history that precedes the extension of patents and plant variety protection to seed in the second half of the twentieth century. This is a history with deep roots in colonial projects to control commodity markets and reshape the materiality and form of living things. Specifically, I demonstrate that the colonial body—comprising people and the seeds they cultivated—provided a space for regulatory experimentation in forms of biocontrol that only later emerge in the colonial metropolis. In this testing ground, the colonial government turned to policy, standardization, agricultural science, and, eventually, law to make seeds (and their human accomplices) behave in a way that was amenable to the needs of European markets. Plants and people emerged as the focus of new biopolitical projects that were at once experiments in the redesign of living materials and experiments in the design of new regulatory techniques.

British colonial Gambia was not alone in this experimentation. In the early twentieth century, states developed a variety of juridical mechanisms to control the reproduction and circulation of biological materials.[5] In such schemes, which were often directed at specific economically important crops, controlling the seed was often a key component of broader programmes to control labour, trade, and the transformation of peasant societies.[6] Such schemes have included, among other interventions, national varietal registers for potatoes in Nazi Germany, authorized varietal lists and seed contracts in Vichy France, and the use of contracts for groundnut seed production in colonial Senegal.[7] While some early schemes were

[4] Jane Guyer, 'Toiling Ingenuity: Food Regulation in Britain and Nigeria' (1993) 20 *American Ethnologist* 797, 798; on plants as central to biopolitical projects see Kregg Hetherington, *The Government of Beans: Regulating Life in the Age of Monocrops* (Duke University Press 2020) 4.

[5] Susannah Chapman and Brad Sherman, 'Finding a Place for Agriculture in Intellectual Property Law' (2018) 49 *International Review of Intellectual Property and Competition Law* 759.

[6] Maria Fedorova, 'Seeds as Technology: The Russian Agricultural Bureau in New York and Soviet Agricultural Modernization, 1921–26' (2021) 80 *The Russian Review* 210; Hetherington (n 4); Lino Camprubi, 'One Grain, One Nation: Rice Genetics and the Corporate State in Early Francoist Spain (1939–1952)' (2010) 40 *Historical Studies in the Natural Sciences* 499; Christophe Bonneuil and Frederic Thomas, 'Purifying Landscapes: The Vichy Regime and the Genetic Modernization of France' (2010) 40 *Historical Studies in the Natural Sciences* 532; Angela Zimmerman, *Alabama in Africa: Booker T Washington, the German Empire, and the Globalization of the New South* (Princeton University Press 2010).

[7] Tiago Saraiva, *Fascist Pigs: Technoscientific Organisms and the History of Fascism* (MIT Press 2016); Bonneuil and Thomas (n 6); Christophe Bonneuil, 'Penetrating the Natives: Peanut Breeding, Peasants and the Colonial State in Senegal (1900–1950)' (1999) 4 *Science, Technology, and Society* 273.

formative of specific regulatory metrics (such as measures of purity, uniformity, stability, and distinctness) that would become important components of some later intellectual property protections, other schemes were testing grounds for regulatory techniques that enabled the removal of the state from the direct provisioning of seeds. Like contemporary instantiations of plant intellectual property, these indirect schemes flexed their grip over the movement and reproduction of living materials by intervening in social and agronomic practices concerning seed; that is, they sought to influence the circulation and reproduction of seed by regulating how farmers saved and accessed planting materials.

Whereas contemporary intellectual property law uses technologies of property to structure the reproduction and circulation of plant reproductive material, early indirect provisioning schemes turned to other means. In The Gambia, after trialling a series of direct seed-lending schemes, the colonial administration eventually turned to law and a reformulated model of indirect rule to *regulate* seed 'at a distance'.[8] This 'distance' was not so much a removal of the colonial state from matters concerning seed provisioning as a reorganization of state techniques for governing living populations. As with intellectual property law, with the seednut storage laws came new forms of audit and discipline for farmers and plants alike, new definitions of licit and illicit activity, and new insinuations as to who owned the groundnut seed that farmers cultivated, harvested, and saved. The devolution of responsibility effected by these laws entailed an extension of regulatory power into domains of social life that previously operated largely outside the remit of state regulation, a legal intervention that nonetheless reshaped, for a short while, relations and articulations of property in plants. In these regulatory shifts, projects to reshape biological life provided a space in which new types of claims over biological materials would emerge.

In the sections that follow, I trace three related shifts in the colonial administration's attempts to govern the reproduction and circulation of plant materials. First, in the early twentieth century, plant reproductive material emerged as what Peter Miller and Nikolas Rose described as an 'intelligible field': a preferred and governable site of regulatory intervention in the colonial administration's quest for a 'minimum economic crop'.[9] Second, it was only after a series of failed regulatory experiments directed at regulating plant reproductive material that the law came to be seen as an ideal mechanism for managing seed interventions. Finally, following the shift to the law, new articulations of property in plants began to take shape. Even as the colonial state sought to absolve itself of responsibility for seed provisioning, it often treated farmers' own seedstocks as if they were state property. Following these shifts takes the narrative from early colonial efforts to

[8] Michel Foucault, *Security, Territory, Population: Lectures at the Collège de France, 1977–1978* (Graham Burchell tr, Palgrave Macmillan 2007).

[9] Peter Miller and Nikolas Rose, 'Governing Economic Life' (1990) 19 *Economy and Society* 1, 6.

induce farmers to grow more nuts, to the founding of produce inspection, field trials, and distribution schemes under the first Department of Agriculture, and, finally, to the reformulation of indirect rule amid the international trade depression of the early 1930s.

Inducements to Groundnuts: Credit, Taxes, and Seed Distribution

Early twentieth-century colonial seed policy in British Gambia emerged out of nineteenth-century transformations in production, trade, and labour practices along the river. Before the British took an interest in commercial groundnuts, the crop had a long history in West Africa. Groundnuts (*Arachis hypogaea*), a South American domesticate, first arrived in West Africa in the sixteenth century with Portuguese traders. From outposts in Cape Verde, Angola, and São Tomé and Principe, the Portuguese traded groundnuts with African merchants from the Niger and Senegal basins in exchange for henna, indigo, and other items.[10] As groundnuts spread through regional trade networks, they were adopted by farmers living along the Gambia River, many of whom were already cultivating an indigenous 'ethno-botanical equivalent', the subterranean-ripening legume called Bambara groundnut (*Voandzeiz subterranean*).[11] By the early eighteenth century, farmers living along the lower Gambia River were growing *Arachis hypogaea* as a source of food and fodder, offering the leafy tops to their livestock.[12]

Early cultivation of groundnuts thus rose to prominence outside the sphere of commercial production. It was not until the end of the Atlantic slave trade in the early nineteenth century that farmers began to cultivate groundnuts as a cash crop. Although precise production records are scarce, historians have noted that the regions where commercial groundnuts first took hold were those that had been centres of trade for both enslaved humans and the locally cultivated grains that were purchased to provision ships travelling across the Middle Passage.[13] It was during this period also that the British began to re-establish and expand their presence on the Gambia River. After the British Parliament formally outlawed the slave trade in 1807, the British established a settlement on Banjul Island in 1816, which they named Bathurst. From this small holding at the mouth of the Gambia River,

[10] Kenneth Swindell and Alieu Jeng, *Migrants, Credit, and Climate: The Gambian Groundnut Trade, 1834–1934* (Brill 2006) 14.

[11] Kenneth Swindell, 'Serawoollies, Tillibunkas, and Strange Farmers: The Development of Migrant Groundnut Farming along the Gambia River, 1848–95' (1980) 21 *Journal of African History* 93.

[12] George E Brooks, 'Peanuts and Colonialism: Consequences of the Commercialization of Peanuts in West Africa, 1830–1870' (1975) 16 *Journal of African History* 29.

[13] Assan Sarr, 'Gender, Spirituality, and Economic Change in Rural Gambia: Agricultural Production in the Lower Gambia Region, c. 1830s–1940s' (2017) 45(2) *African Economic History* 1; Judith Carney, *Black Rice: The African Origins of Rice Cultivation in the Americas* (Harvard University Press 2001) 11.

the British sought to control trade and procure new markets for British manufacturers among the peoples of the lower Gambia River.[14]

Amid these shifts in trade and power, groundnuts emerged as a potential commercial export. In 1830, British traders sent a small shipment of Gambian groundnuts to the British Institute for Tropical Agriculture in the West Indies. Then, in 1834, 213 baskets of Gambian groundnuts were shipped to the London-based firm Forster and Smith. One year later, Forster and Smith built a mill in London to render groundnut oil, and exports of Gambian nuts to Great Britain rose steadily thereafter.[15] By the 1850s, over 10,000 tons of groundnuts were being exported from The Gambia annually.[16] Groundnuts offered a new source of income for farmers of the lower Gambia River, many of whom were already enmeshed within the market economy of Atlantic trade networks. As households along the lower Gambia River sought to navigate changing world markets, they turned to growing groundnuts commercially.[17]

The expansion of commercial groundnut production was nonetheless constrained by a number of factors, two of which would become key concerns for the British in their efforts to induce farmers to cultivate more of the crop.[18] First, commercial groundnut production required large pools of labour to bring harvests to market. In the early decades of commercial production, some of this labour was provisioned through domestic slavery, but it was also drawn from members of extended families and their servants. By the 1850s, however, the opportunities offered by commercial groundnut cultivation had also fostered the rise of long-distance migration among young men from other parts of West Africa.[19] On arrival in their seasonal destinations, migrants would find a local host who would provide them with access to the land, tools, and seed required for groundnut cultivation, in addition to housing and social support.[20] The specifics of the contracts between migrants and their hosts varied, but in general they required migrants to work a set number of days on the host's farm and to pay a percentage of their harvest to the host and local leaders.[21]

[14] Donald Wright, *The World and a Very Small Place in Africa: A History of Globalization in Niumi, The Gambia* (2nd edn, ME Sharpe 2004) 125–26. The British had previously controlled a fort on James Island, located in the lower mouth of the Gambia River, which was destroyed by the French in 1779.

[15] ibid 139–40.

[16] Swindell and Jeng (n 10) 19.

[17] Wright (n 14) 141.

[18] Assan Sarr has shown how access to land was also a key constraint in the expansion of commercial groundnut production, despite long-standing arguments that in sub-Saharan Africa labour was scarce while land was plentiful. See Assan Sarr, *Islam, Power, and Dependency in the Gambia River Basin: The Politics of Land Control, 1790–1940* (University of Rochester Press 2016).

[19] Wright (n 14). See also Sarr (n 18).

[20] In Mandinka, migrant farmers are called *samaalalu*, which refers to their arrival during the rainy season. In the colonial archives, these farmers are often referenced as 'strange' farmers.

[21] Swindell and Jeng (n 10) 58.

The rise of migrant farming from the mid-nineteenth century propelled the expansion of commercial groundnut production, particularly along the north bank of the Gambia River, but it also made visible a second major constraint of commercial cultivation.[22] Commercial groundnut production diverted labour from other crops that had historically been cultivated for foodstuffs, particularly coarse grains. In expanding the area dedicated to groundnuts, men moved away from the production of staples such as millet, rice, and sorghum that had helped provision home pantries. This shift put local food supplies under stress, placing most of the responsibility for household grain production on women, and turning areas that had been long sufficient in food into places with a distinct 'hungry season'. By the late 1850s, the incidence of local hunger in centres of commercial groundnut production was on the rise, made more acute by the seasonal influxes of migrants arriving to cultivate groundnuts.[23]

Whereas colonial powers in some parts of Africa used coerced labour and overt violence to force the production of commodity crops, colonizers sometimes pursued more subtle forms of coercion through the manipulation of markets or the control of key points in the chain of production.[24] With many farmers already growing commercial groundnuts in The Gambia, the British largely pursued the latter strategy, first looking to manipulate market relations and later turning their attention to the movement and materiality of seed. Foremost among the early strategies the British used to induce farmers to produce more groundnuts—amid constraints on labour and food—was to encourage an existing system of credit. Under this system, European traders advanced imported trade goods and cash to farmers at the start of each planting season. At harvest, these loans were to be repaid in cash or kind, with interest. As debt mounted, farmers were forced to expand groundnut production. This cut into the ability of households to produce sufficient food and when the incidence of hunger started to rise among debt-strapped farmers, merchants also began importing rice and advancing it on credit.[25]

Among farmers who were not already tied to these markets, the adoption of commercial groundnut production was slower, with places along the south bank of the river showing very little groundnut cultivation even in the last decade of the nineteenth century.[26] In 1894, the British brought the independent kingdoms that flanked the Gambia River under formal control of the colonial administration, a

[22] Sarr (n 13) 143–44.

[23] Donald Wright, 'The Foundations of Modern Gambia: British Rule, 1816–1965' in Abdoulaye Saine, Ebrima Ceesay, and Ebrima Sall (eds), *State and Society in The Gambia Since Independence, 1965–2012* (Africa World Press 2013) 6.

[24] Saraiva (n 7); Zimmerman (n 6); Allen Isaacman and Richard Roberts (eds), *Cotton, Colonialism, and Social History in Sub-Saharan Africa* (Heinemann 1995); on other forms of market coercion see Jonathan E Robins, 'Coercion and Resistance in the Colonial Market: Cotton in Britain's African Empire' in Jonathan Curry-Machado (ed), *Global Histories, Imperial Commodities, Local Interactions* (Palgrave Macmillan 2013) 101.

[25] Wright (n 23).

[26] Sarr (n 18).

territorial addition that they designated as a protectorate of the colony in Bathurst. Soon thereafter, the British implemented a series of taxes throughout the protectorate, first on traders' licences and migrant farmers, and then on extended family compounds. Taxation, as in other colonies, forced farmers to expand the production of the major export commodity.[27] By the first decades of the twentieth century, commercial groundnut cultivation had spread to almost all areas along the south bank of the river, bringing the peoples living there into the sphere of cash cropping, replete with its seasonal influxes of migrant labour, the hungry season, and cycles of loans and debts.[28]

Between roughly 1900 and 1920, British efforts to regulate groundnut seed took shape within this production milieu. The solvency of the colonial government depended upon the production of a sufficiently large crop that could fetch a good price on European markets.[29] Yet questions of how to increase groundnut production were enmeshed with concerns about how to attract more migrant farmers and how to make up for the resulting shortfalls in the production of local foodstuffs. From a very practical standpoint as well, producing more groundnuts also meant that it was necessary to have enough seednuts to plant a sufficiently large crop. Seed was a tricky factor in this equation because farmers not only needed to have enough seednuts to plant their own fields, but they also needed to have sufficient seed to lend to any migrant farmers who might arrive unannounced to cultivate a groundnut farm. Furthermore, unlike other commodity crops in colonial Africa such as cotton or oil palm, seednuts were also a tasty and protein-rich source of food, long tied to local foodways. In other words, from the perspective of the administration, when hunger hit, seednuts might be eaten.

In 1901, the colonial administration entered the credit system developed by merchants and began directly to advance rice and seednuts to farmers.[30] Under this system, every year, travelling commissioners distributed rice (for eating) and seednuts (intended for planting), payment for which was collected after harvest alongside taxes and other rents. Travelling commissioners' reports indicate that farmers were often required to repay twice the amount (in volume or cash value) of seednuts they had received for planting, a rate of repayment that farmers and headmen alike had started to complain was unfairly high.[31] Kenneth Swindell and Alieu Jeng have argued that loans of rice were not a form of welfare as much as they were 'a policy instrument to support the groundnut trade through ensuring a

[27] Swindell and Jeng (n 10); Robins (n 24) 103.

[28] Sarr (n 18) 145.

[29] Wright (n 23).

[30] Kenneth Swindell, 'Enter the Experts: Environmental and Agrarian Change in The Gambia, 1900–1951' in Abdoulaye Saine, Ebrima Ceesay, and Ebrima Sall (eds), *State and Society in The Gambia Since Independence, 1965–2012* (Africa World Press 2013) 34; Bonneuil (n 7).

[31] CSO 2/89 Monthly Diaries, South Bank District 1906, The Gambia National Archives.

sufficient influx of Strange Farmers'.[32] A similar motivation was at play in the loan of seed to farmers. A persistent concern of the colonial administration was that if migrant farmers arrived in The Gambia only to find no seed to plant, they would relocate to groundnut-growing areas in French-controlled Senegal. Even if sufficient seed was not a guarantee that migrant farmers would arrive, insufficient seed seemed to ensure migrant farmers would depart for more opportune places.[33] In addition to drawing farmers into commercial production through cycles of credit and indebtedness, seednut loans were the prime way for the colonial state to attract migrant labour in the quest for a growing export crop. Controlling the movement of plant reproductive material emerged as a key strategy for influencing the movement of people.

For over two decades, the colonial administration used government-issued loans of rice and seednuts to spur on the production of commercial groundnuts. Not only were the debts that resulted from these loans of food and seed difficult, time-consuming, and costly for the colonial administration to collect, but groundnut production continued to grow tenuous amid an increasingly competitive European market, unpredictable commodity prices, and the vagaries of a changing climate.[34] In Gambia, the decade from 1910 to 1920 was wrought with major crop losses—for both groundnuts and foodstuffs—due to increased incidences of drought (1913–1914, 1917–1919), disease, and flooding (1912–1919). Under the credit system, these losses often prompted further distribution of rice and seed, which exacerbated farmer debt. Then, in 1921, the value of groundnuts on the world market crashed and the price paid to Gambian farmers was cut by almost two-thirds.[35] With so little return on their crop, people were unable to repay their loans and, by 1925, the colonial administration was forced to write off a sum of over £32,000 in rice and seednut debt.[36] Thus began the administration's search for alternative strategies to manage the circulation and reproduction of groundnut seed so as to produce a 'minimum economic crop'.

[32] Swindell and Jeng (n 10) 225. Travelling commissioner reports often referenced food shortages in terms of their effect on groundnut cultivation. For example, a 1919 report from one travelling commissioner described acute food shortages due to crop failures, noting that: 'If help is not forthcoming from the Government then there will be little or no Nuts grown and there will certainly be a famine.' See CSO 2/253 Foodstuff in the Upper River Province, Gambia National Archives.

[33] Reports from travelling commissioners underscore the perception of this link at the local level. For example, in June 1919, the travelling commissioner to South Bank Province relayed that: 'The Chief of Fuladu West reported . . . [that] there is a shortage of seednuts which will mean a decrease in the number of strange farmers, with a consequent loss of revenue.' See CSO 2/528 Monthly Diary 1922, South Bank Province, Gambia National Archives.

[34] In 1912, Nigeria entered the groundnut trade and, by the interwar period, India and Senegal were the world's first and second largest exporters of groundnuts, respectively; Swindell (n 30).

[35] ibid.

[36] Swindell and Jeng (n 10) 225. All monetary values cited in the text are original figures and reflect a pound sterling calculated at twenty shillings in a pound and twelve pennies in a shilling.

As the colonial government sought new techniques of seed distribution, it also grew increasingly attentive to issues of seed quality and varietal selection. In the second and third decades of the twentieth century, groundnuts from India, Senegal, and Nigeria began to flood European markets. Although The Gambia could not compete with the scale of production achieved by these larger producers, the colonial administration sought to nurture the colony's standing in export markets by building a reputation for Gambian nuts as high quality and well-suited to European industry standards. Attaining this quality entailed attention to both the material quality of the harvested seednut and the selection and 'improvement' of groundnut cultivars. On the one hand, within the colonial administration, the quest for seednut quality manifested as concern about how cultivation, post-harvest storage, and seed stock management affected the fullness of nuts, free fatty acid content, moisture content, and the prevalence of rotten or diseased kernels. Attention to varietal quality, on the other hand, entailed concerns about the identification, selection, and stabilization of varietal characteristics that influenced properties such as yield, nut size, average oil quantity, and disease resistance. In the early decades of the twentieth century, it was not always clear how, or if, these two concerns were distinct. Unravelling the locus of quality—and how to ensure that quality from farm to market—emerged as one of the major questions to be addressed by Gambia's first Department of Agriculture.

A Series of Early Schemes: Standards, Mass Selections, and a New System of Seed Provisioning

By the 1920s, the colonial administration had been trialling crops, accessed through imperial botanic networks, for decades. In 1894, the British established a botanic station at Kotu, located close to the coast, where Kew-trained staff planted and observed potential economic crops, including coffee, cotton, indigo, and rubber.[37] Although the colonial administration experimented with food crops such as rice and maize, groundnuts received the greatest attention in early trials due to their significance to the colonial government.[38] By 1910, groundnut varieties from Senegal, Fiji, and elsewhere were being planted at experimental farms throughout the colony. Alongside these introductions and trials, the colonial administration experimented with measures that would influence the quality of the harvest. These measures manifested largely as ad hoc campaigns to encourage farmers to use

[37] Lynn Parker and Kiri Ross-Jones, *The Story of Kew Gardens in Photographs* (Arcturus Publishing 2013).

[38] CSO 2/138 Maize Seed, As to the issue of during 1909 rainy season, Gambia National Archives.

specific cultivation and post-harvest practices, such as the implementation of post-harvest stacking to reduce spoilage caused by late-season rains.[39]

Despite these efforts, by the early 1920s, there were looming questions dogging Gambia's groundnut production: the international market price for groundnuts was growing more volatile, rice and seednut debts were soaring, the incidence of disease within the groundnut crop was on the rise, and there was growing concern about the reputation of Gambian nuts within the European market. In 1921, the colonial government commissioned a report on the Agricultural Conditions and Needs of The Gambia from Morley Thomas Dawe (1880–1943), the Inspector of Forests and Agriculture for West Africa. Among Dawe's many recommendations was that the colony establish a Department of Agriculture to address its mounting agricultural needs.[40] Within a year, Archibald J Brooks (1881–1976), who had trained at Kew, had taken up the post of Director of Agriculture for the colony. Brooks came to the Gambia from the West Indies, where in his capacity as the Officer in Charge of the Agricultural School in Dominica and then the Assistant Agricultural Superintendent (and later Agricultural Superintendent) at St Lucia he had carried out, among other work, research on the control of fungal diseases in groundnuts.[41]

After trekking the protectorate on foot in 1923, Brooks produced his first report on agricultural conditions, in which he outlined the course of action he would pursue as Director of Agriculture. He heralded the promise of free trade and the prospect that a more productive commercial agriculture could 'raise the spending power of the native'. The Gambian farmer, Brooks wrote, 'cannot buy until he can sell, and he cannot sell until he can produce. We have therefore to increase his productivity, and this must be the ultimate aim of our agricultural policy'. However, for Brooks, merely increasing productivity was not a sufficient route to sustained colonial profits. In addition to increasing the tonnage of groundnuts for export, Brooks argued for 'immediate attention with a view to the improvement of the quality of the nut grown, and the condition in which it is exported; thereby raising the standard of the produce grown and placing the industry on a sound business-like foundation'.[42] Towards these ends, Brooks turned his attention to three issues concerning seed: the material quality of the harvested seednut, the identification and selection of disease-resistant varieties, and the design of new programmes for the distribution of selected seed.[43]

[39] ibid.

[40] Swindell (n 30).

[41] AD Cotton, 'Archibald J Brooks, FCS, FLS' (1943) 6 *Journal of the Kew Guild* 126; FW South, 'Fungus Diseases of Ground nuts in the West Indies' (1911) 11 *West Indian Bulletin: The Journal of the Imperial Department of Agriculture for the West Indies* 157.

[42] Report on the Agricultural Position and Requirements of the Gambia, 1924, Kew Archives.

[43] Brooks wrote: 'With a view to this end, I hope that the Agricultural Department will be developed on lines which will enable it to raise and distribute seed-nuts of improved quality, showing resistance to disease; and to provide agricultural instructors who will be travelling constantly in the Protectorate

One of the first initiatives pursued by the Department of Agriculture was an overhaul of the system of produce inspection that had been implemented in 1920. The 1920 Adulteration of Produce Ordinance created a system whereby local inspectors were granted the authority to check any produce destined for market for admixture of sand, sticks, and stones. But, by 1924, following a steep decline in the number of migrant farmers in The Gambia, Brooks started to blame this system as a deterrent. Instead, Brooks recommended compulsory screening of all nuts at the point of purchase. On 6 June 1924, at Brooks' urging, the Ordinance to Amend the Law Relating to the Adulteration of Produce came into effect. The new law not only drastically reduced the number of buying stations available to farmers—which Brooks heralded as improving 'the control which can be maintained in protecting the buyer from adulterated produce'—but it set a standard size for the spacing on the rotary screens.[44] This standard spacing eliminated 'foreign' matter, but it also sifted out shrivelled or immature nuts that would otherwise reduce the value the crop fetched on the European market. In this way, the adulteration of produce measures reworked the quality of the export crop en masse (at least for a time), but it also worked upon the seed.[45] As it was common for the colonial government to repurchase seed from European merchants for distribution under the loan system, any screening that removed shrivelled or diseased nuts provided a type of rudimentary mass selection for seed stocks.[46] Although such selection would not produce intergenerational effects, Brooks was aware that it could improve germination rates and the initial growth of the subsequent crop.[47]

Where produce inspection provided a kind of incidental seed selection, much of the early work of the Department of Agriculture was focused specifically on the trial, selection, and bulking of groundnut varieties, with a particular focus on the identification of disease resistance.[48] In the early 1920s, two groundnut diseases were on the rise in farmers' fields: the fungal disease *Cercospora personata* (leaf spot) and a viral disease known as Rosette. Both diseases threatened to reduce the

for the sole purpose of teaching the farmers, and supervising the various operations throughout the year'; ibid.

[44] Annual Report of the Department of Agriculture, The Gambia, for the year ended 31 December 1924, Kew Archives.

[45] Screening reduced the average adulteration of the crop to about 2 per cent by 1928 (from 8 per cent in the early 1920s). In the late 1920s, after a drop in the price paid for nuts, farmers began adding mud to the nuts destined for sale, which increased the weight of the crop but was impossible to eliminate with the rotary screens; CSO 2/967 Report on the Agricultural Department for the Year 1928–29, Gambia National Archives.

[46] On recourse to repurchasing seed from merchants see CSO 2/711 Seednut Scheme for Distribution, 1926, Gambia National Archives and MCR/10/4/1 Annual Report of the Department of Agriculture, the Gambia, for 1927–1928, Kew Archives.

[47] CSO 2/1095 Report on the Agricultural Department for the year 1930–1931, Gambia National Archives.

[48] 'Agricultural Position' KA (n 42); 1927–1928 Annual Report KA (n 46).

yield and quality of Gambian groundnuts.[49] In its first year, the department ran trials on yield, disease resistance, and manurial dressings for varieties imported from Nigeria, Senegal, and the Philippines, in addition to what Brooks referred to as the 'Gambian' type. By 1925, nine varieties were under trial at the departmental headquarters at Cape St Mary.[50] By 1928, the number had grown to eighteen and, by 1930, the total came to forty-five.[51]

Selections made in these early trials most often entailed mass selection, with varietal types based on slight variations in skin colour, growth habit, or disease resistance. For the first six years of Brooks' tenure, selections on groundnuts continued largely in this way, via the 'careful selection of locally-grown seednuts . . . and by the raising of disease-resistant strains'.[52] The three varieties that would form the core of the department's trials were all selected using these methods. Philippine White and Philippine Pink, named for variations in their nut colour, were selected from a single shipment of the variety Tennessee Red that Brooks had received from the Philippines. Basse, however, was collected from a farmer's field in the town of Basse and was a selection of the widely cultivated Gambian type.[53] All three varieties showed good, but varied, resistance to Rosette and *Cercospora*.

By 1928, Brooks reported that 'no case of absolute immunity has yet been obtained but these three varieties are highly resistant, and efforts are being continued towards raising further resistant strains'.[54] Yet, despite successes in the identification of disease resistance and high-yielding varieties, the selection programme was not achieving intergenerational change in the groundnuts under trial. For example, Basse was one of the department's most promising varieties and for decades was used as the standard against which other varieties were evaluated.[55] It possessed good oil quality and disease resistance, and it travelled through Kew's imperial networks to groundnut-breeding programmes around the world.[56] However, following six years of trials and selection by the department, when it came to bulking the variety for distribution to farmers in the protectorate, European staff mixed it back into the general 'Gambian' stock, citing too little differentiation between Basse and the local type to justify keeping them separate. Departmental selections on farmer-bred varieties had not generated significant intergenerational change (despite regular claims made by European staff as to the superior selection

[49] CSO 2/1233 Report on the Agricultural Department for the year 1931–1932, Gambia National Archives.

[50] 1924 Annual Report KA (n 44).

[51] CSO 2/967 GNA (n 45); CSO 2/1095 GNA (n 47).

[52] 'Agricultural Position' KA (n 42).

[53] MCR/10/4/1 Annual Report of the Department of Agriculture, The Gambia, for the period 1 January 1926 to 31 March 1927, Kew Archives.

[54] 1927–1928 Annual Report KA (n 46).

[55] CSO 2/1703 Department of Agriculture Annual Report 1938, Gambia National Archives.

[56] Tad Brown, personal communication about his thesis research on peanut breeding in the US peanut industry.

methods they used, contrary to those of Gambian farmers). By the late 1920s, the methods of selection used in these early programmes would come under criticism by advocates of pure-line selection.

Nonetheless, the department counted early successes in varietal introductions. This was particularly true of Philippine Pink, which became one of the most widely cultivated varieties in The Gambia in the second half of the twentieth century.[57] Yet these successes meant little for the aims of the colonial administration if farmers had few reliable means to access the seed. Likewise, purer, more standard produce was only part of what the colonial administration sought: the government wanted a crop of a particular size—a 'minimum economic crop'—and this meant that the department needed to find a way either to boost yields per acre or induce more farmers to grow more groundnuts. With the varietal selection programme showing little change in average yield per variety (and manurial trials that might boost yield not faring much better), the most immediate option was the latter one. But getting more farmers to grow more groundnuts was a long-standing dilemma, compounded by household labour dynamics and the unpredictable arrival of migrant farmers.[58] Amid this sea of factors, two solutions rose to prominence in the early 1920s: the need to attract more migrant farmers and the need to ensure the distribution of sufficient, selected seed so that when those farmers arrived, they would have something to plant.[59]

Achieving these goals seemed to rest on dismantling the older system of seed loans. In 1923, there was a sharp drop in the number of migrant farmers settling along the Gambia River.[60] Brooks saw this decline as the cumulative result of the twin burdens produced by the old system of produce inspection and the repayment of rice and seed debts: 'The strange farmer is the milch cow of the Colony', he wrote, 'and he is being milked dry.'[61] To fix the problem of migrant farmer decline, Brooks argued that the balance of the rice and seednut debt be written off. In 1925, the colonial administration did just that, and the following year Brooks unveiled a new scheme for the distribution of seednuts.[62] Central to his new plan was the establishment of twelve seed farms across the protectorate, each consisting of at least ten acres of land for seed multiplication, as well as a seed storage, constructed of galvanized iron and concrete, and capable of holding 100 tons of seednuts. These

[57] S Drammeh, 'Groundnut Improvement, Production, Management, and Utilization in the Gambia' in Savitri Mohapatra and Usha Raman (eds), *Summary Proceedings of the First ICRISAT Regional Groundnut Meeting for West Africa, 13–16 September 1988* (International Crops Research Institute for the Semi-Arid Tropics (ICRISAT) 1990) 41.

[58] Assan Sarr has traced how the expansion of groundnut production also relied upon opening up land previously inhabited by powerful spirits; see Sarr (n 18).

[59] 1924 Annual Report KA (n 44); CSO 2/518 Strange Farmers, Gambia National Archives.

[60] Swindell and Jeng (n 10) 168.

[61] 1924 Annual Report KA (n 44).

[62] CSO 2/711 GNA (n 46); CSO 2/739 Report on the Agricultural Department for 1925, Gambia National Archives.

farms would not only serve as training centres for field demonstrations, but also as trial and multiplication stations for promising varieties of groundnuts initially tested at the departmental headquarters.[63] All of the trials run at the farms were to use local cultivation methods to mimic the growing conditions of local farms. It was hoped that this would enable and encourage the cultivation and distribution of varieties well-suited to Gambia's many growing conditions, of which the coastal departmental headquarters was just one. By 1927, all twelve farms were in operation and were trialling the department's core varieties: Basse, Philippine Pink, Philippine White, Gambia, Zaria, Senegal, and Mauritius.[64]

These farms would be central to the new system of seed distribution. Dubbed the Government Groundnut Seed Supply Scheme, the scheme was envisioned as a replacement for the seednut component of the credit system. The goal of the scheme, which was to be controlled entirely by the colonial government, was to 'guarantee sufficient seed being reserved each year to raise 40,000 tons of ground nuts, i.e., 40 tons for every ton of seed sown'. Under the scheme, the government was to purchase seed directly from farmers during the buying season. This would be stored in the seed depots, where it could be further selected and bulked with selected varieties cultivated on the seed farms. Seed would then be resold to farmers at the beginning of each season, with projected profits of £3,925 accruing to the government annually.[65]

A query about the proposed scheme sent to travelling commissioners, the district-level officers who had managed the seed and rice loans, was met with scepticism. Some commissioners baulked at the prospect of any policy that would encourage farmers not to save their own seed. Others questioned the logic of a policy based on buying and selling seed outright, noting that localized seed exchange worked not through purchase but through in-kind loans.[66] Despite initial scepticism from some in the colonial ranks, the governor decided to proceed with the scheme, citing his desire to avoid the accrual of further debt with farmers and his dissatisfaction with the prices that private European trading firms were charging the colonial government to repurchase seed for distribution. Brooks' distribution scheme promised to avoid this undesirable position for the government by coordinating mass seednut selection and seed distribution within a single project, run by a common arm of the colonial government: the Department of Agriculture. Even more enticing, because the scheme was tied to the seed farms, it not only enabled the selection of good-quality, heavy seed, but also provided a distribution system for the department's top-performing selected varieties.[67] In other words,

63 CSO 2/518, GNA (n 59).
64 1926–1927 Annual Report KA (n 53).
65 CSO 2/711 GNA (n 46).
66 ibid.
67 ibid.

within a single project, it provided an opportunity to coordinate the provision of selected seed stock and the infusion of new varieties into the seed supply.

In the scheme's first year, almost ninety-three tons of seed of selected varieties were raised and distributed from the provincial farms. Not only did this generate over £3,000 in profit for the colonial government, but it also represented a massive infusion of varieties selected by the colonial Department of Agriculture into farmers' seed stocks.[68] Even so, the travelling commissioners continued to advertise the scheme as a secondary option to farm-saved seed.[69] Travelling commissioners were reporting problems with the practicalities of the government scheme: 'Government distribution is difficult, expensive, cannot ensure a really general distribution of the seed everywhere, [and] entails an enormous amount of carrying', wrote one travelling commissioner. Others reported that depots were still too few and far between, making travel to access seed cumbersome. In other cases, farmers were getting seed from the scheme and either selling it at a profit or, where seed was distributed too far in advance of the sowing season, eating it when food was scarce. Where people could not purchase seed outright, government seed issues seemed still to be carried out on credit, only adding to the debts incurred for ongoing distribution of rice.[70]

The problems and expenses of centralized seed distribution were compounded by growing concerns that farmers might sell their nuts over the border in Senegal, where farmers were being offered a higher price.[71] The British needed to find a way to reduce the expenses associated with production, including seed distribution, while increasing the size of the crop. By the end of the year, a new course of action began to take shape. On 5 December 1929, Frank Arthur Stockdale (1883–1949), Agricultural Adviser to the Secretary of State for the Colonies, filed a report on Gambia's agricultural needs with the governor as part of a larger tour of British West Africa.[72] Trained at Cambridge, Stockdale was 'representative of a new breed of scientific expert who was interested in objective experimentation'.[73] His report set out a vision of a professionalized colonial agricultural service, one using the most up-to-date methods of controlled experimentation. He also hoped to build a communication system across the British colonies that would provide a basis for the harmonization of quality grades and standards for commodity exports across the region.[74]

[68] 1927–1928 Annual Report KA (n 46); CSO 2/967 GNA (n 45).
[69] CSO 2/711 GNA (n 46); CSO 2/967 GNA (n 45).
[70] CSO 2/892 Seasonal Reports and Crop Prospects, Gambia National Archives.
[71] CSO 2/954 Groundnut, As to Cultivation, Gambia National Archives.
[72] Charles Jeffries and Elizabeth Baigent, 'Stockdale, Sir Frank Arthur (1883–1949)' *Oxford Dictionary of National Biography Online* (23 September 2004) https://doi.org/10.1093/ref:odnb/36308 (accessed 28 October 2021); CSO 2/993 Visit and Report of FA Stockdale, Agricultural Adviser, Gambia National Archives.
[73] Swindell (n 30) 42.
[74] CSO 2/993 GNA (n 72).

On the specifics of seed improvement and distribution, Stockdale's report was highly critical of Brooks' handling of groundnut trials and his plan for seed distribution.[75] Stockdale requested that 'steps … be taken at once to reduce the number of seed farms', proposing a single up-river station be established in their stead. The reduction and simplification of these farms were to be coupled with the commencement of line breeding for the selection of high-yielding groundnuts, with a view to building a hybridization programme that could produce a variety that was both high yielding and disease resistant. Given the centrality of the seed farms to Brooks' seednut distribution scheme, Stockdale's recommendation would require that a new system of distribution be established. What such a system would entail would 'require further investigation', but whether the seed supply would be selected from government farms, or whether farmers would keep their own seed, Stockdale requested that 'steps should be taken to organize a system which will ensure that the best nuts are retained for seed the following season'.[76]

From the germ line to the market exchange, the aim was to make seed more pure, more stable, and more predictably available. But whereas standardized metrics, screening, and the emerging science of line breeding could provide guidance on how to achieve quality and purity, questions of distribution (and the reproduction of seed once it had been distributed) were inherently questions of how seed was saved, accessed, and exchanged by farmers. These were factors that were also influenced by unpredictable movements of people, the needs of household pantries, and the social and economic decisions that influenced keeping or transacting groundnuts. If the various schemes of the previous three decades were any indicator, to influence the circulation of selected seed at little cost to the administration, the colonial government would need to move beyond the buying and breeding stations and into the personal seed stores and the economic (and often moral) decisions of Gambian farmers.

A New Plan for Seed Reproduction and Distribution: Law and a Reformulated System of Indirect Rule

Less than two months after Stockdale filed his report, a majority of the seed farms throughout the protectorate were ordered to be closed.[77] Brooks' response to the report set out a plan for the closures of the selected seed farms and the establishment of a line-breeding programme.[78] However, he made a case for the continuation

[75] Swindell (n 30).
[76] ibid.
[77] ibid.
[78] Brooks would retire by the end of 1932, before the line-breeding programme he instituted following Stockdale's report produced results. This programme was downsized in the economic cuts made following the onset of the Great Depression.

of his seed distribution scheme at the newly envisaged central, up-river station. In defence of his scheme, he provided figures demonstrating the steady increase in the size of the export crop from 46,583 tons in 1925 to 74,442 tons in 1928. Acknowledging a sharp drop in the 1929 crop, which he attributed to an inexplicable decrease also witnessed in Portuguese and French territories, he argued that from his scheme, 1930 was on track for a crop of up to 80,000 tons.[79]

The gains under Brooks' scheme were to be short-lived, however. In 1931, amid widespread trade depression, the market price paid for groundnuts fell below the cost of production. Gambian farmers decided not to sell below the rate of one shilling per bushel. With so little trade, the colonial government put a halt on the collection of seed and rice debts, but also warned farmers that there would be no further distribution of rice or seednuts on credit (although the reserve fund established under Brooks' scheme was used to distribute some seed for free).[80] By 1932, the colonial administration was so concerned about a possible shortage of seednuts that the administration considered prohibiting the sale of groundnuts to anyone other than a commissioner, with sales punishable by a fine or imprisonment.[81] Although this plan was ultimately rejected, the government in Bathurst advised chiefs to place local prohibitions (called *tongs*) on the sale of seednuts for set periods of time, in efforts to ensure that farmers saved larger quantities of nuts for seed.[82]

At the same time, the United Africa Company, one of the major firms dealing in Gambian nuts, was beginning to raise questions about the measures being taken to ensure that sufficient quantities of good-quality seed were being saved.[83] Representatives in its London office felt that the new governor, Sir Herbert Richmond Palmer (1877–1958), had severely underestimated the quantity of seed that was needed for the coming season. In response to these queries, Palmer released a memorandum outlining what he saw as the only two options for controlling the quality and quantity of groundnut seed: such regulation could be done by a well-organized Department of Agriculture, coupled with a system of produce inspection, or it could be carried out via local leaders themselves, particularly chiefs and the village heads. As the colonial administration could no longer afford the former (and had already taken measures to reduce operations of the Department of Agriculture), the latter, he argued, was the only option.[84]

[79] CSO 2/871 Visit and Report of Stockdale, FA, Agricultural Adviser to the Secretary of State of the Colonies, Gambia National Archives. Brooks was not too far off in his estimate: the crop that year came in at 74,6761 tons; Swindell and Jeng (n 10) 201.

[80] CSO 2/1095 GNA (n 47); CSO 2/1233 GNA (n 49).

[81] CSO 2/1203 Order by the Governor Council Regulating Sale of Groundnuts in the Gambia, Gambia National Archives.

[82] NGR 1/13 Trade, Agriculture, Cattle, Gambia National Archives; CO 87/235/8 Groundnuts, The National Archives, UK.

[83] CSO 2/1134 Groundnut Trade Matters, Gambia National Archives; CO 87/235/8 TNA (n 82).

[84] ibid.

Palmer had been appointed as governor of the Gambia in 1930, but his first posting within the colonial service had been in Nigeria under Sir Frederick Lord Lugard (1858–1945). Lord Lugard, the author of *The Dual Mandate*, had argued for a system of indirect rule as the preferred governance strategy for Britain's African colonies. Palmer seemed to carry a vision shaped by his experience in Nigeria into his administrative approach to the Gambia, where he sought to pare down the administrative overhead of colonial operations. In a January 1932 letter to the Secretary of State for the Colonies regarding economic stabilization and the provision of seednuts, he argued for a reorganization of the protectorate so as 'to place the administrative and legal machinery . . . on a more secure basis than it at present enjoys'.[85] By February 1932, Palmer had sent a dispatch to the colonial office outlining his proposed legal reform: to reformulate the 1894 Protectorate Ordinance in line with the model of governance used in Tanganyika and to establish a separate local tribunal system based on Kenya's Native Tribunal Ordinance. In Palmer's account, the reforms would imbue local authorities (namely chiefs) with greater power to legislate and oversee local disputes. Specifically, the governor had 'come to the conclusion that the only practicable way of controlling the quality of nuts for export purposes is to get the Chiefs to regulate the trading season, and to give them power to do so under the Native Authority Ordinance' for 'at present [they] have not the legal power to enforce their decisions'.[86]

While Palmer sought approval for structural changes to the protectorate's legal order, he also began a search for the specifics of a new seed distribution scheme. By November 1932, the possibility of implementing some form of compulsory enforcement of seednut storage across the protectorate was circulated among members of the administration. The circular was accompanied by a description of a voluntary seednut scheme implemented by Emilius Hopkinson (1869–1951), the travelling commissioner to the North Bank Province in the early 1920s. Under the scheme, Hopkinson had collected three *tentengs* (a local measure of volume of about one bushel) from each farm and distributed two *tentengs* back at the start of the next season. The third *tenteng* formed a reserve, which was given to the landlords of migrant farmers as needed. Any loan made from the reserve would be repaid doubly at the end of the season. In the description accompanying the circular, Hopkinson wrote: 'So much for seed stores and my ideas. Let the people work it themselves, but make the distribution yourself . . . Otherwise leave it to the Headmen not the Chiefs. The seed belongs to the towns not to the districts.'[87]

Following the circular, members of the colonial administration met in early December 1932 to discuss the conversion of Hopkinson's system into a compulsory

85 ibid.
86 CO 87/235/9 Proposed Legal Reform, TNA.
87 CSO 2/1291 Hopkinson Seednut Storage Plan and application thereof in North Bank Province for the years 1932–1933, Gambia National Archives.

scheme for the entire protectorate. After acknowledging the great variety of ways in which different farming communities of the protectorate managed the storage and exchange of seednuts, their conclusion was that 'every farmer, including strange [migrant] farmers, and irrespective of the size of the farm, should put aside for planting ... one four-bushel bag of *selected* seed' in addition to contributing one *tenteng* to a provincial reserve. Such a system, they added, should still leave room for flexibility in how seed would be retained and monitored, an issue they turned over to the governor for consideration. The writer of the opinion further clarified: 'I emphasize the word *selected* as I am of [the] opinion that we should bear constantly in mind the in-breeding of nuts.'[88]

On 31 December 1932, drafts of both the Native Authority Ordinance and the Native Tribunal Ordinance (along with a third bill, the Subordinate Courts Ordinance, which complemented the judicial changes produced by the reorganization of the tribunal system) were published in the official government gazette.[89] After a period of deliberation and revision, the three ordinances were passed by the Legislative Council on 21 February 1933, alongside amendments to a number of other ordinances (including the 1925 Registration of United Kingdom Patents Ordinance).[90] Just one month later, the colonial secretary sent a letter to all commissioners asking that they make sure that each chief make a rule for the storage of seednuts under section 16 of the Native Authority Ordinance. The rule for each district was to follow, *verbatim*, the model rule published in the government gazette the previous December. To ensure uniformity across the protectorate, the colonial secretary enclosed a copy of the rule for reference.[91]

Palmer's legal reform was awash in narratives of fostering greater self-governance, but the changes he sought provided the colonial government with new forms of oversight in local affairs, establishing channels of approval whereby local leaders had to consult the governor and commissioners on issues that were previously matters of local concern.[92] This tension was clear in the passage of the seednut storage rule, which was inspired by the voluntary scheme of one travelling commissioner, adapted by the colonial administration, and mandated to be passed across all districts by the governor. Under the new rule, every cultivator of groundnuts was to 'deposit, after winnowing of the crop which he has cultivated ... one bag of four bushels and three *tentengs* of seednuts of good quality' with the village

88 ibid (original emphasis).

89 CO 87/237/7 Proposed Legal Reform, TNA.

90 ibid.

91 CSO 2/1357 Rules made under s 16 of Native Authority Ordinance Regarding Seed Nuts Storage, Gambia National Archives.

92 Hassoum Ceesay, 'Chiefs and Protectorate Administration in Colonial Gambia, 1894–1965' in Baba G Jallow (ed), *Leadership in Colonial Africa: Disruption of Traditional Frameworks and Patterns* (Palgrave Macmillan 2014) 34.

leader.[93] All village leaders were to be 'personally responsible to the *Seyfu* [Chief] and Commissioner for the safe custody of seednuts so deposited' until the following season, at which time the farmer could withdraw the four-bushel bag. The three *tentengs* would become part of the village reserve, which if issued for planting were to be repaid at a ratio of 2:1. Any farmer who failed to comply with the terms of deposit or repayment could be fined up to £1.[94] Farmers who failed to pay the fine could also be imprisoned for a period deemed acceptable by the local tribunal.[95] The chain of responsibility for enforcement started with the village head, who was overseen by the district chief, who, in turn, had to answer to the travelling commissioner.[96]

The new seednut laws not only regulated seednut availability, but also influenced how farmers accessed and repaid additional planting material, all the while setting a minimum, though undefined, threshold for seed selection. While varietal introductions and trials (and, for a short time, line-breeding and hybridization research) would continue under a whittled-down Department of Agriculture, the law also created a centralized, auditable point at which new varieties and selections could be injected into the local seed supply. In years when the commissioners deemed the seeds within seed stores to be of poor quality, the entire stock was sold off and replaced with heavy, selected seed from elsewhere, an undertaking that sometimes occurred with the support of local leaders, but not always.[97] Alongside the seednut storage rules, some native authorities also passed rules governing the commencement of harvest and post-harvest stacking practices, both of which the colonial administration saw as key factors in the production of both a good-quality export crop and the selection of good-quality nuts. The law could now regulate the quality and quantity of seed by drawing a line between licit and illicit agronomic practices, and mandating how farmers were to save and access planting material.[98]

Despite repeated assertions by colonial administrators that farmers and local officials were complying with the new seednut storage laws, commissioner reports and provincial court records show that these laws were neither unanimously accepted nor observed by farmers. In the years following the passage of the seednut storage law, farmers across the protectorate were prosecuted in the native tribunals for either

[93] Under the law, three *tentengs* was defined as one bushel; PUB 5/26 Ordinances, Rules, and Regulations 1933, Gambia National Archives.

[94] To give a sense of the measure of this fine, in 1933 the average price paid to farmers per tonne of groundnuts was £4. See CO 554/454 Report for the Department of Development and Agriculture for the Period 1 June 1951 to 31 May 1952, TNA.

[95] PUB 5/26 GNA (n 93).

[96] CSO 2/1489 Government Provincial Reserves of Seednuts and Improvement of Seed, Gambia National Archives.

[97] ARP 29/6 Provincial Administrations Annual Reports 1938, Gambia National Archives; CSO 2/1471 General Position in Regard to Locally Produced Foodstuff Supplies, Gambia National Archives; CSO 2/1579 Native Authorities Reserves of Seednuts 1936, 1937, 1938, 1943, 1944.

[98] ARP 29/5 Provincial Administrations Annual Reports 1937, Gambia National Archives; ARP 29/6 GNA (n 97).

failure to comply with the law's statutory deposit of five bushels or the repayment of seed loans at 2:1. In 1934, in one administrative region alone, the Upper River Province, 302 farmers were tried for either refusal to deposit or failure to return their seednuts to village stores, as required under the law.[99] That year, in MacCarthy Island Province, the commissioner complained of 'large-scale evasions of the rule', after which he required village leaders to begin keeping written records of all deposits.[100] Two years later, his reports on local enforcement of the rule were similarly lacklustre. Making the law work entailed placing new pressure and oversight on local leaders. Where the colonial government deemed village leaders lacking in their enforcement, they were removed from their positions, while district chiefs, some of whom were considered too lax in their policing, were levied with fines.[101]

Notwithstanding this resistance, from the perspective of the colonial administration, the law was still working *well enough*. After some concerns that the rule—like other seed distribution schemes—was also driving away migrant farmers, it was amended at the end of 1933 to allow returning migrants to withdraw their statutory deposits, provided they returned to the same district (rather than the same village).[102] More importantly for the British, most districts were reporting sufficient quantities of seed even where farmers refused to comply with statutory deposits and repayments. As a result, issues of nuts from the centralized stores (which had come to be called the 'provincial reserves') were small compared with the government-led distributions of previous years. Districts that had distributed thousands of bags of seed from centralized government depots were now dealing in measures of dozens, and mostly these distributions were due to emergencies, such as the loss of seed to fire.[103] Districts were reporting such surpluses of nuts in village stores that, by 1939, the provincial reserves coordinated by the colonial government for direct distribution by government had been phased out.[104]

Where seednuts remained in village stores after distribution, they were handled in a variety of ways. After the closure of the provincial reserves, surplus nuts were sometimes lent to neighbouring towns that had experienced seed losses due to fire or crop failure, a kind of village-to-village provisioning that emerged in the wake of direct provisioning by the government. In other cases, surplus seed was distributed for food after sowing was complete. In still other cases, surpluses were sold for cash. These

[99] ARP 29/2 Provincial Administrations Annual Reports 1934, The Gambia National Archives. All specific numbers were reported by commissioners as infractions of the seednut storage rule, often as asides in their qualitative descriptions of legal activity in each district. However, these infractions were tracked in variable ways in the case of returns for each province. Some commissioners report only on 'offences against Native Authority ordinances', while other report only 'other offences', rather than crimes such as theft and assault. This means that the number of cases cited potentially reflects a minimum number of infractions.

[100] CSO 2/1357 GNA (n 91).

[101] CSO 2/1579 GNA (n 97); NGR 1/13 GNA (n 82).

[102] CSO 2/1489 GNA (n 96).

[103] CSO 2/1471 GNA (n 97); CSO 2/1620 Report on the South Bank Province for the year 1936, The Gambia National Archives.

[104] CSO 2/1579 GNA (n 97); CSO 2/1489 (n 96).

funds were not returned to farmers who had cultivated and deposited the seednuts, but were placed in the newly established provincial emergency development fund, which was used to finance the administrative costs and public works in each district. Sometimes, the funds were earmarked for the village that had sold the nuts, but such a decision was left to the discretion of the governor, who insisted that 'such an apportioning [of funds] is in no way to be regarded as based on a prescriptive right'.[105]

Surpluses of seed in village stores did not keep the colonial government from complaining of non-compliance. In 1939, one travelling commissioner reported that 'in many villages there is surplus [seed] over and above the local requirements'. He was wary, however, of potential non-compliance, writing that:

> [a] careful watch is being kept by the Native Authorities to guard against an abuse which was observed last year whereby after the distribution of seed farmers sell their allotments to traders or barter them for imported rice: such a procedure is, of course, extremely undesirable and would appear to be criminal conversion since seednuts from village stores are 'entrusted' to the prospective farmer to 'apply to the purpose' of raising a further crop.[106]

Another commissioner wrote of the need to be constantly 'alert to see that seednut stocks are adequate and not misappropriated to other purposes'.[107] In the creation and enforcement of the seednut law, the colonial administration sought to reduce the extent to which it was involved in the distribution and selection of seed, even as it experimented with more intense forms of control. New ideas and articulations of attachments between farmers and seed emerged in the process. Farmers could misappropriate seed they had grown, saved, and procured themselves. Seed became their legal responsibility, but not entirely theirs.

Conclusion: Genealogies of Plant Intellectual Property

The seednut laws were relatively short-lived. They did not last twenty years before being scrapped in favour of interventions that more closely resembled the direct-provisioning policies of post-Second World War agricultural development. The move away from the decentralized control of the seednut storage law was partly the result of the difficulties posed by a new groundnut pest. By the late 1940s, the bruchid beetle was infesting village seed stores and causing major losses to seed stocks. At first, some within the colonial administration felt that the best course of action would be to reduce the concentration of seed in case of infestation. In 1947, the native authorities repealed the 1933 rule and passed a new one that required

105 CSO 2/1579 GNA (n 97).
106 ibid.
107 CSO 2/1489 GNA (n 96).

farmers to deposit only the three *tentengs* of seed into stores, which would only be used as a reserve.[108] Farmers were to retain all the seed they would need for their own fields as they saw fit, while the penalty for failure to make the reserve deposit was raised to £10 or two months' imprisonment.[109]

Only two years later, with losses of reserve nuts still an ongoing problem, the colonial administration was mulling over an entirely new plan. The new seed distribution scheme under consideration resembled the centralized government scheme proposed by Brooks years earlier, although it would be run by the newly created, semi-autonomous Gambia Oilseeds Marketing Board. Under the new scheme, seed would be stored in centralized stores run by the board, nuts would be treated with pesticide, seed would be distributed on credit and repaid in cash, and all participating farmers would be registered in a central ledger (Fig 4.1) . Unveiling this new scheme, however, was contingent upon the repeal of the seednut laws. By 1951, the colonial administration informed local authorities that they were to rescind the compulsory seed storage rules.[110]

Figure 4.1 Groundnuts being stacked into a large pile at a centralized buying station in The Gambia *circa* 1951–1952.
Huxley Collection, Four Guinea's Prints, file 1995/076/5/2/4, Bristol Archives.

[108] SEC 1/338 Seednut Distribution by GOMB, The Gambia National Archives.
[109] SEC 1/666 Jarra West District, District Authority Rules and Orders, The Gambia National Archives.
[110] SEC 1/339 Seednut Stores and Seednut Purchases/Seednut Distribution by GOMB, The Gambia National Archives.

To the extent that the seednut laws were a failed regulatory experiment, they were still productive in other ways: they revealed mechanisms for controlling biological materials that did and did not work; they redefined, for a time, licit and illicit agronomic practices; and they provided a trial in how to capture, regulate, and shape life's productivity beyond spaces directly controlled by the state. They were legal experiments, in other words, in methods of regulating life at a distance. In regulating farmer practice and farmer relations concerning seed, the seednut laws more closely resemble the property-based systems of intellectual property law than the more direct schemes based on lending or purchase. Under the seednut laws, farmers and local leaders—some of whom had families that had been growing groundnuts and saving their own seed for centuries—found themselves answering to new authorities when it came to deciding how much seed to save, how to access seed, and how best to exchange seed with their migrant guests. This was a not-so-subtle shift in the articulation of claims over biological materials and in the techniques of power used to control them. The seednut storage laws marked a strategic turn to decentralization that nonetheless enabled new and, in many ways, more intensive forms of control.

Christophe Bonneuil and Frédéric Thomas have argued that seeds and varietal improvement first became an object of compulsory state policy in the colonial peripheries, where it was possible for the state to enforce a planned seed economy. Only later, with the technocratic provisioning for wartime food and agriculture, did similar regimes emerge within the colonial metropolis, particularly under fascist and proto-fascist regimes.[111] Thus, the compulsory seed reproduction schemes in Senegal predated similar projects in Vichy France by a decade. Likewise, Gambia's compulsory seednut storage law, with its minimum mandate on selected seed, preceded the United Kingdom's involuntary wartime schemes to produce and bulk certified seed domestically, along with the specification of production zones to reduce the incidence of cross-pollination.[112]

These compulsory seed regimes—some of which were backed by the force of the law—provide an interesting counterpart to histories of plant intellectual property. Much of what has been written on the extension of intellectual property protection to plants has focused on the incorporation of plants into already-abstracted intellectual property domains (such as patents, trademarks, or plant variety protection), or has retraced the private strategies used by breeders and companies to exert control over biological inventions before patents or plant variety protection were options (such as the use of hybridization to discourage seed saving or the use of reputation to promote one source of seed over others).[113] These are histories that

[111] Bonneuil and Thomas (n 6).

[112] AF Kelley and JDC Bowring, 'The Development of Seed Certification in England and Wales' (1990) 3 *Plant Varieties and Seeds* 3.

[113] Glenn Bugos and Daniel J Kevles, 'Plants as Intellectual Property: American Practice, Law, and Policy in World Context' (1992) 40 *Osiris* 74; Cary Fowler, 'The Plant Patent Act of 1930: A Sociological History of Its Creation' (2000) 82 *Journal of the Patent and Trademark Office Society* 621; Christine

either directly follow the extension of intellectual property law to plants or that point to the private strategies that, in one way or another, anticipated intellectual property law. There is space in these histories to consider the broader techniques of state power used to control the form and movement of plant reproductive material, a genealogical counterpart to the specific histories of patents and plant variety protection that might just lend new insight into the making of plant intellectual property and the role of the law in designing nature.[114] From the vantage of crop-specific legal histories, plant intellectual property looks less like a novel tool for exerting control over life than a project with deep structural roots in the biopolitical projects of the early twentieth century.

Such a shift in perspective is consequential for understanding the unique history of biological subject matter, but it is also significant for how colonial histories of intellectual property—for Africa and elsewhere—are told. To trace the history of intellectual property law in these places only through the extension of already-abstracted legal forms misses the ways in which the colonies were testing grounds for European juridical experiments and the extent to which those experiments, even those focused on the reproduction of plant life, came to shape the 'juridico–political structures of the West'.[115] Colonies may not have only been the recipients of already-formed intellectual property laws, but also the sites of experimentation in which techniques of governing plant life that came to shape abstracted intellectual property were first trialled.

MacLeod and Gregory Radick, 'Claiming Ownership in the Technosciences: Patents, Priority, and Productivity' (2013) 44 *Studies in the History and Philosophy of Science* 188; Berris Charnley, 'Seeds Without Patents: Science and Morality in British Plant Breeding in the Long Nineteenth Century' (2013) 64 *Revue économique* 69.

[114] Chapman and Sherman (n 5).

[115] Michel Foucault, *Society Must Be Defended: Lectures at the Collège de France, 1975–1976* (David Macey tr, Picador 2003) 103; Aimé Césaire, *Discourse on Colonialism* (Joan Pinkham tr, Monthly Review Press 2000).

5

Some Outlandish Legal Tales

The Debate over Plant Propagation[1]

Marie-Angèle Hermitte

Introduction

On the eve of sedentary agriculture, peasants and labourers started taking care of plant propagation: they would select the most relevant items from crops or from nature and combine them in order to obtain better products. Building on these principles, this practice was formalized and improved in the beginning of the twentieth century to form a specific technological field. Following a fifty-year struggle, those who developed these technologies gained a specific property right to secure the reward for their creative labour: namely the 'plant variety right' which protects (somewhat but not quite like a patent) the breeder of any new plant variety as long as the latter is distinct, uniform, and stable. The granting of this limited right was soon followed by major biological breakthroughs: since the 1960s, large numbers of discoveries and application techniques, known as biotechnologies, have developed rapidly. There is every reason to expect that plant propagation will be possible by modifying the genes and cytoplasm of plant cells directly, thus bypassing some of the constraints resulting from the heredity process. The firms developing such techniques claim that their endeavours should be protected by patenting genes and cytoplasm, whereas those who still work with breeding, grafts, and cuttings strongly oppose this claim. By examining the different elements at play in this exchange, it is possible to predict what the outcome of this conflict will be, although this is somewhat hard to do: the people involved belong to different generations; some are Europeans, while others are North Americans; some of them work for long-standing firms, while others are employed by multinational pharmaceutical or oil companies.

[1] Translated by Laurence Coutrot. This contribution was first published in Bernard Edelman and Marie-Angèle Hermitte (eds), *L'homme, la nature et le droit* (Christian Bourgois 1998) 40–82. A previous version was published in Jean-Claude Fritz and Philippe Kahn (eds), *La Gestion des ressources naturelles d'origine agricole* (Librairies techniques 1983). A follow-up of the story is to be found in Marie-Angèle Hermitte, 'La construction du droit des ressources génétiques: Exclusivismes et échanges au fil du temps' in Marie-Angèle Hermitte and Philippe Kahn (eds), *Les ressources génétiques végétales et le droit dans les rapports Nord–Sud* (Bruylant 2004) https://independent.academia.edu/MarieAngeleHermitte/Books and *L'emprise des droits intellectuels sur le monde vivant* (Éditions Quae 2016).

Marie-Angèle Hermitte, *Some Outlandish Legal Tales* In: *Intellectual Property and the Design of Nature*.
Edited by: Jose Bellido and Brad Sherman, Oxford University Press.
DOI: 10.1093/oso/9780192864406.003.0005

While the technological, legal, and ethical aspects of this conflict are easy to identify, its philosophical dimension is mostly overlooked. On the basis of historical elements, it is argued here that in dealing with biological innovations the human relationship with nature is crucial. While humans once projected their craving for eternity and wilderness into nature, that relationship has been redesigned by the progress of science. By isolating DNA, nucleic acids, and enzymes within cells, biologists have loaded the natural realm with a material reality that in no way corresponds to the fantasized image. However, law must be able to evolve in accordance with a non-traditional model of nature, compatible with the latest scientific developments. Regardless of the scientific pattern, the relevant technology triggers the claim for an ownership right that may be viewed as the primary legal gesture. Assuming a link does exist between humans, nature, and law on the one hand, and the development of scientific knowledge on the other, it is argued that by analysing the first equilibrium, speculation as to what the second would be follows as a consequence.

Historical considerations are crucial to grasp the current status of intellectual property: under the *ancien régime*, there was no such thing as 'labour property': the king 'granted the power of labour', that is, he would either grant or deny a privilege.[2] The implementation of private property, as opposed to feudal property (intellectual property, as opposed to privilege) was a central feature of the revolutionary process. According to Articles 2 and 17 of the French Declaration of Human Rights (1789), everything can be deemed property; not only material goods, but also without restriction the creations of the human mind. The Declaration of 1793 stated: 'The right of property is that which belongs to every citizen to enjoy, and to dispose at his pleasure of his goods, income, and of the fruits of his labour and his skill.' Such a comprehensive understanding of private property was short-lived. Gradually, the following areas were declared non-patentable: in 1792, credit plans and schemes; in 1844, scientific theories and teaching methods; and in 1911, therapeutic methods. In 1906, legal scholars, perplexed by the methods used in agriculture, declared that they could not be owned. At this time, however, the design of new plant varieties—for food or ornamental purposes— reached the pre-industrial stage: plant breeders immediately asked for legal protection[3] and on 23 March 1921, the Tribunal de Commerce in Nice ruled on the claims of a local horticulturist who had been robbed during the 1914 war of 1,000 cuttings of a variety of carnation he had created, known as 'Aline Bouvard'. The plaintiff asked for exclusive ownership of the flower he had created, which he meant to use as breeding material, but his request was rejected: 'Considering, indeed, that no legal text asserts that a person having created a flower holds exclusive ownership over such plant, it is in consequence

[2] Gustave Huard, *Traité de la propriété industrielle* (Marchal & Billard 1906) 18.

[3] *Revue Propriété industrielle* (1911) 91. Tribunal de Commerce de Nice (23 mars 1921) Sirey, 1923, II, 153, note by Étienne Hippolyte Perreau.

impossible to establish by witness testimony a floral ownership right that does not exist.'[4] Such a blunt conclusion triggered a swift reaction: on 3 June 1921, Mr Ricolfi presented a Bill to the House of Representatives on the creation and protection of *horticultural ownership*. This Bill (which never passed into law), which pertained to a 'horticultural patent', was taken up again in 1928, and was rejected once more. These serial rejections did not result by chance: they convey the traditional idea that nature cannot be deemed private or even public property; in order to ensure the profitability of plant-breeding companies, a violent impulse from the profession would be necessary as well as genuine legal 'trickery': a new form of intellectual property was designed in such a restricted mode that the term 'property' would become irrelevant. Such was the first legal arrangement that was scrutinized extensively under its technological, philosophical, and legal aspects. However, such a balance would prove short-lived: in the 1960s, the spin-offs from the biological revolution led to a wholly different vision of nature: owing to new scientific and industrial considerations, the notion of the sacred character of the natural environment faded out. Under this new scheme, private property was no longer restricted. Hence, the industrial entrepreneur was to become a sort of demiurge, able to perform scientific experiments at will. The making of this emerging industrial culture is addressed below. However, in the meantime, since the current disruption is still in progress, the first chapter of the story proceeds as follows: when the tensions between the cultural and scientific representations of nature happen to be eased by the legal apparatus.

The Myth that Nature Cannot Be Owned

'Those things embedded in our huge universe, and over which God has', according to Pothier,[5] 'sovereign dominion', cannot all be part of the human heritage; indeed, some of them, by their very nature, are not suitable for exclusive private or even public ownership: namely, those labelled as 'common' by legal scholars.[6] This has been the case since Roman times with respect to eternal nature, the air we breathe, the streaming waters, 'this gorgeous Sea on which men are unable to leave their mark'. As late as the nineteenth century, the legal scholar pronounced Xerxes mad in claiming to act as 'owner of the sea'. Until recently, the reproductive process of living creatures was almost completely beyond comprehension: the

[4] See Jean-Noël Jeanneney, 'La fleur et l'utérus' *Le Monde* (20 August 1987); the author concludes as follows: 'By ruling against him in this way, the court suspended our humanity for a moment on the edge of unfathomable chasms.'

[5] Robert Joseph Pothier, *Traité du droit de domaine de propriété* (Debure Frères 1772); quoted in various sources as *Treatise on the Right of Dominion or Ownership of Property*.

[6] *Répertoire méthodique et alphabétique de législation, de doctrine et de jurisprudence* (Dalloz 1857) 203.

mysterious origins of life were conceived of in terms of divine creation, or of spontaneous generation, and in the sixteenth century, zoology was full of elaborate hybrids—'dogs with fish heads, men with chicken legs or women with multiple snake heads'.[7] Obviously, such a baroque nature was impossible to conceive of in terms of property. Plant-breeding professionals would struggle for a long time before they could translate into an adequate legal arrangement the notion that their trade consists of combining human creativity with the mere interplay of natural forces, and in making the long-standing dream to domesticate nature come true. To this day, merely mentioning seeds triggers a magical echo: for eons, the dead were buried with a handful of seeds as provision for the journey. This might explain why Mendel's work was overlooked for a long time and why it was only in the early twentieth century that plant reproduction escaped from the weird combination of pragmatism and magic that had prevented its development. In any case, by 1920 the myth was still fully effective, leading to a rejection of the idea of 'horticultural property' among both judges and law-makers. However, this drastic rejection was unsustainable, since the need for high-quality seed was increasing and the techniques of agronomists were improving; for lack of a legal framework, this new market was the ground for 'appalling practices among seed growers, horticulturists and nurserymen. It is not uncommon, for example, to see in the catalogues of one company the creations of another producer without any mention of the breeder'. In the absence of a property right, compensatory channels were set up. Time was available for reflection, making it possible to identify both the natural and legal consequences of cultural obstacles that served as an excuse for repealing the Bill.

Compensation mechanisms to balance the fact that nature cannot be owned

The first companies dedicated to plant breeding in France were set up at the end of the nineteenth century; until then, plant propagation had been performed by peasants and labourers, along with a few freelance amateurs who from the seventeenth century onwards experimented with various selections and cross-breeds, mostly with poor results. In addition, a few castles and abbeys maintained collections, mostly of ornamental plants and fruit trees; however, since the mechanisms of heredity remained unknown, the possibilities for improvement were limited. With the surge of proto-industrialization, the need to discipline this extremely anarchic market emerged: in this domain, where the best rubbed shoulders with the worst, quality standards had to be established by regulation. Compensation mechanisms had to be created, so that breeders' financial rewards were sufficient to allow them

[7] François Jacob, *Le Jeu des possibles* (Fayard-Livre de Poche 1981) 9.

to invest in new research and to monitor the quality of their products. To that end, the professional community had to get organized, both to self-regulate and, less formally, to inform the government's rule-making.

A self-regulating community

From 1920 to 1960, the profession created a number of institutions based on contractual procedures. The resulting system, which is reflected in the current legal framework, began after the Tribunal de Nice ruling. In 1923, a short article was published in the journal *Propriété industrielle* under the title 'France: copyright in horticulture' (1923). It referred to an article by Louis Chasset pointing out that discussions regarding copyright in agriculture happened to be more and more frequent: 'As a result, the National Office of Horticultural Property was founded; it provides forms, registers, a dedicated office, in short, everything is in place, but the new items to be protected have not yet shown up.' This organization was thus created spontaneously, even before the community was ready to submit to its innovations. On the other hand, Chasset also mentions the example of a farmer who designed a new *bigarreau* (variety of cherry) that he distributed on an experimental basis to his pomologist colleagues, who in return pledged not to sell this new item 'without referring to Mr Hautin, who remains free to determine the compensation to which he is entitled'. After pointing out similar experiments, this time in the area of roses, Chasset launches into a discussion of the ethics of these procedures, which is illuminating for the subsequent evolution of the profession:

> Once we [have] managed to police ourselves, we will attempt to police our neighbours and then police the whole world of producers on a legal basis; setting an example is still the best way to achieve a result. Such a cooperative spirit between two companies that might seem competitive at first glance is a small-scale example of further possible action. Granted, more can be done, but let us start on a small-scale basis, so that the long path towards national and then international recognition could be enlightened by the results we achieved, instead of being travelled too quickly to the top, at the risk of getting lost in the many detours or falling into the precipices that inevitably exist on the edge of the most spectacular roads![8]

This superb text clearly indicates the agenda: to define, between like-minded individuals, practices that would make it possible to balance the different interests at stake; these practices would then be adopted first at the national level and later at the international level in accordance with the rule that what is appropriate for oneself is also appropriate for others. Since the creation of learned societies and the National Office of Horticultural Property, which was some sort of legal offshoot, a

[8] He was proved right: thirty-eight years later, an international convention on the protection of new plant varieties was signed.

very large number of associations emerged. They gathered producers on a regional, national, or specialized basis, and included ASSINSEL (Association internationale des sélectionneurs pour la protection des obtentions végétales), FIS (Fédération internationale du commerce de semences), and CIOPORA (Communauté internationale des obtenteurs de plantes ornementales de reproduction asexuée). Within this framework, the professional community managed to 'police' its action, directly or indirectly taking part in the design of international and national solutions. National solutions were devised to meet short-term needs: although the earliest seed producers controlled the entire production process, this changed rapidly; the three typical phases of production—breeding, maintenance breeding, and multiplication—were increasingly performed by separate companies.

Such division of the production line involved some form of contractual arrangement to govern the relationship between the parties. As a result, there was a licence agreement between the plant breeder and the agent in charge of maintenance breeding, and a second contract between the latter and the farmer in charge of seed multiplication. This was a relatively confidential type of private market organization, even though it contributed to the technological locking up of the system at least as much as, if not more than, plant breeders' rights would do later. It is beyond the scope of this chapter to give an overview of these contractual practices, insofar as they vary according to the propagation method, but a brief example is as follows: carnation farming is based either on contracts pertaining to the renting of cuttings which, owing to their restrictive clauses, ensured the variety's designer effective protection, even in the absence of any intellectual property system, or on cultivation concession contracts: this latter contract type imposes on the licensee some onerous obligations:

- they may sell nothing but cut flowers;
- they may not sell any reproductive elements;
- they must limit themselves to a specific number of plantings;
- they must comply with very strict cultivation rules that imply heavy supervision;
- should the contract be terminated, they should destroy the plantations;
- . . . and they must of course pay the royalties.[9]

In Italy, the government agreed to endorse such practices. As early as 1949, the Chamber of Commerce, Industry, and Agriculture in Imperia had compiled these various contract drafts and summarized them in the form of a 'copyright in floral varieties', which acknowledged an exclusive right of exploitation, the possibility of granting it, and the possibility of signing 'publishing contracts'.[10] One might

[9] Lodo Lodi, 'Les usages, les coutumes et les contrats dans le domaine de la diffusion des nouvelles variétés végétales' (1976) 92 *Propriété industrielle* 189.

[10] For Imperia's customary practices see Tribunal Civil de Grasse, 3 mai 1962, JCP, 1962, II, 12823.

wonder whether these earlier practices are still relevant. Indeed, the institutions are still in place, both at the national and international levels, and the contractual arrangement is relatively stable. The informal structure revealed an occupational community that had been relatively easily self-disciplined. It seems that this is reflected today in the almost absence of appeal to the courts: the 'Comité pour la protection des obtentions végétales', composed of experts selected from the community, makes decisions solely on the basis of technical criteria (colour, shape, hairiness) that serve to assess the 'distance' between two varieties. A variety may be protected under the condition that the 'distance' between two sub-strains is sufficient; in the opposite case, they refuse to grant the right. Granting a right may be inconvenient for breeders of closely related varieties, whereas rejecting it is a source of inconvenience for the applicant. Any decision is therefore potentially open to challenge. However, the few suits that were brought did not raise any salient element (a blank endorsement and a nullity attributable to a breach of procedure). In fact, challenges are infrequent because the plaintiffs, defendants, and experts all belong to the same community. This harmonious balance could, of course, be disrupted when varieties with similar characteristics become so numerous that there is no space for new creations. Currently, this is the case with barley. Disputes against the contractual organization itself, although not visible in court, might turn out to become more heated. It appears that in the case of plant licences, licence holders find their obligations too demanding for their activity to be sufficiently profitable. However, no such revolt has yet emerged.

The regulating organization

The first French initiative dates from 5 December 1922, shortly after the Tribunal de Nice ruling and the introduction of the Ricolfi Bill. This regulation provides for the protection of the person who either created or discovered a species or variety (over a twelve-year period). The species or variety had to be new and have unquestionable cultural merits. If these two conditions were met, the species or variety could be registered in the directory of selected plants created for this purpose, and granted a certificate, initially on a provisional basis and subsequently on a definitive basis, granting it the status of an official brand.

There is no mention, as is the case today, of conditions of uniformity and stability, but a variety that deteriorated after a certain number of multiplication cycles was removed from the list. The system relied heavily on a supervisory committee, which provided advice on the approval or rejection of the certificate, carrying out crop trials, examining complaints, etc. All the committee's members were professionals working for the public or private sector. No disposition for legal recourse was planned.

Although the Ricolfi Bill on horticultural property had not yet been approved, various administrations continued their efforts to maximize seed quality, at least in the case of selected field crops. Thus, on 26 March 1925, a decree was promulgated regarding the repression of fraud in the trade of wheat seeds. On 16 November 1932, a decree was issued initiating 'a register of species and varieties of cultivated plants and a register of selected crop plants', which repealed the 5 December 1922 decree. It resumed the former registration system and confirmed the authority of the Control Committee. However, it stressed the idea of crop improvement, which was partially rejected in a later scheme. Subsequently, decrees were drafted, implementing the August 1905 Law on Fraud Repression regarding the trade in wheat, oat, and potato seeds (decree of 23 September 1934). As this experiment turned out to be successful,[11] its scope was extended to maize seeds. At this point these regulations included: 'a partial protection scheme for the breeder of a registered plant variety; and

> a series of obligations imposed on seed trading, related to germination capacity and minimum purity (indications of origin, calibration etc)'.

This desire to find a balance between protection and quality-related requirements provides us with a hint of what the future French system would become (protection of any distinct, uniform, and stable variety, and certification, ie marketing authorization granted exclusively to those varieties that are of agronomic interest). As a result, it can be assumed that the period between the first claim (1904) and the adoption of the law (1970) was not a legal vacuum. This corresponds to the time lapse dedicated to setting up a legal framework. Social roles evolved, actors gained some sort of industrial status, their tasks became more specialized, and they became organized on an international basis. The public authorities defined precise objectives with regard to agronomy, identified species, and varieties, and developed their assessment methods—the private contractual organization became more elaborate. Here, all the prerequisites for the development of customary law are present. This is indeed what happened: when the law was finally passed, it found a slot that had been carefully prepared. The reasons for the reluctance to pass the 1921 Bill into law is therefore under scrutiny here. Often viewed as a symptom of misunderstanding or lack of interest, it has mostly paved the way for the reception of a new right, whose content had to be balanced and consolidated before it could be enshrined in a legislative framework. This is a characteristic feature of economic law: as soon as a need arises—as soon as it is expressed in a legal form—the profession demands some kind of unambiguous legislation that is the unrefined expression of its short-term interests. The idea is launched throughout the legal system, which then offers several solutions. The most expedient solution is usually of a contractual nature: professionals design contracts to make up for the absence of any legal framework: the contents being similar, they will soon end up

[11] Report of the President of the Republic, JO Lois et décrets (7 avril 1937) 4737.

as standard contracts. Another response is provided by the courts, at a different level of the legal order, with different partners. The courts address the issue in contradictory terms, in compliance with the adversarial principle. Furthermore, addressing doctrine helps to inform and renew the debate. Legal intervention reflects the government's view of the general interest. This whole intellectual movement is embedded in the dialectical timeframe of the law: while it unwinds its contradictions, the professional community builds up its network of solidarities and antagonisms, both at the international and national levels. The final legislative outcome will display more complex and more general solutions than the initial drafts. The discrepancy between the initial and ultimate arrangements results from the operation of the legal timeframe over the cultural, economic, and scientific basis. This inertia of the legal order, this meandering of legal time, is often criticized both as a barrier hindering the march of progress and as a product of reactionary forces. This chapter will focus on this delayed process in the case of plant breeder's rights: what are the underlying forces? Which social representations are at stake? Such representations are traced by looking at the various attempts to impose property rights on the natural environment, namely on its most crucial, vital process: plant breeding.

Cultural Barriers that Limit the Appropriation of Nature

Since Lucretius contended that atoms form the structure of matter, philosophers have devoted a great deal of attention to the concept of nature. Currently, it seems that the natural and life sciences are able to identify the major mechanisms of the logic of nature. However, Western mentality does not reflect this precise knowledge of the physical aspects of nature: it sticks to trivial assumptions supporting the notion that no legal appropriation of nature is possible.

Nature is eternal: what is likely to change and what is not

When looking at nature, one must come to terms with seemingly conflicting notions, such as eternity versus finite time spans and the idea of eternity versus the experience of birth and death. The Greeks were searching for the universal order of nature through its constantly renewed productions, yet identifying the universal with the gods (and later with God) does not shake the belief in motionlessness. The idea of progress itself will not change anything: progress will become the invariant of nature. Similarly, the alchemists believed that the very movement of nature conferred permanence: 'Nature always tends to produce from a given seed an individual similar to that from which the seed is issued; however, it may happen that the process is curbed and it ends up as a different species'.[12] Some alchemists, however, readily stretched the meaning of their findings to solve the problem of the horrifying begetting of 'imperfect animals and monsters' in a kind of retrospective fixity:

> Then all alterations and vicissitudes of corruptions and generations must cease in nature; and all the forms of the universe will remain eternally in their existence; because the ordinary movements and alterations in the system of the world tend only to the fixation of spirits, subsisting and maintained only by volatiles, so that nothing will change any more as soon as they have acquired this fixity.[13]

Today, knowledge of the 'writing of heredity'[14] provides a comparable vision of this interplay between universal and contingent elements, between what is permanent and what is not. Indeed, since it is known that the reproduction of living matter is subject to infinite variations, if humans know that they are the offspring of chance, chance is itself subject to the rules of probability. In a way, science fulfils the Greek dream, since the genetic code may appear from a certain point of view as the locus of chance: 'the genetic code is universal and its key (seems) to be known to the whole living world'.[15] Apparently, therefore, there is no discrepancy between the Greek world and contemporary biologists' model. Yet these systems of thought are incompatible, insofar as biologists accept the balance of 'chance and necessity', whereas it was once believed that deviations were merely accidents of essence. Nature, unchanging in essence, is exclusive of human intervention: humankind cannot claim ownership over it.

The laws of nature are immutable

When searching for the permanence of natural movement, one was bound to discover the 'laws of nature'. At the end of the early Middle Ages, Western civilization becomes aware that nature is not a

> [h]idden power, beyond the reach of human reason, and a dangerous rival for the creator: it encompasses all the laws that God has imposed on the physical world. Thus, the philosophers believe that they are simultaneously laying the foundations of science as such and paving the way for a 'natural religion'. God's existence brings evidence that the universe is intelligible; conversely, the intelligibility of the universe makes it possible to gain access to the First Engine, to a clockwork universe corresponds a Watchmaker God.[16]

12 Jean Ehrard, *L'idée de nature en France à l'aube des lumières* (Flammarion 1970) 31.
13 ibid.
14 François Jacob, *La Logique du vivant* (Gallimard 1970) 284.
15 ibid 297.
16 Ehrard (n 12) 45.

Thus, there was a shift from a magical universe, where nature brought fertility and peace as well as disasters and death, to a mechanical and linear universe. Since then, humans have been subjected to the 'laws of nature' in the name of scientific reason, instead of being submitted to them by divine will. The laws of nature set clear limits to the demiurge who is testing its power. Any human legislation subsides before the inflexibility of the laws of nature: all over the world, the sun rises and sets according to an invariable schedule and no legislator is able to modify or appropriate the law of nature. But, strangely enough, the rationale backfired: if the laws of nature can be viewed as inescapable, then anything inescapable is encompassed in nature. Such was the case with some legal principles: deemed inescapable, they came to be regarded as a 'natural law'. People came to think that beyond natural elements, nature also encompassed some human institutions that shared similar characteristics with nature.

Nature is complex and indivisible

Nature is viewed as permanent, eternal, sacred, inescapable. These characteristics are so powerful in the collective imagination that they soon extended beyond the natural world, which was their initial realm. From the eighteenth century onwards, the idea of nature came to pervade all discourse: virtually every statement was based on the 'nature of things', from Oriental despotism to the enslavement of Africans or the corruption of the air as the cause of the Black Death.[17] Anything could be referred to as nature, since nature was intertwined with what defines it. As a result, there is a permanent human nature, physical laws, inescapable, and the nature of things that steers political systems. This list is obviously not complete and everything with the required characteristics may be related to the untouchable realm of nature. Permanent, inescapable, multi-functional—such is the somewhat hazy image of nature in Western society. These same features that secured its survival, regardless of historical events, philosophical debates, or scientific breakthroughs, make it challenging from a legal standpoint.

Legal Representations of Nature

The current representations of nature underlying the legal system are complex. On the one hand, humans still think of themselves as powerless beings facing natural forces, while on the other hand, they are part of a 'techno-nature':[18] nature is shaped by technological efforts, according to Hegel's scheme. The current legal system pertaining to nature reflects this tension. In the former legal system, no one could be granted property rights over nature. Today, although this principle

[17] ibid 365; Jean Delumeau, *La Peur en Occident* (Fayard 1978) 171.
[18] Philippe Roqueplo, *Penser la technique: pour une démocratie concrète* (Seuil 1983) 18.

is not formally rejected (nor is it even discussed for that matter), nature's scope is consistently reduced, owing to the deceptive clarity of scientific knowledge. Before addressing the specific case of 'natural nature', a few clues are provided, based on the case of the legal approach to nature and human nature.

The laws of nature and the legal system

Scientific knowledge is a type of objective knowledge that 'achieves concrete universality' and that therefore 'may virtually expand indefinitely ... through the publication of pragmatic protocols (both experimental and theoretical) so that each individual (provided that individual has the relevant competence) may reproduce scientific concepts unequivocally and check its laws and theories'.[19] However, the universal character of scientific laws, of the laws of nature, has a consequence: the scientist loses control over the findings, and this exclusion has in turn a major consequence: as objective knowledge, knowledge is strictly speaking nobody's knowledge. It is posited as knowledge in itself, 'appropriated by no one, appropriable by all'.[20] Science is viewed as the factual disclosure of the laws of nature, as reflected in a legal system that refuses to patent 'theoretical or purely scientific principles, discoveries and conceptions' (Laws of 1844, 1968). A scientific law, such as the law of universal gravitation, cannot be claimed as property: it is 'a manifestation of nature, belonging to all men and cannot be appropriated by anyone'.[21] No natural phenomenon can be deemed private or public property, even when it is directly applicable; thus, as early as 1852, the French Court of Cassation ruled that 'the application to a specific use of a natural phenomenon, which produces a result by itself and without the use of any particular process to obtain it, is not patentable, no matter how useful this application may be'.[22] This produces the following paradox: currently, technological breakthroughs that are pivotal to society are considered as property; in turn, the profits they yield serve to fund other investments and future investigations. Nevertheless, scientific discoveries, which are the basis of technology, cannot be recognized as anyone's property. No law of nature can be appropriated, because that would freeze the number applications that might be derived from it.

Science is only one step away from knowledge. When reflecting upon property rights regarding knowledge, legal scholars impose a lull, just as they did for science. Thus, when considering whether an archaeologist should be viewed as the 'author' of the findings or whether these could be used by a writer as a plot for a fiction, the Court of Marseilles in Southern France ruled that:

[19] ibid 29.
[20] ibid.
[21] As acknowledged much later in *Diamond v Chakrabarty* 447 US 303 (1980).
[22] Sirey, 1852, II, 595.

> In archaeology, the scientific rules and methods of research and knowledge, as well as the data resulting from excavations, findings and technical elements drawn from other sciences, must be considered as belonging to the common heritage of mankind, as soon as they are presented to the general public. Therefore, knowledge, as well as science should be viewed as free and cannot be appropriated by anyone.[23]

The *Tribunal de première instance* in Marseilles further elaborated on the point by stating that, besides *knowledge* and *scientific data* (which are perceived as objective), the archaeologist builds '*hypotheses*, explanations or reconstructions which remain his own personal property' (1957). When analysing science and knowledge, the legal framework is fully in line with social representations: 'Science is thus split into two entities: an objective one, which belongs to the public, and a "hypothetical" body, which is of a private nature since it involves some creative elaboration of objective data.' Science thus gains a more personal character: the author shapes knowledge in a certain way to the point at which she becomes its 'owner'. The author's idea no longer reveals the objectivity of the world, but its reconstruction. It falls out of the public domain; it is a switch from science to knowledge. The Tribunal of Marseilles' ruling, by underscoring the role of hypothesis, presents the opportunity to move on from pure knowledge to reasoning. Scientific assumptions may be deemed property because they largely result from individual intuition: in a way, they cannot be viewed as universal, as opposed to the logic of scientific reasoning, equated to a law of nature, contrary to the randomized mechanisms of intuition. Such a distinction is useful when addressing the issue of patenting computer software. At first, lawmakers refused to accept them as patentable (1978 Bill). However, the courts were under pressure from professionals seeking to challenge the ruling by citing the 1957 Copyright Law. In this respect, the statement of the Paris Court of Appeal about the type of skill required to develop software is of some interest:

> Considering that developing a software is an original creation of the mind, both in its composition and its expression, far beyond a simple automatic and compelling logic, considering that there is no one best way for that kind of intellectual process, that analysts and developers have to choose, just like translators do, between various presentation and expression modes, in consequence it appears that their personal decisions bear the mark of their personality.[24]

In the light of what happened with plant breeders rights, the outcome of the debate on software protection seems obvious in the medium term: under the pressure of a well-organized professional community at international level (at the request of the World Intellectual Property Organization (WIPO), a committee of experts was

[23] Bernard Edelman, 'La main et l'esprit' [1980] *Recueil Dalloz*, chronique, 44.
[24] 'Cour d'appel de Paris, 2 novembre 1982' *Revue internationale du droit d'auteur* (Janvier 1983) 148.

organized in 1976) who were willing to prevent the spread of anarchic contractual protection, law-makers were very likely end up supporting a form of protection that was neither a patent—since software is not of a technical nature—nor copyright. Indeed, such solutions would doubtless divert this set of laws from its initial purpose. However (although there is no consensus on this last point), the form of expression of software is generally viewed as predetermined by its content and, consequently, individuals only have limited capacity to express their own personality through software creation.[25] Nevertheless, the reasoning behind the decision of the Paris Court of Appeal is interesting since it posits that the compelling development of a certain logic, the truly inescapable nature of some intellectual mechanisms bind them together making them similar, in a way, to the laws of nature. The rules of logic, the rationality of reasoning that have a purely conventional basis, are assimilated in 'nature', insofar as they are by convention binding and hence cannot be treated as property.

Law and human nature

The discussion here is brief, since this issue is only indirectly connected with the main concerns here. Unlike the laws of nature, human nature cannot be viewed as 'objective', although some aspects of its subjectivity are so consistent that they are almost immutable. The courts' statements on human nature are largely based on literature: they managed to make a distinction between the part that can be related to its author and the part related to 'heritage' which the author has borrowed from the common treasure of humanity: theatre plays, cinema, musical composition, etc. In the meantime, by scrutinizing literary and other creative works, legal scholars identified the mechanisms and situations specific to human nature. The author may draw inspiration from this common heritage, although she cannot prevent anyone else from doing the same. Here again, the legal system imposes a limit on what can be viewed as a property and what cannot. No author can protect the parts of her work that are part of human nature: 'death, love, hatred, desire . . ., adultery, violence, the collapse of a couple'.[26] Such are the views that the legal system offers of the laws of nature and of human nature. They provide a certain degree of coherence that will serve as a basis for the detailed analysis presented here of the relationship between legal systems and natural nature.

Law's Trickeries and the Appropriation of Natural Nature

The legal system meanders through 'natural Nature': it defines the line between wild nature and domesticated nature; it opens some doors, while closing others,

[25] The 1985 Bill introduced the protection of software authors under copyright legislation.
[26] Bernard Edelman, 'La création et la banalité' [1983] *Recueil Dalloz*, chronique 7.

allows or forbids people to be appropriated through slavery, allows or forbids animals to be held accountable for their actions. Some phenomena remain outside the legal order, only to be brutally drawn back into it. This was the case with plant breeding. A detailed study of the path followed by law in this matter should make it possible to define the specific relationship between law and 'natural Nature', as well as the legal consequences of human intervention by way of selection. Here again, the historical process is retraced; step-by-step, legal time unwinds and it influences the economic and technological agendas. In legal terms, this chapter will retrace the history of the qualification process, ie the path followed in order to identify in the legal order these categories and concepts that best fit the actual practices in agronomy.

The legal qualification of plant breeding

Our investigation stretches from the period when the first claims were made to the preparation period of the UPOV Convention in the mid-twentieth century. It involves a paradox: on the one hand, breeders' work tends to be dealt with as if it were comparable to industrialists' or composers' creations, since it already enjoys protection; on the other hand, in order to obtain a specific type of protection, since patents rapidly appeared to be inadequate, the specific nature of varietal creation tends to be emphasized. Hence, the emphasis on the horticulturist's 'gift', their 'personal craft', as opposed to the universal and objective nature of scientific knowledge.[27] It was argued that as far as plant breeding was concerned, the link between the process and the outcome was not as deterministic as in some other technical fields: in order to perform identical cross-breeding to obtain the same final result, it is not sufficient to reproduce the same genealogy exactly (as one may end up with similar but not perfectly identical varieties). This ambivalence regarding patent rights—both claimed and rejected—gave way to great legal uncertainty throughout the period that preceded the UPOV Convention. A search for precedents performed by the doctrine following the Nice Tribunal ruling bears the mark of this uncertainty.[28] References were thus made to:

- a ruling of the Paris Court of Appeal qualifying as unfair competition a misleading advertisement posted by a horticultural establishment for the propagation of asparagus in Argenteuil (1840);[29]

[27] B Frey-Godot, *Propriété industrielle* (1923) 31.
[28] Tribunal de Commerce de Nice (n 3).
[29] *Annales de la propriété industrielle* (1922) 366.

- a ruling of the Paris Court of Appeal declaring a new process for dyeing artificial flowers to be patentable (1855);[30]
- a ruling of the Paris Court of Appeal refusing to patent a process for distilling alcohols from a 'mucor Boulard n° 5' mushroom. The Court pointed out that the distillation of alcohols from mushrooms is a perfectly well-known process; the simple fact of using a more efficient variety of fungus than the previous ones is not in its nature sufficient to demonstrate the reality of a new industrial process (1922).[31]

'Misleading advertising, artificial flowers, industrial mushrooms'—the chaotic nature of this list betrays a certain degree of perplexity. Such a totally new issue was difficult for legal experts to deal with. As long as the law-makers did not acknowledge the existence of plant-variety right protection, professionals 'invented' a relatively effective indirect protection device, by randomly combining various legal texts that, in turn, reflect the prevailing lack of straightforwardness:

- law on trademarks (Law of 1857);
- decrees of 16 March 1932 and 11 June 1949, which required anyone selling seeds registered in the official catalogue to use the name listed in the directory; and
- law of 1 August 1905 on fraud repression.

The French Court of Cassation finally rejected this scheme in 1964,[32] at the very moment when, driven by the UPOV Convention of 1961 to pay more attention to new varieties of plants, the French courts were starting to acknowledge the patentability of a variety of carnation:

> If the products of nature, whether mineral or vegetal, cannot be the subject of an invention or a discovery as defined in Article 1 of the law of July 5, 1844, the same may not be held true regarding the combination of raw materials or the application of certain natural phenomena in order to obtain a new composite product, as soon as the intervention of man is such that, without human intervention, it would be inconceivable that such products could be created as a result of the sheer operation of natural forces.[33]

[30] Jules Pataille, *Code international de la propriété industrielle artistique et littéraire; guide pratique des inventeurs, auteurs, compositeurs, artistes et fabricants français et étrangers* (Marescq et Dujardin 1855) 80.

[31] *Annales de la propriété industrielle* (n 29).

[32] Chambre criminelle de la Cour de cassation (20 février 1964) JCP 1964, II, 13788.

[33] JCP 1963, II, 13297, JCP 1965, II, 14263.

This line of reasoning, which parallels the one applied by copyright law to computer software reflects the change in the legal attitude towards the mechanisms of varietal invention: it does not imply any ownership over nature since it only pertains to the artificial creation of a new element of nature. However, this belated acceptance, post-UPOV Convention, was pointless: it did not match the professionals' expectations for a more flexible protection regime adapted to their needs. In this respect, the professional community rejected the 'industrial model' of nature that would have resulted from the patentability of varietal creation.

The preliminary drafts of the UPOV Convention still reflect these concerns, and some of the preliminary papers discounted the role played by nature in varietal propagation and claimed that a patent system would be sufficient;[34] however, the prevailing trend focused on showing how this particular type of creation requires a specific type of protection. The selected features fell under three categories:

a. The process that creates a new variety is not directly linked to the product it generates: the same breeder, using the same genes, will obtain similar, but not totally identical, varieties. Since implementation takes from five to twenty years, it is of no commercial relevance to describe the process.[35] The sole valuable part of the process is the ownership of the finished, fully replicable product (cuttings, seed). As opposed to what happens in industry, the technology to be protected does not stem from the process per se, but from the know-how used to conduct the process. Counterfeiting consists in multiplying the finished product from itself and not from the process, which loses its relevance as soon as the product has been created.
b. The resulting product is never perfectly stable: it has to be 'maintained' so that it does not deteriorate. This is why seeds of a given variety must be sorted at each generation, even if the stability criterion is met (there is no such thing as 100 per cent stability). This is why a seed that is reproduced on the farm in breach of the precise standards of propagation will degenerate rapidly. Such degeneration processes may happen even among self-pollinated plants, which somewhat blurs the distinction frequently established between self-pollinated and cross-pollinated plants.
c. Finally, the product may vary according to the place where it is grown: the same reproductive material, bred in different locations, will yield different results, even in the case of plants that reproduce asexually, ie in principle exactly

[34] UPOV, Acte final du 11 mai 1957, 28 et rapport du 18–19 janvier 1960, 50–51.

[35] 'Such descriptions may sometimes be useful; however, the plant material is too unstable and its varieties are in many cases too closely related for us to assign rights to breeders on the sole basis of written records. Any dispute regarding plant identity can ultimately only be resolved by reference to the plants themselves. This is all the more true for cross-pollinated plant varieties. Consequently, it seems that, requiring, from the breeder an accurate description of those characteristics likely to define and distinguish his varietal innovation would be inconsistent with the very nature of living plants.' Actes UPOV, 88; see also 34, 55, 74, 81.

> identically. A mere variation in soil or climate might produce widely differing results.

The specificity of natural phenomena had to be emphasized, while demonstrating that varietal creation involves a great deal of effort and does not merely consist of the exploitation of natural phenomena. Given these unpredictable characteristics, this tight combination of nature, intuition, and the work of assessing the phenomenon and qualifying it in legal terms was a complex task. In 1954, Chavanne skilfully summarized this tension: 'Plant invention is the result of a creative activity that can only succeed with the active participation of nature. For this reason, a total monopoly covering this product would perhaps be excessive.'[36]

Legal qualification at the 1961 UPOV Convention: The design of a limited monopoly

The qualification of plant propagation results from a legal trade-off: the concept of 'horticultural ownership', dating back to the 1920s, was abandoned and replaced by the concept of 'restricted monopoly', which corresponded to a trade-off between a strictly natural vision and a strictly industrial vision of the process of plant propagation. The resulting balance is as follows:

a. The breeder may exercise his [sic] right against any person using the reproductive material for reproduction as propagating material (namely marketing seeds or cuttings).
b. The breeder may not, of course, object to the use of his material to obtain the transformed product (consumer grain versus seed grain).
c. The breeder may not prevent another breeder from using his material to develop a new variety; nor may he collect royalties from that breeder, who will then use the new variety freely. Such is the phrasing of this limited monopoly:

> The permission of the breeder, or of his successor in title, is not required for the use of the new variety as an initial source of variation for the purpose of creating other new varieties, nor for the marketing of such varieties. Conversely, such authorization shall be required where the repeated use of the new variety is necessary for the commercial production of another variety.

So, here is the core of the current legal status for the European model of nature: it echoes the idea of a restricted monopoly. The monopoly is strict enough to secure

[36] Albert Chavanne, 'La protection des obtentions végétales' [1954] *Recueil Dalloz* 48.

the profitability of long-term investments, but flexible enough to allow for the endless variation that, within the pattern of repetition through which nature perpetuates itself, constitutes the very essence of life. The model of law developed at the time offers a way to merge two conflicting elements under a single law: the monopolistic aspect corresponds to man's creation, whereas the limitation of such monopoly parallels the independent play of natural forces. It is unclear whether the experts in charge of drafting the UPOV Convention had such a clear vision of the legal scheme they were designing. The preliminary drafts for the Convention swarm with ambiguities. This is clearly visible in two sets of preliminary documents: the debate on the nature of plant breeders rights (which was never properly formalized) and the attempt to define the breeder's labour. For some time, the experts attempted to find an agreement over the nature of the breeder's legal right; however, given the complexities, the attempt to provide a definition was abandoned. At the second meeting of the Expert Committee in 1958, the first item on the agenda was a discussion on the nature and content of the breeder's right. This issue was so perplexing that it was quickly settled:

> The preceding discussions make it clear that the breeder's legal right has such distinctive features that it cannot fit into any existing legal provision ... The Expert Committee agrees that the Bill relates to an intangible object which, as any by-product of the human brain pertains to the domain of intellectual property . . . or at least to the intellectual activities framework . . . Ultimately, it seems preferable not to define the nature of this legal right on the basis of similarities or differences with other pre-existing rights . . . It is therefore appropriate to confine oneself to a statement of principle and to focus on defining the content of the legal right and of its implementation.

While it sometimes takes decades to develop a new variety, a natural mutation may occasionally be of immediate agricultural and therefore economic benefit. The preliminary drafts of the UPOV Convention reveal a protracted debate on this issue: as natural mutation did not, by hypothesis, require any effort, should it receive the same protection as any other new varieties? Does this constitute an improvement comparable to some sort of industrial improvement? However, it should be noted that the notion of improvement is much vaguer in plant propagation than in other domains: any new variety is desirable just because by virtue of being new it is likely to transmit a new genetic code, regardless of its agronomic value. In some way, propagation by way of natural mutation has its own merits, whether or not it involves any kind of 'improvement' in the strict sense of the term. The simple shift from the patent system to plant propagation would therefore not be appropriate. It may happen that the parties, on a purely conventional basis, might manage to agree on a co-licensing arrangement. However, such a solution, which has the merit of being flexibile, depends too much on the goodwill of the parties to be acceptable.

Unclear about the exact nature of their trade, professionals were never able to make a sharp distinction between genuine creation and mere improvement. It took more than half a century to clear up these ambiguities, for they did not result from chance but from the cultural obstacles that had to be dealt with.

Some barriers that had to be removed to design the restricted monopoly system

One of these impediments, namely nature, was mentioned above, and is taken up again here only to report on the solution that was found. However, two other items remain in the shade: life in its relations with the law and the fear of famine.

Food insecurity and abundance: or technology as opposed to fear

It is unusual for legal scholars to find in the legal texts they are analysing a reference to one of humankind's greatest fears. The word of law tends to ignore fear. Consequently, it is remarkable that both Michel Cointat, addressing the National Assembly, and Octave Bajeux, addressing the Senate, mentioned food insecurity and its impact on the need to provide seed producers with some kind of protection (Session 1969–1970). After defining briefly what a plant breeder was, Cointat asked why after centuries when amateurs were simply indulging in their passion without claiming any rights, it had suddenly become necessary to provide a legal framework to protect plant breeding. In order to address this question, he declared:

> If I may, I would like to recall this amusing detail: as late as 1885, the government did officially declare in this assembly that France was no longer threatened by food insecurity ... So an empirical approach was the rule and the prospect of famine led decision-makers to refuse to grant a monopoly of sorts over the exploitation of agricultural varieties that could be crucial for the nation. It was vital that any discovery should fall within the common heritage. This state of facts (food priority and empirical approach) explains why the notion of providing legal protection to plant breeders, so that they can safely exploit the results of their labour, emerged at a relatively recent time, the end of the nineteenth century. Indeed, this era marks the beginning of a rapid shift of economic, technical and social conditions that created a new spirit. The great fear of hunger gradually receded thanks to more appropriate cultivation techniques, as well as fertilizers and mechanization.[37]

The report to the Senate closely echoed this speech:

[37] Assemblée Nationale, Séance du 4 décembre 1969, 4638; Sénat, Session 1969–1970 n° 164, 1–53.

From an economic standpoint, the possibility of an exclusive right raised a number of serious objections. Some were ready to accept it, but only for ornamental plants. Regarding edible plants, viewed as crucial to human life, the idea of a monopoly, be it limited in time, seemed unacceptable. Such argument is surprising since it does not hold against close scrutiny. How could breeders be expected to make costly investments, vital to their professional practice, if they are not confident that they will be able to retrieve their investment, and how could they be confident they would, unless they are granted exclusive rights over the results of their time-consuming trials? Not only is their personal interest at stake, but also the general interest. Indeed, progress is as closely linked to discoveries in agriculture as in industrial matters.[38]

It is obvious that whoever controls the seed controls one of the elements most crucial to human survival. In the explanatory memorandum to the Property Act of 1791, Portalis pointed out that this power has a long-standing history: during the 'famine that struck Egypt under the ministry of Joseph, the labourers gave up their lands in order to get the seeds necessary to feed their kins, and as a result the king became the owner of his subjects' land, which he then gave to them for farming upon payment of an annual royalty'. No one could find a more striking metaphor to illustrate the links between grain and the total alienation of individuals. This is how fear—and revolt—towards the one who holds the keys to subsistence were assimilated. Jean Delumeau describes the speculations on grain during periods of hunger and the farmers' revolts against the 'monopolists'.[39] He highlights the long-standing link between the idea of monopoly (at that time, a de facto monopoly) and periods of starvation. Given the link between hunger and monopoly, and the willingness to promote the idea of a monopoly over plant variety creation, the doctrine was bound to flip it, to invert it. The point was to argue that the breeder's achievements should be protected by a monopoly, precisely in order to promote new varieties whose high yields would bring food insecurity to an end. Thus, Freda Wuesthoff wrote:

In the course of our discussions, Baur had convinced us that the creation of new varieties of plants might play a great role in the future development of mankind. The importance of the problems involved can be assessed by simply considering the possibilities of overcoming the recurring periods of starvation which plague hundreds of millions of men in the Far East.[40]

[38] For similar reflections see Kléber Loustau's opening speech on 7 May 1957 at the UPOV Convention, Actes UPOV, 21.

[39] Delumeau (n 17) 213.

[40] Freda Wuesthoff, *Propriété industrielle* (September 1956) 176, 179; Franz Wuesthoff and Freda Wuesthoff, *Protection of New Varieties of Cultivated Plants* Report of the German Group to the Vienna Congress of the International Association for the Protection of Industrial Property (1952). This report was also reprinted in Stephen A Bent and others, *Intellectual Property Rights in Biotechnology Worldwide* (Stockton Press 1987) 81–98.

> A situation where the idea of monopoly suggested starvation produces the opposite situation: a given technology, sheltered under a monopoly, will make it possible to beat starvation all over the world. Such was the first obstacle that had to be removed in order to make it possible for the qualification of a restricted monopoly to be accepted. It left a number of marks that are easily traceable in the current system. Two types of provisions relate directly to the willingness to take 'food security risk' into account as a matter of public interest, one of the targets of the UPOV Convention. First, certain provisions allow the State to impose a compulsory exploitation right whenever the variety is vital to human or animal life. Secondly, national plant variety legislation, which forbids reference to the agronomic value of varieties, is backed up by regulations (both national and international) that impose various quality standards on the commercialization of reproductive field-crop material; the range of these standards amounts to the reintroduction of the requirement of agronomic value.

The preliminary drafts of the Convention specified that while a distinction between edible and ornamental plants was not allowed in terms of the recognition of the breeder's right, such a distinction was allowed regarding the enforcement of this right. By and large, this proposition was accepted except by the Organisation for Economic Co-operation and Development (OECD), which having already introduced its certification system to boost the circulation of high-quality seed, tried to promote the idea that agronomic interest should prevail in all cases; ultimately, OECD's position did not prevail.

Thus, there are basically two intertwined systems: the first relating to the creation of new plants which gives protection to any creator of a distinct, uniform, and stable variety: in that case, the concern for food is not mentioned. The second system relates to sales, where sales in a given country and circulation in the Common Market or in OECD countries are allowed, providing the variety is of agronomic interest. The food concern thus reappears for field-crop varieties through the certification and registration process. The two systems remain independent, in the sense that a given variety may be protected without being registered and vice versa. The PBR system aims to reward invention, whereas the registration system aims to allow commercialization when a given seed meets certain quality standards, which are verified at the producer's premises and being of agronomic interest. Thus, a variety that is new enough to be protected by a PBR may not be registered in France for lack of agronomic interest since it is able to resist a certain type of disease currently unknown in France. It would neither be registered nor marketed in France, but might be of interest under different pedoclimatic conditions and therefore may be registered in other countries enjoying a different climate.

We may therefore end up with a variety that is protected by plant breeders rights in France that cannot be commercialized in France, although it can be commercialized in a third country. Conversely, some varieties that long ago ceased to be eligible for protection may be registered, since they have not lost any of their agricultural relevance. Similalry, some very old varieties of historical value, no matter how unprofitable they are, may also be registered. This trend, which is consistent regarding fruit trees and likely to result in tastier apples! Only field-crop varieties and certain vegetable plants may be registered, at least so far. This is a clear indication of the specific regime applicable to edible varieties as opposed to ornamental varieties. The main consequence of this dual certification and registration system is that forgery is rare. Indeed, to qualify for sale the seed's origin has to be specified, as certified by the official services. Before granting certification, the authorities check both the pedigree and the quality of seed. This complex system has turned out to be effective, as evidenced by the small number of infringement actions. The few disputes that have arisen were resolved through settlements, as the profession remained extremely disciplined. Counterfeiting is much more frequent in the case of ornamental plants, where the living material may be subject to garnishment orders. The material is handed to the official services to be examined, but more often than not, the conflict is settled out of court.

The drift of the living matter

The salient quality of the living lies in its ability to reproduce. Performing actions that involve reproducing the living matter and acknowledging a monopoly right in this domain should have raised ethical obstacles, yet this does not seem to be the case. This newer empowerment over life, on the contrary, was asserted and emphasized with the precise aim of gaining protection different from that provided by patents. In the opening speech for the UPOV Convention, Kléber Loustau, Under-Secretary of State for Agriculture, made this statement about breeders: 'Their work is now based on firm foundations and their knowledge enables them to create living machines as drastically new as the inventions of their colleagues in industrial mechanics.'

In calling for specific protection the experts also invoked the reproductive capacity of plants: the patent, designed for lifeless matter, relies on the link between process and product. To the contrary, the staffers in charge of drafting the UPOV Convention emphasized that: 'the usefulness of a new plant depends on its capacity to reproduce as a pure race and not on whether the process of breeding can be replicated; because in practice, the replication of the breeding process takes ten years and costs millions of francs.'

At first sight, the fact that the living character of plants was emphasized rather than concealed appears to be paradoxical. This makes sense, however, if it is recognized that the idea of owning living nature would have been an obstacle at the beginning of the twentieth century, since legal experts dealing with industrial or intellectual property issues were uncomfortable when reasoning about living as opposed to inert matter. However, the period when claims to a monopoly were first voiced coincides with the time when scientists discovered the structure of life. The basic cogs of life were seen as components whose logic became intelligible. At that time, publications in biology commonly referred to an 'industrial pattern' of living nature.[41] Joël de Rosnay accounts for the photosynthetic process by comparing the cell's chloroplast to a 'photosynthesis factory' including a 'chemical synthesis unit'.[42] In his chapter 'D'étranges objets', Jacques Monod described living beings as objects endowed with a purpose, as machines able to build and reproduce themselves.[43] Finally, François Jacob wrote that 'everything urges to compare the logic of heredity to that of a computer', and that bacteria work like 'a small chemical factory' capable of performing about 2,000 reactions.[44] In parallel with the sacred vision of life, a new scientific vision was being developed that removed a number of cultural barriers to extending ownership to life. The organic vision of nature and of the state as biological bodies gave way to a vision of nature as a set of molecules—units of production—and to the 'new industrial state'.[45]

There is no such thing as nature

I have already argued extensively that nature cannot be owned. It is now time to explain how these barriers were removed and what traces they left in the law.

How wilderness came to be appropriable

'The antithesis to ownership is not communism but the savage state.'[46] This anti-communist joke may be applied to the work accomplished by Roman law when drawing a line between what is wild and what is not, between what is free and what is not. Given its origins, such distinction may seem archaic, but it is still of practical use. When Dolly Darmon reminds us that micro-organisms existing in nature—the 'wild strain'—are not patentable, this recalls the legal status of game and domestic animals in Roman law, allowing a challenge to Darmon's conclusion: 'Law does not precede the dream, it is born of day-to-day realities.'[47] Given that untamed nature is meant to escape the law, the unseasoned jurist will be surprised to read the opening sentence of the French law of 1970: 'For the implementation of this law, a new plant variety, created or *discovered*, is called a "plant variety".'

Traditionally, a discovery alludes to a wild, natural state, thereby precluding ownership. The plant breeders right's system, conversely, makes it possible to obtain protection for a variety that as long as it meets the legal criteria of being distinct, uniform, and stable (DUS), even if the breeder's work solely involves discovering

[41] Bernard Edelman, 'Vers une approche juridique du vivant' *Les Temps Modernes* (février 1981) 1434 (also in Edelman and Hermitte (n 1) 27–39).

[42] Joël de Rosnay, *Les origines de la vie* (Le Seuil 1996) 56–57.

[43] Jacques Monod, *Le hasard et la nécessité* (Le Seuil 1970) 19.

[44] François Jacob, *The Logic of Life* (Gallimard 1970, Princeton University Press 1993) 274.

[45] John Kenneth Galbraith, *The New Industrial State* (Princeton University Press 1967).

[46] D Dalloz, *Répertoire de jurisprudence générale*, 1857, v° Propriété, 179.

[47] Dolly Darmon, 'Protection juridique des inventions biotechnologiques' (1981) 18(4) *Revue d'économie industrielle* 93, 102.

the variety in nature. It should be noted that this hypothesis is extremely unlikely. Indeed, if a plant with notable genetic characteristics is discovered in nature, it will nearly always need to be redesigned in order to add other features, to adapt it to other growing conditions, to make it sufficiently uniform and stable. However, even if the actual conditions of its implementation make this hypothesis unlikely, infringement remains a possibility.

The explanation is still the same: by investigating the way plants reproduce, scientific research tends to reduce the impact of the traditional humanistic model of nature. Nature is constantly shaping, inventing, and recreating itself; in a way, the primal savage is no longer part of it, and humans will only ever know their offspring. Does this mean that we need to endorse such a far-fetched line of reasoning without further reflection? The problem does not really arise for developed countries, and seldom arises in the relationship between developed and developing countries. Experts from developed countries go in search of wild plants that have notable characteristics (perennial instead of annual, resistant to a disease). With or without permission from the local authorities, they take plants away, redesign them, and then end up selling the processed products back to their country of origin. For a long period of time, this did not cause any conflict, as plants (with the exception of fragrant plants and spices) as opposed to mineral resources were not considered a source of potential wealth. These genetic resources may nevertheless add to the pool of all exploitable natural resources for the developing countries that detain them. Granted, it is currently difficult to figure out a way in which this claim may fit into a new balance of rights. However, there is an urgent need to acknowledge the legitimacy of the compensation that private companies may have to pay when they are engaged in such appropriation. This issue might become more challenging in the years to come. Indeed, most of the reserves of genetic diversity are located in developing countries, such as the 'Vavilov centres' for cultivated species, or the 'Pleistocene refuges'. These undiscovered botanical reserves represent a potential source of unassessable value, to which developing countries should pay greater attention in order to avoid destroying it by uncontrolled clearing. Plant genetic resources are the equivalent of a commodity that locals should learn to shield and develop on a local basis, unless they receive fair compensation in exchange for their use. These local resources should be viewed as being in *public* ownership, based on the principle of sovereignty over natural resources (this was implemented by the Convention on Biological Diversity). The lesson must be heard: so far, the argument has remained within a framework playing on the appropriable or non-appropriable character of plant propagation. It now moves to a different perspective: the globalization of the phenomenon and the acuteness of the problems resulting from development—namely two of its essential components, health and nutrition—compelling consideration of the type of property that should be adopted to project the principles of development law into a sector that has so far remained unrelated, and to define what mutual relationships these different modes of appropriation should maintain.

Permanence and variations

Among the main features that characterize the concept of nature in Western culture is the sensation of permanence, the sense of eternity. The laws of nature are immutable, even though the body of scientific knowledge concerning nature is evolving: human nature appears to be immutable in its most fundamental aspects, and the process of plant reproduction is arguably an essential part of the sustainability of the environment. Disturbing such permanence would be sacrilege. However, nature is not quite as permanent as that. Nature's apparent immobility rests on the stability of vegetal *species*, a category designed on purpose to bring under a single umbrella a number of varieties of different and changing items. Consequently, speaking of the stability of species is a tautology, a trick that supports the appearance of immobility. In fact, nature constantly unwinds the thread of time, playing on its dual capacity to reproduce in an identical manner and to evolve. In a way, one might say that after copying nature by creating a new variety and thus taking part in the process of perpetual evolution, the breeder breaks away from it when they stop evolution by artificially maintaining the variety. The framing of this stability is one of the key elements of the legal system.

In order to be protected, a variety should be distinct, uniform, and stable: distinct, ie sufficiently distant from the closest varieties; uniform, in that all individuals of the same generation are identical; and stable, in that populations are identical from one generation to the next. The degree of stability required depends on the mode of reproduction; almost total stability can be expected for self-pollinated plants compared with cross-pollinated plants. Stability is achieved after several years of experiments (fixity has to be achieved by self-fertilization and by systematically discarding all individuals that are different to the chosen type). This procedure makes it possible to fix the variety, ie to put an end to its natural variability. Breeders first play along with nature's game by initiating variation or using natural variation; they then oppose it by blocking evolution, by artificially creating immobility. However, varietal creations experience instability, whether unintended or systematic.

A breeder presents a variety that is granted a plant variety right, since it meets the legal requirements, and notably the stability standards. However, after several years on the market, genetic instability resulting from the presence of a hybrid parent in the pedigree may occur. This is the case with certain varieties of wheat in France, whose pedigree contains a hybrid wheat–rye parent. It is of course possible to discard these varieties. In fact, when such varieties offer an agricultural benefit, an official waiver is granted that allows commercialization to continue (we see here the issue of 'agronomic relevance' re-emerges in the case of edible plants).

The main task of a large number of organizations—mostly national and international research institutes—is not to create finished varieties that meet the established DUS criteria, but rather so-called semi-finished products that comprise more or less improved populations, or parent material. This material constitutes a basic gene pool that is impossible to protect and is therefore free of appropriation: in principle, it is the subject of totally free exchange within the international scientific community. Only some additional work is required, to be conducted by private companies or more often than not in developing countries through national cooperation programmes. This additional work consists of transforming a flexible, semi-finished material into a finished, protectable product, adapted to the specific agricultural conditions in which it is to be cultivated. It is clear that this system, based on humanistic objectives, is controversial, for only the most competent companies can benefit from it, which does not help to reduce technological inequalities.

Once the breeder has created a new, uniform, and stable variety, their mission is not over. If not properly bred, a variety will degenerate, regaining its natural variability. National laws (and the UPOV Convention) therefore compel the breeder to maintain the variety in its original state, which entails an effort somewhat comparable to that required to achieve stability. The breeder is therefore obliged both to keep a vegetative collection of the protected variety, and to maintain the variety created to match the control sample. This demanding obligation has a two-fold objective: to maintain a sample that will make it possible to prove a possible infringement since the description is not sufficient; and to ensure throughout the lifetime of the variety, the stability and uniformity required initially, qualities that are essential to users to establish their cultivation plans. Should breeders fail to meet this obligation, they may be stripped of their rights; this is a major element of the system. Such obligation involves stopping natural variability, for the duration of the protection and, in the case of field crops, for the duration of the listing in the register. This duty to maintain stability and uniformity is a source of economic problems. Indeed, maintaining collections requires land and skilled resources, which represent a significant cost. Not only does the maintenance of commercial varieties represent a financial burden for breeders, but it is also to some extent ineffective. Indeed, maintaining collections requires land and skilled resources, which represent a significant cost. This duty to maintain commercial varieties that represents a burden for breeders, is also largely ineffective. The world's genetic legacy is a natural resource essential to human survival. It has not been possible to demonstrate as some have claimed that the existence of plant variety rights leads to genetic attrition. However, variety creation definitely involves selecting a finite number of genetic combinations; intensive cultivation practices and mechanization definitely lead to using but a limited number of varieties; and finally, the structure of the seed industry is definitely all the more geared towards mass production, in that it is held by multinational industrial groups. All these factors tend to undermine the world's genetic heritage. It is therefore urgent that governments and the international community take over from private collections so that varieties with little or no current commercial interest, which nonetheless carry valuable genetic information, are preserved. There is momentum in this direction, but it is difficult to hope that this trend will help curb the process. The demand for long-term stability therefore leads to a complete reversal of appearances: nature, far from being motionless, operates as a discrete process. To the scientist's eye, there is no such thing as nature in the cultural sense of the term.

Conclusion

This tale of plant breeders' right, as just told, came to an end in the mid-1980s. Reviewing it in 2022 brings back a distant sound, something similar to a flute solo. It is swiftly being covered by the brass instruments of patent law, followed by the violins of plant genetic resources, the percussion instruments of risk law and the cellos of biodiversity law that join the orchestra. Is this an orchestral score, where the instruments are introduced in disorder and then rearranged? As it stands, it is nothing but a cacophony.

Let us return to the flute solo. At the beginning of the 1960s, a fairly homogeneous professional community attempted to industrialize agriculture. It rejected patent law, which was unsuited to the cumulative nature of progress in the plant sector, and invented a sui generis intellectual property right, plant breeders rights, which combined exclusivism for the variety with free access to the biological resources it harboured.

This community is self-confident and pays little attention to what is happening in the Council of Europe, where a harmonization of European patent rights is in the making. The community believes that it fixed the problem in 1963 by accepting the rules that would be taken up in 1973 by the European Patent Convention: that plant varieties and the essentially biological processes used for obtaining plants were excluded from patentability, which is their sole concern. The community was not impacted by the claim that microbiological processes and the products thus obtained are patentable. All this was be confirmed by the 1998 European Directive on the patentability of biotechnological inventions. At first, this error was not perceived as such.

As early as the mid-1970s, the Food and Agriculture Organization of the United Nations (FAO) started playing its violins, forecasting the loss of biological resources adapted to the agro-ecosystems in developing countries: new varieties would replace local varieties whose genetic resources would be irretrievably lost: these had to be kept (mostly in so-called *ex situ* collections). Repeatedly, in 1981, 1983, and 1989, the FAO attempted to turn 'plant genetic resources useful to agriculture' into a 'common heritage of humanity', preserved and accessible to all. All of them? Not quite, since farmers are kept apart, even though in 1989 the notion of a 'farmer's right' emerges albeit without any precise content. The flute and violins play an interesting but questionable score, because it transforms resources into the undivided property of the sector's professionals alone.

From the end of the 1970s onwards, the brass instruments of the patents covered other sounds. Genes became patentable at the end of the 1970s, followed by micro-organisms in 1981, plants in 1985, and animals in 1988. The impetus, begun by the United States, immediately spread to the European Patent Office and then to the entire industrialized world. Free invention was stopped, and farmers who used their harvest for seeds became infringers. The various voices of the farming world were overlaid by the trumpets of the chemical industry's biotechnology: 'Let's do away with your gardeners' rights!' Yet, as early as 1990, it was clear that patent law was still unsuitable for a cumulative invention process: without free access, possibly for a fee, inventors would quickly be locked in, as they are all dependent on each other. No one was listening.[48]

However, in 1990, Europe's right brain called on the percussion section of the law of risk and its so-called precautionary principle by adopting Directive 90/220: no genetically modified variety, with its share of patents, could be brought to market without prior authorization. This had a chilling effect on these markets, which were already weighed down by patents. Most consumers disliked these plants and only North American law-makers were enthusiastic about them. Twenty years later, in 2010, the Cartagena Protocol on Biosafety brought the risk issue to the international level.

The complex situation of the 1990s provided an opportunity for plant breeders to regain a place in the orchestra. On 19 March 1991, they amended their Convention by introducing the notion of 'essentially derived variety' to protect themselves from those who might use their varieties free of charge to modify them with a patented gene. The amendment to the Convention also formalized the 'farmer's privilege' and 'farm-saved seed', which helped to seduce many farmers. Plant breeders rights regained steam in Europe by creating specific institutions and a Europe-wide plant-variety right in 1994. In addition, at the beginning of the 1990s two new instruments came into play: development law with its principle of permanent sovereignty over natural resources, and biodiversity law, created in 1992 in Rio. Since industries from northern countries patent genes and the organisms in which they are found, developing countries were to recall that the organisms living on

[48] A French Member of the House of Representatives understands the problem but is unable to make his point. Rapport de Daniel Chevallier, député, Office parlementaire d'évaluation des choix scientifiques et techniques, No 1827 (Assemblée Nationale), No 148 (Sénat), législature 1990–1991 https://www.senat.fr/rap/r90-148-1/r90-148-1.html in M-A Hermitte, *La protection de l'innovation en matière de biotechnologie appliquée à l'agriculture*, in D Chevallier, Rapport sur les applications des biotechnologies à l'agriculture et à l'industrie agro-alimentaire (Office parlementaire d'évaluation des choix scientifiques et technologiques 1990), vol II, Annexes, 115–290.

their territories, which have now become potential resources, must be covered by the principle of permanent sovereignty over natural resources: so much for the common heritage. Thus, the cellos of biodiversity give a voice to 'indigenous peoples' and to some arcane 'local communities', who are already suing to overturn patents that lack novelty because they are based on their traditional knowledge. WIPO took up the issue in 1998 to attempt—at the pace of a strolling snail—to design an intellectual property right for these communities, a task that is still in progress. Twelve years later, this led to the Nagoya Protocol, which encourages states to draw up legislation organizing access to these traditional resources and know-how, provided that it is agreed and that it organizes the sharing of benefits, in an equitable manner of course.

In 2001, the FAO successfully urged states to sign the International Treaty on Plant Genetic Resources (ITPGRFA). The seed companies took the wheel, promoting *ex situ* collections of old local varieties, claiming an eased access for research and breeding, but with no possibility of claiming patent rights. The International Seed Federation still emphasizes this point: protection of innovations, the ITPGRFA, rather than Nagoya, and a 'scientific' conception of risk. However, at the beginning of the twenty-first century patent law continued to gain ground, including in Europe where, in 1998, it was decided to authorize the patentability of organisms and components, even if merely isolated from the natural environment. At the legal level, it seems that the question has been settled. On the commercial level, however, the picture is mixed. Depending on the species (since the transgenic varieties cultivated mainly cover soya, maize, canola, and sunflower) and depending on the region of the world (since genetically modified organisms (GMOs) are an almost total failure in Europe), which allows traditional breeders to pursue technical progress without resorting to transgenesis.

The last twenty years of this story is rich with paradoxes. Transgenic varieties, the only marketable items, are affected by an increasing stacking of patents, which challenges the economic viability of the sector, already undermined by safety issues. As soon as a specific problem seems to be fixed, such as the question of the patentability of essentially biological processes,[49] others emerge, such as the question of patented native genes or native traits. Hope had seemed to come from the announced overcoming of the old transgenesis by 'gentler' processes, including CRISPR-Cas and various forms of mutagenesis. In the name of such gentleness, business and political circles are trying to convince people to drop the precautionary principle and forget about the cumbersome prior authorization measures. While this issue remains uncertain, politicians appear keen on 'disruptive modernity'. And yet, unintended effects, which were supposed to be non-existent, are no longer debated. Moreover, the issue of gene patentability remains open, leading

[49] See Veit Braun, 'The Essence of Biology: Tomatoes, Broccoli, and European Patents on Native Plant Traits' in this volume.

to long-lasting legal warfare. The problem of unmanageable patent thickets has resurfaced with such intensity that some breeders, although active in this war, are looking for varieties that are free of patents, and some are even turning their attention to work on new species that are likely to be domesticated more freely. Meanwhile, the concentration of the agrochemical industry is being reinforced with the help of inventive start-ups for whom safety is not the primary concern: the process is an endless story.

6

Novelties, Frauds, and Protections

The Seed and Nursery Business in Nineteenth-century America

*Daniel J Kevles**

Pioneering the Seed and Nursery Enterprise

In the North American colonies and, later, the United States of the late eighteenth century, only a handful of seed houses and fruit nurseries dotted the landscape, most occupying a few acres of land and cultivating a paltry diversity of stock.[1] Whatever their size, virtually all these firms relied heavily on importations from abroad for new plants, trees, or vines that they then sold directly or as next-generation seedlings. They also obtained advantageous new varieties from among their own plantings or from local farmers and orchardists. Rather than intentionally bred, most were chance finds in the fields, natural hybrids produced by the cross-pollination of birds, bees, and the wind, which the proprietors then propagated from cuttings or seeds, harvesting the resulting plants, seeds, or seedlings for sale. Nurserymen offered, for example, the Bartlett Pear, which originated in England but was imported, grown, and renamed by Enoch Bartlett on his farm in Dorchester, Massachusetts, and the Jonathan Apple, which was named after Jonathan Hasbrouck, a teenager who found it growing on a farm in Kingston, New York.[2]

* I am grateful for the help of the staff at each of the archives mentioned below, and to the editors of this volume and Mario Biagioli for their comments and encouragements. I am also indebted to J Stephen Casscles for making available to me a copy of his study in progress of the Prince Family and their nurseries. This chapter draws on work supported by the Books Program of the Alfred P Sloan Foundation, the National Science Foundation, the Cullman Center for Scholars and Writers at the New York Public Library, and the Humanities Institute at the LuEsther T Mertz Library, New York Botanical Garden. My thanks to all.

[1] HAS Dearborn, 'Historical Sketch' (1847–1851) 1 *Transactions of the Massachusetts Horticultural Society* 84; Ulysses P Hedrick, *Horticulture in America to 1860* (Oxford University Press 1950) 208, 230.

[2] Daniel J Kevles, 'Fruit Nationalism: Horticulture in the United States—from the Revolution to the First Centennial' in Marco Beretta, Karl Grandin, and Svante Lindqvist (eds), *Aurora Torealis: Studies in the History of Science and Ideas in Honor of Tore Frangsmyr* (Science History Publications 2008) 129, 131–32; Ulysses Prentiss Hedrick, *A History of Agriculture in the State of New York* (New York State Agricultural Society 1933) 381–82; Philip J Pauly, *Fruits and Plains: The Horticultural Transformation of America* (Harvard University Press 2008) 104–05.

Daniel J Kevles, *Novelties, Frauds, and Protections* In: *Intellectual Property and the Design of Nature.* Edited by: Jose Bellido and Brad Sherman, Oxford University Press. © Daniel J Kevles 2023. DOI: 10.1093/oso/9780192864406.003.0006

In the revolutionary era, a few plant and seed houses were themselves beginning to originate new varieties.[3] Leading the way was the Prince Nursery, which had been established around 1720 at Flushing Landing, Long Island, by Robert Prince and which, in 1745, his son William began to turn into a prominent innovative enterprise. William understood that plant seeds are the products of sexual reproduction (a process that had been identified in a few plants in the 1690s and abundantly confirmed in many others by the mid-eighteenth century). The trees and vines that grew from them varied widely in quality, including in vigour, resistance to disease, and merit, as well as in abundance and merit of fruit. These reproductive habits prompted William to devise a method—apparently independently of innovators in Europe—of breeding superior trees. He planted in close proximity a large number of high-quality fruit trees of the same variety, and selected from the offspring any of superior particular qualities. He then reproduced them asexually—that is, to use the current term, he 'cloned' them—by grafting cuttings onto root stock or buds onto the branches of other trees. As asexual reproductions, they were identical to the original and constituted a new variety that could be propagated by the same method in indefinite numbers. About 1790, employing this method, William planted the pits of twenty-five quarts of the greengage plum and obtained trees yielding together a rainbow of fruits, including the white gage, red gage, and prince's gage plums, all of which became standards in the American fruit basket.[4]

The Prince Nursery flourished, tripling in size to twenty-four acres by 1790, aided by offering trees reliably true to the superior original and its expanding diversity of stock, especially flowering and ornamental plants. The nursery was within convenient boat-reach of Lower Manhattan, via north from Flushing Creek into Flushing Bay and then south down the East River. With such quick water transportation to the city and its ports, it steadily extended its reach to farmers, orchardists in the city, its environs, and, increasingly, other colonies. The British occupation of New York City and much of western Long Island during the American War for Independence had cut off most of its wider market, but British troops protected the nursery—the Princes may have been Loyalists—and peace brought unfettered access to the rest of the United States. Beginning in 1793, William's two sons took

[3] No doubt typical of the local purveyors were Hannah and Jacob Dubre, who sold seed and fruit trees from their thirty-five-acre farm near Philadelphia between the 1750s and the 1770s. See *D Landreth's Seed Company Newsletter, The Period: 1784–1800*. This was the first of twelve newsletters covering successive periods, issued by Landreth's beginning in January 2009 under the title: *What It Means to Have Been a Part of America for 225 Years* (D Landreth Seed Co 2009–2010), in author's possession. These commemorative newsletters are based largely on the company's holdings of sixty Landreth's seed catalogues dating from 1839 to 1945, including a complete set for 1852 to 1893.

[4] J Stephen Casscles, *A History of the Prince Family & Nurseries of Flushing, NY and Their Influence on American Horticulture (1720–1869)* (in draft; copy in author's possession,34–36, 55–56, 59, 66, 68; William Prince, *A Short Treatise on Horticulture: Embracing Descriptions of a Great Variety of Fruit and Ornamental Trees and Shrubs, Grape Vines, Bulbous Flowers, and Green-House Trees and Plants, &c., Nearly All of which at Present Comprised in the Collections of the Linnaen Botanic Garden at Flushing, New York* (New York 1828) 24–25.

over and divided the family enterprise, with one, William, Jr, calling his portion the Linnaean Botanic Garden and Nursery. The Garden, shipping to customers in the Hudson Valley and along the East Coast, became perhaps the most prominent nursery in the nation. Early in the 1790s, taking time away from their duties in New York, then the seat of the new federal government, George Washington, Thomas Jefferson, John Jay, and other high-ranking officials day-tripped to Flushing to see the Prince Nursery and, in Jefferson's case, to purchase large quantities of stock.[5]

Philadelphia was the home of several widely known plant and seed firms, notably Bartram's Garden, located on the Schuylkill River, and the downtown seed house of David and Cuthbert Landreth, both recent immigrants from England. Bartram's had been founded in 1731 by John Bartram, whose trade had won notoriety on both sides of the Atlantic, and was now run by his children.[6] While continuing in the international seed trade, they expanded their domestic operation, searching for new plants in the North American wild and adding part of the family farm to the commercial enterprise.[7] Landreth's, which opened in 1784, prospered as a local business, winning a large contract from the city to line its central streets with trees. It soon began attracting customers from afar, including Washington, Jefferson, and Napoleon's brother Joseph. By the 1820s, the firm, which had opened a branch in Charleston, South Carolina, was known from Boston to New Orleans and was shipping sizeable quantities of seeds to British India. It was perhaps the largest seed house in the nascent industry, with a farm on the city's outskirts for the production and testing of seed and a five-storey, three-storefront-wide warehouse at its centre.[8]

In their early days, the seed houses and nurseries tended to advertise in local newspapers, a practice they continued into the late nineteenth century. Initiating their own advertisements, in 1771 William Prince issued a one-page list of the fruit trees available at his nursery, and in 1783, William Bartram, one of John's sons,

[5] Casscles (n 4) 56–57, 61, 63, 69.

[6] Kevles (n 2) 129, 131; Pennsylvania Horticultural Society, *From Seed to Flower Philadelphia, 1681–1876: A Horticultural Point of View* (1976) 'Introduction' 22; 'Preface' [1801], reprinted in *A Catalogue of Trees, Shrubs, and Herbaceous Plants, Indigenous to the United States of America, Cultivated and Disposed of by John Bartram & Son, at Their Botanical Garden, Kingsessing, near Philadelphia* (1807) 2, 7; *Periodical Catalogue of Fruit and Ornamental Trees and Shrubs, Green House Plants, Etc., Cultivated and for Sale at Bartram's Botanic Garden* (1828–1830) 3; Archives, Bartram's Garden (ABG), Kingsessing, PA.

[7] *Periodical Catalogue of American Trees, Shrubs, Plants, and Seeds, Cultivated and for Sale at the Bartram Botanic Garden, Near Philadelphia* (1831) 83–84; [Bartram's] *Periodical Catalogue* (1828–1830) 3–4, Index; Joel T Fry, 'John Bartram Carr, the Unknown Bartram' (John Bartram Association 1994) 1–2, 4; ABG (n 6).

[8] Landreth's, *Part of America* (n 3) 'The Period 1784–1800'; 'The Period 1800–1820'; Landreth & Son, *Kitchen-Garden Priced List of Landreth's American Pedigree Seeds* (1886) 31, in Special Collections, Manuscripts and Archives Department, University of Delaware Library (UDEL), Newark, Delaware. In Charleston, Landreth's originally used slave labour hired at between US$100 and US$160 per man per season. It ceased doing so in 1833. Landreth's *Part of America* (n 3) 'The Period 1830–1850'.

put out a one-page broadside of the stock for sale at the family's Linnaean Botanic Garden. From the turn of the century, purveyors of seeds and plants added more sheets and turned them into bound catalogues.[9] In content, these publications tended to comprise bare lists of the seeds, plants, and fruits available for purchase. Amid the dominant localism of the markets, there was little competition and thus little need for product and brand differentiation. In this period, what counted as a selling point was much less any special botanical merit and much more that the stock was imported from many regions of the world.[10] In a newspaper notice promoting the opening of his seed business, David Landreth announced '[a] fresh IMPORTATION of Choice Garden Seeds'. The firm continued to tout its stock of imports, telling customers in 1824, for example, that it had gone to 'considerable expense' to procure useful and ornamental trees and plants not only from the United States, but also from Europe, China, the Cape of Good Hope, New South Wales, India, Mexico, and South America.[11]

Bernard McMahon, another Philadelphia seedsman, considered the emphasis on imports a disservice to the American plant business. Irish by birth and a radical Jeffersonian by conviction, he was an American plant nationalist, devoted

[9] Joel T Fry, 'Inside the Box: John Bartram and the Science and Commerce of the Transatlantic Plant Trade' in Pamela H Smith, Amy RW Meyers, and Harold J Cook, *Ways of Making and Knowing: the Material Culture of Empirical Knowledge* (University of Michigan Press 2014) 197–98, 200; Pennsylvania Horticultural Society, *From Seed to Flower* (n 6) 14; Irwin Richman, *Seed Art: The Package Made Me Buy It* (Schiffer Publishing Ltd 2008) 8–9; *To Be Sold, by William Prince, at Flushing-Landing, on Long-Island, Near New York, a Large Collection of Fruit Trees, as Follows* (CH Gaine 1771); *Catalogue of American Trees, Shrubs, and Herbaceous Plants, Most of Which Are Now Growing, and Produce Ripe Seed in John Bartram's Garden, Near Philadelphia* (1783); ABG (n 6). Other broadsheets include *A Catalogue of Kitchen-Garden, Field, and Flower-Seeds, Plants, etc. for Sale by S Grundy* (undated); and *A Catalogue of Fruit Trees for Sale, in the Fall of 1806, by Daniel Smith and Company, at Burlington, State of New Jersey, Near Philadelphia* (1806)ABG (n 6); Newspaper advertisements: 'American Seeds and Plants, for Sale at Bartram's Botanic Garden'; 'Bartram's Botanic Garden, Near Gray's Ferry'; Bartram's Botanic Garden, Near Philadelphia; 'For Sale as Usual, At Bartram's Botanic Garden, Near Gray's Ferry Kingsessing'; 'Fresh American Seeds, for Sale, at Bartram's Botanic Garden', *Paulson's American Daily Advertiser* (26 October 1818, 19 October 1819, 18 June 1820, 13 March 1827, 19 March 1832, 13 March 1813, and 2 December 1817)ABG (n 6); John Bartram, 'Bartram's Garden Kingsessing'; John Bartram, 'Seeds and Plants'; 'Kingsessing Gardens, Near Gray's Ferry, Four Miles from the City' *The Aurora* (27 June 1811, 24 November 1810, 17 April 1810)ABG (n 6). Bartram's Garden issued its first bound catalogue in 1801, responding to 'repeated' requests from friends at home and abroad. See *Trees, Shrubs, and Herbaceous Plants* (1807) 2. Examples of bound catalogues include *A Catalogue of American Seeds Sold by Bernard McMahon, Seedsman, Philadelphia* (Bartholomew Graves 1804).

[10] See *A Catalogue of Garden, Grass & Flower Seeds, Roots, Plants, etc. Constantly for Sale Wholesale and Retail by Goldthwait & Moore, Corner of Second and Walnut Street* (Thomas Beadford 1796); UDEL (n 8); [Bartram's] *Periodical Catalogue 1828–1830*.

[11] Landreth's *Part of America* (n 3) 'The Period 1784–1800'; D Landreth Seed Company, *Our History, in Possession of D Landreth's Seed Co* (Shelburne undated) http://www.landrethseeds.com/history.html (accessed August 2012); David Landreth and Cuthbert Landreth, *Catalogue of Greenhouse Plants, Hardy Trees, Evergreen Shrubs, Flowering Shrubs, Bulbous Rooted, and Herbaceous Plants* (1824) iii; UDEL (n 8). Extolling imports was a regular practice of the firm. In a circular in 1836, it stressed that the company obtained seeds from 'extensive collections in Europe' and 'direct from the East and West Indies and South America'. See *Catalogue of the Principal Garden Seeds Cultivated at the Horticultural Gardens of David Landreth & Co* (William Stavely 1836) 14; UDEL (n 8).

to supplementing imports with native seeds.[12] Among his admirers was Thomas Jefferson himself, who that same year arranged for McMahon to be given a large portion of the seeds and plant specimens obtained by Meriwether Lewis and William Clark during their expedition through the newly acquired Louisiana Territory. What they brought back spotlighted the vastly increased native sources now available. In 1806, McMahon published the *American Gardener's Calendar*, the first comprehensive handbook for growers in the United States and, in part, a celebration of native varieties that deplored neglect of 'the profusion of beauties so bountifully bestowed upon us by the hand of nature'. The embargo that Jefferson had imposed against trade with Britain in 1807 added a timely lustre to McMahon's home-grown admonition and to the popularity of his book, which enjoyed steady sales for many years.[13]

In March 1812, McMahon advertised several new species of currant in the *Aurora*, a pro-Jefferson newspaper, making a selling point of the special provenance of the plants:

> The seeds of those shrubs were collected by Messrs. Lewis and Clark . . . on their expedition to the Pacific Ocean, and sent to the advertiser by Thomas Jefferson, Esq. then President of the United States, to whose love of country and science, the advertiser is indebted for several hundred important species of plants, now in his possession, and in a successful state of cultivation.[14]

Demand for plants and seeds grew as Americans moved West, for example, from New England to New York state, which in settlers' leases required the planting of orchards, and then into the Ohio and Mississippi valleys. Land grants made under the Northwest Ordinance, which the US Congress passed in 1787 to establish rules for settlement of the Northwest Territory (now the states of Ohio, Indiana, Illinois, Michigan, and Wisconsin), required that every homesteader plant at

[12] Peter Hatch, 'Bernard McMahon, Pioneer American Gardener' *Twinleaf* (1993) http://www.monticello.org/site/house-and-gardens/bernard-mcmahon (accessed 22 September 2021); Robert S Cox, '"I Never Yet Parted": Bernard McMahon and the Seeds of the Corps of Discovery' in Robert S Cox (ed), *The Shortest and Most Convenient Route: Lewis and Clark in Context* (American Philosophical Society 2004) 102, 109–14. In 1804, McMahon informed prospective customers that he offered: '[F]or sale, an extensive variety of Asiatic, South-Sea Islands, African and European Seeds, of the most curious and rare kinds; and is daily adding to his collection, as he avails himself of every opportunity to procure seeds from all parts of America, as well as from every part of the world, to which the enterprize [sic] of American commerce extends.' See *A Catalogue of American Seeds Sold by Bernard McMahon, Seedsman, Philadelphia Sold by Bernard McMahon, Seedsman, Philadelphia,* (n 9) 1, ABG (n 6); see also 1807 *Garden, Herb, Flower* 3.

[13] Cox (n 12) 115–17, 119–21, 123–24; Hatch (n 12). In 1804, Lewis sent Jefferson several cuttings of the Osage orange tree, which he had obtained from the Osage tribe in Missouri. Jefferson sent the slips to William Hamilton, a friend who owned a large estate in Philadelphia and who gave some of them to Landreth's. See ibid 107–109; McMahon, *Gardener's Calendar* vii, 72.

[14] Bernard McMahon, 'Fragrant Currant' *Aurora & General Advertiser* (11 March 1812)ABG (n 6).

least fifty apple or pear trees.[15] The demand escalated with the further westward migrations out to the Great Plains and the Far West of California, Oregon, and Washington. People settled on and began cultivating millions of acres of land that, with the aid and protection of the federal government, they appropriated from the Native Americans who had long occupied them. By the mid-nineteenth century, the United States had become a continental nation, having acquired vast additional lands by annexing Texas, winning California in the Mexican War, and negotiating possession of the Oregon Territory below the 49th Parallel with the British.

All elements of the nation's commerce, including agriculture, were facilitated by the transportation revolution that had begun in the early nineteenth century. Public and private developers had established steamboat services on the major rivers and Great Lakes, built roads and canals, and laid down railroad tracks. The steel ribbons eventually linked settlements to distant towns and cities across regions. After the first transcontinental railroad was completed in 1869, the connections extended across the continent, expanding regional markets, and ultimately creating a national one, not only for the produce from the farms, but also for the resources, including seeds as well as fruit trees and vines, that enabled them. Farmers and orchardists became all the more accessible to nurseries and seed houses with the establishment, in 1863, of the US postal category of third-class mail, which among other provisions authorized the mailing of 'seeds, cuttings, bulbs, roots and scions'.[16]

Demand for seeds was somewhat limited by the tendency of farmers to save seed from one crop for planting the following year. But new farms and gardens required new seed, which offset the market dilution of seed saving. Demand was also probably sustained by the biological economy of sexually reproducing plants. The farmer's or gardener's seeds, themselves the products of random sexual reproduction in the field or garden, would yield a next generation that might decline in quality and yield.[17] Thus, to maintain the vitality of their crops, farmers and gardeners faced a recurrent need for fresh, high-quality seed that they might obtain from neighbours or seed houses or both.

In sum, Americans wanted diverse trees, seeds, and vines to establish and sustain their farms, orchards, home gardens, and families with grains, vegetables, fruits, and medicinal plants. In the 1840s, judging by the content of seed catalogues, demand for flower seed began rising, led by the country's rapidly expanding cities, emerging suburbs, and proliferating civic cemeteries; residents devoted less of their gardens to

[15] Emily Pawley, *The Nature of the Future: Agriculture, Science, and Capitalism in the Antebellum North* (University of Chicago Press 2020) 166; Michael Pollan, *The Botany of Desire: A Plant's-Eye View of the World* (Random House 2001) 16.

[16] Cheryl Lyon-Jenness, 'Planting a Seed: The Nineteenth-Century Horticultural Boom in America' (2004) 76 *Business History Review* 394.

[17] The tendency to reversion was common knowledge among seedsmen. See eg *Landreth's Rural Register and Almanac 1887*, 49; UDEL (n 8); see also Charles Darwin, *The Variation of Plants and Animals under Domestication* (John Murray 1868).

growing vegetables and more of them to cultivating ornamental trees and flowers, especially roses, for both the decoration of their homes and the shielding of their outhouses. In 1875, a leading nursery noted that such ornamentals have become 'a necessity' for 'everyone who has a garden' and for parks and pleasure grounds as well. The increasing urbanization also gave rise to market gardens, which drew on nurseries and seed houses to supply nearby cities with fresh fruits, vegetables, and flowers and which proliferated significantly in the latter half of the century.[18]

The combination of rising demand and better transportation greatly stimulated expansion in the seed and nursery industry.[19] The number of nurseries mushroomed from a few dozen clustered around the major cities at the beginning of the nineteenth century to more than 1,000 by 1850, selling more than fifteen to twenty million trees a year. Western New York state exemplified the story. Beginning in the 1830s, new nurseries and seed houses sprang up in the region, with business boosted by the Erie Canal. Completed in 1825, the canal facilitated the movement of goods between New York City and Buffalo, and the region's location on Lake Erie gave it access to the markets of the developing Midwest. By the late 1850s, thirty-five nurseries were operating in and around Rochester, and the city was on its way to becoming a centre of national trade in fruit trees and vines. In 1856, the *Genesee Farmer* declared that 'more nursery trees were grown in Monroe County than in all the United States besides'.[20]

As a result of changing family circumstances, Bartram's Garden and McMahon's closed, but Landreth's, a robust survivor, emerged as a national leader in the seed business, and the Prince Nursery remained a pacesetting horticultural player. Eventually acquiring part of his brother's land, William Jr expanded the Linnaean Botanical Garden into a botanical as well as commercial showplace, greatly increasing the varieties under cultivation both by breeding and importation. He was advantaged in knowledge and importation by his standing as a corresponding member of the London Horticultural Society, which gave him free access to the several thousand fruit varieties that it grew in its garden at Chiswick. He tested and evaluated the imported plants and trees for quality and local viability, amassed an extensive library on horticulture and agriculture, and published several treatises of his own on the subject. He combined business and science, emphasizing the value of the latter to the former, in a fashion that his son, William Robert Prince, already the author of the first

[18] Lyon-Jenness (n 16) 382; 'Preface to 23rd Edition', *No 2 Descriptive Catalogue of Hardy Ornamental Trees, Shrubs, Roses, Etc. Ellwanger and Barry, Proprietors* (1875) 2, EB, Box 194, file BC1934, CCMHSD; Landreth's *Part of America* (n 3) 'The Period 1890–1900'; Pawley (n 15) 167.

[19] Hedrick (n 1) 208, 230–33, 241. According to a knowledgeable observer, between seventy and eighty nurseries were operating in the United States that were celebrated for their abundant variety of plants, and many others were newly under way; Dearborn (n 1) 84–85.

[20] Pawley (n 15) 168; Camden Burd, 'The Ornament of Empire: Plant Nurserymen and the Making of the American Landscape' PhD Thesis (Rochester University 2019) 11, 133, 149. The first significant nursery in Western New York was established by Lewis Fallen in 1827 on Grand Island, in the Niagara River area near Buffalo; Hedrick (n 1) 238–39, 245.

authoritative book on American viniculture, continued after he took control of the nursery in 1835. By then, it covered some forty acres, contained about 10,000 species and varieties of plants and trees, and employed a sizeable workforce. A number of the employees went on to start their own nurseries, carrying with them the knowledge of the Prince methods and model of science and business. Despite a disastrous investment in mulberry trees, William Robert managed to pursue the model until his death at the end of the 1860s. The nursery died with him.[21]

Among the standout new contenders were several firms, including, notably, in the northeast, Hovey & Co, in Cambridge, Massachusetts, and in Rochester, New York, George Ellwanger & Patrick Barry's Mount Hope Nursery. Both nurseries started small and young. Charles M Hovey, a Boston native, had taken to horticulture as a teenager, keeping detailed notes on pears, apples, and peaches. In 1832, aged twenty-two, he founded Hovey & Co, with his older brother Phineas, on a one-acre site in Cambridgeport, about half a mile east of Harvard on the road from Boston to Mount Auburn. Specializing at the outset in vegetables, shrubs, and small fruits, the company sold its products through a store on Cornhill Street in Boston that was just below the meeting hall of the Massachusetts Horticultural Society.[22] George Ellwanger was an enterprising native of Germany and Patrick Barry an immigrant from Belfast, Ireland, and a graduate of several years with Prince's Linnaean Botanical Garden and Nursery. In 1839, Ellwanger bought out his employer's five-acre nursery and the next year, he and Barry, both aged twenty-four, partnered to open The Mount Hope Botanical and Pomological Garden.[23] Together with Landreth's and the Prince Nursery, the two enterprises would eventually take their places among the most prosperous and influential companies in the nation's seed and nursery business.

In New York, a cluster of nurseries made Flushing a vital centre of horticulture; in Philadelphia and Boston, several new firms achieved prominence by catering to the burgeoning urban and suburban demand for flower seeds as well as ornamental plants. In the upper Midwest, many smaller nurseries, a number founded by veteran employees of Ellwanger & Barry's, formed a network of regional nurseries, supplying fruits, flowers, and vegetable seeds to farmers, orchardists, and

[21] Pawley (n 15) 170; 'Inoculations', 'Prince Account Books', [c 1816–1846], Prince Nursery Records, Item SB218, LuEsther T Mertz Library, New York Botanical Garden; *Catalogue of American Indigenous Trees, Plants, and Seeds Cultivated and for Sale at the Linnaean Botanic Garden, William Prince, Proprietor* (1820) Catalogue Collection, Massachusetts Horticultural Society Depository, Franklin, MA (CCMHSD), Box 621; Hedrick (n 1) 208–10; Casscles (n 4) 55, 69, 76–77, 82, 95, 98, 101–102, 113–14, 120–21, 123, 186–87, 198–99, 219–20, 226–27.

[22] *A Descriptive Catalogue of Fruits Cultivated and for Sale by Hovey & Co, at their Cambridge Nurseries, Cambridge, near Boston, Mass. (only two miles from the city) for the Autumn of 1844 and the Spring of 1845*, 4, Box 380, Hovey Pt 1; CCMHSD (n 21); BJ Hutchinson, 'A Taste for Horticulture' (1980) 40(1) *Arnoldia* 31, 36; Pauly (n 2) 59. Hovey maintained the practice of note-taking, recording such data as the time of budding or fruiting of particular plants in his nursery. See 'Horticultural Memoranda for 1838' in Hovey Horticultural Memoranda, Hovey files, CCMHSD (n 21).

[23] Hedrick (n 1) 243–45; on Ellwanger & Barry see Burd (n 20).

home gardeners around Chicago and Bloomington, Illinois, Detroit, Cincinnati, Columbus, and Toledo.[24]

In 1850, the US Census found 8,479 nurserymen, seedsmen, and florists operating in the country; in 1860, 21,788; in 1870, 32,520; in 1880, 56,032; and in 1890, 72,691.[25] The proliferation of firms—whether large or small, or national, regional, or local in reach—transformed the far-flung enterprise into a business essential to the increasingly specialized economy. It also generated an intensifying competition that steadily altered the business' character and orientation.

To the end of meeting competition, both the surviving companies and the new entrants placed a premium on offering multiple plant varieties every year and—especially important—each year, a number of what the trade called 'novelties', or what would be termed 'innovations': in the main, new varieties of vegetables and fruits, but also varieties for nurserymen of greater hardiness or earlier bearing and for the higher-end urban market of enhanced flavour and appearance.[26]

However, the impersonality that came with the vastly expanding market also generated unscrupulous competitors—thieves of names and novelties. Legitimate seed houses and nurseries grew increasingly absorbed with safeguarding their brands and obtaining a return on their investments in their innovations, the effort in labour, and the dollars required to turn them into marketable products. Increasingly, the firms came to recognize that the novelties as such represented a kind of property—what is called 'intellectual property'—that they needed to protect. While they did not have such terminology, they came to possess the concept, understanding well the economic advantage of preventing others from undercutting, appropriating, reproducing, and selling their new productions.

Innovation: Incentives and Practices

At the time, US patent law provided no incentive for the innovation of plant novelties because plants were assumed to be ineligible for patents. Since the Patent Act in 1793, statutory law had defined, in language written by Thomas Jefferson, what might be granted a patent: 'any new and useful art, machine, manufacture or composition of matter, or any new and useful improvement on any art, machine, manufacture or composition of matter, not known or used'. In 1836, Congress

[24] Casscles (n 4) 15–17, 25, 50. For example, Joseph Breck & Co, in Boston; Peter Henderson & Co, in New York; Henry A Dreer in Philadelphia. See the catalogues in CCMHSD (n 21); Lyon-Jenness (n 16) 385–86, 392; Hedrick (n 1) 243–45. In 1858, Marshall Wilder, a prominent Boston nurseryman, noted that fewer than forty years earlier not a nursery in New England was entitled to the name, but that now some 'contain nearly as great a variety of fruit trees as the most extensive in England and France'. Marshall Wilder, 'President's Address' [1858] *American Pomological Society Proceedings* 20.

[25] Lyon-Jenness (n 16) 389; *Eleventh Census [1890]—Volume 1 (Part I & Part II) Report on Population of the United States* (1895) 'Occupations' 304 Table 78. The category in 1890 was 'gardeners, florists, nurserymen, and vine growers'.

[26] Pawley (n 15) 167.

overhauled the Act by requiring that patent applications be examined for novelty and originality—which they had not been since the 1790s—and by equipping the Patent Office to carry out both the statutory law and court interpretations of it. The Act left unchanged Jefferson's definition of what was patentable, and the requirement of novelty implied that naturally occurring products such as plants were not patentable because they were neither made by human beings nor new compositions of matter, machines, nor manufactures.[27]

The courts had, early on, begun turning implication into law by establishing unequivocally that imported technologies did not qualify for patents because they were not new, which meant that imported plants were also ineligible. The Supreme Court took a major step towards defining novel native varieties as similarly patent-ineligible when in 1852, in the landmark case of *Le Roy v Tatham*, it held that principles of nature were not patent-eligible because they were not made by human beings, and that such principles extended beyond natural laws and forces to properties of natural matter. It was a short step from there to the doctrine that products of nature as such could not be enclosed by patents. That doctrine lurked implicitly in several Supreme Court decisions in the latter half of the nineteenth century, and it was articulated explicitly in 1889 by Commissioner of Patents Benton J Hall in an internal ruling in the matter of *Ex parte Latimer*.[28]

Nursery and seed-house proprietors found alternative incentives to innovation in their local communities. As they prospered, they became pillars of civic society in their towns and cities, the recipients of social approbation for both the economic and aesthetic improvements entailed in their production and sale of novel fruits, vegetables, and flowers. They commanded respect as upright men, paragons of trustworthy practices in both life and business, exemplars of a trade that not only brought profits to its practitioners, but also enhanced the beauty of town and countryside alike. Both professional and amateur horticulturalists could subscribe to the belief of the famed nurseryman and landscape architect Andrew Jackson Downing: 'We are inclined to claim ... for horticultural pursuits, a political and moral influence vastly more significant and important than the mere gratification of the senses.'[29]

The leading nurserymen joined with amateur devotees of fruits and flowers to establish local horticultural societies that sprang up in a number of cities, beginning in the 1820s. Prominent among these were the New York Horticultural Society, the Pennsylvania Horticultural Society, and the Massachusetts Horticultural Society, of which Charles M Hovey was an energetic member. Starting in the 1850s, as horticulture moved west, similar organizations cropped up in the new regions of cultivation; for example, in Rochester, the Fruit Growers' Society of Western New York (renamed

[27] *United States Statutes at Large, Volume I, Ch 11* [21 Feb 1793] 318; Daniel J Kevles, 'Invention, Yes; Nature, No: The Birth of the Products-of-Nature Doctrine from the American Colonies to the US Courts' (2014) 23 *Perspectives on Science* 24.

[28] *Le Roy v Tatham* 55 US 156 (1852) 176; *Ex parte Latimer* (Decisions of the Commissioner of Patents 1889) 124, 126. Both are discussed in Kevles (n 27) 29–31.

[29] Casscles (n 4) 14; Burd (n 20) 3–4, 42, 48–52, 65, 78–79, 83–84, 100.

the Western New York Horticultural Society in 1870), in which Patrick Barry held sway as president after 1865 for the better part of a quarter century, and the State Pomological Society of Michigan. These provided a means to cultivate customers as well as to exchange information on multiple horticultural matters, including native and foreign fruits, ornamental trees and plants, fertilizers, pests, and pesticides. They also offered opportunities for conviviality and celebration of achievements. The Massachusetts Horticultural Society hosted sumptuous dinners with copious wine and Madeira, where members and guests extolled the uplifting value of their products and praised each other's accomplishments. The centrepiece of its meetings comprised lengthy tables laden with new fruits, vegetables, and flowers. Judges evaluated them in different categories of competition and awarded prizes to the best. The awards were highly coveted and constituted a major incentive to innovation. They amounted to a seal of recognition and attested to the quality of the product, both of which could be turned to advantage in the competitive market.[30]

Among the topics of discussion at the societies was the production of novelties. A few of the business' leaders urged that fruit- and seeds-men create these through deliberate hybridization, which involved taking the pollen from one plant variety and using it to fertilize another. However, such effort was discouraged by the difficulty of the manual procedure—the need for tweezers, magnifying glass, and a sure hand—and by biology and economics. Sexual crosses of plants, trees, or vines yielded, in the main, unpredictable results, including often vegetables and fruits unworthy of table or market. Furthermore, while hybridized vegetables might appear in the first year after they were seeded in the ground, fruit trees only tended to bear after as long as three to nine years after planting. In the vegetable case, especially with fruits, the outcomes were too uncertain to warrant the investment of land, time, and labour that hybridization required.[31] Most domestic plant innovation thus continued to arise from the plots of cultivators who found new varieties in their fields or gardens, the products of natural hybridization that they selected and propagated.[32]

The dependence on natural hybridization no doubt favoured the larger producers; the greater the number of trees or plants, the more likely the occurrence of such chance hybridization. Landreth's exemplified the large producer's advantage in seeds. Starting with seven acres, the firm expanded the grounds devoted to seed production during its first century to several thousand acres—more, it averred, than any other seed establishment in the world—including some 600 acres in Bloomsdale, on the banks of the Delaware near Bristol, Pennsylvania. Several of the fields were in different parts of the country to allow the selection of seeds

[30] ibid 150–52; Lyon-Jenness (n 16) 410; Dearborn, (n 1); New York Horticultural Society, 'Minutes, 1821–1829' (New York Horticultural Society MSS, LuEsther T Mertz Library).

[31] Landreth's *Part of America* (n 3) 'The Period 1870–1880' 4.

[32] This is evident from the reports in multiple catalogues of the origins of new varieties of fruits and seeded plants. Daniel J Kevles, 'New Blood, New Fruits: Protections for Breeders and Originators, 1789–1930' in Mario Biagioli, Peter Jaszi, and Martha Woodmansee (eds), *Making and Unmaking Intellectual Property: Creative Production in Legal and Cultural Perspective* (University of Chicago Press 2011) 253, 259–60.

suitable for different climates and soils.[33] Landreth's obtained novelties from natural crosses that were by-products of its mass production of seeds. When an advantageous new vegetable or flower cropped up, the company selected its seeds and multiplied them through successive plantings.

Landreth's process generated several money-making novelties from its fields, notably varieties of peas, cabbages, and pearl onions that, by maturing early, gave the farmer an advantage in the produce market. In 1799, the firm had listed seventy-one varieties of vegetables; in 1852, ninety-three; and in 1884, 251, making for an increase in the first fifty-three years of about 24 per cent, but in just the next thirty-two years of almost 170 per cent. In 1847, Landreth's advertised some 165 varieties of flower seeds; in 1886, more than 250.[34]

A similar process produced novelties among the nurseries that cultivated trees and plants by the thousands. In 1872, Ellwanger & Barry, a huge producer, announced that it had obtained 'a seedling of ours', a remarkable bicolour geranium combining 'a brilliant yellow color with a broad chocolate zone' that it called 'The Pride of Mount Hope' and said was destined 'to become one of the most desirable and popular plants for borders and edges'.[35]

But the adventurous proprietor of a small nursery might generate an advantageous hybrid in his field and propagate and sell it himself, using an extended version of William Prince Sr's method of origination. By the early 1830s, Prince Jr and his son William Robert had extended the method, planting together high-quality trees of not just one variety but two. William Robert said that his views accorded closely with the remarks of the British nurseryman John Lindley on 'amelioration and propagation', which William Robert and his father quoted at length in their *Pomological Manual* of 1831, that the '"intermixing" of pollen and stigma of different varieties could produce fruits of an advantageous "intermediate nature"'.[36] While the long period of time it took for fruit trees to reach first bearing made the process unsuitable for some of them, it was practical for fruiting vines because they bore within a year or two: if the new vinous variety proved exceptionally popular, it could earn the firm a fortune, just as later a blockbuster drug would turn the future of a biotechnology start-up into gold.

Production by this process of a hardy and luscious strawberry launched Hovey as one of the period's most prominent and wealthy nurserymen. A long-time collector

[33] Landreth & Son, *Kitchen-Garden Priced List of Landreth's American Pedigree Seeds* (n 8) 2, 31; *Landreth's Rural Register and Almanac 1886*, 2, 31; UDEL (n 8).

[34] David Landreth & Sons, *Descriptive List of Landreth's Pedigree Turnip Seeds and Other Seasonable Seeds* (1883) 9, 11–12, 14; *Landreth's Rural Register 1886* (n 33) 26; Landreth & Son, *Kitchen-Garden*, 1886 (n 8) 14–16, 26; Landreth's, *A Catalogue of the Principal Garden Seeds Cultivated by David Landreth, Philadelphia* (1847) 15–18; UDEL (n 8); Landreth's *Part of America* (n 3) 'The Period 1870–1880'.

[35] *Wholesale Catalogue of the Mount Hope Nurseries, Rochester, N.Y. for the Spring of 1872 No 4–1872*, 16; Ellwanger & Barry Catalogues, Box 193, file BC1933; CCMHSD (n 21).

[36] William Robert Prince, aided by William Prince Jr, *The Pomological Manual; or A Treatise on Fruits: Containing Descriptions of a Great Number of the Most Valuable Varieties for the Orchard and Garden* (T & J Swords 1831) Pt II: 'Preface' viii–ix; 'Pomological Reform' (1847–1848) 2 *The Horticulturist and Journal of Rural Art and Rural Taste* 176. Various methods of hybridization originated in Europe. For a discussion of how and why they were used in the United States see Pauly (n 2) 65–75.

of strawberry plants, Hovey knew from experience that some of the finest specimens from abroad would die off in the New England climate, burned by summer heat or killed by winter cold. The difficulty of cultivating strawberries made the fruit a luxury in the market and compelled most Americans to harvest them laboriously from the wild. In the summer of 1832, Hovey began developing improved strawberries by planting different varieties in proximity, aiming for crosses with the merits of better hardiness, productivity, size, flavour, and appearance. The next year he selected seed from promising plants, planted the seeds in February 1834, and, on scrutinizing the crop when it came into full bearing in the summer of 1836, plucked a particularly appealing strawberry from among some thirty plants of note. Hovey recalled that in 1838, the runners from this single plant produced 'one of the most remarkable crops of remarkable strawberries we ever saw'. The fruits were very large, often 5.5 inches in circumference, with firm, shining red flesh and yielding to the palate 'a most agreeable acid, and exceedingly delicious and high-flavoured juice'. Between 1838 and 1854, Hovey's Seedling Strawberry, as he named it, received the Massachusetts Horticultural Society's annual premium for strawberries at least twelve times. It was so widely cultivated as to become the principal market and table strawberry for several decades.[37]

The leading fruit and flowermen also obtained novelties from smaller nurseries and farmers' commercial orchards.William Prince Jr compiled a list in his account books of 'New sorts of fruits, etc. that may be obtained', noting their qualities and distinguishing features.[38] While the small fanciers and nurseries each cultivated only a limited number of fruit trees and vines, when combined together, the operations of each comprised a distributed form of mass production that might yield advantageous hybrids by chance or by the process that Hovey had used, that could, in turn, be sold to a larger, more established company for mass propagation and marketing.

American horticulture was, in this way, gifted with the Concord grape by Ephraim Bull, the proprietor of a small nursery in Concord, Massachusetts. Bull planted the seeds of a chance seedling that he found in a corner of his garden. After it fruited, in 1843 he planted the seeds from the fruit and selected the most promising vines for propagation, then repeated the cycle over several years. Bull's new variety ripened two weeks earlier than the earliest then known and yielded large clusters of delicious fruit, good for the table and for wine. It caused a sensation in the horticultural world after it was first exhibited at the Massachusetts Horticultural Society in 1853. The next year, Hovey, under contract with Bull, began marketing the grape nationally.[39]

[37] Hutchinson (n 22) 41; Charles M Hovey, *The Fruits of America, Containing Richly Colored Figures, and Descriptions of all the Choicest Varieties Cultivated in the United States* (D Appleton 1852) 25–28; Pauly (n 2) 70–72.

[38] 'Prince Account Books' [c. 1816–1846], Prince Nursery Records, Item SB218, LuEsther T Mertz Library, New York Botanical Garden.

[39] Marshall Wilder, 'President's Address' [1867] *American Pomological Society Proceedings* 43, 44; Albert Emerson Benson, *History of the Massachusetts Horticultural Society* (Plimpton Press 1929) 107–108; Pauly (n 2) 74–76; Edmund A Schofield, '"He Sowed; Others Reaped": Ephraim Wales Bull and the Origins of the "Concord" Grape' (1988) 48 *Arnoldia* 9.

For all the merits of Landreth's peas, Hovey's strawberry, and Bull's grape, the production of native new varieties was at best chancy, irregular, and uncertain. Small regional nurseries in the upper Midwest, reluctant to rely on chance, ordered new or unusual varieties from eastern nurseries. The leading firms—notably Prince, Hovey, and Ellwanger & Barry— went further east, to Europe and Asia, not only continuing the longstanding introduction of new varieties from abroad, but also, amid the intensifying competition and demand from other nurseries, even heightening their reliance on the practice.[40]

Hovey's catalogue for 1847, acknowledging the rising interest in the cultivation of flowers, especially of new varieties, announced that the company had enriched its offerings with 'all the new and choice kinds that have been introduced to notice in Europe'.[41] Landreth's added a premium to importations from Asia after the mid-1850s, when the US Navy sent Commander Matthew C Perry to Japan. The federal government signed a contract with Landreth's to pack hundreds of pounds of seed into sealed glass containers to be sent with the expedition as gifts to the Japanese people. Upon his return in 1855, Perry gave Landreth's hundreds of varieties of Japanese trees, plants, and shrubs, the first such major importation into the United States, for cultivation and distribution.[42]

After Perry's return, Hovey added Japanese varieties to his list of flowers, featuring, for example, Japan lilies. Ellwanger & Barry followed suit, telling its customers that its extensive collections were kept 'fully up to the times' by 'the importation of the most interesting foreign "novelties"' as well as 'by the acquisition of valuable home productions'. Foreign pears loomed large in the market. Both Hovey and Ellwanger & Barry made a point of featuring them, with Ellwanger & Barry reporting that its pipeline of experimental pears had been 'enriched by a large number of new foreign varieties', including particularly 'interesting novelties' from China and Japan.[43] Beginning in the 1840s, however, Landreth's made a point of declaring that it was now offering as few imported vegetable seeds as possible, claiming in its catalogues that while foreign seeds might be cheaper, American seeds were 'far more reliable, more certain to give satisfaction, and better adapted to our climate'.

[40] Lyon-Jenness (n 16) 392; Burd (n 20) 73–74, 76, 99; Hovey & Co, *Descriptive Catalogue of a large and selected assortment of Seeds: … Containing … New, Rare, and Beautiful Varieties or very recent Introduction Received Direct from the Most Celebrated Florists in England, France and Germany, and Many of the Choicest of Our Own Cultivation* (1859) Box 380 Hovey Pt 1; CCMHSD (n 21).

[41] *Catalogue of Annual, Biennial and Perennial Flower Seeds, for sale by Hovey & Co* [1836] 1; *A Descriptive Catalogue of a Choice Collection of Flower Seeds; comprising, in all, upwards of five hundred species and varieties … Among the seeds are many new, rare and splendid varieties, well worth the attention of florists and amateur cultivators. For sale by Hovey & Co, Seedsmen and Nurserymen* (1847); *A Descriptive Catalogue of Pears Embracing Many New and Choice Varieties … Hovey & Co* (1849) 3–8, Box 380, Hovey Pt 1; CCMHSD (n 21).

[42] Landreth's, *Part of America* (n 3) 'The Period 1850–1860'; *The D Landreth Seed Co Historical Timeline.*

[43] *Catalogue of Annual, Biennial and Perennial Flower Seeds* (n 41) 1; *A Descriptive Catalogue of a Choice Collection of Flower Seeds; … For sale by Hovey & Co* (1847); *A Descriptive Catalogue of Pears* (n 41) 3–8; CCMHSD (n 21), *No 1 Descriptive Catalogue of Fruits 1880*, Ellwanger & Barry, EB, Box 194, file BC1934; CCMHSD (n 21).

After the Civil War, Landreth's added an increasingly strong nationalist note to its brand identification, emphasizing in its advertisements that it provided 'American seeds for the American climate'. In its 1886 catalogue, the company called itself 'preeminently the AMERICAN SEED HOUSE', adding that '[we] at all times fly the American Flag'. By then, capitalizing on its origins in Philadelphia in the period of the Revolution, it had adopted the Liberty Bell as its graphic logo.[44]

Advertising and Promotion

The mounting competition prompted the leading nurseries and seed houses to expand their use of advertising and catalogues not only to gain market share, but also to establish and promote brand names. They advertised in newspapers, some in thousands of them, and in agricultural journals. They branded their novelties by naming them after themselves or their firms, sending to market, for example, 'Hovey's Cherry', 'Landreth's Extra Early Peas', and 'Landreth's Bloomsdale Spinach'; and the strawberries 'Charles Downing', 'Longworth's Prolific', and 'Peak's Emperor'. They reinforced the brands by transforming their catalogues, replacing the bare lists of fruits, vegetables, and flowers with selling descriptions of their productions that might include reference to shape, taste, and colour, time to maturity, fecundity, and hardiness, and by presenting their firms as the grower's helper and friend. Distributing their catalogues by the tens of thousands, they made themselves well known among farmers, orchardists, and fanciers, foreshadowing the catalogue marketing of Sears, Roebuck and Co that began in the mid-1890s.[45]

Landreth's was in the vanguard of the catalogue transformation. Beginning in 1847, it replaced its plant lists with an annual *Rural Register and Almanac*. The publication comprised not only a seed catalogue, but also extensive advice about gardening and farming, basic facts about the US government (including the names of the presidents and cabinet members), schedules of astronomical events, reports of recent scientific discoveries (particularly those related to farming), and new gardening tools. Demand for the new catalogue was strong, stimulating an increase in the first year's print run of about 13,000 to some 600,000 by the late 1850s. Perhaps mindful of the publication's popularity, other companies expanded their catalogues in a similar fashion. Landreth's kept the *Rural Register and Almanac* up to date with

[44] Hovey & Co, *Descriptive Catalogue of a large and selected assortment of Seeds* (1859) cover, 16, Box 380, Hovey Pt 1; *Landreth's Rural Register 1887* (n 17) 18 and back cover; *Landreth's Pedigree Turnip Seeds* (n 34) 13; Landreth's, *A Catalogue of the Principal Garden Seeds* (1847) cover; Landreth & Son, *Kitchen-Garden* (n 8) 16; CCMHSD (n 21).

[45] Burd (n 20) 125; *Descriptive Catalogue of Fruits ... 1876, Ellwanger & Barry* 60–61, EB, Box 194, file BC1934; CCMHSD (n 21). In 1867, James Vick, the proprietor of a leading seed house in Rochester, advertised in more than 3,000 newspapers nationwide, and in the early 1870s distributed more than 200,000 catalogues annually. Lyon-Jenness (n 16) 384, 387, 397–98.

an eye not only to the information it contained, but also to the ethnicities of the domestic customers it was trying to reach, many of them immigrants, by publishing it in the mid-1880s in English, German, French, Spanish, and Swedish.[46]

Prince, Hovey & Co, and Ellwanger & Barry issued some half dozen or more catalogues a year, each devoted to a different category of plants, including vegetables, flowers, and root and bulbous plants, as well as fruit trees, ornamental trees, and shrubs. Hovey & Co tended to extravagant descriptions, especially in promoting its new varieties. The company described the Hovey Cherry as 'one of the largest and most beautiful cherries known. It measures more than an inch in diameter and is produced in clusters of twenty or thirty cherries each. The colour is amber, beautifully shaded with deep coral red. Flesh firm, sweet and rich'. Grandiloquent selling was common in the seed and nursery catalogues of the day. Ellwanger & Barry tended in its descriptions to judicious restraint, tempering its advertisement of Kenrick's Autumn apple: 'Large, round striped, crisp, juicy, rich, first rate', with the caution, 'tree rather a poor grower, but a good bearer'. Similarly, an advert of the Spitzenberg Esopus apple added to the luscious description: 'tree rather a feeble slow grower, and moderate bearer'. The *Michigan Farmer* commended Ellwanger & Barry's catalogues as models of what others might well emulate.[47]

A number of nurseries extended the range of their markets by advertising and selling their productions through itinerant agents. William Prince Jr sold his plants through an army of salesmen operating out of ports from New Orleans to Mobile, Alabama, and up the Eastern Seaboard to Boston. Ellwanger & Barry, eager to sell to the vast reaches of the settling West, were early and prominent in the use of agents, employing sixty-nine of them by the 1860s. Eastern firms followed suit with the aim of competing for Midwestern trade. The agents covered vast territories, some of them hired by the companies, some acting as freelance representatives. Companies tended to give their designated agents some horticultural training, which enabled them to provide customers with reliable advice on the plants they were selling and how to cultivate them. They equipped the agents with catalogues, plant lists, descriptions, and order forms. The agents not only drummed up business; they also served as the nurseries' eyes and ears on the distant ground, providing firms with information about demand, preferences, prices, competition, and relevant circumstances from weather to transportation. They also offered a

[46] Landreth & Son, *Kitchen-Garden* (n 8) 4; 1830–1850; Landreth's *Part of America* (n 3) 'The Period 1850–1860'.

[47] Hovey & Co, *Descriptive Catalogue of a large and selected assortment of Seeds: ... Containing ... New, Rare, and Beautiful Varieties or very recent Introduction Received Direct from the Most Celebrated Florists in England, France and Germany, and Many of the Choicest of Our Own Cultivation* 1859; *New and Choice Fruits*, Hovey & Co, No 7 Merchant Row, Boston [1854] 1–2, Box 380, Hovey Pt 1; *No 1 Descriptive Catalogue of Fruits ... 1868 ... Ellwanger & Barry*, 12–13; *Descriptive Catalogue of Fruits ...* 1876, Ellwanger & Barry, 44, Box 193; EB, Box 194, file BC1934; CCMHSD (n 21); Lyon-Jenness (n 16) 399.

degree of protection against defaults on orders and bills by gathering intelligence on the creditworthiness of customers and the soundness of banks.[48]

The novelties, the advertising and catalogues, and the travelling agents all combined to generate enormous growth in the leading seed and nursery firms. Landreth's continued to expand, while Hovey & Co and Ellwanger & Barry earned places among the powerhouses in the trade.

Hovey realized the ambition that he set out in his catalogue for 1836: that the company was intended to become 'a complete repository for every variety of Garden, Flower and agricultural seeds'. In the course of developing the Seedling Strawberry, Hovey nurtured another new and popular variety: the Boston Pine. Drawing on the profits from the two vines, the Hovey brothers enlarged their nursery, buying forty acres of woodland in Cambridge and expanding into the cultivation of fruit trees, especially pears, a particularly coveted fruit. During the 1840s, along with obtaining new pear varieties from local fanciers, Hovey introduced his own Boston Pear and the Hovey Cherry, both of which other nurserymen held in exceptionally high regard for their beauty, fine quality, and luscious taste.[49]

In the half-century following the company's founding, Hovey built multiple greenhouses—one of them, at 96 feet by 30 feet, being the largest such structure in the country at the time of its construction—eventually covering an acre with glass. His stock came to comprise nearly 60,000 pear trees and thousands of young trees of other fruit, representing dozens of varieties. It also included 20,000 geraniums and, according to Hovey, collections unequalled elsewhere in the United States of camellias and azaleas. In the mid-1860s, RG Dunn and Company, then emerging as one of the country's leading assessors of creditworthiness, rated Hovey as 'rich and growing richer all the time'.[50]

Ellwanger & Barry, the flagship nursery in Rochester, situated at the nexus of the Erie Canal, the Great Lakes, and railroads running east and west, reached a vast market. By the 1850s, it had expanded to 500 acres, and by 1880 to 650 acres, in addition to including extensive greenhouses and graperies, making it, as the catalogue for that year boasted, 'the most extensive and complete' nursery in the country. The company cultivated 2,000 varieties of pears, plums, cherries, apples, peaches, quinces, currants, and more than one million grape vines. It raised comparably extensive ornamental trees and shrubs, making its total stock greater than that of any other two

[48] Casscles (n 4) 198; Burd (n 20) 103–105, 109–11, 123–24; Lyon-Jenness (n 16) 401–403.

[49] *New and Choice Fruits. Hovey & Co., No. 7 Merchant Row, Boston* [1854], 1, Box 380, Hovey Pt 1, CCMHSD (n 47) 1; Hutchinson (n 22) 39, 45; Pauly (n 2) 59. See the sketch and description of the local pear provided by JG Cabot in 1843 in Hovey Horticultural Memoranda, CCMHSD (n 21).

[50] *Catalogue of Annual, Biennial and Perennial Flower Seed for sale by Hovey & Co.* [1836] 11; *A Descriptive Catalogue of Fruits Cultivated and for Sale by Hovey & Co., at their Cambridge Nurseries . . . for the Autumn of 1844 and the Spring of 1845* 4; *A Descriptive Catalogue of a Choice Collection of Flower Seeds; comprising, in all, upwards of five hundred species and varieties . . . For sale by Hovey & Co*, 184, Box 380, Hovey Pt 1; Hovey, 'To Our Old Friends and Customers' *Hovey's Illustrated Catalogue of New, Rare, and Beautiful Plants, Fruit Trees, Shrubs, Roses, Etc.* 1886, [3], Box 383, Hovey Cat; CCMHSD (n 21); Hutchinson (n 22) 39, 45; Pauly (n 2) 59.

nurseries combined. The owners had begun annual importations of ornamentals valuable for the country 'quite in advance of the demand' for them, they noted in 1875, believing 'that at no distant day a country so wealthy and enterprising as ours is, would offer a market for such productions'. In 1877, noting the 'greatly increased attention' to roses, it started issuing a catalogue devoted to the flower, multiplied propagation of it tenfold, and made it 'a leading feature of our business' (Fig. 6.1).[51]

Ellwanger & Barry found its major profit centre in the states of the Great Lakes region, which lacked natural good nursery stock, but it expanded into Canada, Pennsylvania, several southern states, and the Far West. It provided California with many of its cultivated trees, shipping them via the Isthmus of Panama until it could send them via the transcontinental railroad. Over the years, Ellwanger & Barry sold plants to forty-five states and seven countries. Its business practices provided models to the numerous firms in and around Rochester eager to reach markets beyond the state of New York. In the nation's centennial year, a journal of the rural home turned effusive, declaring that Ellwanger & Barry had made virtually every 'city, town or hamlet in this country ... more beautiful and enjoyable'.[52]

Charles Hovey, Patrick Barry, and several other nurserymen gained national influence as authoritative pomologists by publishing or editing journals and, like the Princes, writing books for practitioners.[53] Particularly influential was Hovey's *Magazine of Horticulture, Botany, and All Useful Discoveries and Improvements in Rural Affairs*, which he established in 1835 and edited until it merged with the *American Journal of Horticulture* in 1868. It was the first national magazine in the subject and in its day, one of the most influential in the field.[54] From 1844 to 1852, Barry edited the horticultural section in the widely read *Genesee Farmer*, which took its name from the Genesee Valley in western New York, and for two years in the mid-1850s he edited *The Horticulturalist and Journal of Rural Art and Rural Taste*, succeeding its founder, Andrew Jackson Downing, who had died in a steamboat explosion. A temperance advocate and moral reformer, Barry took advantage of both editorships to promote the Mount Hope Nursery and the merits of horticulture as a civilizing counterpoint to ugly materialism and indulgent habits, declaring that it would 'contribute towards the improvement of soil and its products, the culture of the mind, and the encouragement and elevation of men'.[55]

51 Hedrick (n 1) 243–45; *No 6 Catalogue of Select Fruit and Ornamental Trees, Small Fruits, Shrubs, Roses, Etc ... Ellwanger & Barry* [1880] 'Preface to 23rd Edition', *Descriptive Catalogue of Hardy Ornamental Trees, Shrubs, Roses, Etc. ... Ellwanger and Barry ... No. 2, 1875*, 2; 'Preface to the First Edition', *A Descriptive Catalogue of Roses offered for sale by Ellwanger & Barry ... No 5*; 1st edn, 1877, EB, Box 194, file BC1934; CCMHSD (n 21).

52 *No 6 Catalogue of Select Fruit and Ornamental Trees, Small Fruits, Shrubs, Roses, Etc ... Ellwanger & Barry* [1880] Box 194, file BC1934, EB; CCMHSD (n 21); Burd (n 20) 92–93, 99, 122–23, 130, 135.

53 Pawley (n 15) 171.

54 The magazine ceased publication in 1868, its cumulative pages comprising what the Cornell plant scientist Liberty Hyde Bailey later described as a record of 'the budding stage of New World Horticulture'. Its name, design, and layout were originally borrowed from *The Gardener's Magazine*, which was edited by JC Loudon and was probably the first such journal in England. See Hutchinson (n 22) 31–37; Pauly (n 2) 59.

55 Lyon-Jenness (n 16) 388, 409; Burd (n 20) 44, 112–13.

Figure 6.1 Ellwanger & Barry Feature Hybrid Roses.

Source: New Roses, 1880.

Courtesy of the Archives of Massachusetts Horticultural Society.

Hovey kept up with European horticultural literature, touting some of it for sale in his catalogues, and Barry accumulated a comprehensive working library of the major pomological works in several languages.[56] In the journals they edited, the two men dispensed pomological news from both sides of the Atlantic, notices of new and rare fruits and flowers introduced into the United States, the activities of horticultural societies throughout the country, and pomological gossip. They also called for honest practices in the plant business and warned against deception and fraud.

Honesty and Deception

In the local areas in and around towns and cities, the proprietors of seed houses and nurseries knew each other, not least from the gatherings of their horticultural societies, and often enjoyed personal ties. An etiquette of trustworthiness coloured their business relationships. Ephraim Bull counted on it when he began promoting the Concord grape before release, along with the White Concord, a novelty that soon followed, by inviting various nurserymen to test them.[57] The strategy posed risks to Bull's control of the vines. Nurserymen and gardeners propagated fruit trees, vines, and some flowers such as roses using asexual means—that is, by grafting cuttings, scions, or buds onto root stock or, in a number of cases, by planting them directly into the ground. Under comparable environmental conditions, the process would yield faithful reproductions of the originals that would bear fruits or blossoms virtually identical to those on the stock from which they had been derived. Competitors who obtained possession of Bull's vines could generate identical copies of his grapes and capture sales that might otherwise have been his own.

The nurserymen in the Boston area refrained from such practices, holding to a code of honour that respected the interests of originators.[58] Those to whom Bull sent his Concord vines or who later asked for test vines from his White Concord revealed several of the code's specific tenets. One or another pledged or swore on his honour that he would keep confidential the characteristics of any new fruit or even that the vines were in his possession until Bull had authorized the release of the information; that he would not propagate the vine for sale until one or two years after Bull had put it on the market; and that he would not compete with Bull by

[56] Hedrick (n 1) 243–45.

[57] 'Bull to JM Jewett' (18 April 1854); 'Bull to P[atrick] Barry' (6 March 1854) Box 1, folder 14, Ellwanger and Barry Nursery Records (EBNR), Special Collections, Rush Rhees Library, University of Rochester, Nursery Company Correspondence.

[58] The code adumbrated present-day practices, exemplified by, for example, stand-up comics who have established a system of social norms for the protection of the intellectual property in their material. See Dotan Oliar and Christopher Jon Sprigman, 'There's No Free Laugh (Anymore): The Emergence of Intellectual Property Norms and the Transformation of Stand-Up Comedy' (2008) 94 *Virginia Law Review* 8, *Law and Economics Research Paper Series No 2009–04* (revised 2009) http://ssrn.com/abstract=1138376 (accessed 4 August 2022).

underselling him. William Kenrick, a nurseryman who was an uncle of the novelist Nathaniel Hawthorne, offered to pay a reasonable cash price for evaluation samples of the White Concord, noting that he 'perfectly understood that it never is customary to sell the plants of a new fruit, so readily multiplied, except only for cash on delivery'. Kenrick sweetened the offer by promising that 'at proper time, and at your bidding I should publish far and wide the exact truth. If it is really what I hope it is'.[59]

However, the impersonal nature of expanding national markets allowed honour to diminish and die with distance. Distance enabled the entry into the market of sellers who lacked the personal ties and common values of the circles around a Prince, a Hovey, a Landreth, or an Ellwanger & Barry. A noticeable number of the new breeds cared far more about turning quick profits than about transforming the landscape and society. Profiteers, charlatans, and frauds: they knew little about the trade or its plants, or their names, benefits, and growing requirements, especially after the 1850s, when so many new varieties were being introduced. They misrepresented their products, supplying customers with plants and seeds that did not live up to their advertisements of hardiness, healthiness, quality of fruit, or colour of flowers. Critics in the trade called them 'imposters', 'careless' in their nurseries, and 'evil' overall. One customer implored the industry: 'Cannot some plan be devised to put a stop to vegetable and fruit humbugging? It puts money in the hands of unprincipled men to the serious cost and disappointment of the cultivator'.[60]

Among the worst perpetrators of fraud were freelance plant agents who offered purchasers cheap but usually unreliable stock, promiscuous mixes of varieties whose identity and quality they misrepresented. Dubbed 'plant peddlers', some falsely claimed to be agents of reputable nurseries. Ellwanger & Barry found that it had to 'caution the public against certain persons who are in the habit of using our Catalogues, and representing themselves as our agents, but who in reality have no dealings with us'. Most commonly, others got a bona fide certificate of agency from a nursery, sold enough of the nursery's productions to maintain the certificate, and on the side, as the *American Agriculturalist* noted in 1863, sold 'inferior and untrue trees picked up here and there at nominal prices'. James Vick, a leading seedsman in Rochester, admonished customers for spending their money on the 'worthless wares of these swindlers' and leaving themselves few dollars for the honest dealer. The fact of the matter, he said, was that 'truly, many people like to be humbugged'.[61]

Buyers of all goods were vulnerable to fraud and misrepresentation, but the practice was facilitated with plants and seeds by the nature of these products. As Landreth's noted, unlike staple goods such as sugar or cotton, seeds did not convey their bona fides on their face: 'the character of Garden Seeds cannot be determined

[59] 'Samuel Miller to Bull', 30 March 1861, 10 April 1861; 'Ambrose F Page to Bull', 20 October 1856; 'William Kenrick to Bull', 24 December 1856, 16 July 1859, Box 1, folder 13, EWB.

[60] Lyon-Jenness (n 16) 383, 385, 390–91; Burd (n 20) 66–67.

[61] *Abridged Catalogue of Select Fruit and Ornamental Trees, Cultivated and Sold by Ellwanger & Barry* [c. 1870], Anderson Horticultural Library, University of Minnesota, Minnesota Landscape Arboretum, Chaska, MN (AHL); Lyon-Jenness (n 16) 402–404, 419; Pawley (n 15) 174.

by inspection, an entire season must pass before their respective values are determined', that is, to say what plant or what quality of plant it would yield.[62] That fact made deception easy to accomplish at the time of sale.

Compounding the problem, a good deal of seed was sold by commission houses. They bought seed from farmers and seed growers and mixed them together into undifferentiated accumulations. They reportedly sold stores, farmers, and gardeners bags, boxes, and paper packages that contained seeds of varieties different from those on the labels or that were adulterated with weeds, or seeds that could not be counted on to germinate, and that, if they did, produced low-yielding or low-quality crops.[63]

The Horticulturalist found honest nurserymen undercut by fraudsters who could palm off 'indifferent and worthless varieties of fruits and flowers, as something new, extraordinary, and valuable, at the most exorbitant prices'.[64] Buyers would be none the wiser at the time of the sale, given that the identity and character of, say, a hibernating rose or a quiescent vine did not reveal themselves for some months, and that the fruit of a seedling tree often did not become manifest until five or six years after planting. Cautioning against an absorption with the low end of the price range, William Prince, Jr. warned that buyers of seedlings who paid attention only to 'cheapness' found 'not infrequently, after the toil and expense of years,' that when the trees arrived at bearing they were 'absolutely worthless'. In 1854, *The Prairie Farmer* stated the disadvantaging truth to its readers, who were accustomed to purchasing at a distance: 'A fruit, untrue to name, makes no revelation of the fact, often for some years'.[65] Whether buying seeds or plants, purchasers faced a hazard similar to that of the wine fancier upon buying a bottle labelled, say, *Chateau Lafitte*, that, upon drinking, proved to be a blend of mediocre varietals or worse. Some seed houses and nurseries brazenly sold their goods under someone else's nursery or brand name. In 1841, a former Prince clerk had the shameless temerity to issue a fruit catalogue claiming that he was now the proprietor of the Linnaean Botanic Garden and inviting orders to an address in Flushing. 'FRAUD AND DECEPTION', William Robert Prince announced on the cover of his next year's catalogue, warning customers against the clerk's 'spurious', wholly fabricated advertisement.[66] Charles Hovey discovered a firm doing business under the name Hovey & Co with which his nursery had no connection. Hovey warned his own customers about the firm's claims—that the plants and trees came from its 'extensive nurseries at Cambridge' and that it had been 'awarded more than three hundred first-class prizes'—charging that these were outright falsehoods 'only intended to deceive our old friends and customers'.[67] In 1883, a man named Albert

[62] *Landreth's Rural Register 1887* (n 17) 17.

[63] The commission system and its flaws are described in *The History of a Cabbage Seed*, reprinted in Landreth & Son, *Kitchen-Garden* (n 8) 28–29.

[64] Editor, 'Hints to the Purchasers of Trees, Seeds, etc' *Horticulturalist and Journal of Rural Art and Rural Taste* (1 June 1855) 252.

[65] ibid 252; Pawley (n 15) 174; Lyon-Jenness (n 16) 381–82.

[66] Casscles (n 4) 130–31.

[67] Hovey, 'To Our Old Friends and Customers', Hovey's Illustrated Catalogue of New, Rare, and Beautiful Plants, Fruit Trees, Shrubs, Roses, Etc. 1886, [3], Box 383, Hovey. Cat., CCMHSD (n 21).

Landreth moved from Philadelphia to Manitowoc, Wisconsin, to undertake the growing of peas for the production of seed. Perhaps he had some connection to the Landreth firm or family, but when he started selling seeds as 'Landreth's', the company in Philadelphia sued him for misappropriation of its name.[68]

The Naming Evil

Misuse of names plagued the fruit business far more than it did the seed houses, not least because its products could be propagated identically. Since seeds derived from a sexual process, the features of plants grown from them would differ from those of the parental plants, much as human children differ from their parents. But fruit innovators suffered from the kind of appropriation faced by today's originators of digitized music and film. The capacity of fruit trees or vines to be reproduced identically by asexual means offered multiple opportunities for those who might cheat. They could obtain valuable varietal stock by purchase or conveyance of orchard land, or by picking up cuttings by the side of the road, as well as by invading an orchard to steal them in the dead of night. Such practices were sufficiently widespread—and threatening to nurserymen—as to stimulate the passage, beginning in the 1840s, of state laws against 'fruit theft'.[69] The scavengers or thieves could then propagate the trees or vines and sell them under the original names, taking advantage of the brand's reputation, or under a name of their own devising. A good apple sold by another name would taste just as sweet.

Fruits in the United States were, in fact, bought and sold under a riot of synonyms; in the eighteenth century, most fruit varieties had no particular names. They were identified by their colour or place of origin, and over time they underwent multiple, unregulated, and unregistered rechristenings, reflecting new habitats and local whim. For example, the Bahia navel orange, which the Department of Agriculture imported from Brazil in the late 1860s, became known in the 1870s as the Washington navel orange and the Riverside navel, names derived from the areas in California where it had been established. One popular apple, the Ben Davis, was also called Kentucky Streak, Carolina Red Streak, New York Pippin, Red Pippin, Victoria Red, and Carolina Red. One critic pointed out that a customer who ordered twenty-five differently named pears would find herself with only two types of the fruit. In 1875, William Howsley, of Leavenworth, Kansas, a compiler of apple synonyms, reported that twenty-nine varieties were known by 370 names, including seventeen for the Ben Davis, twenty-seven for the Ortley, and thirty-six

[68] Timothy R Eggen, *History of Lakeside Packing Company 1887–1987: A Century of Quality* (Occupational Monograph 62 1987) 1 http://images.library. wisc.edu/WI/Efacs/MTWCImages/OccSeries/Monograph62/reference/wi.monograph62. i0001.pdf (accessed 4 August 2022).

[69] Pawley (n 15) 167.

for the Nickajack, one of the most widely consumed apples of the day. He added that the designation 'pippin', meaning a seedling, was used so frequently—207 times in one catalogue—as to be 'meaningless'. Howsley called the tendency of 'so many old and fine varieties' to be referenced in horticultural publications under new names 'an intolerable evil, and grievous to be borne'.[70]

Variant nomenclature had plagued botany for several centuries, and the fruit and seed business in the United States from its beginnings. By way of clarification, in the early nineteenth century, nurseries and seed houses provided in their broadsheets and catalogues both the common English and Latin botanical names for the advertised goods, and some, including Bartram's Garden, identified them by their Linnaean nomenclature. In the 1820 catalogue for his Linnaean Botanic Garden, William Prince identified the plants and trees he offered for sale solely by their Latin names.[71] The practice of joint English and Latin naming declared the degree to which the seed and nursery businesses straddled the worlds of commerce and botanic learning; it also expressed an eagerness to specify the plants with certainty for customers amid the increasing Babel of common names. At the head of the list of seeds in his catalogue for 1810, McMahon, a devotee of the Linnaean system of classification—he called his 20-acre garden 'Upsal', after Uppsala, Linnaeus' city in Sweden—said that he provided the scientific names as well as the common ones for people who wished to become acquainted with them, but also 'to prevent misconceptions of the articles required by purchasers'.[72] Hovey followed suit in his first catalogues, listing the annuals by a common name and the Latin name, for example 'Blue Amethus/*Amethusea caerulea*'. However, enthusiasm for using the Linnaean system as a means of specifying plants in commercial catalogues had by then declined significantly; even William Prince published his later catalogues in English. By the 1840s, the rising use of common names and brand names had driven out many of the Latin plant designations as well (see Fig. 6.2).[73]

[70] Casscles (n 4) 64; William Saunders, Superintendent of Gardens and Grounds, *United States Department of Agriculture Annual Report 1887*, 688; 'Report of the Committee on Apples' [1867] *American Pomological Society Proceedings* 138–39 and appended 'Catalogue of Fruits', vi; 'Report of Dr Howsley on Nomenclature of Apples' [1871] *American Pomological Society Proceedings* 79–80; William Howsley, 'The Confused Nomenclature of the Apple' [1875] *American Pomological Society Proceedings* 90–93; Pawley (n 15) 173; see also Charles Downing, 'Names and Synonyms' [1875] *American Pomological Society Proceedings* 67; Kevles (n 2) 133.

[71] *Catalogue of American Trees, Shrubs, and Herbaceous Plants, in John Bartram's Garden, Near Philadelphia* (1783) 2; ABG (n 6); David Landreth and Cuthbert Landreth, *Catalogue of Greenhouse Plants* (n 11) iii.

[72] *A Catalogue of Garden, Herb, Flower, Tree, Shrub, and Grass Seeds: Gardening Agricultural, and Botanical Books, Garden Tools, etc. Sold by Bernard McMahon*, 1810, 2. In his first broadsheet, McMahon noted that he included along with the common names of the plants the '*Generic* and Specific Names and Distinctions, according to the Sexual System of the celebrated LINNAEUS' for the use of 'such *Ladies, Gentlemen*, and *Gardeners*, as wish to become scientifically acquainted with the Plants they cultivate'. *A Catalogue of Garden, Herb, Flower, Tree, Shrub, and Grass Seeds: Gardening, Agricultural and Botanical Books, Garden Tools, etc. etc., Sold by Bernard McMahon, Seedsman, No 129 Chestnut-Street, Philadelphia*, 1803, 1, ABG (n 6).

[73] *Catalogue of Annual, Biennial and Perennial Flower Seeds for sale by Hovey & Co.* (n 41) 1. Hovey included the Latin name as late as 1847. See *A Descriptive Catalogue of a Choice Collection of Flower Seeds* (n 41); CCMHSD (n 21).

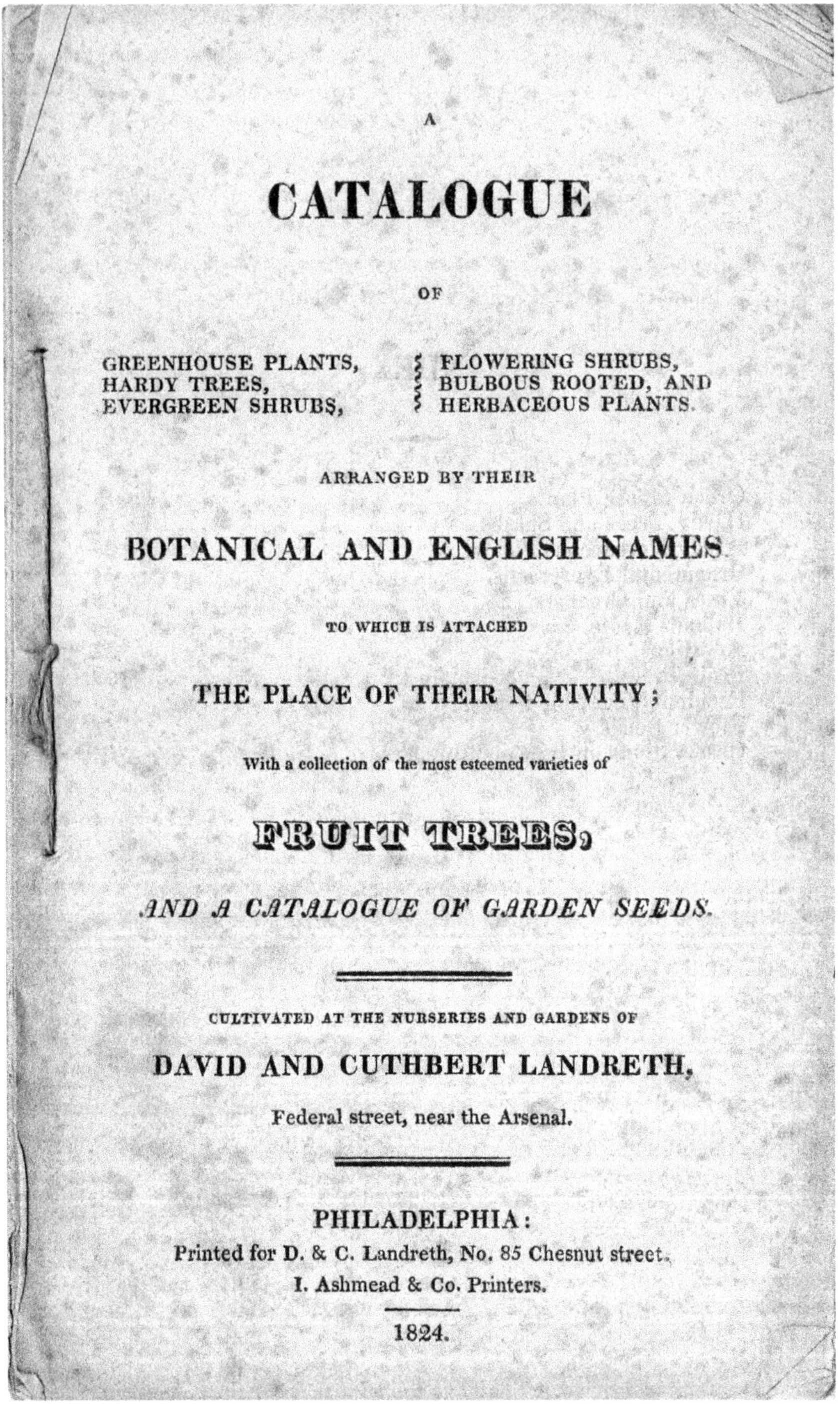

A

CATALOGUE

OF

GREENHOUSE PLANTS, HARDY TREES, EVERGREEN SHRUBS, FLOWERING SHRUBS, BULBOUS ROOTED, AND HERBACEOUS PLANTS.

ARRANGED BY THEIR

BOTANICAL AND ENGLISH NAMES

TO WHICH IS ATTACHED

THE PLACE OF THEIR NATIVITY;

With a collection of the most esteemed varieties of

FRUIT TREES,

AND A CATALOGUE OF GARDEN SEEDS.

CULTIVATED AT THE NURSERIES AND GARDENS OF

DAVID AND CUTHBERT LANDRETH,

Federal street, near the Arsenal.

PHILADELPHIA:

Printed for D. & C. Landreth, No. 85 Chesnut street.

I. Ashmead & Co. Printers.

1824.

Figure 6.2 Landreth's Catalogue, 1824, showing the Latin botanical and English names of their offerings.

Special Collections, Manuscripts and Archives Department, University of Delaware Library.

The proliferation of common fruit names now prompted passionate objections less because it gave rise to misconceptions and far more because it aided misrepresentation and fraud. As early as 1855, *The Horticulturalist* associated the confusion with 'the extraordinary growth of horticultural commerce in the past few years'. While the country was filled with many 'honest and honorable' dealers in trees and plants, the journal stated, 'very many of them lack honesty, and will not hesitate to misrepresent and deceive wherever they consider deception necessary to success'. Faced with so much deception, Howsley thought it 'imperative that the original and true name of every fruit should be known', and he expected that if nurseries were to adhere to a uniform list of names in their advertising, they would be patronized to a much greater extent than 'if their varieties were veiled under suspicion of inaccuracy'.[74]

Ensuring Brand Quality

The leading proprietors of both nurseries and seed houses recognized the merits in the advice offered in 1857 by a horticultural commentator: profits would come to those who issued 'catalogues containing more truth than falsehood; attend diligently to the commands of correspondents . . . [and] avoid clap-trap and humbug'.[75] During the middle third of the century, they devised a variety of means both to protect their brands and to foster consumer confidence in their offerings, whether novel or not.

Reputable sellers such as James Vick nurtured trust via familiarity, salting its catalogues with chatty observations, business gossip, and practical advice. In 1847, Landreth's provided homey and accessible planting and harvesting instructions for each of its forty-one vegetable seed offerings—it ran the alphabetical gamut from artichoke to turnip—explaining in one case, for example, which variety was best for family use, and, in another, which was most appropriate for pickling. In its listing of aromatic and sweet herbs, it assured customers that these could last for years if stored in tightly corked containers. Ellwanger & Barry guided users through the techniques of transplanting and planting seedling fruits, and cautioned rose growers against transferring young stalks grown in pots too quickly into the spring soil. A number of the leading nurserymen commended themselves to their clientele by publishing books on horticultural practices, among them Barry's own *Treatise on the Fruit Garden*, published in 1851 and long one of the best books on pomology in the United States.[76]

[74] Editor, 'Hints to the Purchasers of Trees, Seeds, etc' (n 64); Howsley (n 70) 90–93.

[75] Burd (n 20) 89.

[76] Lyon-Jenness (n 16) 398; *Catalogue of the Principal Garden Seeds Cultivated by David Landreth* (1847) 3–14; UDEL (n 8); Ellwanger & Barry, *Descriptive Catalogue of Fruits Cultivated and for Sale at the Mount Hope Nurseries* (1857) [3], Box 193, BC1933; *A Descriptive Catalogue of Select Roses, Mount Hope Nurseries* (1882) 2–3, Box 195, BC 1935, EB CCMHSD (n 21); Hedrick (n 1) 243–45.

Proprietors sought to instil not only confidence in their firms, but trust in their products, an impression given not only by the size and success of their companies but by the reports of their managerial practices that appeared in their books, journals, and catalogues.[77] William Prince, Jr told his customers that he deployed methods in propagating desirable varieties that enabled him 'to pledge himself for the identity and correctness of all the fruits obtained from him', adding that he 'guarantees the identity of every tree . . . sent from his establishment'. Hovey assured customers that a large portion of his domestic plants were raised 'under our own observation', and that the rest came from unquestionably reliable domestic sources on whom 'we can rely for their genuineness and vitality'. He reported that he travelled to England, Scotland, and France to choose the best pear trees, sparing no expense to make his collection 'one of the most complete in the country'. All the plants and seeds he obtained from abroad came from growers with gold-standard reputations or with the imprimaturs of leading horticultural societies. He included in his catalogue almost 'none of the fruits neglected as inferior, in the best choices of the London Horticultural Society's Catalogue of Fruits'.[78]

Like Hovey & Co, Landreth's emphasized that the firm sold only fresh seed that it grew itself, explaining that only in this way could 'the quality of Garden Seeds be fully known, nor purchasers honestly assured the articles are such as they purport to be, inasmuch as *neither texture nor complexion is an index of age or quality*'. Customers were invited to see the grounds in Bloomsdale, and later editions of the catalogues included pictures of the extensive Bloomsdale installations.[79] Landreth's also touted the freshness of its seeds, reporting that it burned whatever stock remained unsold at the end of the planting season. It thus differentiated itself from the commission houses, which were said to take back unsold seed from merchants, to repackage them and offer them for sale the next year. In 1887, Landreth's offered to burn even its unsold seed still in the possession of merchants, reimbursing the merchants for the cost. In 1903, the year after its seed house at Bloomsdale burned down, the firm turned tragedy to its advantage by advertising that customers could be 100 per cent certain that all Landreth's seeds the next season would be indisputably fresh.[80]

[77] Pawley (n 15) 172.

[78] *Annual Catalogue of Fruit and Ornamental Trees and Plants . . . Cultivated at the Linnaean Botanic Garden, William Prince, Proprietor . . .* (New York 1825) v; *Catalogue of Annual, Biennial and Perennial Flower Seeds for sale by Hovey & Co.* (n 41) 11; *A Descriptive Catalogue of Fruits* (n 22) 3; *A Descriptive Catalogue of Pears* (n 41) Box 380, Hovey Pt 1; CCMHSD (n 21).

[79] Landreth's *A Catalogue of the Principal Garden Seeds* (n 44) 2 (italics in the original). The firm had begun making this point as early as 1824. Landreth and Landreth' *Catalogue of Greenhouse Plants . . .* (n 11) 47; Landreth's, *Part of America* (n 3) 'The Period 1890–1900'; Landreth & Son, *Kitchen-Garden*, (n 8) 32; *Landreth's Rural Register 1886* (n 33) 32, 39.

[80] See Landreth & Son *Kitchen-Garden Priced* (n 8) 28–29; *The History of a Cabbage Seed* (n 63) 28–29; *Landreth's Rural Register 1886* (n 33) 18; D Landreth & Sons, *Landreth's Seed Catalogue* (1903) 1; UDEL (n 8).

In a retrospective on his fifty years as a nurseryman, Hovey noted that he had subjected his seeds to yearly test trials in his greenhouses. The quality of novelties obtained from others might rest when first introduced 'upon the reputation of the originators'; Hovey had recommended them only 'after a trial in our own grounds, even if holding up a high standard had led to the rejection of "many really good things"'.[81] From the outset of business, Ellwanger & Barry, following in the Prince family's footsteps, maintained a large portion of its nursery for experiment, by which it meant testing for quality and reliability specimens of novel fruit trees, vines, and flowers that it had obtained from foreign and domestic sources. In 1871, its specimen fruit grounds comprised nearly 2,000 varieties, not counting grapes and small fruits, and its specimen ornamental grounds contained 'the most complete collection in this country'. There could be 'no progress' in fruit culture 'without experiment', it was explained: 'it is only by experiment that we can find out what is valuable and what is worthless'. Ellwanger & Barry reported in a fruits catalogue that tests of a long list of 'so-called Russian apples', a number of them from the Imperial Gardens of Russia, concluded for the most part with 'considerable disappointment'; in a catalogue of ornamentals that the firm had 'discarded such trees and plants as in our opinion lacked the necessary characteristics of hardiness and vigor'; and in its catalogue of roses that those plants failing to 'answer to expectations' were 'at once stricken from the list'.[82]

Ellwanger & Barry refrained from offering 'a long list of varieties, many of which are of little value'. By culling failed or disappointing plants, it provided instead 'a selection of the very best'. The process required time, money, and patience, but the firm was 'well pleased with the investment', saying that it enabled the business to operate with a 'degree of intelligence', satisfying to itself and providing its patrons with 'a reasonable guarantee of our accuracy'. In 1878, the firm decided to offer for sale two grape varieties, the sole survivors of twelve years of seeds taken from more than 100 vines that it had grown and progressively selected as they fruited each year. Even then, these were 'not the best of all grapes', the catalogue forthrightly acknowledged, but their features—resistance to heat and cold, hardiness, good quality, and earliness and certainty of ripening—placed them 'among our most valuable grapes'.[83]

[81] Hovey, 'To Our Old Friends and Customers', *Hovey's Illustrated Catalogue of New, Rare, and Beautiful Plants, Fruit Trees, Shrubs, Roses, Etc.* 1886, [3], Box 383, Hovey. Cat., CCMHSD (n 21).

[82] 'Preface to 23rd Edition', *Descriptive Catalogue of Hardy Ornamental Trees, Shrubs, Roses, Etc. . .. Ellwanger and Barry...* No. 2 (n 18) 2; *No 1: Descriptive Catalogue of Fruits... 1878–79* Ellwanger & Barry 3, 'Preface to the First Edition', *A Descriptive Catalogue of Roses offered for sale by Ellwanger & Barry... No 5; 1st edn* (1877) 1; *No 1 Descriptive Catalogue of Fruits,* Ellwanger & Barry, (n.p.), EB, Box 194, file BC1934 (n 43); CCMHSD (n 21); 'Special Notice', *Descriptive and Illustrated Catalogue of Bulbous Flower Roots, Etc. for sale by Ellwanger & Barry... No 5,* 1871, 16; 'Preface to 20th Edition, 1871', *Descriptive Catalogue of Fruits... No 1,* 1871, Ellwanger & Barry, EB, Box 194, file BC1933; CCMHSD (n 21).

[83] *Descriptive and Illustrated Catalogue of Bulbous Flower Roots, Etc. for sale by Ellwanger & Barry... No 5* (1877) title page; E&B, 'Advertisement' (August 1857) *Descriptive Catalogue of Fruits* (1857) 2, Box 193, file BC1933; *No 1: Descriptive Catalogue of Fruits* (n 82) ... *1878-79. Ellwanger & Barry;* 61–63, EB, Box 194, file BC1934; CCMHSD (n 21).

Landreth's similarly stressed that it culled plants of low quality from its fields, acknowledging that it charged higher prices to cover the costs, but contending that the prices signalled the merits of its seeds. The demand for low-priced goods by some merchants has led to 'miserable stocks' on the market, one of its catalogues noted:

> [C]ommon and low-grade plants of every form are more productive of seed than those of high breeding. Some seed growers, to meet this call for low prices, let the crops go without the eradication of the sports and maldevelopments, thus saving themselves the labor, while at the same time securing a larger return of seed.[84]

Some competitors faulted Landreth's for playing excessively on its reputation and longevity, adding complaints about its prices.[85] Landreth's derided the accusation, analogizing its selective practices to the measures used by growers of other sexually reproduced organisms to maintain the strength of their stocks. 'PURITY PRESERVED', its 1883 catalogue proclaimed, explaining:

> It is natural, both in animal and vegetable life, for stock to run out. The cattle-breeder, understanding this, purchases new animals; the wool-grower buys expensive bucks; the horseman breeds to noted studs. If this were not observed, our boasted herds and flocks would become worse than unprofitable. So it is with seeds; and such has always been our practice. Peas are not an exception, but need the watchful eye and ready hand to remove all degenerate vines. It may be said that others can do this; sometimes they do; but in ninety-nine cases in one hundred they do not, as the process of selection takes time, and the diminished yield seems money out of pocket.[86]

Landreth's warned seed consumers against allowing price alone to determine their purchases, noting, 'It would be as unwise as for a sick man who wanted to get well, to purchase cheap medicines'. In the long run, Landreth's put it, the higher-priced 'BEST is certainly the CHEAPEST'.[87]

The quality assurances of the seed—and nurserymen were reinforced by inclusion in the catalogues of endorsements by leading journals and testimonials from satisfied buyers certifying the merits and reliability of their plants. In its fruits catalogue for 1878–1879, Ellwanger & Barry introduced the Sharpless Seedling Strawberry, which had been raised in 1872 by JS Sharpless, in Catawissa, Pennsylvania, and then tested for several years by Ellwanger & Barry. The firm, touting it as 'the largest and *best strawberrry* now in cultivation' certified its

[84] *Landreth's Rural Register 1887* (n 17) 9.
[85] ibid 17.
[86] *Landreth's Pedigree Turnip Seeds* (n 34) 15.
[87] *Landreth's Rural Register* (1887–1889).

own judgment with a local newspaper's encomium that it was the 'Prince of Strawberries' and the praise from the editor of *The Country Gentleman* that it produced fruit of 'enormous size, some of the largest berries weighing about an ounce and a half each'. In its *Kitchen-Garden Catalogue* for 1886, Landreth's published a sample of what it said were 2,000 commendations from nine states and the District of Columbia, including an endorsement of Landreth's Winter Wheat, then in its fourth season of trial: 'Hundreds have been to see the Wheat, all say it beats any Wheat they ever saw'. The authors of most of the endorsements were identified by name and place, and one testimonial—praise for the yield of Landreth's several varieties of cabbage—was described as signed and witnessed.[88]

The catalogues of the leading houses also showcased the prizes and accolades won by their productions. Awarded in annual competitions sponsored by state and local horticultural societies, both served as independent warrants of the merits of the fruits and flowers. Ellwanger & Barry regularly reported the prizes and premiums won by its fruits from various state fairs and societies—more than ninety firsts in 1879 alone—and recounted the multiple awards given to its grapes, plums, and apples at the US Centennial Exhibition in Philadelphia in 1876, not only for their quality, but also because, as the citation for the grapes put it, they were 'properly named'.[89]

Hovey listed his numerous garlands from the Massachusetts Horticultural Society that followed the triumph with his Seedling Strawberry. These were, for example, for the Hovey Cherry, which the society's fruit committee predicted in 1850 would 'take a high rank, and become an established favorite' and for which in 1854 it awarded Hovey & Co the Appleton Gold Medal for its sustained standing as 'a new and superior cherry'; and for the Boston Pear, which in the early 1850s the fruit committee commended repeatedly. In 1886, Hovey proudly noted that the Massachusetts Horticultural Society had awarded his fruits and flowers '*fifty* gold, silver, and bronze medals and pieces of silver plate and more than one thousand prizes … twice the number ever awarded to any other horticulturalist in the country'.[90]

The sales pitches of the travelling agents in essence reflected on the veracity of the nurseries and catalogues they represented, and fraudulent peddlers exercised reputable nurseries such as Ellwanger & Barry, which declared around 1870 that 'the reputation of our establishment has already been injured in several parts of

[88] *No 1: Descriptive Catalogue of Fruits* ...1878-79. Ellwanger & Barry, (n 82) 19–31, 61–63, EB, Box 194, file BC1934; CCMHSD (n 21); Landreth & Son, *Kitchen-Garden*, (n 8) 27; Lyon-Jenness (n 16) 398.

[89] *No 1 Descriptive Catalogue of Fruits* ...1880. Ellwanger & Barry (n 43) 4; *No 6 Catalogue of Select Fruit and Ornamental Trees, Small Fruits, Shrubs, Roses, Etc.*... Ellwanger & Barry [1880], EB, Box 194, file BC1934; CCMHSD (n 21).

[90] *New and Choice Fruits. Hovey & Co., No. 7 Merchant Row, Boston* [1854], 1, Box 380, Hovey Pt 1; Hovey, 'To Our Old Friends and Customers', *Hovey's Illustrated Catalogue of New, Rare, and Beautiful Plants, Fruit Trees, Shrubs, Roses, Etc. 1886*, [3], Box 383, Hovey. Cat., CCMHSD (n 21).

the country by such parties'. Upstanding nurserymen were at pains to discredit the misrepresentations they often advanced. Individually and through their societies, these nurserymen denounced the tree peddlers as ignorant and dishonest, and as practitioners of deception. One nurseryman held that it was imperative to 'brand the swindler in such plain characters that all may know and avoid him', and another warned members of the Illinois State Agricultural Society in 1860: 'Never buy trees of a peddler. Buy your trees of the regular, educated nurseryman, near you, or order them from a distant one, in whom you have confidence.'[91]

Few leading nurserymen were willing to abandon the use of travelling agents; such agents were too valuable for marketing. They sought instead to enlist agents who were honest, reliable, and likely to command the public's confidence. Ellwanger & Barry assured its customers with italicized emphasis that their agents were '*men of well known integrity, who are bound to act faithfully and impartially for the interests of their customers as well as of their employers*'. Yet many established nurseries declined to rely on character alone. They provided their agents with evidence of official certification, including signed certificates, printed order forms with company logos, and confirmations of the agent's identity. Ellwanger & Barry summarily declared: 'All our agents and those who purchase from us extensively to fill their orders, have certificates bearing our signature. Those who have no such certificates are to be regarded as imposters'.[92]

Descriptive Integrity: Words

Like Howsley, the reputable nurseries attached special importance to reliable nomenclature. Various nurseries—for example, the Oak Grove Nursery in Jackson County, Michigan—advertised its products as true to name; Ellwanger & Barry counted names important enough to declare on a catalogue cover that the firm spared no pains 'to insure complete accuracy in the nomenclature' of its offerings and invited all nurserymen to its grounds to see for themselves. When George Ellwanger and Patrick Barry were stocking their fledgling firm with fruit trees from other nurseries, they stressed to suppliers that they must send only such plants 'as will prove *true* to their names', warning that otherwise they would not want them.[93]

[91] Lyon-Jenness (n 16) 414–15, 418.

[92] *No 6 Catalogue of Select Bear Fruit and Ornamental Trees, Small Fruits, Shrubs, Roses, Etc …* . Ellwanger & Barry [1880]; *Abridged Catalogue of Select Fruit and Ornamental Trees, Cultivated and Sold by Ellwanger & Barry* [c. 1870], AHL (n 61); Lyon-Jenness (n 16) 414–16, 418.

[93] Ellwanger & Barry, *Wholesale Catalogue No 4, for Autumn of 1855 and Spring of 1856*, cover; 'Preface to 23rd edition' (n 18); *Descriptive Catalogue of Hardy Ornamental Trees, Shrubs, Roses, Etc… Ellwanger and Barry… No. 2*, 1875 2; AHL (n 61); Ellwanger & Barry to B Hodge (29 September 1842; to Bryant, 11 October 1842, Letterbook, vol I, EBNR (n 57); Lyon-Jenness (n 16) 395.

However, the leading proprietors recognized that veracity in nomenclature was by itself insufficient. If true names were to carry any weight, they had to be linked to reliable descriptions of the fruits and flowers they designated. By the 1840s, descriptions were becoming a common feature of fruit and flower catalogues. Hovey helped pioneer the trend, telling customers in the mid-1840s that his detailed and accurate descriptions would assist them in selecting 'trees suitable for their purposes'. Two years later he pointed to the special value of descriptions for the choice of flower seed: 'Their kinds are so numerous, their habits so unlike, their colors so dissimilar, and the height to which the different kinds attain, so varied, that to individuals unacquainted with them, a descriptive catalogue will be of great value in making their selections, either for a small or large garden.'[94] He made the fruit descriptions a luscious selling point as well, portraying the Concord grape, which Bull had consigned to him for sale, as:

> a most vigorous growing vine, perfectly hardy, with bunches of large size, handsomely shouldered, often weighing a pound and with large roundish oval berries, frequently measuring an inch in diameter; color very dark, covered with a thick blue bloom; flesh free from all pulp; flavor very rich and luscious, with a fine sprightly aroma.

In its prize citations, the Massachusetts Horticultural Society assisted the identification effort, describing Hovey's Boston Pear in 1851, for example, as 'a fruit of medium size, round oblong shape, yellow color, with a fine blush in the sun, and russet at the stem; skin smooth; flesh melting, juicy, of a very rich pleasant flavor, resembling in general appearance the Golden Beurre of Bilboa'.[95]

Ellwanger & Barry's testing programme aimed not only at determining the quality of plants, but also, in the case of roses, at comparing the descriptions provided by the original 'raiser' with the blossoms they could observe with their own eyes. If necessary, it altered the descriptions.[96] Yet not all nurserymen were so scrupulous. The leading fruit growers complained that some nurserymen misrepresented the new seedlings that appeared in their fields and gardens, claiming that they were worthy of attention when in fact, as a contributor to *The Horticulturist* charged in 1847, they

[94] *A Descriptive Catalogue of Fruits* (n 22) 3; *Descriptive Catalogue of a Choice Collection of Flower Seeds; comprising, in all, upwards of five hundred species and varieties . . . Among the seeds are many new, rare and splendid varieties, well worth the attention of florists and amateur cultivators. For sale by Hovey & Co, Seedsmen and Nurserymen* (1847) Box 380, Hovey Pt 1; MHS Depository. The 1847 catalogue also identified each plant by one or more of eight numbers that designated the scientific name, the common name, the period of duration of the plant, hardiness, color of the flowers, height of the plant, period of blooming as well as price per packet.

[95] *New and Choice Fruits*. Hovey & Co., No. 7 Merchant Row, Boston [1854], 1-2, Box 380, Hovey. Pt.1; CCMHSD (n 21).

[96] 'Preface to the First Edition' *A Descriptive Catalogue of Roses offered for sale by Ellwanger & Barry . . . No 5*; 1st edn, 1877 1–2, EB, Box 194, file BC1934; CCMHSD (n 21).

were 'either of too indifferent quality to be worth notice, or they are second-rate; or they are inferior, or only equal to many sorts already in cultivation'. The contributor called for 'pomological reform', declaring that its establishment 'will protect the public against a flood of new varieties of little or no value'.[97]

The contributor had in mind 'restricting the right to describe, name, and publish, a new fruit, to competent pomologists'.[98] In 1849, a number of such pomologists—half from nine states and Canada, the rest from New York state—met in Buffalo, New York, with the aim of establishing a national organization intended, in no small part, to regulate fruit names and descriptions. John Kennicott, the editor of *The Prairie Farmer*, noted that objective appraisal of fruit quality was crucial to supplanting the 'vanity of their originators or disseminators', since an industry standard would assist nurserymen in culling 'hundreds of 3rd and 4th rate fruits' that swelled 'every nursery catalogue'. The Buffalo meeting led to the establishment, largely at the initiative of Marshall P Wilder, a prominent nurseryman in the Boston area, of the first national organization of fruit innovators and sellers—the American Pomological Society, its name drawn from Pomona, the Roman goddess of fruits.[99]

The society promptly appointed a committee on synonyms and created a catalogue of fruits, giving the preferred name of each, and identifying the synonyms by which it was also known. It tried to link the name with the specific fruit by providing verbal descriptions of its size, shape, and other distinguishing features, including taste. The catalogue listed varieties that its compilers in their wisdom judged worthy or unworthy, designating the latter for rejection by cultivators, in an attempt to suppress inferior fruits.[100]

Joseph Cabot of Boston, a stalwart in the Massachusetts Horticultural Society and a supplier of novel pears to Hovey, had a good deal to do with initiating the rejection list. He noted that public announcement of such a list was 'a matter of some delicacy, as private interests may feel themselves to be thereby injuriously affected'. But in his view, 'public necessity' overrode such disadvantage. The catalogue of fruits, Marshall Wilder held, was 'the best means of preventing those numerous impositions and frauds which, we regret to say, have been practiced upon our fellow citizens, by adventurous speculators or ignorant and unscrupulous venders . . . greatly to the injury of the purchaser and fruit grower, to the dealer and the nurseryman, and to the cause of pomology'.[101]

However, the American Pomological Society's verbal descriptions of fruits were no more exact or reliable than those in the nursery catalogues it aimed to regulate.

[97] 'Pomological Reform', *The Horticulturist* (July 1847) 175; Pawley (n 15) 162.

[98] ibid.

[99] Lyon-Jenness (n 16) 411; Pawley (n 15) 180. The Society was formed from two groups, the North American Pomological Convention and The American Congress of Fruit-Growers, both founded in 1848. In 1849, the two agreed to consolidate as the American Pomological Congress, which in 1852 renamed itself, agreed to meet biannually, and adopted a constitution and by-laws. See Wilder (n 39) 29–32.

[100] 'Fruit Catalogue of the American Pomological Society'; Constitution and Bylaws [1858] *American Pomological Society Proceedings* 237–45, 247–48.

[101] Joseph S Cabot, 'Report of the Committee on Synonyms and Rejected Fruits'; Wilder (n 24) 214–17.

For example, there was the apple Autumn Seek-no-further, which was described in the society's *Proceedings* as 'a fine fruit, above medium size; greenish white, splashed with carmine. Very good'. Or the pear Clapp's Favorite: 'Very large; similar to Bartlett in form, but less musky in flavor; vinous, melting, buttery, and juicy; fine texture'.[102] Any number of varieties could conform to those characteristics.

In the judgement of some number of pomological critics, words were simply not up to the task of capturing varietal differences. As one of them put it to his fellow horticulturalists in New York state, 'Varieties pass into each other by insensible shades; or often differ so slightly and by such variable characters, that it becomes exceedingly difficult to discriminate. Even experienced cultivators find it necessary to place different varieties of fruit together before the eye, which, when taken apart, might be pronounced identical.'[103]

Descriptive Integrity: Pictures

Hovey himself recognized the inadequacy of verbal descriptions, whether published in the American Pomological Society's catalogue or in nursery catalogues, including his own. He told his customers in the mid-1840s that it was inexpedient 'in the limits of a Catalogue, to undertake to describe minutely and accurately, every variety of fruit'. Those who wanted descriptions sufficiently precise 'for the purpose of detecting synonyms' would have to 'refer to works of authority'—by which he meant the publications of the London Horticultural Society or comparable works by horticultural specialists in the United States—'rather than to a mere Catalogue'.[104]

Hovey was himself exercised by the proliferation of synonyms, believing that it created 'a confused nomenclature which has greatly retarded the general cultivation of the newer and more valuable varieties'. To guide himself in achieving correctness in nomenclature, Hovey planted more than 1,000 specimen trees representing upwards of 600 varieties along more than a mile of the border walks in his nursery. As the trees came into bearing, he said, they afforded 'a fine opportunity … for a careful inspection of the fruit, the detection of synonyms, and for insuring *accuracy* in the propagation of each variety'. He invited friends and pomologists to inspect the trees for themselves.[105]

Although recognizing the limitations of on-site inspection, Hovey was, at the time, planning a far more accessible means of dealing with fruit names and synonyms: the dissemination of accurate illustrations of the fruits themselves. A number of mid-nineteenth-century nursery catalogues included black-and-white etchings or

[102] 'Report of Native Fruit Committee' [1860] *American Pomological Society Proceedings* 115–23.

[103] John H Thomas, 'Hints on Describing Fruits' (1843) 63 *Transactions of the New York State Agricultural Society* 269, 270.

[104] *A Descriptive Catalogue of Fruits* (n 22) 3.

[105] Hovey 'Preface', *Fruits of America* (n 37) v; *A Descriptive Catalogue of Pears* (n 41); CCMHSD (n 21).

lithographs of vegetables, fruits, and flowers, some of them showing—in an evident attempt to add specificity to the depictions—cut-away drawings of the fruit's interior structure. James Vick illustrated his catalogues by employing artists and engravers. Hovey himself was no stranger to fruit illustration, regularly publishing black-and-white fruit drawings in *The Horticultural Magazine*. Indeed, during the first twenty years of his editorship, the illustrations would accumulate to more than 500, plus another 1,500 engravings for the multiple subjects discussed in its pages.[106]

However, now Hovey was keen to identify fruits by illustrating them in colour. Paintings and coloured etchings had long been used to identify botanical specimens, including fruits. During the early nineteenth century in Britain and France, heightened attention was given to the practice of coloured illustration in response to the proliferation of different names for the same fruits. But even if beautiful, as many of the illustrations were, they did not lend themselves to the widespread identification of fruits, even in small markets, let alone the steadily enlarging ones of the United States. Most were hand-painted. Oils and hand-coloured etchings of lithographs were laborious and expensive to produce in any number.[107]

Hovey, who kept up with European horticultural publications, fastened on a new technology to accomplish his purpose. Devised in Europe in the 1830s, the technology promised to enable the production of multiple faithful copies of coloured fruit portraits. It involved impressing different colours on the same lithograph in successive printings, sometimes as many as a dozen. It soon crossed the Atlantic to several cities in the northeastern United States. William Sharp, an English painter, drawing teacher, and lithographer, brought it to Boston in 1838 and promptly opened a shop to produce what he called 'chromo-lithographs'. In 1847, Hovey enlisted Sharp to begin publishing a series of chromo-lithographs of the nation's fruits.[108]

In 1853, Hovey brought out the series in a compendium that he titled *The Fruits of America, Volume I*, which was followed by *Volume II* in 1856. Together, the two volumes comprised ninety-six vibrant chromo-lithographs, each handsomely depicting a different fruit with its stem and leaves. Hovey declared in the Preface to the first volume that he felt 'a national pride' in 'beautifully' portraying the 'delicious fruits in our own country, many of them surpassed by none of foreign growth' and thus demonstrating the rapidly developing 'skill of our Pomologists' to the 'cultivators of the world'. He was unembarrassed to tout his own skills by including a chromolithograph of his Seedling Strawberry in Volume I (Fig. 6.3). But

[106] *New and Choice Fruits. Hovey & Co., No. 7 Merchant Row, Boston* [1854], 1-2, Box 380, Hovey. Pt.1; CCMHSD (n 21); Lyon-Jenness (n 16) 387. See eg the luscious black and white engravings of the American Seedling Gooseberry, Binckley's Orange Raspberry, the Purple Leaved Maple in *No 1 Descriptive Catalogue of Fruits ... 1868 ... Ellwanger & Barry* 14–15, 47–49, EB, Box 193, file BC1933; CCMHSD (n 21).

[107] Dearborn (n 1) 84–85.

[108] Jay T Last, *The Color Explosion: Nineteenth-Century American Lithography* (Hillcrest Press 2005) 19–20, 143–44.

his aims transcended patriotic celebration. He averred that his 'principal object' in publishing the work was to 'reduce the chaos of names to something like order'.[109]

Hovey held that Sharp's plates showed that the 'art of chromo-lithography produces a far more beautiful and correct representation than that of the ordinary lithograph, washed in color, in the usual way. Indeed, the plates have the richness of actual paintings, which could not be executed for ten times the value of a single copy'. However, some critics found chromo-lithographs dissatisfying, and lacking fidelity to the delicate tints of nature characteristic of the best plates done by hand. Chromo-lithography was a complex, demanding process, an art in and of itself. It required a sophisticated understanding of colour, the inventive use of inks, and perfect registration of the print with a different coloured stone in each of a number of successive impressions.[110]

In the coming decades, chromo-lithographs would greatly improve in quality, their cost would decline, and they would become more widely used in the nursery trade. But around the middle of the nineteenth century, users of fruit illustrations counted as superior those portraits produced by the well-established technique of printing black and white lithographs or etchings that were then water-coloured manually.[111]

A much-admired practitioner of the genre was an artist named Joseph Prestele, a German immigrant from Bavaria who had been a staff member at the Royal Botanical Garden in Munich, where he practised the scientific illustration of botanical specimens. Prestele belonged to the Inspirationists, an ascetic, communitarian offshoot of Lutheranism, and had been driven by religious harassment to the United States in 1838, settling in the sect's enclave in Ebenezer, New York. In 1858, he moved to Iowa, where a vanguard of Inspirationists had migrated to establish the Amana Colonies. In the 1850s, he pioneered the production of water-coloured lithographs for nurserymen, omitting the matter-of-fact features of scientific illustration—seeds, roots, and cross-sections of blossoms—in favour of presenting commercially appealing compositions of blossoms and fruits. His standards were high and the work was tedious and slow, but he had three sons, all of them talented artists, and he managed to produce multiple plates for several nurseries with the sustained help of one of them and the short-term assistance of another. The third, William, likely participated in the enterprise for a time, but he was a creative spirit and restive in the Inspirationist community. Sometime before 1858, not yet aged twenty, he left for New York and pursued a successful career in fruit illustration using his father's methods.[112]

Joseph Prestele's clients were glad to have his colour plates, valuing them as a means to identify and promote their fruit varieties in the market. Copycat entrepreneurs followed his example—some even appropriated his plates—establishing atelier-like

[109] Hovey, 'Preface', *Fruits of America* (n 37) v–vi.

[110] ibid; Charles van Ravenswaay, *Drawn from Nature: The Botanical Art of Joseph Prestele and His Sons* (Smithsonian Institution Press 1984) 58–60.

[111] Last (n 108).

[112] Ravenswaay (n 110).

facilities where lithographers and water-colourists produced the fruit plates in volume. The use of such plates by commercial nurseries rose steadily after the Civil War, amid the ongoing expansion of the fruit industry, and so did the demand for plates produced by chromo-lithography as that technique grew better and cheaper.[113]

Figure 6.3 Charles M Hovey, 'Hovey's Seedling Strawberry', Drawn from Nature by Sharp & Son, *Fruits of America*, vol I (1852).
Special Collections, General Library, University of California, Davis.

[113] ibid.

Fruit nurseries relished and relied on the coloured plates. These not only added pictorial definition to different fruit varieties; they also served as a reliable means of brand identification in the competitive national market. In their catalogues, both nurseries and seed houses coupled selected verbal descriptions with one or another type of coloured plates, especially of flowers. It was an effective way of arousing consumer demand and for identifying what the branded plant would yield.[114]

Ellwanger & Barry exemplified the practice. The firm kept in its office several dozen coloured fruit lithographs, a number of them by Prestele, and a sample book of sixty-five hand-coloured plates, mostly of fruits, some of flowers, in a handsome bound volume, gold-lettered on its black cover: 'Album of Fruit/ Ellwanger and Barry/ Mt. Hope Nurseries/ Rochester, NY'. The nursery enhanced its catalogues with coloured plates, many by the Rochester lithographer George Frauenberger (firms like his, employing artists and lithographers, proliferated in such number in response to the demand for fruit illustrations as to make the city a national centre of such productions). Produced expressly for Ellwanger & Barry, the plates depicted fruits and flowers in which it took special pride, notably the Sharpless Seedling Strawberry, which formed the frontispiece of its 1878–1879 fruits catalogue.[115]

Ellwanger & Barry similarly frontispieced coloured fruit and flower plates in a number of their other catalogues. Many were gorgeous, for example the Waterloo Peach, muted red overall with voluptuous whitish cheeks; the Japan Snowball, a bursting ball of white petals; the Hydrangea Paniculata Grandiflora, its pinkish flowers crowding the bush; five roses clustered together in an explosion of white, purplish red, blood, red, and yellow; the Madame Lemoine Pelargonium, a round ruffle of dark green leaves clustered at the base of the stem, and a globular packet of pinkish red flowers at the top; and the Weigela, in Ellwanger & Barry's words, 'an elegant shrub, with fine rose colored flowers, introduced from China'.[116]

[114] For two-coloured illustration of vegetables see Landreth's (n 3) 'The Period 1850–1860'. For black and white engravings see eg James M Thorburn & Co, *Annual Descriptive Catalogue of Seeds* (1881); UDEL (n 8) 8; and Richman (n 9) 8–10. Richman's book includes many samples of colour and black-and-white illustrations in seed catalogues. On the development and the use of colour lithography in plant and seed catalogues and elsewhere in the United States; see Last (n 108).

[115] EBNR (n 57) vol 19 and 'Horticultural Prints' flat boxes; Burd (n 20) 145; *No 1: Descriptive Catalogue of Fruits . . . 1878–1879*, EB, Box 194, file BC1934; CCMHSD (n 21).

[116] *Ellwanger & Barry, No 7 Summer and Autumn of 1879. Descriptive Priced List of Strawberries . . . Ellwanger & Barry*; *No 1 Descriptive Catalogue of Fruits* (n 43); *No 2 Descriptive Catalogue of Hardy Ornamental Trees, Shrubs, Herbaceous Perennial Plants, Etc. Mount Hope Nurseries . . . Ellwanger & Barry* [1880]; *A Descriptive List of New Roses, for 1880 . . . Ellwanger & Barry*; *No 2 Descriptive Catalogue of Hardy Ornamental Trees, Shrubs, Roses, Etc., . . . Ellwanger & Barry, Proprietors* (1876) Box 194, file BC1934; *Catalogue of Green House and Hot-House Plants, Select Bedding Plants, Chrysanthemums, Dahlias, etc. . . .* 1864, EB, Box193, file BC1933; CCMHSD (n 21).

Reputable nurseries provided their travelling agents with fold-out books of coloured plates to bolster their trustworthiness. Several Rochester lithographic firms supplied them, but the dominant producer was Dellon Marcus Dewey, in Rochester, which provided customized coloured plates of fruits, flowers, and ornamental trees. One of the most widely used was Dewey's *Colored Fruit Book for the Use of Nurserymen*, first published in 1859, which included seventy coloured prints. Dewey declared that the plates had been meticulously drawn and coloured from nature, and that their purpose was to 'place before the purchaser of Fruit Trees, as faithful a representation of the Fruit as is possible to make, by the process adopted'.[117]

By the 1870s, the Dewey company offered more than 2,300 illustrations. Agents picked which plants they wanted to sell and Dewey would provide a box of relevant plates or a fold-out of loosely connected plates. In the 1870s, Dewey developed a pocket-sized plate book. Other Rochester firms used Dewey's books and plates and so did a few Midwestern nurserymen. Deluxe editions of Dewey's plate books, edged in gilt and bound in Morocco leather, served as prizes at horticultural fairs and as parlour-table books. Dewey employed some thirty people, including several capable German, English, and American artists. In 1875, he published the *Tree Agents' Private Guide*, which advised salesmen to impress customers that they were God-fearing, upright, and moral.[118]

Strategies of Protection: The Turn to Protection by Marketing and Law

All the measures taken by the seed houses and nurseries to protect their brands were aimed at encouraging consumer confidence or at forestalling consumer deception. The measures were inevitably vulnerable to the ingenuity and brazenness of frauds and cheats. Even illustrations could be made to lie. One reviewer, while praising the call for honesty in the *Tree Agents' Private Guide*, expressed apprehension that deceivers would not be swayed by its arguments. In 1879, a critique of the travelling-agent industry warned purchasers to beware of 'oily-tongued fellows with florid prints of impossible fruits faithfully depicted between richly bound lids'. Anyone could obtain the plates and anyone could prey on gullible farmers, showing them plates of strawberries

[117] For example, the Stecher Lithographic Co, which provided plates for the sample book of JW Thompson and Co in the 1880s. Electronic copy of sample pages in author's possession. I am grateful to Markley Boyer for calling this plate book to my attention. On Stecher and Rochester see Last (n 108) 150–55, 272–73; Ravenswaay (n 110) 78–80, 122.

[118] Ravenswaay (n 110) 78–80, 122; Lyon-Jenness (n 16) 405.

grown on trees or blue roses, and what the *American Agriculturalist* called 'astonishing fruit'.[119]

More importantly, if they safeguarded the brands to some degree, the measures served only indirectly to protect the innovator against appropriation of his or her novel vegetable, fruit, or flower, which meant from theft of his or her intellectual property. The American Pomological Society had no police power. Its only weapon was moral suasion, which is to say that it had little authority to enforce uniformity in fruit names, descriptions, or qualities. Thieves could still clone fruit trees and vines and sell them by different names. Cheats might be unable to reproduce sexually reproducing vegetables or flowers, but they could still offer their own seeds under reputable brand names. In the face of these circumstances, the reputable seed houses and nurseries turned increasingly in the latter half of the nineteenth century to claim and to devise direct protections for, their rights as originators, partly by marketing strategies but also through the federal trademark law of 1881.[120]

Landreth's strategy comprised a combination of packaging and fierce protection of its name. In 1847, the firm began selling its seed in packets and boxes with warrants of freshness on the labels. The practice of purveying seeds in small paper envelopes had been pioneered by the Shaker communities, which brought them sizable income from their agricultural enterprises. By the 1880s, Landreth's was dating its packages, a practice it thought should be used by the entire seed trade, noting that not until it was adopted would the seed business 'be conducted upon a healthy basis, as packets not bearing the date of issue may be offered to planters years after the seeds have lost all vitality' (Fig. 6.4).[121]

The firm was eager to protect the several varieties of vegetables it had originated in its proof farms, including Landreth's Bloomsdale Spinach and Landreth's Winter Wheat. It was passionate about protecting Landreth's Extra Early Peas, a kind of heirloom for the firm that it had introduced in 1823 and, so it noted in an 1883 catalogue, had 'since kept in their original *purity* by unceasing labor and attention'. Landreth's aimed 'to check the enormous fraud practiced by irresponsible parties who alike injured the conscientious merchant, the consumer, and ourselves by palming upon the public as LANDRETHS' EXTRA EARLY PEAS, stock of which we had no knowledge, and [is] of doubtful quality at best'.[122]

[119] ibid 407.

[120] See eg 'Protection for Fruit Evolvers', editorial, *California Fruit Grower*, quoted in Luther Burbank, Burbank's Experiment Farms, *The 1899 Supplement to New Creations in Fruits and Flowers* (Luther Burbank Papers, Library of Congress, Washington, DC, Box 14).

[121] *Catalogue of the Principal Garden Seeds Cultivated at the Horticultural Gardens of David Landreth & Co* (n 11) 12; Landreth and Landreth, *Catalogue of Greenhouse Plants ...* (n 11) 47; Landreth & Son, *Kitchen-Garden* (n 8) 3; Richman (n 9) 9; *Landreth's Rural Register 1886* (n 33) 3; *Landreth's Rural Register 1887* (n 17) 18; Landreth's *A Catalogue of the Principal Garden Seeds* (n 44) cover.

[122] *Landreth's Pedigree Turnip Seeds* (n 34) 14.

Taking advantage of federal law, it trademarked the Liberty Bell logo and the brand names 'Landreth' and 'Landreth's'. Beginning in 1878, it had begun selling each of the three varieties in distinctively labelled packets, boxes, and bags. The pea and spinach seeds, moreover, were shipped in red and blue muslin bags respectively, and the wheat in white duck bags. All came to be fastened, as an 1887 catalogue said, with a 'wire and lead seal (a Bell), bearing the stamp, "Landreth, Phila., Trade Mark" '. The firm claimed that its system—both of selling the peas and spinach seeds in sealed bags of special colour and of bearing the trademark—was itself registered with the Commissioner of Patents, and it put readers on notice that 'all infringements will be prosecuted under the law'.[123]

In 1883, Landreth's sued Albert Landreth's firm in Wisconsin for misappropriation of its trademarked name. Landreth's won and touted its victory in a 'CIRCULAR' printed in its *Rural Register and Almanac* for 1887, declaring that it had gained a ruling in a trademark case in the US Court of the Eastern District of Wisconsin under which it was 'protected in the exclusive use of the seed-dealing designation of "LANDRETH OR LANDRETH'S" ... as attached to a seed package, circular, price-list or advertisement'. The firm made clear 'that any one selling or advertising seeds as LANDRETH'S, without authorization', would be 'subject to injunction and damages', adding that the firm would 'not hesitate to take steps to enjoin all who improperly make use of our name'.[124]

'This decision is of value to every Seedsman of reputation, as it equally protects others with ourselves', Landreth's declared of its victory. The protection covered every reputable seedsman's brand name—Landreth's called it 'his recognized Firm designation as an indicia of his issue'—and safeguarded him 'somewhat in the enjoyment of his skill and application'.[125] The phrase 'skill and application' was shorthand for the investment of time, knowledge, and effort in the selection and propagation of new varieties that would advantage both growers in their production for market and seed houses in the profits of their businesses.

Packaging was not a practical option for producers of novel fruit trees, vines, or cloneable flowers such as roses. They sought instead to protect returns on investment in their novelties by reliance on a pricing strategy. They might command a monopoly—and a monopoly price—over the novelty when it was first introduced, but the originator could not maintain market control over succeeding generations of the plant. The monopoly would thus end in the short time it took competitors to

[123] *Landreth's Rural Register 1887* (n 17) 49, 61.

[124] ibid 49, 61, 65.

[125] ibid. Albert Landreth switched from raising and selling pea seeds to canning peas, starting the highly successful Lakeside Packing Company, itself a well-known brand; see Eggen (n 68) 1.

begin identically reproducing and marketing the product. Its price would fall rapidly and so would the innovator's revenues.

Under the circumstances, originators forged a strategy of protection that centred on selling the first release of new varietals at high prices. The price level reflected the fact that at first introduction, the supply of a novelty was limited. But the price was also intended to capture in the first several years of sales what economists would later call all the downstream revenues of which other propagators, authorized or not, might deprive the fruit innovator.

The nursery catalogues of the day reveal the pricing practice. Ellwanger & Barry was evidently content to derive income from high-volume sales of common varieties. In 1857, the firm's wholesale prices for apple, pear, cherry, plum, and peach trees ranged from ten cents to thirty-six cents each if bought in lots of 100. Its retail prices similarly varied, reaching only fifty cents a specimen depending on the maturity, bearing quality, and root stock. But its pricing strategy differed for new varieties. When after twelve years of coaxing it derived two compelling new grapes, the Monroe and the Rochester, it priced them at US$2 each for a one-year-old plant and US$3 each for a two-year-old one. (By comparison, it offered 'Select Foreign Grapes' at US$1 per plant.) When its fields generated the new Pride of Mount Hope geranium, it disclosed the price —which was presumably too offputtingly high for its general catalogue—in a special circular that had to be obtained by special request.[126]

Hovey first offered his new Seedling Strawberry at US$5 (about US$164 in 2023) for a dozen plants, then several years later at US$2 per dozen, a decided premium over the US$2–US$4 for 100 plants at which common varieties were ordinarily sold. When in 1854 he first listed Bull's Concord grape for sale, he priced it at US$5 per cutting.[127] Hovey's catalogue in 1845, informing customers of the prices for trees at different stages of maturity, added that a higher rate would be charged for larger trees and for trees 'of new and rare varieties of recent introduction'. Hovey advertised similar pricing for his new Cherry tree and his Boston Pear tree, including a few of large size and abundant in buds at US$10 each.[128]

[126] 'New Seedling Grapes Raised by Ellwanger & Barry', *No 1: Descriptive Catalogue of Fruits... 1878–79;* Ellwanger & Barry 50–51; Ellwanger & Barry, *Wholesale Catalogue for Autumn of 1857,* 2–3; *Wholesale Catalogue of the Mount Hope Nurseries* (n 35) 16, EB, Box 193, file BC1933, CCMHSD (n 21); Burd (n 20) 90.

[127] Pauly (n 2) 70–72; Hutchinson (n 22) 41; EB, *Descriptive Catalogue of Fruits* (1864) [reprint of 1863] 55, EBNR (n 57); *New and Choice Fruits. Hovey & Co., No. 7 Merchant Row, Boston* [1854] 2, Box 380, Hovey Pt 1; CCMHSD (n 21).

[128] *A Descriptive Catalogue of Fruits* (n 22) 4; *New and Choice Fruits* (n 47) 1; *A Descriptive Catalogue of Pears* (n 41); CCMHSD (n 21).

15

THEIR PURITY.

Uniformly the *purest* of any so-called Extra Early in the market. This we say, whether as respects one bushel or ten thousand—whether as respects the past or present. Occasionally some other stocks may be found which are satisfactory, but there is no assurance that the next bushel purchased will be the same. The *proof is against it*—dearly bought experience raises a doubt not to be disregarded. With Landreths' Extra Early, our thousands of bushels are, as compared one to the other, like needles in a paper, or coins from the mint, *always the same.*

PURITY PRESERVED.

It is natural, both in animal and vegetable life, for stock to run out. The cattle-breeder, understanding this, purchases new animals; the wool-grower buys expensive bucks; the horseman breeds to noted studs. If this were not observed, our boasted herds and flocks would become worse than unprofitable.

So it is with Seeds; and such has always been our practice. Peas are not an exception, but need the watchful eye and ready hand to remove all degenerate vines. It may be said that others can do this, sometimes they do; but in ninety-nine cases in one hundred they do not, as the process of selection takes time, and the diminished yield seems money out of pocket. Again, we have another process by which we renew or rejuvenate our stock. This we cannot make public, but will state that it is of wondrous efficiency!

CONFIDENCE WELL PLACED.

A CARD.

PEDIGREE STOCK.

Introduced by us in 1823.

LANDRETHS' CELEBRATED EXTRA EARLY PEAS

are put up in lead-sealed bags of one bushel, halves, quarters, and eighths—no extra charge for bags.

We will sell them in this form *alone*, introduced by us in the Autum of 1878, to check the enormous fraud practiced by irresponsible parties, who alike injured the conscientious merchant, the consumer, and ourselves by palming upon the public as LANDRETHS' EXTRA EARLY PEAS, stock of which we had no knowledge, and of doubtful quality at best.

Purchasers of *sealed bags* can plant the contents with confidence, and rest satisfied to abide the result.

MAKE NO DOUBTFUL PURCHASE.

Occasionally a bushel or two of some other stocks may be met with which proves early, and fairly good, but the probabilities are that other stocks will prove *late* mixed with *runners* or *rogues*, and producing pods *small in size* and *poor in form*, thus bringing to the planter, when too late to correct the error, disappointment and vexation, and, worse still, a *loss of time* and *money*. Verily, "a bird in the hand is worth two in the bush."

D. LANDRETH & SONS,
Seed Growers,
Philadelphia.

Figure 6.4 Landreth's Emphasis on Purity and on Protection by Sealed Packaging, from a Landreth's catalogue, 1883.

Special Collections, Manuscripts and Archives Department, University of Delaware.

The first season's sales of Bull's Concord grape totalled US$3,200 (the equivalent of almost US$104,000 in 2023), a sizable sum, but, faced with the rapid dissemination of the grape, Hovey had to reduce the price from US$5 to US$3 a cutting, and just four years later, his contract with Hovey having ended, Bull sold them in bulk at deep discounts, as low as 20 cents each for 100 yearlings.[129] Nurserymen contended, often invoking Bull, that their high first-sale prices could not be maintained long enough against copycat competitors to recoup their investments. In 1900, a knowledgeable originator of fruits summarily noted: 'The usual attempt to secure compensation from the first sales alone nearly always fails, afterward the variety is the common property of the trade, when the introducer's opportunity for profit is gone forever.'[130]

In the late 1890s, the prolific California plant innovator Luther Burbank fulminated to the readers of *Green's Fruit Grower* that he had:

> been robbed and swindled out of my best work by name thieves, plant thieves and in various ways too well known to the originator … A plant which has cost thousands of dollars in coin and years of intensest [sic] labor and care and which is of priceless value to humanity may now be stolen with perfect impunity by any sneaking rascal. Many times have I named a new fruit or flower and before a stock could be produced some horticultural pirate had either appropriated the name, using it on some old, well-known or inferior variety or stealing the plant and introducing it as their own, or offering a big stock as soon as the originator commences to advertise the new variety.[131]

Now that pricing or any other private strategy seemed increasingly ineffective, nurserymen began in the 1870s, with mounting intensity from the 1880s, to call for assistance from government, notably through patent and trademark law, in safeguarding what they now commonly called the 'rights of originators'. However, patents on plants were foreclosed by the 1889 ruling in *Ex Parte Latimer*; Commissioner Hall had said there explicitly that it would be 'unreasonable and impossible' to allow patents 'upon the trees of the forest and the plants of the earth'. Well into the twentieth century the Commissioner's decision was not cited in court

[129] Bull to P[atrick] Barry (6 March 1854) Box 1, folder 14; 'Agreement between EW Bull and Hovey & Co' (4 December 1854) Box 2, folder 23; 'John W Curtis to Bull' (2 May 1859); 'Joseph Breck & Sons to Bull' (11 March 1857) Box 1, folder 13; EWB, 'The Concord Grape', Sales circular (March 1859) Special Collections, Concord Library, Broadsides; Schofield (n 39) 13.

[130] Jacob Moore, 'Plea of the Originator' (1900) 8 *National Nurseryman* 5, 58.

[131] 'Burbank to Jacob Moore' (4 May 1898) published in *Green's Fruit Grower* (June 1898), clipping in Luther Burbank Papers, Luther Burbank Home and Gardens, Archives, Santa Rosa, CA, Scrapbooks, vol 2, 45. See also 'Jacob Moore to Chas A Green' (20 April 1898); 'Protection for Fruit Evolvers', editorial, *California Fruit Grower* (nd); 'Moore to Peter Gideon' (nd), *Green's Fruit Grower*, Scrapbooks, vol 2, 44, 47, 115.

decisions on the patentability of natural products, but it did figure in the thinking of leading nurserymen.[132] Fruit innovators thus pinned their hopes on trademarks, tacitly assuming that the mark would not only protect the name of the novel plant or tree, but also secure to the originator the exclusive right to the living organism itself and to its propagation.

However, that assumption was severely undercut in 1895 by the ruling of a federal Appeals Court in the case of *Hoyt and Others v JT Lovett Co.* James Hoyt and Edwin Hoyt, nurserymen in Connecticut, had sued the JT Lovett Nursery in New Jersey for selling a grape that had been found in the Green Mountains in Vermont. The Hoyts believed they had bought the grape wood with exclusive rights and they had trademarked it as the 'Green Mountain Grape'. The Court found against the Hoyts partly on grounds that certain facts in the case contradicted the tenets of trademark law as it had been judicially interpreted. However, its decision also addressed the scope of trademark protection for living products.[133]

Apparently, Lovett's lawyer had raised the issue, contending, in the words of the Court, 'that the protection of a trade-mark cannot be obtained for an organic article which, by the law of its nature, is reproductive, and derives its chief value from its innate vital powers, independently of the care, management, or ingenuity of man'. The Court, while noting that the question was 'novel and unprecedented', agreed:

> The Hoyts did not make the Green Mountain vine, nor, strictly speaking, did they produce it. It grew out of the earth, was fashioned by nature, and endowed with powers and qualities which no human ingenuity or skill could create or imitate. If such protection as that now claimed by the complainants was allowed, a breeder of cattle could with equal propriety and reason demand like protection for the natural increase of his herd. In every aspect such claims would seem to be impracticable and inequitable.[134]

Over the course of the nineteenth century, the seed and horticultural enterprise had come to place a premium on protecting brand-named novelties as such. By the end of the century, that effort had generated the aim of protecting the

[132] *Le Roy v Tatham* (n 28); *Ex Parte Latimer* (n 28); Christopher Beauchamp, 'Patenting Nature : A Problem of History,' 16 *Stan. Tech. L. Rev.* 257 (2013), 273-276.
[133] *Hoyt and Others v JT Lovett Co* 71 F 173 Circuit Court of Appeals, Third Circuit (3 December 1895).
[134] ibid.

intellectual property in the seeds, trees, vines, and flowers that the brands represented. Landreth's and the Hoyts' resort to the new trademark law was emblematic of the drive, then emerging, towards the protection of intellectual property by multiple means, but especially through the law, in the material objects of the living world.

7

Brands Matter

Nature, Economy, and the Gift

Annalisa Colombino and Paolo Palladino[*]

Introduction

In this chapter, we propose that the relationship between intellectual property right and the appropriation of nature is best understood by shifting the focus of attention from production to the consumption of commodified organic matter, proposing also that the eating of meat offers an instructive site of enquiry. The analysis moves from diverging accounts of the transformations wrought by the contemporary appropriation of nature to their shared presuppositions about political economy. We argue for a shift from Marx to Mauss. As a result, we suggest, obligation displaces exploitation as the pivotal relationship around which current understanding of intellectual property rights and the appropriation of nature might productively be recast.

Contemporary modes of appropriating organic matter and the development of intellectual property rights are closely intertwined. As Birch and Tyfield have argued, however, the historical significance of this relationship stems from financial investment in the promise of transformation, rather than the matter transformed, thus raising questions about the proliferation of references to the nature of the matter involved, ranging from 'biotechnology' to 'bioeconomy' and 'biocapital'.[1] While we think that there is much merit to the argument, the allure of bioeconomy also seems inseparable from the reproductive capacities of organic matter itself. Indeed, if one were to bring into the conversation the consumer who looks to the products of biotechnology to transform themselves and their relations with others the focus would return to the materiality of the bioeconomy. We are then attracted to Haraway's more materially grounded argument that there is something distinctive about the bioeconomy and that this stems from the encounter between different organic species. From a theoretical standpoint, the resultant notion of

[*] We would like to thank Oron Catts and Ionat Zurr, as well as Heide Bruckner, Maan Barua, Petr Jehlicka, and Teresa Young, for their help in developing the argument advanced in this chapter.

[1] Kean Birch and David Tyfield, 'Theorizing the Bioeconomy: Biovalue, Biocapital, Bioeconomics or . . . What?' (2013) 38(3) *Science, Technology and Human Values* 299.

Annalisa Colombino and Paolo Palladino, *Brands Matter* In: *Intellectual Property and the Design of Nature.* Edited by: Jose Bellido and Brad Sherman, Oxford University Press.
DOI: 10.1093/oso/9780192864406.003.0007

'encounter value' has helped greatly to better understand how Marx's labour theory of value might be extended to the appropriation of nature and in a way that would appear to overcome its anthropocentrism.[2] It also seems to us, however, that this notion does not in fact overcome an anthropocentric understanding of economic relations. This, we suggest, might lend weight to Birch and Tyfield's further claim that much of the literature on the bioeconomy conflates moral and economic considerations, but we argue instead that this is precisely the site where intellectual property right and the contemporary appropriation of nature can be fruitfully rethought.[3]

The eating of meat as a visceral encounter with the complexities of the world is the terrain on which our enterprise unfolds.[4] While the attention devoted today to the development of synthetic meat clearly illustrates the operation of the bioeconomy, even in its more conventional guises meat often arrives on the plate as a branded product that is protected by a variety of trademarks referring to either history or place of origin. Trademarks are ubiquitous and are the means through which intellectual property rights insinuate themselves and permeate everyday life, attached more or less visibly to most, if not all, of the commodities that sustain our material existence, connecting producers, ourselves, and our imagination in very complicated ways.[5] Partaking in eating meat, or not, as the case may be, involves

[2] Donna J Haraway, *When Species Meet* (University of Minnesota Press 2007).

[3] In what follows, we work with and against the distinction between human, animal, and stone, which Heidegger employed to articulate humans' supposedly distinctive capacity to imagine things as being otherwise than they are; that is, the capacity to engage in 'worlding'; see Matthew Calarco, 'Heidegger's Zoontology' in Matthew Calarco and Peter Atterton (eds), *Animal Philosophy: Essential Readings in Continental Philosophy* (Continuum 2004) 18. Here, Ingold's extension of worlding to the stone is mobilized to position the animal at the centre and both the stone and the human at the polar extremes, thus problematizing not so much the notion of worlding, but rather the kinds of worlding to which one might aspire; Tim Ingold, 'Materials Against Materiality' (2007) 14(1) *Archaeological Dialogues* 1. Such reframing seeks to test some of the most deeply embedded presuppositions about humanity's place in the world; see Alain R Pottage, 'Introduction: The Fabrication of Persons and Things' in Alain R Pottage and Martha W Mundy (eds), *Law, Anthropology, and the Constitution of the Social: Making Persons and Things* (Cambridge University Press 2004) 1; and Yan Thomas, 'Res Religiosae: On the Categories of Religion and Commerce' in Alain R Pottage and Martha W Mundy (eds), *Law, Anthropology, and the Constitution of the Social: Making Persons and Things* (Cambridge University Press 2004) 1, 40.

[4] The complexity of all that meat involves is conveyed very powerfully in the Wachowski brothers' *The Matrix* (1999), in the scene where Cypher agrees to betray Zion and meat stands ironically for the reality of the world and the subject's relation to such reality; see also Sushmita Chatterjee and Banu Subramaniam, 'Introduction: How to Think with Meat' in S Chatterjee and B Subramaniam (eds), *Meat! A Transnational Analysis* (Duke University Press 2021) 1.

[5] For an overview on how the meaning of branding originates in the practice of marking bodies of livestock, slaves, or criminals to signify ownerships see Andy Pike, *Origination: The Geographies of Brands and Branding* (John Wiley & Sons 2015) 4. The complexity of branding strategies is evinced by the way in which corporate ventures are today financed on the promise that they will revolutionize the agro-alimentary production system by marketing edible protein that, in every imaginable regard, looks like meat, but is not meat. While these ventures' strategies invite potential consumers to imagine a product that is wholly compatible with their chosen lifestyle, be it vegan or dedicated to environmentally sustainable consumption, they cannot do so except by referring to the animal origins of the thing called 'meat'. For an important account of the interplay between branding and the bodies from which meat is carved in the production of value see Nicole Shukin, *Animal Capital: Rendering Life in Biopolitical Times* (University of Minnesota Press 2009).

complex negotiations about who and what we are that are not readily reduced to a matter of economic exchange. Indeed, it is this very complexity that led 'The Tissue Culture & Art Project' to turn to synthetic meat to 'bring into question deep rooted perceptions of life and identity, concepts of self, and the position of the human in regard to other living beings and the environment'.[6]

Figure 7.1 'Tissue Engineered Steak No.1' 2000, A study for 'Disembodied Cuisine'. Artists: The Tissue Culture & Art Project (Oron Catts and Ionat Zurr). Medium: Prenatal sheep skeletal muscle and degradable PGA polymer scaffold. Date: 2000–2001.

Part of Oron Catts and Ionat Zurr's Research Fellowship in the Tissue Engineering and Organ Fabrication Laboratory, Harvard Medical School, available at https://tcaproject.net/ (accessed 28 July 2022).

This leads us to reconsider the notion of encounter value. The importance of this notion, we argue, lies in its oscillation between moral and economic perspectives, and the attempt to hold on to a Marxian understanding of value limits its utility. Simply put, we regard the production of value as involving affective work in crafting both ourselves and our relations with others, including non-human animals, and we disagree that Marxian analyses can account for these relations. Marx,

[6] 'The Tissue Culture & Art Project' https://tcaproject.net/about/ (accessed 28 July 2022).

however, is not the sole theoretical resource to rethink economic relationships between human and non-human animals. Although our argument turns to Mauss, one could equally well turn to Weber, who once wrote that:

> Insofar as the behavior of animals is subjectively understandable it would be theoretically possible to formulate a sociology of the relations of men [sic] to animals, both domestic and wild. Thus, many animals 'understand' commands, anger, love, hostility, and react to them in ways which are evidently often by no means purely instinctive and mechanical and in some sense both consciously meaningful and affected by experience.[7]

We propose that current debates over the contemporary appropriation of nature may benefit from a shift in attention away from Marx and processes of production, to focus instead on acts and practices of consumption, as viewed through Mauss' understanding of the gift as conceptually prior to exchange.[8] This has important implications for any understanding of the appropriation of nature and intellectual property right, which we reconsider by attending to practices of commoning and usufruct. Importantly, it is not our intention to articulate the details of any alternative understanding of the appropriation of nature and intellectual property right. It is instead to highlight the contingency of the present configuration and to point to promising sites of enquiry into contemporary experiments in reframing the relationship. This we do by drawing on empirical research on the Piemontese breed of cattle in Piedmont, on attitudes towards eating meat among consumers in Styria, and on the development of new relations between sheep, shepherds, and land use in Catalonia.[9]

[7] Max Weber, *The Theory of Social and Economic Organization* (Free Press 1947) 104; see also Bob Carter and Nickie Charles, 'The Animal Challenge to Sociology' (2018) 21(1) *European Journal of Social Theory* 79.

[8] Marcel Mauss, *The Gift: The Form and Reason for Exchange in Archaic Societies* (Routledge 2002).

[9] Although we draw on very specific and situated examples, our mode of engagement with the relationship between intellectual property right and the appropriation of nature has been shaped by a reading of Foucault, particularly 'Nietzsche, Genealogy, History' in Donald Bouchard (ed) *Language, Counter-Memory, Practice: Selected Essays and Interviews by Michel Foucault* (Cornell University Press 1977) 139. Furtrhermore, our approach to rethinking the economy is indebted to Bataille's reading of Mauss (n 8), and his understanding of 'general economy', which involves criticism of all forms of 'restricted economy', including Marx's labour theory of value; see Georges Bataille, *The Accursed Share: An Essay on General Economy* (Zone Books 1988). As such, our approach does not seek to engage with normative definitions of the bioeconomy, such as those emerging, for example, from within the European Union, but to articulate a more abstract and general understanding of the appropriation of nature. This serves to bring to the fore common assumptions about how more concrete problems are approached and how we might think about them outside normative frames of reference such as those proposed by the likes of the the European Union.

Intellectual Property Right, Financialization, and Embodied Consumption

The contemporary appropriation and commodification of biological resources, arguably from *Diamond v Chakrabarty* onwards, are the subject of wide-ranging critical enquiry.[10] Intellectual property right is, however, much more than just an operating device of the contemporary capitalist economy among others.[11] It is instead involved centrally in the appropriation of nature by facilitating dematerialization and the removal of economic relations from the contingencies of affect and spatio-temporal location. At the same time, such dematerialization also finds its limit in contemporary forms of consumption that are tied to affect and spatio-temporal location. What follows begins to explore the contours of this difficulty.

Much of the literature on the contemporary appropriation of nature suggests that the extraction of value from biological resources is so distinctive as to merit its own label, the bioeconomy. Drawing on autonomist Marxism, Birch and Tyfield observe that the productive capacities of living organisms have been exploited throughout the historical development of capitalism and that more recent manipulations at the molecular level introduce no qualitative break.[12] It is cognitive labour, aided by intellectual property right and financial speculation on the promise of its fruits, that produces value. Copyright has long been fundamental to the operation of capital, by enabling property and the production of value through the reproduction of the object appropriated, but contemporary intellectual property right differs insofar as it seeks to secure property and right of reproduction over processes rather than products.[13] This contributes greatly to broader dynamics

[10] *Diamond v Chakrabarty* 447 US 303 (1980). While the historical conditions of possibility for the extension of intellectual property right to encompass living organisms are discussed usefully in Melinda Cooper, *Life as Surplus: Biotechnology and Capitalism in the Neoliberal Era* (University of Washington Press 2008), the relationships between living substance, ownership, and law have long been intertwined, and this is important to any critical consideration of property and its limits; see Yan Thomas, 'Imago Naturae. Note sur l'Institutionnalité de la Nature à Rome' in *Théologie et Droit dans la Science Politique de l'État Moderne. Actes de la Table Ronde de Rome* (12–14 Novembre 1987) (École Française de Rome 1991) 201.

[11] Given the manifold ways in which intellectual property is entangled in the operation of the contemporary economy, it can be regarded usefully as a *dispositif*, the Foucauldian collection of physical, institutional, administrative mechanisms, and forms of knowledge that secure and maintain the exercise of power; see Michel Foucault, 'The Confession of the Flesh' in Colin Gordon (ed), *Power/Knowledge: Selected Interviews and Other Writings* (Pantheon 1980) 194. Consequently, we employ the term 'intellectual property right', rather than its plural, 'intellectual property rights'.

[12] Autonomists emphasize the ability of the working class to force changes to the organization of the capitalist economic system independently of state, party, or trade union. In so doing, they expand participation in class struggle beyond the confines of wage-earning collectives, to encompass all forms of unwaged work. Hardt and Negri further articulate this expansion by developing the concept of 'multitude', aiming thus to encompass all forms of life previously excluded from the more general struggle of the oppressed; see, most recently, Michael Hardt and Antonio Negri, *Assembly* (Oxford University Press 2017).

[13] On the history of copyright and the appropriation of organic matter see Jean-Paul Gaudillière and Daniel J Kevles, 'Introduction' in Jean-Paul Gaudillière, Daniel J Kevles, and Hans-Jörg Rheinberger (eds), *Living Properties: Making Knowledge and Controlling Ownership in the History of Biology* (Max

of dematerialization. Indeed, Birch and Tyfield also draw on autonomist analyses of the role that financial markets play in the evolution of the contemporary economy.[14] Autonomists argue that in the contemporary, post-industrial economy, profit is generated by exploiting the labour of the 'general intellect' and the extraction of surplus value from the cultivation of consumers' attachment to particular brands, both of which are then turned into shares on financial markets.[15] In this context, profit no longer depends on the exchange of material commodities, but on affective relationships. Investment of affect is not only what the worker is required to employ in delivering the services for which they are paid, but is also what brands try to elicit from potential consumers. In other words, the creation of value rests on corporate capacity to connect affectively with both consumers and employees, by strengthening brand recognition and corporate culture. Such capacity, in turn, depends on how well corporations connect with and enrol consumers in both processes of innovation and the enhancement of corporate reputation on financial markets. Viewed from this vantage point, the principal driver of the bioeconomy is, as Birch and Tyfield propose, corporate speculation on the promise of technological development, rather than the materiality of the commodity itself.

This said, Birch and Tyfield's argument also rests on Morini and Fumagalli's more specific reflections on the emergence of the bioeconomy, whereby value is created by appropriating the affective work invested in crafting ourselves and our relations to others, including in relation to decisions about what to consume.[16] Our own reading of the same text leads us to observe how, just as with many other discussions of the contemporary transformation of labour, the relationship between producer and consumer is too readily detached from the materiality of bodies and material cultures that have long sustained the political appeal of the autonomist perspective. The inextricable connection between formative notions such as 'more work for mother' and the role of material technologies developed supposedly to relieve the tedium of housework is lost.[17] It seems evident to us that, despite the

Planck Institute for the History of Science 2009) 1. The issue of historical periodization is discussed helpfully in Philip Mirowski and Esther-Mirjam Sent, 'The Commercialization of Science and the Response of STS' in Edward J Hackett and others (eds), *The Handbook of Science and Technology Studies* (3rd edn, MIT Press 2008) 635, and, more generally, in Fabienne Orsi and Benjamin Coriat, 'The New Role and Status of Intellectual Property Rights in Contemporary Capitalism' (2006) 10(2) *Competition & Change*, 162.

[14] See Christian Marazzi, *The Violence of Financial Capitalism* (MIT Press 2011).

[15] Historically, the general intellect is the knowledge that the working class generates in the totality of its existence. Autonomists argue that, today, value is extracted from the activities of networked consumers by transforming general intellect into collective, unpaid work. The contemporary intellectual property regime secures and regulates such appropriation of human understanding. On the concept of 'general intellect' see Paolo Virno, 'Notes on the General Intellect' in Saree Makdisi, Cesare Casarino, and Rebecca Karl (eds), *Marxism beyond Marxism* (Routledge 1996) 265.

[16] See Cristina Morini and Andrea Fumagalli, 'Life Put to Work: Towards a Life Theory of Value' (2010) 10(3–4) *Ephemera* 234.

[17] The phrase 'more work for mother' is borrowed from Ruth Schwartz Cowan, *More Work for Mother: The Ironies of Household Technology from the Open Hearth to the Microwave* (Basic Books

dematerializing impulses of contemporary capitalism, including its investments in the appropriation of nature, the credibility of its speculative ventures, if not the very possibility of resistance, rests on the circulation and use of commodities. For example, Italy is today a site of diverse experiments in agricultural production, food consumption, and participatory democracy. Cooperative purchasing groups such as the Gruppi di Acquisto Solidale ('communal purchasing groups') illustrate how consumers can sometimes become conscious of their consumption and act as a class confronting its exploitation by challenging modes of ownership, production, and distribution of food.[18] Not only is eating one of the principal sites of encounter between consumers and the products of the contemporary bioeconomy, but it also discloses the limitations of the framing of contemporary labour as immaterial. Such framing overlooks the conceptual implications of situations such as eating, where there is the fullest, co-constitutive, and reciprocal relationship between bodies and networks of consumption. At the very least, the failure to explore the notion that 'der Mensch ist was er isst' ('Man is what he eats'), Feuerbach's playful pun on humans being essentially what they eat leaves the ambitions of the autonomist perspective to encompass all aspects of social existence unfulfilled.

In sum, while the critique of thinking about the contemporary appropriation of nature as blind to the more general, dematerializing tendencies of contemporary financial capital is very persuasive, we also suggest that this underestimates the importance of the materiality and agency of bodily, if not visceral, existence, without which investment in the bioeconomy and the intellectual property regimes that sustain it would cease to make sense.[19] If there is nothing material about the contemporary economy, only financial speculations on the future value of promises and dreams realized, materiality returns as the very stuff that sustains these dreams. This more complex understanding of who or what actors are involved in the articulation of the contemporary appropriation of nature can be examined very fruitfully by focusing on eating meat and the non-human animals from whom it is carved.

1985). While Cowan's focus on women and their material conditions of existence exemplifies the concerns of second-wave feminism, the contrast with Morini and Fumagalli's more abstract understanding of affective labour draws attention to a cognitivist drift within autonomism whereby analyses such as Marazzi's raise questions about the relationship between general intellect and embodiment. Marazzi's understanding of 'bare life' suggests that the body is a wholly passive site where the violence of capitalism is inscribed, rather than the site of potential to be otherwise; see Marazzi (n 14) 39, 42.

[18] Cristina Grasseni, 'Direct Food Provisioning: Collective Food Procurement' in JK Gibson-Graham and Kelly Dombroski (eds), *The Handbook of Diverse Economies* (Edward Elgar Publishing 2020) 223; see also Kevin St Martin, Gerda Roelvink, and JK Gibson-Graham, 'Introduction: An Economic Politics for Our Times' in K St Martin, G Roelvink, and JK Gibson-Graham (eds), *Making Other Worlds Possible: Performing Diverse Economies* (University of Minnesota Press 2015) 1.

[19] For an analysis of how eating may be viewed as a visceral experience that shows how 'food is never ingested by itself' see Allison Hayes-Conroy and Jessica Hayes-Conroy, 'Visceral Difference: Variations in Feeling (Slow) Food' (2010) 42 *Environment and Planning A*. 2956.

Rethinking Nature, Culture, and the Production of Value

The work of rethinking the relationship between the contemporary appropriation of nature and intellectual property right begins by first considering the merits and limitations of Haraway's recasting of Marx's labour theory of value. The focus then turns to animal husbandry as the site where to begin crafting an alternative perspective on human entanglement with non-human animals and the production of value that is more attuned to Mauss' understanding of the social bond.

A long-standing critic of the separation of nature and culture, Haraway responds to Marx's understanding of value as stemming from use and exchange, aiming to forge a definition that allows for a more porous relationship between the two. Haraway introduces the notion of 'lively commodity' to bring into the analysis how the bioeconomy rests ultimately on the exploitation of non-human animal organisms and hence always entails an encounter between species. Haraway labels the value attached to this relationship 'encounter value'. To better understand what is at stake in Haraway's proposition, especially in relation to Marx, it is helpful to consider Franklin's analysis of the contemporary isolation and mobilization of the organism's reproductive capacities.[20] Franklin observes how wealth is today produced in a manner very similar to that which Marx once attributed to agriculture, but Franklin also maintains that Marx failed to appreciate the full importance of reproduction to the origin of capital. The productive circuit upon which the accumulation of agricultural capital rests is inseparable from the reproductive capacities of the biological organism and it is this very capacity that contemporary capital exploits. In other words, the present situation highlights how reproduction is the ultimate source of value and what enables capital. The site of Franklin's critique of Marx is, however, the laboratory, and so the critique neglects the many other sites where reproduction is put to work today. Haraway arguably expands the conceptual vocabulary, adding encounter to use and exchange as sources of value, and does so in a way that extends the analysis of the contemporary appropriation of nature outwith the laboratory.[21]

There still remains, however, a sense in which Birch and Tyfield are right to suggest that, more often than not, scholarly engagement with the distinctiveness of

[20] Sarah Franklin, *Dolly Mixtures: The Remaking of Genealogy* (Duke University Press 2007).

[21] Barua disputes this reading of Haraway, preferring to cast encounter value as extending the labour theory of value to encompass the lives of non-human animals; Maan Barua, 'Lively Commodities and Encounter Value' (2017) 34(4) *Environment and Planning D: Society and Space* 725. For a further discussion of Marxism and the conceptual difficulties it confronts when it comes to relations between human and non-human animals see Massimo Filippi, Michael Hardt, and Marco Maurizi, *Altre Specie di Politica* (Mimesis 2016). Significantly, Hardt and Negri's notion of the multitude, which aims to encompass all forms of life, should allow for the inclusion of non-human animals. Their formative reading of Spinoza is, however, often at odds with more materialist alternatives, most notably Deleuze's, thus allowing little room for any great attention to relations between human and non-human animals. See also Susan Ruddick, 'The Politics of Affect: Spinoza in the Work of Negri and Deleuze' (2010) 27(4) *Theory, Culture & Society* 21.

the bioeconomy, which the notions of lively commodity and encounter value seek to capture, blurs, if it does not confuse, boundaries between moral and economic considerations.

Firstly, as Birch and Tyfield have argued, there is nothing obviously lively about the materials nourishing the bioeconomy, including the reproductive capacities fuelling its speculative dynamics, because these are not actualized through any intrinsic property, but through human intellectual labour. At best, then, there is an imaginative leap linking inert organic materiality and the organism or its vital capacity, such as in branding and labelling as PGI (Protected Geographical Indication), which forges links between product, life, and place, or the 'happy' and 'organic' attributions to meat products.[22] Agency remains with the embedding of human imagination into what is otherwise a conventional economic exchange. There simply is no difference between this situation and other economies that capitalize on the production and circulation of brands. From this perspective, encounter value is an unnecessary concept.

Secondly, in strictly Marxian terms, production exists beyond questions of justice or ethics, beyond questions of morality, except where the bodies put to work resist and this resistance is acknowledged as such. Production only becomes a matter of justice and ethics once work and life are separated, and workers find themselves having to contest the expropriation of their productive power. When it comes to eating meat, questions of justice or ethics arise when consumers reject the object of consumption because its production ignores the plight of the animals transformed. Arguments may ensue as to what animals want and how this might be known, which are fundamentally questions of justice and ethics. While the answer to these questions might challenge human profit-making and could bring economic production to a halt, there is no animal labour involved or any animal revendication of the expropriation suffered.[23]

In the light of these considerations, the notions of lively commodity and encounter value must be regarded as moral revendications on behalf of non-human animals and other organic species exploited in the process of appropriating and commodifying nature, so diverging from Marx's original understanding of work and labour. These otherwise important notions might even be regarded as involving some form of anthropomorphism, so defeating the ambition to overcome the restrictions imposed by the separation and distinction between nature and culture. It may be, however, that the problem lies with the insistence on a Marxian reading of

[22] See Pike (n 5).

[23] While Hribal and others have drawn attention to phenomena resembling labourers' resistance to exploitation, these do not meet the requirement of consciousness and class formation critical to Marxian analyses of labour; see Jason Hribal, *Fear of the Animal Planet: The Hidden History of Animal Resistance* (AK Press 2011). Also, Dinesh Joseph Wadiwel 'The Working Day Animals, Capitalism, and Surplus Time' in Charlotte E Blattner, Kendra Coulter, and Will Kymlicka (eds), *Animal Labour: A New Frontier of Interspecies Justice?* (Oxford University Press 2019) 181; and Maan Barua, 'Animating Capital: Work, Commodities, Circulation' (2019) 43(4) *Progress in Human Geography* 650.

work and the creation of economic value. There may be other ways of articulating the conceptual utility of encounter value. We broach one possible alternative by turning to Porcher's critique of both industrial meat production and vegetarian responses to such production.[24]

Porcher offers a series of ethnographic reflections attentive to the lives of non-human animals, to the relations between these animals and those who tend to them, from birth to death, and to the consumers who would reject the forms of life leading to the slaughterhouse. The resultant diagnosis is that animal husbandry has been humanity's principal form of life with non-human animals, but that it is currently under threat. The threat to this form of life stems not just from industrialized production, but also from vegetarian responses such as the search for forms of meat consumption that do not involve the killing of non-human animals. Yet, as Porcher observes, husbandry is what enables not just the lives of the farmers involved in the practice, but also the lives of the non-human animals on which the activity depends, so much so that, were husbandry to disappear, so would the non-human animals for whom vegetarians claim to care. From this point of view, the emergence of synthetic meat intimates that 'factory farming' and 'animal rights activism' are not nearly as opposed as might be imagined and that the 'de facto alliance of industrialists and animal rights activists is the result of a common vision of modernity as a wrenching away from nature'.[25] Porcher then seeks to articulate an understanding of husbandry that will answer the challenge that the emergence of synthetic meat encapsulates. To this end, Porcher turns to Mauss' account of sociality as rooted in the exchange of gifts to displace Marx's focus on labour, because, as observed earlier, it is very unclear how this understanding of work can be extended to non-human animals.[26] Porcher also thinks that Marx provides an account of work that is insufficient to understand the complex structures of feeling involved in our relationship to the working lives of animals, human and otherwise.[27] As a result, Porcher proposes that Mauss provides a more useful framework to explain why animal husbandry is in fact an ethical form of life, even where it ultimately involves the slaughter of the animals tended, seeking thus to bypass the

[24] Jocelyne Porcher, *The Ethics of Animal Labour: A Collaborative Utopia* (Palgrave MacMillan 2017).

[25] ibid 99.

[26] Mauss' understanding of the gift and reciprocity allows for encounters that cross boundaries of species, as opposed to use and exchange value, which are clearly anthropocentric concepts. As a result, *The Gift* is sometimes said to have dealt a blow to the entire enterprise of anthropology from which it has never fully recovered. As Ingold puts it, Mauss succeeded in demonstrating the possibility of interpenetration as a durable condition by showing how the gift given is incorporated into the very being of the other, and yet remains fully conjoined to the being of the gift-giver; Tim Ingold, 'On Human Correspondence' (2017) 23(1) *Journal of the Royal Anthropological Institute* 2. True to this understanding, Porcher opens the possibility of an encounter that is meaningful to the other-than-human participants.

[27] To explore the question of how domestic animals work, Porcher extends to non-human animals the conceptual framework drawn from the psychodynamics of work articulated by Dejours, which focuses on understanding work as a collective, intelligent achievement and experience.

language of exploitation and its oversimplifications of our relationship to animal life, both human and otherwise.[28] Porcher argues that the slaughtered non-human animal should be regarded as enabling the continuation of the life shared with humans by donating its own. Citing Caillé, Porcher writes that 'the tie [between the human and the non-human] means more than the commodity ... the value of the tie is of more importance than the value of the usage and the value of the exchange'.[29] Put differently, the affective ties between human and non-human animals that are built up over the course of working lives lived together, from birth to death, are a source of value that exceeds the separation of work and life on which Marx's labour theory of value is predicated.

One consequence of the shift from Marx to Mauss is a convergence between Porcher's argument about animal husbandry and the complexities involved in eating meat that Bruckner's interviews with 'conscientious meat consumers' have disclosed.[30] If Porcher concludes that the affective ties between human and non-human animals established over the course of working lives lived together, from birth to death, are the true source of value, Bruckner's interviews disclose an equally complex relationship to the meat eaten. There is a complex interplay of connection and disconnection between consumers and both the non-human animals slaughtered and the forms of life associated with these animals up to their death. This is very different to the moral and material purity that industrial producers of synthetic meat and animal rights activists seek to advance. Following Porcher's example, the question becomes how to theorize this complex understanding of eating meat, and how to do so in a way that responds to the questions about the generation of value that the appropriation of nature poses. We explore this question by turning to a debate between Esposito and Nancy over the Eucharist and the meaning of embodiment, which invites us to read Porcher's argument as drawing attention to the flesh and the complexities of the relationship between what we consume and who we are.[31]

[28] Scholars in the field of critical animal studies argue that there is no difference between husbandry and industrial production, and that humanity's relationship to the animal world is so antagonistic that, as Wadiwel puts it, it is best characterized as a 'war against animals'; Dinesh Joseph Wadiwel, *The War Against Animals* (Brill 2015).

[29] Porcher (n 24) 104.

[30] Heide K Bruckner, 'Beyond Happy Meat: Body Mapping (Dis)connections to Animals in Alternative Food Networks' (2018) 50(3) *Area* 322; Heide K Bruckner, Annalisa Colombino, and Ulrich Ermann, 'Naturecultures and the Affective (Dis)entanglements of Happy Meat' (2019) 36(1) *Agriculture and Human Values* 35.

[31] Roberto Esposito and Jean-Luc Nancy, 'Dialogo sulla Filosofia a Venire' in Jean-Luc Nancy, *Essere Singolare Plurale* (Einaudi 2001) vii; see also Thomas F Tierney, 'Roberto Esposito's "Affirmative Biopolitics" and the Gift' (2016) 33(2) *Theory, Culture & Society* 53.

From Eating Meat as Empirical Fact to Meat as Metaphor

As Bruckner observes, when we examine how consumers speak about their choices to eat locally as opposed to industrially produced meat, we discover an understanding of eating as not just a metabolic process, but as also involving a physiological connection with other forms of life and the moral order in which these other lives unfold. As one participant in Bruckner's project put it:

> I think about animals when I'm eating meat, how they lived, how they were treated ... if they suffered, or if they had a good life, we eat that, too. This is something you can't see through labels, you can't see the big picture. The whole interconnection between the animal and you, it becomes a part of you when you eat.

In other words, in the moment of eating, an act of appropriation takes place, but, at the same time, the condition of possibility for such appropriation is the blurring of the separation between the subject of appropriation and the object appropriated. Value, according to Haraway's encounter theory, emerges where there are two separate living bodies, but their encounter is not as symmetrical as is required by a situation where the separation is as blurred as occurs in eating. Eating involves one organic body incorporating another, but how one should think about this is complicated. The incorporation could be regarded as a quantitative subtraction leading from two bodies to one, but also as a qualitative transformation producing a third body. In other words, eating invites consideration of the encounter between two bodies as producing a third and wholly new one, even perhaps that of Bruckner's 'conscientious consumer'. This connection, we suggest, moves the exploration from Porcher's turn to Mauss and the economy of the gift to Esposito and Nancy's debate over the Eucharist. Their debate over the relationship between meat, flesh, and the founding of the community enables a more-than-human understanding of the flesh as bringing together human and non-human animals in a pre-discursive relation of commensality. This understanding points to ways of developing a more complex framing of the relationship between production, consumption, and our animal existence. It shifts the frame away from the dominant focus on exchange and the forms of exploitation involved in the commodity form. This dominant focus is inescapably anthropocentric, and so it is blind to that which differentiates the appropriation of nature from other forms of exploitation, namely our being entangled intimately and viscerally in the relationship between producer and object produced, between consumer and object consumed.

The Eucharist is the Christian, ritual commemoration of Christ's last supper before the crucifixion, at which he is said to have given his disciples bread and wine with the words 'this is my body' and 'this is my blood'. Christian orthodoxy understands the celebration as an earthly anticipation of the banquet that is to come with the realization of the Kingdom of God. In more secular terms, it is a symbolic exchange in which mundane things such as wine and bread acquire meaning and value beyond themselves, becoming symbols for the founding of a community. As Merleau-Ponty once noted, the common distinction between meat and flesh reflects how things always are more than themselves. In the Preface to the Italian edition of Nancy's *Being Singular Plural*, Esposito and Nancy engage in an extended argument over the exact relationship between these two terms and the Eucharist. Nancy is suspicious of the distinction between meat and the flesh because, in his view, the flesh is a discursive concept that captures and enframes the freedom of the primordial being-with-others. Esposito argues instead that the body is in fact an atomizing, historical configuration of the flesh, the figure for the very same primordial being-with-others. The flesh, according to Esposito, is the point where the body is no longer the integrity and interiority of our being who we are, but where we open onto others and onto that which we have always shared: the 'common'. As Esposito observes, in the incarnation, Christ transcends his divine nature and becomes something other than himself, and this is precisely why the concept has persisted beyond the end of the Christian religion. The incarnation touches on the question of the common in the most profound way, on our being as the 'flesh of the world'.[32]

In sum, if the flesh lies at the intersection of competing visions of the relationship between bodies and the common, the question is where humans stand in relation to the two opposing perspectives and how humans understand the consumption of meat. If the eating of meat triggers the discovery of new relations, the question is what kind of relations these are.

One might begin by asking what is on the figurative plate. One might answer that it is calories and protein, in the sense posited by some breeders of the Piemontese cattle, when they refer to its meat as containing 'fewer calories, less fat, and higher protein per ounce than beef from other breeds'.[33] Alternatively, one might answer that it is the encounter with the common, in the sense posited by other breeders when they refer to their association, La Granda, as engaged in the 'cultivation of the earth to produce the meat so as to create a virtuous, symbiotic food chain wherein everyone benefits the other: the earth, the animal, the human. One should not even overlook bacteria and their healthy role'.[34] In other words, eating can be understood as a metabolic function, or as a commensal and communitarian practice, which could be expanded to include the non-human animals eaten. It is in this last sense that we find the arguments over the Eucharist and the distinctions between body and flesh particularly resonant.

[32] Esposito and Nancy (n 31) xxvii (our translation).

[33] 'Certified Piedmontese Real Nebraska Beef' www.piedmontese.com (accessed 10 March 2021); see also Annalisa Colombino and Paolo Giaccaria, 'Breed Contra Beef: The Making of Piedmontese Cattle' in Jody Emel and Harvey Neo (eds), *Political Ecologies of Meat* (Routledge 2015) 161.

[34] 'La Granda' http://www.lagranda.it/turismo-del-gusto/ (accessed 10 March 2021).

We suggest that it is Esposito's account of the relationship between body and flesh that is closest to our understanding of commensalism. Agamben's imagery of the banquet on the Day of Judgement seems useful to capture the situation. On the occasion of this banquet, the righteous in the guise of human figures crowned with non-human heads, so marking the reconciliation of humanity with its animal nature, share the flesh of the Leviathan. The Leviathan could be regarded as being eaten or appropriated, but only by overlooking how, on the Day of Judgement, the law ceases to apply and to the extent that the violence of distinction, ownership, and incorporation is suspended. Agamben writes: 'Perhaps there is still a way in which living beings can sit at the messianic banquet of the righteous without taking on a historical task and without setting the anthropological machine into action.'[35] It must also be remembered, however, that every historical actualization of the common, be it commensal or otherwise, will take on the discursive form that leads Nancy to be suspicious of the flesh.

The difficulty involved in the process of historical actualization is instantiated by the ways in which the ideals that informed the revitalization of the Piemontese have fallen back into conventional and exploitative forms of agro-alimentary political economy. Specifically, the emergence of the Piemontese as an international gastronomic phenomenon is the result of tensions between two groups. One is led by ANABORAPI (National Association of Breeders of the Piemontese Bovine Breed) and COALVI (Consortium for the Protection of the Piemontese Breed), two breeders' associations supported by Piedmont's regional government. These organizations sought to frame the Piemontese as embedded in the region, aiming thus to create a more valuable local source of meat. The other group involved an alliance between La Granda, Slow Food, and Eataly.[36] This second alliance has instead sought to reframe the same Piemontese as a distinctive local product to be sold on metropolitan markets, focusing particularly on North America. This reframing has then led to the proliferation of different brands, ranging from the Vicciola, the Italian answer to Kobe beef, to North American Certified Piedmontese and Texas Piedmontese beef. These enterprises are sustained by a mostly transatlantic circulation of genetic material seeking to corner and capitalize on the qualities that a patented mutation of the myostatin gene lends to the meat.[37] In other words, regional and national public funding for ANABORAPI and COALVI seems to have proved most profitable to a small number of capitalist ventures operating primarily outside the confines of Piedmont region. The latter ventures are far more invested

[35] Giorgio Agamben, *The Open: Man and Animal* (Stanford University Press 2002) 92.

[36] Eataly is an international chain of food halls retailing Italian food specialties; see Annalisa Colombino, 'Becoming Eataly: The Magic of the Mall and the Magic of the Brand' in Ulrich Ermann and Klaus-Jürgen Hermanik (eds), *Branding the Nation, the Place, the Product* (Routledge 2018) 67.

[37] See also Annalisa Colombino and Paolo Giaccaria, 'Dead Liveness/Living Deadness: Thresholds of Non-Human Life and Death in Biocapitalism' (2016) 34(6) *Environment and Planning D: Society and Space* 1044.

in the potential of a more exclusive relation to the Piemontese's genetic constitution, duly tracked by different proprietary regimes, than in the common and its distinctive forms-of-life.[38]

In this understanding, then, the common exists in the oscillation between Esposito's hope and Nancy's suspicion of the flesh, between ANABORAPI, COALVI, and La Granda's original intention 'to create a virtuous, symbiotic food chain wherein everyone benefits the other' and the outcome of their operations, a highly mobile and profitable biological construct. The challenge is how to move from this understanding of the common back to the more general arguments over the appropriation of nature.

Gifts, Debts, and the Violence of Forgetting

Having grounded the philosophical and theological abstractions of Nancy and Esposito's debate, we now turn to their implications for economic theory. If the understanding of eating meat evoked thus far recollects Agamben's banquet, it is because it reconnects what has long been framed as separate: the meat, the flesh, and the body. The question then is how to assign an economic value adequate to the life surrendered. Some have tried to re-read Marx to develop such an answer, be it in the form of animal labour or encounter value, but this is not persuasive because it fails to recognize the founding violence that underpins Marx's understanding of value, namely the separation of work from life and the transformation of concrete into abstract labour, which can only be experienced by a conscious political subject. If the re-reading is to be effective, it needs to be framed in a way such that the understanding of the violence shifts onto the separation between the human and the animal. We propose to articulate such a framing by moving from debt to the violence of forgetting indebtedness.[39]

[38] This drift is consistent with Legendre's claim, in his genealogical investigations of the modern state and its juridical foundations, that contemporary liberal society has replaced the ritual of communion with the fusion of consumption; Pierre Legendre, *God in the Mirror: A Study of the Institution of Images: Lessons III* (Routledge 2018). The issue is, however, to understand what such fusion entails and what boundaries are left intact. As Pottage once suggested, Legendre shared in structuralist scepticism about Maussian understanding of exchange; Alain Pottage, 'Crime and Culture: The Relevance of the Psychoanalytical' (1992) 55(3) *Modern Law Review* 421.

[39] Some discussions of the gift and the founding of the community, important to understanding the contemporary appropriation of nature, have framed the gift as a sacrificial gesture; see Margaret Lock, *Twice Dead: Organ Transplants and the Reinvention of Death* (University of California Press 2001). The following discussion is closer to Bataille's reading of Mauss, whereby the sacrificial economy, which the gift inaugurates, is always at risk of becoming a restricted version of the more general and foundational economy of expenditure. Fascist rituals are the prime example. See Bataille (n 9). There can be no resolution of the tension inherent in the quest for subjectivity and sovereignty, and thus the defining issue becomes how to reconcile oneself with the cost of being oneself. Bataille sometimes addresses this issue by focusing on eating meat and becoming vegetarian.

As Grossberg, Hardin, and Palm observe in their analysis of valuation and the contemporary changing understanding of debt, Maussian theory of the gift can be understood as installing 'obligation' as the fundamental mode of existence.[40] From this point of view, obligation is no longer the moral condition presupposed by prevailing discussions of debt, but a precondition of social existence, and value—including use and exchange value— are historical constructs that draw upon and reconfigure this prior, generative mode of existence.[41] As Grossberg, Hardin, and Palm put it:

> For us, this structure of feeling of obligation can be understood as a multiplicity of invisible hands of mutual and collective organization, holding people together not merely in terms of rendering social the effects of the pursuit of individual self-interest but more as an active organizing of relationality, constituting the possibility of sociality itself. This multiplicity of invisible hands is the condition of possibility of various trajectories and apparatuses of value transformation.[42]

This understanding of obligation is consistent with Nancy and Esposito's understanding of existence as being-in-common, that is, a form of being beyond ethical or moral imperatives, so we are attracted to it as a resource for the articulation of a more persuasive conception of encounter value than Haraway's reliance on Marx. From our perspective, however, this understanding of obligation also suffers from a major limitation, namely that it restricts the bond to 'people'. Following Mauss, the gift exchange exceeds any boundaries between the human and the non-human, so that the restriction of obligation to people alone is not one that Mauss himself would have drawn. As Mauss says of the potlatch, the primordial congregation:

> [p]roduces an effect not only upon men [sic], who vie with one another in generosity, not only upon the things they pass on to one another or consume at it, not only upon the souls of the dead who are present and take part in it, and whose names have been assumed by men, but even upon nature.[43]

In other words, the bond is forged in exchanges that exceed any boundaries between either the living and the dead or the human and the non-human. We would therefore rephrase obligation as the condition of possibility for the emergence

[40] Lawrence Grossberg, Carolyn Hardin, and Michael Palm, 'Contributions to a Conjunctural Theory of Valuation' (2014) 26(3) *Rethinking Marxism* 306; see also Elettra Stimilli, *Debt and Guilt: A Political Philosophy* (Bloomsbury 2018).

[41] As Foucault once observed, the question of what constitutes value is by and large a historical one; see Michel Foucault, *The Order of Things: An Archaeology of the Human Sciences* (Vintage Press 1994).

[42] Grossberg, Hardin, and Palm (n 40) 318.

[43] Mauss (n 8) 18.

of diverse types of value, not only use value and exchange value, but also encounter value.

Having come through something comparable to Lewis Carroll's looking glass, use value and exchange value have always been regarded as referring to human productive activity and thus are anthropocentric. Encounter value aims to be less anthropocentric, but it also rests on an insufficient examination of the relationship between those involved in the encounter. The issue is most evident when Haraway engages with Deleuze's notion of 'becoming animal'.[44] As Haraway notes, Deleuze distinguishes between 'actual' organisms and the proliferative powers of life in its most amorphous 'molecular' form. Here the term 'molecular' is not employed in the sense intended by any distinctions between animal lives on the farm and configurations of life emerging from the experimental laboratory—both dealing with thoroughly ordered and codified 'molar' forms—but as a way of capturing the primordial state out of which 'actual' forms are forged. While Haraway is sceptical about Deleuze's distinction, the disagreement nonetheless draws attention to the possibility of a form of existence before the separation between human and non-human animals, and to Haraway's presumption of formed, separate organisms encountering each other. This raises another possible reading of encounter value. The state of debt that mutual dependence entails means that encounter value could be regarded as a form of valuation radically different from either use or exchange value. The notion of encounter value points to conditions of possibility for the emergence of use and exchange value and the inescapable violence involved in their emergence. It could then be said that all valuation involves a violence of separation and distinction. In Marx, the distinction between use and exchange value rests on a prior separation of work and life such that the worker finds, as Marx stated in the *Economic and Philosophical Manuscripts*:

> Not only that his [sic] labor becomes an object, an external existence, but that it exists outside him, independently, as something alien to him, and that it becomes a power on its own confronting him. It means that the life which he has conferred on the object confronts him as something hostile and alien.[45]

Viewed from this vantage point and paraphrasing Marx, the founding violence of bioeconomic structures is not the failure adequately to compensate the work that animals and nature more generally do for us. Following Porcher's critical disposition towards Marxian interpretations of human relations with non-human animals, it is instead the failure to acknowledge how the appropriation of nature

[44] Haraway (n 2) 29; see also Alain Beaulieu, 'The Status of Animality in Deleuze's Thought' (2011) 9(1–2) *Journal for Critical Animal Studies* 69.

[45] 'Estranged Labour' https://www.marxists.org/archive/marx/works/1844/manuscripts/labour.htm (accessed 10 March 2021).

involves life becoming an object, that is, an external existence and a power on its own confronting humanity. This rupture erases the inextinguishable debt that binds humans, animals, and all other forms of organic life.

In sum, if the appropriation of nature has generated great interest and debate, it is because it involves the semblance of separate subjects and objects involved in networks of use and exchange, but it also involves the consumption of ourselves and our shared modes of life, our animal existence.[46] It may be that the latter cannot be valued economically, but its ethical and political value is still important to the very possibility of contemporary modes of consumption, where the materiality of the commodities that are consumed matters in defining who and what we are, as in the choices made about eating meat or not. On this alternative understanding of valuation, obligation displaces exploitation as the pivotal existential relationship.

Commoning, Creative Commons, and Usufruct

We close our argument by offering an example of commoning and shared investment in the fruits of labour across the species, asking what this might mean for intellectual property right. We answer the question by proposing that usufruct displaces the notion of property underpinning intellectual property right, and that the 'creative commons' can be reimagined as a system of distributed usufruct.

Since Hardin's famous essay on 'the tragedy of the commons' was first written over half a century ago, it has proved profoundly influential in scholarly and policy-making debates over the management of natural resources.[47] In contemporary neoliberal economies, measures to forestall the exploitation of these resources to the detriment of present and future generations have entailed the enclosure of these resources and their management through public—private partnerships. Ostrom has, however, demonstrated that local communities have long been able to allocate natural resources in sustainable ways and without any recourse to either the market or the state.[48] More recently, Ostrom has inspired scholars such as Fournier to rethink the notion of the common and shift the focus onto processes of 'commoning'.

[46] Calarco, in a discussion of Deleuze's writings on Francis Bacon, argues that the flesh offers an understanding of human and non-human animals as caught up in a shared space of embodiment and exposure; Matthew Calarco, 'Identity, Difference, Indistinction' (2011) 11(2) *CR: The New Centennial Review* 41; see also Matthew Calarco, 'Being Toward Meat: Anthropocentrism, Indistinction, and Veganism' (2014) 38(4) *Dialectical Anthropology* 415. Thinking about eating as a visceral experience connecting us with the world closely resonates with this understanding of the flesh. If eating illuminates how we taste the vulnerability of the world, the eating of meat is a particularly troubling site because we bite into our existence as and with animals.

[47] Garrett Hardin, 'The Tragedy of the Commons' (1968) 162 *Science* 1243.

[48] Elinor Ostrom, *Governing the Commons: The Evolution of Institutions for Collective Action* (Cambridge University Press 1990). For an overview of the work inspired by Ostrom's research see Ismael Vaccaro and Oriol Beltran, 'What Do We Mean by "the Commons?" An Examination of Conceptual Blurring Over Time' (2019) 47(3) *Human Ecology* 331.

Thinking in terms of 'commoning' avoids transforming the commons into a primitive form of organization somehow lost to the present and focuses attention instead on the creative work involved in constructing alternative modes of managing shared resources.[49] This performative understanding implies that the commons are the product of participatory processes and entail both rights and obligations to one another, which can also bind humans and non-humans.[50] Understood in this way, commoning becomes useful to any re-examination of how contemporary social relations and practices might be mobilized to transform the world and make it otherwise. Yet, as the evolution of creative commons also suggests, it is difficult to imagine how the notion of commoning might be extended to the fruits of the general intellect. Creative commons has attempted to resist the inroads of privatization by devising a system of licences regulating the use and sharing of the works of those authors who choose to distribute and make their work freely available to the public, but it has only succeeded partially in securing the free sharing of knowledge, largely because this initiative is constrained by the presumption that there is no alternative to enclosure.[51] Prompted by Agamben's return to the institution of usufruct, however, we propose that a revised notion of this device, which extends it to immaterial forms of knowledge, might provide a way out of the impasse that intellectual property regimes present for any sharing and use of the common.[52]

Usufruct invests the property of things in a fictive person and then assigns temporary rights over the uses to which the things are put. It thus effectively sets the issue of ownership aside and focuses instead on protecting beneficiaries, but only so long as the substance of the things used is not altered or dissipated to the

[49] See Valérie Fournier, 'Commoning: On the Social Organisation of the Commons' (2013) 16(4) *M@n@gement* 433. In a review of the literature on the commons and commoning, Turner points to a primitivism in Ostrom's and others' arguments whereby the majority of examples are situated in an imagined Global South, blind to the complexities and hybridities of common holding. Turner refers to Fournier as exemplifying a more studied engagement with the process of securing common holding; Matthew D Turner, 'Political Ecology III: The Commons and Commoning' (2017) 41(6) *Progress in Human Geography* 1; see also Pierre Dardot and Christian Laval, *Common: On Revolution in the 21st Century* (Bloomsbury 2019).

[50] On more-than-human understating of commoning see Marta Nieto-Romero and others, 'Historical Commons as Sites of Transformation: A Critical Research Agenda to Study Human and More-Than-Human Communities' (2019) 107 *Geoforum* 113; see also JK Gibson-Graham, Ann Hill, and Lisa Law, 'Re-embedding Economies in Ecologies: Resilience Building in More Than Human Communities' (2016) 44(7) *Building Research & Information* 703.

[51] Hardt and Negri note the difficulty that some theorists of intellectual property rights confront when seeking to free their projects from the notion of property. See Hardt and Negri (n 12) 91, 310 n 17.

[52] In *The Highest Poverty*, Agamben examines monastic practices, chiefly Franciscan relations to ecclesiastic property, to further his exploration of what might constitute a form-of-life beyond the understanding of bio-political modes of governance; see Giorgio Agamben, *The Highest Poverty: Monastic Rules and Form-of-Life* (Stanford University Press 2013). Drawing on shared intellectual resources, namely Thomas's essay on usufruct and the slave's body, Monod considers instead how the relation between production and consumption might be redrawn by rethinking of goods-as-services and the bonds between producers and consumers; see Jean-Claude Monod, 'From Abuse to Usufruct' (2010) 1 *Esprit* 152; Yan Thomas, 'L "Usage" et les "Fruits" de l'Esclave' (1998) 7 *Enquête* 203. The history of usufruct is also considered very helpfully in Terence Ball, '"The Earth Belongs to the Living": Thomas Jefferson and the Problem of Intergenerational Relations' (2000) 9(2) *Environmental Politics* 61.

detriment of future beneficiaries. Usufruct entails the right to use a thing without owning it, but also entails responsibility for the maintenance of the thing used.[53] Practices of commoning, such as those that have been at work around the Xisqueta trademark, illustrate this alternative understanding of sharing the fruits of work and the land.[54]

Over the past decade, a local non-governmental organization has drawn young people, artisans, and sheep owners to work together for the social and economic recovery of the communities of the Catalan Pyrenees.[55] Their aim has been to re-establish shepherding as a profitable activity by enabling the payment of a fair price to the shepherds working with the Xisqueta sheep.[56] The result of such work is incorporated in the Xisqueta trademark, which is applied to wool products marketed and sold in urban areas. The collective creation and circulation of this trademark have rendered possible a professional activity that the global markets for inexpensive textiles and meat had marginalized. What is important for those involved in this communal enterprise is to keep shepherding and wool production as viable activities in the present and the future. There is little doubt that the liveness of the initiative depends on a wide range of networking activities. These range from local associations to other like-minded enterprises such as Big Brother Bio Farming, a social platform connecting producers, retailers, and consumers interested in partaking in social experiments that eschew corporate production. What makes the Xisqueta a viable, reproducible, alternative experiment in production and trade is the form of life that underpins it. Rearing the Xisqueta has offered graduates of the Escola de Pastors de Catalunya (Shepherding School of Catalonia), the school created in the context of this experiment, a way of life in which working with

[53] Riparian right is the most ancient and commonly encountered form of usufructuary arrangement; see Anthony Scott and Georgian Coustalin, 'The Evolution of Water Rights' (1995) 35(4) *Natural Resources Journal* 821. While such arrangement is well established with respect to other natural resources, Claeys refers to the riparian precedent to reconsider intellectual property right; Eric R Claeys, 'Intellectual Usufructs' in Shyamkrishna Balganesh (ed), *Intellectual Property and the Common Law* (Cambridge University Press 2013) 404. Equally important to the present discussion is Thomas' argument that the concept of 'nature' can be regarded as having first emerged as one of the many fictive persons of Roman Law; see Thomas (n 10). This said, and as the editors have observed, it is not clear how usufruct applies with respect to fungible goods, a distinction that, as Thomas also notes, was important to articulation of Roman law; Yan Thomas, 'La Valeur des Choses: Le Droit Romain hors la Religion' (2002) 57(6) *Annales:. Histoire, Sciences Sociales* 1431. Resolving such legal complexities is beyond our expertise.

[54] The language of persons and things employed here is indebted to its discussion in Pottage (n 3).

[55] See Paolo Palladino, 'What's in a Name? On Affect, Value and the Bio-Economy' (2020) 15 *BioSocieties* 70.

[56] The enterprise evolving around the Xisqueta rests on ambitions to reorder the movement of global capital. As Ploeg observes, the difficulties confronting contemporary agricultural producers worldwide have led many to either abandon production or to minimize their engagement with the market. The latter response effectively returns the producers to the status of peasants. Some have actively embraced this process of global repeasantization, aiming to reappropriate the agro-ecological commons and forge a new socio-economic order; Jan Douwe van der Ploeg, *The New Peasantries: Struggles for Autonomy and Sustainability in an Era of Empire and Globalization* (Earthscan 2008). The participants in the Catalan experiment follow in these steps, sometimes employing the phrase 'we are peasants' as their slogan.

sheep exceeds the monetary value of the income generated in animal husbandry. Shepherding becomes attractive to young people because, as some of them have argued: 'It is another life! . . . It's a very strange kind of connection because you suddenly start to feel as if you, the sheep and the landscape are one.'[57] The graduates' accounts of their work also show how their profession engenders duties and obligations towards the animals they raise:

> You get to know each sheep, you see how they grow and you become attached to them. It's different . . . [But] . . . You cannot invest too much affection in animals who you will have to sell or sacrifice. Since they ultimately are commodities, all that you can offer them is the best life possible, feeding them well, being patient and not making them bear the brunt of your own limitations.[58]

In contrast to industrial farming systems, this work pivots on knowing closely and caring for the lives of animals, on balancing the affective investments between human and non-human animals while working together and offering animals the possibility of living 'the best life possible'. In other words, the Xisqueta initiative works not only thanks to a network of producers and consumers who partake in alternative economic formations, but also because the traded products incorporate a way of life that binds humans, other animals, and landscape into affective communities where exploitation is displaced by obligation. If Xisqueta™ is a valuable brand, it is valuable because it is the fruit of being-in-common.[59]

In sum, in seeking to regenerate the local ovine economy, the activities around Xisqueta™ foster an alternative way of life which, as Porcher might put it, is more attuned to lived relations with non-human animals than to the imperatives undergirding industrial animal production, which truncate, rather than foster, life with non-human animals. Xisqueta™ is understood to be the collectively created trademark used to share the fruit of this work across species. Viewed through this lens, usufruct is the process of distributing rights to use knowledge that is collectively produced. It assists practices of commoning, understood as forms of social organization through shared use and entailing relations of obligation between all those involved, be they human or non-human. Insofar as the flesh of Xisqueta™ is also eaten, consumption then becomes a practice of remembering the gift of the common viscerally.[60] Eating the flesh of Xisqueta™ also serves to demonstrate the contingency of the present, that the contemporary relationship between

[57] Laia de Ahumada, *A Cel Ras: Converses amb Joves Pastors* (Pagès Editors 2013) 25, 30.

[58] ibid 76, 78.

[59] This constitutive moment in which an entirely new ordering of the world comes into being calls into question the countervailing power invested in the multitude, which, as intimated earlier (n 17) with regard to the concept of general intellect, tends to dissolve into mind rather than the flesh that all forms of life share.

[60] As Bataille would put it, fleeing the violence of this scene is no answer because, just as Porcher sets out, the price to be paid for the 'accursed share' is simply displaced elsewhere.

intellectual property right and the appropriation of nature could be framed otherwise, and points to promising sites of further enquiry into contemporary experiments in reframing this relationship.[61]

Conclusion

In a series of reflections on political economy and the contemporary understanding of debt, Stimilli calls on readers to think about bonds of obligation beyond the terms set by contemporary economic theory. Stimili writes: 'Since it cannot be subtracted or traded, the gift is ... at the margins of the logic of classical economy; however, as a social fact resulting from benefits that create bonds, it instead becomes part of a formulation aimed at redefining economy's contours'.[62] This understanding of obligation is important to a critical re-examination of thinking about intellectual property right and the appropriation of nature.

We have examined the relationship between intellectual property right and the appropriation of nature by looking at how it is articulated in its most mundane guise. While much scholarly debate on the bioeconomy focuses on technological enterprises, we have instead attended to the consumption of branded products, particularly those constructed around the recollection of specific forms of life. Brands, after all, incorporate intellectual property rights into the most quotidian practices. Our exploration of the subject has been inspired by Birch and Tyfield's perceptive critique of the bioeconomy. Yet, while bringing the role that finance plays to the fore, their critique also dispenses with the notion that the materiality of organic existence plays any constitutive and defining role in the evolution of this same economic formation. Such dispensation is closely aligned with the autonomist Marxian tradition, which has proved very influential in advancing the evermore orthodox notion that the contemporary economy has become immaterial. This autonomist analysis proposes that capitalism today creates wealth not from the extraction of any surplus from the labours of industrial workers, nor from the exchange of commodities on the market. Wealth stems from the exploitation of the affective relations that the contemporary corporation entertains with the consuming public to produce innovative products and so enhance its corporate reputation on financial markets. Viewed from this perspective, the consuming public is the unwaged productive force enrolled in the circuit of contemporary capital through its consuming habits and practices. As such, the autonomist tradition grants consumption a pivotal role in shaping capitalism. We concur. Yet, in

[61] While it is beyond the scope of the present exploration, it is worth noting how Agamben connects usufruct and the slave's body to question how the abstraction that is labour is constituted; see Giorgio Agamben, *The Use of Bodies* (Stanford University Press 2016). This seems to be a particularly promising line of enquiry.

[62] Stimilli (n 40) 38.

framing the current situation as 'cognitive' and in emphasizing how profits are obtained by appropriating knowledge and affective relations, the autonomist argument frames consumption as dispersed through networks of disembodied and atomized individuals. Overlooking how consumption is in fact the material, embodied, and collective practice sustaining the contemporary economic formation not only runs the risk of downplaying its environmental impact, but also is politically disempowering. These risks and consequences, however, are the product of the analytical framework employed, one that divides our relationship to the world into matters of economy and matters of morality. What is needed is an alternative way of viewing the world that overcomes these divisions and reasserts the bonds of obligation that will enable future generations to enjoy the fruits of the stewardship required to ensure the continuity of life on this fragile planet.

Our counterproposal has been articulated, almost paradoxically, by turning to the consumption of meat, which has today come to symbolize the failure of stewardship of the planet. We have focused on such consumption as the mundane, prandial practice that tests the limits of understanding of the appropriation of nature and intellectual property right. The examination has unfolded in two parts. In the first part we have followed Haraway by insisting upon the fundamental importance of the difference that the reference to nature entails, of the matter that is lost in emphasizing contemporary capitalism's dematerializing impulse. Simply put, it is impossible to understand either the development and contradictions of the Piemontese proprietary regime or the affective investments of Styrian conscientious consumers of meat, or the creation of the Xisqueta™ trademark, without referring to both organisms and forms of life lived. Brands matter, but not if there is no one to consume the branded product. Every dematerialization on financial markets involves forms of rematerialization, here at the site of consumption. In the second part of the argument, we have sought to move beyond Haraway's articulation of encounter value to capture these distinctive features of the contemporary appropriation of nature because, in our view, the concept remains trapped by the anthropocentrism of orthodox economic thought. We have done so by revisiting the very foundations of economic relationships and focusing on the question of exploitation, here of our being in and of the natural world. We have articulated how Mauss allows us to reconsider, in less anthropocentric terms, of the original violence that is key to Marx's pivotal notion of alienated labour, namely the separation of work and life. We have proposed that Mauss' notion of the gift allows for a shift in the analytical terms from the violence of separation to that of forgetfulness, specifically forgetfulness of the relationship between humanity and nature. In other words, our response to autonomist arguments about the dematerializing features of contemporary financial capital is to recover how the distinctiveness of the bioeconomy rests with its distinctive violence. This is the erasure of the debt and obligation owed to the world in which we live. We have then sought to recover a more positive and affirmative understanding of the bioeconomy. From the encounter with the world of Xisqueta,TM we have learned how obligation is not as a matter of moral duty, but a framing of the bond binding the world with which to reconfigure the boundaries of the economy, or as Stimilli puts it, the bond that 'redefin[es] economy's contours'. So, when we close by writing that we exist in this world as a result of a gift, and that by appropriating the conditions of our existence, material and immaterial, we forget this gift and destroy the world, we are simply observing how obligation is in fact the most fundamental aspect of our being in and of the world, a relationship today recovered in the work of commoning and the reaffirmation of usufruct.[63]

[63] While further analysis again exceeds our expertise, the present exercise leads to a concept of obligation as more than just an ethical comportment and a mode of existence in relation to others—human and non-human—and more as a strategy of contesting the present 'order of things'. The argument that the organic matter at the heart of the bioeconomy 'matters' rests on disclosing how blindness to such entanglement involves understanding how we come to relate to ourselves and others in those ways that supposedly distinguish modern, liberal cultures from other ways of being in the world. It's about disclosing how we come to divide the world between 'people and things'. Undoing this is no easy task. It would be nice to believe that obligation pre-exists right, but, as others have shown, the parsing of the world we seek to contest is deeply rooted in the legal and governmental structures shaping our very lives and ways of thinking about what is fair and just; see Alain Pottage 'Finding Melanesia in Ancient Rome: Mauss' Anthropology of Nexum' in Sinclair W Bell and Paul J du Plessis (eds), *Roman Law before the Twelve Tables: An Interdisciplinary Approach* (University Press Scholarship Online 2020). The best that can be said is that the reminder of the obligations all around us may dilute the hold of our subjectivity; see also Annalisa Colombino and Paolo Palladino, 'In the Blink of an Eye: Human and Non-Human Animals, Movement, and Bio-Political Existence' (2019) 6 *Angelaki* 24 168.

8

Copyright, Nature, and Travel Narratives

Publishing Cook's Voyages

Isabella Alexander[*]

... as the sea,
Far thro' his azure turbulent domain,
Your empire owns, and from a thousand shores
Wafts all the pomp of life into your ports;
So with superior boon may your rich soil,
Exuberant, Nature's better blessings pour
O'er every land, the naked nations cloathe,
And be th'exhaustless granary of a world![1]

Introduction

In his 1730 landscape poem, *The Seasons*, James Thomson weaves together the themes of nature, empire, trade, and ocean travel. Although another of his poems, *Rule Britannia!*, has been enduringly popular since being set to music by Thomas Arne in 1740, Thomson's name is largely forgotten today outside eighteenth-century literary studies.[2] Thomson and *The Seasons* are, however, well known by name to copyright historians for the starring role they played in the landmark common law copyright decisions of *Millar v Taylor*[3] and *Donaldson v Becket*.[4] Yet,

* I am grateful to Jose Bellido, Brad Sherman, Tomás Gómez-Arostegui, and Katherine Biber for reading this chapter in draft and their very helpful suggestions. All errors of course remain my own.

1 James Thomson, *The Seasons: Spring* (A Millar 1744) 6.

2 The patriotic and empire-celebrating tone of *Rule Britannia!*, as well as its reference to slaves, have made it the subject of controversy in the wake of #BlackLivesMatter, leading to more critical attention being paid to Britain's imperial past and its contemporary portrayal. See eg 'A Row Erupts in Britain over "Rule, Britannia!" at the Proms' NPR *All Things Considered* (11 September 2020) https://www.npr.org/2020/09/11/912045003/a-row-erupts-in-britain-over-rule-britannia-at-the-proms/ (accessed 2 February 2022); 'Rule, Britannia! Is Out of Tune with the Times' *The Guardian* (26 August 2020) https://www.theguardian.com/music/2020/aug/25/rule-britannia-is-out-of-tune-with-the-times/ (accessed 2 February 2022).

3 *Millar v Taylor* (1769) 4 Burr 2303.

4 *Donaldson v Becket* (1774) 4 Burr 2408, 2 Bro PC 129.

Isabella Alexander, *Copyright, Nature, and Travel Narratives* In: *Intellectual Property and the Design of Nature*. Edited by: Jose Bellido and Brad Sherman, Oxford University Press. © Isabella Alexander 2023.
DOI: 10.1093/oso/9780192864406.003.0008

despite the reams of paper scholars have devoted to these cases and their significance in relation to the existence or otherwise of a perpetual common-law copyright, little attention has been paid to the poem at the heart of them. Almost as little attention has been paid to a third case, brought before the courts in the same year as *Donaldson v Becket*, that dealt with a work exploring similar themes in a very different genre, and that raised similar questions in relation to the scope of copyright. This was the greatly anticipated, commercially successful, yet critically disparaged, work written by John Hawkesworth recounting James Cook's first and most famous Pacific voyage.

It is not simply coincidence that, at a time when booksellers, lawyers, and legislators were struggling to work out the parameters of a comparatively new legal regime, the works selected to test these parameters should have the natural world as a central theme. This chapter sets out to explore the intersections between copyright and nature, and their relationship with empire, during the formative years of the modern, statutory regime of copyright law through the genre of travel writing. Including within the scope of 'nature' flora and fauna, as well as landscape, marine, and celestial features and (in line with contemporary thinking) indigenous peoples, the chapter focuses closely upon the publication of the accounts of Captain James Cook's three Pacific voyages. As will be explored in more detail, travel writing depends on the visualization of nature as well as representing an attempt to master it, through measurement, classification, illustration, and depiction. It also encapsulates many of the paradoxical tensions that characterize copyright's assertion of property through authorship: fact/fiction; mutable/immutable; subject/object; public/private; author/owner; artificial/natural.

This chapter examines how the interactions between sailors, naturalists, booksellers, and institutions sought to produce authoritative accounts of both voyage and nature, as well as their relationship to empire, how these accounts were ushered into print, and how ownership was exerted over them. It seeks to draw out the pivotal role played by copyright law in the way in which the printed accounts of Cook's voyages were produced and circulated, and thus by extension in the construct of nature that these accounts produced. Copyright draws nature into the commodity form when it is systematized, narrated, visualized, and made infinitely reproducible. Copyright works to stabilize the text and allows its authority to be asserted and reasserted. This chapter observes the close parallels between the ways in which travel narratives enable nature to be valued for its exploitable potential, and the ways in which copyright law also allows nature to be 'authored', and thus appropriated as an object of copyright.[5]

[5] Bernard Edelman, 'The Law's Eye: Nature and Copyright' in Brad Sherman and Alain Strowel (eds), *Of Authors and Origins: Essays on Copyright Law* (Clarendon Press 1994) 79–91.

Travel Narratives, Nature, and Empire

When Captain James Cook set off on his famous first voyage in 1768, the natural historian John Ellis wrote to renowned Swedish taxonomist Carl Linnaeus that: 'No people ever went to sea better fitted out for the purpose of Natural History, nor more elegantly.'[6] Voyages of discovery and exploration had been concerned with uncovering and reporting the wonders of nature since the fifteenth century, but this practice reached its apotheosis in Cook's three Pacific voyages.[7] The uniqueness of Cook's voyages arose from a confluence of factors. First, the recently established ability to determine longitude accurately represented a significant shift in how Europeans could know the world.[8] Secondly, Cook was himself a gifted navigator and close observer of marine, terrestrial, and astronomical phenomena, and moreover was accompanied by a range of skilled naturalists, astronomers, draughtsmen, and artists, who worked tirelessly to identify, classify, describe, and depict nature in its multitude of variations: plant; mineral; meteorological; and human. The texts and images they produced captured the imagination of Britons and fed a large and growing interest in the natural world and exotic locations.

Enlightenment science had begun to be assimilated into progressive ideologies from the end of the seventeenth century, and by the late eighteenth century was finding expression in the systematizing of nature. A European culture of collecting gave birth to the field of natural history.[9] Carl Linnaeus' system of classifying all the earth's plants according to the characteristics of their reproductive parts, first set out in *Systema Naturae* in 1735, was to play an important part in this totalizing construction of nature, as Linnaeus' disciples spread across the globe, collecting, measuring, describing, preserving, drawing, recognizing, and naming plants and insects, and bringing them back home in the best condition possible.[10] Along with Linnaeus, the work of others, such as Buffon, Cuvier, and Saint-Hilaire, sought to bring order to the natural world, training a 'scientific gaze' upon landscapes both known and newly encountered.[11]

Published accounts of exploration voyages were integral in transforming public attitudes to the natural world and constructing a new concept of nature in the late eighteenth century. Travel writing brought together these descriptions, visualizations, and collections. It imposed order and structure on nature through its narrative form and accompanying diagrams and illustrations, just as the ability to

[6] Ellis to Linnaeus (19 August 1768), quoted in JC Beaglehole, *The Life of Captain James Cook* (Adam & Charles Black 1974) 146.

[7] Lorraine Daston and Katharine Park, *Wonders and the Order of Nature, 1150–1750* (Zone Books 1998).

[8] Brian W Richardson, *Longitude and Empire: How Captain Cook's Voyages Changed the World* (UBC Press 2005) 6.

[9] Paul Smethurst, *Travel Writing and the Natural World, 1768–1840* (Palgrave Macmillan 2012) 2.

[10] Mary Louise Pratt, *Imperial Eyes: Travel Writing and Transculturation* (Routledge 2007) 24–26.

[11] Smethurst (n 9) 16–42.

determine longitude at sea imposed navigational order upon the oceans.[12] These impulses also formed part of a project that was imperialist, capitalist, and racialist. Scholars including Paul Smethurst, Mary-Louise Pratt, and Beth Fowkes Tobin have made powerful cases for the close links between travel writing, natural history, and imperial objectives.[13] Smethurst argues that travel writing helped 'to instill forms of order and structure, such as museum order and the picturesque, in the abstract space of nature', and this in turn reflected 'power relations implicit in imperialism, territorialisation and mercantilitism'. In this way, argues Smethurst, nature came to be valued for its 'usefulness and potential as an exploitable resource'.[14] Indeed, it was not simply factual travel accounts that had this effect, as Tobin observes:

> The intellectual and visual mastery of the tropics, as exercised in genres as different as georgic verse, botanical illustrations, and garden views, preceded and accompanied such material appropriations of land, labour, and natural resources as the Pacific voyages of discovery, the sugar plantations in the West Indies, and the indigo, cotton, and tea estates in Bengal.[15]

Pratt has argued that travel writing was an essentially imperial project, which 'gave European reading publics a sense of ownership, entitlement, and familiarity with respect to the distant parts of the world that were being explored, invaded, invested in, and colonised'.[16] For Pratt, the natural history produced by travellers and travel writers turned on 'a great longing: for a way of taking possession without subjugation and violence'.[17]

Late eighteenth-century print technology brought together the navigator, the naturalist, the state, and the public; it produced and conferred authority upon the travel account, and created and regulated the market in which it circulated, and the audience that consumed it. Crucial to achieving this was the law of copyright. Copyright emerged in 1710 as a statutory right in books initially owned by an author, but was more frequently wielded by a bookseller, and gradually developed through case law and further legislation over the course of the century.[18] By the latter part of the eighteenth century, it was sufficiently developed to operate as an important technological apparatus within what Latour has described as 'a cycle of accumulation' emanating from London, the 'centre of calculation'.[19] As he explains,

[12] ibid (n 9) in particular.

[13] ibid; Pratt (n 10); see also the contributions in David Phillip Miller and Peter Hanns Reill (eds), *Visions of Empire: Voyages, Botany, and Representations of Empire* (Cambridge University Press 1996).

[14] Smethurst (n 9) 15.

[15] Beth Fowkes Tobin, *Colonizing Nature: The Tropics in British Arts and Letters, 1760–1820* (University of Pennsylvania Press 2011) 13.

[16] Pratt (n 10) 3.

[17] ibid 56.

[18] An Act for the Encouragement of Learning by Vesting the Copies of Printed Books in the Authors or Purchasers of such Copies, during the Times therein mentioned (1709) 8 Anne c 19 (Statute of Anne).

[19] Bruno Latour, *Science in Action: How to Follow Scientists and Engineers through Society* (Harvard University Press 1987) 215–57.

with illustrations from the voyages of La Perouse, dominating other parts of the world through central accumulation of knowledge required distant events, places, and people to be rendered mobile, stable, and combinable.[20] Achieving this depended on various techniques, as well as a range of conditions that were woven together to work towards the same goal. As Latour warned, there is always a chance that the accumulation will fail since the cycle made up of these conditions 'may leak at the seam'.[21] Copyright was one of these conditions, but evidently could also be a point of leakage.

Moreover, the relationship between copyright and nature was not simply one in which copyright operated as a technology assisting in the ordering and unifying of nature within an imperial context and for imperial aims. The parallels between them run more deeply. As Blackstone explained in his *Commentaries* (1765–1770), copyright can be seen as 'being grounded on labour and invention' and justified according to the right of occupancy.[22] Just as the eighteenth-century practices of natural history have been viewed as a way of asserting power and mastery over both nature and territories, so too does copyright work to assert ownership over something that was previously unowned. Examining the publication of the official accounts of Captain James Cook's three voyages, focusing upon the disputes they generated in relation to authorship, authority, and copyright law, allows an exploration of these parallels and connections.

As is well known, Cook's three voyages into the Pacific were ostensibly aimed at addressing three scientific questions of the time. The aim of the first voyage was to observe the transit of Venus, part of a global enterprise to determine the distance between the earth and the sun, with a secret side project of discovery in the south. The second voyage's aim was to determine the existence or otherwise of a great southern continent, while the third voyage sought to establish the existence or otherwise of a Northwest Passage between the Pacific and Atlantic Oceans. While at sea, Cook carried instructions from the Admiralty as to where he should sail and what he should do on the voyage. The instructions required him to note and record all manner of maritime data, including ascertaining the latitude and longitude of points, tides, draughts of coasts, ports etc, depth markings, wind changes, and so on.

The practice of requiring voyages of discovery to make and record observations of nature using mathematics and empirical methods dated back to 1665, when the Royal Society had issued its 'Directions for Sea-Men'. The Directions asked travellers to keep an 'exact diary' of their observations, copies of which would be made available upon return to both the Admiralty and the Royal Society and set

[20] ibid 223.
[21] ibid 222.
[22] William Blackstone, *Commentaries on the Law of England, Book the Second* (Clarendon Press 1766) 406.

out the technical navigational data to be observed. The Directions were later supplemented by further instructions drafted by Robert Boyle, which emphasized the observation of 'productions of nature'.[23] In this tradition, Cook's 'Additional Instructions' for the first voyage, contained in a sealed packet, directed him to discover new lands or attain 'a Knowledge of distant parts which though formerly discover'd have yet been imperfectly explored' as this would 'redound greatly to the Honour of this Nation as a Maritime Power as well as to the Dignity of the Crown of Great Britain, and may tend to the advancement of the Trade and Navigation thereof'. If he should discover any new country, he should 'take possession' of it in the name of the king.[24]

In addition, the instructions requested:

> You are also carefully to observe the Nature of the Soil, and the Products thereof; the Beasts and Fowls that inhabit or frequent it, the fishes that are to be found in the Rivers or upon the Coast and in what Plenty; and in case you find any Mines, Minerals or valuable stones you are to bring home Specimens of each, as also such Specimens of the Seeds of the Trees, Fruits and Grains as you may be able to collect, and Transmit them to our Secretary that We may cause proper Examination and Experiments to be made of them.[25]

Instructions in similar terms were provided for each of the following two voyages (although not in sealed packets), and they reveal how closely intertwined were scientific knowledge, imperial ambition, and commercial advancement. That these instructions were secret also, as Pratt observes, points to the 'ideological dialectic' between scientific and commercial exercises that were, on the one hand, seen to mirror and legitimate each other, while on the other hand displayed a conflict between the interests of commerce and the disinterestedness of science.[26]

Richardson argues that Cook's voyages were transformative in relation to Britons' understanding of the world, reworking political and economic relations through their accumulation of information, and helping to create the institutions that manage the accumulation of such data. He goes on to state that 'the ability to publish all of the elements of this account in books organized around a single authoritative voice allows the world and the different ways of understanding it to be unfolded through the text as a single, coherent narrative'.[27] But while Cook may have been the single authoritative narrator in name, a closer examination of the ways in which the narrative was brought into print reveals a more disaggregated

[23] Smethurst (n 9) 23–26.
[24] Beaglehole (n 6) 148–49.
[25] JC Beaglehole (ed), *The Journals of Captain James Cook on His Voyages of Discovery: The Voyage of the Endeavour 1768–1771* (Boydell Press 1999) cclxxxii–iii.
[26] Pratt (n 10) 34
[27] Richardson (n 8) 199.

and complex state of affairs. Where other fields of contemporary literary production may have been witnessing the rise of the Romantic author, Craciun has pointed out that in the case of exploration literature, authorship was still inextricably bound up with naval regulation and obligations of military obedience, as well as through loose ties with institutions such as the Royal Society.[28]

Indeed, Cook's Instructions as to the required observations could only be realized through a collaboration of different individuals with different skills. Accompanying him on his voyages were those with the scientific skills to make the 'correct' types of observation, and artists with the skills to visualize what was observed and discovered. Even amongst these broad categories, different skills were found in different persons—some were particularly skilled in astronomy, taxonomy, botany; some in depicting landscapes, plants, people. Those with literary skills were needed to write the tale of the voyage; printers and booksellers and engravers were required to bring the material form into being. Copyright and contract law were required to organize the contributions into official and authorized accounts, and to protect that official account from being adulterated in a marketplace saturated with unofficial accounts. The practices and processes involved in bringing these accounts into print, and exerting control over them once they were there, were not straightforward, and it is to these we now turn.

Publishing the First Voyage: Individualizing Nature and the Boundaries of Copyright

The commitment of Cook's voyages to natural history may to a great extent be attributed to the role played by Sir Joseph Banks. Indeed, the importance of the role played by Banks in relation to the shape of all three voyages can scarcely be underemphasized. On the first voyage, Banks was able to leverage his social status and wealth, his friendship with Lord Sandwich, and his Royal Society fellowship to gain a berth on the *Endeavour*.[29] Furthermore, he had arranged to be accompanied by four assistants: the botanist and Linnaean disciple Daniel Solander, another Linnaean student Herman Diedrich Spöring (who would be his secretary), and two artists, Sydney Parkinson and Alexander Buchan. The naturalists further carried with them an extensive library of around sixty reference books and scientific equipment, including storage chests, specimen bottles, and instruments such

[28] Adriana Craciun, *Writing Arctic Disaster: Authorship and Exploration* (Cambridge University Press 2016) 23 (hereafter Craciun, *Writing Arctic Disaster*); John Gascoigne, *Science in the Service of Empire: Joseph Banks, the British State and the Uses of Science in the Age of Revolution* (Cambridge University Press 1998)

[29] David Phillip Miller, 'Joseph Banks, Empire and "Centers of Calculation" in Late Hanoverian London' in David Phillip Miller and Peter Hanns Reill (eds), *Visions of Empire: Voyages, Botany, and Representations of Empire* (Cambridge University Press 1996); Glyn Williams, *Naturalists at Sea: Scientific Travellers from Dampier to Darwin* (Yale University Press 2013) 73–74.

as telescopes and microscopes.[30] In spite of the fact that they did not survive the voyage, Parkinson, Buchan, and Spöring nevertheless managed to produce over 950 botanical drawings, 200 coastal views and 200 drawings of Pacific peoples and their artefacts and dwellings, before their untimely deaths.[31] Banks and Solander had collected thousands of botanical specimens, and both Banks and Cook had filled journals with descriptions of their discoveries and observations. So had other crew members, as will soon be seen.

When the voyagers returned to London, British society clamoured to hear stories of their explorations and to see the curiosities that they had brought back.[32] But initially it was Banks and Solander who were most fêted in the press.[33] Banks urged the timely publication of an account of their travels so that 'our own countrey shall have the honour of our Discoveries!'[34] It does not appear to have been considered that Cook would write up the account himself: indeed, the plan developed by the Admiralty was to produce a volume that covered not only Cook's voyage but also those of three earlier navigators, Byron, Wallis, and Carteret. Searching for someone to write the story, the First Lord of the Admiralty, Lord Sandwich, apparently consulted his friend Dr Charles Burney, who suggested John Hawkesworth for the task, and David Garrick supported the choice.[35] The Admiralty apparently had no view as to the appropriate publisher for this important work, leaving it to Hawkesworth to decide. With no shortage of offers, Hawkesworth settled on William Strahan, who offered him the astronomical sum of £6,000 as well as copies worth £75.[36]

The choice of Strahan led to a breach with Garrick, who had wanted Hawkesworth to choose his own bookseller, Becket.[37] But, of all London booksellers, it is likely only Strahan could afford such a generous offer. Holder of the lucrative law patent, and official printer to the king since 1770, Strahan operated or owned part of three separate printing houses and ran at least twenty-five presses.[38]

[30] Williams (n 29) 74; Bernard Smith, *Imagining the Pacific in the Wake of the Cook Voyages* (Melbourne University Press 1992) 43.

[31] Smith (n 30) 43.

[32] Beaglehole (n 6) 273.

[33] Williams (n 29) 88.

[34] Philip Edwards, *The Story of the Voyage: Sea Narratives in Eighteenth-century England* (Cambridge University Press 1994) 83.

[35] ibid 83.

[36] Beaglehole (n 6) 290. According to the historical currency calculator on the UK National Archives website, the value of this in 2017 was £523,531.80, or 60,000 days of wages for a skilled tradesman: https://www.nationalarchives.gov.uk/currency-converter/#.

[37] Edwards (n 34) 85.

[38] Patricia Hernlund, 'William Strahan (1715–1785) printer' *Oxford Dictionary of National Biography Online* (23 September 2004) https://doi.org/10.1093/ref:odnb/26631 (accessed 26 June 2022). The law patent was the royal privilege to print books concerning the common law of England. It was first granted to Richard Tottel in 1557, and had changed hands many times before being purchased by Strahan and Henry Woodfall in 1761. See Adrian Johns, *The Nature of the Book* (Chicago University Press 1998) 299; Tariq A Baloch, 'Law Booksellers and Printers as Agents of Unchange' (2007) 66(2) *Cambridge Law Journal* 389, 402.

It is also important to note here what Strahan was apparently purchasing, namely a licence to print and publish Hawkesworth's book in perpetuity. The Court of the King's Bench had recently held, in the decision of *Millar v Taylor*,[39] that a perpetual common law copyright survived the passage of the Statute of Anne (providing for a maximum of twenty-eight years' protection). Strahan was a staunch defender of this position, but his publication of *Voyages* was to become a plank in the argument of those who opposed it, and the position that was so favourable to the established, copyright-owning booksellers such as Strahan was not to last long.[40]

Hawkesworth began work in 1771, drawing on the journals of Byron, Wallis, Carteret, and Cook, as well as those of Joseph Banks, which Banks lent him for the purpose.[41] The Admiralty had stipulated (as was usual on such voyages) that all other journals and diaries made by members of the *Endeavour*'s company be surrendered and it was thus expected by all concerned that Hawkesworth's account would be the sole version on the market. However, notwithstanding this order, some diaries did find their way into the hands of publishers. Only two months after the *Endeavour* had docked, the booksellers Becket and de Hondt published *A Journal of a Voyage round the World*, an account based, probably, on the work of a midshipman.[42] This work had been labelled by one of Cook's correspondents, Captain Bentinck, as 'so interesting that there is no putting the book down', but that its inaccuracy was 'most tiresome' and 'provoking'.[43]

Having started work on the journals, Hawkesworth was clearly unimpressed to find that his scoop was threatened by the potential appearance in print of yet another account of the voyage. This was the diary of Sydney Parkinson. As noted above, Parkinson had died on the voyage, leaving his notes, observations, and personal diary in the possession of Banks, who, as Parkinson's employer, considered himself their owner. Parkinson's brother and sister, however, wished to recover both his possessions and his unpaid salary. Stanfield Parkinson, Sydney's brother, was appointed administrator of his estate. Sydney's patron, the influential physician and botanist Dr John Fothergill, arranged a mediation between Banks and the family, which resulted in Banks paying Stanfield Parkinson the sum of £500 in return for all Sydney's 'works and performances' relating to the voyage, on 31 January 1772. The previous day, Banks had assigned all his rights in Sydney Parkinson's notes, papers, and writings to Hawkesworth.[44]

39 *Millar v Taylor* (n 3).

40 For Strahan's efforts see Robert Dale Harlan, 'William Strahan: Eighteenth Century London Printer and Publisher' PhD Thesis (University of Michigan 1960) 197–98.

41 John Hawkesworth, *An Account of the Voyages Undertaken by Order of His Present Majesty for Making Discoveries in the Southern Hemisphere, 3 vols* (Strahan and Cadell 1773) vol 2, xiii.

42 For a discussion of the work's possible authorship see Beaglehole (n 25) cclvi–cclxiv.

43 Beaglehole (n 6) 289–90.

44 Mark Leeming, 'Hawkesworth's Voyages: The First "Australian" Copyright Litigation' (2005) 9 *Australian Journal of Legal History* 160, 161; Complaint of John Hawkesworth, C12/1624/8, m1 (26 January 1773); TNA.

After having made the agreement, Stanfield requested that Banks allow him to look over the papers to satisfy his curiosity, and Banks agreed to deliver them 'under the Express Injunction that no other use should be made of them'. Parkinson, however, entered into an agreement with two Fleet Street printers, Charles Clarke and John Jacquery, to publish the journals.[45] On 20 January 1773, Hawkesworth placed a notice in a number of newspapers, stating that an account of the voyages of Cook, as well as those of Byron, Wallis, and Carteret, was in press and due to be published in April. He further warned that 'there is some reason to believe that an imperfect Account of Part of the Voyage of the Endeavour, is surreptitiously printing' and that he ought to warn the public that 'there are no Materials for such an Account, but some loose and unconnected Papers of the late Mr. Sidney Parkinson'. He therefore advised members of the public to 'suspend their Curiosity till the Work now advertised is published'.[46]

On 26 January 1773, Hawkesworth followed his warning by bringing a Bill of Complaint in Chancery, seeking an injunction against Parkinson, and retained Alexander Wedderburn, the Solicitor General, to argue his case.[47] Dr Fothergill provided an affidavit confirming his role in the mediation and that Stanfield Parkinson had confessed to him that he had arranged for the papers to be copied with the object of having them published. Fothergill was 'much Hurt at the Deceitful and Ungrateful Behaviour' of Parkinson, telling him it reflected poorly upon both. He offered to reimburse Parkinson for his expenses in making the copies if he would deliver them up to him, an offer that Parkinson refused, having determined to publish.[48] Armed with this affidavit, and one from Hawkesworth, Wedderburn sought and obtained an interlocutory injunction on 4 February 1773.[49]

Parkinson retained Edward Thurlow, the Attorney General. Wedderburn and Thurlow were regular courtroom rivals and appeared in most of the major copyright cases of the period, Wedderburn for the copyright owner and Thurlow for the alleged infringer.[50] As discussed below, they were shortly to appear on opposing sides of the most significant copyright case of the era, *Donaldson v Becket*. Stanfield Parkinson submitted his Answer on 11 May 1773. The Answer accepted that his brother had been employed by Banks to make 'paintings or Drawings, delineations and lineary descriptions' of the sights, peoples, animals, and plants they encountered, but claimed that his tasks for Banks did not include keeping a journal or diary of 'remarkable or other Incidents or occurrences'. Rather, Sydney had risen early in the morning or stayed up late at night so that he could write notes of his

[45] Complaint of John Hawkesworth, C12/1624/8, m1 (26 January 1773); TNA.
[46] *Public Advertiser* (20 January 1773); *London Evening Post* (19–21 January 1773); *St James Chronicle or the British Evening Post* (28–30 January 1773).
[47] C12/1624/8, m1. For a detailed account of the litigation see Leeming (n 44).
[48] C31/187 ff3–4 (28 January 1773); TNA.
[49] C33/439 f159r–159v (4 February 1773); TNA.
[50] Leeming (n 44) 162.

observations 'for his own private Use and Enjoyment', some of which he presented to his intimates, relations, and acquaintances, and others he kept for his own use. Therefore, Parkinson argued, Banks could assert no title over such writings. In a lengthy response, he denied most of Hawkesworth's allegations and asked for the injunction to be lifted.[51]

On 28 May 1773, after further argument, the Lord Chancellor ordered the injunction be dissolved.[52] No reasons are recorded for the decision, but Mark Leeming has plausibly argued that the Court likely found that the series of transactions between Parkinson, Banks, and Hawkesworth had not properly transferred title to the copyright in the unpublished manuscript.[53] The preface to the *Journal* suggested the problem was the defect in Hawkesworth's title and, in addition, noted that 'the alleged date of the assignment of such property, from Banks to Hawkesworth, was prior to that of the receipt of the £500 before-mentioned, given by Stanfield and Britannia Parkinson to Banks, on which the pretended right of the latter to such manuscript was founded'. This, wrote the author, was a circumstance that 'might reasonably suggest some collusion'.[54]

Despite his legal victory, Parkinson aired his displeasure at the delay caused by the legal proceedings in the press, promising his book would include an account of the 'extraordinary means' taken by Hawkesworth, Fothergill, 'and Others' to 'delay and suppress' his publication.[55] The proceedings had indeed given Hawkesworth and Strahan time to catch up with Parkinson's publication plans. After having been advertised as appearing first in April and then in May, Hawkesworth's *Voyages* was eventually published on 9 June 1773.[56] Two days later, Parkinson's *Journal* appeared, in a handsome folio volume, illustrated with a number of original engravings taken from Sydney Parkinson's shipboard sketches and paintings.[57] It also included lists of plants and their medicinal uses, as well as language glossaries from the various islands visited on the voyage. The *Journal* was reviewed briefly in *Monthly Review*, which noted the writer 'seems to have been a well-disposed young man' and that it was illustrated by twenty-seven plates 'which may perhaps be thought to constitute the most valuable part of it'.[58]

[51] Answer of Stanfield Parkinson, C12/1624/8 m2 (11 May 1773); TNA.

[52] C33/439 f304v (28 May 1773); TNA.

[53] Leeming (n 44) 165–66.

[54] Sydney Parkinson, *A Journal of a Voyage to the South Seas in His Majesty's Ship Endeavour* (London, printed for Stanfield Parkinson, and sold by Richardson and Urquhart, Evans, Hooper, Murray, Leacroft, and Riley 1773) xxii.

[55] *Public Ledger* (3 June 1773).

[56] *Public Advertiser* (20 January 1773); *London Evening Post* (19–21 January 1773); *The Morning Chronicle and London Advertiser* (3 May 1773); *The Morning Chronicle and London Advertiser* (9 June 1773). In a letter to Hawkesworth, Banks admitted that announcing a publication date that could not be met was a strategy to divert sales from Parkinson's *Journal*: 'if a short time for instance two or three months is fixed many who would otherwise buy Parkinsons work will say we can well stay so Long & when disappointed at the end of the time will probably have forgot that such a book exists of these maybe some after two disappointments may not chuse to go to the third expense.' Banks to Hawkesworth (12 January 1773), quoted in R Joppien and B Smith, *The Art of Captain Cook's Voyages*, vol 1: *The Voyage of the Endeavour* (Yale University Press 1985) 54.

[57] *London Evening Post* (10–12 June 1773).

[58] *Monthly Review, or Literary Journal*, vol 50 (May 1774), 411.

A review in the *Westminster Magazine* likewise complimented Parkinson on the accuracy of the prints (in respect of corresponding to the written descriptions), as compared with those in Hawkesworth's *Voyages*. The reviewer observed that although the inhabitants of Terra del Fuego are described in both works as uncouth, wretched, and living in despicable conditions, only Parkinson depicted them accordingly (see Fig 8.1).

Figure 8.1 View of a Village in the Bay of Good Success in the Island of Terra del Fuego, Plate II in *A Journal of a Voyage to the South Seas in his Majesty's Ship, The Endeavour* (London, printed for Stanfield Parkinson, and sold by Richardson, Evans, Hooper, Murray, Leacroft, and Riley 1773). The associated text, on page 8 of Parkinson's *Journal,* notes: 'These poor Indians live in a village [see pl. II] on the south side of the bay, behind a hill; the number of their huts is about thirteen, and they contain near fifty people, who seem to be all the inhabitants of this dreary part of the island, which is very cold, even in the middle of summer.'
Reproduced from the collections of the State Library of New South Wales, Q78/11 (Dixson Library).

In Hawkesworth's *Voyages* (Fig 8.2), 'they are presented in a picturesque view, delineated by Cypriani, as well-limbed and fair-featured beings, by no means so contemptible and miserable'.[59]

59 *The Westminster Magazine* (June 1773) 337.

Figure 8.2 The image of the inhabitants of Terra del Fuego that appears in Hawkesworth's *Voyages*, delineated by Cipriani, and engraved by Bartolozzi, appears in a very different style to that drawn by Parkinson.
From an *Album of plates and charts from an account of the voyages undertaken by the order of His Present Majesty for making discoveries in the southern hemisphere—drawn up by John Hawkesworth and from the official accounts of Captain Cook's second and third voyages.*
Reproduced from the collections of the State Library of New South Wales, X980/27 (Dixson Library).

The Preface to Parkinson's *Journal*, narrated as though by Stanfield but in fact by his editor, William Kenrick, levelled several accusations against Banks, including that Banks had stolen Sydney's more valuable effects. It also accused Fothergill of 'pernicious counsel' and 'officious meddling', as well as colluding with Banks and Hawkesworth against Parkinson.[60] Stanfield died later that year, having been declared insane. It seems possible that this illness or disability may have influenced his earlier conduct, or that the stress of taking on Banks and the Admiralty took a toll on his mental health, or perhaps some combination of the two. Dr Fothergill did, perhaps surprisingly, return to the family's good graces. Despite everything that had occurred, he attended Stanfield on his deathbed and was bequeathed the copyright in the *Journal*. On Fothergill's death, his editor John Coakley Lettsom reissued the *Journal*, adding an abstract of Cook's second and third voyages, as well

[60] Parkinson (n 54) viii–xxiii.

as accounts of voyages of Byron, Wallis, Carteret, and Bougainville.[61] Lettsom included an 'advertisement', explaining that the transfer of the copyright to Fothergill evinced 'a thorough dependence on him, and the most unequivocal acknowledgment of his rectitude'.[62] Lettsom also included Fothergill's written response to the original preface, allowing him to assert his good intentions, and a letter from Banks thanking him for his assistance in mediating the dispute.[63]

While Fothergill's reputation survived the dispute and publication of rival texts, Hawkesworth was not so fortunate. The litigation tarnished his reputation 'as a high-minded moralist', and his *Voyages* was attacked on all sides: for its depictions of the South Sea Islanders' sexual practices; for impiety by including a challenge to the doctrine of providential intervention in the introduction; and, for his writing style.[64] Cook himself was 'mortified', particularly by the 'nautical blunders' made by Hawkesworth.[65] Hawkesworth died on 17 November 1773, his health apparently destroyed by the vilification he had received.[66]

The success of the book from its publisher's perspective is unclear. Despite being sold at the relatively high price of three guineas, all 2,000 copies of the first edition of *Voyages* sold out, and a second edition of 2,500 copies was printed within months. But twelve years later, 610 copies were still unsold, and some commentators on the controversy consider the publication one of Strahan's rare failures.[67] Nevertheless, the book proved popular in libraries (it was, for example, the most borrowed book in the Bristol Library between 1773 and 1784), and unauthorized reprints quickly appeared in Dublin and New York. It was also translated into French, Dutch, and German.[68] However, Strahan's significant investment in the copy was under attack on two fronts: not only from unauthorized copies, but also from a renewed attack on the booksellers' monopolies in the courts.

As already noted, in the 1769 case of *Millar v Taylor* involving Thomson's *The Seasons*, the Court of the King's Bench had found in favour of the existence of a perpetual, common law copyright that existed independently of the Statute of Anne and the limited copyright terms found therein.[69] However, the debate was

[61] JC Lettsom, *Advertisement to A Journal of a Voyage to the South Seas in his Majesty's Ship Endeavour* (Charles Dilly and James Phillips 1784).

[62] ibid.

[63] 'Explanatory Remarks on the Preface to Sydney Parkinson's Journal of a Voyage to the South Seas by John Fothergill MD FRS' in JC Lettsom, *A Journal of a Voyage to the South Seas in his Majesty's Ship Endeavour* (Charles Dilly and James Phillips 1784).

[64] Karina Williamson, 'Hawkesworth, John (bap. 1720, d. 1773), writer' *Oxford Dictionary of National Biography Online* (25 May 2006) https://doi.org/10.1093/ref:odnb/12658 (accessed 26 June 2022); Leeming (n 44) 166.

[65] Beaglehole (n 6) 439.

[66] Williamson (n 64).

[67] Harlan (n 40) 193.

[68] WH Pearson, 'Hawkesworth's Voyages' in RF Brissenden, *Studies in the Eighteenth Century II: Papers presented at the Second David Nichol Smith Memorial Seminar, Canberra, 1970* (University of Toronto Press 1973) 239.

[69] *Millar v Taylor* (n 3).

soon reopened and, in 1771, Thomas Becket commenced proceedings against Alexander and John Donaldson in respect of the same work at issue in the earlier case. The case went to the House of Lords, where it was argued in February of 1774.[70] As mentioned above, Wedderburn was acting for Becket, arguing in favour of common law copyright, while Thurlow opposed him for Donaldson. The House of Lords voted to uphold the supremacy of the Statute of Anne, with the result that once a book was published, it was subject to the time limits of that Statute.[71] Strahan had been involved on the sidelines, providing financial support as well as exerting his influence where he could.[72] The result on a personal level was that Strahan had paid £6,000 for the right to print a work forever; now, he would only have whatever remained of the statutory term of fourteen years from publication.

By this time, Strahan had purchased the property in *Voyages* outright from Hawkesworth, transferring half of the copyright to his partner Thomas Cadell.[73] It may have suddenly seemed much more important to assert that right during the considerably more limited statutory term and, on 4 November 1773, several weeks before Hawkesworth's death, Strahan and Cadell sought an injunction in Chancery. Their target was the bookseller Francis Newbery, who had published a compilation of accounts of all the English circumnavigators, including parts of Hawkesworth's *Voyages*, as well as Parkinson's *Journal*.[74] Newbery's compilation was to appear in forty-eight weekly parts, at fourpence halfpenny a part, of which fifteen had so far appeared.[75] Like Hawkesworth, Strahan retained Alexander Wedderburn to act for him. Wedderburn argued that Newbery's publication was in breach of the Statute of Anne because it copied exact words and sentences from Hawkesworth's *Voyages*, as well as copying one of the prints.[76] Unsurprisingly, Newbery retained Edward Thurlow. In his Answer, Newbery explained that the use he had made of Hawkesworth's book was 'common and customary with Compilers and Authors of Collections and Abridgements' and that without the liberty of doing so 'no Histories Dictionaries Compendiums Epitomes or other Books of General Instruction and Improvement could be Compiled for the use of the Publick'.[77]

[70] *Donaldson v Becket* (n 4).

[71] For detailed discussion of the case, its findings, and implications see H Tomás Gómez-Arostegui, 'Copyright at Common Law in 1774' (2014) 47 *Connecticut Law Review* 1; Ronan Deazley, *On the Origin of the Right to Copy* (Hart Publishing 2004); Mark Rose, 'The Author as Proprietor: Donaldson v Becket and the Genealogy of Modern Authorship' (1988) 23 *Representations* 51.

[72] Harlan (n 40) 196–97.

[73] According to the Bill of Complaint, Strahan purchased the right from Hawkesworth in May 1773 and assigned half to Cadell on 4 May 1774: C12/1629/11 (4 November 1773); TNA.

[74] Complaint of William Strahan C12/1629/11 (4 November 1773); *An historical account of all the voyages round the world performed by English navigators: including those lately undertaken by order of His present Majesty: the whole faithfully extracted from the journals of the voyagers: Drake, undertaken in 1577–80, Cavendish, 1586–88, Cowley, 1683–86, Dampier, 1689–96, Cook, 1708–11, Rogers, 1708–11, Clipperton and Shelvocke, 1719–22, Anson, undertaken in 1740–44, Byron, 1764–66, Wallis, 1766–68, Carteret, 1766–69, and Cook, 1768–71* (F Newbery 1773–78). See Leeming (n 44) 170.

[75] C12/1629/11 (4 November 1773); C33/442 f1v-2r (11 November 1773); TNA.

[76] ibid.

[77] Answer of Francis Newbery C12/1629/11 m4; TNA.

The matter was referred to a master in Chancery to assess whether the book was 'a fair abridgment'.[78] In earlier cases, the Court of Chancery had held that a genuine abridgement would not amount to infringement.[79] Although the Master's report does not seem to have survived, it appears from Strahan and Cadell's exceptions, which have, that the Master found that the first fifteen numbers were a fair abridgement.[80] When the exceptions came on to be argued, Lord Chancellor Apsley postponed ruling on them and continued the injunction in respect of the first fourteen numbers, but stated Newbery was at liberty to publish the fifteenth number and subsequent numbers (which were not extracts from Hawkesworth and thus not the subject of Strahan and Cadell's complaint).[81] According to the published report, Apsley LC consulted privately with the prominent jurist William Blackstone.[82] Blackstone convinced Apsley LC that: 'an abridgment, where the understanding is employed in retrenching unnecessary and uninteresting circumstances, which rather deaden the narration, is not an act of plagiarism upon the original work, nor against any property of the author in it, but an allowable and meritorious work'.[83] The book Newbery produced fell within this definition and so it was not an infringement.

It is important to set this case alongside that of *Donaldson v Becket*, which was in the courts at the same time and involved many of the same players. The text at issue in that case, the popular landscape poem *The Seasons*, was not an apparently fact-based travel narrative, but it was a work with descriptions of the natural world at its heart. *Donaldson v Becket* has attracted considerable scholarly debate owing, in large part, to the judicial format adopted, uncertainties over how the various judges involved voted on the different questions being asked, and the lack of a definitive judgment that addressed the issues and decided the case. Its significance has also been the subject of debate. For Mark Rose, the arguments made in the case were important in that they developed the representation of the author as a proprietor and the literary work as an object of property.[84] However, as Kathy Bowrey points out, 'while numerous philosophical conceptions were called upon as "common sense" by advocates for and against literary property, the collision of ideas was chaotic, with proponents largely talking past each other'.[85] Importantly, and despite the significance long ascribed to the case, *Donaldson v Becket* did not

[78] C33/442 f179v (11 April 1774); TNA.

[79] See Isabella Alexander, *Copyright and the Public Interest in the Nineteenth Century* (Hart Publishing 2010) 165–74.

[80] C40/3; TNA. See Leeming (n 44) 171.

[81] C33/442 f.368v (5 August 1774); TNA.

[82] *Strahan v Newbery* (1774) Lofft 775; Leeming (n 44) 171.

[83] (1774) Lofft 775, 775.

[84] Mark Rose (n 71) 69–70.

[85] Kathy Bowrey, 'Law, Aesthetics and Copyright Historiography: A Critical Reading of the Genealogies of Martha Woodmansee and Mark Rose' in Isabella Alexander and H Tomás Gómez-Arostegui (eds), *Research Handbook on the History of Copyright Law* (Edward Elgar Publishing 2016) 42.

establish a 'universal legal endorsement of philosophical criteria by the nature or limits to which this authorial property could be discerned'.[86]

The case of *Strahan v Newbery* raised similar questions from a different angle. As with Thomson's *The Seasons*, Hawkesworth's *Voyages* extolled the virtues of trade and empire, and sought to describe and delineate nature. Yet as a travel narrative it presented itself not as a work of poetic authorship, but as a work of fact, science, and information, and its authorship was complex, diffuse, and obfuscated. The legal issue in dispute was not one of simple reprinting but of abridgement, thus raising the question of whether the publisher of a work could trace ownership into an altered text and putting again at issue what exactly it was that could be owned in relation to a book.

The finding that Newbery's publication was an abridgement did not rely on a new principle; nor was it specifically adapted for travel narratives. However, the case and the judge's decision highlight two important themes. First is the interplay between authorship, authority, and authenticity. Hawkesworth's *Voyages* was to be the official, or authorized, account of the voyages of Cook and the other captains. While not produced *by* the Admiralty, it acquired authority through the Admiralty's prevention of the publication of alternative accounts (as far as possible), and from Lord Sandwich's involvement with its production, through the choice of Hawkesworth, and through his relationship with Banks, whose involvement in turn imparted scientific authority. But the question of authorship was more complex. Hawkesworth had not been on the voyages, so he relied on the written accounts of others to produce an account that interweaved perspectives, in particular those of Banks and Cook.[87] As Edwards points out, Hawkesworth's introduction reveals he was 'as confused as anyone about the purpose of the published voyage-narrative, who its readers were to be and what they required'.[88] Hawkesworth awkwardly explains his dilemma over whether to write in the first or third person, concluding that he will write in the first person but that 'the manuscript would be submitted to the Gentlemen in whose names it would be written … and nothing published without their approbation'.[89] Neither Cook nor Carteret was, in fact, happy with much of the manuscript, but their objections do not appear to have resulted in alterations.[90] Further, Hawkesworth made no acknowledgement of his use of Parkinson's materials at the urging of Banks.[91]

In her work on the construction of the identity of 'the Explorer' through proprietary authorship models in the early nineteenth century, Craciun claims that in the earlier period:

86 ibid 43.
87 Edwards (n 34) 87–92.
88 ibid 87.
89 Hawkesworth (n 41) vol 1, iv–v.
90 Edwards (n 34) 88.
91 Joppien and Smith (n 56) vol 1, 54.

> Authorial rights, whether a tactical invention deployed by booksellers or an outgrowth of the modern self's capitalist self-possession (or both) are largely invisible and find little purchase within the corporate and naval polities producing writings on exploration[92]

It is true that there is little evidence of authorial agency to be found in the disputes, which coalesce more around questions of authorization and non-authorization. But authorship was far from irrelevant. The attacks on Hawkesworth raised questions over his authorial qualifications and abilities. Walpole wrote that he had to 'wade through' *Voyages* and complained that 'the entertaining matters would not fill half a volume'.[93] Perhaps more seriously, Hawkesworth's ability to convey accurate scientific information was also attacked. William Dalrymple, still smarting from having been overlooked in favour of Cook to lead the voyage, wrote an extended pamphlet complaining of the treatment of his own work, but with some broader objections, including as to the accuracy of the illustrations:

> The plates of your work seem to be on the plan of La Chappe and some of the worst French Voyages, where fancy and imagination eclipse truth and nature; *Buchan's drawings* of the people of Terra del Fuego convey a perfect idea of *their costume*; your *engraving* shews what they *may be* when a French dancing master has *taught* them *attitudes*: the plates at N 21 and 22 are disgraceful to an *English* Book, and would put even a Gascoon to the blush.[94]

Similarly, the question of whether Newbery's publication was a breach of Strahan's exclusive rights also turned, to an extent, on its own authorial claims. Apsley LC considered that Newbery's edition was 'conveyed in language as good or better than in the original, and in a more agreeable and useful manner', that a true and valuable abridgement was 'an act of understanding' and that in this abridgement Newbery had employed 'understanding' in 'retrenching unnecessary and uninteresting circumstances'.[95] Thus, Newbery himself is portrayed as an author and, indeed, one who had improved upon the earlier work of Hawkesworth.

The second theme that emerges from the case against Newbery is the same interplay between private rights and the claims of the public to have access to information about the natural world. The tension between exclusive rights and the competition that would place more books in the hands of more members of the reading public was already playing out in the common law copyright debates.[96]

[92] Craciun (n 28) 23.
[93] Quoted in Leeming (n 44) 166.
[94] *A Letter from Mr Dalrymple to Dr Hawkesworth* (J Nourse, T Payne, B White, J Robson, P Elmsly, T Davies, and S Leacroft 1773) 26.
[95] *Strahan v Newbery* (n 82).
[96] See Deazley (n 71), in particular chs 7 and 8.

As Leeming has pointed out, Strahan's overpricing of Hawkesworth came to form a plank of Edward Thurlow's rhetorical attack on common-law copyright in the case of *Donaldson v Becket*. Replying to Wedderburn before the House of Lords', Thurlow asked:

> If one court's determination in favour of the common law rights had given three guineas for such a work as Hawkesworth's Voyages, what would not a determination of the House of Lords give? Six guineas at least, so that the public would be materially injured if the monopoly contended for by the respondent was ratified and confirmed. That it was a monopoly tending to distress the public, injure literature and contrary to every spring of natural justice.[97]

One month later, Thurlow addressed the House of Commons to argue against the booksellers' bill attempting to extend the statutory term of copyright, calling them 'a set of impudent monopolising men' and stating that 'Hawkesworth's books, which was a mere composition of trash, sold for three guineas by their monopolising'.[98] There appears to be something of a logical flaw in Thurlow's argument that the public was injured by having their access to such 'trash' restricted. However, this was not the end of either the public interest in, or the litigation over, publications about Cook's voyages: Thurlow would soon get another opportunity to consider the question of who should profit from such publications. Before this could occur, however, more contests over authorship, authority, authenticity, and the depiction of nature arose in relation to the publication of Cook's second voyage.

The Second Voyage: Authorial Antagonists and Competing Visions

The fall-out from the Hawkesworth affair led the Earl of Sandwich and the Admiralty to take a different approach when it came to publishing the account of Cook's second voyage. However, they were not the only parties who had taken lessons from Hawkesworth. The enormous sum his work had raised from Strahan demonstrated the financial attractions of publication, thereby making it something worth fighting over and, indeed, a bitter dispute emerged between Sandwich, Cook and two naturalists, Johann Reinhold Forster and his son George. The roots of this dispute can be traced back to Joseph Banks, and his withdrawal from the second voyage.

[97] W Cobbett, *Parliamentary History of England from the Earliest Times to the Year 1803* (Hansard 1813) xvii, 970.

[98] ibid xvii, 1086; see also Leeming (n 44) 168–69.

Both Banks and Solander had planned to join Cook's second expedition, now in two ships, the *Resolution* and the *Adventure*. Banks had assembled a team of scientists, artists, and secretaries, as well as two horn players, to accompany them, but, when Cook rejected Banks' alterations to the ship, Banks withdrew. Replacements were required and the Admiralty selected the Prussian naturalist Johann Reinhold Forster, who requested his son George be allowed to accompany him. Johann Forster was 'widely regarded as one of the most knowledgeable and competent scholars of his day', and his inclusion on the voyage was welcomed by Linnaeus, who wrote, 'it is to you that all who love and treasure natural science should look'.[99] Also contributing to the progress of scientific observation on the voyage were the astronomers William Wales and William Bayly and the artist William Hodges. Hodges' artistic specialty was landscape, and his drawings and paintings on the voyage came to pay particular attention to weather, light, and atmospheric conditions.[100] Later, Forster recruited the Swedish physician and botanist Anders Sparrman to join the voyage at the Cape of Good Hope.[101]

The terms of the agreement between the Admiralty and the Forsters came to form the basis of the subsequent dispute. According to the Forsters, it was agreed that they should be granted the sum of £4,000 (which Parliament had already allocated for the naturalist Lind, who was to accompany Banks), but that Johann Forster, knowing this would have to be used to cover their expenses, in addition proposed two conditions: first, that he should 'be employed to write the history of the voyage, and enjoy all the profits of the publication … in the same manner as (the late) Dr Hawkesworth)'; secondly, that a place be made for him after the voyage so he could continue to support his large family'.[102] Daines Barrington, who was carrying out the negotiations, apparently agreed to the terms, and noted that one of the chief aims of sending Forster was to write up the voyage as 'Captain Cook had pleaded his inability to write an account of his circumnavigation in the Endeavour and had entirely given up thoughts of becoming an author'.[103] The conflict between Banks and the Admiralty that had led to Forster's inclusion on the voyage, and the tension this perhaps indicated in relation to the desired outcomes for the voyage, seem to have been appreciated by Forster, who wrote to the naturalist Thomas Pennant: 'I shall do for Natural History whatever lies in my power; my efforts will be great, as I have great Antagonists & the Expectations of my Patrons and Friends are likewise great.'[104] The statement was to prove prophetic.

[99] Michael E Hoare, *The Tactless Philosopher: Johan Reinhold Forster (1729–1798)* (Hawthorn Press 1976) v, 76.

[100] Smith (n 30) 45.

[101] Williams (n 29) 99.

[102] *A Letter to the Right Honourable the Earl of Sandwich, First Lord Commissioner of the Board of the Admiralty, &c, From George Forster, FRS* (G Robinson 1778) 3–4.

[103] ibid 4.

[104] Michael Dettelbach, '"A Kind of Linnaean Being": Forster and Eighteenth-Century Natural History' in Nicholas Thomas, Harriet Guest, and Michael Dettelbach (eds), *Observations Made during a Voyage Round the World, by Johan Reinhold Forster* (University of Hawai'i Press 1996) lxv.

Forster's experience of the voyage was evidently not a happy one. Willing to endure considerable hardship in the collection of specimens, his prickly personality led to conflict with his shipmates.[105] However, he and his companions collected 330 plant specimens, 220 of which had not been previously identified, as well as 104 birds and 74 fishes new to science. They also sketched around 500 plants and 300 animals.[106] Upon returning to England, Forster did not receive the same rapturous reception as had Banks and Solander. Nevertheless, he quickly completed a large folio work, *Characteres generum plantum*, containing descriptions and drawings of many of the botanical specimens collected on the voyage, which was published and presented to the king in November 1775. His intention of producing a narrative account of the voyage, however, was soon frustrated.

According to his son George's later account, as they reached the Cape of Good Hope on their homeward journey, Cook received a copy of Hawkesworth's *Voyages*, as well as news of Hawkesworth's 'prodigious profits'. This inspired in Cook a desire to 'obtain a share in the emoluments of the history of the voyage' and, according again to George, a plan was hatched between Cook and Sandwich to renege on the agreement with Forster.[107] It seems that first Sandwich developed a scheme that would give two-fifths of the profits of the work to Cook (whose journals were to be used), one-fifth to Hodges, whose drawings would be used for the engraved plates, and two-fifths to Forster. The latter agreed, but was required to submit a specimen of work, which Sandwich found unsatisfactory. In April 1776, a new plan was formulated. Sandwich summoned Cook and Forster to the Admiralty and they signed an agreement according to which the work would be split into two: Forster would produce the 'philosophical' part, and Cook the 'nautical' part, with the profits split equally. The engraved plates would also be split—Cook was to have charge of finding 'proper persons' to engrave maps, charts, and surveys, while Forster would arrange for engraved plates of natural history, utensils, implements of war, and 'the natives'. The Admiralty would cover the cost of engraving the plates, but reserved the right to distribute the plates between the two volumes. Afterwards, the plates would become the property of Cook and Forster.[108]

The agreement would not hold for long. Forster submitted a second specimen of writing to Sandwich who, again, found it unsatisfactory and insisted it be edited (or 'corrected'). Richard Owen Cambridge was engaged to do the corrections, overseen by Daines Barrington.[109] The changes made were entirely unacceptable to Forster, who considered his manuscript 'mutilated'. Indeed, he considered his authorial persona at stake, even emasculated, as George later explained:

[105] Edwards (n 34) 108–12; Williams (n 29) ch 5.
[106] Williams (n 29) 116–17.
[107] Forster (n 102) 12.
[108] ibid App II, 5.
[109] Beaglehole (n 6) 467.

> Where is the man of such finished impudence, who will consent freely to be represented to the world as in a state of insanity? And yet this was the only light in which an author could appear, who should have ventured to publish such a manuscript as my father's after it had been castrated by Mr Barrington.[110]

Having reached this impasse, Forster offered to sell his own manuscripts to the Admiralty for £200 and to forgo his promised profits for a lump sum of £1,000. While it seems Cook was in favour of accepting the offer, Sandwich approached the king, who commanded Sandwich to expedite the publication of Cook's narrative only, if Forster would not submit to the corrections.[111] Forster attempted to acquire proofs of the copperplates, some of which were based on his own drawings, knowing their commercial value to any book of the voyage, but was prevented by the Admiralty, which demanded they be returned.[112] Furthermore, the final element of the agreement, namely that Forster would be given early copies of Cook's proofs to translate into French and German, was also denied.[113] In imminent need of finance, Forster accepted 400 guineas from Banks for George's drawings.[114]

It was now settled that Cook himself would produce the narrative, authorized and supported by the Admiralty, with editorial assistance from Dr John Douglas, Canon of Windsor. However, his was still not the first account of the voyage to appear on the market. In 1775, shortly after the *Resolution's* return, an anonymous publication, *Journey of the Resolution's Voyage* (apparently written by Joseph Marra, a gunner's mate), was published by Newbery. Cook does not seem to have been overly concerned, writing to the Secretary of the Admiralty: 'If this is the only account of the Voyage that is printing, I do not think it worth regarding; I have taken some measures to find out if there are any more'.[115] A second anonymous publication, *Second Voyage Round the World*, appeared in 1776.[116]

The third publication to beat Cook to market was by George Forster. George framed his authorship efforts as being compelled 'to alleviate if possible, in some measure, the difficulties to which [Lord Sandwich's] arbitrary proceedings had reduced my father and his unhappy family'.[117] George Forster's two-volume work, *A Voyage Round the World*, was published in March 1777 by the London booksellers White, Robson, and Elmsly and sold at the price of two guineas. Without being subject to the delays occasioned by engravings, and by dint of hard work, Forster was able to beat Cook into print by six weeks. His victory, however, was

110 Forster (n 102) 14–15.
111 ibid 17; see also Hoare (n 99) 161.
112 Hoare (n 99) 163; Forster (n 102) 17.
113 Beaglehole (n 6) 469–70; Forster (n 102) 19.
114 Hoare (n 99) 164.
115 Quoted in Edwards (n 34) 103.
116 ibid 105n.
117 Forster(n 102) 17.

short-lived. In May 1777, Strahan and Cadell published Cook's *A Voyage Towards the South Pole and Round the World*. The two volumes contained sixty-three engraved plates, but were sold at the same price as Forster's two volumes. George accused the Admiralty of interfering to lower the price to below cost, which would normally have been four guineas, so that the work could compete with George's on price. Further, he added that to ensure that Cook's own profit margins were not affected by the strategy, the Admiralty had covered the expenses of paper and print and made him a gift of the plates.[118]

Indeed, the plates also formed a site of aesthetic conflict. The plates were taken from paintings made by William Hodges, the artist on the voyage. Hodges specialized in landscape painting, but was required to engage also in portraiture for representing Pacific peoples. Bernard Smith suggests that the problem arose when Hodges returned and felt obliged to recast the paintings executed for the Admiralty and exhibited in the Royal Academy to reflect conventional neo-classical, picturesque, and romantic themes. He was roundly attacked by George Forster for the engraving of the peoples of 'Eua, which Forster protested did 'not convey any adequate idea' of the 'Euan people. Forster went on to complain that: 'The connoisseur will find Greek contours and features in this picture, which have never existed in the South Sea.'[119] However, as Tobin points out, it could also be argued that 'in applying classical tropes to Pacific Islanders, Hodges thought he was dignifying his subject matter, making a claim for the significance of these interactions that would go beyond detailing the exotic to articulating universal truths about encounters between disparate peoples'.[120] This outburst indicates the complex nature of the 'antagonism' between all parties. At stake was not just the ability to profit from written and graphic accounts of the voyage, but the way that the voyage itself, and its natural history, would be framed. Whose imprint upon nature would succeed in the marketplace; whose authorial voice, and whose aesthetic vision, would command most authority?

The various contractual relations, both spoken and written, entered into by the parties clearly recognized the importance of the narrative as a valuable commodity in the marketplace. The journals upon which each man based their published narratives were seen as significant only as source material (although both Cook's journals and those of Johann Forster were subsequently edited and published as distinct offerings). Both Cook's and George Forster's *Voyages* were to a large extent collaborative works. Cook had significant editorial assistance from Douglas and drew on the journal of the astronomer, William Wales. George Forster's work was heavily based both on his father's journals and those of Cook.[121] Indeed, one

[118] ibid 18–19.
[119] Smith (n 30) 72.
[120] Tobin (n 15) 148.
[121] Ruth Pritchard Dawson, 'Georg Forster's Reise Um Die Welt: A Travelogue in its Eighteenth-Century Context' PhD Dissertation (University of Michigan 1973) 30–37.

of George's biographers points to further contributions by the Oxford astronomer, Thomas Hornsby, and the German scholar, Dr Raspe.[122]

Nevertheless, each man was at pains to develop a distinct authorial voice. Cook framed his introduction by listing the navigators who came before him, beginning with Magellan, before moving to establish his technical expertise with an explanation of the kind of ship, equipment, and manpower required for such a journey. He explained the editorial assistance he had received as being necessary due to his imminent departure on another voyage and being provided by 'some friends'. The account was designed 'for information, and not merely for amusement'. Cook's authority as an author would not lie in his literary style or education; indeed, he requested the reader overlook 'inaccuracies of style' from one who, having spent his life at sea 'has had no opportunity of cultivating letters'. Rather, they should value his account as one emanating from 'a plain man, zealously executing himself in the service of his Country, and determined to give the best account he is able of his proceedings'.[123] Cook himself valued the book as both a truthful account and as an object with commercial value. He also emphasized the contribution of the imagery supplied by Hodges. On the verge of setting off on his third voyage, he wrote to a friend:

> The Journal of my late Voyage will be published in the course of the next winter, and I am to have the sole advantage of the sale. It will want those flourishes which Dr Hawkesworth gave the other, but it will be illustrated and ornamented with about sixty copper plates, which, I am of opinion, will exceed every thing that has been done in a work of this kind; as they are all of them from Drawings made on the spot, by a very able artist.[124]

Forster, meanwhile, pinned his colours to the claims of science and regal patronage, commencing his work with the grand claim that: 'History does not offer an example of such disinterested efforts, towards the enlargement of human knowledge, as have been made by the British nation, since the accession of his present Majesty to the Throne.'[125] He located his authority to write the voyage in the Admiralty's initial arrangement with this father (subsequently, as he explained, revoked), the journals of his father (a man 'prompted by his natural love of science') and his own participation in the voyage. Here he compared his own account to that of Hawkesworth, which had 'incurred universal censure' as a result of having been 'compiled by a person who had not been on the voyage'.[126] He further cast doubt

[122] ibid 37–43.

[123] James Cook, *A Voyage Towards the South Pole and Round the World* (Strahan and Cadell 1777) xxxvi.

[124] Beaglehole (n 6) 505.

[125] Georg Forster, *A Voyage round the world in His Britannic Majesty's Sloop, Resolution, commanded by Capt James Cook, during the Years 1772, 3, 4, and 5*, vol 1 (B White, J Robson, and P Elmsley 1777) iii.

[126] ibid ix–x.

on Cook's authorship, observing that 'The active life of captain Cook, and his indefatigable pursuits after discoveries, have made it impossible for him to superintend the printing of his own Journals; and the public, I am much afraid, must again converse with him by means of an interpreter'.[127] He went on to suggest that Cook's version would be subject to censorship, which would further undermine 'the authenticity of the performance'.[128]

George's own authorship would be subsequently queried by William Wales in another pamphlet in which Wales accused George of placing his name on a book written by his father in order to avoid the Admiralty's prohibition on Forster publishing such a narrative.[129] In pursuance of the agreement of April 1776, the elder Forster did eventually publish his own 'philosophical' work, *Observations Made During a Voyage Round the World*, in 1778. This would be Forster's most important work and it was received as a significant contribution to natural history in the scientific community.[130] In this work, Forster transformed empirical observations of both nature and the people of the South Seas into 'elaborate arguments concerning the progress of happiness, education, and civility'.[131]

Lacking the authority of the Admiralty's support, the publishing networks of Strahan, and the naval authority and growing popular fame of Cook, the Forsters turned to the court of public opinion. George set out details of the quarrel in the Introduction to his work, arranged for publication of his reproachful letter to the Earl of Sandwich, and also published his response to William Wales.[132] They did not entirely eschew the law, going to the trouble of swearing oaths before the Court of the King's Bench as to the veracity of their complaints and appending these, along with the text of the agreement entered into with Lord Sandwich, to the published letter.[133] Indeed, reputations of all sorts were at stake, as can be seen in a letter Lord Sandwich wrote to Daines Barrington on 11 June 1776:

> Dr Forster must allow me to say that, although his reputation as a writer is materially concerned in this publication, mine also as a judge of good and bad writing, is concerned, if the performance is to appear before the public. I will therefore not give any sanction to it till you tell me that you think it such as ought to appear under the approbation of the Admiralty.[134]

[127] ibid x.

[128] ibid x.

[129] William Wales, *Remarks on Mr Forster's Account of Captain Cook's last Voyage round the World, in the Years 1772, 1773, 1774, and 1775* (J Nourse 1778) 9.

[130] Hoare (n 99) 183–84.

[131] Nicholas Thomas, 'John Reinhold Forster and His Observations' in Nicholas Thomas, Harriet Guest, and Michael Dettelbach (eds), *Observations Made During a Voyage Round the World* (University of Hawai'i Press 1996) xx.

[132] *Reply to Mr Wales's Remarks by George Forster FRS* (B White, J Robson, and P Elmsly 1778).

[133] Forster (n 102).

[134] Sandwich to Barrington (11 June 1776), quoted in Hoare (n 99) 182.

Whatever the truth of the matters underlying the dispute, there was certainly a growing concern at the Admiralty for the 'authoritative' nature of the account to be published at its expense.

Publishing the Third Voyage: Nature Depicted and the Death of the Author

Cook's third voyage is distinguished from the previous two in that there were no civilian naturalists sent aboard the ships, although the astronomer William Bayly would travel on board the *Discovery*. Cook selected James King as second lieutenant of the *Resolution* upon the recommendation of Thomas Hornsby, an Oxford professor of astronomy. In a well-known but not well-substantiated story, Cook responded to King's regret that there were no naturalists on the voyage with the comment: 'Curse the scientists, and all science into the bargain.'[135] William Anderson, the *Resolution*'s surgeon, had an interest in natural history that he could be expected to pursue, and David Nelson, a gardener from Kew, was sent to assist, his wages being paid by Banks.[136] Most significantly, Cook chose John Webber as the voyage's artist, at the suggestion of Daniel Solander. Webber was trained as both a landscape artist and a figure draughtsman, and he provided a comprehensive visual record of the voyage, producing drawings of landscapes, encounters with local peoples and natural history drawings, mostly of birds.[137] Webber's role was clearly set out in the introduction to the official account of the voyage, with the narrator (ostensibly Cook) stating:

> Mr Webber was pitched upon, and engaged to embark with me, for the express purpose of supplying the unavoidable imperfections of written accounts, by enabling us to preserve, and to bring home, such drawings of the most memorable scenes of our transactions, as could only be expected by a professed and skilled artist.[138]

Cook had intended to write the account of his third voyage, but he did not return with his ship, having been killed in Hawai'i.[139] The Admiralty had given the usual

[135] Williams (n 29) 123.
[136] ibid 125.
[137] Smith (n 30) 73; Williams (n 29) 125.
[138] James Cook and James King, *A Voyage to the Pacific Ocean: Undertaken, by the Command of His Majesty, for Making Discoveries in the Northern Hemisphere … Performed under the Direction of Captains Cook, Clerke and Gore, in His Majesty's Ships the Resolution and Discovery: in the Years 1776, 1777, 1778, 1779, and 1789* (Nicol 1784) 5.
[139] John Douglas recounted in his Introduction to the account of Cook's third voyage that: 'Captain Cook, knowing, before he sailed upon this last expedition, that it was expected from him to *relate*, as well as to *execute*, its operations, had taken care to prepare such a journal as might be made use of for publication.' ibid lxxvii.

instructions to Cook that upon his return to England, he should immediately report to the Admiralty Office to lay before the Lords Commissioners a full account of his journey, as well as his surveys and drawings, taking care to include the log books and journals of his officers as well. He was to instruct them not to divulge where they had been until they had permission to do so.[140] The ships returned under the command of Captain James King, arriving in London on 4 October 1780, and the requested materials were deposited with the Admiralty.

Preparations for publication were soon under way, directed again by Lord Sandwich and Banks. The work was to form three volumes. The first two volumes, which covered Cook's voyage, were prepared for publication by Canon John Douglas from Cook's journals, supplemented by those of William Anderson, surgeon on the *Resolution*, which were made available to Douglas by the Admiralty. The third volume was based upon the journals of Captain James King.[141] Again, the authorship of the volumes was diffuse. With one author of the underlying source material deceased, and the other having departed on a new voyage, Douglas was at pains to emphasize Cook's authorial contribution, stating that 'this journal, which exists in his own hand-writing, has been faithfully adhered to', but adding that he had also made use of Anderson's journal in relation to matters 'imperfectly touched, or altogether omitted' by Cook.[142] The third volume, Douglas states, 'was completely prepared for the press by Captain King himself'.[143] It is soon clear, however, that significant other contributions, enumerated by Douglas in the Introduction, have been made to the volumes: by Henry Roberts who drew up the charts, by the shipboard artist John Webber, the engravers of the charts and plates (see Fig 8.3), through additional consultation with King and others, including William Wales.[144] While authorship was aggregate, authority for the volumes was clearly articulated in two respects: first, with His Majesty, under whose direction and encouragement the voyage was made; and, secondly, with the Admiralty, which for the first time explicitly claimed it on the title page with the words 'Published by Order of the Lords Commissioners of the Admiralty'.[145]

[140] Secret instructions for Captain James Cook, Commander of his Majesty's Sloop the Resolution, 6 July 1776, reproduced in Cook and King (n 138) xxxv.

[141] Cook and King (n 138)

[142] For a detailed discussion of Douglas' contribution see Ian S MacLaren, 'Exploration/Travel Literature and the Evolution of the Author' (1992) 5 *International Journal of Canadian Studies* 39; also Tobin (n 15) 156–58.

[143] Cook and King (n 138) lxviii.

[144] ibid lxxiv–lxxv.

[145] The many advertisements for the upcoming publication likewise emphasized that the book was published by order of the Admiralty.

Figure 8.3 'Sea Horses', drawn by J Webber, engraved by E Scott, figures by J Heath, engraved plate 52 in James Cook and James King, *A Voyage to the Pacific Ocean: undertaken, by the command of His Majesty, for making discoveries in the northern hemisphere . . . : performed under the direction of Captains Cook, Clerke and Gore, in His Majesty's ships the Resolution and Discovery: in the years 1776, 1777, 1778, 1779, and 1789* (Nicol 1784).
Reproduced from the collections of the State Library of NSW, F78/5 (Dixson Library).

Transforming the voyages from an expedition of lofty aims into a literary product for the marketplace was, however, a slow process and hampered in several respects. In 1782, Douglas wrote to Banks stating that he had finished inscribing, arranging, and numbering the plates.[146] However, there were still delays, in reducing the charts, and in finding engravers, and there was difficulty in obtaining the appropriate quality and thickness of paper.[147] The publisher of the work was no longer William Strahan, but George Nicol (or Nichol) with Thomas Cadell. The firm of W and A Strahan remained involved, but on this occasion was credited as printer.[148] George Nicol had been appointed as bookseller to the king in 1781, and

[146] Letter from Dr Douglas, Amen Corner, to Sir Joseph Banks (5 November 1782) (Auckland Heritage Collections GMS 57).

[147] Cook and King (n 138) lxxxi–lxxxii; Letter from G Nicol to Sir Joseph Banks (10 October 1783) (Auckland Libraries Heritage Collections GMS 58).

[148] Other printers were clearly also involved, as mentioned in Nicol's letter to Banks in October 1783, where he names Mrs Haddile and Kaynes currently undertaking the work as 'the best printers in London', but urges the employment of more printers to speed up proceedings. Letter from G Nicol to Sir Joseph Banks (n 147).

his involvement might indicate His Majesty's growing interest and involvement in the publication.

Authority and authorship were one thing, but ownership of the copyright was quite another. In June 1782, Cook's widow wrote to Lord Sandwich asking if he might be able to make some provision for her and her family 'upon the presumption that the History of the Voyage in which my dear Husband lost his Life will soon be laide before the Public'.[149] The Admiralty was content to do so. In his introduction, Douglas requested indulgence from the reader for his own role, 'having engaged in a very tedious and troublesome undertaking upon the most *disinterested* motives; his only reward being the satisfaction he feels, in having been able to do an essential service to the family of our great navigator'.[150] The distribution of profits would not occur until 1785 but, in the meantime, the question of copyright raised more pressing issues.

Despite the Admiralty's and the Captain's orders, the booksellers could hardly ignore the vacuum created by the delay in the official publication. One account of the voyage was published anonymously in 1781 by Newbery, authorship later being claimed by John Rickman, lieutenant on the *Resolution*.[151] While no legal action was taken, it does appear that the Admiralty sought to interfere in relation to the former, with Rickman claiming in the Preface to the second edition that his work had been maligned by the Admiralty out of 'jealousy ... which this work might excite, lest the sale of that account which is one day or other to be published by authority might be affected'.[152] A second account was written by William Wade Ellis, surgeon's mate on the voyage, and published by London booksellers Robinson, Sewell, and Debrett in 1782.[153] This work included a folding chart and 21 plates engraved from Ellis' own artworks. He sold the work for 50 guineas, but incurred the wrath of Banks for doing so. Banks wrote to Ellis that he was 'sorry you have Engaged in so impudent a business as the publication of your Observations', and added that although he might have helped Ellis in the future, he would no longer be able to do so.[154]

[149] Beaglehole (n 6) 691.

[150] Cook and King (n 138) lxxix.

[151] *Journal of Captain Cook's last Voyage to the Pacific Ocean, on Discovery; performed in the Years 1776, 1777, 1778, 1779, illustrated with Cuts, and a Chart, shewing the Tracts of the Ships employed in this Expedition. Faithfully Narrated from the original MS* (F Newbery 1781).

[152] John Rickman, *Journal of Captain Cook's last Voyage to the Pacific Ocean, on Discovery; performed in the Years 1776, 1777, 1778, 1779, illustrated with Cuts, and a Chart, shewing the Tracts of the Ships employed in this Expedition. Faithfully Narrated from the original MS* (2nd edn, F Newbery 1781).

[153] W Ellis, *An Authentic Narrative of a Voyage performed by Captain Cook and Captain Clerke, in His Majesty's ships the Resolution and Discovery, during the years 1776, 1777, 1778, 1779, and 1780, in search of a North-West passage between the Continents of Asia and America* (G Robinson, J Sewell, and J Debrett 1782). A second edition was published in 1783, and a third in 1784.

[154] Quoted in James Taylor, *Picturing the Pacific: Joseph Banks and the Shipboard Artists of Cook and Flinders* (Adlard Coles 2018) 54. See also JC Beaglehole (ed), *The Journals of Captain James Cook on his Voyages of Discovery: The Voyage of the Resolution and Discovery 1776–1780* (Boydell Press 1999) ccvii.

Two years later, the Admiralty's 'official' version, including maps, charts, and illustrative prints, was published by Nicol and Cadell. It appeared under the title *A Voyage to the Pacific Ocean undertaken by the Command of His Majesty for making Discoveries in the Northern Hemisphere*. The Lords Commissioners registered it with the Stationers' Company on 28 May 1784, but no statement as to the author was made and the party registering was named as the Lords Commissioners of the Admiralty. Eventually published on 4 June 1784, the three quarto volumes were sold at a price of £4 14*s* and 6 pennies *(d)*. The decision to 'give the work to the Public at little more than prime costs' was later rued by Nicol, who wrote to Banks in 1801 complaining that the popularity of the work (by then in its third edition) could have produced a profit of £12,000 rather than £4,000 to that date.[155]

Notwithstanding efforts to keep the price down, it was not long before new and unauthorized publications began to appear. In June 1784, *The Universal Magazine of Knowledge and Pleasure* began to publish extracts from *A Voyage to the Pacific Ocean*, including as illustrations 'many Cuts copied from those published by Direction of the Lords of the Admiralty'.[156] On 31 July 1784, George Kearsley announced the publication of *An Abridgement of Captain Cook's Last Voyage performed in the Years 1776, 1777, 1778, 1779 and 1780; undertaken by command of His Majesty for making Discoveries in the Northern Hemisphere*.[157] In his advertisement, Kearsley helpfully explained that:

> The splendid edition of this entertaining work, just published by the Lords of the Admiralty, is sold for Four Guineas and a Half. This Compendium is faithfully extracted from it, to accommodate such as cannot make so expensive a purchase, however their curiosity may be excited. All the Nautical and Astronomical Parts are entirely omitted.[158]

Kearsley had already published abridgements of the earlier voyages and promised to reissue them to accompany his new volume. In the Introduction to his work, he doubled down on his public-spirited motivation for the venture, and—possibly with a view to framing his defence to the copyright suit he was about to confront—he explained:

> The price of the splendid and elegant quarto Edition lately printed by order of the Lords of the Admiralty, under the patronage of His Majesty, is unavoidably (from the numerous and expensive engravings) so very high, that the majority of the Public are excluded from the pleasure of reading it: and it is an undoubted

155 Letter from G Nicol to Sir Joseph Banks (14 January 1801) (Auckland Libraries Heritage Collections GMS 71).
156 *General Evening Post* (1–3 July 1784) 5.
157 *Whitehall Evening Post* (31 July–3 August 1784) 1.
158 ibid.

fact, that not one person in fifty can with convenience, or propriety, make the purchase, however eager their curiosity to peruse it.

To accommodate the great number who are included in this description, has been the principal aim in printing this Epitome ... His Majesty's motives in projecting these long and hazardous voyages, were truly laudable, as they had the general benefit of society without distinction, and the honour of Great Britain in particular, for their objects. This Abridgement will considerably contribute to the accomplishments of those desirable pursuits; pursuits worthy of a great King, reigning over a great People.[159]

Gesturing towards *Strahan v Newbery*, Kearsley added:

> Abridgements of such large works as are either useful or entertaining, have ever been encouraged, for the reasons already mentioned; and likewise, because they give the mind a bias to rational amusement, and (what is of still more importance) contribute to the extension of useful knowledge, without the inconvenience of incuring (sic) an expence (sic) amounting almost to a prohibition.[160]

Upon hearing about Kearsley's intentions, the Lords Commissioners asked him to desist from publishing and deliver up to them any profit he had made and any copies remaining. Kearsley refused, claiming first that they did not have good title, and secondly that his book was not the same but contained many material alterations. On the day of publication, 31 July 1784, the Attorney General, Richard Pepper Arden, brought a complaint in Chancery on behalf of the Lords of the Admiralty against Kearsley. Arden claimed that the book Kearsley had published was 'in very near the same words or however of the same purport or effect' as the official account and so was in breach of the Statute of Anne.[161] The Lord Chancellor was now Edward Thurlow. He held that the Bill of Complaint had failed to mention 'the charitable purpose' of the publication and there was nothing to establish that the property was held by the Lords Commissioners. In fact, he said, 'for any thing appearing the Voyage was published as a present to the public'.[162]

To remedy this situation, a further complaint was brought to the Court on 11 August 1784 by Nicol, stating that the Lords Commissioners did 'authorise and empower' him to print and publish the book, for which he would receive a reward but pass on the profits to the Admiralty.[163] Lord Chancellor Thurlow heard the

[159] *Abridgment of Captain Cook's Last Voyage Performed in the Years 1776, 1777, 1778, 1779 and 1780; Undertaken by Command of His Majesty for Making Discoveries in the Northern Hemisphere* (Kearsley 1784) iii.

[160] ibid iv.

[161] Complaint of Richard Pepper Arden, C12/964/2 (31 July 1784).

[162] GT Exch Ch Reports 324.

[163] Complaint of George Nicoll, C12/135/18 (11 August 1784).

complaints of all the parties together on 16 August 1784 and granted an injunction until Kearsley should put in an Answer.[164] The injunction was still in force when, on 11 December 1784, Nicol sought a second injunction against the booksellers John Stockdale, James Scatcherd, Isaac Whitaker, John Fielding, and John Hardy.[165] They had begun in August to publish by monthly numbers a book, in octavo, which they called 'a Copious Comprehensive and Satisfactory Abridgment of Cook and King's *Voyage to the Pacific Ocean*'. By December, the defendants had printed off between 3,000 and 4,000 copies of each number, of which 54,000 copies had been sold at £36 per 1,000.[166]

Nicol again charged that this work was 'in very near the same words however of the same purport or effect' as the official account.[167] It appears an interim injunction was granted, but in this case the defendants did put in an Answer.[168] They claimed that, upon realizing the huge demand for the work, Nicol and the Lords Commissioners 'formed a Design of monopolising that Edition' to the prejudice of the public and those who had subscribed to it. Stockdale himself had subscribed for 100 sets but had only fifteen delivered to him, while other booksellers who had subscribed for similar amounts had none delivered. After publication, two of the defendants, Scatcherd and Whitaker, had approached Nicol to buy twenty sets at £4 14 shillings (*s*), the non-trade price, rather than the trade price of £3 12*s* a set. However, despite having copies in stock, Nicol refused. The defendants further alleged that those prices were 'very unreasonable and extravagant' given that the plates in the book were 'engraved at the Expence of His Majesty or paid for out of the public Money and were meant and intended as a present to the public and not for the private advantage of the Complainant', while the expense of printing and publishing did not exceed 28*s* per set.[169]

They admitted having published nineteen numbers, but denied their volume was the same as Nicol's, saying it contained many differences and was 'a fair Abridgement' and not a 'colourable Abridgement'. They added that they had paid someone to carry out the abridgement and that it 'is written in much better Stile and Language' than Nicol's books, as well as commissioning their own engraved plates 'at a great expence'. They published this book on account of the 'great Price and Scarcity' of Nicol's works, which by then were being sold to the trade at six to nine guineas and were still difficult to purchase. They also added that, even if the

[164] C33/462/461r; *Nichols v Kearsley* [1784] Dickens 645.

[165] *Nichols v Kearsley* [1784] Dickens 645; C12/135/18 [1784]; *Nicol v Stockdale, Scatcherd, Whitaker, Fielding, and Hardy* [1784] C12/132/23; 3 Swans 687; Lincoln's Inn Misc MS 109, 211 *Nicol v Stockdale and Others* (15 January 1785) from Mr Romilly's Notes.

[166] Answer of Stockdale, Scatcherd, Whitaker, Fielding, and Hardy C12/132/23 m2 (19 January 1785).

[167] Complaint of Nicol C12/132/23 m1 (11 December 1784).

[168] In the defendants' answer, they claim they were served with the injunction on 20 December 1784: Answer of Stockdale, Scatcherd, Whitaker, Fielding, and Hardy C12/132/23 m2 (19 January 1785).

[169] ibid.

Court found they had copied the work, Nicol did not have any property in either the book or the prints contained in it.[170]

In addition to the abridgement question, a second legal problem for Nicol and the Admiralty lay in the charitable arrangement they had made with Cook's widow and the other heirs, as well as their failure to properly construct the issue of ownership in their Bill of Complaint. Nicol's Bill of Complaint stated that the Lords Commissioners were entitled to profits from the sale, but did not state that Nicol had paid for the printing and publishing. The Lord Chancellor concluded that Nicol could therefore only be seen as a servant acting at the direction of the Admiralty and not as either a proprietor or assignee. Not holding exclusive title, he could not be entitled to an injunction and Thurlow LC ordered that the injunction be dissolved. He added that if the Bill had stated the object of the publication, then he would have considered Nicol to be a trustee and granted the injunction on that basis.[171]

Stockdale and his partners were not above using the legal case for advertising purposes. On 1 January 1785, they placed a notice in *The Times*, complaining about the injunction having been brought *ex parte*, without notice to the defendants, and not delivered until it was too late for them to put in an Answer. They promised that the numbers now stopped would be printed in the 'same stile of elegance' as the preceding ones that had 'stimulated the envy of Mr Nicoll'. Further, they put the public benefits of their addition front and centre, adding that Nicol by

> [p]utting an exorbitant price upon the edition partially vended by him, frustrates the intention of Parliament, which granted a supply of public money for the purpose of disseminating nautical and philosophical knowledge among all classes, and who did not mean to confine it to the opulent, or bury it in dusty libraries to which the public have no access.[172]

On 18 January 1785, they were undoubtedly delighted to place additional advertisements informing the public that the injunction had been dissolved and subscribers could receive the remaining numbers, along with two copperplates and a general chart of the three voyages.[173]

Although ownership could not be established satisfactorily for the purposes of the infringement suit, the Admiralty made good on its commitment to Mrs Cook, although she was not to have sole rights to the profits. On 28 July 1785, a memorandum was drawn up in the presence of Lord Sandwich, Lord Howe (who had succeeded Sandwich as first Lord), Sir Joseph Banks and Admiralty Secretary

[170] ibid.
[171] GT Exch Ch Reports 325.
[172] *The Times* (1 January 1785) 3.
[173] *Morning Post* (18 January 1785).

Philip Stephens. It stated that the profits would be divided as follows: one half to Cook's family, with Mrs Cook holding the principal during her life, and after her death, being divided equally amongst surviving children; one-quarter to the heirs of Captain King, who had died the preceding October; and one-eighth to the legal representatives of Captain Clerke. The final eighth, after a sum was deducted for Mr Anderson's executors, was to go to 'Mr Blyth' (identified by Cook's biographer Beaglehole as William Bligh)[174] in recognition of his surveying and cartographic services.[175] Despite the Admiralty's failure to close the door on competing abridgements, the work generated considerable profits, as noted above. By 1801, it was in its third edition and producing about £40 profit a year.[176]

Conclusion

It is hardly surprising that exploration narratives became embroiled in copyright disputes during formative periods of modern copyright law. Travel writing was the most popular literary genre of the period, responding to and fuelling popular interest in science, the natural world, the exotic, trade opportunities, and the prestige of imperial acquisition. In examining the construction of different accounts and visions of the natural world, and how those accounts were ushered into print, and then reproduced, altered, and circulated in different ways, it can be seen that copyright law becomes an important part of the cycle of accumulation of knowledge. Copyright (as well as contracts based on copyright) were used to marshal, control, and make official specific constructions of nature, which in turn aligned with imperial ideologies and imperatives. But the cycles, as Latour noted, could also 'leak at the seam'. The legal disputes that arose over abridgements could be seen as examples of such a leakage, so that the accounts do not remain stable, but are retold and reimagined, reaching different audiences and performing different purposes.

There are other parallels that emerge in the relationships between travel writing and nature, and between copyright and nature. One such parallel is the role played by labour in reducing something held in common into something that can have commercial value and be subject to ownership. As Sherman and Bently have observed, the common law copyright litigation known as the 'battle of the booksellers' was instrumental in developing a justification for copyright as a property right that rested upon a version of Locke's possessive individualism and, in particular, the role of (mental) labour.[177] In copyright doctrine, it is thus human labour or action

[174] Memorandum for the division of profits arising from the sale of the book of Captain Cook's late voyage (28 July 1785) (Auckland Heritage Collections GMS 59).

[175] Beaglehole (n 6) 692.

[176] Letter from G Nicol to Sir Joseph Banks (n 155).

[177] Brad Sherman and Lionel Bently, *The Making of Modern Intellectual Property Law* (Cambridge University Press 1999) 23–24.

that gives rise to the copyright work, moving it from the realm of unowned ideas to owned expression. What happens then if the unowned ideas are found in nature? Can a description or depiction of nature then be owned? As Bernard Edelman asks, 'under what conditions can one consider oneself to be the "author" of nature?'[178] For him, the answer is when 'the stamp of personality is imposed upon it'.[179] And who is the author? 'The author is someone who "augments"; who is involved in the artistic translation of the action of "man" upon nature'.[180] Edelman's examples are drawn from French law, but in the common law tradition, a similar approach can be discerned. In the 1740 case of *Blackwell v Harper*, Lord Hardwicke LC had no trouble finding that Elizabeth Blackwell's botanical prints were 'inventions' and within the Engravings Act's protection despite being 'taken from nature'.[181]

Likewise, what the explorers and scientists valued in nature was either the product of labour or its potential to be so.[182] Describing the western coast of Australia, Cook wrote in his journal:

> We are to Consider that we see this Country in the pure state of Nature, the Industry of Man had had nothing to do with any part of it and yet we find all such things as nature hath bestow'd upon it in a flourishing state. In this Extensive Country it can never be doubted what most sorts of Grain, Fruits, Roots, &c of every kind would flourish.[183]

However, as more recent scholarship has sought to emphasize, far from being naturally picturesque and untouched by human hand, this was a 'highly artificial aboriginal landscape', manipulated over long periods by indigenous fire management and agricultural practices.[184] In line with his earlier works and lectures on natural history, Forster's *Observations* sought to offer insights into how forces that shaped the earth could be employed to further 'the moral advancement of the human species'.[185] Where Cook failed to see how the labour of humans shaped nature, Forster was scathing about nature that did not appear to have yet been laboured upon, writing:

[178] Edelman (n 5) 82.

[179] ibid 83.

[180] ibid 86.

[181] *Blackwell v Harper* (1740) Barn C 210, 212. For a discussion of this case see Isabella Alexander and Cristina S Martinez, 'The First Copyright Case under the 1735 Engravings Act: The Germination of Visual Copyright?' in Marie-Stéphanie Delamaire and Will Slauter (eds), *Circulation and Control: Artistic Culture and Intellectual Property in the Nineteenth Century* (Open Book Publishers 2021) 39–76.

[182] Smethurst (n 9) 56–57.

[183] Beaglehole (n 25) 397.

[184] Paul Carter, *Road to Botany Bay: An Exploration of Landscape and History* (University of Minnesota Press 2010) 342; Bruce Pascoe, *Dark Emu: Aboriginal Australia and the Birth of Agriculture* (Scribe 2018).

[185] Dettelbach (n 104) lxxi.

> Where man the lord of creation on this globe, has never attempted any change on it, there nature *seems* only to thrive; for in reality it languishes, and is deformed by being left to itself... how beautiful, how improved, how useful does nature become by the industry of man![186]

Travel writing occupied an uncertain space within copyright law because of its status as a mixed literary genre. Mazzeo has argued that travel writing presented itself 'on the one hand, as implicitly authorless material knowledge, as objective, truthful, and even scientific records of the facts of geography and cultural difference'. However, on the other, she states, it emphasized 'personal experiences, insights, and emotional responses of an individual narrator' and 'clearly exploited literary strategies'.[187] As discussed above, different accounts offered different authorial perspectives and voices, and were accompanied by images with different aesthetic approaches. Travel narratives' claim to factual objectivity exposed them to being abridged by contemporaries, and later to being plundered by Romantic writers.[188] The uncertain place of the author put the text's ownership into doubt, unsettling its stability and authority.

The official printed accounts of Cook's voyages 'became the ideal representation of scientific exploration literature'.[189] Cook became the central actor around whom the entire technological apparatus of the voyage coalesced, in name if not in reality. On board ship, Cook's authority as captain was absolute, at least over the naval officers. He narrated the published accounts of his voyages, and his personal journals were the chief source of data and information. And yet Cook was the 'author', in the sense of being the person who shaped the narrative and fixed it upon paper, of only his second voyage. Circulating around him was an aggregation of authorial contribution, from the Admiralty's directions shaping his voyage, to the crucial role played by Joseph Banks (travelling on the ship, funding people and equipment, and pulling strings in London), to the journals of crew members and scientists on board the ship, to the additional authors and editors engaged to ensure the resulting work could reach the desired audiences, to the printers and booksellers whose expertise brought the material form into being and whose trade networks ensured its circulation, and the laws that shaped and regulated the books and their marketplace. It was copyright law that drew the contributions together so that the particular construction of nature could take shape and circulate, but nature itself that ensured the law could not fix that construction into a single, authored, and authoritative form.

186 Johan Reinhold Forster, cited in Nicholas Thomas, Harriet Guest, and Michael Dettelbach (eds), *Observations Made during a Voyage Round the World* (University of Hawai'i Press 1996) 99.

187 Tilar J Mazzeo, *Plagiarism and Literary Property in the Romantic Period* (University of Pennsylvania Press 2007) 124.

188 ibid ch 5.

189 Richardson (n 8) 7.

9

Artificial Flowers

Plastic Nature, Synthetic Biology

Jose Bellido and Brad Sherman

Introduction

Intellectual property law has been protecting biological innovations for over a century. This has been accompanied by a growing body of academic literature that has looked at the role of intellectual property law in a range of areas from micro-organisms and asexually reproduced plants through to animals and human genes.[1] However, one type of 'biological' innovation that has been overlooked by intellectual property scholars is artificial flowers.[2] This is despite the fact that this 'economically important and geographically diverse group of plants'[3] has been protected, at least in the United States which is the focus here, by patents since the mid-nineteenth century, by copyright since the 1960s, and by trademarks from the 1920s or thereabouts. In part, this oversight may be because artificial flowers were until recently an unrecognized taxon.[4] The neglect may also be explained by the fact that there is something not quite right about artificial flowers. No matter how much they may have improved over time and how much more realistic and lifelike they may have become, artificial flowers still seem odd, out of place, and from another less tasteful age.

[1] See eg Glenn E Bugos and Daniel J Kevles, 'Plants as Intellectual Property: American Practice, Law, and Policy in a World Context' (1992) 7 *Osiris* 75; Cary Fowler, 'The Plant Patent Act of 1930: A Sociological History of Its Creation' (2000) 82 *Journal of the Patent & Trademark Office Society* 621; Alain Pottage and Brad Sherman, 'Organisms and Manufactures: On the History of Plant Inventions' (2007) 31(2) *Melbourne University Law Review* 539.

[2] There are some notable exceptions. See eg Gregg Oppenheimer, 'Originality in Art Reproductions: Variations in Search of a Theme' (1978) 26 *Bulletin of the Copyright Society of the USA* 1; Jerome H Reichman, 'Design protection after the Copyright Act of 1976: A Comparative View of the Emerging Interim Models' (1984) 31(3) *Journal of the Copyright of the Society of the USA* 267, 271.

[3] In 1961, more than '$112 million worth of plastic flowers and plants were sold in the United States, while only $16 million worth were sold in the rest of the world'; see Kirsten Hardfie, 'But They're Only Imitation …? Plastic Flowers That Can Disgust and Delight' in Susan Lambert (ed), *Provocative Plastics: Their Value in Design and Material Culture* (Palgrave Macmillan 2020) 177, 182.

[4] Artificial flowers pose a 'genuine scientific conundrum' since the 'taxa lacks genetic material, appears virtually immortal, and have the ability to form intergenetic crosses with ease, despite any evident mechanism for cross-fertilization'; see Nat Bletter, Kurt A Reynertson, and Julie Velasquez Runk, 'Artificae Plantae: The Taxonomy, Ecology, and Ethnobotany of the Simulacraceae' (2007) 5 *Ethnobotany Research and Applications* 159..

Jose Bellido and Brad Sherman, *Artificial Flowers* In: *Intellectual Property and the Design of Nature*. Edited by: Jose Bellido and Brad Sherman, Oxford University Press.
DOI: 10.1093/oso/9780192864406.003.0009

The creation and use of artificial flowers has a long history, reflecting the enduring quest to replicate life.[5] While artificial flower-makers have occasionally created imaginary plants and flowers, they have largely been preoccupied with creating flowers that mimic nature. This has included attempts to replicate the look and feel of parts of plants such as leaves, petals, bark, stems, pistils, and calices. It has also involved attempts to create lifelike artificial plants and trees (or at least those parts that are above ground). There have also been attempts to develop artificial flowers that smell like natural flowers,[6] artificial flowers that open and close to replicate (repeatedly) the life cycle of a flower,[7] and artificial flowers that are waterproof, washable, and thus more hygienic.[8] Like their natural counterparts, artificial flowers have a varied ecology. A recent ethnobotanical study of artificial plants found that artificial flowers exist in a range of different ecotypes from houses, fish tanks, home gardens, costumes, cemeteries, concrete gardens, parades, and restaurants through to museums, dentists' offices, supermarkets, igloos, hotel rooms, zoos, hats, and lobbies of buildings.[9]

While they may get dusty and fade, artificial flowers do not wilt or die. Nor do they require weeding, fertilizing, watering, or pruning. It is their ability to thrive in environments where fresh flowers cannot survive that has made artificial flowers so popular as indoor decorations in clubs, hotels, restaurants, and homes.[10] As an 1883 patent for a new type of flowerpot for artificial flowers proclaimed:

> Artificial flowers and plants have to a great extent taken the place of natural flowers for house-decoration, and the demand for these is constantly increasing, because they possess the advantage of remaining fresh for a very long time and require no attention other than an occasional dusting.[11]

[5] Montagu Browne, *Artistic and Scientific Taxidermy and Modelling* (Adam and Charles Black 1896) 297–379.

[6] William Eggert, 'Artificial Flower' US Patent No 355,982 (11 January 1887); Solon Palmer, 'Perfumed Artificial Flower' US Patent No 369,878 (13 September 1887); Jesse Redwine, 'Artificial Flowers and Combinations Therewith', US Patent No 1,989,883 (5 February 1933); Benjamin Gilowitz, 'Aromatic Ornament' US Patent No 2,492,039 (20 December 1947); Maxine Pesu and others, 'Fragrant Artificial Flower Apparatus' US Patent No 6,391,398 (21 May 2002); see Edith Beeson, 'Seven-Year Cycle Brings Fake Blossoms Out Again; Fashion Sprouts Flowers That Never Saw Soil' *The New York Times* (29 March 1957) 15.

[7] Stacy Potts, 'Artificial Flower that Blooms' (1877) 37(4) *Scientific American* 1. Peter Marlow, 'Animated Artificial Flower' US Patent No 7,861,444 B2 (4 January 2011) (device which simulates natural flowering actions including growth and efflorescence).

[8] Doris Munn, 'Artificial Flowers' US Patent No 45,439 (21 March 1925); see also 'Italian Plastic Flowers Washable and Lifelike' *The New York Times* (21 January 1958) 32; Wilfrid Blunt, *Of Flowers and a Village: An Entertainment for Flower Lovers* (Hamish Hamilton 1963) 86.

[9] Bletter, Reynertson, and Velasquez Runk (n 4) 161.

[10] Sherwood Kohn, 'The Flowering of Fake Flowers', *The New York Times* (23 August 1964) 54, 58, 60; see also Jeffrey L Meikle, *American Plastic: A Cultural History* (Rutgers University Press 1995) 255.

[11] Benjamin Lowy, 'Flower-Pot for Artificial Flowers' US Patent No 281,706 (24 July 1883).

Their longevity has also made artificial flowers attractive to milliners, tailors, and dress-makers.[12] Artificial flowers also appeal to the film industry where the intense heat of the lamps and the fact that the scenes that flowers appear in may take weeks to film means that fresh flowers wilt and die and need to be replaced.[13] The problems of continuity that this creates are avoided through the use of artificial flowers which are freeze-frames of nature at a particular point in time.[14] In this sense artificial flowers are, like type specimens, historical snapshots that retain their original shape and appearance regardless of variations in climate, temperature, and time.[15]

As well as serving decorative and ornamental purposes, artificial flowers perform functional roles. The fact that plastic and fabric plants are sometimes scientifically accurate, with the 'correct number of petals, sepals, stamens, and pistil parts', has facilitated their use as teaching aids for learning about botany and nature.[16] Artificial flowers also have a long history of disguising or camouflaging things that people find unattractive or want to hide such as solar panels, cell-phone towers, barometers,[17] osmosis machines,[18] and 'insect-destroyers'.[19] Artificial flowers also play an important ceremonial role. Perhaps the most well-known is the poppy, which became the symbol of commemoration of the loss of life after and during the world wars.[20] The production and sale of blood-red poppies also served to provide ex-service men and war widows with employment.[21]

[12] 'Vogue of artificial flowers' *The New York Times* (24 April 1927) 12; 'New artificial flowers appear' *The New York Times* (4 August 1929) 10. Such an interest can also be seen in the patent specifications; see eg Agnes C Fliegel, 'Millinery' US Patent No 622,429 (2 March 1923); Elizabeth V Dillon, 'Flowers for Millinery Purposes' US Patent No 234,673 (5 May 1922). Mollie E Bingaman, 'Method of Producing Transferable Embroidery-Patterns' US Patent No 277,665 (15 May 1883); Henry W Fishel, 'Boutonniere' US Patent No 489,671 (10 January 1893).

[13] Anthony Jenkinson, *America Came My Way* (Arthur Barker 1936) 128.

[14] Andrew R Boone, 'Hollywood Improves on Nature in Making Outdoor Movies' (1987) 130(2) *Popular Science* 58; see also Vic Ball, 'Plastic Flower Boom' (1961) 25 *Grower Talks* 1, 8.

[15] Frank Zeimet, 'Artificial Flower' US Patent No 1,970,625 (14 August 1931). Natural flowers were said to 'share many of the advantages of artificial flowers and, if cared for appropriately are capable of growing and blooming in a pleasing way, many thousands of people enjoy receiving flowers in one form or another on a daily basis throughout the world'; see eg Peter Marlow, 'Animated Artificial Flower' US Patent No 7,861,444 B2 (4 January 2011) (device which simulates natural flowering actions including growth and efflorescence').

[16] David Hipply, 'Faux Flowers' (Sept 1995) *The Science Teacher* 79; see also Francis C Bowen, 'Artificial Trees and Flowers' US Patent No 206,387 (7 January 1878).

[17] Leighton Macdonald Perveil, 'Barometrical Rose' US Patent No 456,498 (21 July 1891).

[18] Andrew Peterson, 'Machine for Ozonizing Air' US Patent No 1,239,515 (11 September 1917) (external structure designed to conceal the true function of the machine).

[19] Robert L Lynch, 'Insect-Destroyer' US Patent No 571,925 (24 November 1896); Joel B Hamilton, 'Tobacco-Fly Exterminator' US Patent No 251,222 (20 December 1881).

[20] Selling these replica poppies thus served to raise money for the welfare and support of war veterans and widows. Interestingly, copyright and trademarks began to play a significant role fuelling these charitable endeavours. One particularly important reason for this can be traced to their function as guarantee of origin to provide a platform for merchandising activities Nicholas J Saunders, *The Poppy: A Cultural History from Ancient Egypt to Flanders Fields to Afghanistan* (Oneworld Publications 2013) 101–103, 120.

[21] 'Scarlet Petals' (1927) 30(5) *The Rotarian* 34.

However tempting it might be to dismiss artificial flowers as botanical, cultural, and legal curiosities, things are rarely what they seem with artificial flowers. While there is a sense in which intellectual property law's engagement with artificial flowers, like artificial flowers themselves, is frivolous and inconsequential, in other ways it deserves to be taken seriously; not least because it raises a number of questions that are at the very heart of the way intellectual property law engages with nature. This chapter focuses on one of these, namely the role that life plays in the way intellectual property law interacts with nature, and how that role changes in the context of artificial or synthetic biology.

Living Subject Matter

Life plays an ambiguous and somewhat contradictory role when it comes to artificial flowers. While life acts as a role model, it is also absent. Indeed, one of the selling points of artificial flowers is that while these 'permanent botanicals'[22] may become dusty and fade, they are not living or, more importantly, they cannot die. As a result, while artificial flowers may be designed to replicate nature, these 'genomically challenged plants' are not quite natural: they are life-like but not living. While their lack of vitality often provides artificial flowers with a commercial advantage, it is sometimes seen as a liability. As Peter Marlow said in his 2011 patent for animated artificial flowers, 'natural flowers have certain advantages over artificial flowers'.[23] One of the most important was that 'if cared for appropriately, natural flowers are capable of growing and blooming in a pleasing way'. While natural flowers may have many benefits over artificial flowers, Marlow felt that natural flowers were still in need of improvement. This was because with natural flowers as 'vitality progresses very slowly; it is difficult to observe'. Furthermore, the beauty of natural flowers quickly fades. Because they are so commonplace, natural flowers, like static artificial flowers, are generally not objects of sustained or exceptional interest'.[24] To overcome the problems that vitality creates—it is either absent, too quick, or soon forgotten—Marlow invented an 'artificial flower that gradually grows, blooms and delicately reveals a surprise gift from within its corolla'. The result was a form of artificial vitality that would satisfy the 'continuing human need for objects that delight and enchant by their ability to transcend expectation'.

As with artificial flowers, life occupies an ambiguous position in the way patent law engages with nature. For much of the twentieth century, the fact that biological material was living was of little consequence for intellectual property law. The situation changed in 1980, however, following the Supreme Court decision of

[22] Daryln Brewer, 'Trees to Fool the Senses' *The New York Times* (26 March 1987) 2.
[23] Marlow (n 15) 3.
[24] ibid.

Chakrabarty.[25] This is because at the same time as the Supreme Court confirmed that modified biological subject matter was potentially patentable, biological subject matter was also stripped of any vital force. As the Supreme Court said in its judgment, 'the relevant distinction for purposes of [patentable subject matter] is not between living and inanimate things, but between products of nature, whether living or not, and human-made inventions'.[26] The position remained unchanged until the beginning of the twenty-first century when the US Supreme Court handed down its decision in *Association for Molecular Pathology v Myriad Genetics*.[27] In deciding that isolated human genes were not patentable subject matter, the Supreme Court rejected the argument that genes should be construed as chemical compounds. Instead, the Supreme Court said that genes formed the basis for hereditary traits in living organisms and were to be judged accordingly. Following *Myriad*, the quality that defines biological material in patent law is its capacity for reproduction. As a result, life now lies at the core of biological subject matter.

While the Supreme Court may have vacillated about the role vitality plays in deciding subject matter eligibility, one constant across the twentieth century was the difficulty that living subject matter posed for patent law. Even when the Supreme Court in *Chakrabarty* shifted the focus of attention away from whether or not the subject matter was living, there was no escaping the fact that living subject matter, even when it qualified as a human-made invention, created problems for the law. Furthermore, while the shift to a molecular understanding of plant subject matter may have resolved many problems, many remained. One of the most important was that no matter how much breeders and scientists tried, they were unable to explain why plant innovations occurred. While breeders may have been able to stimulate change by crossing plants or subjecting plants to extreme conditions, they could not explain the reasons why the biological innovation had taken place. In these situations, breeders were forced to distil what went on inside a plant from what occurred on the outside. As with other empirical sciences, breeders, scientists, and farmers were forced to work backwards from the end-results in an attempt to explain what had happened.

As well as being secretive, living plant-based subject matter is also fluid, malleable, and unstable. One consequence of this was that breeders were unable to describe plant inventions with the specificity and detail demanded by intellectual property law making it difficult, if not impossible, to apply the existing rules and procedures to plant-based inventions.[28] This was particularly the case where

[25] *Diamond v Chakrabarty* 447 US 311 (1980).
[26] ibid 313.
[27] *Association for Molecular Pathology v Myriad Genetics* 569 US 576 (2013).
[28] Joseph Rossman, 'The Preparation and Prosecution of Plant Patent Applications' (1935) 17 *Journal of the Patent Office Society* 632, 635–38. Harry C Robb, 'Plant Patents' (1933) 15(10) *Journal of the Patent Office Society* 752, 753. Robert Starr Allyn, *The First Plant Patents: A Discussion on the New Law and Patent Office Practice* (Educational Foundations 1934) 18.

the novel characteristics of a plant lay in its odour, flavour, or taste.[29] One of the reasons often given to explain why plant-based subject matter was initially not protected by intellectual property was that breeders lacked the ability to describe their inventions in a way that would have allowed the intangible to be identified, demarcated, and distinguished. As the Supreme Court explained in *Chakrabarty*, one of the reasons why plants were thought to be unpatentable for so long was that they were not amenable to the written description requirement that the patent 'contain a written description of the invention ... [in] clear, concise, and exact terms'.[30] The problems that arose in describing plants with the specificity demanded by intellectual property law were compounded by the fact that certain types of plants—namely, those that reproduced sexually—were non-uniform and unstable and therefore thought to be ineligible for protection. As Joseph Rossman said, a 'machine, once made, stays put: it cannot grow or change. But it is impossible to determine whether a Baldwin apple is like the original Baldwins that grew on the first tree of that variety when it was discovered in 1793'.[31]

The secretive, unruly, and changeable nature of living subject matter not only defined biological subject matter, it also shaped the way patent law engaged with that subject matter. In accommodating plant-based subject matter, intellectual property law-makers changed the way that the process of invention was configured. Instead of using the asymmetrical relationship between nature and invention favoured by a mechanical view of intellectual property, plant-based subject matter forced the law to draw on a different conception of agency. The starting point for the reconfiguration of the process of invention was the recognition of the positive role that nature plays in the creation of plant inventions.[32] As well as altering the notion of agency that underpins the inventive process, patent law also reversed the roles played by the participants involved in the creation of the invention. While under the mechanical view of creation nature provides the underlying material which the human inventor then shapes into the resulting invention, with patent law nature does the inventing and the breeder is relegated to the task of identifying and then reproducing nature's creations. As the Supreme Court said in *Chakrabarty*, in producing a new plant the breeder worked 'in aid of nature' to bring about the resulting invention.[33] In this sense, in dealing with plant based subject matter patent law developed a notion of agency that saw the breeder and nature working together as joint inventors in the development of plant inventions. As neither breeder nor nature could operate independently of each other to develop a novel plant invention, it was only when the skill and effort of the two were combined that a plant invention's existence could be guaranteed. In this sense, nature

[29] Allyn (n 28) 46.
[30] *Diamond v Chakrabarty* (n 25).
[31] Joseph Rossman, 'Plant Patents' (1931) 13 *Journal of the Patent Office Society* 7, 15.
[32] Robb (n 28) 753.
[33] *Diamond v Chakrabarty* (n 25) 312.

and breeder operated like Siamese twins in the creation of plant inventions The fact that the plant invention would not have occurred in nature without the efforts of the breeder meant that plant inventions, like artificial flowers, were simultaneously both natural *and* artificial. Importantly, the fact that the plant invention did not exist in a natural state meant, at least for patent law purposes, that it was not a 'product of nature' and thus potentially patentable.

Patent law adopted a range of strategies to deal with the unstable and fluid nature of living subject matter. In some ways, the simplest and most straightforward response was the decision to exclude sexually reproduced plants from the scope of the 1930 Plant Patent Act. Another strategy that was used to accommodate living subject matter was to craft the intangible property so that it was coextensive with the plant as a whole rather than specific parts of a plant such as fruit or flower. Defining the intangible in this way helped to define the scope of what was protected. For example, based upon the practice developed for design patents, plant patent law limited applicants to a single claim that set out the distinguishing characteristics of the plant as a whole. While the form of the claim varied, they followed a similar pattern whereby, after linking the claim to 'the plant as described', applicants would highlight the distinct features of the biological invention. While protection may have indirectly covered the novel and commercially valuable parts of plant (such as seed), the intangible interest was framed in such a way that it covered the plant as a whole.

Another technique used to deal with living subject matter was to limit protection to the *external surface* rather than the internal workings of individual plants. In more technical terms, protection was limited to the phenotypical traits and characteristics rather than the underlying reasons for or causes of these characteristics. While it was recognized that 'varietal characteristics were caused by the genetic complements of the cells', the secretive nature of plant-based subject matter meant that it 'was impossible to determine the genetic constitution by examination of the cells'.[34] As a result, breeders had to rely on the external seed and plant characteristics when talking about plant subject matter. At the same time, the intangible did not extend to plants that were similar to the protected plant nor to more abstract groups or classes of plants. The plant's intangible property was limited to and coextensive with the external characteristics of the protected material plant. In this sense, the plant-based intangible property was treated as if it was coextensive with its tangible instantiation or form. The upshot of this was that in accommodating the peculiarities of living plant-based subject matter, the intangible property recognized by patent law was configured in such a way that it coincided with

[34] Alain Pottage and Brad Sherman, *Figures of Invention: A History of Patent Law* (Oxford University Press 2010) 191; see also Walter A Davidson and Benjamin E Clark, 'How we try to measure trueness to variety' in *Seeds: The Yearbook of Agriculture* (US Government Printing Office 1961) 448–52, 450. The focus on the surface of the plant was enshrined in the legislation that established plant patent law and plant variety protection in the United States.

the external features of individual plants rather than with the more abstract groupings such as genus or species.[35] The intangible was treated, in effect, like a legal hologram of a physical plant.

Another technique that patent law used to manage living subject matter was to view the subject matter through a botanical lens. This built upon the fact that across the twentieth century plant breeders developed an increasingly sophisticated and effective range of techniques to describe and identify plants. This included the standardization of naming practices, a growing agreement about how plants were classified and ordered, and the development and adoption of species-specific criteria to describe plant traits and characteristics (including the use of identification aids such as colour charts to describe flower or leaf colour). Importantly, the various techniques and practices that breeders developed across the twentieth century to describe plants, and the information this generated, was not something that was external to plant subject matter. Rather, plant subject matter was an informed material that was constituted in relation to the informational and material environments in which it was generated.[36] As a result, the environment entered into the constitution of the entity as it was folded into and became part of the subject matter.

Nature and copyright

Given the type of subject matter that is traditionally associated with copyright, it is not surprising that little attention has been given to the use of copyright to protect nature. In the rare situations where the courts have been called on to do so, the law has found itself grappling with similar issues to those that arose in patents. This can be seen for example in the 2011 decision of *Kelley v Chicago Park District*.[37] In 1984, Chapman Kelley, an artist known for his representational paintings of landscapes and flowers, was given permission by the Chicago Park District to install a permanent wildflower display on a grassy area on top of the underground Monroe Street parking garage in Grant Park, Chicago. When it was finished the garden, known as 'Wildflower Works', consisted of two very large elliptical flower beds (totalling around 66,000 square feet) that were planted out with a variety of native wildflowers and edged with borders of gravel and steel (Figure 9.1). Promoted as living art, the garden was very popular. Despite this, in 2004 the Park District modified the garden by halving its size, changed the oval flower beds into rectangles, and replaced some of the plants with different varieties. Kelley sued the Park District claiming that this breached his moral right of integrity in the garden under the Visual Artists Rights Act of 1990.

[35] *Kim Bros v Hagler* 167 F Supp 665, 120 USPQ 210 (SD Cal 1958).

[36] See Isabelle Stengers, *Power and Invention: Situating Science* (University of Minnesota Press 1997); Alfred N Whitehead, *Process and Reality: An Essay in Cosmology* (Macmillan 1978).

[37] *Kelley v Chicago Park District* 635 F 3d 290 (7th Cir 2011).

Figure 9.1 Chapman Kelley, 'Wildflower Works', (non-commissioned) watercolor, 1984–2004.
Courtesy of the Estate of Chapman Kelley.

After the district court handed down a split judgment, the case was appealed to the Court of Appeals for the Seventh Circuit which rejected Kelley's claim for breach of moral rights. Unlike the district court, the Court of Appeals said that the impediment to copyright protection was not that Wildflower Works failed the test for originality. Instead, echoing the problems that patent law experienced in dealing with living subject matter, the Court of Appeals said that the reason why Wildflower Works was not protected by copyright was because 'a living garden lacks the kind of authorship and stable fixation normally required to support copyright' and that '[a] living garden like Wildflower Works is neither "authored" nor "fixed" in the senses required for copyright'.[38] As such, it did not qualify for moral rights protection under the 1990 *Visual Artists Rights Act.*

Adopting a view of creation that mirrors the mechanistic view of invention that dominates in patent law, the Court of Appeals said that 'authorship is an

[38] See also *Toney v L'Oréal USA* 406 F 3d 905, 910 (7th Cir 2005) ('A person's likeness—her persona—is not authored and it is not fixed').

entirely human endeavor'.[39] On the basis that a 'work must be the product of human authorship' and not 'the forces of nature', the Court said that 'works owing their form to the forces of nature cannot be copyrighted'.[40] The problem that Kelley faced was that the Court believed that the creativity that shaped 'what we see and experience in a garden — the colors, shapes, textures, and scents of the plants — originates in nature, not in the mind of the gardener'.[41] The problem here was that at 'any given moment in time, a garden owes most of its form and appearance to natural forces, though the gardener who plants and tends it obviously assists. All this is true of Wildflower Works, even though it was designed and planted by an artist'.[42] While patent law had been willing to reconfigure the invention to accommodate and recognize the inventive role that nature plays in biological innovation, copyright law was not willing to do so. Instead, it clung to a human-centric view of creation. On the basis that 'authorship is an entirely human endeavor' and that the 'essence of a garden is its vitality'[43] the Court of Appeals said that 'simply put, gardens are planted and cultivated, not authored'.[44]

As well as highlighting the authorship problems that living subject matter creates for copyright law, the Court of Appeals also drew attention to the problems that an unruly and changing living subject matter creates.[45] When a landscape designer reduces a plan for a garden to writing, the intangible intellectual property will be embodied in a fixed and tangible form. However, as the Court of Appeal said, the 'same cannot be said of a garden, which is not a fixed copy of the gardener's intellectual property'.[46] Although the planting material is tangible and can be perceived for more than a transitory duration, the court said it was not stable or permanent enough to be called 'fixed'. The problem here was that 'seeds and plants in a garden are naturally in a state of perpetual change; they germinate, grow, bloom, become dormant, and eventually die. This life cycle moves gradually, over days, weeks, and season to season, but the real barrier to copyright here is not *temporal* but *essential*'. A garden 'may endure from season to season, but its nature

[39] *Kelley v Chicago Park District* (n 37) 304.

[40] *Citing* U.S. Copyright Office, *Compendium II: Copyright Office Practices* § 503.03(a) (1984); § 202.02(b); § 3:19 n 1.

[41] *Kelley v Chicago Park District* (n 37) 304.

[42] ibid.

[43] ibid 305.

[44] The problems that were identified in relation to gardens also arose with seeds and seedlings. As the Court of Appeal said, to the 'extent that seeds or seedlings can be considered a "medium of expression," they originate in nature, and natural forces—not the intellect of the gardener—determine their form, growth, and appearance'. See ibid 304.

[45] This gives rise to subsequent questions such as 'at what point has fixation occurred?' 'When the garden is newly planted?' 'When its first blossoms appear?' 'When it is in full bloom?' 'How—and at what point in time—is a court to determine whether infringing copying has occurred?' See ibid 305.

[46] ibid.

is one of dynamic change'.[47] Likewise, 'a garden is simply too changeable to satisfy the primary purpose of fixation'.[48] The reason for this was that a 'garden's constituent elements' were 'alive and inherently changeable'.[49] The 'forces of nature—the varying bloom periods of the plants; their spread habits, compatibility, and life cycles; and the weather—produced constant change'.[50] One of the consequences of this was that a garden's appearance was too 'inherently variable to supply a baseline for determining questions of copyright creation and infringement'.[51]

The upshot of this is that while copyright law has been willing to accommodate representations of nature such as pictures of roses, plans for gardens, and maps, it was not willing to protect nature itself.[52] The chief reason for this is that nature is living. In this sense it could be said that life plays an important but somewhat different role in the way copyright law deals with living nature than it does in patents. While biological patents post-*Myriad* are defined by their capacity for reproduction, gardens are excluded from copyright because they are living. In contrast, the representations of nature that are protected by copyright law are defined by their absence of life. No matter how evocative or lifelike a painting may be, it is not possible to recreate plant life from a paper representation: it is biologically sterile. In this sense, life operates as a boundary object that helps to manage the distinction between patent and copyright.

Inventing Artificial Flowers

Patents granted for artificial flowers since the mid-nineteenth century fall into two general categories. The first group of patents were for the machines used to manufacture artificial flowers. For example, US Patent No. 96,582 from 1869 was for a 'new and improved machine for securing branches, leaves, or flowers or other ornaments to the stem of artificial flowers by means of two layers of thread applied to the wire system'[53] (Figure 9.2).

[47] ibid.
[48] ibid.
[49] ibid.
[50] ibid 294.
[51] ibid 305. A 'garden is simply too changeable to satisfy the primary purpose of fixation'. See ibid 304–305.
[52] See also *Margarete Steiff Inc v Bing* 215 F 204 (1914), where it was held that 'in so far as the [plaintiff's] animals copy or reproduce nature, so far they can claim no protection, for every one can do that'.
[53] Ambose Giraudat, 'Machine for Branching Artificial Flowers' US Patent No 96,582 (9 November 1869).

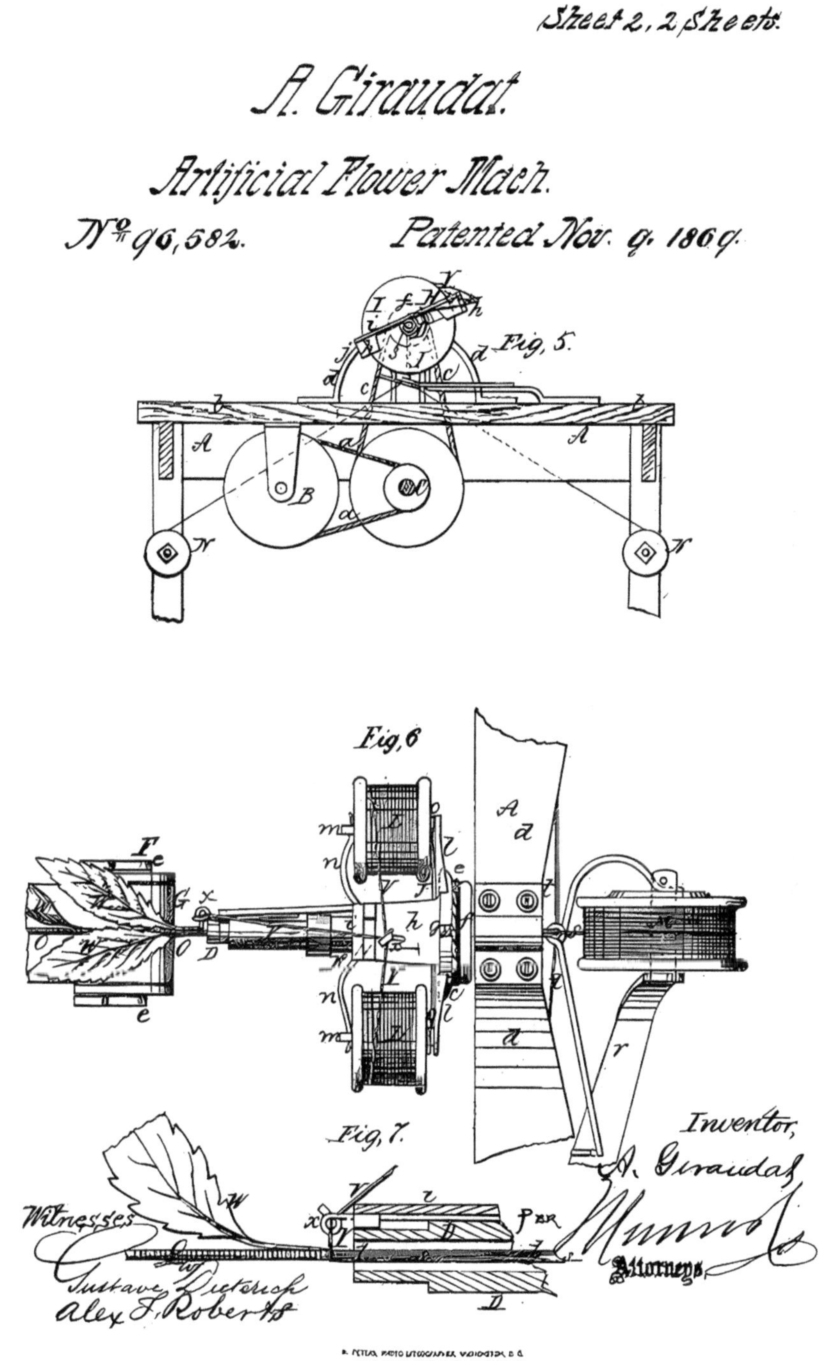

Figure 9.2 'Machine for branching artificial flowers' US Patent No. 96,582 (1869).
Courtesy of the National Archives at Kansas City.

Other patents claimed things such as an apparatus for making artificial bark,[54] an apparatus that produced 'long and short branches and sprays of flowers, piquets, seed or tassels, fringes, trimmings, fruit etc',[55] and a machine that crimped textiles or other materials for use in making artificial flowers.[56] As well as claiming the machines used to manufacture artificial flowers, patentees also claimed the methods and the materials used in their manufacture. They also claimed new and improved articles of manufacture resulting from those processes: the artificial flowers themselves. In many cases, the inventions were relatively straightforward. Thus, for example, a 1925 patent claimed an 'artificial flower formed of ribbon having wire on the edge thereof, the wire and ribbon being bent and crimped to simulate petals'.[57] In other cases, the processes were more complicated. For example, a 1922 patent for a 'Decorative Plant Product' claimed:

> Claim 1: An artificial flower including in combination a flower center and a series of milk weed pods arranged liked petals thereon, said flower center and milkweed pods being of natural growth.
>
> Claim 2: A manufactured flower comprising a stem, leaves of natural growth fastened to said stem, a tape wound around said stem in spiral form and covering the connections between said stem and leaves, a discoidal-seed pod mounted on one end of said stem, and a plurality of mature milkweed pods connected to the periphery of said discoidal pod and arranged radially with the stem ends of said milkweed pods pointed outwardly, said pods being of natural growth and combined to simulate a poinsettia.[58]

In many cases, patents were granted for parts of flowers and plants. These included the veined look of natural drooping leaves, petals, flower stems, pistils, calices, twigs, reeds, branches, vines, and stems.[59] Patents also covered artificial plants as

[54] Dominick Rossi, 'Method of and apparatus for making artificial bark' US Patent No 401,548 (28 February 1922).

[55] Isidore Birge, 'Apparatus for Branching Artificial Flowers' US Patent No 418,489 (31 December 1889).

[56] Gioachino Molla, 'Crimping-Machine' US Patent No 613,069 (25 October 1898); Harry L McKain, 'Machine for Manufacturing Artificial Flowers, Vines etc' US Patent No 754,084 (8 March 1904).

[57] Guadalupe Rosas, 'Artificial Flower' US Patent No 45,219 (22 July 1925); see also the patent for 'a process of using rice paper to preserve natural flowers in such a way that they were pliable enough to be moulded into a permanent shape' made by ES Harris, 'Improvement in the Manufacture of Artificial and Preservation of Natural Flowers' US Patent No, 96,587 (9 November 1869).

[58] Leopold Kropp and Victor F Bergman, 'Decorative Plant Product' US Patent No 1,412,008 (4 April 1922).

[59] For early examples see Francis C Bowen, 'Artificial Trees and Flowers' US Patent No 206387 (7 January 1878); Bernard W Gates, 'Structural Imitation of Natural Objects' US Patent No 1.150,027 (17 August 1915); Louise Malstrom, 'Method of Producing Artificial Flower Petals' US Patent No 1400691 (22 March 1921); Dominick Rossi, 'Artificial Flower-Stem' US Patent No 1,204,905 (14 November 1916); Dominick Rossi, 'Artificial Flower Stems', US Patent No 116999 (26 August 1916); Patents also extended to include the materials that underpinned artificial flowers and wreaths; see eg Jules Lambert, 'Gage for Forming Foundation for Artificial Flowers' US Patent No 276,430 (24 April 1883).

a whole (minus the roots). For example, an 1885 patent claimed an 'artificial glass flower consisting of the calyx *h*, with its hollow stem *i*, and the head *f*, with its stem *g*' (each part individually described).[60] While patentees tended to claim individual flowers and plants (or parts thereof), they sometimes claimed groups of flowers. In line with the treatment of artificial flowers as objects of manufacture, these abstract groupings were not for species or genus of (artificial) plants. Instead, patentees claimed artificial groups using abstract non-botanical terms such as 'imitation bouquets'.[61]

Over time, patentees also claimed a range of different materials to manufacture artificial flowers. This included processed or manufactured materials such as steel and other metals, papier-mâché, fabrics (ribbons), and chenille. More recently, this extended to plastics, polymers, and polyethylene.[62] The later more modern materials had a considerable impact on the artificial flower industry. The use of plastics allowed artificial flowers to be mass produced at a relatively low cost.[63] Plastic could also be coloured to imitate the colour tones of fresh flowers and bent or folded so that the artificial flowers retained their shape. This material property, often described as plastic memory, provided durability, longevity and uniformity to artificial flowers.[64] These attributes, which the artificial flower industry cherished, have had a detrimental impact on the environment.[65] As well as building artificial flowers from processed materials, patentees also used 'one natural object for the imitation of another'.[66] To this end, artificial flower-makers have claimed a range of different biological materials to craft artificial plants and flowers from milkweed pods, the cocoons of the silkworm (which were cut, shaped and dyed), and reed grasses, through to everlasting flowers, broom corn sprigs, the cells of conch spawn, sea-shells, and fur.[67]

60 Rudolf Georgi, 'Artificial Flower' US Patent No 322,367 (14 July 1885).

61 Roy E Tilles, 'Imitation Bouquet' US Patent No 1,583,505 (24 June 1925).

62 See eg André Emile Decamp, 'Artificial Flowers' US Patent No 2,881,545 (12 March 1956); Lino Bosco, 'Process of Manufacturing Plastic Flowers and Leaves in Multicolor Design' US Patent No 2,908,942 (6 August 1957); Annelie Flynn, 'Artificial flower construction (1961)' US Patent No 3,137,610 (2 May 1961). For an interesting overview see Roy A Larson, 'The Impact of Plastics in the Floriculture Industry' (1993) 3(1) *Hort Technology* 28 29.

63 'The flowers that bloom' *Hong Kong Trade Bulletin* (July 1963) 308–12.

64 'Some recent developments in the Plastic Flower Industry' *Hong Kong Trade Bulletin* (May 1961) 198.

65 Andreas Folkers, 'Fossil Modernity: The Materiality of Acceleration, Slow Violence, and Ecological Futures' (2021) 30(2) *Time & Society* 223, 230.

66 Edwin King, 'Artificial Flower' US Patent No 259,871 (20 June 1882).

67 Catherine E Howard, 'Improvement in the Manufacture of Artificial Flowers' US Patent No 100,293 (1 March 1870); Edwin King, 'Artificial Flower' US Patent No 259,871 (20 June 1882); Carl Hartman, 'Artificial Flower Made of Fur' US Patent No 666,522 (22 January 1901); Louise F Welch, 'Artificial Flower' US Patent No 451,209 (18 April 1922); Leopold Kropp and Victor F Bergman, 'Decorative Plant Product' US Patent No 1,412,008 (4 April 1922); Carl C Foldessy, 'Manufactured Flower' US Patent No 674,819 (15 November 1923); Robert Morris, 'Miniature Trees' US Patent No 685,402 (10 January 1924).

While most artificial flowers and plants attempt to copy nature as closely as possible (with differing degrees of success),[68] artificial flower-makers occasionally rejected this approach and set out instead to develop 'unnatural' flowers; that is, artificial flowers that were 'not known to approximate any known flower in nature'.[69] Producing artificial flowers that were the product of human imagination rather than natural evolution was seen as the best way to develop an artifice that could lay claim to novelty. In some cases, the novelty of the fanciful plant or flower was in its form or shape. In other cases, artificial flower-makers experimented with unnatural colours to produce fanciful plants and flowers (Figure 9.3).

Figure 9.3 'Method and means of producing artificial flower leaves' US Patent No. 2,467,572 (1949).
Courtesy of the National Archives at Kansas City.

While artificial flower patents usually included drawings of a particular flower variety, sometimes described the invention with reference to specific plants such as sunflowers and poinsettias, or used botanical language to describe the natural materials they used to make their artificial flowers, these botanical references did

[68] Artificial flower factories such as CALART in California, had gardens that functioned as studios or workshops to make accurate reproductions; see *Prestige Floral Société Anonime, AE Decamp, and AJ Fristot v California Artificial Flower Company Inc and Calart Inc (Prestige Floral v California Artificial Flower Co)* 61 Civ 2240: 'Transcript of proceedings, D'Agnillo—Direct Examination' (11 December 1961).

[69] Lina Prager Weber, 'Design for an Artificial Flower (1900); D-33993; Leopold Kropp and Victor F Bergman, 'Decorative Plant Product' US Patent No 1,412,008 (4 April 1922). This was also a suggestion made decades later. See Blunt (n 8) 233.

not become part of how inventions were claimed. Instead, what was claimed was the (artificial) article of manufacture, which was described accordingly. While the overarching aim of patented artificial flowers and plants was to imitate nature, what was claimed were new and improved *articles of manufacture*. In line with this, instead of using scientific taxonomic names, patentees used non-botanical terms such as 'artificial flower', 'imitation tree' or 'miniature trees' to describe their inventions.[70] For example, while Harriet Adams' 1925 patent for 'Artificial Flowers' included a drawing of a group of flowers labelled 'lupines' and the description referred to 'flowers such as blue-bonnets or lupines or other legumes', the patent claimed the 'process of making artificial flowers of a leguminous type'.[71] In a similar way, while US Patent No. 1,749,526 for 'Artificial Flowers' used a botanical reference to describe the invention—it was for 'improvements in artificial flowers in which the elements of the flower, as petals, leaves, etc. are capable of being made up into tubular shape, as for instance the chrysanthemum'—ultimately, the patents used abstract and broad language to claim all artificial flowers made using the method of manufacture and/or material outlined in the patent.[72] The upshot of this is that while in many cases the end result may have been a lifelike reproduction of nature, artificial flowers were not claimed botanically. Instead, they were consistently claimed as non-living articles of manufacture.[73]

Recognizing that artificial flowers were treated as objects of manufacture helps to explain why they did not fall foul of what is now called the 'product of nature' doctrine.[74] It can explain, for example, why artificial flowers made up of natural material did not suffer the same fate as the patent in the 1931 decision of *American Fruit Growers v Brogdex*, where the Supreme Court held that an orange dipped in a solution of borax to render the skin mould-resistant was not a manufactured article and thus not patentable subject matter.[75] What is it about artificial flowers that distinguishes them from the modified orange in *American Fruit Growers*? What is the difference, for example, between a patent for an orange dipped in borax and US

[70] Robert Morris, 'Miniature Trees' US Patent No 685,402 (10 January 1924); Harry L Berman, 'Artificial Tree' US Patent No 1,636,981 (26 July 1927); Theodore Kirchen, 'Artificial Flower', US Patent No 2,282,657 (5 July 1940).

[71] Harriet E Adams, 'Artificial Flower' US Patent No 1,731,089 (8 October 1929).

[72] W Compton, 'Artificial Flower' US Patent No 1,749,526 (4 March 1930). See also Robert Morris, 'Miniature Trees' US Patent No 685,402 (10 January 1924).

[73] A rare exception to this was a 2013 patent for a scented artificial flower which used hybrid botanical language in the patent claims. After claiming a method for manufacturing artificial flowers having a lifelike look, feel and scent, using a specific polymeric material, the patentee also stated that the artificial flower was to be 'selected from the group consisting of a rose, calla lily, tulip, poppy, lily, magnolia, peony, orchid, water lily, Japanese lantern, Chinese lantern, amaryllis, gardenia, lotus, dahlia, hydrangea, daisy, aster, and single bud'. Sheila Meta, 'Scented Artificial Flower' US Patent No 2008/0311315 A1 (31 January 2013).

[74] On the history of this doctrine see Daniel J Kevles, 'Imitation, Yes; Nature, No: The Products-of-Nature Doctrine from the American Colonies to the U.S. Courts' (2015) 23 *Perspectives on Science* 1, 13–34.

[75] *American Fruit Growers v Brogdex* 283 US 1 (1931).

Patent No. 1,405,786, which claimed a lotus seed pod treated with a preservative solution of glycerine, water, and formalin which was then painted and varnished?[76] Or US Patent No. 1,484,656, which claimed a 'decorative product comprising a natural plant part having a varnish-like coating with particles of pigment severally more or less dissolved and spread therein and with the remained set firmly in the coating'?[77]

While the differing legal fates of these patents might be explained by the fact that no one cared enough about artificial flower patents to challenge them, there are other factors that account for the difference. The reason why Brogdex's patent for the modified orange failed was because there had not been a 'change in the name, appearance, or general character of the fruit'.[78] That is, there had not been a change of kind. As the US Supreme Court said, the modified orange 'remains a fresh orange fit only for the same beneficial uses as theretofore'.[79] In contrast, the reason why artificial flower patents for preserved lotus pods and varnished plant parts did not fall foul of the product of nature doctrine was that the underlying natural product was transformed into something new. Unlike the case with Brogdex's modified orange, with artificial flowers the inventor brings about a change of kind. The appearance of the underlying natural product changes and it is given a new name, a new character, and a new use. As the patent for the lotus-based plant product said, the invention 'consisted of an improved method of cutting and decorating a lotus seed pod (torus) or the like of natural growth so as to form an *artistic plant product* simulating a natural growth of different design and appearance from the lotus plant'.[80] What was claimed was an 'article of manufacture compromising a seed pod of natural growth having proportions thereof cut away to produce a certain *predetermined ornamental appearance*, said pod being decorated artificially'.[81]

Plastic botanists

Following the rapid growth in the plastic artificial flower industry in the late 1950s several manufacturers and distributors started to register artificial flowers with the US Copyright Office. These registrations proliferated following *Mazer v Stein*;[82] the landmark US Supreme Court decision that affirmed the shift in registry practice that had taken place earlier[83] and held that three-dimensional articles could

[76] Richard Lloyd Johnston and John S Wallner, 'Decorative Plant Product' US Patent No 1,405,786 (7 February 1922).
[77] Leopold Koroff, 'Plant Product' US Patent No 1,484,656 (26 February 1924).
[78] *American Fruit Growers v Brogdex* (n 75) 12.
[79] ibid 11–12.
[80] Johnston and Wallner (n 76).
[81] ibid.
[82] *Mazer and Endicter v Stein* 347 US 201 (1954).
[83] Alan Latman, 'Fifteen years after *Mazer v Stein*: A Brief Perspective' (1969) 16 *Bulletin of the Copyright Society of the USA* 278, 281; see also Editors, 'Copyright Protection for Mass-Produced,

be copyrighted, permitting the overlapping of copyright and design patents.[84] The decision confirmed that commercial use did not invalidate copyright and thus that copyright registration for items such as dolls, jewellery, textile fabrics, and artificial flowers was allowed. By the early 1960s, hundreds of artificial flowers including gardenias, dahlias, violets, roses, hyacinths, and lilies had been registered at the US Copyright Office as sculptures[85] (Figure 9.4). This trend did not go unnoticed in the Copyright Office, which acknowledged that the number of deposits had increased spectacularly.[86]

Figure 9.4 'Gardenia Flowers, Inc.' US copyright registrations GP-30588 and GP-30795 (1961).
Courtesy of the National Archives at Kansas City.

Commercial Products: A Review of the Developments Following *Mazer v Stein*' (1961) 38(4) *University of Chicago Law Review* 807.

[84] FA de Moleyns, Commercial Department, British Embassy, Washington DC to HA Angus, Commerce & Industry Department, Hong Kong (10 March 1961); HKRS163–1-2713; PRO HK.

[85] For example, 'Sculptured Dahlia' Copyright registration Gp 26063; class 'G', 14 June 1960 ('Cactus Dahlia') and see *Prestige Floral Société Anonyme v Zunino-Altman Inc* 203 F Supp 649, 650 (SDNY 1962). A quick glance at the registry for the late 1950s and early 1960s shows there was some coexistence of protection in relation to artificial flowers, epitomised by inventors such as Alfred-Jean Fristot and André Emile Decamp, who were also listed as authors of floral creations. André Emile Decamp, 'Artificial flowers' US Patent No 2,881,545 (14 April 1959) and Alfred-Jean Fristot, 'Artificial Dahlia-like flower'; US Patent No 3,039,220 (10 April 1961); see also 'Current Registrations' in *Catalog of Copyright Entries*, vol 15, works of art (Library of Congress 1962) 21, 93, 181, 207, 263.

[86] Sixty-Fourth Annual Report of the Register of Copyrights for the Fiscal Year ending 30 June 1961 (Library of Congress 1962) 5. Around the same time, the British Patent Office noticed an increasing number of applications to register artificial flowers as designs; see Patents, Designs, and Trade Marks, *Seventy-Eighth Report of the Comptroller-General of Patents, Designs and Trade Marks, with Appendices, for the year 1960* (HMSO 1961) 10.

Many of the registered plastic flowers were made outside of the United States because of the inexpensive labour costs and because their plasticity and durability made them suitable for long-distance shipping. Although artificial polyethylene flowers and foliage were manufactured in France, Italy, Puerto Rico, and Japan,[87] Hong Kong, the 'the world's largest nursery of plastic flowers',[88] was the main exporter. In part this was because of the uncertain status of copyright in Hong Kong, which was a result of the fact that the British Copyright Act 1956 had not been extended to the territory, and which therefore created the perception that the plastic flower trade offered genuine business opportunities.[89]

In the first case dealing with the copyrightability of artificial flowers *Prestige Floral v California Artificial Flower Company* (1962) Judge Feinberg held that 'although a flower, like a dog, is a creation of nature, a likeness of it may be copyrighted'.[90] In this sense, the approach adopted by copyright law in relation to artificial flowers was similar to how it engaged with living nature. While copyright law has been willing to accommodate representations of nature such as pictures of roses, plans for gardens, and maps, it was not willing to protect nature itself.[91] This is, however, where the similarities ended. As seen above, copyright law treated representations of nature as sterile artistic works. In contrast, when copyright law engaged with artificial flowers it treated the three-dimensional sculptural representations of nature as if they were living (in much the same way as patent law approached living biological subject matter). This is reflected in the way the creativity of artificial flowers was construed, in the way the intangible property was configured, and in the way artificial flowers were viewed (namely, as botanical entities).

Unlike in patent law, where the role of the human agent (as inventor) was reconfigured to accommodate the secretive nature of plant subject matter, copyright law was not willing to change the way it thought about authorship and agency in its dealings with living plants. The consequence of this was that living subject matter was deemed to be outside the scope of copyright.[92] However, copyright law's engagement with artificial flowers followed a distinct path: one that reached a similar

[87] Jane Waddell, 'Flowers that Dazzle and Deceive' (1967) 4 *Seattle Magazine* 28.

[88] 'Hong Kong Annual Report 1959 (Hong Kong 1960) 29; CO 1071/173; TNA; see also 'Plastic flower industry blossoms' *The New Scientist* (18 August 1960) 445; and Richard Hughes, *Hong Kong: Borrowed Place—Borrowed Time* (André Deutsch 1968) 25.

[89] See eg John O Farrer to William Wallace, Board of Trade (25 July 1961); BT 209/1174; and William Wallace to PA Tilley, Colonial Office (8 May 1963); CO 1026/254; TNA.

[90] *Prestige Floral SA v California Artificial Flower Co* 201 F Supp. 287, 291 (SDNY 1962) and *Prestige Floral SA v Zunino-Altman Inc* (n 85) 651. See also *Fristot v First American Natural Ferns Co* 251 F Supp 886 (SDNY 1966); *Florabelle Flowers Inc v Joseph Markovits Inc* 296 F Supp 304 (SDNY 1968), *Gardenia Flowers Inc v Joseph Markovits Inc* 280 F Supp 776. (SDNY 1968); *First American Artificial Flowers Inc v Joseph Markovits Inc* 342 F Supp 178 (SDNY 1972).

[91] Sixty-Fifth Annual Report of the Register of Copyrights for the Fiscal Year ending 30 June 1962 (Library of Congress 1963) 9 (giving an explanation to the denial of preliminary injunctions 'on the ground that the similarities between the works might be the result of their both being reproductions of living flowers').

[92] *Prestige Floral and Others* (n 68). But see *Gardenia Flowers v Joseph Markovits* 62 Civ 1713 (18 December 1967) (where authorship was precisely raised not in relation to the floral creations per se but regarding the corsages).

result to the approach taken in patents towards natural plants, but by a different means. Rather than reconfiguring the role that the author played in creating the final product, authorship was simply ignored or presumed. While this was in part a result of the labour practices used to create artificial flowers (notably in Hong Kong) and the difficulty of tracing and bringing foreign designers to court but it might also have been a consequence of the invisibility of the gendered division of labour on which the making of these flowers depended.[93] Perhaps the most important reason for the effacement of authorship was that it reflected the way that artificial flowers were imagined and commercialized. It was rare, for example, to see any credit given to designers or authors in artificial flower catalogues (Figure 9.5). Artificial flowers were designed to be creations of nature and their most important attribute was that they were nature-like effects, and not the result of human ingenuity and skill. While in other contexts this effacing of authorship may have been fatal to claims to copyright, this was not the case with artificial flowers.[94]

Figure 9.5 'Catalogue (exhibit)', *A J Fristot et al and Others v First American Natural Ferns Co.*, (1966).
Courtesy of the National Archives at Kansas City.

[93] By the early 1960s, it was estimated that 10,000 workers, mainly women, were employed in the local plastic flower industry in Hong Kong; see Arthur Wong, 'Plastic Paradise' *Far Eastern Economic Review* (6 August 1964) 253–355; and 'Plastic Flower Boom' *Hong Kong Standard* (12 February 1961); HKRS70-3-385; PRO HK.

[94] *Prestige Floral SA v Zunino-Altman Inc* (n 85) 652.

Another similarity between the way copyright law treated artificial flowers and the way that patent law dealt with living biological subject matter was in terms of how the subject matter was viewed. Instead of looking at artificial flowers as mass produced designs, objects of manufacture, or works of artistic craftsmanship, copyright law treated artificial flowers *as if* they were living botanical entities. This can be seen, for instance, when botanists were called upon to help judge artificial flowers or when custom authorities described artificial flowers as articles that had to look 'enough like a flower'.[95] When shipments of plastic roses and geraniums were impounded by customs officers in the United States,[96] these officers were called upon to consider whether the imported artificial flowers were copies or substantial reproductions of copyrighted articles.[97] As often happens with living flowers, the customs officers found it difficult to determine whether the impounded flowers were infringing. To assist with their deliberations they submitted samples of the artificial flowers to botanists for examination.[98]

In making their arguments before the courts, litigants also treated artificial flowers as if they were natural flowers. As well as arguing that the seasonal character of artificial flowers (they were more popular at different times of the year) meant that the law needed to respond quickly to calls for injunctions,[99] in support of their 'horticultural contentions'[100] parties often drew upon botanical literature, upon marketing catalogues where artificial flowers were presented as if they were botanical varieties[101] (Figure 9.6) and used botanical language to describe their creations in court.[102]

[95] *Marshall Field & Co v United States* 45 CCPA 72 (1958).

[96] 'US Copyright hits Fake Flowers Imports' (1961) 136 *Florist & Nursery Exchange* 12; 'Hong Kong' (1961) 65(8) *Foreign Commerce Weekly* 2; and 'Copyrights and Copycats' *Far Eastern Economic Review* (16 March 1961) 491–92. See also an interesting account of the controversy in Matthew Turner, 'Hong Kong Design and the Roots of Sino-American Trade Disputes' (1996) 547 *The Annals of the American Academy of Political and Social Science* 37, 48.

[97] *Norwood Imports v United States* 132 USPA 216 (Cust Ct 2d Div 1961). The authority for the collector's action of exclusion derived from the Copyright Act of 30 July 1947, 61 Stat 663, Ch 391 (17 USC § 106).

[98] John F Atwood, 'Importing and Copyrights: The Role of the United States Bureau of Customs' (1970) 18(1) *Bulletin of the Copyright Society of the USA* 1. However, these controversies faded away because customs authorities became increasingly reluctant to exercise complicated analyses that went beyond their competence; see Frank W Sheaffer, Department of State Instruction to the American Consulate General, Hong Kong (27June 1961); RG 59; Box 2534; NARA, College Park, Maryland. This change took place after the Federation of Hong Kong Industries recommended that their members file statements denying that the flowers were piratical copies; see Hong Kong Chamber of Commerce, *Annual Report* (1961) 51 and 'HK's Plastic Flower Industry Bounces Back' *China Mail* (17 July 1961); HKRS70-3-385; PRO HK.

[99] *First American Artificial Flowers v Joseph Markovits Inc* (n 90) and *Prestige Floral v California Artificial Flower Co* (n 90).

[100] Sixty-Ninth Annual Report of the Register of Copyrights for the Fiscal Year ending 30 June 1966 (Library of Congress 1967) 23.

[101] *Rico v Hub Floral Mfg Co* 206 F Supp 192, 193 (SDNY 1962) (referring to the catalogues); *Prestige Floral and Others* (n 68) (also referring to the ways in which the catalogues were made).

[102] *First American Artificial Flowers Inc v Joseph Markovits Inc* (n 90) 186; see also the 'Affidavit by Isidor Abrams in opposition to motion for a preliminary injunction'; *Prestige Floral SA v Zunino Altman Inc* 61 Civ 3929 (9 February 1962).

Figure 9.6 'Artificial Flowers (exhibit)', *Rico Ltd v Hub Floral Manufacturing Co.*, (1962). Courtesy of the National Archives at Kansas City.

Because these floral creations were based on natural resemblance, the courts also treated artificial flowers like they were living natural flowers in reaching their (copyright) decisions. In some situations, real flowers literally stood in for artificial flowers as legal arguments depended on the specific flowers they intended to simulate. For example, in infringement actions the courts focused on the living flowers that were used to form the artificial flowers moulds, rather than either the moulds or the artificial flowers themselves. In these instances, vitality played a direct role in the way artificial flowers were assessed.[103] Taking into account the changeability of nature, the courts also reasoned that it was highly unlikely, for example, that parties in Hong Kong and France could use identical lilacs as models to build their replica flowers.[104] Given that it was too much of a coincidence for a plaintiff and a defendant to use the same lilac, rose, or geranium for their floral creations, proof of similarity of form was taken as proof of copying.[105]

[103] See eg *Gardenia Flowers v Joseph Markovits* (n 92) (asking whether such a flower grows from a stem in a normal daisy flower).

[104] *Prestige Floral and Others* (n 68) 'Michele D'Agnillo: Redirect Examination'. It was also unlikely that they could both come up with the same idea of only including two sizes of flower petals, one size of bud, and two sizes of leaves.

[105] *Prestige Floral SA v Zunino-Altman Inc* (n 85).

In other situations, the courts also engaged with artificial flowers as if they were living. For example, as well as calling on botanical experts to help them deliberate on the legal fate of artificial flowers, the courts utilized botanical methods to identify artificial flowers.[106] One of the problems that often arises in botanical taxonomy is how to distinguish plants that are very similar. To deal with this problem, botanists tend to focus on one or two distinctive traits that differentiate a particular variety from related varieties. The courts and customs officers often adopted a similar approach to determine whether an artificial flower was infringing a copyright registered flower. Based upon the fact that the most distinctive feature of plastic flowers was the way that the petals were arranged, courts and customs officers often resorted to a 'petal test' which looked at the way petals fitted together, vein for vein, to decide whether artificial flowers were the same.[107] This paradoxical relationship whereby the natural and the artificial coalesced in copyright cases was noted by a contemporary commentator who said that 'the copyright of flowers and plants belongs to Mother Nature. But you can hold a copyright on a flower that nature did not design but then is not an artificial flower'.[108]

Conclusion

Vitality plays an important role in the way intellectual property law engages with biological subject matter. While vitality lies at the heart of the way patent law interacts with nature-based subject matter (both in terms of how the subject matter is defined and in terms of how the law was changed to deal with an unruly, secretive, and changing subject matter), copyright law was not willing to make significant changes to accommodate nature. At best, copyright law was only willing to protect a sterile and unchanging representation of nature. One of the interesting things about the way intellectual property law interacted with artificial flowers is how this logic was blurred. The question of whether the subject matter was alive or dead simply did not arise in relation to patents for artificial flowers. It did not matter that plants are inherently unruly, secretive, and changeable. Instead, patents for

[106] *Prestige Floral and Others* (n 68) 'D'Agnillo:Direct Examination'. The 'petal test', as a way of demonstrating 'the precise way in which the leaves nest into each other,' was also used in the 'Statement of Philip T Dalsimer, Attorney, New York, Patent Law Association' *Design Protection: Hearings on S. 1884 Before the Subcommittee on Patents, Trademarks, and Copyrights of the Committee on the Judiciary United States Senate* (US Government Printing Office 1961) 68.

[107] Atwood (n 98) 8; see also Ball (n 14) 3. The manufacture of plastic flowers involved two main processes. The basic components such as buds, cores, petals, calyces, stems, and leaves were formed by injecting polythene into moulding machines. A variety of moulds were used to reproduce the shapes and sizes of natural flowers and foliage. See 'Artificial Flowers' [April 1964] *Hong Kong Trade Bulletin* 69, 69; see also Fred York-Sung Yao, *United States Market for Hong Kong Artificial Flowers* (University of Pennsylvania Press 1962) 12–14.

[108] Vaun Willmott, 'Legal Advice on US Customs Decision' *South China Morning Post* (2 March 1961); HKRS70-3-385; PRO HK.

artificial flowers treated the subject matter in the same way that patentees treated machine parts or mechanical inventions: that is, they treated the subject matter as if it was fixed, inanimate, and stable. In this sense, the focus in those patents was on the artificial part of *artificial* flowers.

In contrast, the focus in copyright shifted to the flower part of artificial *flowers*. Practically speaking, copyright law treated artificial flowers as if they were living entities. In this sense, copyright treated artificial flowers in the same way as patents dealt with living plants. As seen above, to accommodate the secretive nature of plant subject matter, the role of the human agent (as inventor) was reconfigured in patent law. In its dealings with living plants, copyright law was unwilling to change how it thought about authorship and agency. The consequence was that living subject matter was deemed to be outside the scope of copyright. Interestingly, copyright law's engagement with artificial flowers was similar to the way patent law interacted with natural plants, but by a different means. Rather than reconfiguring the role that the author played in creating the final product, it was simply ignored. The upshot of this is that whereas life is a defining feature for patents for plants, it is absent from copyright. In contrast, when it comes to artificial flowers, life is absent in the assessment of patentability but present in copyright.

One could conclude from this that the manner in which intellectual property law has engaged with artificial flowers resembles the way it has treated plants more generally: they are unconventional, awkward, and out-of-place. However, one of the things that this chapter has shown is that despite the similarities, artificial flowers should not be lumped in with plant-based subject matter. The main reason for this is that artificial flowers are not biological entities. At the same time, and despite their copyright registration as sculptures, they are not simply artistic objects (not least because of the way that they are treated as botanical objects). Instead, artificial flowers are hybrid objects that span different worlds. As objects created by 'botanists in plastic'[109] artificial flowers are at once artificial and at the same time extrinsically intertwined with nature. In this sense, the lineage of artificial flowers within intellectual property is closer to synthetic biology than it is to biology; to a subject matter that is inspired by nature but takes up engineering standards and techniques to build nature from scratch.

[109] Kohn (n 10) 54.

10

Modified Pearl Oysters and Repeatable Peaches

Cultivation, Invention, and the Laws of Nature in Twentieth-century Japan

Kjell David Ericson[*]

Introduction

In early 2002, Japan's prime minister Koizumi Jun'ichirō announced plans to promote Japan as a 'nation based on intellectual property' (*chiteki zaisan rikkoku* and, in slogan form, *chizai rikkoku*). Later that year, the Diet (Japan's bicameral legislature) passed a piece of legislation that designated the prime minister's cabinet as responsible for overseeing strategy related to intellectual property or *chiteki zaisan*.[1] The 2002 Intellectual Property Basic Act's namesake category encompassed, among other things, 'inventions, devices, new varieties of plants, designs, works and other property that is produced through creative activities by human beings (including discovered or solved laws of nature or natural phenomena that are industrially applicable)'.[2] This formulation of intellectual property brought together concepts that have at times existed in tension, whether invention versus discovery, or living organisms (here in the Basic Act, explicitly in the form of plants) versus non-living entities. The law instead proposed a logic of ownership based on a looser grouping of 'creative activities', all the while guided by a criterion of industrial applicability.

* I would like to extend thanks to John DiMoia and the editors of this volume, all of whom read versions of this chapter and provided much-appreciated feedback.

[1] Kobayashi Tadashi, 'Shubyōhō no enkaku to chiteki zaisan hogo' (2005) 55(8) *Refarensu* 17, 38–40. Japanese language glosses of 'intellectual property' did not suddenly appear in the early 2000s. Formulations of intellectual property appeared after the 1893 administrative merging of the Paris Convention for the Protection of Intellectual Property with the Berne Convention for the Protection of Literary and Artistic Works to form the Bern-based United International Bureaux for the Protection of Intellectual Property. Terms such as *chiteki zaisanken* or *chiteki shoyūken* appeared from time to time in Japanese language legal discourse throughout the twentieth century, particularly from the 1980s within corporate research divisions and following Japan's accession to the 1994 Agreement on Trade-related Aspects of Intellectual Property Rights (TRIPs), although in general subordinated to law-by-law treatments of patents, copyrights, trademarks, and designs.

[2] These English language translations of passages in the Intellectual Property Basic Act can be found in the Japanese Law Translation Database System http://www.japaneselawtranslation.go.jp (accessed 1 March 2022).

Kjell David Ericson, *Modified Pearl Oysters and Repeatable Peaches* In: *Intellectual Property and the Design of Nature.* Edited by: Jose Bellido and Brad Sherman, Oxford University Press. © Kjell David Ericson 2023.
DOI: 10.1093/oso/9780192864406.003.0010

The twenty-first-century Intellectual Property Basic Act, however, is just one part of a longer history of intersections between monopoly rights systems and living organisms in Japanese legal circles. Indeed, questions about the limits of inventive claims and 'industrial' applications have persisted for well over a century, and have extended beyond national contexts.

This chapter examines the historical circumstances and aftermaths of three patent-related episodes that spanned the twentieth century. The first episode centres on the early twentieth-century question of whether the surgical modification of living, pearl-bearing shellfish was subject to patent protection under Japanese industrial property law. The 1910s' judicial interpretation of pearl cultivation as a patentable application of the 'laws of nature' would echo in other discussions about the limits of industrial property in the Japanese empire. Discussions about the relationship of plant and animal cultivation (including micro-organism cultivation) to patent law in Japan lasted long after 1959, when bureaucrats and law-makers redefined the still-employed legal basis of invention in terms of manipulations involving the 'laws of nature'. The second episode retraces the historical outlines of plant variety protection in Japan by focusing on the intensification of plant patent lobbying in the 1970s, which was shaped by ongoing debate over the legal boundaries of patentable invention. In particular, competing jurisdictional claims between Japan's Ministry of Agriculture and Forestry (MAF) and the Japanese Patent Office (JPO) left residual institutional mandates to govern plant-related matters. The third episode follows Kurakata Eizō, a Japanese fruit breeder who started his career in colonial Korea in the 1930s and who later became a key player in the 1970s plant-patent lobby. Kurakata's 1977 application for a Japanese patent covering what he claimed as a new variety of peach was, over two decades later in 2000, the subject of the first-ever High Court ruling on plant patents in Japan.

These three episodes suggest how the imperial and trans-war East Asian contexts of agricultural breeding and industrial property have continued to shape disputes over biopatenting and intellectual property in Japan, well into the twenty-first century.[3] Narrating the conceptual and legal transformations of what has

[3] Works that have explored longer twentieth-century agricultural linkages include Tatsushi Fujihara, 'Colonial Seeds, Imperialist Genes: Hōrai Rice and Agricultural Development' in Hiromi Mizuno, Aaron S Moore, and John DiMoia (eds), *Engineering Asia: Technology, Colonial Development, and the Cold War Order* (Bloomsbury 2018); Tae-Ho Kim, 'Making Miracle Rice: Tongil and Mobilizing a Domestic "Green Revolution" in South Korea' in Hiromi Mizuno, Aaron S Moore, and John DiMoia (eds), *Engineering Asia: Technology, Colonial Development, and the Cold War Order* (Bloomsbury 2018); Kaori Iida, 'Genetics and "Breeding as a Science": Kihara Hitoshi and the Development of Genetics in Japan in the First Half of the Twentieth Century' in Denise Phillips and Sharon Kingsland (eds), *New Perspectives on the History of Life Sciences and Agriculture* (Springer 2015); Hiromi Mizuno, 'Mutant Rice and Agricultural Modernization in Asia' (2020) 36 *History and Technology* 360; Manyong Moon, 'The Dual Green Revolutions in South Korea: Reforestation and Agricultural Revolution under the Authoritarian Regime' (2012) 21(3) *Historia Scientiarum* 161; Victoria Lee, *The Arts of the Microbial World Fermentation Science in Twentieth-Century Japan* (University of Chicago Press 2021); Lisa Onaga, 'Toyama Kametaro and Vernon Kellogg: Silkworm Inheritance Experiments in Japan, Siam,

counted as 'industrial' property, in other words, brings longer histories of law and empire in East Asia into view.[4] The disputes discussed here direct attention to the shifting geopolitical boundaries of 'Japanese' law, by including East Asian spaces at the edges of the pre-1945 Japanese empire and legal reforms of the post-1945 state.[5] By highlighting episodes across the twentieth century—all of which were entangled with trans-war developments spanning the ostensible dividing line of 1945—this chapter attempts to reconcile strands of institutional history and legal commentary that have at times been told separately. Geographical transformations have in turn been connected to conceptual ones. All three episodes were bound up with knotty problems of justifying the authorship of inventive claims on living organisms and their by-products. In different ways, all revealed transregional and multi-institutional trajectories of ideas about cultivation and ownership that complicate more recent invocations of Japan as an IP nation.

The Boundaries of 'Industrial' Property in Early Twentieth-century Japan

This section examines the conceptual malleability of 'industry' in early—to mid-twentieth-century Japanese debates over the patentability of processes involving living creatures. It opens at the turn of the century, a moment when IP—in the form of *industrial* rather than *intellectual* property—brought concerns about the legal relationships among patent protection, invention, and nature into focus.

and the United States, 1900–1912' (2010) 43 *Journal of the History of Biology* 215; David Fedman, *Seeds of Control: Japan's Empire of Forestry in Korea* (University of Washington Press 2020).

[4] See Alexis Dudden, *Japan's Colonization of Korea: Discourse and Power* (University of Hawai'i Press 2006); Asano Toyomi, *Teikoku Nihon no shokuminchi hōsei: hōiki tōgō to teikoku chitsujo* (Nagoya Daigaku Shuppankai 2008); Turan Kayaoğlu, *Legal Imperialism: Sovereignty and Extraterritoriality in Japan, the Ottoman Empire, and China* (Cambridge University Press 2010); Pär Kristopher Cassel, *Grounds of Judgment: Extraterritoriality and Imperial Power in Nineteenth-Century China and Japan* (Oxford University Press (OUP) 2012); Susan Burns and Barbara J Brooks (eds), *Gender and Law in the Japanese Imperium* (University of Hawai'i Press 2014); Lauren Benton, Adam Clulow, and Bain Attwood (eds), *Protection and Empire: A Global History* (Cambridge University Press 2018).

[5] With regard to the history of industrial or intellectual property in East Asia, past research includes Asano (n 4); Toyomi Asano, 'Regionalism or Imperialism: Japan's Options toward a Protected Korea after the Russo—Japanese War, 1905–1910' in Pedro Iacobelli, Danton Leary, and Shinnosuke Takahashi (eds), *Transnational Japan as History: Empire, Migration, and Social Movements* (Palgrave Macmillan 2015); Eiichi Motono, 'Anglo–Japanese Trademark Conflict in China and the Birth of the Chinese Trademark Law (1923), 1906–1926' (2011) 37 *East Asian History* 9; Jung Lee, 'Invention without Science: "Korean Edisons" and the Changing Understanding of Technology in Colonial Korea' (2013) 54 *Technology and Culture* 782; Eugenia Lean, *Vernacular Industrialism in China: Local Innovation and Translated Technologies in the Making of a Cosmetics Empire, 1900–1940* (Columbia University Press 2020); Harald Fuess, 'Das Ringen um staatliche Souveränität und das Wirtschaftsrecht des Stärkeren: Europa und der Markenschutz in Japan und Ostasien, 1884–1923' (2018) 9 *Zeitschrift für Japanisches Recht: Sonderheft* 23; William P Alford, *To Steal a Book Is an Elegant Offense: Intellectual Property Law in Chinese Civilization* (Stanford University Press 1995).

Pearl Oyster Modification as Industrial Property

The question of what was or was not 'industrial'—and, as a result, patentable or unpatentable—acquired new resonance upon the Meiji Japanese state's accession to the Paris Convention for the Protection of Industrial Property in 1899. In *fin de siècle* European and North American legal circles, industrial property was a category that could, in principle, extend to the realms of the agricultural and mineralogical. In 1899, the same year that Japan joined the Paris Convention, a US commentator noted that industrial property extended 'not only to the productions of industry properly so called, but equally to the productions of agriculture (wines, grains, fruits, cattle, etc.), and to mineral productions used in commerce (mineral waters, etc.)'.[6] Agriculturally-tinged understandings of industrial property did not, however, translate smoothly into the language of imperial Japanese law. One reason for this was the very term chosen as the Japanese-language gloss for the 'industrial' of the Paris Convention's *propriété industrielle*: *kōgyō* 工業. In Japan, the industry of *kōgyō* denoted a field that stood in contrast to agriculture or *nōgyō* 農業. Depending on the context, industrial *kōgyō* could even serve as agricultural *nōgyō*'s binary opposite.

The boundaries of *kōgyō* in early twentieth-century Japanese industrial property law came into dispute in a handful of cases that involved attempts to take out patents on inventive claims with agricultural and fisheries applications. One early impetus for rethinking industrial property's relationship to living creatures concerned a method for deliberately inducing the formation of semi-spherical pearls in shellfish. The patent covered a step in the production of what were then sold as 'culture pearls', namely the preparation and treatment of nucleating objects that would be inserted between the inner layer of a pearl oyster's shell and its soft flesh. The patent's owner, Mikimoto Kōkichi, had submitted a claim over the process in 1894. He received approval for a fifteen-year patent nearly two years later in 1896. Mikimoto's first patent was at the centre of the largest domestic patent dispute in pre-1945 Japan. Starting around 1908, Mikimoto brought criminal patent infringement charges against three competitors. In response, the trio challenged the basis of Mikimoto's inventive claims in patent tribunals and civil courts.[7]

[6] Arthur Philip Greeley, *Foreign Patent and Trademark Laws: A Comparative Study with Tabular Statements of Essential Features of Such Laws* (J Byrne 1899) 216.

[7] For more on this case see Kjell Ericson, 'The Life and Times of Patent No. 2670: Industrial Property and Public Knowledge in Early Twentieth-Century Japan' in Graeme Gooday and Steven Wilf (eds), *Patent Cultures: Diversity and Harmonization in Historical Perspective* (Cambridge University Press 2020). For considerations of ideas of invention and patenting practices in late nineteenth- and early twentieth-century Japan see Ruselle Meade, 'Popular Science and Personal Endeavor in Early-Meiji Japan: The Case of *Hatsumei Kiji*' (2017) 26(2) *Historia Scientiarum* 77; Tom Nicholas and Hiroshi Shimizu, 'Intermediary Functions and the Market for Innovation in Meiji and Taisho Japan' (2013) 87(1) *Business History Review* 121.

Changes to the geopolitical boundaries of industrial property protection accompanied the life of Mikimoto's pearl cultivation patent, which, after receiving the first-term extension ever granted in Japan, would last from 1896 to 1921. Mikimoto obtained his patent just before Japan joined the Paris Convention for the Protection of Industrial Property in 1899. Mikimoto's patent was issued under a post-1885 patent system that restricted applicants to Japanese imperial subjects. By the early 1890s, however, Euro–US negotiators were adamant that extending patent and trademark protection to claimants outside the Japanese empire would be a condition for renegotiating the advantageous commercial treaties they had signed from 1858 onwards. The legal regime after 1899 allowed people outside the Japanese empire to apply for patents through the mediation of Japanese patent lawyers. The transformation of post-1899 industrial property law in turn led to efforts in Japanese courts to circumscribe the range of inventions that could be patented by foreign claimants. Such was the case in 1903, when Japan's *Daishin'in* High Court ruled that a claim could not receive a patent as a novel invention if it had been 'publicly known or publicly used' within the Japanese empire.[8]

Dispute over the pearl patent began in earnest in 1908, when Mikimoto had three nearby entrepreneurs arrested on criminal charges of patent infringement. The criminal trials turned on the spatial boundaries of public knowledge in the Japanese empire. The trio of would-be pearl cultivators argued that they themselves had made use of published materials that had circulated in Japan well before Mikimoto's patent application in 1894. Earlier publications described a process that had been practised in southern China for inducing hemispherical pearls in freshwater molluscs. They contended that this publicly accessible 'Chinese method', not Mikimoto's patented claims, was what had guided them. Criminal court judges sympathized with their arguments, finding the trio not guilty of prisonable patent infringement. The acquittal of the alleged patent infringers in criminal court occurred alongside the formation of new anti-Mikimoto alliances and the spread of non-Mikimoto pearl farms elsewhere in the Japanese empire. As such, historians in Japan have identified the trio's victory in the criminal trials over Mikimoto's first patent as a formative moment in the spread of pearl cultivation practices.[9]

A parallel series of arguments unfolded outside the criminal patent infringement trials, in JPO tribunals and in civil courts. Judges said that evidence of methods 'publicly known' prior to Mikimoto's application was not admissible for

[8] Ericson (n 7) 325–27; Hanaoka Toshio, *Kosodewata seizōki tokkyo mukō shinketsu fufuku jōkoku jiken hyōron* (Yūhikaku 1903). On legal practice more generally see Darryl E Flaherty, *Public Law, Private Practice: Politics, Profit, and the Legal Profession in Nineteenth-Century Japan* (Harvard University East Asia Center 2013).

[9] See Ōbayashi Hideo, 'Shinju yōshokugyō sōsetsuki no shomondai: Mikimoto no dokusen to sore e no tatakai' (1962) 12(2–3) *Chihōshi kenkyū* 141; Ōbayashi Hideo, *Mikimoto Kōkichi* (Yoshikawa Kōbunkan 1971). Questions of priority in subsequent pearl patents are discussed in Kuru Tarō, *Shinju no hatsumeisha wa dare ka?: Nishikawa Tōkichi to Tōdai purojekuto* (Keisō Shobō 1987); and Yamada Atsumi, *Shinju no sekaishi: tomi to yabō no gosen-nen* (Chūō Kōron Shinsha 2013).

the purposes of considering whether the patent should be invalidated. On top of that, Mikimoto's legal counsel Kishi Seiichi pushed the boundaries of the patent's scope. The patent's written claims did not mention any direct claims over shellfish or their biological functions. Rather, the claims were limited to processes for preparing objects that would thereafter be inserted into living pearl oysters. Nevertheless, Kishi pressed the idea that Mikimoto's claim was patentable because it made use of 'laws of nature' (*shizen no hōsoku*). He compared Mikimoto's process to earlier patents issued in Japan for the brewing of alcohol and soy sauce. As Kishi put it, if brewers added yeast or *tane kōji* mould starters to make alcoholic beverages, so too had Mikimoto made use of bivalves to produce pearls.[10] Kishi's central argument was as follows: 'Both make use of artifice in order to aid nature's powers. It therefore goes without saying that both are industrial processes'. The JPO and *Daishin'in* High Court agreed. Echoing Kishi's arguments, a High Court ruling held in 1911 that Mikimoto's patent could count as an industrial process that 'makes use of natural side effects through human artifice'.[11] The civil trials in the Mikimoto patent dispute reinterpreted industrial property in terms of the application of human artifice to the 'laws of nature'. It was a logic that would resurface in ensuing attempts to justify industrial property in the realms of agriculture and fisheries.

Patentable Industry from *Kōgyō* to *Sangyō*

Amid cases such as the Mikimoto pearl cultivation patent dispute, some legal commentators in Japan began to criticize the ambiguous connotations of the 'industry' encompassed by *kōgyō* in Japanese patent law. In the late 1930s, one Japanese jurist described the term as 'an infelicitous word choice bordering on mistranslation'.[12] By that time, an alternative Japanese-language formulation of 'industrial' property had in fact already been proposed—not in the metropole or the formal colonial empire, but rather by a team of legal officials sent from Tokyo in the mid-1930s to the Japanese puppet state of Manchukuo, in what is today part of north-east China.

The 1936 Manchukuo Patent and Invention Law (*Tokkyo hatsumeihō* [J]/*Texu famingfa* [C]) introduced a conception of industrial property that its drafters intended to go beyond patent law in the formal Japanese empire.[13] The first clause of the new law specified that patents could be applied for 'industrially usable

[10] On intersections of brewing and fermentation craft practices with microbial sciences see Lee (n 3).

[11] Ericson (n 7) 330–32. Some of Kishi's collection of papers related to the case are published in Kishi Dōmonkai (ed), *Kishi Seiichi soshō kirokushū gyōseihen dai 1-shū* (Ganshōdō Shoten 1939).

[12] Suehiro Izutarō, *Kōgyō shoyūkenhō* (Nihon Hyōronsha 1939) 1.

[13] On law in Manchukuo more generally see Thomas David DuBois, 'Inauthentic Sovereignty: Law and Legal Institutions in Manchukuo' (2010) 69(3) *The Journal of Asian Studies* 749; Asano (n 4); Shin'ichi Yamamuro, *Manchuria under Japanese Domination* (Joshua A Fogel tr, University of Pennsylvania Press 2006).

inventions' (*sangyōjō riyō shiubeki hatsumei*) consisting of either products or processes.[14] Notable was the law's wording of 'industry' as *sangyō* 産業, rather than *kōgyō*, as in Japanese imperial law. Two Japanese men involved in drafting the Manchukuo legislation, Mutō Tomio and Hanabusa Masami, explained their choice of *sangyō* by noting that 'when one limits invention to industrial (*kōgyōteki*) things, inventions without a direct connection to industry (*kōgyō*), such as . . . cultivating plants without using soil or gathering pearls will not be patentable'. The existing terminology of 'industry' as *kōgyō* had what Mutō and Hanabusa described as a 'narrow meaning'. By contrast, they stressed that the Manchukuo law employed the 'comprehensive phrasing' of industrial invention denoted by the term *sangyō*.[15]

Outside Manchukuo, the legal status of patents in the wartime Japanese empire was shifting as well. Amid calls for total mobilization, many inside and outside the government attacked the logic of privately held patent rights. In 1943, a special directive ordered the suspension of patent and trademark activity, including applications and evaluations. The wartime state (including the Army and Navy ministries) reclassified over 1,500 patents as military secrets and cancelled many other foreign-claimed rights. In post-1945 Japan, American-led Occupation authorities pushed for the rehabilitation of the patent as a mode of property protection and pursued restitution for patents that had been revoked during the war.[16] But post-1945 patenting was neither a legal blank slate nor a return to an imagined pre-war status quo. Earlier questions about invention and industry persisted after 1945, albeit in ways that had been transformed by total war and the economic reorganizations of the 1930s and early 1940s.

Patent disputes in post-1945 Japan raised further possibilities for rethinking the scope of industrial property law. In the early 1950s, for example, a trial over the patentability of a commercial process for the encryption of telegraph messages recalled discussions about the vocabulary of invention and industry. The Tokyo High Court ruled in 1950 that a method for rearranging Roman letters and Arabic numerals was not patentable. Yet even as judges denied the patent in question, they brought up the scope of industry encapsulated in *kōgyō*: 'Is the scope of "industrial invention" limited to inventions based on *kōgyō*, whose meaning is in opposition to things like agriculture and commerce?' If that were the case, the Court noted:

> [a]s for inventions that dramatically speed up the growth of vegetables or inventions related to pearl cultivation, which are both tied to agriculture and fisheries, if one started from the premise that these were not inventions based in industry

[14] Hanabusa Masami and Mutō Tomio, *Manshū teikoku tokkyo hatsumeihō kaisetsu* (Manshū Gyōsei Gakkai 1936) 1.

[15] ibid.

[16] Tomita Tetsuo, 'GHQ to Nihon no tokkyo seido' in Nakayama Shigeru, Goto Kunio, and Yoshioka Hitoshi (eds), *Tsūshi Nihon no kagaku gijutsu: Senryōki 1945–1952* (Gakuyō Shobō 1995).

(*kōgyō*), then none of them would have been able to receive protection under patent law.[17]

The ruling suggested that invention should not be limited to fields of arbitrarily non-agricultural industry. Rather, invention in a broader sense took place 'through the domination of nature and the use of natural forces'. Such an understanding of invention, the Court suggested, should cover agricultural applications, too.[18]

A broadened conception of industry made its way into the 1959 Patent Act, the first wholesale revision of Japanese industrial property legislation since 1921. The 1959 law, which remains on the books in an amended form, reflected earlier changes inside and outside the Japanese empire. It began with an explicit definition of invention as 'the highly advanced creation of technical ideas utilizing the laws of nature'. The protection of invention was, in turn, framed to support 'the development of industry', here expressed in terms of *sangyō* rather than *kōgyō*. The rewording and its potential re-envisioning of industry were notable. Pre-war Manchurian patent law served as a precedent for industrial property-related legal reforms in post-1945 Japan, well over a decade after the Manchukuo state apparatus had been dismantled. As the Patent Office's 100th anniversary in-house history put it, the post-1959 choice of *sangyō* for 'industry' had 'borrowed from the example of the establishment of Manchukuo's patent law'.[19] Several generations of researchers have outlined the deep connections between Japanese bureaucrats who used Manchukuo as a laboratory for industrial policy in the wartime Japanese empire and post-war Japan.[20] Added to continuities in industrial policy were shards of Japanese-language Manchukuo legal terminology in the reformulation of industry's conceptual boundaries towards a more direct embrace of agricultural applications. Concepts including *sangyō* found a home in the Ministry of International Trade and Industry (MITI, *Tsūsan Sangyōshō*), where a coterie of former imperial bureaucrats played roles in the regulation of post-war technology licensing agreements, in concert with the MITI-housed Patent Office.[21]

Patent protection in post-1945 Japan continued to be shaped by past legal disputes and institutional remnants of war and empire, in ways that would have ongoing implications for inventive claims that purported to be both industrial and agricultural (or, for that matter, aquacultural). As in cases such as the early

[17] 'Kōkoku shinpan no shinketsu torikeshi seikyū jiken' (1950) 1(7) *Gyōsei jiken saiban reishū* 1071–72.

[18] ibid.

[19] Tokkyochō [JPO] (ed), *Kōgyō shoyūken seido hyakunenshi*, vol 2 (Hatsumei Kyōkai 1985) 266.

[20] Chalmers Johnson, *MITI and the Japanese Miracle: The Growth of Industrial Policy, 1925–1975* (Stanford University Press 1982); Louise Young, *Japan's Total Empire: Manchuria and the Culture of Wartime Imperialism* (University of California Press 1999); Janis Mimura, *Planning for Empire: Reform Bureaucrats and the Japanese Wartime State* (Cornell University Press 2011).

[21] MITI was reconstituted in 2001, along with several other agencies, as the *Keizai Sangyōshō* or Ministry of Economy, Trade, and Industry (METI).

twentieth-century Mikimoto pearl patent dispute, certain methods of cultivation had already been fair game for inventive claims before the 1959 rewriting of the Patent Act.[22] Yet both before and immediately after 1959, cultivation was circumscribed in terms of processes for raising plants and animals—or, in the case of pearl cultivation, for modifying living shellfish. From the mid-twentieth century onwards, the idea of extending patent protection to living organisms, whether *in toto* or in part, would bring additional and still-unresolved questions about the social and legal boundaries of industrial property. Nowhere was the situation more vexed than with plants.

Plant Protection and Horticultural Histories

This section introduces the problem of registering and protecting plant varieties in late twentieth-century Japan. It does so by following strands of lobbying and debate about the ownership and authorship of plant varieties in the Japanese empire and the post-1945 Japanese state. It traces criticisms of the Japanese plant variety registration system that was implemented in 1947, as well as later proposals for alternative modes of plant protection in terms of patentable 'industrial' property.

Trans-war plant protection debates and Japan's 1947 Agricultural Seeds and Seedlings Law

Agricultural scientists, lawyers, and horticultural breeders in Japan took notice of legal changes in the early twentieth-century world. In particular, the 1930 American Plant Patent Act inspired curiosity and critique in Japan (and elsewhere) almost immediately after the law's passage. The Act, which created rights protecting the asexual or vegetative propagation of plant varieties, appealed to fruit and especially flower breeders in 1930s' Japan. Proponents such as the Tokyo Imperial University agricultural geneticist Noguchi Yakichi introduced Japanese-language readers to the law and suggested that Japan adopt a plant protection system along similar lines.[23]

The sporadic conversations of the 1930s about plant patenting in the Japanese empire took on new dimensions after the 1945 start of what would become a nearly seven-year American-led occupation. In February and May 1946, the reconstituted Patent Office hosted two conferences that floated the idea of introducing

[22] Later in the twentieth century, patent officials would also return to the Mikimoto pearl patent ruling as a way to signal the extent of industrial property and its limits. See the passage in 'Tokkyohō semina' (1963) 286 *Jurisuto* 286 31, quoted in Ericson (n 7) 339.

[23] Noguchi Yakichi, 'Shokubutsu shinhinshu no tokkyo tōroku (tsuiroku)' (1933) 8(3) *Nōgyō oyobi engei* 130; Noguchi Yakichi, *Nō no kagaku* (Kawade Shobō 1947) 167–72.

an American-style system along the lines of the Plant Patent Act.[24] Among the attendees was the geneticist Noguchi. Officials in attendance from the JPO and the MAF gestured at the possibility of implementing patent protections for plants at an unspecified time in the future, but the meetings concluded with the recommendation that, amid widespread and persistent food shortages in Japan, it was too early to install a comprehensive plant patent law.[25]

Instead, a plant protection system took shape in post-war Japan under the 1947 Agricultural Seeds and Seedlings Law (*Nōsan Shubyōhō*), which offered up a framework for registering the names of new plant varieties through the MAF. The law had not emerged from concerted plant breeder lobbying. There had not, for example, been any notable plant breeder voices in support of patent-like plant protection at the previously mentioned 1946 conference (there were, however, requests for measures such as state-sanctioned breeder prizes).[26] Contemporaneous explanations of the Agricultural Seeds and Seedlings Law stressed goals of promoting the distribution of high-quality seeds and the stamping out of so-called 'unscrupulous seed dealers' (*akushitsu gyōsha*), rather than the protection of breeders per se.[27] MAF official Matsunobu Yōhei would later describe the law as something akin to a trademark registration system, albeit with protections that lasted between three and ten years, a shorter period of time than for a trademark.[28]

Debates over plant patent protection unfolded amid longer-standing divisions between publicly funded staple crop breeding and private horticultural research. The Japanese state promoted research into staple crop variety improvement and the distribution of seeds before and after 1945. Historians have shed light on connections between the Japanese empire and the intra-imperial and post-1945 spread of crop cultivars. Such work has revealed the central role of agriculture in the Japanese empire and post-colonial East Asia to conventional understandings of the Green Revolution. Research laboratories attached to prefectural and colonial governments as well as the MAF (the *Nōrinshō*) pursued several strands of staple crop improvement, including the widely adopted *Hōrai* (*Ponlai*) rice strain.[29] Another project led to the development of shorter-stalked wheat plants that grew quickly and could survive in cold, windswept areas. One product of this research was *Nōrin*

[24] Shisa Makoto Sensei Tsuitō Kinen Shuppankai (ed), *Engei kenkyū kara baiteku no kiso-zukuri e* (Shisa Makoto Sensei Tsuitō Kinen Shuppankai 1986) 226–32.

[25] ibid 231–32.

[26] ibid 229.

[27] See Diet discussions about the law in Kokkai kaigiroku, Sangiin, honkaigi 27-gō (26 August 1947).

[28] See Matsunobu Yōhei, 'Nōgyō gijutsu no hatten to tokkyo seido' (1967) 22(5) *Nōgyō gijutsu* 231. Matsunobu had recently returned to a position at the MAF after studying agricultural economics at Cornell University.

[29] Fujihara (n 3); Fujihara Tatsushi, *Ine no Daitōa kyōeiken: Teikoku Nihon no 'Midori no Kakumei'* (Yoshikawa Kōbunkan 2012); Mizuno (n 3). On rice research in South Korea see Moon (n 3); Fujihara (n 3).

10 ('Agriculture and Forestry 10'), a high-yielding wheat variety that later became part of Norman Borlaug's hitherto better known wheat-breeding research.[30]

The 1947 Agricultural Seeds and Seedlings Law treated staple crop research in public research institutions separately from other kinds of plant-breeding activities. Notably, the new law came to exclude rice, wheat, barley, soy, and other plant organisms classified as 'staples' under the 1952 Main Crop Seeds Law (*Shuyō Nōsanbutsu Shushihō*), which specified prefectural government-level regulation of staple seed certification and sales.[31] To be sure, divisions between staple and ornamental breeding were not always clear-cut in state-funded academic research. At institutions such as Kyoto Imperial University, agricultural scientists had investigated a wide variety of plant organisms. For example, geneticist Kihara Hitoshi had worked with plant organisms including wheat and watermelon in his well-known research into polyploidy.[32] This kind of public research continued, but the post-1947 legal framework of plant protection—along with formalized post-1952 divisions between staple crops and other plant varieties—would shape commercial plant-breeding interests through the 1980s (and to some extent beyond). The largest private Japanese seed companies such as Takii and Sakata continued to focus, for the most part, on fruits, garden vegetables, and flowers.[33]

The plant patent movement in Japan in the 1970s

By the late 1960s, hints of dissatisfaction with the plant varietal registration system outlined in the 1947 Agricultural Seeds and Seedlings Law (and further circumscribed by the 1952 Main Crop Seeds Law) had grown louder. Calls for a new formulation of plant ownership crystallized with the publication of a special feature in the March 1970 issue of the magazine *Nōkō to Engei* (a title its editors styled in English as *Agriculturist and Horticulturist*).[34] Editor Uemura Naoyuki convened a roundtable discussion including a plant breeder, an executive at the Sakata seed company, MAF horticultural official Haga Akiyo, and JPO patent examiner Ikenoya Kin'ichi. Aside from Haga's protestations that the existing law was, in its own right, 'a form of plant patent', the other participants discussed what they saw as

30 Fujihara (n 3); Jonathan Harwood, 'The Green Revolution as a Process of Global Circulation: Plants, People and Practices' (2018) 75 *Historia Agraria* 7, 11–12.

31 Nishimura Masami, '"Nōsan shubyōhō" to wa dō iu mono ka' (1970) 25(3) *Nōkō to engei* 104.

32 Iida (n 3).

33 For a broader survey see Hisano Shūji, 'Shubyō jigyō no kōzō to kinō ni kansuru ichi kōsatsu: yasai shubyō o chūshin ni shite' (1998) 54 *Nōkei ronsō* 21. The two companies Takii and Sakai, for example, together controlled 'nearly all' of the American market for broccoli and cauliflower seeds by the 1980s, as noted in a weekly tabloid article entitled 'Europe dominates wheat, America monopolizes corn: What will become of rice?': 'Komugi wa Yōroppa ga sei shi, tōmorokoshi wa Amerika ga dokusen, kome wa dō naru ka?: Nihon ga shushi sensō ni sankaku suru hi' (1984) 143 *Shūkan hōseki* 66, 69.

34 'Tokushū: Wagakuni ni mo hoshii "shokubutsu tokkyohō"' (1970) 25(3) *Nōkō to engei* 98.

a deeply flawed Agricultural Seeds and Seedlings Law.[35] Contributions from a half dozen other breeders concurred. Plant breeders contended that the many years and high costs required to develop new varieties deserved a longer period of protection. The existing system, they said, did little to restrict the cultivation and sale of registered plants. The special feature pressed the case for an alternative, conveniently encapsulated in its title: 'What our country also wants: a "plant patent law" '.[36]

The 'also' in the title was not trivial. Calls for a new approach to plant protection strengthened in Japan amid transformations in North America and Europe. In Western Europe, the Convention of the International Union for the Protection of New Varieties of Plants (UPOV) had gone into effect in 1968, nearly seven years after the union's formation. In the United States, the Department of Agriculture-administered Plant Variety Protection Act would extend protection, starting in December 1970, to sexually reproduced plant varieties, not just the asexual methods encompassed by the 1930 Plant Patent Act. In the early 1970s, then, the range of possibilities encompassed by the colloquial notion of a 'plant patent' was beginning to include a wider variety of protection systems, including some that existed outside patent bureaucracies and the legal form of the utility patent. Following the 1970 special issue of *Agriculturist and Horticulturist*, Ikenoya began a survey of foreign plant variety protection systems in an eighteen-part series in the same journal.[37] What followed was a flurry of additional publications, meetings, and lectures.[38]

In July 1971, a coalition of some sixty members formed the *Shokubutsu Tokkyohō Seitei Sokushin Kyōgikai*, a lobbying group known in English as the 'Japan Campaign for the Promotion on [sic] a Plant Patent Law' (JCPPPL).[39] The group was led by Shisa Makoto, a retired Nagoya University agricultural scientist with long-standing academic interests in floral biology. Shisa's most prominent recruit to the JCPPPL was his former schoolmate Sakomizu Hisatsune, a well-connected bureaucrat and politician who would serve as the group's chairman. Sakomizu had worked in the highest echelons of the Japanese empire's wartime bureaucracy, overseeing financial control policies (alongside formerly Manchukuo-posted officials) as a section chief in the Public Finance Bureau (*Rizaikyoku*) of the Finance Ministry.[40] In a briefly concurrent role as cabinet secretary under Prime Minister Suzuki Kantarō, Sakomizu had been involved in the drafting of the 14 August

35 'Zadankai: Kaisei semarareru "Nōsan shubyōhō": Shokubutsu tokkyo to no chigai wa doko ni' (1970) 25(3) *Nōkō to engei* 98.

36 'Tokushū' (n 34).

37 The first article appeared as Ikenoya Kin'ichi, 'Shokubutsu tokkyo e no michi (1): Shokubutsu tokkyohō wa naze hitsuyō ka' (1970) 25(4) *Nōkō to engei* 188. The final part was Ikenoya Kin'ichi, 'Shokubutsu tokkyo e no michi (18): Kaigai no hinshu hogo' (1971) 26(9) *Nōkō to engei* 114.

38 'Shokubutsu tokkyohō' seitei o: ikushu gakusha-ra ga shinpojiumu' *Mainichi Shinbun* (10 April 1971).

39 'Hana, kudamono ni mo tokkyoken o: kyō sokushinkyō sōritsu sōkai' *Mainichi Shinbun* (20 July 1971).

40 Mimura (n 20) 142.

1945 speech, famously broadcast by radio at noon the following day, during which Emperor Hirohito had announced Japan's unconditional surrender.[41] Along with other wartime imperial 'reform bureaucrat' officials like Kishi Nobusuke, Sakomizu returned to substantial leadership roles in post-war Japanese economic planning.[42] Moreover, Sakomizu was, along with several other JCPPPL participants, a member of the Japan Rose Society (*Nippon Bara Kai*), a body chaired in the early 1970s by retired University of Tokyo physicist Kaya Seiji, who had taken over the role upon the passing of his predecessor, the former prime minister Yoshida Shigeru.[43]

JCPPPL's membership came from several sources. Contributors to the 1970 special issue of *Agriculturist and Horticulturist*, including editor Uemura Naoyuki and the patent official Ikenoya Kin'ichi, took active roles in the organization. Prominent too were fruit and vegetable-focused horticulturists, such as the tomato breeder Kataoka Setsuo.[44] Shisa's connections also included academic and industry scientist–breeders, some of whom would participate in the group. Kihara Hitoshi, the then-retired Kyoto University professor who had been a central figure in the formation of genetics as a discipline in Japan, in large part through studies of wheat and other agricultural plants, joined the JCPPPL as an adviser.[45]

The 'Shisa Group' (as at least one MAF official would later refer to the JCPPPL) had at its core a vocal community of commercial flower breeders.[46] One of the JCPPPL's loudest voices was Suzuki Seizō, a breeder later known in Japan as 'Mister Rose'.[47] Shisa and Suzuki argued that Japanese horticulturists were developing an international reputation as purveyors of 'pirated' (*kaizokuban*) flowers that had been propagated in bulk using cuttings of varieties protected in the United States and Europe. Without a strong plant patent law, they argued, legal imports of new floral varieties from abroad would dry up.[48]

The JCPPPL's leaders were conscious of the prominent roles played by plant-breeder and seed-company lobbies in the creation of plant protection laws elsewhere, particularly in the United States. During the 1970s, the group enlisted figures in the American horticultural trade in a push for plant protections in Japan. Among them was Paul Ecke, the 'Poinsettia King' of California, who amplified the

[41] Tsuyoshi Hasegawa, *Racing the Enemy: Stalin, Truman, and the Surrender of Japan* (Harvard University Press 2009) 215–52.

[42] Mimura (n 20) 29–35; Andrew Levidis, 'Politics in a Fallen Empire: Kishi Nobusuke and the Making of the Conservative Hegemony in Japan' in Barak Kushner and Andrew Levidis (eds), *In the Ruins of the Japanese Empire: Imperial Violence, State Destruction, and the Reordering of Modern East Asia* (Hong Kong University Press 2020) 178.

[43] Saishō Hazuki, *Aoi bara* (Shōgakukan 2001) 402.

[44] Kataoka Setsuo, 'Shokubutsu tokkyohō seitei sokushin kyōgikai ni tsuite' (1972) 22(3) *Ikushugaku zasshi* 186.

[45] Shuppankai (n 24) 217.

[46] Matsunobu Yōhei, 'Nōgyō gijutsu to shokubutsu shinhinshu hogo seido (2)' (1980) 35(8) *Nōgyō gijutsu* 337, 339.

[47] For more on Suzuki see Saishō (n 43).

[48] Shuppankai (n 24) 123.

piracy narrative by condemning what he saw as the rampant illicit propagation of flowers in Japan.[49] The JCPPPL marshalled foreign critics such as Ecke to reinforce their claims that internationally legible mechanisms of plant protection were necessary. At the same time, Shisa stressed to Japanese-speaking audiences that, under different legal circumstances, accusations of piracy from figures like Ecke might have gone in the opposite direction. Stronger plant protection, said Shisa, offered a way for fruit—and ornamental-flower breeders to avoid repeating the vast and largely unremunerated transfers of germplasm that had moved to California and elsewhere in the late nineteenth—and early twentieth-century world.[50]

The JCPPPL featured members with close ties to (and employed positions in) the JPO, such as Ikenoya Kin'ichi, but many in the group considered the MAF as the agency that would continue to administer a reformed plant protection system. Between 1972 and 1975, JCPPPL members, including Shisa and Ikenoya, were part of a MAF-hosted study group on plant variety protection.[51] In January 1975, Sakomizu delivered a petition to the MAF that described the JCPPPL's proposal for a new plant protection law. Sakomizu stressed to MAF officials that the group's requests were based on 'five years' of research on 'advanced countries' laws and their application'. The petition gestured toward the 1968 ratification of the UPOV Convention in Western Europe and the 1970 passage of the Plant Variety Protection Act in the United States. With some exaggeration, the JCPPPL petition lauded the establishment elsewhere in the world of plant protections with 'rights identical to those for industrial patents and copyrighted works', but lamented that 'today Japan is completely isolated from global trends'. The petition went on to state that Japanese agriculture was hampered 'both internally and externally', unable to profit from the export of improved varieties while being hindered from plant importation. The JCPPPL called for the protection of all forms of plant cultivation, whether asexual propagation through cuttings or sexual reproduction involving seeds. In line with systems such as the American Plant Variety Protection Act, the group requested evaluation standards based not on utility but rather 'novelty, uniformity, and stability' over a period of protection that could be extended to up to fifteen years.[52]

[49] '"Hana no kaizokuban" busui desu: Beikoku no engeika, torishimari chinjō' *Asahi Shinbun* (7 November 1971); Shuppankai (n 24) 215–16; Matsunobu (n 46) 339.

[50] 'Shokubutsu tokkyohō seitei sokushin kyōgikai no rijichō Shisa Makoto' *Mainichi Shinbun* (30 October 1972).

[51] The group met six times between October 1972 and April 1975. See Shuppankai (n 24) 222.

[52] Shuppankai (n 24) 220.

The mid-1970s' rise (and apparent decline) of interagency frictions over Plant Patents

The JCPPPL's 1975 petition to the MAF arrived just before an abrupt shift in the JPO's relationship with plant protection. By the mid-1970s, the JPO was pursuing reforms to allow patents for not only processes but also products—a policy shift that would reshape drug-patenting practices in the Japanese pharmaceutical industry after 1976.[53] In November 1975, newspapers carried stories about a related change to JPO evaluation standards. Patent officials announced that plant varieties would be able to receive patent protection, like any other 'industrial' invention. They went so far as to suggest that geneticist Kihara Hitoshi's pre-1945 method for breeding seedless watermelons might have been eligible for global royalty payments rather than freely available for use by growers around the world.[54]

The JPO's declaration that living plants could be patented soon prompted reflection upon 'the persistent question [of] whether biological inventions resemble industrial artifacts and to what extent that resemblance matters'.[55] A key objection to the JPO's newfound push for plant patenting was that practices of breeding did not yield results repeatable enough to count as 'industrial' property claims. The issue had already come to the fore at the 1952 Congress of the International Association for the Protection of Intellectual Property (AIPPI) in Vienna. A report by the West German delegation to the Congress had noted that 'it seemed that a process is not capable of being industrially exploited and therefore patented if it cannot be reproduced'. The report suggested that the only viable option was either to specify the use of seeds, 'provided that the new variety breeds true', or else to make use of asexual, vegetative propagation methods of the sort covered under the 1930 American Plant Patent Act. As the West Germans noted: 'In practice, nobody in such cases has in mind the reproduction of the breeding process, but starting with the new plants obtained from the breeder the invention is utilised in practice by multiplying the said plants sexually (by seeds) or asexually (by cuttings, bulbs, root division, budding, etc)'. In other words, this interpretation held that the starting

[53] Maki Umemura, *The Japanese Pharmaceutical Industry: Its Evolution and Current Challenges* (Taylor & Francis 2011) 65–66; Julia Yongue, 'Origins of Innovation in the Japanese Pharmaceutical Industry: The Case of Yamanouchi Pharmaceutical Company' (2005) 22 *Japanese Research in Business History* 109; Timothy M Yang, *A Medicated Empire: The Pharmaceutical Industry and Modern Japan* (Cornell University Press 2021).

[54] 'Shokubutsu shinhinshu mo tokkyo ga toreru' *Asahi Shinbun* (15 November 1975). Given subsequent developments explored in this chapter, it is also worth flagging up that this statement overlooked post-1945 assertions in South Korea that the Japanese-born Korean scientist Woo Jang-Choon had first engineered the seedless watermelon. See John P DiMoia, 'Providing Reassurance and Affirmation: Masculinity, Militarization, and Refashioning a Male Role in South Korean Family Planning' in Angela Ki Che Leung and Izumi Nakayama (eds), *Gender, Health, and History in Modern East Asia* (Hong Kong University Press 2017) 255.

[55] Alain Pottage and Brad Sherman, 'Kinds, Clones, and Manufactures' in Mario Biagioli, Peter Jaszi, and Martha Woodmansee (eds), *Making and Unmaking Intellectual Property: Creative Production in Legal and Cultural Perspective* (University of Chicago Press 2011) 269.

baseline for industrial patent claims was evidence of a stable-featured variety, not the methods of selective breeding by which the variety had come into being in the first place. In Europe, several cases tested the extent to which breeding processes as such could be patented. In 1953, a Swiss tribunal denied a patent for a new rose variety by pointing out that unless the same flower could be created by someone else following the same procedure, the claims did not constitute a reproducible invention. A later case in West Germany, widely read in Japan and elsewhere, concerned a patent application for a new variety of red dove. The 1969 'Red Dove' decision rejected the patent claim, holding that a breeding process might be patentable only if someone else could reproduce the organism. Following the breeding methods described in a patent was not sufficient on its own. The German court argued that including information about the breeding method as such 'does not ensure a genetically identical repetition of such breeding method [or the obtaining of] ... the same genetic results'. The Red Dove decision indicated a theoretical opening for the patenting of breeding practices. In practice, however, the ruling set the bar of repeatability too high to clear. As a 1987 survey of intellectual property rights in biotechnology put it, 'for all practical purposes, the issuance of patents to plant varieties not covered by West Germany's varietal protection system ceased, with the [West German] Patent Office adopting the general position that varietal inventions, plant or animal, were presumptively irreproducible under the "Red Dove" standard'.[56]

Through the early 1970s, the JPO had likewise made no indication that claims involving the breeding of organisms could be patented. The 1967 edition of the JPO's in-house edited commentary on the Patent Law noted that, while there was debate about where in the text of the law it could be inferred, 'there is no dispute that patentable inventions must have repeatability (*hanpuku keizokusei*)'. As for plants, the JPO's interpretation stressed that 'since at the present moment it is difficult to repeatedly cultivate the same variety, they cannot receive patents'.[57] A practical guide to patenting later advised in 1972 that the repeatability issue would pose problems for a claim involving a new variety of rose. There, JPO examiner Nakamoto Hiroshi noted that exceptions lay in other areas: 'As for patents that target animals and plants, particularly among methods that use biological phenomena for productive purposes, pearl production methods, *shiitake* mushroom cultivation methods, and prawn (*kuruma ebi*) propagation methods have already been patented. However, these kinds of processes are not for the creation of new varieties as such, and in this respect the creation of a new rose variety is a different thing'. As Nakamoto put it, 'Because a new variety of rose or a process for its

[56] Stephen A Bent and others, *Intellectual Property Rights in Biotechnology Worldwide* (Macmillan 1987) 86–87, 221–23. The 'Red Dove' ('*Rote Taube*') ruling can be found at BGH, Beschl v 27.3.1969 X ZB 15/67. (An English-language translation of the 'Red Dove' ruling is in 1 IIC 136 (1970).)

[57] Tokkyochō (ed), *Shin kōgyō shoyūkenhō chikujō kaisetsu* (revised edn, Hatsumei Kyōkai 1967) 71.

cultivation lacks (or has a low level of) reproducibility (*saigensei*) or repeatability (*hanpuku keizokusei*) . . . it has no industrial utility'.[58] Even if pearl cultivation processes could be patented, plant patents were still out of bounds.

Why, then, did the JPO make such a dramatic about-face in 1975? One place to look is to the activities of plant patent lobbyists such as JCPPPL member Ikenoya Kin'ichi—who, one may recall, was himself a JPO patent examiner. Ikenoya chided the JPO's hesitance to accept plant patents due to concerns over reproducibility. To be sure, Ikenoya admitted that it would be no easy task to judge whether two separate plant samples were of the same variety. He agreed with other observers that at least three elements would be necessary in order to implement a system of plant patents: (i) narrowing the scope of relevant features used in defining a 'new' variety; (ii) keeping seeds of a new variety in controlled storage and maintaining its vegetative propagation (through cuttings or other methods); and (iii) judging suspect plants through comparison with (or breeding with) known samples. Ikenoya suggested, however, that all three prerequisites were already feasible. Gesturing toward government patent examiner Nakamoto Hiroshi's earlier dismissal of a hypothetical rose patent, Ikenoya wrote that 'the Patent Office's long-standing position of denying the patentability of plants because, as living organisms, they or their methods of production lack (or have a low level of) reproducibility or repeatability . . . should be reconsidered, and in that sense, it could be seen that there is no longer any reason for [patent] denial'.[59]

Some Japanese politicians also began to support the JPO's approach to plant patenting. A spark came from JCPPPL member Suzuki Seizō when he hosted several Diet members at the Keisei Rose Garden, the urban railway conglomerate-owned nursery park where he was head of research. The politicians, intrigued by the idea of plant patents, invited JCPPPL members to speak in Tokyo and began investigations of their own. One of the politicians who had visited Suzuki, Tanaka Takeo, pressed the head of the JPO Saitō Hideo to explain the agency's stance toward plant patenting during a public hearing in February 1975.[60] If nothing explicitly prevented plant patents under the law, Tanaka wondered, why couldn't the JPO actively publicize their patentability and put out a call for applications? Saitō would later point to Tanaka's questioning at the February hearing as a turning point in the JPO's approach to plant patents.[61] Examiners suggested that replicability was not an insurmountable obstacle to the patenting of claims that involved the manipulation of 'laws of nature' through plant breeding. Applicants could use multiple routes to establish replicability, including explanations based on genetic

[58] Yoshifuji Kōsaku and Mon'ya Nobuo (eds), *Tokkyo ishō shōhyō no jitsumu sōdan* (Yūhikaku 1972) 2.

[59] Quoted in Harima Yoshitsugu, 'Tokkyohō zakkichō: Dai 2-shō shokubutsu tokkyohō to gijutsuteki shisō' (1973) 26(4) *Patento* 29, 34.

[60] Ikenoya Kin'ichi and others, *Shokubutsu tokkyo to shubyōhō* (Kōdansha 1985) 40.

[61] Kokkai kaigiroku, Nōrin suisan iinkai, 4-gō (11 December 1975).

principles or certified evidence of practical results.[62] As JPO official Takemoto Shōji explained, 'if there are no other reasons for denial, it will become a patent'.[63]

The JPO's 1975 announcement prompted MAF officials to speed up the drafting of a competing plant variety protection system. To MAF officials, the JPO's plant variety evaluation standards were an unwelcome bid to play a larger role in agricultural regulation. Some in the MAF floated the fear that one day the JPO might issue patents for new varieties of rice and other staple grain crops that had been excluded under the 1947 Agricultural Seeds and Seedlings Law. In turn, MAF officials wrote draft legislation that they framed as a revision of the earlier law.[64] The Japanese Diet passed the MAF draft in 1978, which went into effect under the shortened title of the Seeds and Seedlings Law (*Shubyōhō*).

The 1978 Seeds and Seedlings Law installed a revised system of plant variety registration that, as with the 1947 law, remained within the bureaucratic orbit of the MAF, not the JPO. Even so, the new law had initial cross-agency support. At the start of the 1980s, some officials in the MAF and the JPO viewed the Seeds and Seedlings Law as an endpoint of the interagency tensions that had defined the previous decade.[65] Plant patent proponents in the JCPPPL, however, were less satisfied. The JCPPPL and the MAF's once-warm relationship, which had included MAF-funded research projects and joint study sessions, had already begun to cool during the second half of the 1970s.[66] Alternative allies were not forthcoming. With the Seeds and Seedlings Law, some JCPPPL members also sensed that the JPO was beginning to lose interest in the prospect of plant patents, even before a single one had ever been affirmed.[67]

The lack of a clear historical narrative about plant variety protection in Japan reflects divergent bureaucratic and breeder interests, particularly from the 1970s onwards. As seen above, debate unfolded amid widespread criticism of the MAF's 1947 Agricultural Seeds and Seedlings Law and the JPO's 1975 declaration that—in contrast to contemporaneous trends in Europe and a decade before the United States Patent and Trademark Office's 1985 *Ex parte Hibberd* ruling that any type of plant could, in theory, receive a patent[68]—it welcomed the prospect of plant variety

62 Murabayashi Ryūichi and others, *Shokubutsu shinhinshu hogo no jitsumu: kenri no shutoku to shingai* (Keizai Sangyō Chōsakai 2004) 355.

63 Takemoto Shōji, 'Sangyōbetsu shinsa kijun "shokubutsu shinhinshu" ni tsuite' (1976) 73(2) *Hatsumei* 10, 12.

64 Former MAF official Matsunobu Yōhei has reflected on his role in the drafting of the law in several publications. See Matsunobu Yōhei, 'Shubyōhō no tanjō monogatari' *Gekkan gendai nōgyō* (September 2018) http://www.ruralnet.or.jp/gn/201809/syubyouhou.htm (accessed 15 March 2020).

65 See 'Shokubutsu shinhinshu hogohō o megutte: Shu to shite shubyōhō ni tsuite (jō)' (1979) 683 *Jurisuto* 15.

66 For example, after 1976 the JCPPPL declined to send representatives to attend some of the later meetings hosted by the MAF. Shuppankai (n 24) 221; Kushibuchi Kin'ya, 'Shokubutsu no ikushuken o megutte: shinpojiumu ni shusseki shite' (1977) 32(2) *Nōgyō gijutsu* 64.

67 Shuppankai (n 24) 223.

68 Glenn E Bugos and Daniel J Kevles, 'Plants as Intellectual Property: American Practice, Law, and Policy in World Context' (1992) 7 *Osiris* 74, 75.

utility patents. One response to the JPO's move, the MAF's revised 1978 Seeds and Seedlings Law, marked what chroniclers have described as a new era in plant variety protection. Nevertheless, the JPO's 1975 plant patent evaluation standards did not disappear with the passage of the MAF's revised law and Japan's subsequent accession to the UPOV Convention in 1982. Nor would the JPO and the MAF ever come to a formal jurisdictional agreement about plant variety protection during the remainder of the twentieth century. On the contrary, MAF-JPO controversies during the 1970s left lasting and mutually unresolved institutional mandates to authorize and govern plant-related claims. Ongoing ambiguity about the patentability of plants, and for that matter other living organisms, left openings for dispute.

Plant Patents on Trial: The Case of the Repeatable Peach

The situation in the late 1970s dissatisfied many in the JCPPPL. Some members were happy with the provisions of the 1978 Seeds and Seedlings Law for longer protection periods than the previous 1947 legislation. But concerns remained that the new MAF-centred system had not been designed with breeder interests in mind. Even so, Japan's plant patent lobby lost steam after the passage of the 1978 law. In 1981, the JCPPPL dissolved after nearly a decade in existence. One of the most disappointed ex-members was a then-75-year-old fruit breeder named Kurakata Eizō.

Kurakata Eizō, colonial Korea, and the 'Ban Kitou' peach

Kurakata had been born to a relatively well-off, landowning Tokyo family in 1906. After his private schooling, he sought to try his hand at growing fruit overseas. He first decided on Argentina, but later abandoned the plan. Around 1933, he joined a tide of colonists from the Japanese archipelago who settled in the Korean peninsula, then part of the Japanese empire.[69] Practices of garden horticulture were a defining feature of early twentieth-century Japanese settler migration, both inside and outside the formal Japanese colonial empire.[70] Fruit and vegetable growing was an important livelihood for Japanese migrants to the Americas, especially

[69] For a broader view of Korea-bound migrants from Japan see Jun Uchida, *Brokers of Empire: Japanese Settler Colonialism in Korea, 1876–1945* (Harvard University Asia Center 2014). On agriculture in the Korean peninsula see Holly Stephens, 'Agriculture and Development in an Age of Empire: Institutions, Associations, and Market Networks in Korea, 1876–1945' PhD Thesis (University of Pennsylvania 2017). On practices and politics of patenting in colonial Korea see Lee (n 5).

[70] Research into the agricultural and horticultural dimensions of Japanese settler colonialism is a burgeoning field. See Eiichiro Azuma, *In Search of Our Frontier: Japanese America and Settler Colonialism in the Construction of Japan's Borderless Empire* (University of California Press 2019); Sidney Xu Lu, *The Making of Japanese Settler Colonialism: Malthusianism and Trans-Pacific Migration, 1868–1961* (Cambridge University Press 2019); Fedman (n 3); Michael Alan Thornton, 'Settling Sapporo: City and State in the Global Nineteenth Century'. PhD Thesis. (Harvard University 2018).

along the Pacific coast of the United States.[71] Kurakata, however, came of age in the years after the 1924 United States Immigration Act had made immigration all but impossible from Japan.[72] He claimed to have chosen to settle in Ulsan County, to the north of the colonial port city of Pusan, after consulting a Japanese library for areas of the Korean peninsula with climates 'similar to that of California'.[73] The means by which he acquired land is unclear, but Kurakata's time in Korea loomed large in his recollections as a time when he undertook breeding experiments for the cultivation of apples, persimmons, and peaches. Kurakata would later say that he had been repatriated from Korea to Tokyo in 1945 with little more than a few hundred-odd seeds, some of which he used to grow a white peach variety that he called his 'early-ripening white peach' (*wase hakutō*).[74]

Kurakata came into public view in Japan as a vocal critic of the 1947 Agricultural Seeds and Seedlings Law. Kurakata recounted difficulties in protecting his claims to the early-ripening white peach, which he had registered under the law in 1951 but had noticed being sold by other breeders without his permission. From his perspective, the MAF was uninterested in enforcing the law within Japan.[75] By the early 1960s, he was calling for more substantial plant protections: 'Since copyright is protected for 30 years after death, this is far too short. Breeders' rights should really be protected for a longer period. That would be a policy that helps the efforts of breeders to improve varieties'.[76]

Kurakata's early-ripening white peach headlined the JCPPPL's lobbying activities in the early 1970s. JCPPPL leader Shisa Makoto brought up the Kurakata peach as an example of the limitations of the Agricultural Seeds and Seedlings Law. Shisa noted that Kurakata had received no compensation for the earlier spread of

[71] On racialized responses to movements of Japanese people and agricultural products see Philip Pauly, 'The Beauty and Menace of the Japanese Cherry Trees: Conflicting Visions of American Ecological Independence' (1996) 87(1) *Isis* 51; Jeannie N Shinozuka, 'Deadly Perils: Japanese Beetles and the Pestilential Immigrant, 1920s–1930s' (2013) 65(4) *American Quarterly* 831; Cecilia M Tsu, *Garden of the World: Asian Immigrants and the Making of Agriculture in California's Santa Clara Valley* (Oxford University Press 2013).

[72] Flows of people, techniques, and seeds moved in multiple directions. See Martin Dusinberre and Mariko Iijima, 'Transplantation: Sugar and Imperial Practice in Japan's Pacific' (2019) 27(3) *Historische Anthropologie* 325. Eiichiro Azuma has shown that Japanese 'transmigrants' arriving in Manchukuo from the United States after the 1924 United States Immigration Act, for example, took with them plans and tools for the implementation of mechanized, American-inspired modes of cultivation; see Azuma (n 70) 153–82.

[73] Aoki Keiichirō, *Nōgyō fūdo jinbutsu shi: Tōkyō* (Dōhōsha 1977) 64; 'Wase hakutō no ikusei: Tōkyō-to Kurakata Eizō shi' in Shūkan Jiji Henshūbu (ed), *Sono hito sono jigyō* 5 (Jiji Tsūshinsha 1963) 53. Holly Stephens has reconstructed the late nineteenth- and early twentieth-century activities of Sim Wŏn'gwŏn, an Ulsan-based Korean rice broker, sometime economic theorist, and cultivator of grains, fruits, and other crops. See Stephens (n 69) 84–130. On Pusan see Hannah Jane Shepherd, 'Cities into Empire: Fukuoka, Pusan, and Japan's Imperial Urbanization, 1876–1953' PhD Thesis (Harvard University 2018).

[74] 'Wase hakutō no ikusei' (n 73) 54.

[75] Kurakata would eventually hire a lawyer to pressure several seed dealers to pay him a small amount in damages. Kokkai kaigiroku, Nōrin suisan iinkai 24-go (24 May 1978).

[76] 'Wase hakutō no ikusei' (n 73) 58.

his varietal in Argentina, where 'most of the peaches are Kurakata early-ripening'. Shisa contended that 'if both countries had plant patent laws, he would have become a very rich man'.[77]

In 1978, with the new Seeds and Seedlings Law about to come into force, Kurakata spoke in front of an Agriculture, Forestry, and Fisheries Diet committee meeting in Tokyo. Kurakata criticized the MAF's continued administration of plant variety protection under the Seeds and Seedlings Law, which he saw as a continuation of the unsettled place of plant breeders' rights under the earlier 1947 Agricultural Seeds and Seedlings Law. He testified that 'breeders' rights are not expressed whatsoever in the MAF's latest plant protection law'.[78]

A key part of Kurakata's 1978 testimony was a narrative of his time as a settler in 1930s' colonial Korea. By the late 1970s, Kurakata credited his Korean interlude not just with the then-well-known Kurakata early-ripening white peach, but also for a newer variety of yellow peach. He claimed to have first obtained the latter in 1977, after '44 years' of breeding work that he timed from his 1930s' sojourn in colonial Korea.[79] He had cross-bred two American varieties of canning peach, the Tuscan and the Elberta, to yield the yellow peach hybrid 'Tusberta'. With the Tusberta he crossed a peach variety that he would refer to in English-language applications as 'Ban Kitou' (a 'late-ripening peach' rendered in his Japanese-language documents with the somewhat idiosyncratic gloss of *ban kitō* for 晩生黄桃). The Ban Kitou was a material legacy of Kurakata's time in the Korean peninsula, where he claimed to have acquired samples of the otherwise undocumented peach. Ban Kitou germplasm was presumably among the seeds he brought back to Tokyo in 1945. At least one specimen of the Tusberta and the Ban Kitou's progeny had yielded yellow fruits with a 'distinctive good flavor'.[80]

Unlike his previous experiences with the early-ripening white peach variety, Kurakata used his 'distinctive' yellow peach as a test organism for alternatives to the MAF-centred plant protection system. Kurakata pursued two avenues for laying claim to the yellow peach. The first was through the JPO, where Kurakata submitted a utility patent application in October 1977 for a 'Kurakata yellow peach', through the representation of fellow JCPPPL member Ikenoya Kin'ichi.[81]

77 Shisa Makoto, 'Seitei nozomareru 'shokubutsu tokkyo' (1973) 45(5) *Nōgyō fumin* 123.

78 Kokkai kaigiroku, Nōrin suisan iinkai 24-go (24 May 1978).

79 'Kairyō 44 nen no ōtō' *Yomiuri Shinbun* (24 December 1985).

80 'Yellow Peach Tree' United States Plant Patent No 4,423 (5 June 1979). On the Elberta peach variety see William Thomas Okie, *The Georgia Peach: Culture, Agriculture, and Environment in the American South* (Cambridge University Press 2016).

81 Japan Patent Application 52–127193 (24 October 1977), opened for public examination on 15 May 1979 under Kōkai tokkyo kōhō 54–60132.

Six months later, he filed a second application in the United States under the 1930 Plant Patent Act, this time for a 'Kurakata yellow peach tree'. Kurakata received approval for an American plant patent in June 1979.[82] The application with the JPO, on the other hand, was only getting started.

Figure 10.1 'Yellow Peach Tree', US Plant Patent No 4,423 (5 June 1979).
Courtesy of USPTO.

[82] 'Yellow Peach Tree', United States Plant Patent No 4,423 (5 June 1979); 'Yellow Peach Tree', file wrapper, PP04423, 20 April 1978 (filing date), 5 June 1979 (issue date), USPTO Archives.

The 1980s' spectre of 'seed wars'

The Kurakata yellow peach patent applications moved through the American and Japanese legal systems amid changes in the geopolitical role of patents as vehicles for making claims on living creatures.

Told from the perspective of the United States, the global history of living organism protections unfolds both in terms of a broadening scope of claims, but also in terms of shifts in the administrative centres of their governance.[83] The spotlight moves from the United States Patent Office-administered 1930 Plant Patent Act to the Department of Agriculture's 1970 Plant Variety Protection Act, and then to a broadening of the JPO's purview following the extension of patent rights to microorganisms, plants, and animals. During the 1980s, a series of US legal decisions stretched patent protection over creatures great and small. In the 1980 *Diamond v Chakrabarty* case, the United States Supreme Court held that whether or not the genetically engineered bacterium in question was alive was irrelevant to the question of its patentability. Supreme Court justices upheld the United States Patent and Trademark Office's acceptance of the bacteria patent application by noting that:

> While laws of nature, physical phenomena, and abstract ideas are not patentable, respondent's claim is not to a hitherto unknown natural phenomenon, but to a nonnaturally occurring manufacture or composition of matter—a product of human ingenuity having a distinctive name, character [and] use'.[84]

Living or not, the bacteria was ruled to have been non-naturally occurring.

The *Diamond v Chakrabarty* judgment dovetailed with the Japanese government's 1982 accession to the international UPOV Convention on plant variety protections to provoke new fears about the effects of monopoly rights on global food supply chains. As in other parts of the 1980s' world, some in Japan used the militarized metaphor of 'seed wars' to describe ambiguously interstate and transnational battles for control of plant germplasm and their effects on farmers who relied upon inexpensive seeds and customary practices of saving seeds for the next planting. In a Japanese context, 'seed war' meant, more than anything, conflict over rice. In 1982, an American company's scuttled attempt to sell hybrid rice seeds in Japan had surprised officials in the Ministry of Agriculture, Forestry, and Fisheries (hereafter MAFF; the fisheries element was incorporated into the MAF's title after 1978). Media reports compared

[83] Foundational contributions include Bugos and Kevles (n 68); and Daniel J Kevles, 'Of Mice & Money: The Story of the World's First Animal Patent' (2002) 131(2) *Daedalus* 78.

[84] *Diamond v Chakrabarty* 447 US 303, 100 S Ct 2204, 65 L Ed. 2d 144 (1980); Daniel J Kevles, 'Ananda Chakrabarty Wins a Patent: Biotechnology, Law, and Society, 1972–1980' (1994) 25(1) *Historical Studies in the Physical and Biological Sciences* 111. On the subsequent *Moore v Regents of the University of California* case see Doogab Yi, 'Who Owns What? Private Ownership and the Public Interest in Recombinant DNA Technology in the 1970s' (2011) 102 *Isis* 446.

the seed firm's overtures to the 1853 Edo Bay 'arrival of the black ships' (*kurofune tōrai*) under American Commodore Matthew Perry that had led Tokugawa officials to sign unequal trade treaties with the United States and other Western powers.[85]

The return of interagency frictions over plant patents

Tensions over the jurisdiction of biotechnology rights flared again in the 1980s between the MAFF and the JPO. The first major dispute concerned the Kyoto-based pharmaceutical company Nippon Shinyaku's patent applications for polyploid varieties of mugwort (*yomogi*) plants that had been bred in order to yield increased quantities of santonin, a chemical used in treatments against parasitic worms.[86] The 1977 mugwort applications were remnants of the period just before the institution of MAFF-administered plant variety protections under the Seeds and Seedlings Law in 1978. When the JPO made the applications public in 1983, the Japan Seeds and Seedlings Association (*Nihon Shubyō Kyōkai*) launched a formal objection, but the dispute ended without a protracted legal battle.[87]

In 1985, the JPO issued Japan's first plant variety utility patent for Nippon Shinyaku's pentaploid mugwort. At the same time, however, MAFF officials wrote off the mugwort patent as a one-off vestige of the pre-1978 situation. They described the resolution of the mugwort case as a barrier to future attempts by foreign companies to gain exclusive control of staple crop varieties through utility patents. The acceptance of the mugwort patents, they said, had paved the way for the implementation of a 'missile intercept' system that would funnel plant variety protection applications through the MAFF and the 1978 Seeds and Seedlings Law, rather than via the JPO and the Patent Act.[88]

After Nippon Shinyaku's polyploid mugwort, the route to additional plant variety utility patents thus appeared to be blocked. In other words, it was not simply the case in the mid-1980s that 'Japan has followed the American lead and granted a patent on a plant', as Jack Kloppenburg described the mugwort case in his pioneering study of plant biotechnology.[89] To be sure, the Japanese government's

[85] 'Shushi sensō, Nihon e no shōgeki (1): kurofune tōrai 'shudan' no kiki: Ō-Bei, chakuchaku to shijō seiha' *Nihon Keizai Shinbun* (16 July 1984).

[86] For more on the company's long-running, global mugwort bioprospecting and santonin extraction activities, including founder Ichinose Hisomu's relationship with Kyoto University geneticist Kihara Hitoshi see Suzuka Osamu, 'Kyoto to santonin kokusanka: Ichinose Hisomu o kaiko shite' (1987) 22(1) *Yakushigaku zasshi* 7.

[87] 'Baio tokkyo keisō (5): shokubutsu baio no kenri hogo (shin tekunoroji no ikkō)' *Nikkei Sangyō Shinbun* (13 November 1985).

[88] 'Shokubutsu tokkyoken, shubyōhō ni ipponka, Tsūsan Nōsui ga gōi' *Nihon Keizai Shinbun* (29 June 1985).

[89] Jack Kloppenburg, *First the Seed: The Political Economy of Plant Biotechnology, 1492–2000* (Cambridge University Press 1988) 273.

food policy in the 1980s showed other signs of a more permissive approach to agribusiness, particularly with the 1986 carving out of an exception to the 1952 Main Crop Seeds Law that made it easier for companies to sell the seeds of rice and other staples to farmers.[90] Yet, far from an emerging American-style trend, the mugwort case indicated to a wide swath of observers, in Japan at least, that no patents for a plant variety would ever again be accepted by the JPO.

Interagency tensions came to a head in 1988, when the JPO approved Kurakata Eizō's revised yellow peach patent, eleven years after Kurakata had filed his initial application with his patent lawyer Ikenoya Kin'ichi. By that time, Kurakata's claims had undergone a transformation. Crucially, the patent's wording had changed by 1984 from a claim over a plant organism, the 'Kurakata yellow peach' itself, into a claim over two cultivation processes, the 'breeding' (*ikushu*) and subsequent 'propagation' (*zōshoku*) of a yellow peach plant.[91] Elsewhere, Jack Kloppenburg has noted that judicial acceptance of the possibility of patent claims on whole organisms was not the only flashpoint of US debate about biopatenting in the 1980s. Process patents involving living creatures also inspired new anxieties about seed monopolies.[92] So too in Japan. It is possible to see in Kurakata's JPO claims elements akin to an asexually propagated US-style plant patent (for which, as the reader will recall, Kurakata had directly applied in the United States just after depositing the Japanese patent application), *and* elements of a plant variety protection claim over an organism obtained through cross-breeding. In Japan, the Kurakata process patent seemed to open a path toward a set of claims that could cover acts of cross-breeding altogether.

The registration of the Kurakata patent concerned other breeders and farmers in Japan precisely because it implied a wider scope of plant protection than anything available under Japan's 1978 Seeds and Seedlings Law, or, for that matter, under US law. Echoing responses in the earlier polyploid mugwort patent case, two plant breeder groups, the Japan Horticultural Nokyo Federation (*Nihon Engei Nōgyō Kyōdō Kumiai Rengōkai*) and the Japan Fruit Tree Seeds and Seedlings Association (*Nihon Kaju Shubyō Kyōkai*), lodged complaints with the JPO. Both contended that the Kurakata patent encompassed traditional cross-breeding methods. Their leaders sent out calls for support from breeders elsewhere in Japan.[93] The groups made it clear that the patent case was about more than just a peach. Rather, they claimed, the dispute held in the balance 'not only the continued existence of the Seeds and Seedlings Law (the plant variety protection system), but also agriculture writ large'.[94]

[90] Hisano Shūji, 'Shuyō nōsakubutsu shushi seidoka no kome shushi shijō to aguribijinesu no jigyō tenkai' (1999) 55 *Hokkaido Daigaku Nōkei Ronsō* 73.

[91] 'Momo no shinhinshu ōtō no ikushu zōshokuhō' Tokkyo kōhō Shō-59–34330 (published 22 August 1984) https://www.j-platpat.inpit.go.jp (accessed 10 September 2020).

[92] Kloppenburg (n 89) 267.

[93] 'Tokkyo mukō no soshō ni goshien o' (1992) 46 *Kaju Shubyō* 19.

[94] ibid 21.

The peach patent goes to court

Dispute over Kurakata's yellow peach patent took place simultaneously as a contest among plant breeders and as an interagency tussle. Both plant breeder groups countering Kurakata had close ties with the MAFF. Kurakata, despite his previous denials of anti-MAFF leanings, had continued to push for JPO approval of the peach application. Media reports framed the case as a bureaucratic 'proxy battle'.[95]

All the while, Kurakata and his peach patent continued to appear in arguments about patented industrial property as an alternative mode of plant variety protection in Japan. In 1991, Kurakata's lawyers Ikenoya Kin'ichi and Katō Eiichi argued that the 1978 Seeds and Seedlings Law did nothing to link the status of plant breeder claims to intellectual property rights. The word 'rights' (*kenri*), they noted, had not shown up anywhere in the revised law. Patent rights, by contrast, provided avenues for restricting the breeding and sale of peaches (or other fruits, vegetables, and flowers) beyond anything envisioned in the Seeds and Seedlings Law.[96]

Opposition to the Kurakata yellow peach patent rested on several different lines of reasoning. One was that Kurakata had rewritten his Japanese patent application, with the advice of a 'former patent examiner' (presumably Ikenoya) to make claims on a breeding process rather than the peach or peach tree itself. Critics saw this as a way to evade the limitations of the Seeds and Seedlings Law altogether.[97] Although restructured as a patent covering cultivation processes of breeding and propagation, some complained that the Kurakata patent would function in practice as a plant variety claim. Critics also argued that the patent violated the dual protection clause of the 1978 UPOV Convention, arguing that separate plant patents were not allowed where plant variety protections, such as those afforded under the Seeds and Seedlings Law, were already available.[98] MAFF officials would continue to cite the dual protection ban through the late 1990s, when Japan acceded to the revised 1991 UPOV Convention, which eliminated the dual protection prohibition altogether. The Kurakata yellow peach patent application also revived questions about whether plant-related claims could be treated as industrial, novel, and repeatable inventions. One agricultural scientist opposing Kurakata noted that there was a vanishingly low likelihood—a probability expressible only with

[95] Madarame Shun'ichirō, '"Kajitsu shinhinshu" gijutsu meguru Nōsuishō Tokkyochō no tokkyo funsō' (1992) 36(8) *Zaikai tenbō* 120.

[96] Katō Eiichi and Ikenoya Kin'ichi, "Shokubutsu shinhinshu no shinsa kijun no kaitei ni yosete," *Patento* 44 no. 8 (August 1991) 52–60

[97] Madarame, 'Kajitsu shinhinshu' (n 95) 121

[98] Margaret Llewelyn and Mike Adcock argue that the dual protection provision has in the past been misinterpreted as an either/or choice, when in fact the provision was intended to allow for the simultaneous operation of multiple legal systems. See Margaret Llewelyn and Mike Adcock, *European Plant Intellectual Property* (Hart Publishing 2006) 25–26

'astronomical' figures—of repeatedly obtaining the variety of yellow peach that Kurakata had claimed to invent through traditional cross-breeding methods.[99]

Despite these objections, Japan's High Court ruled in favour of Kurakata's patent in 2000. The ruling was the first directly to engage with the legacies of the JPO's 1975 attempt to expand the boundaries of patentable invention to include plant varieties. As such, the case attracted wide interest in legal circles.[100] Takabe Makiko, who would later serve as chief judge in Japan's Intellectual Property High Court, noted after the case that 'this is the first ruling on the replicability of plant patents by the *Daishin'in*, so its meaning is significant'. She added that 'in the future, this will extend a large influence over issues including the legal protection of new biotechnologies'.[101]

Even so, the ruling's implications for cultivation-related patents were ambiguous. At issue was the revised wording of the Kurakata patent application, which after 1984 included claims over both the cross-breeding of a yellow peach variety *and* its ensuing asexual propagation. Had the crosses leading to Kurakata's claimed 1977 observance of the yellow peach progeny described in his application constituted 'the highly advanced creation of technical ideas utilizing the laws of nature', as defined under the 1959 Japanese Patent Act? Could the peach plant-breeding process itself be treated as a 'repeatable' invention, as had been debated in different parts of the mid—to late-twentieth-century world? Did the multiplication of plants obtained through cuttings or other forms of asexual propagation count as an invention in its own right?

Judges in Japan parsed the relative contributions of the 'breeding' and 'propagation' portions of Kurakata's inventive claims. An oft-quoted passage in the peach ruling stated that 'If a new variety is bred, after that it can be reproduced through traditionally used propagation methods. If the breeding of a new variety is possible, even if the probability is low, one can offer this up as the technical effect that is the goal of the invention'.[102] In other words, however unlikely the chances of recreating the same peach tree, the fact that it had once existed was sufficient to assume that it could be reproduced in the future.

But in the case at hand, material barriers to the reproduction of the Kurakata yellow peach remained. Quite simply, this was because the Ban Kitou—the parent peach tree that Kurakata had brought back to post-war Japan from his time in

[99] Iwamasa Masao, '"Momo no shinhinshu ōtō no ikushu zōshokuhō" no tokkyo ni omou' (1992) 67[8] *Nōgyō oyobi engei* 867

[100] Itakura Shūichi, 'Hanrei shōkai: Shokubutsu shinhinshu Kurakata ōtō ikushu zōshoku hōhō jiken: Saikō saiban hanketsu ni itaru made' (2000) no. 30 *Tokkyo kenkyū* 34 (hereafter Itakura, 'Hanrei shōkai')

[101] Takabe Makiko, '"Shokubutsu no shinhinshu o ikushu shi zōshoku suru hōhō" ni kakawaru hatsumei no ikushu katei ni okeru hanpuku kanōsei' (2001) no. 1195 *Jurisuto* 111. Japan's Intellectual Property High Court opened in 2005, in the wake of the 2002 Intellectual Property Basic Act.

[102] Quoted in Itakura, 'Hanrei shōkai' (n 100) 35–36.

colonial Korea—inexplicably went missing in 1995.[103] Critics of plant utility patents in Japan had already pointed out that the JPO's sole reliance on paper examinations was insufficient to the task of growing, evaluating, and comparing plants in the ground.[104] Starting in 1980, the JPO had introduced procedures for depositing micro-organism samples as part of the process for obtaining utility patents in Japan.[105] But in the realm of plant-related patents, no seed or seedling storage protocols were in place. The Kurakata patent application—a process patent application, no less—had faced no requirement for the submission of 'Kurakata yellow peach' germplasm to the JPO. The physical unavailability of the Ban Kitou for future breeding experiments meant that the 'low probability' of obtaining a Kurakata yellow peach via cross-breeding would remain a hypothetical approximation.

Although groups opposed to the Kurakata yellow peach patent lost the case, their outcry was muted. Legal affirmation of the Kurakata patent was a blow to those who had opposed it for over a decade, but compared with the situation in the late 1980s and early 1990s, agricultural observers in Japan had begun to see the case less as a harbinger of future monopoly strategies than as a curious outlier.[106] Kurakata Eizō himself passed away in 1996, four years before the *Daishin'in* High Court's ruling. Today, the Kurakata yellow peach cannot be found in seed catalogues. Without the Ban Kitou parent plant, it probably never will be.

Nor did the 2000 ruling on Kurakata's yellow peach patent herald the start of widespread plant variety patenting through the JPO. Efforts at plant protection have, if anything, moved closer to the orbit of the MAFF. Contributing to lukewarm interest in plant patenting has been the strengthening of plant variety protections outside the realm of patent law. This was already apparent by 1998, when Japan adhered to the 1991 version of the UPOV Convention following a substantial revision of the 1978 Seeds and Seedlings Law.[107]

Patent protection in Japan remains an option in theory, but new plant varieties are in practice registered under the Seeds and Seedlings Law. Along the way, further tweaks to the Seeds and Seedlings Law have come with growing lists of plant varieties for which farmers are not allowed to reserve seeds to use in the next season's planting. More recently, the 2017 scrapping of the 1952 Main Crop Seeds Law and 2020 revision to the Seeds and Seedlings Law have led to renewed concerns over the possibility for a wider scope of monopoly ownership claims on crop

[103] ibid 36.
[104] Matsunobu (n 46) 340.
[105] This began with Japan's 1980 ratification of the 1977 Budapest Treaty on the International Recognition of the Deposit of Micro-organisms for the Purposes of Patent Procedure. See Itō Junji, 'Kōgyō gijutsuin biseibutsu kōgyō gijutsu kenkyūjo ni okeru tokkyo biseibutsu kitaku gyōmu no keii to genjō' (1982) 40(2) *Hakkō to kōgyō* 141.
[106] 'Ikushu hōhō wa "hatsumei"' *Nihon Nōgyō Shinbun* (1 March 2000).
[107] Kobayashi (n 1).

plants (including for rice and other grains), particularly when paired with the expanding number of plant varieties for which seed saving has been prohibited.[108]

Conclusion

When framed in broadened terms of 'intellectual' property, the idea that living organisms are subject to monopoly ownership claims can sidestep the questions of human agency and authorship embedded in 'industrial' conceptions of invention. Yet while many governments (along with inter-state and transnational groupings) have come to treat non-patent plant variety protections as forms of intellectual property, there remain divergences over the extent to which claims over plants (and other living organisms) fit alongside ideas of industrial invention and legal mechanisms such as utility patents. At present, for example, although plant varieties are ineligible for patenting under EU law, no such restriction currently exists in Japan.[109] Thus, even with the current lack of Japanese plant patent applications, the hypothetical implications of the Kurakata peach patent case remain a source of intermittent legal speculation.[110]

The Kurakata peach patent ruling also brought attention to an earlier dispute: the Mikimoto pearl cultivation patent trials. Some tried to link the two episodes of patent controversy by considering them together as a referendum on the idea of repeatability as a prerequisite for inventive claims. Had not the pearl patent case also centred on a cultivation process that was less than 100 per cent reliable when attempted on living shellfish? Others, along with some who had been involved in plant patent debates since the early 1970s, pushed against this interpretation.[111] After all, while the pearl patent trials resulted in judicial interpretations of inventions in terms of manipulations that made use of the 'laws of nature', repeatability as such had not factored into early twentieth-century rulings. In fact, the

[108] For reflections on the end of the 1952 Main Crop Seeds Law see the collection of essays in Nōsan Gyoson Bunka Kyōkai (ed), *Shushihō haishi de dō naru? Shushi to hinshu no rekishi to mirai* (Nōsan Gyoson Bunka Kyōkai 2017).

[109] Kawada Atsushi, '"Shokubutsu no hinshu" mata wa "honshitsuteki ni seibutsugakuteki na shokubutsu no ikusei no hōhō" no hogo: Shubyōhō ni yoru hogo to tokkyohō ni yoru hogo to no kōsaku' (2019) 72(12) *Patento* 225

[110] See, for example, Ihara Tomoki, 'Shokubutsu shinhinshu no ikushu katei ni okeru hanpuku kanō: ōtō jiken' in Ono Shōen Sensei Kiju Kinen Kankō Jimukyoku (ed), *Chiteki zaisanhō saikō saibanrei hyōshaku taikei 1 (tokkyo jitsuyō shin'an hō)* (Aobayashi Shoin 2009); Takeshi Tsuru, 'Case No. 2: Definition of an Invention: Repeatability' in Christopher Heath and Atsuhiro Furuta (eds), *Japanese Patent Law: Cases and Comments* (Kluwer Law International 2019).

[111] Hiraki Yūsuke, 'Momo no shinhinshu ōtō no ikushu zōshokuhō no tokkyosei ni tsuite' (2001) 51(4) *Chizai kanri* 571, 586.

association of pearl cultivation with the issue of probability and repeatability only appeared in earnest from the 1960s onwards.[112]

Instead, the Kurakata yellow peach has, like the Mikimoto semi-spherical pearl cultivation method, served as a malleable focal point of legal dispute over claims involving living creatures as 'industrial' property.[113] Such cases illustrate the changing contexts in which the monopoly ownership of cultivation—including the modification of living organisms in the service of commodity production and their reproduction through practices of cross-breeding—has faced new legal challenges and taken on new historical meanings as precedent in different parts of the world. Peaches, like pearl oysters before them, came to serve as test cases for biopatenting in Japan. Both examples hint at deep interlinkages among colonial empire, migration, cultivation, and legal rights regimes in East Asia and beyond that have informed arguments in Japanese courts about the patentability of inventive claims. Both might also be added to the wide range of seemingly unlikely organisms that have been part of twentieth-century debates about the edges of the natural, the patentable, and the possessable.[114]

[112] This included multiple editions of a widely used patent textbook. See eg Yoshifuji Kōsaku, *Tokkyohō gaisetsu* (Yūhikaku 1968) 59.

[113] Nano Hiko, 'Seibutsu ni kakawaru chiteki shōyūken no yukue' (1990) 87(8) *Hatsumei* 54

[114] Kevles (n 83); Christopher Beauchamp, 'Patenting Nature: A Problem of History' (2013) 16(2) *Stanford Technology Law Review* 257.

11

Scientific Activism and Intellectual Property

How UK-based Agroecologists and Plant Synthetic Biologists Have Challenged the Status Quo

Dominic J Berry[*]

Introduction

Combining short periods of ethnography with interviews and participant observation, this chapter analyses ownership and design in biological organisms and materials from the ground up, and from an historically informed perspective.[1] The approach does not privilege or centre extant intellectual property (IP) law or systems of governance, but instead explores the means and meanings of ownership that can emerge amongst groups of biological innovators. The chapter focuses on two specific sets of discontents from two different worlds of science, namely agroecology and synthetic biology (each introduced in more detail below). Historians and sociologists of science have demonstrated the myriad ways in which scientists, lawyers, and policy-makers interact with one another to produce

[*] I am very grateful to everyone who over the course of this research gave their time to talk to me and agreed to participate in interviews. Linda Kahl, Jim Haseloff, Nicola Patron, Jenny Molloy, and Bruce Pearce each gave me very valuable feedback on an initial draft. Obviously, any mistakes concerning the description of the activities of the ORC and OpenPlant (or any other aspect of the chapter for that matter) reside with me. My thanks also to Laura Downey, who provided a very helpful expert outside view on this topic and greatly improved the structure, and to Jocelyn Bosse and Helen Curry, who took time to offer very important comments and criticisms. Parts of this research were funded by the AHRC through Follow-on Funding (AH/L009455/1) and the European Research Council through Consolidator Grant (616,510-ENLIFE). It was written while employed as Research Fellow on the Narrative Science project, supported by the ERC under the European Union's Horizon 2020 research and innovation programme (Grant Agreement No 694,732) and the Everyday Cyborgs 2.0 project supported by a Wellcome Trust Investigator Award in Humanities and Social Sciences 2019–2024 (Grant No 212507/Z/18/Z).

[1] For the agroecological case, over the course of a one-year postdoctoral research fellowship (2014–2015), I collaborated with the Organic Research Centre (ORC) and historians of science at the University of Leeds. This fellowship involved a site visit to the ORC and collaboration with colleagues there on an international workshop on IP in the plant sciences. For more see www.cultivatinginnovation.org (accessed 23 August 2021). For the synthetic biology case, between 2015 and 2017, I contributed to the Engineering Life project, a Science, Technology, and Innovation (STS) project based at the University of Edinburgh: see www.stis.ed.ac.uk/engineeringlife (accessed 23 August 2021). The methods adopted incorporated site visits to numerous UK-based synthetic biology laboratories, interviews with key actors, and participant observation at several synthetic biology meetings. I was given access to a working group organized by the OpenPlant project, the purpose of which was to draft and design an alternative to existing material transfer agreements, which was eventually dubbed the OpenMTA.

Dominic J Berry, *Scientific Activism and Intellectual Property* In: *Intellectual Property and the Design of Nature*. Edited by: Jose Bellido and Brad Sherman, Oxford University Press. © Dominic J Berry 2023.
DOI: 10.1093/oso/9780192864406.003.0011

laws and regulations that attempt to reflect (or produce) scientific—industrial consensuses, albeit imperfectly, and with a bias towards the interests of some actors over others.[2]

When it comes to IP and biology, different IP regimes also privilege certain features and functions of organisms and biological materials, thereby directing the possible futures of biological novelty.[3] This chapter reports on two cases where actors have taken concrete steps to overcome the initial marginalization of the biological features and functions that matter to them, by reforming existing regulations or contracts, so that these better align IP protection with their preferred system of innovation (systems that were otherwise illegal or disbarred). The actors thereby hope to change both the direction of the development of biology and the kinds of biological things that exist, along with the social significance of their biological materials.

A sense of ownership can arise in many contexts, as when we identify with someone or something that we find inspiring, or when we specialize in a field of knowledge, or when we donate to a charity. In each of these cases, we may feel we have a stake in these things in some small way thanks to our emotional, temporal, or financial investment. Of course, not all senses of ownership are worthy of nurturing. But they cannot be dismissed if they point in the direction of alternative ownership regimes that might produce (social, epistemic, financial, political) goods. By interpreting ownership as something sensed in many ways for many reasons, radiating outwards on a larger spectrum than that which is covered by the law, the chapter builds upon the work of historians Christine MacLeod and Gregory Radick, specifically their IP-broad/IP-narrow framework. The novelty of their framework is precisely its ability to recognize that there are more forms of intellectual ownership than can be, or have been, encoded in the law.[4] Legal

[2] Stathis Arapostathis and Graham Dutfield, *Knowledge Management and Intellectual Property: Concepts, Actors and Practices from the Past to the Present* (Edward Elgar Publishing 2013); Mario Biagioli, Peter Jaszi, and Martha Woodmansee (eds), *Making and Unmaking Intellectual Property* (University of Chicago Press 2011); Robert Bud, 'Upheaval in the Moral Economy of Science? Patenting, Teamwork and the World War II Experience of Penicillin' (2008) 24 *History and Technology* 173; Graham Dutfield, *Intellectual Property Rights and the Life Science Industries* (World Scientific Publishing Company 2009); Courtney Fullilove, *The Profit of the Earth: The Global Seeds of American Agriculture* (University of Chicago Press 2017); Graeme Gooday and Steven Wilf, *Patent Cultures: Diversity and Harmonization in Historical Perspective* (Cambridge University Press 2020); Sally Smith Hughes, 'Making Dollars out of DNA: The First Major Patent in Biotechnology and the Commercialization of Molecular Biology, 1974–1980' (2001) 92 *Isis* 541; Daniel J Kevles, 'Patents, Protections, and Privileges: The Establishment of Intellectual Property in Animals and Plants' (2007) 98 *Isis* 323; Christine MacLeod, *Heroes of Invention: Technology, Liberalism and British Identity, 1750–1914* (Cambridge University Press 2007); Shobita Parthasarathy, *Patent Politics: Life Forms, and the Public Interest in the United States and Europe* (University of Chicago Press 2017).

[3] Jean-Paul Gaudillière, Daniel J Kevles, and Hans-Jörg Rheinberger (eds), *Living Properties: Making Knowledge and Controlling Ownership in the History of Biology* (Max Planck Institute for the History of Science, Preprint 382 2009); Charles Lawson and Berris Charnley, *Intellectual Property and Genetically Modified Organisms: A Convergence in Laws* (Routledge 2015); Margaret Llewelyn and Mike Adcock, *European Plant Intellectual Property* (Hart Publishing 2006).

[4] Christine MacLeod and Gregory Radick 'Claiming ownership in the technosciences: Patents, priority and productivity' (2013) 44 *Studies in the History and Philosophy of Science* 188.

instantiations of IP, such as copyright, trademarks, and patents, are referred to by MacLeod and Radick as IP-narrow. The possible broader forms of IP phenomena that can arise include ownership claims (which can be asserted regardless of any instrument of the law recognizing them, as when someone asserts authority over a particular field of enquiry), productivity claims (as when someone claims their novelty or way of doing things produces a better result than an alternative), and priority claims (as when someone claims they arrived at a possible solution—or type of innovation—first). Examples of IP-broad exist in a great many places, including autobiographies, museum artefacts, secured or fenced-off premises, newspaper articles, and, of course, court rooms.[5] Each kind of claim can be asserted and perform social functions regardless of whether the law is thought to support or intervene upon it. Steps towards reforming and expanding what matters for IP-narrow have already been taken by some legal scholars themselves. We see this, for instance, with recognition of the need to include certification schemes, registration systems, and access—and benefit-sharing under the umbrella of IP and its investigation.[6]

Introducing Agroecology and Synthetic Biology

Agroecology is much contested and its history not yet thoroughly developed.[7] The name covers a wide variety of people, including organizers, activists, and researchers, motivated (in general) by a scepticism regarding the value of heavily industrialized agriculture and critical of its effects on farming and the environment.[8] It is most directly associated with agricultural initiatives in the Global South. The UK-based study covered here does not include reference to these significant anticolonial lineages, which therefore makes it unrepresentative of agroecology at large.[9] Synthetic biology is likewise much contested and its history not yet

[5] Louis Volkmer, a PhD student based between the University of Edinburgh and National Museums Scotland, is currently exploring IP in contexts of museum curation, with a particular interest in care.

[6] Brad Sherman and Susannah Chapman, 'Introduction' in Brad Sherman and Susannah Chapman (eds), *Intellectual Property and Agriculture*, vol 1 (Edward Elgar Publishing 2020) 1–5; Graham Dutfield, *That High Design of Purest Gold: A Critical History of the Pharmaceutical Industry 1880–2020* (World Scientific 2020); Laura JS Murray, Tina Piper, and Kirsty Robertson, *Putting Intellectual Property in its Place* (Oxford University Press 2014).

[7] A Wezel and V Soldat, 'A quantitative and qualitative historical analysis of the scientific discipline of agroecology' (2009) 7 *International Journal of Agricultural Sustainability* 3; A Wezel and others, 'Agroecology as a Science, a Movement and a Practice: A Review' (2009) 29 *Agronomy for Sustainable Development* 503.

[8] Miguel A Altieri, *Agroecology: The Science of Sustainable Agriculture* (Westview Press 1995). My thanks to Bruce Pearce for suggesting this text. See also Omar Felipe Giraldo and Peter M Rosset, 'Agroecology as a Territory in Dispute: Between Institutionality and Social Movements' (2018) 45 *The Journal of Peasant Studies* 545; Eduardo Sevilla Guzmán and Graham Woodgate, 'Agroecology: Foundations in Agrarian Social Thought and Sociological Theory' (2013) 37 *Agroecology and Sustainable Food Systems* 32.

[9] My thanks to Helen Curry for emphasizing this point, and for sharing the following resources that further historicize agroecology: Steve Gliessman, 'Agroecology: Growing the roots of resistance' (2012)

thoroughly developed.[10] The name covers a wide variety of people, the majority of whom are researchers, but also including many organizers and activists, motivated (in general) by an ambition to make new things that it is hoped will be profitable and/or provide new knowledge of biology as a subject of engineering (although the nature and extent of these engineering connections are the subject of much debate).[11] In both cases, 'organizer, activist, researcher' can be embodied by the same person. In most respects, these two groups are epistemically, politically, economically, and socially distinct from one another. However, as we shall see, both groups are intent on co-producing alternative means of governance for IP in their industries of interest.[12] They also engage in activist and advocacy work to serve their overall ambitions, hoping to inspire public interest in the changes they seek, while cultivating more targeted support from academic and industrial society. Both are also prone to explaining themselves as motivated by concern for what has happened to the agricultural seeds industry and its consolidation in the hands of a tiny number of large, global commercial actors. Last, the two groups have succeeded in introducing changes to the normal procedures covering international trade of biological materials. For the agroecologists, this has meant securing a special dispensation from the European Commission (EC) to market seeds that would otherwise be prohibited (and which has now been incorporated into EU law). For the synthetic biologists, this has meant creating an alternative material transfer agreement (MTA), one which in many respects is really an *alternative to* an MTA (which has already begun to be used). Investigating agroecologists and synthetic biologists in parallel achieves at least two goods, one that matters for these actors and another that matters for those who study them.

First, recognizing each other's frustrations might inspire these two groups (neither of which is homogenous) to support one another strategically and coherently. Doing so may require further learning from one another, and further changes

37 *Agroecology and Sustainable Food Systems* 19; Marta Astier, 'Back to the Roots: Understanding Current Agroecological Movement, Science, and Practice in Mexico' (2017) 41 *Agroecology and Sustainable Food Systems* 329.

[10] Deborah Scott, Dominic Berry, and Jane Calvert, 'Synthetic biology' in Sahra Gibbon, Barbara Prainsack, Stephen Hilgartner, and Janelle Lamoreaux (eds), *Routledge Handbook of Genomics, Health and Society* (2nd edn, Routledge 2018).

[11] Luis Campos, 'Outsiders and In-Laws: Drew Endy and the Case of Synthetic Biology' in Oren Harman and Michael Dietrich (eds), *Outsider Scientists: Routes to Innovation in Biology* (University of Chicago Press 2013); Fox Keller, 'What Does Synthetic Biology Have to Do with Biology?' (2009) 4 *BioSocieties* 291; Michel Morange, 'Synthetic Biology: A Bridge between Functional and Evolutionary Biology' (2009) 4 *Biological Theory* 368; Pablo Schyfter, 'How a "Drive to Make" Shapes Synthetic Biology' (2020) 44 *Studies in History and Philosophy of Biological and Biomedical Sciences* 632; M Simons, 'The Diversity of Engineering in Synthetic Biology' (2020) 14 *Nanoethics* 71.

[12] Sheila Jasanoff, *Designs on Nature: Science and Democracy in Europe and the United States* (Princeton University Press 2005). Thanks to my colleague Laura Downey for suggesting the appropriateness of this analytical perspective and language when characterizing the activities the actors are engaged in, and why I find them interesting.

within each group. In contrast with synthetic biology, agroecology has existed for many decades, and has developed an extensive discourse on the underlying problems begetting science, society, and industry. This makes them a model for the kinds of epistemic and political community that synthetic biology should seek to emulate. The normative component of this suggestion builds on the fact that synthetic biology has often claimed to appreciate—and indeed has sometimes directly sponsored—interdisciplinary collaboration with social scientists, geographers, anthropologists, and historians, with the intention that such longer-term collaboration would increase their own reflexivity, developing their own discourse concerning problems begetting science, society, and industry. Some of the activities falling under 'responsible research and innovation' (RRI) could be cited here.[13] As these kinds of interdisciplinary arrangement have been developed amongst agroecologists for some time, synthetic biologists can learn from them. At the same time, there are ways in which the most recent techniques developed for plant gene and genome alteration (a suite of methods that rapidly came to be called 'editing') could be of great value to agroecological research and breeding programmes, *provided* that processes and institutions of 'democratization' were pursued.[14] Some of the strongest opponents to these techniques within agroecology would consider it naive to think that any amount of democratization, and any amount of reshaping of the ownership of seed-production systems, might increase the attractiveness of these techniques. That is a matter for agroecologists. Paralleling them with synthetic biology points out that democratization is *supposed* to be something that synthetic biologists particularly care about.[15] It is possible that in pursuing this deeper learning from one another, and making necessary further changes, the two communities could become more than the sum of their parts.

Second, bringing the two together is productive for IP scholars, and other researchers travelling adjacent to agroecology, synthetic biology, and the wider biological sciences, because it allows reflection on why their discourse and difficulties might often appear so similar. Their similarities arise primarily due to a shared structural problem in the law. As Muireann Quigley has argued, the law deals with complex biological phenomena by constructing certain objects (be they human bodies, collections of cells, or plant varieties), and drawing boundaries around them.[16] Rights and responsibilities towards these objects can then be apportioned

[13] Andrew S Balmer and others, 'Five Rules of Thumb for Post-ELSI Interdisciplinary Collaborations' (2016) 3 *Journal of Responsible Innovation* 73.

[14] Maywa Montenegro de Wit, 'Democratizing CRISPR? Stories, Practices, and Politics of Science and Governance on the Agricultural Gene Editing Frontier' (2020) 8 *Elementa: Science of the Anthropocene* 1.

[15] Emma Frow, 'Rhetorics and Practices of Democratization in Synthetic Biology' in Matthias Wienroth and Eugenia Rodrigues (eds), *Knowing New Biotechnologies: Social Aspects of Technological Convergence* (Routledge 2015) 174–87.

[16] Muireann Quigley, *Self-Ownership, Property Rights, and the Human Body: A Legal and Philosophical Analysis* (Cambridge University Press 2018).

to different parties. This can be applied both to the case of plant varieties and also to DNA constructs. The approach adopted here to describe this problem-situation combines two different concepts: boundary objects and boundary-work. As these help to diagnose the nature of the IP problems that agroecologists and synthetic biologists face, they are fleshed out in the next section, before the following sections describe the two case studies. These are then analysed.

Boundary Objects and Boundary-work

Plant varieties and DNA constructs are boundary objects (in a concrete rather than an abstract sense), because they fulfil a stabilizing function across the different social worlds invested in them. This means that as they circulate, they help these social worlds to understand one another, and achieve shared or independently held goals. They do so while still possessing a certain amount of heterogeneity vis-à-vis their identity within different local sites.[17] For plant varieties, the different social worlds that rely on some notion of a 'variety' in order to coordinate between each other include that of farmers, breeders, plant scientists, regulators, seed companies, and consumers (although the latter are so detached from the processes enabling seed production that they are often left out of consideration). The different kinds of 'thing' that might be considered a variety at these local sites include: a pedigree or combination of pedigrees; a genome; a trackable identity code; raw material for future innovation; a catalogue number. The primary means of making varieties into boundary objects (ie primary means of objectification) are tests of their distinctness, uniformity, and stability (DUS), more on which later. For DNA constructs, the different social worlds that rely on some notion of a 'construct' in order to coordinate between each other include synthetic biology labs in particular, molecular biology labs at large, health and biotechnology companies, regulators, administrators of repositories, and consumers (although the latter are so detached from the processes enabling the production of synthetic biology's materials that they are often left out of consideration). The different kinds of 'thing' that might be acknowledged as a DNA construct at these local sites include: a collection of 'parts' with different originators; a tool for experimentation; a trackable identity code; a database number; raw material for future innovation; a case number. The primary means of objectification turning DNA constructs into boundary objects does not involve looking at them (as in the case of plant variety DUS tests), but is instead achieved through standards for their description, more on which later.

[17] Susan Leigh Star and James R Griesemer, 'Institutional Ecology, "Translations" and Boundary Objects: Amateurs and Professionals in Berkeley's Museum of Vertebrate Zoology, 1907–39' (1989) 19 *Social Studies of Science* 387.

This argument combines boundary objects with a second, older, and otherwise unrelated concept, that of boundary-work, more specifically, boundary-work as has been developed by Quigley in the context of the law.[18] Though focused on possible boundaries between persons and things, the way in which Quigley applies the boundary-work concept—by highlighting the consequences that follow from different ways of making boundaries—is much more generally applicable. Both of the cases discussed in this chapter place a different legal boundary under pressure. In the case of agroecology, researchers and regulators had to reorganize the priorities, or values, that motivate the boundary between legal and illegal commercial seed production, which they are doing in the first instance through a trial exemption. In the case of synthetic biology, researchers and regulators had to revise the implications for materials crossing private property boundaries, which they are doing through an 'OpenMTA'.

Because boundary-work helps define the kinds of object recognized by the law, and because the kinds of object sought or used by the law will likely have been—or will be hoped to be—particularly suitable as a boundary object, these two concepts are complementary. Agroecologists interested in trading heterogenous population varieties for the purposes of breeding for diversity, described in above, are intending to trade a boundary object that resists the typical means of objectification. As a result, they are expanding the kinds of object around which boundaries might be drawn, such that there are now not just 'plant varieties' but also 'plant varieties *minus* some otherwise important biological, legal, social, and economic expectations'. Synthetic biologists interested in trading commercializable 'open' DNA constructs for the purposes of distributed innovation, as described above, are intending to trade a boundary object that, although perfectly capable of being objectified, is somewhat unruly (regarding its actual possible uses, which are open-ended) and so resists the typical *meaning* of objectification. As a result, synthetic biologists are expanding the kinds of boundaries that might be drawn, such that there are now not just 'DNA constructs' but 'DNA constructs *minus* some otherwise important legal, social, and economic expectations' (See Table 11.1 below).

The material features of the novelties in question are clearly particularly important, and the processes involved in their production will be given special attention.[19] We are now in a position to say that this chapter addresses the management of IP-narrow and IP-broad accrued by boundary objects, particularly as they perform boundary-work that constructs new cultures of biological design and innovation.

[18] Quigley (n 16).

[19] In this respect I have been influenced by Alain Pottage and Brad Sherman, *Figures of Invention: A History of Modern Patent Law* (Oxford University Press 2010).

Table 11.1 'Comparison between plant varieties and DNA constructs'

Boundary object	Plant varieties	DNA constructs
Novelty	Population varieties	'Open' DNA constructs
Problem	Resists typical means of objectification	Resists typical meaning of objectification
Solution	Create new means of objectification	Create new means of drawing boundaries
Boundary-work	Two alternative boundaries now drawn between legal and illegal seed, one around population varieties and one around everything else	Two alternative ways of drawing boundaries come to exist between commercial and non-commercial DNA constructs, one around open parts and one around everything else

IP and Its Agroecological Discontents

Agroecology established itself as an international community over the course of the twentieth century. It is constituted by activists, organizers, and scientific researchers interested in agricultural productivity, in ways that are particularly sensitive to environmentalist and anti-industrialist concerns. This chapter focuses on their scientific membership in particular, because they have led recent efforts to alter the governance of plant varieties in ways directly connected with IP, while producing their own biological innovations. Another obvious defining feature of agroecology within the space of agricultural science is the inspiration it has drawn from ecology, a science of biology and the environment that has a history of its own.[20] The community and its activities are diverse, ranging across all kinds of farming systems, such that no single definition will be entirely adequate. If we take a narrower view, by focusing on their plant science membership, then agroecologists can be characterized as interdisciplinary researchers dedicated to

[20] Laurent Coumel and Marc Elie, 'A Belated and Tragic Ecological Revolution: Nature, Disasters, and Green Activists in the Soviet Union and the Post-Soviet States, 1960s–2010s' (2013) 40 *Soviet and Post-Soviet Review* 157; Frank N Egerton 'The History of Ecology: Achievements and Opportunities, Part one' (1983) 16 *Journal of the History of Biology* 259; Tom Griffiths and Libby Robin (eds), *Ecology and Empire: Environmental History of Settler Societies* (Edinburgh University Press 1998); Sharon E Kingsland, *The Evolution of American Ecology, 1890–2000* (Johns Hopkins University Press 2005); Ageliki Lefkaditou, Konstantinos Korfiatis, and Tasos Hovardas, 'Contextualising the Teaching and Learning of Ecology: Historical and Philosophical Considerations' in Michael R Matthews (ed), *International Handbook of Research in History, Philosophy and Science Teaching* (Springer 2013); Brian Sewell Lindseth, 'From Radioactive Fallout to Environmental Critique: Ecology and the Politics of Cold War Science' (PhD dissertation, University of California 2013); Paolo Palladino, 'Defining Ecology: Ecological Theories, Mathematical Models, and Applied Biology in the 1960s and 1970s' (1991) 24 *Journal of the History of Biology* 223.

understanding agricultural production in the field, while thinking critically about productivist farming, science, and policy. Productivism in this context refers to farming, science, and policy that make increases in overall agricultural productivity (typically defined by yield) the primary goal—and the ultimate measure—of a farming system's success. Agroecology instead elevates alternative goals, including sustainability, environmentalism, and farmer autonomy. Of course today, the majority of agricultural scientists, no matter their discipline or research community, will assert their own support for sustainability and the environment, and many will gladly share their own concerns about the undesirable effects of industrialized agriculture. The point is that agroecology defines and distinguishes itself in contrast to other cultures of agricultural science by being *more* invested in environmentalism, and *more* dedicated to minimally industrialized and/or organic farming. These distinctions are earned through the kinds of institutional or commercial collaborative partners that they will embrace or reject, the kinds of trial they design, and most importantly, the kinds of questions that they pursue. In the hands of *some* agroecologists, important questions have included 'what kinds of plant variety should be available to farmers?', 'what kinds of plant variety have been prioritized by regulators, policy-makers and IP law?', and 'how should IP protections affect farmers, researchers, and their plant materials?'.

The Organic Research Centre and breeding for diversity

The Organic Research Centre (ORC) is now based just outside Cirencester in the south east of England. It was founded originally in 1980 at Newbury as the Elm Farm Research Centre, reflecting a global trend in the institutionalization of organic farming research centres at that time.[21] At the outset, agroecology (either as a focal point for discourse or an international community) does not appear to have been an interest of the ORC, although it would become one by the time we reach the particular case study focused on in the following section. The most important figure for the ORC's eventual agroecological response to plant varieties and breeding practice, which began in earnest around 2000, was Professor Martin Wolfe. Wolfe was a plant pathologist who, by the time he came to work with the ORC, had more than twenty-five years of experience working at the Plant Breeding Institute (PBI), Cambridge. There he initially became interested in studies of varietal diversity, the potential costs of monoculture, and the pursuit of alternative farming systems. Through Wolfe, we can come to understand the kinds of object that plant breeders are attempting to innovate, the complexity of the phenomena

[21] Philip Conford, *The Origins of the Organic Movement* (Floris Books 2001); Philip Conford, *The Development of the Organic Network* (Floris Books 2011).

that plant IP is expected to create a boundary around, and why the ORC was forced to draw a new one.

Wolfe completed a PhD at the University of Cambridge in 1963, joining the PBI as a plant pathologist shortly thereafter. The PBI was the UK's foremost agricultural plant-breeding establishment and—alongside the John Innes Horticultural Institution—was one of the UK's most significant sites for the institutionalization of genetics.[22] When Wolfe joined, the PBI was a publicly funded institution tasked with (amongst other things) producing commercial varieties of particular value to UK farmers, some of which were exceedingly successful.[23] He also happened to arrive at the PBI a year after the UK had agreed to sign a new international convention, the Union for the Protection of New Varieties of Plants (UPOV).[24] Agreeing to sign the latter necessitated the creation of the UK's first legislation for plant variety IP protection, the 1964 Plant Varieties and Seeds Act.[25] Between the Convention and the Act, the UK formalized a system for identifying varieties over which IP rights might be asserted, the kinds of protection and exemptions that this could entail, and the limits of the rights afforded to breeders. The primary tests of a variety's suitability concerned its Distinctness, Uniformity and Stability. These DUS tests are still applied today and assume that the proposed variety will have a single, uniquely identifiable phenotype and be a pure line. PBI employees were amongst the first and most immediately successful breeders to benefit from this legislation, protecting their plant breeders' rights (PBRs) with few reservations. Such was the freshly governed world of plant breeding into which Wolfe entered.

The methods underlying the breeding of new plant varieties have never been static, and a core aspect of the research efforts at the PBI concerned the exploration of new methods of breeding novel varieties.[26] The neatest snapshot of the

[22] Berris Charnley, 'Agricultural Science, Plant Breeding and the Emergence of a Mendelian System in Britain, 1880–1930' (PhD thesis, University of Leeds 2011); Robert Olby, 'Scientists and Bureaucrats in the Establishment of the John Innes Horticultural Institution under William Bateson' (1989) 46 *Annals of Science* 497.

[23] On the case of the PBI's Proctor barley see Matthew Holmes, 'Crops in a machine: industrialising barley breeding in twentieth-century Britain' in Jon Agar and Jacob Ward (eds), *Histories of Technology, the Environment and Modern Britain* (University College London 2018). On the first varieties released by the PBI see Charnley (n 22).

[24] Graham Dutfield, 'Turning Plant Varieties into Intellectual Property: The UPOV Convention' in Geoff Tansey and Tasmin Rajotte (eds), *The Future Control of Food: A Guide to International Negotiations and Rules on Intellectual Property, Biodiversity, and Food Security* (Earthscan/IDRC 2008) 27–47; Jay Sanderson, *Plants, People and Practices: The Nature and History of the UPOV Convention* (Cambridge University Press 2017).

[25] Dermot J Hayes, Sergio H Lence, and Susana Goggi, 'Impact of Intellectual Property Rights in the Seed Sector on Crop Yield Growth and Social Welfare: A Case Study Approach' (2009) 12 *AgBioForum* 155. For a study of the economic impact of the 1964 legislation see Dwijen Rangnekar, 'Intellectual Property Rights and Agriculture: An Analysis of the Economic Impact of Plant Breeders' Rights' (Action Aid 2000).

[26] Berris Charnley, 'Managing knowledge in "systematised plant breeding": Mendelism and British agricultural science, 1900–1930' in Stathis Arapostathis and Graham Dutfield (eds), *Knowledge Management and Intellectual Property: Concepts, Actors and Practices from the Past to the Present* (Edward Elgar Publishing 2013) 200–15; Jonathan Harwood, *Europe's Green Revolution and Others Since: The Rise and Fall of Peasant-Friendly Plant Breeding* (Routledge 2012).

plant-breeding research undertaken at the PBI during Wolfe's term of employment is a chapter in *Wheat Breeding: Its Scientific Basis*, written by two of the institute's most well-respected breeders, Francis Geoffrey Hugh Lupton and John Bingham, published in 1987.[27] Lupton, also the book's editor, had joined the PBI in 1948, following a term of service during the Second World War, eventually going on to lead the cereals division and becoming deputy director of the PBI in 1978.[28] They provided an overview of the approaches that the PBI had taken towards the production of novel varieties. First emphasizing the pure-line concept as placing the enterprise on a firmer footing, they then provided details as to how variable plant material could be produced in the first place.[29] This included, for instance, the pursuit of 'diallel' and 'half diallel' sets of crosses, in which a set of parent varieties are hybridized systematically between one another, either in both directions (pollen of variety X is used to pollinate variety Y, and pollen of variety Y is used to pollinate variety X), or only in one of these directions, ie half.[30] This was the kind of background breeding activity that a publicly funded research centre could pursue, well beyond the interests or resources of most private breeders.

Earlier in that same volume, the PBI's interests in multiline varieties and the cultivation of mixtures had also been introduced, particularly as methods for resisting disease.[31] Wolfe's own first overview on this topic had been published only a couple of years earlier.[32] It began with concerns about the long-term effects of monoculture, quoting an earlier source, Jack R Harlan, a professor of plant genetics at the University of Illinois. In a 1972 paper titled 'Genetics of Disaster', Harlan had offered a sweeping and anxious review of the current status of agricultural science in relation to industry, focusing in particular on plant genetic resources:[33]

[27] Francis Geoffrey Hugh Lupton (ed), *Wheat Breeding: Its Scientific Basis* (Springer Science + Business Media 1987).

[28] Graham Jenkins, 'Obituary: Dr Francis Geoffrey Hugh Lupton 16 July 1921–23 May 2006' (2007) 43 *Experimental Agriculture* 1.

[29] For a historical account that problematizes the historiographical status of the pure line in ways that clearly inform the present chapter see Dominic J Berry, 'The Plant Breeding Industry after Pure Line Theory: Lessons from the National Institute of Agricultural Botany' (2014) 46 *Studies in the History and Philosophy of Biological and Biomedical Sciences* 25.

[30] Francis Geoffrey Hugh Lupton and John Bingham, 'Production of new varieties: an integrated research approach to plant breeding' in Francis Geoffrey Hugh Lupton (ed), *Wheat Breeding: Its Scientific Basis* (Springer Science + Business Media 1987) 497–98.

[31] Roy Johnson and Francis Geoffrey Hugh Lupton, 'Breeding for resistance' in Francis Geoffrey Hugh Lupton (ed), *Wheat Breeding: Its Scientific Basis* (Springer Science + Business Media 1987) 383–87.

[32] Martin Wolfe, 'The Current Status and Prospects of Multiline Cultivars and Variety Mixtures for Disease Resistance' (1985) 23 *Annual Review of Phytopathology* 251.

[33] Understanding of disaster narratives in connection with contemporary agricultural policy and politics is the subject of Jocelyn Bosse, Xan Chacko, and Susannah Chapman, 'The Cosmopolitics of Food Futures: Imagining Nature, Law, and Apocalypse' (2020) 34 *Journal of Media and Cultural Studies* 840.

> Whatever the [breeding] procedure, the net effect was to narrow the genetic base of the crop as grown in production fields. Generalized adaptation and general resistance to pests were both sharply reduced. A large proportion of the genes of the old landraces was discarded, and modern varieties represent only a fraction of the germ plasm once grown.[34]

A pure-line mentality—convinced that variation was bad, uniformity was good, and off-types in the field somehow immoral—developed. Symptoms of the mental climate could be found in crop-judging contests, ribbons awarded at county and state fairs, crop improvement associations, seed certifying agencies, and in some provisions of state and federal seed acts.

Wolfe and the PBI were therefore interested in exploring the effects of increased field diversity, including through the adoption of multiline varieties. Helen Curry's historical research into twentieth-century scientific anxieties concerning biodiversity loss and its connections with industrialized agriculture, which highlights late-twentieth century interest in the concept of 'genetic vulnerability' in the face of large agricultural disasters, establishes the wider context for the likes of Wolfe and Harlan.[35] Wolfe was immediately interested in the multiline varieties in his capacity as a pathologist, thanks to their potential to survive at least partially when specific pathogens arrived at the field. If intended to be grown in a mixture, the pressure to produce 'pure' versions of the respective lines (ie DUS), is lost. Evidence that the PBI itself attempted to cultivate any multi-lines has not been found. The point is that, as a publicly funded research centre, the PBI at least had resources and mandate to take an interest in these options and could have pursued such a research programme into the background of varietal diversity, should it have wished to do so.

These distinctions between public and private organizations, and between breeding activities that take place 'in the background' rather than in the 'foreground', eventually crystallized in the UK into a new institutional division of labour, between public and private science, and between non-commercial and commercial breeding, all with the closure of the PBI. This took place during the same year in which Lupton's volume was published, precipitating Wolfe's departure for Switzerland.

The Thatcher government's sale of the PBI to the private multinational Unilever in 1987 is a significant milestone in any history of the UK's industrial strategy, let alone plant breeding.[36] What is not often appreciated is how a new

[34] Jack R Harlan, 'Genetics of Disaster' (1972) 1 *Journal of Environmental Quality* 212.

[35] Helen Curry, 'Breeding Uniformity and Banking Diversity: The Genescapes of Industrial Agriculture, 1935–1970' (2017) 10 *Global Environment* 83; Helen Curry, *Endangered Maize: Industrial Agriculture and the Crisis of Extinction* (University of California Press 2021).

[36] Paolo Palladino, *Plants, Patients and the Historian: (Re)membering in the Age of Genetic Engineering* (Rutgers University Press 2002); Colin Thirtle and others, 'The Rise and Fall of Public Sector Plant

institutionalized division of labour, between background and foreground breeding work (or between 'fundamental' and 'near market' research, in the Thatcher government's vernacular), elevated certain kinds of plant variety (and plant-breeding methods) as an ideal commercial model. Where longer-standing cultures of innovation in plant breeding had begun to worry about the effects of monoculture and a too-narrow focus on pure lines, the latter now experienced a fillip. To a large extent, this was thanks to their easy incorporation into an imaginary of innovation focused on transferring publicly funded research into private hands to ensure the maximal exploitation of IP.[37] The pure line, which could be produced in numerous highly distinct, uniform, and stable forms, was thereby encouraged. Researchers in the foreground of variety production had incentives to produce more and more varieties that excelled in terms of meeting DUS tests, and heterogenous varieties or the propagation of seed mixtures were either forgotten or treated as unserious. Many of the plant scientists of the PBI were able to continue their fundamental research by taking up new positions at the John Innes Institute, which in 1994 became the John Innes Centre (JIC) after officially merging with this Cambridge group.[38] The prior expectation (or capacity) to produce marketable cereal varieties went to Unilever and its newly established subsidiary, Plant Breeding International.[39] The boundary between legal and illegal commercial seed production was drawn around varieties as pure lines, with pure lines as the preserve of private actors.

Exemption from EU Council Directive 66/402/EEC

Martin Wolfe returned to live in the UK in the late 1990s. After first setting up his own experimental farm, Wakelyns (a ninety-minute drive from Cambridge, a fifty-minute drive from Norwich), he began to collaborate with the ORC in Newbury (a four-to-five-hour drive). One of their first major collaborations revived all the older connections described above. Deciding to pursue a form of multiline work, referred to as breeding 'composite cross populations' (CCPs), an initial twenty-one distinct varieties were hybridized in a half-diallel by the JIC. The resulting progeny

Breeding in the United Kingdom: A Causal Chain Model of Basic and Applied Research and Diffusion' (1998) 19 *Agricultural Economics* 127.

37 The fortunes of the National Research Development Corporation, and Thatcher's increasing emphasis on ensuring that IP was vigorously exploited, can be followed in Jon Agar, *Science Policy Under Thatcher* (University College London 2019).

38 On the longer history of Cambridge–John Innes relations see Sarah Wilmot, 'J.B.S. Haldane: the John Innes years' (2017) 96 *Journal of Genetics* 815.

39 Andrew Joseph Webster, 'Privatisation of Public Sector Research: The Case of the Plant Breeding Institute' (1989) 16 *Science and Public Policy* 224.

were then organized into six populations.[40] These could be grown on, and environmental influences allowed to affect the survival or otherwise of each plant, an approach dubbed 'evolutionary plant breeding'.[41] Trial crops of the population varieties produced were then planted at Wolfe's Wakelyns site in 2012. But, in order for the ORC and its collaborators to pursue the possibilities of breeding for diversity in agricultural *practice*, they needed to overcome some of the rules that had governed the sale of cereal varieties in Europe since the mid-1960s. Dr Bruce Pearce had particular responsibility for refining and overseeing the ORC's population breeding programme, eventually leading a variety to market. The following description of these most recent developments is based on conversations with Pearce during 2014–2015, and the presentation he gave at the Cultivating Innovation conference.[42]

Passing a DUS test is what defines varieties as varieties in the eyes of the regulator, ie this is the process of objectification through which plant materials pass to become boundary objects.[43] In contrast, population varieties are not intended to be distinct, uniform, or stable. Indeed, they are intended to maximize the potential value of crop diversity (ie their non-uniformity), and also the potential value to be gained from the population undergoing further heritable changes occurring over time, due to being grown persistently in a particular region (ie their instability). This variability is crucial for those pursuing them as a solution to monocrop agriculture and systems of seed production that otherwise expect farmers to purchase new seed stocks each season. After an initial research proposal submitted to the EU was rejected, the ORC eventually found some support for the idea from the UK's Department for Environment, Food, and Rural Affairs (Defra). The latter, as well as the Animal and Plant Health Authority (APHA), worked closely with the ORC on the steps necessary to bring population varieties to market. At the same time, the ORC collaborated with other groups in Europe to create a network of organic and agroecological researchers interested in breeding for diversity. A proposal was put to the EC for a trial exemption, which was agreed, and a temporary experiment in the marketing of population varieties began in March 2014.[44] This exemption was

[40] Hannah Jones, Kay Hinchsliffe, Sarah Pepler, and Martin Wolfe, 'Evolutionary Breeding of Wheat for Low Input Systems' (Elm Farm Research Centre 2005) https://www.organicresearchcentre.com/manage/authincludes/article_uploads/WB%20SUSVAR%20poster%20Jan%202005.pdf (accessed 26 July 2022).

[41] SL Phillips and Martin S Wolfe, 'Centenary Review: Evolutionary Plant Breeding for Low Input Systems' (2005) 143 *Journal of Agricultural Science* 245.

[42] Dr Pearce's presentation, 'Insights from the Temporary EU Marketing Experiment—and the Marketing of—Cereal Populations' https://www.cultivatinginnovation.org/resources.html (accessed 9 April 2021).

[43] For many plant breeders, what defines a variety as a variety is their say-so. Some professional plant breeders have become very angry with me whenever they thought I was suggesting agreement on a variety being a variety was a matter for coordination between themselves and relevant institutions.

[44] 2014/150/EU: 'Commission Implementing Decision of 18 March 2014 on the organisation of a temporary experiment providing for certain derogations for the marketing of populations of the plant species wheat, barley, oats and maize pursuant to Council Directive' 66/402/EEC.

updated in 2018 to extend the trial period to February 2021, the maximum length of time the EU allows for temporary experiments.[45]

The way in which this trial exemption worked was that actors in different member states could apply to participate in the scheme. They would have to apply to their respective seed certification authorities. In England, this was and remains the APHA, although this was itself only formed in 2014, taking over responsibility for seed certification programmes from the earlier Plant Health and Seeds Inspectorate. The experiment specified three possible means by which a population variety would have to be produced for it to be eligible:

(a) crossing five or more varieties in all combinations, followed by bulking of the progeny and exposing the stock to natural selection in successive generations;
(b) growing together at least five varieties of a predominantly cross-fertilizing species, bulking the progeny, repeatedly re-sowing and exposing the stock to natural selection until plants of the original varieties are no longer present;
(c) inter-crossing varieties using crossing protocols different from those in (a) or (b) to produce a similarly diverse population that does not contain varieties.

As for the problems of identification, ie how to make a population variety into a boundary object, participants had to agree to undergo alternative forms of assessment for the identification of seed stocks, and also fulfil requirements for traceability, which the ORC and its collaborators helped to design. Identity could be specified by reference to the original varieties the plants had been crossed from, the particular scheme under which the seed had been multiplied (ie *this* temporary exemption), the region in which they were produced, their degree of heterogeneity, and also descriptions of relevant characteristics of the population (ie yield, quality, performance, etc.).

A very long time has passed since 2015, and it is far from clear what room, if any, the UK government will make for population varieties in its own variety and seed certification legislation post-Brexit.[46] At EU level, the Commission has decided to incorporate provision for population varieties into its new organic regulations (Regulation (EU) 2018/848) and *only* its organic regulations.[47] It has also

[45] Commission Implementing Decision (EU) 2018/1519 of 9 October 2018 amending Implementing Decision 2014/150/EU on the organisation of a temporary experiment providing for certain derogations for the marketing of populations of the plant species wheat, barley, oats and maize pursuant to Council Directive 66/402/EEC.

[46] This paragraph is based upon email communications between Bruce Pearce and Ambrogio Costanzo, forwarded to me on 9 April 2021. My thanks to them both for their generous assistance.

[47] Regulation (EU) 2018/848 of the European Parliament and of the Council of 30 May 2018 on organic production and labelling of organic products and repealing Council Regulation (2018) EC No 834/2007.

adopted more expansive parameters than the original temporary experiment, as this legislation covers any and all organic plants, not just cereals. As such, the EU now recognizes the marketability of seeds termed 'organic heterogenous material'. These are, however, excluded from being awarded PBRs, which means any future payment schemes to original breeders will have to be organized by alternative mechanisms.[48] No evidence has come to light that anyone involved in these discussions has suggested incorporating the tracking system—which had been used throughout the trial exemption to maintain the identity of population varieties—into the plant variety rights legislation as an alternative to DUS, which would allow breeders of population varieties to accrue PBRs. This is a potentially missed opportunity as far as the co-production of alternative governance is concerned. It is true that the exercise of IP rights is a secondary interest for most breeders of population varieties; nevertheless, the possibility is at least worth considering, to avoid population varieties gaining status as 'second-class citizens'. In summary, we can understand the regulatory problems confronting breeding for diversity as having been dealt with by making two boundary objects, around each of which a different boundary can be drawn, one around material marketed *only* to organic farmers and *without* attached PBRs, and another around material not primarily marketed to organic farmers and *with* PBRs attached. The status quo is challenged and made to accommodate something it had previously excluded, but by applying only to organic produce, the greater part of the industry is left unaffected. The situation is quite different for the next case.

IP and Its Synthetic Biological Discontents

Synthetic biology established itself as an international and interdisciplinary scientific community around the year 2000. A defining feature of synthetic biology in the space of the biological sciences is the inspiration it draws from engineering, although the extent of these connections and debts remains contested. The community of synthetic biologists and their activities are diverse, ranging across all kinds of biological organisms and systems, such that no single definition will be entirely adequate. If we take a narrower view, by focusing on their plant science membership, then synthetic biologists can be characterized as interdisciplinary researchers dedicated to understanding plant systems and materials, with general ambitions to better understand (and to make new) productive organisms, biological processes, and materials. Some form of the productivism discussed earlier in the context of agroecology (and which that community regards with deep scepticism) is therefore almost always present in synthetic biology. Yet this need not be the

[48] Prior to the creation of PBRs, breeders looking for remuneration would often rely on certification systems, and the paying of a levy by food processors.

case, and alternative goals and values have been explored by some synthetic biologists, typically in collaboration with social scientists in the context of either RRI or art—science projects.[49] Indeed, synthetic biologists have often defined themselves in comparison to alternative cultures of molecular biology by attempting to incorporate a more openly critical approach to the ethical, social, economic, and legal constituents of their science.[50] Sometimes this includes concern about the influence of IP governance on science and industry. In contrast with the example of agroecology, the IP ambitions of some synthetic biologists are therefore much more central to their identity as a community in the first place. It is an aspect of synthetic biology that has already attracted the attention of scholars based in law, science and technology studies (STS), the history of science, and innovation studies. Rather than relating a survey of this still-expanding literature, select references are made below to some of the most relevant arguments.

A final important point to understand about this case is that—just as agroecology does—synthetic biology intends to differentiate itself from other communities by elevating particular epistemic goals and values, including precision, efficiency, speed, reliability, and standardization.[51] Of course the majority of biological scientists, no matter their discipline or research community, will assert their own support for precision, efficiency, and reliability, just as some will gladly share their own concerns about the ethical, social, economic, and legal constituents of their science. The point is that synthetic biology defines and distinguishes itself in contrast to other cultures of biological science, by being *more* invested in these epistemic goals, and *more* dedicated to RRI, etc. It earns these distinctions through the kinds of institutional or commercial collaborative partners that it will embrace or reject, the kinds of experiment designed, and most importantly, the kinds of questions pursued. In the hands of *some* synthetic biologists, important questions have included, 'what kinds of biological materials should scientists concentrate on making and sharing?', 'what kinds of material have been prioritized by regulators, policymakers and IP law?', and 'how should IP protections operate on scientists and their biological materials?'.

[49] Jane Calvert and others (eds), *Synthetic Aesthetics: Investigating Synthetic Biology's Designs on Nature* (The MIT Press 2017); Claire Marris and others, 'Taking Roles in Interdisciplinary Collaborations: Reflections on Working in Post-ELSI Spaces in the UK Synthetic Biology Community' (2015) 28 *Science and Technology Studies* 3; Emma Frow and Jane Calvert, 'Opening up the Future(s) of Synthetic Biology' (2013) 48 *Futures* 32.

[50] Ken Taylor and Simon Woods, 'Reflections on the Practice of Responsible (Research and) Innovation in Synthetic Biology' (2019) 39 *New Genetics and Society* 127.

[51] Gail Davies, Emma Frow, and Sabina Leonelli, 'Bigger, Faster, Better? Rhetorics and Practices of Large-scale Research in Contemporary Bioscience' (2013) 8 *BioSocieties* 386; Dominic J Berry, 'Chronicle, genealogy, and narrative: understanding synthetic biology in the image of historiography' in Mary S Morgan, Kim M Hajek, and Dominic J Berry (eds), *Narrative Science: Reasoning, Representing and Knowing Since 1800* (Cambridge University Press 2022) 328–50.

The OpenPlant project and circulating synthetic biology's 'parts'

The OpenPlant project is run between three East Anglian research centres: a group of laboratories at the University of Cambridge (with central project facilities run by the Haseloff lab), alongside the JIC and the Earlham Institute, both of which are based at the same science park just outside Norwich. As we will see, they also have some important international collaborators. OpenPlant was one of the UK's flagship synthetic biology research centres and has been funded by various means since 2015. It developed in response to, and in collaboration with, the international community of synthetic biologists, more specifically those who have pursued efforts to make research and innovation 'open'. For the purposes of this chapter, the most important 'open' things that matter are the DNA constructs, which synthetic biologists intend to share amongst themselves as part of a system of distributed innovation, relying on a modular approach to biological design. Earlier scholars have already investigated what forms of openness were imagined by synthetic biologists at its origins.[52] Luis Campos observed that the synthetic biologists who most engaged in IP discourse did not necessarily do so out of a prior direct engagement with IP law, but through a more general discussion about what collaborative and 'open' synthetic biology might be, and how it could work.[53] The case study focused on here and in the section that follows is a direct descendant of the activities that Campos addressed, which took place between 2000 and 2011 and concerned the formation of the BioBricks Foundation (BBF) and the BioBricks Public Agreement (BPA). His description of the problems facing those who would make boundary objects of DNA constructs uses the same kind of parallel thinking explored throughout this chapter, between plants and DNA constructs:

> Although earlier generations of plant breeders and other associated biological engineers had struggled with how to provide IP protection for sexually reproducing species whose continuity of traits could not be assured with the technology of the time, in the case of the Registry [of DNA constructs] not only was the ontological status of the parts it contained unclear, but their *empirical* status was often unclear as well: just what was in the aliquot containers in deep freeze?[54]

Synthetic biology's DNA constructs are open-ended boundary objects, and as such are somewhat unruly. This is thanks not only to how heterogenous the category is, or how many kinds of producer might make them, but also because their possible uses are intentionally very open ended. In these respects, DNA constructs make

[52] Nadine Levin and Sabina Leonelli, 'How Does One "Open" Science? Questions of Value in Biological Research' (2016) 42 *Science, Technology, & Human Values* 280.
[53] Luis Campos, 'The BioBrick™ road' (2012) 7 *BioSocieties* 115.
[54] ibid § 122.

population plant varieties look perfectly disciplined. Campos, writing in 2012, ended on a relatively cautious note with regard to the BBF's IP ambitions. The case study presented here manages to continue the BBF's history with some profound consequences.

Jane Calvert and Emma Frow have made further important observations of IP activity and discourse in synthetic biology, which help contextualize the ambitions of OpenPlant. Emma Frow's incorporation of a moral economies analysis into this space has been very fruitful, and also provides further means by which to think across the two cases of plant breeding and parts building presented here.[55] Calvert, also writing around 2021, was similarly cautious about the future for those trading objects that are both eminently patentable and also intended to be refined and shared in a system of distributed innovation.[56] The case study here concerns an example of synthetic biologists aiming squarely at this problem. While the International Genetically Engineered Machine (iGEM) competition is not discussed here, Calvert's recognition of the role played by that institution, intending to prove principles of biological engineering, should be kept in mind, not least because all the people studied in this case were direct contributors to iGEM.[57] Ten years on, Calvert's warnings that many elements shared through iGEM are already the subject of patent claims, leaving distributors open to potential accusations of infringement, have not yet materialized as legal problems for the organization. In order for the DNA constructs of interest to these actors to circulate as boundary objects, they had to develop standards by which to name and construct them, precisely the kind of activity that both iGEM and the BBF support and inspire. In the case of OpenPlant, this was the specific responsibility of Nicola Patron, who, as we shall see, was also closely involved with the OpenMTA. Last, some members of OpenPlant, such as Jenny Molloy—who worked closely with Linda Kahl throughout the development of the OpenMTA—have also been particularly active in spheres of DIY-bio and citizen science, intending to make scientific resources more easily accessible.[58] How the OpenMTA complements and coordinates some of this work will be discussed in this case. Making a system of innovation work according to values and principles of one's own choosing requires a great deal of work that is not directly concerned with the law, or IP-narrow. Given this array of activity, Massimiliano Simons' observation that DIY-bio communities are often as

[55] Emma K Frow, 'Making Big Promises Come True? Articulating and Realizing Value in Synthetic Biology' (2013) 8 *BioSocieties* 432; Berris Charnley, 'Seeds Without Patents: Science and Morality in British Plant Breeding in the Long Nineteenth-century' (2013) 64 *Revue économique* 69.

[56] Jane Calvert, 'Ownership and Sharing in Synthetic Biology: A "Diverse Ecology" of the Open and the Proprietary?' (2012) 7 *BioSocieties* 169.

[57] Emma Frow and Jane Calvert, '"Can Simple Biological Systems Be Built from Standardized Interchangeable Parts?" Negotiating Biology and Engineering in a Synthetic Biology Competition' (2012) 5 *Engineering Studies* 42; Andrew S Balmer and Kate J Bulpin, 'Left to Their Own Devices: Post-ELSI, Ethical Equipment and the International Genetically Engineered Machine (iGEM) Competition' (2013) 8(3) *BioSocieties* 311.

[58] Ana Delgado, 'DIYbio: Making Things and Making Futures' (2013) 48 *Futures* 65.

much invested in anti-institutionalism as they are in democratization, and thus seek to make resources more accessible and easier to commodify, is also pertinent for characterizing this case.[59]

From this very short tour of the contextual origins of OpenPlant, we can immediately appreciate how many different elements are in play, be they repositories, standards, networks of distribution, or the diverse 'ecologies' of ownership and sharing, to use Calvert's phrase. To approach the case study, we need to narrow our view. While the overall OpenPlant project incorporates very many different researchers, at career stages ranging from postgraduate to professor, each with their own ambitions and interests, only some of them are directly connected to questions of IP. When it comes to the latter, a smaller collection of four key individuals have played the most important roles, and they will be introduced in the following section. However, in terms of providing the background for where OpenPlant came from, there is nevertheless a single contingent factor that helps to explain the particular ambitions of the project with regard to IP and the plant sciences, and that is the leader of the Cambridge contingent, Professor Jim Haseloff.

At precisely the same time that the PBI was being privatized, Haseloff was working in Canberra, Australia, at the Division of Plant Industry within the publicly funded Commonwealth Scientific and Industrial Research Organisation (CSIRO). His first significant engagement with IP occurred there, an episode that received some public interest through *New Scientist*.[60] Haseloff and a collaborator, Wayne Gerlach, had identified RNA enzymes that could be made to cleave specified sites of RNA.[61] Their innovation came to be referred to as 'gene shears', which then became the name of the company that CSIRO spun out on the foundations of Haseloff and Gerlach's work.[62] After CSIRO arranged for an exclusive licence for the technology with Groupe Limagrain (a large French cooperative for agricultural and horticultural seed production) on a pending patent, this deal was undermined by a counterclaim from Thomas Cech at the University of Colorado, who asserted that his own prior patent already covered this technology. The reporting on these matters in the scientific press caused significant controversy, not least thanks to Cech's status as a Nobel Prize laureate, which had been awarded that same year, all of which *Nature* felt it had to address.[63] A US patent was eventually awarded in

[59] Massimiliano Simons, '"Science Without Scientists": DIY Biology and the Renegotiation of the Life Sciences' in Dick Houtman, Stef Aupers, and Rudi Laermans (eds), *Science Under Siege: Contesting the Secular Religion of Scientism* (Palgrave Macmillan 2021) 155–78.

[60] 'Molecular shears to attack viral diseases' *New Scientist* (25 August 1989) 31; 'The controversy that sliced into the growing techniques of "gene shears"' *New Scientist* (21 October 1989) 31–32.

[61] Jim Haseloff and Wayne L Gerlach, 'Simple RNA Enzymes with New and Highly Specific Endoribonuclease Activities' (1989) 334 *Nature* 585.

[62] It is, of course, worth noting for how long a 'scissors' metaphor has existed in molecular biology, establishing a pattern that much CRISPR discourse and litigation have followed, even down to the influence and significance of whether work is recognized as Nobel Prize winning or not.

[63] John Maddox, 'The Great Gene Shears Story' (1989) 342 *Nature* 609.

1993,[64] by which time Johnson and Johnson had also partnered the Gene Shears company on equal terms with Limagrain. Further litigation was to follow in Europe as Gene Shears Pty Ltd again butted up against Cech patents through the latter's licensee Ribozyme Pharmaceuticals, Inc (RPI).[65] In a *PR Newswire* report, the chief executive of RPI, Dr Ralph E Christoffersen, was quoted as saying:

> We do not believe the Gene Shears patent covers those ribozymes that RPI presently has in clinical trials … Moreover, it is RPI's expectation that none of the allowed claims will be determined to cover RPI's chemically-stabilized synthetic ribozymes … We are extremely proud of our strong patent position. We hold over 100 issued or allowed patents worldwide, and we currently have over 100 additional patent applications pending.[66]

Such was the biotechnological world into which Haseloff's first patents entered, although he was not closely involved with the commercial developments of Gene Shears. In 1989, he left CSIRO for a research fellowship at Harvard, working on trans-splicing ribozymes,[67] before moving to Cambridge in 1993, where he became a professor of synthetic biology in 2015. His professorship coincided with the launch of OpenPlant, which was funded as one of the UK's six BBSRC—EPSRC Synthetic Biology Research Centres.[68] One of the most significant strands of the project was the design and launch of a novel MTA, one that, if it functioned as intended, would help more biological scientists contribute to bettering biologically engineered things, and indeed also make these into commercial products if they so wished. However, it would also allow scientists to contribute to the bettering of biologically engineered things *without* having to think at all about the kind of litigation that had plagued Gene Shears, if they preferred. In this case, in contrast with the agroecological one, it was not so much that the boundary objects themselves were all that different from the other DNA constructs already subject to trade and transfer at this time. Rather than a new means of objectification, what was needed was a new way of drawing boundaries between commercial and non-commercial DNA constructs.

[64] James P Haseloff and others, 'Ribozymes' US Patent Office 5,254,678 (1993) http://patft.uspto.gov/netacgi/nph-Parser?Sect1=PTO2&Sect2=HITOFF&u=%2Fnetahtml%2FPTO%2Fsearch-adv.htm&r=22&p=1&f=G&l=50&d=PTXT&S1=Haseloff.INNM.&OS=IN/(Haseloff)&RS=IN/Haseloff (accessed 8 May 2021).

[65] 'Genetic engineering tool patented by Australians' *Reuters News* (21 October 1993) 188 words.

[66] 'RPI Disputes Gene Shears' Claim Regarding European Ribozyme Patent' *PR Newswire* (28 January 2000) 536.

[67] Uwe Köhler and others, 'Trans-splicing Ribozymes for Targeted Gene Delivery' (1999) 285 *Journal of Molecular Biology* 1935.

[68] Their activities are well documented here. See https://www.openplant.org (accessed 8 May 2021).

The OpenMTA

Without diminishing the contributions of too many other people, it is safe to say that the primary driving forces behind the making and shaping of what became the OpenMTA were Dr Linda Kahl, of the BioBricks Foundation (BBF), Prof Jim Haseloff and Dr Jenny Molloy of the University of Cambridge, and Dr Nicola Patron of the Earlham Institute. The latter three each participated in a recorded interview about their ambitions and motivations for the OpenPlant project. There were also numerous opportunities to discuss the OpenMTA with Linda Kahl, although these were informal and not recorded.

The initial proposal to focus on MTAs was brought into OpenPlant at the project's very beginning in 2015, by the BBF's Linda Kahl. From that point onwards, Linda worked closely with Molloy to design an alternative. Kahl brought to the group her research into the effects of MTAs on scientific research practices, the different kinds of MTA currently available, and an initial proposal for what a new one would look like. A draft discussion paper building on this work was written up by Kahl, Molloy, and Haseloff, and presented at OpenPlant's first project conference in July that year. It was also subject to dedicated discussion at this same event through a working group session. MTAs had been on Kahl's radar at least as early as 2013, identified as one of a number of factors making life more difficult for biological engineers who wished to share their DNA constructs around the world while exerting few, sometimes any, rights or expectations concerning their future use.[69] What mattered in particular was that existing MTAs would prevent users from incorporating transferred materials into a commercial product, or prevent users from sharing them with commercial partners. This was the key sticking point and framed the matter in terms of freedom to operate:

> As the scale of commercial biosystems are rapidly increasing, patent 'thickets' and proliferating cross-licensing arrangements are becoming problematic, even for large pharma and agrochemical companies, and can be crippling for small companies. Innovation in a young field like synthetic biology requires freedom to operate. We believe steps to facilitate free exchange of DNA parts and tools will substantially speed the take-up of new technologies in plant synthetic biology, and foster innovation and entrepreneurship in the UK.[70]

[69] Linda J Kahl and Drew Endy, 'A Survey of Enabling Technologies in Synthetic Biology' (2013) 7 *Journal of Biological Engineering* 1. The same wording was then also incorporated into the public report.

[70] Jim Haseloff, Jenny Molloy, and Linda J Kahl, 'IP Discussion Paper' (24 July 2015), shared with members of the OpenPlant IP working group. This same wording was also then incorporated into the public report, 'Towards and Open Material Transfer Agreement: OpenPlant IP Working Group Report' https://www.openplant.org/s/OpenMTA-Report.pdf (accessed 10 May 2021).

Haseloff would also often express concern about how such a system could be made to succeed in the face of large and litigious biotechnology and agricultural companies, often referencing Philip Howard's 2009 study of the seeds industry.[71] Just as agroecologists sought to create legal space for the diversity of value to them, so too did OpenPlant.[72] The language of a 'two-tier' system was developed, a particular contribution of Haseloff:

> The intention of OpenPlant is to promote innovation using a two-tier system for IP management. While freedom to operate is necessary for foundational technologies, the commercial applications and products that will be built upon these foundational technologies require investment in development, production and distribution for which IP protection is usually necessary. This two-tier model for IP management involves a decision about which route is most appropriate for a given technology to achieve its desired impact. Low-level technologies with little commercial value in isolation or with high potential to spur innovation are made available openly, while high-value applications may be patented or otherwise protected.

The logic of a two-tier system maps perfectly onto the 'foundational' versus 'near-market' logic of the 1980s. One could say, then, that the OpenMTA was both a confirmation of—and a reaction against—the steady accretion of near-market concerns into foundational spaces (according to the terms of such a framework). This is because, by 2015, a distributed innovation model of biological engineering had become almost impossible to practise with actual commercial intent. While plant breeders, for instance, had long avoided this problem for themselves through breeders' rights exemptions (which some countries also extend over plant patents),[73] OpenPlant and synthetic biology had no equivalent. While the final form of the eventual OpenMTA was the result of conversation and debate with members of this working group, and it also underwent a global request for comments process, the final adopted version was nevertheless heavily based on Kahl's original.[74]

The OpenMTA was a crucial part of OpenPlant's further plans, to ensure that plant DNA constructs underwent a process of more thorough objectification at this time. In the same year that the project was launched, a new international standard for naming and building with plant DNA constructs was released, an initiative led

[71] Philip H Howard, 'Visualizing Consolidation in the Global Seed Industry: 1996–2008' (2009) 1 *Sustainability* 1266.

[72] Fernán Federici and others, 'Synthetic Biology: Opportunities for Chilean Bioindustry and Education' (2013) 46 *Biological Research* 383.

[73] Viola Prifti, 'The Breeding Exemption in Patent Law: Analysis of Compliance with Article 30 of the TRIPS Agreement' (2013) 16 *The Journal of World Intellectual Property* 218.

[74] https://www.praxisauril.org.uk/news-policy/news/open-material-transfer-agreement-openmta-call-review-and-comment (accessed 23 May 2021).

by Nicola Patron.[75] The availability of such a syntax, inspired by earlier BioBrick standards proposed by Drew Endy and others, is intended to make it easier for those labs that opt in to using it to share their materials with registries and have these travel between a large number of different labs without losing an understanding of precisely what was being shared, or the kinds of thing it was meant to do. Further infrastructural matters also had to be dealt with, including the development of IP-free plasmids for the physical transfer of these constructs, which were themselves dependent on the OpenMTA to function as intended.[76] This is to say nothing of the numerous initiatives Molloy pursued in parallel, including the Open Enzyme Collection and the Public Domain Gazette, co-founded with Kahl, which were intended to increase IP transparency for smaller commercial actors.[77] There is vastly more that could be discussed concerning this overall project, and the hope is that future researchers will give the case further attention.

The final version of the OpenMTA was eventually launched in 2018. It can be found easily online and the authors remain open to receiving comments.[78] The most significant terms for those adopting the OpenMTA are those concerning distribution and licences:

> Distribution: The Recipient may distribute the Material and substances created by the Recipient through use of the Material, including Progeny, Unmodified Derivatives, and Modifications, without requesting consent from the Provider. Recipient agrees to notify the Provider of any distributions of the Material to third parties as requested by the Provider. Any request for notification will be specified in an implementing letter.
>
> No Implied License: Except for the rights expressly granted herein, the Recipient agrees that no other rights or licenses, whether express or implied, are granted to the Recipient under any patent, patent application, or other proprietary right of the Provider. As between the parties, each retains all right, title, and interest in works and inventions made by its personnel, and nothing herein shall be construed to transfer ownership of any invention, patent, patent application, or other proprietary right.

Here in a nutshell are the terms that enable a 'two-tier' model to function, so that those wanting to dip into and work on materials that have some proprietary interest attached to them can do so, and likewise, ship them out of their own lab to someone else's, while leaving paths to eventual patents open. The matter for

[75] Nicola J Patron and others, 'Standards for Plant Synthetic Biology: A Common Syntax for Exchange of DNA Parts' (2015) 208 *New Phytologist* 13.

[76] Bernardo Pollak and others, 'Loop Assembly: A Simple and Open System for Recursive Fabrication of DNA Circuits' (2018) 222 *New Phytologist* 628.

[77] https://publicdomaingazette.org/ (accessed 21 May 2021).

[78] Linda Kahl and others, 'Opening Options for Material Transfer' (2018) 36 *Nature Biotechnology* 923.

working out what, when, where, and how to apportion IP interests when patents do come to be sought, is largely left for the community of researchers to determine between one another, just as plant breeders are expected to keep one another honest about derivative varieties. In summary, we can understand the regulatory problems confronting the sharing of DNA constructs as having been dealt with by drawing two different kinds of boundary: one for material transferred *only* by users of the OpenMTA and *without* the requirement that they be used exclusively with non-commercial intent, and the other around material transferred by some other MTA, with all the usual caveats as to commercial use.

Last, by the time of launch, the freedom to operate framing had taken on a further gloss, emphasizing that this freedom was being secured on behalf of smaller, less well-funded actors around the world—including non-profits such as the GrowMore foundation—which can redistribute open parts at lower cost and without concerns for licences.[79] It remains the case that the most pressing aim is to cultivate a larger number of smaller businesses, removed from the shadow of big biotech. If in these ambitions there is some underlying hope for democratization, then there exists a pressure-point on which scholars and publics can rightly press, regarding what democratization might mean and what else it might require.

Conclusion: Constructing New Cultures of Innovation

The two cases of agricultural and biological innovation from recent history presented here might each be considered illustrative or significant in numerous ways. From this perspective, understanding why these things happened as they did builds on the insights of MacLeod and Radick, which inspired this investigation in the first place.[80] The anxieties of the actors in both of these cases stemmed from the fact that existing laws, regulations, protocols, etc did not sufficiently recognize, nor consider, the kinds of materials, values, and behaviours that these communities recognized as important. Instead—these actors might now say—parts of IP-narrow were occluding parts of IP-broad. This is the case whenever a pure-line variety is treated more seriously than a population variety because the 'design' of populations is so open ended, in contrast with a pure line. Effort, planning, investment, and assessment go on in both. The capacity of IP-narrow to occlude IP-broad is all the clearer in synthetic biology cases whenever, for instance, a licence agreement picks out a particular individual as a DNA construct's originator, regardless of whatever labour from others had gone into characterizing it in the first place. Alternatively, our actors might say that the ways in which aspects of science and biology have come to be defined for the purposes of IP-narrow have marginalized

[79] My thanks to Nicola Patron for this example of the kind of non-profit that OpenPlant has in mind.
[80] MacLeod and Radick (n 4).

or diminished aspects of science and biology that are otherwise readily recognized, if we make sure to also look for IP-broad. This would be the case for biological variability and genetic heterogeneity in the case of agroecology, and for the kinds of organism or system that can be created if we emphasize biological modularity and standardization in synthetic biology. Heterogeneity does not fit into the imagined world of commercial plant breeding defined by existing international regulations, just as a swappable, modular distributed collection of commercializable DNA constructs does not fit into the imagined world of MTAs. Cultures of innovation recognize more IP than only that codified in law. In unpacking these cases through the terms of IP-broad, we see that ownership claims, productivity claims, and priority claims were front and centre in both cases.

For the agroecologists, ownership claims concerned the background breeding work that went into producing population varieties, an effort shared with the JIC. Investing in these biological materials with the intention of selling them to farmers placed the ORC and Pearce in a novel situation, requiring that they work out the marketing and begin planning for whatever longer-term commercial activity might be possible beyond the trial exemption. Regarding productivity claims, we look to their critiques of large multinational companies, concerning the damage that monocrop agriculture does to the environment, its threats to the future of biodiversity, and the productive potentials bound up with breeding for diversity. Diverse population varieties, so the argument goes, will be better able to adapt to local climates over many years of growth, and will produce more diversity as they are propagated over time. The way in which priority plays out is particularly interesting, given that the intention is not to assert priority for some key contributors, but instead to acknowledge that varietal material is decidedly (and valuably) unfinished: in other words, a distributed innovation model all of its own.

For the synthetic biologists, ownership claims were of course very important, as they wished to increase the number of people in distinct laboratory spaces working with materials that *might* go on to become the subject of IP-narrow claims. But, not knowing which, when, or why any given DNA construct might make this transformation, they sought to create greater flexibility, 'opening up' ownership to increase the number of potential future commercial actors. Productivity claims are central to everything that the synthetic biologist does, and moreover, also matter for how they characterize their science as a science. Organizing things by standards, reducing the friction involved in transferring materials between groups, and so on, are all intended to make a more productive science, not just valuable innovations. Finally, priority claims are rife, but are by and large played out in publications and presentations rather than necessarily through IP-narrow. Given the way in which this system of distributed innovation is intended to work, it remains to be seen whether synthetic biologists will be aggrieved or satisfied by their participation in the development of innovations in which they may or may not gain explicit stakes or recognition. As a field, however, synthetic biology has often increased effort to recognize kinds of labour (such as the making of protocols or designing laboratory workflows) that other cultures of molecular biology typically overlook. Thus, there is a chance that things can be made to work as intended, and the heat kept out of priority disputes by asserting different norms.

Agroecology and synthetic biology are both dealing with legacies of regulation and policy that took shape between the mid-1960s and the 1980s. They are also both ostensibly dealing with historical interpretations of those periods, and the lessons they are thought to hold. This chapter has emphasized the non-naturalness of a firm distinction between fundamental and near-market breeding, and the need to consider plant breeding and seed production as a large, integrated system. On these terms, the ORC's activities in the early 2000s have been cast as something of a strange and unexpected revival of public-sector plant breeding in the UK, even if only on a very small scale. Likewise, the synthetic biologists are dealing with legacies of the Thatcher era, and the emphasis placed on exploiting potential IP to the maximum possible extent. Rather than challenge this logic entirely, their strategy has been to reform things from within. In their eyes, it is too often the case that large commercial actors have been able to exert control on research that is both somewhat fundamental and yet also potentially near market. The OpenMTA acts as a pressure valve for DNA constructs, much as the breeder's exemption does for varieties.

If breeding for diversity attracts further practitioners, and comes to be a sustainable contributor to seed production systems around the world, then there may come a need to address the disparity that now exists in EU law regarding PBRs. If it were possible to trace population varieties for the purposes of the trial exemption, it is difficult to see why such a system could not also be used to help organize and collect royalty payments. Of course, given their aims for acclimatization, population varieties also open up a vast array of possibilities concerning how ongoing breeding and multiplication work is organized, and who is primarily responsible for it, making the farmer a much more central figure. Policy-makers dealing with agriculture might do well to conceive of such farmers as contributing to a system of distributed innovation, much like synthetic biologists.

12

Creating New Values in Animals in the Era of Mendel's Rediscovery

Brendan Matz

Introduction

North Americans began to import purebred livestock in large numbers during the first half of the nineteenth century. These so-called improved breeds were often crossed to produce new varieties or used to transform domestic stock through grading.[1] However, a growing group of agriculturalists maintained the breeds in their purity by only mating animals whose ancestry could be traced back to the breed's foundational families and geographic origins. Breed histories were often murky and definitions of purity changed over time, but standards for genealogical documentation and the outward appearance of animals had begun to take shape by the middle of the century. This system of evaluation based on pedigree and physical form developed out of a need to establish the identity of breeding animals in the marketplace.

Without some guarantee of authenticity, purebred livestock could not be properly differentiated from other animals and would therefore not garner appropriate prices. In the years following the Civil War, the problem of obtaining remunerative prices for skilled breeding work became more acute, as deliberate misrepresentation of pedigrees increased. Breeders' associations were created primarily to address the issue of fraud, and they succeeded to some degree in promoting higher prices for certified stock. Yet the prevalence of market fads and fluctuations eventually led to calls for more objective approaches to the selection of breeding animals. During the first decade and a half of the twentieth century, breeders began to advocate for evaluation based on the measurement and experimental testing of clearly defined performance characteristics. The rise of breeders' associations and the shift to a performance ideal following 1900 demonstrate an increasing awareness among American agriculturalists of the

[1] Crossing involved the breeding of two distinct breeds that were believed or known to 'breed true', or produce offspring with a clearly defined set of physical characteristics. Grading involved the breeding of a distinct breed, usually introduced from abroad, with local, unpedigreed livestock.

Brendan Matz, *Creating New Values in Animals in the Era of Mendel's Rediscovery* In: *Intellectual Property and the Design of Nature.* Edited by: Jose Bellido and Brad Sherman, Oxford University Press.
DOI: 10.1093/oso/9780192864406.003.0012

need for what would now be called intellectual property, such as protection in the domestic market for purebred livestock. Although animal breeders did not use the term 'intellectual property' during the period considered here, the arrangements that they devised suggest that they often recognized the importance of protecting their investment of breeding skill and knowledge within competitive markets. The growing body of literature on the history of animal breeding supports the position that agriculturalists within various national contexts developed their practices with a concept of intellectual property in mind.[2] The aim here is to show that in order to be in a position where this was possible, breeders first had to develop mechanisms that allowed them to identify and differentiate the innovative results of their breeding efforts. As will be seen below, while the systems of evaluation based on pedigree and physical form, and the corresponding shift to a performance ideal, may have provided the framework to allow this to happen with certain types of animals, for others the process was incomplete.

Livestock Prices, Pedigree Fraud, and the System of Breeders' Associations

In 1846, Lewis F Allen, an uncle of Grover Cleveland, successful insurance agent, arborist, and livestock enthusiast with 800 acres of land on Grand Island, New York, established the first registry for purebred livestock in the United States.[3] During the 1830s, American Shorthorn breeders had to submit their pedigrees to a British herd book if they wanted their animals publicly registered. Allen saw that, by the early 1840s, a sufficient number of purebred, high-quality Shorthorns and their breeders existed in the United States to sustain a public record at home. With the support and help of other Shorthorn men, he created a registry that allowed Americans to avoid the expense, inconvenience, and logistical difficulties of British registration. This American Herd Book promised to improve the nation's herds and provide domestic buyers with certified animals bred or owned by Americans.[4]

[2] See eg Daniel J Kevles, 'Patents, Protections, and Privileges: The Establishment of Intellectual Property in Animals and Plants' (2007) 98 *Isis* 323 (hereafter Kevles); Glenn Bugos, 'Intellectual Property Protection and the American Chicken-breeding Industry' (1992) 66 *Business History Review* 127.

[3] 'Obituary Lewis Falley Allen' *The New York Times* (3 May 1890) 4.

[4] Lewis F Allen, 'An American Herd Book' *The Cultivator* (May 1844) 158.

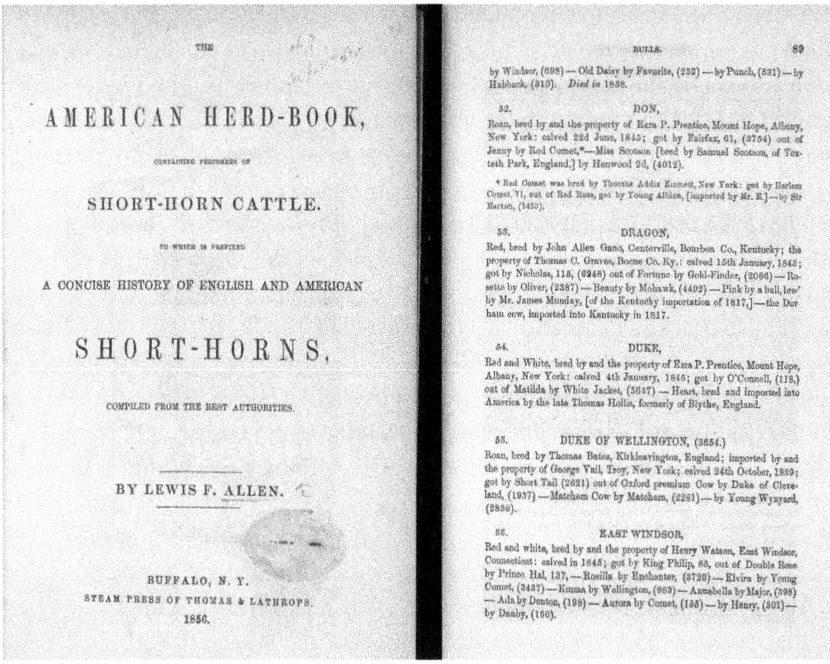

THE

AMERICAN HERD-BOOK,

CONTAINING PEDIGREES OF

SHORT-HORN CATTLE.

TO WHICH IS PREFIXED

A CONCISE HISTORY OF ENGLISH AND AMERICAN

SHORT-HORNS,

COMPILED FROM THE BEST AUTHORITIES.

BY LEWIS F. ALLEN.

BUFFALO, N. Y.
STEAM PRESS OF THOMAS & LATHROPS.
1856.

BULLS. 89

by Windsor, (698) — Old Daisy by Favorite, (252) — by Punch, (531) — by Hubback, (319). *Died in* 1838.

52. DON,

Roan, bred by and the property of Ezra P. Prentice, Mount Hope, Albany, New York: calved 22d June, 1845; got by Fairfax, 61, (3754) out of Jenny by Red Comet,*—Miss Scotson [bred by Samuel Scotson, of Toxteth Park, England,] by Henwood 2d, (4012).

* Red Comet was bred by Thomas Addis Emmett, New York: got by Harlem Comet, 71, out of Red Rose, got by Young Albion, [imported by Mr. E.]—by Sir Marton, (1453).

53. DRAGON,

Red, bred by John Allen Gano, Centerville, Bourbon Co., Kentucky; the property of Thomas C. Graves, Boone Co. Ky.: calved 15th January, 1845; got by Nicholas, 115, (6248) out of Fortune by Gold-Finder, (2066) — Rosette by Oliver, (2387) — Beauty by Mohawk, (4492) — Pink by a bull, bred by Mr. James Munday, [of the Kentucky importation of 1817,]—the Durham cow, imported into Kentucky in 1817.

54. DUKE,

Red and White, bred by and the property of Ezra P. Prentice, Mount Hope, Albany, New York: calved 4th January, 1845; got by O'Connell, (118,) out of Matilda by White Jacket, (5647) — Heart, bred and imported into America by the late Thomas Hollis, formerly of Blythe, England.

55. DUKE OF WELLINGTON, (3654.)

Roan, bred by Thomas Bates, Kirkleavington, England; imported by and the property of George Vail, Troy, New York; calved 24th October, 1839; got by Short Tail (2621) out of Oxford premium Cow by Duke of Cleveland, (1937) —Matchem Cow by Matchem, (2281) — by Young Wynyard, (2859).

56. EAST WINDSOR,

Red and white, bred by and the property of Henry Watson, East Windsor, Connecticut: calved in 1845; got by King Philip, 85, out of Double Rose by Prince Hal, 137, — Rosilla by Enchanter, (3729) — Elvira by Young Comet, (3437) — Emma by Wellington, (683) — Annabella by Major, (398) — Ada by Denton, (198) — Aurora by Comet, (155) — by Henry, (301) — by Danby, (190).

Figure 12.1 Lewis Allen's *American Herd Book* (cover and page 89) 1856.
Courtesy © The British Library Board.

Perhaps more importantly, it established a degree of protection for the investment of craft skill by breeders. Allen recognized the significance of this latter aspect of his project and stressed that successful breeders invested *intellectual* as well as physical labour in the shaping of their animals: 'To breed successfully, requires skill, talent, research, observation; and all of these of a high order'. However, unless breeders received proper incentives for innovation and the preservation of valuable breed characteristics, the quality of animals and the integrity of the business of breeding would be compromised. On this key point he wrote: 'Talent and labor of this kind cannot be had for nothing; and without remunerating prices be maintained, the downfall of the Short Horns in America will sooner or later be at hand.'[5] For Allen and like-minded breeders of purebred livestock, the creation of animals with distinct, desirable, features required a carefully policed registry that ensured some monetary reward for meticulous research and skill.

[5] Lewis F Allen, *The American Herd Book, Containing Pedigrees of Short Horn Cattle*, vol 1 (Press of Jewett, Thomas & Co 1846) 84. Allen was not alone in his concern about Shorthorn prices. See eg 'The American Herd-Book' *The Western Farmer and Gardener* (October 1844) 59.

Purebreds were valuable not only for the characteristics they exhibited—such as early maturity, ease of fattening, and high milk production—but also for their ability to pass on those characteristics reliably to offspring. Herd books were designed to help establish prices in the marketplace commensurate with this inherent value by publicly identifying individual animals by name, date of birth, distinctive markings, breeder, owner, and pedigree. Theoretically, no other animal could have the same published profile and actual genealogy, so business transactions over long distances could be conducted with a guarantee of authenticity. Herd book registration assured buyers that they had the genuine article; as a result, they were more likely to buy from breeders who used only the purest blood and could prove it with documentation. The high demand for a limited supply of pure specimens would therefore lead to sufficient compensation for the skilled breeder's knowledge work. The key components of this work were the identification of superior breeding animals, the culling of offspring that deviated from a breed standard or individual ideal, and the fixing of characteristics in the herd through a combination of inbreeding and out-crossing. Success in the profession required skilled eyes and hands and a craft-based understanding of the principles of biological heredity.[6]

Yet the maintenance of remunerative prices for skillfully bred animals remained a serious problem for breeders, motivating them to develop new forms of what can be viewed as intellectual property protection. By the time of the Civil War, fraud was becoming a persistent problem in rural America, as traditional social relationships in the country were strained by industrialization. During what historians have referred to as the 'golden age of deception', rural Americans became prey to an array of deceptive business practices. Arriving from afar on new types of transportation like the railroad and the steamboat, perpetrators of fraud were not known by the members of the community and often disappeared after making their sales.[7] In addition to travelling peddlers of bogus fruit trees and seeds, rural Americans encountered unscrupulous animal breeders and dealers who tried to palm off their inferior specimens as high-quality purebreds. After the Civil War, the disruption of provincial, community-centred life became more acute. Political unity gave rise to a national market for the exchange of goods and services, and the agricultural economy began to grow dramatically. In the midst of this shift towards a more

[6] The understanding here of the knowledge work performed by American breeders during the second half of the nineteenth century is based on a reading of numerous breeding handbooks and treatises published at the time. See eg SL Goodale, *The Principles of Breeding, or Glimpses at the Physiological Laws Involved in the Reproduction and Improvement of Domestic Animals* (Crosby, Nichols, Lee and Company 1861); and Manly Miles, *Stockbreeding: A Practical Treatise on the Applications of the Laws of Development and Heredity to the Improvement and Breeding of Domesticated Animals* (D Appleton and Company 1879).

[7] On the problem of fraud in rural America during the second half of the nineteenth century see Earl W Hayter, *The Troubled Farmer 1850–1900: Rural Adjustment to Industrialism* (Northern Illinois University Press 1968), quotation at 10.

atomistic capitalist economy, agriculturalists formed voluntary associations to protect their interests and foster a degree of cooperation.[8]

The creation of the first breeders' associations took place within this dynamic context, as breeders of purebred animals called for greater protection against misrepresentation in the market. It was well known that the sale of a grade or a scrub as purebred diminished the value of genuine animals sold by scrupulous breeders.[9] Moreover, the deceptive introduction of such animals into competitions at agricultural fairs took away their rightful prize money and bragging rights. Buyers often paid higher prices for prizewinning animals and their descendants, so breeders used such distinctions in their marketing.[10] To combat fraud, the associations collected and carefully vetted pedigrees and published them in association herd and flock books. Buyers could refer to the books in making their decisions, and through this public documentation they received proof of an animal's identity, ancestry, and, theoretically, its quality. Associations sought to establish a business climate of trust and integrity and appealed to the moral character of their members. By joining the association, one declared common interest with other breeders and gained incentive to report genealogical information truthfully.[11] Membership fees and fees for each registered animal (and, in some cases, the requirement that prospective members be recommended by an established breeder) provided added assurance that all but the most serious and upright men would be included in the cooperative enterprise.[12] One agricultural journalist emphasized the 'irresistible moral power' of breeders' associations and described their efforts as the 'only available means of security against fraud both in blood and pedigree'.[13] Indeed, in the absence of more formal IP protection, these communities and their respective animal registries provided breeders with a sense of security and allowed for some control of market prices.

[8] The classic treatment of the shift away from the community-centred society of the early nineteenth century to a modern industrialized society is Robert H Wiebe, *The Search for Order 1877–1920* (Hill and Wang 1967). On the development of the American agricultural economy in the years following the Civil War see Alan L Olmstead and Paul W Rhode, *Creating Abundance: Biological Innovation and American Agricultural Development* (Cambridge University Press 2008) 1–16; and Sidney Ratner, James L Soltow, and Richard Sylla, *The Evolution of the American Economy: Growth, Welfare, and Decision Making* (Basic Books 1979) 255–74. On the proliferation of agricultural voluntary associations see Wayne Caldwell Neely, *The Agricultural Fair* (Columbia 1935) 102–103.

[9] See eg 'Cattle Breeders' Convention' *American Farmer's Magazine* (May 1859) 272. Grades were the product of a cross between a domestic and a purebred animal; 'scrub' was the name given to the often poorly performing domestic livestock.

[10] See eg 'Pure Bred Stock at Private Sale' *Ohio Cultivator* (15 April 1854) 127.

[11] See Barbara Orland, 'Turbo Cows: Producing a Competitive Animal in the Nineteenth and Early Twentieth Centuries' in Susan R Schrepfer and Philip Scranton (eds), *Industrializing Organisms: Introducing Evolutionary History* (Routledge 2004) 179. Orland argues that breeders' associations encouraged the breeding community to regulate and discipline themselves. See also Kevles (n 2) 327. Kevles refers to 'the collective IP of the cartel of breeders'.

[12] See 'Constitution of the American Jersey Cattle Club' in *Herd Register of the American Jersey Cattle Club*, vol 1 (1871).

[13] 'Cattle Breeders' Association' *American Farmer's Magazine* (May 1859) 269. The cattle breeders' appeal to morality suggests that the constitution of any body of knowledge—in this case, genealogical

In addition to investigating the accuracy of pedigrees, associations established scales of points, or standards for the appearance of the breed. These exacting descriptions of the proper conformation of purebred animals served as a guide to breeders, buyers, and judges at fairs.[14] The rich visual culture of which the standards were a part helped to educate the attention of breeders and buyers and provided models of good breeding.[15] With the establishment of herd books and associations, breeders also began to pay artists to produce engravings suitable for inclusion along with pedigrees. These mass-produced images served to further identify, differentiate, and advertise specific animals and their descendants in the marketplace.[16]

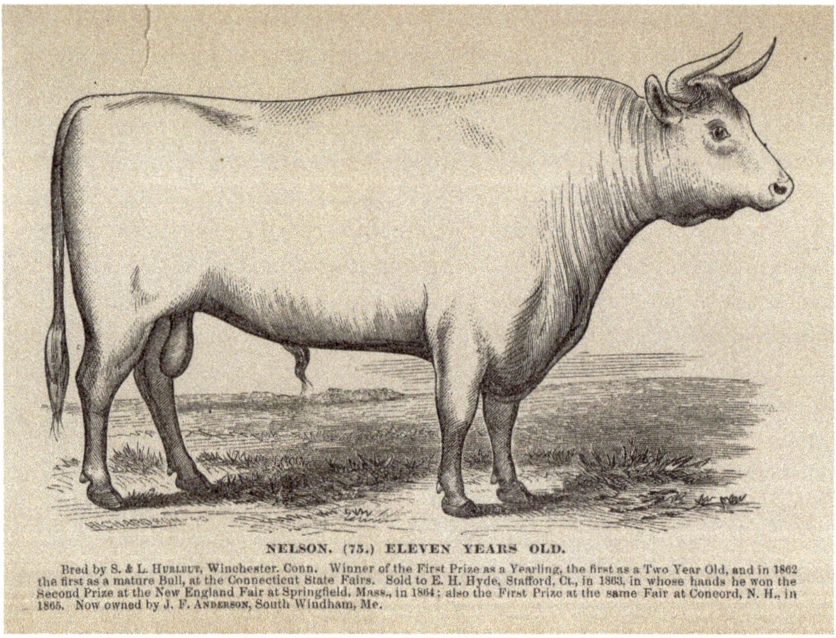

Figure 12.2 'Nelson Bull' *American Devon Herd book*, vol 1, 1863.
Courtesy of the New York Public Library.

information about purebred livestock and the theory of heredity used to make sense of it—requires the identification of trustworthy agents. See Steven Shapin, *A Social History of Truth: Civility and Science in Seventeenth-Century England* (University of Chicago Press 1994), esp xxv–xxxi.

14 Conformation is the shape, size, and symmetry of an animal's visible parts and its overall structure.

15 See Cristina Grasseni, 'Good Looking: Learning to be a Cattle Breeder' in Cristina Grasseni (ed), *Skilled Visions: Between Apprenticeship and Standards* (Berghahn Books 2007) 53–54; Ron Broglio, *Technologies of the Picturesque: British Art, Poetry, and Instruments, 1750–1830* (Bucknell University Press 2008) 174–81.

16 See Association of Breeders of Thorough-Bred Neat Stock, *American Devon Herd Book*, vol 1, frontispiece. The *American Devon Herd Book* included two images in its first volume: an etching of a bull

Figure 12.3 'Devon Cow' *American Devon Herd book*, vol 1, 1863.
Courtesy of the New York Public Library.

Associations and their herd books provided moderately strong intellectual property protection for honest breeders. Although more research is necessary in this area, it appears that exclusive associations, with their committee-supervised vetting of pedigrees, did in fact diminish fraud and establish remunerative pricing of animals in many cases. For example, a representative of the Vermont Merino Sheep Breeders' Association remarked in 1877: 'Already great benefit has been realized by owners of flocks that have been accepted for registration, as such sheep now command at least twice the price of sheep of equal apparent quality, but of doubtful pedigree.'[17]

and one of a cow. Inscriptions included beneath the etchings provided details about the animal's ancestry, its owner, and breeder, and prizes awarded at fairs. See also 'Portraits of Animals' *Prairie Farmer* (September 1854) 353; and E Hersey Derby, 'The "Oakes Cow" and her Portrait' *The Cultivator* (January 1859) 30.

[17] Albert Chapman, 'The Vermont Merino Sheep Breeders' Association' in *Fourth Report of the Vermont Board of Agriculture for the Year 1877* (J & JM Poland 1877) 203.

Figure 12.4 'Vermont Merino Sheep' *Trade Card, circa* 1906.
Courtesy of the Vermont Historical Society.

The IP protection afforded by the association model goes a long way towards explaining its spread in the late nineteenth century and its persistence up to the present day. By 1945, eighteen breed associations for cattle, eighteen for sheep, and nine for swine had been formed in the United States. Headquartered largely in the Northeast and Midwest, the associations gradually aligned themselves with the meat, dairy, and wool production industries.[18]

Market Fads, the Performance Ideal, and State Intervention

Although the system of breeders' associations helped combat fraud and promoted higher prices for certified animals, purebred breeding remained a risky enterprise. Purebred sales results that began to appear in the press by the late nineteenth and early twentieth centuries reveal no set pattern of values, suggesting a volatile and unstable market.[19] Booms and busts had long been a feature of livestock breeding.

[18] On the spread and geographic distribution of the associations see Olmstead and Rhode (n 8) 289–91.

[19] For a discussion of this market volatility in Canada see Margaret Derry, *Ontario's Cattle Kingdom: Purebred Breeders and Their World, 1870–1920* (University of Toronto Press 2001) 50–52. A survey of press on American sales suggests that American breeders experienced the same problem. See eg 'Purebred Livestock Sales' *The Breeder's Gazette* (22 November 1883, 710–711; and 'Supreme Shorthorn Sales', *Colman's Rural World* (29 August 1900, 4. For a discussion of the close relationship between corn and swine prices (the so-called 'corn-hog cycle') see Fred A Shannon, *The Farmer's Last Frontier: Agriculture, 1860–1897* (Rinehart and Company Inc 1945) 165–69.

For example, wild speculation in Merino sheep during the first decade of the nineteenth century drove prices up to thousands of dollars in some cases. Because the value of the animals was based on their continued scarcity, the speculative bubble burst when sheep imports flooded the market in 1810.[20] Speculation in other breeds over the course of the nineteenth century, including Poland China swine, led to similar market crashes where those who did not cash in early enough lost sizable investments.[21] Even during less frenzied times, the market for fine stock was characterized by shifting fashions. Buyers' preferences for characteristics like colour and for certain families within breeds played a significant part in determining sales and fixing prices.[22]

By the beginning of the twentieth century, the prevalence of fads and market volatility led many commentators to call for more objective standards of evaluation. To be sure, it was widely recognized that a breeder had to sell stock to stay in business and therefore had to satisfy the expectations of the customers. But buyers could be educated and shown that the application of science to breeding could pay. Eugene Davenport, the Dean of the College of Agriculture at the University of Illinois, and an influential commentator on livestock breeding, advised:

> In the matter of applying scientific principles to the business of practical breeding, one economic fact must be reckoned with—stock must be bred that will sell, and if that is done then the breeders must produce what people want. The desires of the buyer may all be wrong, and if so he should be educated to sane standards with as little delay as possible; but until he is corrected, he must be dealt with on his own terms.[23]

Davenport criticized the prevailing reliance of breeders on an animal's conformation in selection, arguing that the supposed correlations between external form and internal function were often spurious. Thinking like a Mendelian, he identified the 'single character' rather than the 'individual as a whole' as the 'real unit of study in all problems of heredity'.[24] By focusing on clearly defined performance

[20] See Carroll W Pursell, Jr., EI DuPont and the Merino Mania in Delaware 1805–1815' (1961) 36(2) *Agricultural History* 92, 95. During the Peninsular War, military juntas in Spain decided to sell the country's great flocks of Merinos, leading to the export of numerous breeding animals.

[21] See 'The Swine Pedigree Craze' *The Breeder's Gazette* (17 March 1897) 203.

[22] On colour and pedigree crazes among cattle breeders see Derry (n 19), 41–46. A good example of these shifting fashions was the refusal of American breeders of Shorthorns to buy white and roan animals because of a preference for red coat color.

[23] Eugene Davenport, 'The Breeding of Animals' in Liberty Hyde Bailey (ed), *Cyclopedia of American Agriculture*, vol 3 (The Macmillan Company 1908) 27.

[24] ibid 25. Jonathan Harwood points out that late nineteenth-century theories of heredity conceived of the individual as an integrated whole rather than as the sum of discrete traits. See Jonathan Harwood, 'Linkage before Mendelism? Plant-breeding research in Central Europe, c. 1880-1910' in Hans-Jörg Rheinberger and Jean-Paul Gaudillière (eds), *Classical Genetic Research and Its Legacy: The Mapping Cultures of Twentieth-Century Genetics* (Routledge 2004).

characteristics and on function rather than form and pedigree, the breeder could more objectively choose the breeding animals and judges could reward truly exceptional achievement at fairs. Whereas breeding based on form and pedigree tended to follow fashions and was conservative, breeding based on demonstrated performance was scientific and innovative. The latter also brought the enterprise of fine stock breeding into closer alignment with the requirements of industrial production of animal products. If buyers could be shown that purebreds increased one's profits in the production of commercial stock through grading, a strong market for high-quality surplus breeding animals could be guaranteed (further raising and stabilizing prices).[25]

It was hoped that breeders' associations would play a major role in educating buyers and engineering a shift towards the performance ideal. Associations for dairy cattle took the lead in this endeavour. As early as the 1880s, Solomon Hoxie, the Secretary of the Dutch Friesian Herd Book, began to experiment with alternatives to the standard form of animal registration. Rather than registering livestock based on purity of blood alone, his 'Advanced Registry' included only those animals that had demonstrated special individual merit. For bulls, merit was demonstrated by a series of measurements performed using instruments specially designed by Hoxie himself; for cows, tests of milk yield, and later, with the introduction of the Babcock method in the 1890s, butter fat content were conducted. Hoxie viewed the system as a tool for identifying superior breeding animals in a more objective manner. Moreover, he saw the compilation of reliable performance data as the necessary precursor to a science of cattle breeding.[26] Other breeders' associations instituted similar systems, providing breeders with a way to differentiate their animals further in the marketplace and buyers with valuable information about performance that probably influenced investment decisions.[27]

Associations for animals bred for meat took advantage of economic conditions around 1900 to further consolidate and expand the market for fine cattle, swine, and sheep. By the end of the nineteenth century, the meat production industry and its allies in Washington started to identify a looming problem: Livestock production was not keeping pace with the rapid increase in human population. With the

[25] For discussions of the shift to performance-based evaluation and the importance of selling purebred stock to commercial breeders for grading see Davenport (n 23) 27; Eugene Davenport, *Principles of Breeding: A Treatise on Thremmatology or the Principles and Practices Involved in the Economic Improvement of Domesticated Animals and Plants* (Ginn and Company 1907) 654–77; and Herbert W Mumford, *Beef Production* (Published by the Author 1907) 162–64.

[26] On Hoxie and the Advanced Registry see Jane L Hoxie, *Solomon Hoxie* (Published by the Author 1922) 72–87; and Frederick Lowell Houghton, *Holstein-Friesian Cattle: A History of the Breed and Its Development in America* (Press of the Holstein-Friesian Register 1897) 269–71.

[27] See William H Caldwell, 'Relation of Advanced Registry Work to Improvement in Breeding' in *American Breeders' Association Annual Report*, vol 2 (1906) 104–105; CM Winslow, 'Methods Used by the Ayrshire Breeders' Association in Perfecting the Breed' in *American Breeders Association Annual Report*, vol 4 (1908) 29–31.

closing of the frontier, the geographic area of production could not be extended.[28] As a result, industrialists and government officials began to call for a more intensive use of production capacity. A key element of this agenda was the encouragement of livestock feeders, producers of commercial stock, and small-scale farmers to use better breeding material. The breeders' associations argued that only purebred animals, which had always comprised only a small percentage of the total livestock population, could help the industry achieve the necessary efficiency and standardization.[29]

Along with representatives from the agricultural colleges, the agricultural press, and the railroad and livestock market interests of Chicago, the breeders' associations established the International Live Stock Exhibition at the Union Stock Yards in Chicago as a 'comprehensive means of forcibly presenting to the farmer and feeder the folly of producing inferior animals'.[30] The massive show, which took place annually and was financed in large part by the Union Stock Yard and Transit Company of Chicago, included a grand breeders' prize exhibition with daily sales of all breeds. The breeders' associations maintained their offices on the exhibition grounds and played a major role in establishing the standards of judging. Working with the agricultural colleges, the practical breeders devised a sophisticated system of animal evaluation that emphasized performance and the specific needs of industrial meat production. These needs included more comprehensive distinctions between different grades and classes of livestock. Winners of a yearly collegiate livestock judging competition were awarded an impressive trophy for 'the most efficient work in judging horse, cattle, hogs, and sheep'.[31] The exhibition was hailed as a success from its beginning, with the editors of the famed *Breeders' Gazette*

[28] The superintendent of the US Census had announced in 1890 that 'there can hardly be said to be a frontier line'.

[29] For an excellent discussion of the origins of intensive livestock production in the US see William Cronon, *Nature's Metropolis: Chicago and the Great West* (WW Norton and Company 1991) 207–62. However, Cronon places little emphasis on breeding. The meat packing industry's emphasis on efficiency and standardization coincided with the progressive reform agenda of the time. See eg David B Danbom, 'Rural Education Reform and the Country Life Movement, 1900-1920' (1979) 53 *Agricultural History* 462. According to the Bureau of Animal Industry Report for 1904, registered animals made up the following percentages of the total population: horses, 1.8 per cent; dairy cattle, 1.27 per cent; beef cattle, 1.04 per cent; sheep, 0.49 per cent, and hogs, 0.38 per cent. See *Bureau of Animal Industry Annual Report, 1904* (Washington 1905) 514. On the performance testing of animals bred for meat see 'Report of the Committee on Breeding for Meat Production' in *Proceedings of the American Breeders' Association*, vol 4 (1908) 180–81; and Andrew Boss, 'Testing Meat Producing Animals' in *Proceedings of the American Breeders' Association*, vol 2 (1906) 53–58. For a discussion of the various grades and classes of livestock in the meat industry see Rudolf Alexander Clemen, *The American Livestock and Meat Industry* (Ronald Press 1923) 481–86.

[30] See *Review and Album International Live Stock Exposition*, (Union Stock Yard 1913), quoted at 5. For a comprehensive history of the International see Alvin Howard Sanders, *The Story of the International Live Stock Exposition* (International Live Stock Exposition Association 1942).

[31] *Review and Album International Live Stock Exposition* (n 30) 33. On agricultural judging contests see LJ Briggs, 'Grading in Agricultural Judging Contests' (1907) 3 *Proceedings of the American Breeders' Association* 260.

remarking: 'Conjured up from the resources of a continent, the International Livestock Exposition sprang full-rounded into an astonishing existence.'[32]

Secretary of Agriculture James 'Tama Jim' Wilson represented the federal government at the International's second meeting in 1902 and voiced his enthusiastic support for the endeavour. The exposition fitted well into Wilson's agenda at the USDA, which included an effort to strengthen the scientific work of the department.[33] Indeed, he viewed the International as a welcome addition to the vast agricultural education and research infrastructure that America had built up since the establishment of the USDA in 1862. During his speech at the formal opening of the show, he remarked:

> [f]or the education of farmers and farmer's sons through experimental stations and agricultural researches we have more money at Washington than Harvard, Yale, the University of Chicago, and Stanford combined. We are trying to help the man everywhere in every part of the United States who raises things out of the ground.[34]

As important members of this group of agricultural producers, breeders of new plant varieties and pedigreed livestock received significant attention from the state.[35] The plant geneticist Willet Hays, who was appointed Assistant Secretary of Agriculture in 1905, became a vocal advocate for a more scientific approach to artificial selection, arguing that biologists and practical breeders would benefit mutually from cooperation. Hays was also a key figure in the American Breeders' Association, which was founded for this very purpose.[36] Yet, Hays was realistic about the importance of market forces and recognized the need for proper incentives to encourage biological innovation. Like the inventors of useful machines, Hays said at the 1903 St Louis meeting of the ABA, creative breeders deserved remunerative compensation for work that greatly benefited society:

[32] Quoted in ibid 11.

[33] On Wilson's scientific agenda at the USDA see Jack Ralph Kloppenburg, *First the Seed: The Political Economy of Plant Biotechnology, 1492–2000* (University of Wisconsin Press 2004) 70.

[34] Quoted in *Review and Album International Live Stock Exposition* (n 30) 13.

[35] The USDA had promoted hybridization and varietal crossing since the 1880s to diversify the country's agricultural product base. The rediscovery of Mendel's work in 1900 was met with remarkable enthusiasm by the American agricultural research establishment, largely because Mendel's way of thinking about heredity in terms of discrete units that could be traced from generation to generation coincided with these earlier efforts. See Diane B Paul and Barbara A Kimmelman, 'Mendel in America: Theory and Practice, 1900-1919' in Ronald Rainger, Keith Benson, and Jane Maienschein (eds), *The American Development of Biology* (University of Pennsylvania Press 1988) 281–310.

[36] On Hays' tenure at the USDA see Andrew Boss, 'Willett Martin Hays' (1919) 20 *Journal of Heredity* 507. For a discussion of his role in the ABA see Barbara A Kimmelman, 'The American Breeders' Association: Genetics and Eugenics in an Agricultural Context, 1903–1913' (1983) 13 *Social Studies of Science* 163.

> Inventors who create new values, and creative breeders who add to the transmitting efficiency of plants and animals, are alike in that they too often do not secure for themselves reasonable remuneration. It is to the interest of the manufacturer, the grower of pedigreed seeds or pedigreed animals, and the general public that a liberal share of the new values go to the inventor and to the creative breeder.[37]

Hays' vision for ensuring that breeders received proper remuneration involved subsidizing breeding with public money in lieu of patent rights.[38]

Conclusion

The shift away from form and pedigree towards a performance ideal in agricultural breeding was not complete. The documentation of genealogical information remained an important part of breeding not only because it was a powerful marketing tool but also because it helped establish the ability of a given animal to breed true. A long line of distinguished ancestors did, in fact, help breeders select profitable animals, especially when pedigree certification was combined with performance and progeny tests. Evaluation of animals based on conformation also retained its value as an aid in selection. Performance testing worked extremely well for dairy breeds, but it was more difficult to implement for animals bred primarily for meat. In many cases, the visual and tactile evaluation of animals grounded in craft knowledge and an aesthetic sensibility offered more assistance to the practical breeder than the new performance-based approaches and Mendelian theory. The incomplete nature of the shift away from form and pedigree towards a performance ideal in animal breeding not only offers an insight into agricultural history, but it also offers a potential explanation as to why animal breeding has largely been overlooked by intellectual property law.

[37] Willet M Hays, 'Distributing Valuable New Varieties and Breeds' *Proceedings of the American Breeders' Association*, vol 1 (1905) 58.

[38] See Willet M Hays, 'American Work in Breeding Plants and Animals' in *Proceedings of the American Breeders' Association*, vol 2 (1906) 159. At the time, animals and plants were not viewed as patentable material by the courts because they were 'products of nature'. See Lori Andrews and Jordan Paradise, 'Genetic Sequence Patents: Historical Justification and Current Impacts' in Jean-Paul Gaudillière, Daniel J Kevles, and Hans-Jörg Rheinberger (eds), *Living Properties: Making Knowledge and Controlling Ownership in the History of Biology* (Max Planck Institute for the History of Science Preprint 382 2009) 143–48.

13

Conceptualizing Nature as Information

Rendering South Asian Genetic Resources and Associated Knowledge Searchable and Legible

Allison Fish

Introduction

One of the dominant concerns regarding the application of intellectual property claims to natural resources in the global south is the issue of biopiracy - or the unauthorized taking, development, transformation, and commercialization of local genetic resources and associated knowledge,[1] typically via patent claims. Within these discussions, India has emerged as a site of global standard-setting—both in terms of identifying biopiracy as a problem, as well as generating possible solutions. This chapter does not recapitulate the well-trod discourse concerning the political, economic, and historical power imbalances that give rise to biopiracy, nor the Indian state and civil society efforts to ensure the problem receives global attention. Instead, the following discussion explores the Indian central government's decades-long, iterative use of information technologies to monitor, track, and manage the use of South Asian biocultural resources in response to these issues.

In exploring this topic, the chapter describes the evolution of three interlinked projects championed by the Indian central government and designed to distinguish *legitimate* bioprospecting from *illegitimate* biopiracy. These projects include:

(1) the Traditional Knowledge Digital Library, an Indian central government project inspired by prominent instances of biopiracy from the 1990s and designed to reflect the International Patent Classification, a hierarchical ordering system designed and managed by the World Intellectual Property Organization, a United Nations body;
(2) the recent attempt of the Indian National Biodiversity Authority (NBA) to monitor compliance with the Nagoya Protocol via a purpose-built machine learning system, dubbed the IT Monitoring Tool, which collates and analyses

[1] The terms 'biocultural resources' or 'biocultural heritage' are used to refer to the intertwined concept of local ethnobotanical knowledge and related genetic resources throughout this chapter.

Allison Fish, *Conceptualizing Nature as Information* In: *Intellectual Property and the Design of Nature*. Edited by: Jose Bellido and Brad Sherman, Oxford University Press. © Allison Fish 2023. DOI: 10.1093/oso/9780192864406.003.0013

existing digital information resources describing biocultural heritage utilization; and

(3) a recent partnership between the Indian NBA, the United Nations Development Programme, and PricewaterhouseCoopers Turkey and India to design a pilot project employing blockchain technology to track and trace the utilization of Nagoya-protected resources, as well as the distribution of resulting financial benefits.

What emerges is a picture of a techno-legal system in-the-making over the *longue durée*; a system that has been developed under the auspices of the Indian central government and that is configured to reflect the shifting and varied requirements of intellectual property mechanisms governing genetic resource management; a system that is made interoperable via its reliance on scientific taxonomy and nomenclature as the key organizational device and whose implementation is imagined according to the logics of value creation and possessive accumulation inherent to biocapital.[2] Further, a temporal reading of this system reflects the conceptual transformation of biocultural resources—from a regional South Asian heritage, to a national patrimony under contemporary threat of biopiracy, through to a future economic resource subject to the potential exploitation of the Indian developmental state.

Managing South Asian biocultural heritage and transforming nature into an economic resource of the modern Indian nation-state did not emerge suddenly or as an intentional, fully formed objective from the outset. Rather, it is a systemic approach that has evolved gradually over several decades through the layering of different technologies, tools, and databases—some of which were explicitly designed to *identify* unauthorized acts of biopiracy, some of which were designed to *distinguish* illegitimate activities from legitimate and authorized acts of bioprospecting, and some of which were created for other purposes. In this sense, the Indian state's systemic approach conceptualizes biopiracy as a problem of identification that, with adequate and accurate information, can be rendered visible via techno-scientific surveillance and, ideally, resolved through recourse to the law. As such, the Indian approach to the problems created by biopiracy has historically relied upon a methodology that uses technology to fill the gaps in patent [and adjacent forms of] law that allow biopiracy to occur.

[2] Biocapital is a term coined by Kaushik Sunder Rajan, *Biocapital: The Constitution of Postgenomic Life* (Duke University Press 2006), which argues that advances in genomic sciences and the associated fields of biotechnology can only be understood in relation to the economic markets from which they emerge. Jean-Paul Gaudillière applies an alternative reading of biocapital to describe how the Indian state's approach to managing the 'traditional knowledge of life-derived entities is mobilized to build markets through a close and nonetheless highly problematic conjunction of data collection, material production, and property rights'. See Jean-Paul Gaudillière, 'An Indian Path to Biocapital? The Traditional Knowledge Digital Library, Drug Patents, and the Reformulation Regime of Contemporary Ayurveda' (2014) 8(4) *East Asian Science, Technology and Society: An International Journal* 391.

In relaying the history surrounding the Indian state's techno-legal approach to preventing biopiracy, this chapter aims to contribute to a larger discussion regarding how legal forms, technological infrastructures, and scientific taxonomy and nomenclature increasingly function to regulate biocultural heritage access and use via a transactional economic imaginary. It also looks to the particular way that nature has been configured and described in these accounts, how this has changed over time, and what this means for the way intellectual property law conceptualizes nature and engages with its elements.

The Traditional Knowledge Digital Library: An Early Use of Technology to Combat Biopiracy and Organize Bio-cultural Heritage

In the late 1980s and early 1990s stories about patent claims pertaining to local ethnobotanical knowledge from Indigenous communities and/or the global south began to proliferate. Among these stories, patent claims relating to the therapeutic uses of the neem plant and the turmeric root, as well as the fragrant taste and smell of basmati rice gained significant global attention provoking indignation from influential figures such as Vandana Shiva and members of the Indian Parliament. This sentiment eventually materialized into challenges against several of these patent claims, most of which were lodged on behalf of the Indian state and pursued in the United States and Europe in the 1990s and early 2000s. While a number of these challenges were successful, such as the challenge spearheaded by the Indian Council of Scientific and Industrial Research in relation to US Patent No. 5,401,504 for the wound healing uses of turmeric, some challenges were not. Moreover, the cost of each patent challenge was substantial, rising to upwards of US$1 million or more. In addition, studies undertaken on behalf of the Indian government around this time estimated that thousands of patent claims involving the biopiracy of South Asian ethnobotanical knowledge were filed each year in jurisdictions around the world. As a result, leading Indian government officials became convinced that, given the scale of the problem and the enormous potential costs, a successful campaign against biopiracy required pivoting away from individual patent challenges. Instead, a proactive and preventative strategy to the problem was desirable.

It is against this backdrop that officials from various Indian government agencies, including the Council for Scientific and Industrial Research and the Department of Indian Systems of Medicine and Homeopathy,[3] developed the Traditional Knowledge Digital Library (TKDL) project. The TKDL project is

[3] This has since been renamed the Ministry of Ayurveda, Yoga, Unani, Siddha, and Homeopathy.

a state-sponsored online digital archive that documents several major systems of South Asian classical medicine, most of which emphasize a holistic approach involving treatments relying on plant and mineral based therapeutic compounds. Launched in 2001,[4] the primary objective of the TKDL is to prevent future instances of biopiracy related to South Asian classical medical knowledge by making related prior art available to patent claims examiners at intellectual property agencies in various jurisdictions around the world.

To accomplish this objective, the TKDL has been designed in response to lessons learned through the experience of the turmeric patent challenge at the US Patent and Trademark Office and the neem patent challenge at the European Patent Office.[5] A key takeaway for Indian officials involved in these challenges was that South Asian ethnobotanical knowledge was already well-documented and known throughout the region. However, most texts documenting this prior art were only available in hard copy form in India and the vast majority were recorded in South Asian languages. Practically speaking, patent examiners working in intellectual property agencies in North America, Europe, and East Asia could not physically access the prior art and, in the rare case that they could, did not have the linguistic or cultural fluency required to understand them. Thus, for Indian officials tasked with resolving the issue, the key problem was that patent examiners required *legible* and *accessible* translations of the relevant ethnobotanical knowledge made available to them in their respective jurisdictions.

Designed to remedy this twinned problem of legibility and access, the TKDL design involves two steps. The first step involves a three-part translation process in which South Asian nature is rendered linguistically, scientifically, and legally *legible*. To accomplish the translation, the TKDL contents are curated through a multi-step process involving:

- digitization of existing records documenting prior art of South Asian classical medical knowledge, such as medical texts, the vast majority of which document the use of plant-based compounds in therapeutic treatments;
- translation of these texts from South Asian languages, such as Sanskrit and Urdu, into the languages most commonly used by patent examiners internationally such as English, French, German, and Japanese; and
- reformulation of plant-based compounds and therapeutic diagnostics described in South Asian classical medical ontologies into formulas and processes legible to the plant and biomedical sciences and thus to the patent system.

[4] The TKDL project was formally conceived and proposed in 1999 before its 2001 launch.

[5] See Allison Fish, 'The Place of "Culture" in the Access to Knowledge Movement: Comparing Creative Commons and Yogic Theories of Knowledge Transfer' (2014) 30(5) *Anthropology Today* 7; and Gaudillière (n 2).

This tripartite translation is then made digitally *accessible* to patent examiners in intellectual property agencies around the world who have entered into contractual agreements with the Indian government to access the TKDL for the purpose of patent review.

The result of this process is an online digital archive whose contents are theoretically searchable along numerous parameters—from means of diagnosis either via South Asian or allopathic terminologies, the original textual location and author of the knowledge, formula for preparation of therapeutic compound, method of treatment delivery, as well as the local and botanical names of materials used in the treatment. In practice, however, patent examiners, the intended users of the TKDL, tend to query the database using basic Boolean search methods involving Linnaean botanical taxonomies or common plant names.[6] This is for two reasons. First, and perhaps most importantly with respect to the original purpose of the TKDL, botanical taxonomy is what allows the TKDL to speak across other informational resources that examiners use in their search for prior art when plant-based materials are implicated in a patent application.

Secondly, and this is perhaps most significant for a future imaginary of the TKDL, the key design feature enabling search is the Traditional Knowledge Resource Classificatory system. The classificatory system is structured along the same hierarchical logics as the International Patent Classification system. When the TKDL was in its early design stages, its leading architect, V.K. Gupta, noted that at that time the International Patent Classificatory system only contained a single category describing plant-based therapeutics (A61K 35/68[7]). Given the diversity of knowledge and resources that could be described within such a singular category, Gupta conceived the Traditional Knowledge Resource Classificatory system as a means to explode this single category into multiple classificatory devices, each one tailored to a specific South Asian classical medical system documented within the TKDL and devolving from the International Patent Classification system.

Thus, there is a separate classificatory device for each of the traditions documented within the TKDL archive—one for Ayurveda, one for Unani, one for Siddha, one for Sowa Rigpa, and one for Yoga. Ostensibly, these classificatory systems are organized according to the unique logics of the therapeutic system described. However, because the TKDL is intended to function interoperably across the individual therapeutic systems documented, as well as articulate with the International Patent Classification—the archive's emphasis remains on describing therapeutic compounds and their biomedical efficacy. Theoretically, this breakdown would allow TKDL users potentially to reformulate and innovate upon the therapeutic knowledge that is documented within the TKDL. This potential has

[6] ibid.

[7] The International Patent Classification has been reorganized and this category has changed since the inception of the TKDL.

created a future imaginary for the TKDL as a site from which new innovations based on Indian traditional knowledge might emerge. What is interesting is that this imaginary has haunted the project since its inception, but, to date, has not been realized.

While the TKDL has only ever been explicitly allowed to be used in the course of patent examinations, the idea that the database would serve as a resource for both academic and industrial research and development with partners from both the public and private sectors has always been an implicit aspect of the project's development. Since 2005, the original lead of the TKDL, VK Gupta has envisioned that such third-party access would be based upon 'joint ownership and licensing of the intellectual property rights of the products to be created based upon the contents of the TKDL.' For Jean-Paul Gaudilliere, Gupta's vision signals that the TKDL 'remains above all a tool in intellectual property rights management'[8] of Indian innovation and biocapital. In this sense, and according to this logic, the TKDL marks an early, if not the earliest, turning point in the use of digital technologies to harness biocultural heritage as an economic resource falling within the state's remit to develop.[9]

A contemporary approach for combating biopiracy

The TKDL was initially envisioned as a proactive and preventative solution to biopiracy at a time when the only alternative was to challenge individual patent fillings suspected of unauthorized takings of widely established practices. In essence, the TKDL signals an important strategic move and the Indian central government devotes significant financial resources and skilled personnel towards achieving this objective.[10] However, the TKDL has been subject to critique owing to the publicly funded archive's gated access restrictions, as well as the fact that it does not automatically prevent biopiracy-based claims nor does it yield the promised efficacy or results.[11] Critics, for example, note that patent examiners are not regularly

[8] See n 2 above.

[9] In August 2022, as this chapter was going to press, the Union Cabinet in India formally announced a plan to open access of the TKDL to other users. At the time of publication there is little formal evidence as to what this increased accessibility means in practice.

[10] According to a request for information filed by T Prashant Reddy, in May 2012 the TKDL employed eighteen personnel and, up to that point, had cost the Indian central government just under 16 crore INR, approximately US$3,053,000 given exchange rates at that time. Reddy is an intellectual property law academic and practitioner located in India, as well as a regular contributor to the *SpicyIP: De-Coding Indian Intellectual Property Law* blog series. Prashant Reddy, 'The budget for TKDL and also its focus on Indian patent applications' (2012) https://spicyip.com/2012/05/budget-of-tkdl-and-also-its-focus-on.html (accessed 12 December 2022).

[11] In the last decade, the *Spicy IP* blog has published a number of contributions critically analysing the development, implementation, and efficacy of the TKDL. Key contributors include T Prashant Reddy, Balaji Subramanian, and Madhulika Vishwanathan. These critiques are reiterated by Sunil Abraham in his report to the Association of Progressive Communication on 'Economic, social and cultural rights in India: Opportunities and advocacy in intellectual property rights: The Traditional Knowledge Digital

accessing the TKDL during examinations, nor are they significantly or regularly relying on TKDL contents as key pieces of evidence in rejecting offending claims. Instead, critics point out that Indian officials need to monitor patent filings regularly and then provide the relevant patent office with documentation of prior art contained within the TKDL.

Whether or not these criticisms are merited, it has become clear that the digital archive is incapable of fully preventing the biopiracy activities that are of concern to Indian state officials and activists. Moreover, since the TKDL's first release, new regulatory instruments have appeared at both the domestic and international level for managing bioprospecting and preventing biopiracy. Chief among these is the Nagoya Protocol on Access to Genetic Resources and the Fair and Equitable Sharing of Benefits Arising from their Utilization, an international legal instrument falling under the Convention on Biological Diversity.

The Nagoya Protocol is an international agreement ratified by 140 countries that aims to establish a standardized framework allowing potential users to access and use biocultural resources in a manner that providers deem appropriate.[12] It also aims to ensure that any benefits arising from the use of protected are shared fairly and equitably with providers. The protocol does this by requiring member states to adopt measures that ensure users obtain prior informed consent from resource providers[13] and that there are benefit sharing agreements in place.[14]

India became the fifth country to ratify the Nagoya Protocol in 2012. In doing so, the country's obligations were assigned to the NBA, an autonomous statutory body under the Ministry of Environment, Forestry, and Climate Change, that is tasked with implementing and coordinating the national-level response to the Convention on Biological Diversity. Shortly after ratification, a press release from the NBA noted that as a megadiverse country, India:

> [h]ad been a victim of misappropriation, or biopiracy, of our genetic resources and associated traditional knowledge, which have been patented in other countries (well-known examples include neem and haldi [turmeric or *Curcuma longa*]) … and it is expected that the ABS Protocol is a key missing pillar of the CBD [that] would address this concern.[15]

Library' (2016) https://www.apc.org/sites/default/files/ESCRsIndiaCaseStudiesTKDL_final.pdf (accessed 22 December 2022). See also T Prashant Reddy and Sumathi Chandrashekaran, *Create, Copy, Disrupt: India's Intellectual Property Dilemmas* (Oxford University Press 2017), particularly the ch 9 entitled 'The Traditional Knowledge Trilogy'.

[12] Tom Dedeurwaerdere, Paolo Melindi-Ghidi, and Arianna Broggiato, 'Global Scientific Research Commons Under the Nagoya Protocol: Towards a Collaborative Economy Model for the Sharing of Basic Research Assets' (2016) 55 *Environmental Science and Policy* 1.

[13] Nagoya Protocol, art 6.1.

[14] ibid art 5.1.

[15] Intellectual Property Watch, 'India Ratifies Nagoya Protocol on Biodiversity Access and Benefit-Sharing' (2012) https://www.ip-watch.org/2012/10/05/india-ratifies-nagoya-protocol-on-biodiversity-access-and-benefit-sharing (accessed 24 November 2021).

Interestingly, this sentiment is almost identical to the public proclamations surrounding the allocation of public resources to the TKDL projects.

The Nagoya Protocol contains several interesting and unique features when compared with other international legal instruments. For example, unlike many international legal agreements which only apply in the country where they are enacted, the Nagoya Protocol also regulates behaviour outside of the countries where it has been adopted into national law. This is because ratifying countries are under an obligation to both ensure resources obtained and used in the country are Nagoya complaint, as well as any materials *imported* into the country.[16] To demonstrate compliance, the import of Nagoya protected materials should be accompanied by evidence documenting; appropriate access permits, prior informed consent from authorities and providers, and benefit sharing agreements.[17] To facilitate the international circulation of Nagoya Protocol-protected materials, the Protocol supports another innovative feature—the online ABS Clearing House which digitally issues and archives internationally recognized certificates of compliance (IRCCs).[18] These certificates of compliance allow provider countries to digitally document and publicize who has been authorized to utilize which resources and for what purposes.[19] These digital certificates also function as easily accessible proof that a user has complied with the provider country's implementation of the Nagoya Protocol.

The IRCCs listed on the ABS Clearing House website flag the Indian state's leadership in establishing global best practice in the implementation of the Nagoya Protocol. Significantly, in early 2022, twenty-three member states had lodged approximately 3,413 IRCCs . Of this number, 2,413 IRCCs (more than 70 per cent of total number of certificates filed) had been filed by India.[20] Recent work on the explanatory power of quantitative indicators in global governance is helpful in understanding the significance of India's utilization of the IRCCs feature.[21] Most scholarship on this topic tends to focus on how quantitative indicators of legal governance are produced, disseminated, and used in a manner that reduces complex social phenomena and relationships into simple, quantifiable and ranked terms. The overriding presumption is that these simple-to-read indicators of global

[16] Nagoya Protocol, arts 5.1, 6.1.

[17] ibid art 17.1.

[18] ibid art 14.

[19] There is an additional indicator that tracks the circulation of the genetic resources across the global value chain known as the 'Check Point Communiqué'. However, this mechanism has not been widely utilized at this time.

[20] Secretariat to the Convention on Biological Diversity, 'Access and Benefit-sharing Clearing-house' https://www.cbd.int/abs/en/ABSCHGuide.pdf (accessed 25 February 2022). France, the state with the next highest numbers of certificates, had filed 353.

[21] Kevin Davis, Benedict Kingsbury, and Sally Engle Merry, 'Indicators as a Technology of Global Governance' (2012) 46 *Law and Society Review* 71. Sally Engle Merry, *Seductions of Quantification: Measuring Human Rights, Gender Violence and Sex Trafficking* (University of Chicago Press 2016).

governance are shaped by experts in the global north and are mobilized to measure the rule of law (or lack thereof) in the global south.

The Indian state's dominance in the utilization of the IRCC mechanism belies an interesting twist on this presumption about the dynamics of global governance. In doing so, India emerges as a site of global standard-setting and decision-making of how soft international law can be implemented, monitored, and enforced. The following sections describe how the Indian state has achieved this feat in relation to monitoring compliance with Nagoya and also indirectly with patent law, rapidly implementing and synchronizing domestic legal interpretations and technological tools with those operating at the international level. Specifically, the Indian state has done this by creating: (1) a federal administrative structure that has sole authority for authorizing access; (2) an online system that tracks and archives all documentation related to access and use permits (including prior informed consent and access and benefit sharing agreements); and (3) a machine learning tool that monitors for compliant and non-compliant usage of Nagoya Protocol-protected materials in online materials.

Using New and Old Technologies to Implement the Nagoya Protocol in India

The Indian strategy for implementation of the Nagoya Protocol operates across three tiers of government. These include: a single national biodiversity authority, a central government agency headquartered in Chennai;[22] a state biodiversity board or union territory council governing activities in each state or territory;[23] and approximately 270,000 biodiversity management committees that operate at the level of the local community.[24] The National Biodiversity Authority is responsible for coordinating across the three tiers of government in the implementation

[22] The NBA functions include issuing central guidelines on access and benefit sharing requirements and procedures, granting official approvals for access, advising both central and state governments, and contesting intellectual property claims on any Nagoya Protocol-protected resources that are lodged in foreign jurisdictions: Biological Diversity Act 2002 (India) s 18.

[23] State biodiversity boards receive applications that have been duly filed with the NBA and act as mediator with the appropriate local committee in negotiating and monitoring resource ABS; in doing so, the state boards can form expert committees to assist in the review of the matter; and once a state board has been satisfied that an appropriate access and benefit sharing agreement has been struck, then it sends this on to the NBA for further processing: Biological Diversity Act 2002 (India) ss 22–25. See National Biodiversity Authority, *Operational Guidelines to the State Biodiversity Boards for Processing of Applications for Access to Biological Resources Received Under Section 7 of the Biological Diversity Act, 2002* (National Biodiversity Authority 2019).

[24] These registers have been subject to recent criticism for pitting state, non-governmental organizations, universities, and local community interests against one another: see Bahar Dutt, 'The Peoples' Biodiversity Register, Meant to Empower Local Communities, Is Leaving Them Out' *The Hindu* (18 October 2020).

of Nagoya.[25] In addition, the national authority manages the permit system for all foreigners using protected biocultural resources, the transfer of research results to foreign entities, and any intellectual property claims related to resource use and/or development.[26]

In describing the mammoth task facing the NBA, the chairman, Dr Vinod Mathur, said: '[I]t was when we started implementing [the Nagoya Protocol] that we realized that there were major gaps and we started asking how information technology could help us in plugging this gap and that is perhaps the origin of... the role of [information technology] in the kind of monitoring tool that we have tried to develop.'[27] According to Mathur, the first step was to use technology to create a single, centralized permitting system—the ABS E-filing System. This system is an online portal supported by the NBA that digitally connects and coordinates the various government bodies and processes involved in the authorized use of a protected resource.[28] This repository also archives the requisite documentation and is accessible to state authorities and stakeholders. A prospective provider can use the ABS E-filing System to lodge bioprospecting applications that detail information such as the resource to be utilized, the purpose of use (eg commercial, or non-commercial), and area of use (eg pharmaceutical, agricultural, etc.). After lodging an application, the request is referred to the relevant state biodiversity board, the entities charged with mediating prior informed consent and benefit sharing agreements with relevant local biodiversity management committees.[29] The resulting documentation is then attached to the application and the whole package is reviewed by expert panels, the relevant state biodiversity board(s), and the NBA. Once relevant approvals are received, the NBA can authorize the application and a permit will be issued and this automatically triggers the Indian National Authority to file an IRCC in the international ABS Clearing House system.[30] Most countries only provide IRCCs in their own domestic language. In contrast, India, in order to enhance global accessibility and, in a move similar to the TKDL effort to make local knowledge available in the 'five most common patent languages', publishes IRCCs in all official United Nations' languages.[31]

[25] The state biodiversity boards are responsible for permits by domestic entities for domestic research and commercialization purposes and also coordinate with the local committees to establish an access and benefit sharing agreement: Biological Diversity Act 2002 (India) ss 23–25.

[26] Additionally, there are numerous legislative, administrative, and policy measures for which the NBA is responsible and which empower the authority to act.

[27] Vinod Mathur, 'ABS-IT Monitoring Tool: Relevance of Access and Benefit Sharing in India' Presentation at the Webinar on IT Tool for Monitoring Access and Benefit Sharing in India (United Nations Development Programme's Global Access and Benefit Sharing Project 12 February 2020) https://vimeo.com/417263942> (accessed 25 November 2021).

[28] National Biodiversity Authority, 'ABS e-filing' https://absefiling.nic.in/NBA/login/auth (accessed 30 May 2023).

[29] In some instances, resource access will require agreements with multiple local committees: see National Biodiversity Authority Operational Guidelines (n 23) [3].

[30] ibid.

[31] The United Nations has six official languages, including Arabic, Mandarin Chinese, English, French, Russian, and Spanish. According to clearing house guidelines, IRCCs should be published in

The Indian scheme allows for the coordinated review of applications resulting in a single point for authorization, thereby avoiding the problem of applicants obtaining permits at some levels of government, but not others. It also provides a mechanism by which approved bioprospecting activities are domestically and internationally legible and accessible through a multilingual publication process. To do this, the Indian state had to create an entirely new techno-legal regulatory structure to track the movement of bioprospecting decisions across the three-tiers of this administrative hierarchy via a centralized ABS E-Filing System.[32] Significantly, in creating this centralized system, the NBA operates both conceptually and literally as the ultimate arbiter of decisions governing the use of biocultural heritage resources in India. This reinforces the notion that, while the management of such resources should proceed according to cultural norms,[33] which in India are often at the sub-national or regional level, they are ultimately under the jurisdiction of the Indian central government and the province of national patrimony. This notion of an Indian biocultural patrimony is further reinforced outside the state and globally broadcast via the registration of certificates of compliance at the ABS Clearing House.

Identifying Non-compliance by Tracking Unauthorized Uses via Machine Learning: The Role of Botanical Taxonomy in Allowing the TKDL to Articulate with the IT Monitoring Tool

Having established a unified pathway for authorizing and documenting permissible utilization of Nagoya Protocol-protected resources, state officials turned their attention to the task of determining how to police unauthorized utilization. Dr Aeshita Mukherjee, a scientist working at Deutsche Gesellschaft für Internationale Zusammenarbeit (GIZ) India, undertook research that was significant to outlining this issue and creating a solution. After studying the Indian access and benefit sharing scheme for four years and comparing findings across patent applications filed in various jurisdictions, Mukherjee concluded that only a 'miniscule' amount

one or more of these to ensure legibility. The Indian approach, which is unusual, is to publish IRCCs in all six languages.

[32] Although conceptually straightforward, there have been reports that there have been barriers affecting the roll-out of the ABS e-filing system. See Shalini Bhutani and Kanchi Kohli, 'Despite Landmark Judgment, Issues of Regulation Remain in India's Biodiversity Regime' *The Wire* (5 March 2019) https://thewire.in/law/divya-pharmacy-india-biodiversity-act (25 November 2021); Lakshmi Supriya, 'How Laws to Protect Biodiversity Backfired on Scientists Trying to Save It' *The Wire* (26 July 2018) https://thewire.in/the-sciences/how-laws-to-protect-biodiversity-backfired-on-scientists-trying-to-save-it (accessed 25 November 2021).

[33] Significantly, in a post-colonial country as diverse as India, locating biocultural heritage within national identity as opposed to local or regional (South Asian) identity is a politicized move.

of benefit sharing was taking place in comparison to the vast amount of Indian-origin resources that were being used and exploited. According to Mukherjee, there were numerous reasons for this, but two factors were paramount. First, most users were outside of India and, therefore, outside the NBA's remit.[34] Secondly, there was no easy way to monitor, identify, and police the misuse of Indian biocultural heritage. Mukherjee, an academic scientist by training, was particularly frustrated that there were many instances of misuses hiding in plain sight. For Mukherjee, publicly accessible scientific journals and patent filings in various jurisdictions clearly indicated thousands of instances where Indian-origin biocultural resources were being utilized. Further, the vast majority of utilizations were clearly unauthorized (eg low numbers of access permits granted by NBA). However, the sheer scale of materials available (eg number of journal articles and patent filings) meant that searching, identifying, and tracing misuse was impossible using the available methods.[35] As a result, Mukherjee and others working on the issue increasingly accepted that if the access and benefit sharing scheme was to work effectively, the Indian state had to be able to monitor use and misuse of Nagoya Protocol-protected resources. In thinking about how Nagoya Protocol compliance might be monitored, machine learning and data science approaches quickly emerged as potential solutions.

Mukherjee's journey, from her realization of the scale of biopiracy to her understanding that instances of prior art were available but not accessible, through to her inspiration to use new and emerging information technologies to create a solution is almost indistinguishable from the narrative that VK Gupta, the designer of the TKDL, related regarding the creation of this earlier project. There are, of course, significant points of departure. Namely, Mukherjee and Gupta were working at points in time where the laws regulating bioprospecting activities were different, as were the available technologies for information storage, search, and retrieval. For Gupta the question was whether a patent filing included prior art, thereby invalidating the novelty requirement. In contrast, Mukherjee's work took place at a point in time after the Nagoya Protocol and, therefore, the first legal question was whether access and use of biocultural heritage was properly authorized. The next question, for Mukherjee then, was whether authorized usage satisfied the requirements of patent law in that it represented a novel and inventive step. Therefore, the materials documenting misuse of biocultural heritage expanded from a discrete body of texts, patent filings, to a much larger corpus that included academic papers, biological repositories, and other reports. Additionally, the technological capacity that Mukherjee could call on and deploy was fundamentally different than that upon which the TKDL was built.

[34] Aeshita Mukherjee, 'Global Capacity Building Workshop on the Monitoring and Utilization of Genetic Resources Under the Nagoya Protocol' (30 September 2019–2 October 2019, Germany).

[35] As Dr Vijay Kumar of Chennai's Centre for Advanced Computing and Dr Paul Odlham of One World Analytics said, this is simply a problem of scale.

The task of building the computational tool for monitoring Nagoya Protocol compliance was undertaken by a public-private collaboration that included the NBA, the Centre for Advanced Computing in Chennai, GIZ India, and One World Analytics in London. Once completed, the tool was piloted at State Biodiversity Boards in Maharashtra, Tamil Nadu, and Uttarakhand in 2019. The resulting effort, named the IT Monitoring Tool for Access and Benefit Sharing in India,[36] provides a means to identify when Indian-origin Nagoya Protocol-protected resources are being used, assess whether those uses have received the appropriate approvals, and flag any suspicious cases for follow-up. The IT Monitoring Tool brings together a wider infrastructure involving pre-existing technologies and data repositories that are built upon legal and scientific classificatory systems, as well as new software tools (see Fig. 13.1 below for a diagram representing the workflow of the IT Monitoring Tool).[37] Significantly, the wider knowledge infrastructure enabled by the IT Monitoring Tool has the potential to identify both the legitimate (bioprospecting) and illegitimate (biopiracy) use of Nagoya Protocol-protected resources—although its current orientation focuses upon the latter.

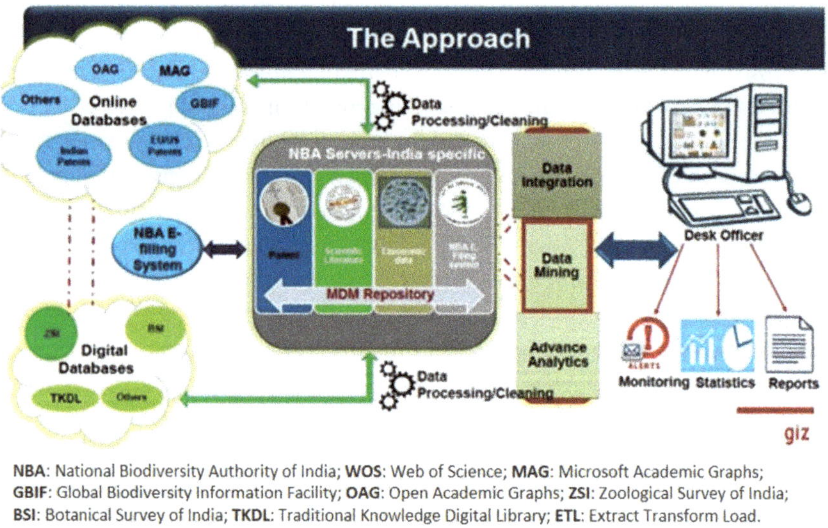

Figure 13.1 Diagram of Information Technology Enabled ABS Monitoring System. IGBP, ABS, GIZ, India. India-German Biodiversity program.
Courtesy of Aeshita Mukherjee-Wilske.

[36] See n 8 above.

[37] In analysing framing knowledge infrastructures, it is important to trace the context from which they emerge, identify which parties contribute to its fabrication, examine how they are sustained and maintained, and note the wider political opportunities and challenges that are associated with their development. See Helena Karasti and others, 'Knowledge Infrastructures: Part 1' (2016) 29 *Science and Technology Studies* 2.

To determine whether a Nagoya Protocol-protected resource of Indian origin has been used appropriately, the IT Monitoring Tool scours online informational repositories—both those that are openly accessible and subscription-based—pertaining to patent applications and filings, as well as scientific research publications (eg journal articles located in the Web of Science) and biodiversity resources (eg Global Biodiversity Information Facility). For each document, the IT Monitoring Tool algorithm asks three subsidiary questions: Is 'use' of a Nagoya Protocol-protected resource indicated?[38] Does that use involve resources of Indian origin? and, has that use been 'approved' by the appropriate Indian authority (is that use ABS compliant)?

Assessment of the first question, which involves a simple 'yes' or 'no' response to whether biodiversity use has occurred, is complicated primarily due to the scale of materials available—more than a billion taxonomic records, and hundreds of millions scientific publications and patent filings. With this done, the IT Monitoring Tool then moves to a more complex assessment of whether biocultural resources of Indian origin are implicated. To do this, the IT Monitoring Tool draws upon pre-existing databases such as the Botanical Survey of India, the Zoological Survey of India, the Traditional Knowledge Digital Library, and other collections that point to India as a possible 'origin' for the materials. Finally, to determine whether a use has been 'approved' (or is Nagoya Protocol compliant), the IT Monitoring Tool compares the findings of the previous two steps against information found within the NBA's ABS e-filing system, which contains a list of authorized bioprospecting activities and authorized users. If there are doubts about whether usage has been authorized, the publication or patent filing is flagged for desk-review by an officer at the NBA for attention. In this respect, the IT Monitoring Tool is not intended to operate as a fully autonomous decision-making system as it is anticipated that there is always a human-in-the-loop to render final judgment.

The operation of the IT Monitoring Tool is underpinned by a shared set of interlinked assumptions surrounding the usage of Nagoya Protocol-protected resources. First, there is an assumption that biological resources can be identified according to a common and consistent language—biological taxonomies and scientific classificatory systems that have developed as a feature of scientific communication over time. Secondly, this shared language of taxonomy and classification can be deployed to link biocultural resource usage across informational repositories such as scientific literature, patent filing systems in jurisdictions around the world, online and digital databases surveying animal and plant life, and the Indian ABS e-filing system. And, finally, the integrated techno-legal infrastructure

[38] On a related matter see Paul Rabinow, *French DNA: Trouble in Purgatory* (University of Chicago Press 1999).

drawn together in the IT Monitoring Tool presumes that the origin of biocultural resources is discoverable and can be traced to, or mapped neatly upon, a specific political-geographic jurisdiction—India.

The Role of the TKDL in India's Implementation of Nagoya

The TKDL provides an interesting basis of comparison to understand the IT Monitoring Tool for five reasons. First, both tools, while aimed at resolving similar problems, are the product of experimental collaborations across different Indian central government ministries focusing on information technology and biocultural resource management. In doing so, they offer a unified and influential account that positions local and regional biocultural heritage as Indian national patrimony. In this sense, both projects employ nature and culture as key resources that contribute to the larger nation-making project in which the Indian nation-state is engaged. Secondly, both projects utilize a parallel approach to resolving a similar problem. Specifically, the TKDL and the IT Monitoring Tool are both bespoke technological systems that have been built to address the legal gaps that result in the inadequate regulation of bioprospecting and, as a result, allow biopiracy to occur. To do this, the TKDL and the IT Monitoring Tool both attempt to make the sources and uses of Indian biocultural patrimony accessible (ie digitally available online and, thus, searchable and discoverable) and legible (ie scientifically and linguistically translated into the language of international intellectual property law). Thirdly, both projects use technology, in as simplistic a manner as possible, to resolve a similar legal challenge. In order to achieve this resolution, both projects coordinate existing tools and layer these with novel computational approaches to arrive at a possible, even if imperfect, solution. Fourthly, and perhaps most tangibly, the IT Monitoring Tool literally draws upon the TKDL as a source of data.

Finally, when taken together as part and parcel of an emergent phenomena, it is clear that both projects have changed in various ways over time. For example, the TKDL has expanded at different points in time to include new medical systems deemed to be under threat of piracy, such as yoga in 2008 and Sowa Rigpa around 2018.[39] Additionally, there has been a continued, if never quite realized, discussion to use the TKDL as a platform for commercial and non-commercial scientific research and development. This discussion has most recently culminated in a decision by the Union Cabinet in August 2022 to expand user access to the

[39] See Traditional Knowledge Digital Library, 'Major Milestones' http://tkdl.res.in/tkdl/LangGerman/Common/milestones.asp?GL=Eng> (25 November 2021). The initiation of digitzation activities related to yoga began in January 2008. There is no specific date listed for initiation of activities in relation to Sowa Rigpa, however, the CSIR-TKDL Unit did recruit various positions to work on the Sowa Rigpa portion of the TKDL in early 2018.

database, however, details are sparse as to what this means. Similarly, discussions are already in play regarding potential future uses of the IT Monitoring Tool and, like the TKDL, these uses may imagine Indian biocultural patrimony as some sort of economic resource with commercial potential the state can not only survey, but also harness.

Interestingly, the TKDL not only serves as a conceptual template for the IT Monitoring Tool but is also integrated into its operation as a key pre-existing database documenting South Asian traditional knowledge. Thus, the TKDL figures as a central resource in the operation of the IT Monitoring Tool's evaluation of South Asian biocultural heritage. This utilization is a reminder that emerging techno-legal solutions are not always, or even regularly, built-for-purpose from the ground up. Rather, they often involve an aggregation and coordination of existing resources. As such, emerging solutions such as the IT Monitoring Tool may be constrained by the logics and structures of the pre-existing technologies that make up their component parts. Given this, as well as the publicity and significant critique the TKDL has attracted—whether merited or not—India's earlier experience with the use of technology to fill the gaps in the law may be instructive for understanding the future imaginaries that will guide the IT Monitoring Tool.

Given this larger context, the TKDL and the IT Monitoring Tool present less as isolated, individual projects and more as different facets of a techno-legal informational infrastructure that has been developing within and across the Indian central government over the last twenty years. While the purpose of this infrastructure has shifted over time it has, to date, remained primarily oriented around distinguishing between the *legitimate* use of Indian biocultural patrimony (bioprospecting) and the *illegitimate* appropriation of these resources (biopiracy). Despite this consistency, the creators of the IT Monitoring Tool have suggested that when fully scaled up and comprehensively trained it will able to be used for more than simply monitoring bioprospecting activities and flagging suspected instances of biopiracy for review.[40] In addition, the IT Monitoring Tool may have the capacity to generate reports about where, when, and how Indian and/or South Asian resources are used around the world, who is involved in this research, and how the benefits that flow from this work are distributed. There is also a possibility that this may eventually lead to more precise information about the use of biocultural resources between countries, particularly between developed and developing countries, and how foreign researchers are collaborating with or involving their Indian counterparts. If done well, this could be an important tool for understanding how biodiversity research is taking shape, how the benefits that flow from this work are being distributed, as well as generating scientific insights more broadly. However, if

[40] Paul Oldham, 'Global Capacity Building Workshop on the Monitoring and Utilization of Genetic Resources Under the Nagoya Protocol' (30 September 2019–2 October 2019, Germany).

done poorly, such statistics can be vectors of misinformation that, once produced, are opaque, unregulated, and difficult to contest.[41]

Finally, the IT Monitoring Tool, like the TKDL, has begun to move beyond South Asia to other countries throughout the world where it is increasingly being discussed as an exemplar of global best practice regarding the implementation of the Nagoya Protocol.[42] A reason for this is that the IT Monitoring Tool offers both a means to monitor compliance within a jurisdiction, as well as the potential to monitor compliance globally. Additionally, a growing number of non-state actors—universities, journals, and funding bodies have made or are considering making Nagoya Protocol-compliance a precondition for working with them. The upshot of this is that non-compliance with the Nagoya Protocol carries global consequences. In the context of the IT Monitoring Tool, this means that if India were to identify a non-compliant use of a Nagoya Protocol-protected resource and issue a public notice of non-compliance, then there would be a much greater possibility that this would carry consequences even if the misuse occurred outside of India. Flagging non-compliant uses should, in theory at least, mean that products based on resources accessed without approval would not be eligible for import into any of the 140 countries that have ratified the Nagoya Protocol.[43] This would also, again in theory, apply to any non-state actors who have elected to comply with the conditions of the Nagoya Protocol. Further, this might give investors reason to pause and consider whether they should invest in products derived from the use of resources accessed without appropriate approval.

A Possible Future: Application of Blockchain Technologies to Trace Biocultural Resource Circulation and Value Creation

Interestingly, while the IT Monitoring Tool is the subject of significant future imaginaries, there is already the potential that it will be replaced before it has been fully deployed. Significantly, in early 2021 the Indian NBA, United Nations Development Program partnered with PricewaterhouseCoopers (Turkey and India) to discuss the use of blockchain technologies and smart-contracting to

[41] See Cathy O'Neil, *Weapons of Math Destruction* (Crown Books 2016) for a discussion of the difficulties and dangers inherent in algorithmic decision-making. While O'Neil references socio-political examples and the IT Monitoring Tool purportedly draws its data from research in the natural sciences, a similar argument might apply here in understanding how the reporting function of the tool might operate.

[42] This is also something that happened with respect to the TKDL. The format for the TKDL has been adopted by countries and Indigenous communities throughout the world to varying degrees. For example, IP Australia both uses the TKDL in their review of patent applications and is considering building something similar for Australian indigenous communities. Additionally, Australian indigenous communities are considering their own databasing projects to protect language and ethnobotanical knowledge.

[43] See Nagoya Protocol, art 15.1.

tag, trace, and make transparent ABS relationships involving Nagoya Protocol-protected resources. It is anticipated that this project, while still in the design stages, will be piloted in India in the near future once funding has been secured and proper government authorizations obtained.

In a panel discussion on the blockchain pilot, Dr. Vinod Mathur, chairman of the NBA, expressed deep enthusiasm stating, 'I am a great believer in technology ... in what can be achieved, what needs to be done, and where we are'. Mathur unequivocally stated that: '[w]e [the NBA] want this pilot to happen. We want to partner with this pilot ... I feel that the government should take it as an investment. Invest in process, invest in an infrastructure.' In describing the attraction of the blockchain approach to ABS tracking, Mathur noted that it was the simplicity that appealed to him. According to Mathur:

> [y]ou can't live without understanding a financial transaction ... so we are trying to build up the principles of a financial transaction and we are trying to take it to the way that ecology operates. And in your way you have made it simpler ... From a theoretical construct [this blockchain technology] ... will work ... What is challenging is to create an inventory, to create a system and take this technology to a grass roots level ... So we have a lot of work to do, but the good part is we know what that work is x.

Further in the discussion, Mathur also affirmed the notion that the blockchain program drew conceptual parallels between financial and ecological transactions and that such an approach was in line with the country's *Digital India* campaign. According to Mathur, 'I can share with you that the Government of India is committed to a Digital India. So this activity and this pilot of ours fits in the minds of the top leadership'. Mathur then went on to note that while such campaigns digitally track and make transactions transparent they were incredibly expensive, there was evidence from other sectors that they would quickly pay for themselves. Citing the example of income tax, Mathur noted that:

> it is a computerised process now. Hundreds of millions of rupees have been spent on that. But now it is getting its return. We can now understand who is giving funds, where that is coming from, who is paying and who is not ... so the same thing ... we need to pick up, we need to partner [to do this for access and benefit sharing].

Mathur's enthusiasm for a project using blockchain and smart contracting technologies to track biocultural resource utilization is based upon an anticipation of potential future economic benefits. Significantly, a similar vision animates the historic design and contemporary policy surrounding both the TKDL and the IT Monitoring Tool. In this sense, all three techno-legal projects imagine that biocultural resources are part of Indian national patrimony, that these resources are being misused owing to a gap in patent law that allows biopiracy to go unchecked, that this legal gap can be resolved via processes of digital translation and tracking, and that such processes also have the potential to yield a financial return to the Indian state and its people. This future imaginary endures despite the fact that none of the techno-legal projects described above have realized their stated goals of proactively preventing biocultural piracy or of generating a down-stream economic benefit. Furthermore, the implication of this imaginary tends to position biocultural heritage as an economic resource and the potential subject of a financial transaction. While still operating as an imaginary, the consequences of framing biocultural resources as a latent commodity is likely to be something that will continue to haunt access and benefit sharing in the future.

Conclusion

The interaction between intellectual property law and natural resources has long been negatively marked by the spectre of economic exploitation and biopiracy. This is only exacerbated when such engagements are physically located in the global south. Moreover, the dominant narrative in this space presumes such exploitation comes via actors, such as multi-national corporations, that hail from the global north and who deploy scientific practice and labours in an effort to disassociate plant genetic resources from local peoples and traditional knowledges. Further, it is often imagined that these issues can be resolved and related power imbalances can be rectified through appropriately tailored legal interventions at the international and local levels; enter the Nagoya Protocol.

The Indian state's approach to the techno-legal regulation of South Asian natural resources that fall within—and at times exceed—its national borders offers another account of the relationship between intellectual property, nature, and society. This account offers a vision through which technological innovations offer regulatory solutions to legal problems that legal institutions, on their own, cannot resolve owing to doctrinal and administrative failures. In creating this solution, the Indian central government has developed an approach that relies upon online information technologies to plug perceived gaps in the global operation and enforcement of intellectual property law. This approach is structured around certain presumption of how to make knowledge about nature, the human ability to innovate upon nature, and the societal right to intervene in nature *legible* and *accessible*.

A key component of making this knowledge *legible* and *accessible* is in rendering it as information that can be systematically captured, ordered, and described in a manner that can be translated uniformly across time and space. The key classificatory device that accomplishes this move, and which is embedded in all three projects described above, is biological taxonomy and nomenclature. In addition, there are also a number of other presumptions at play that animate these projects and their applications. First, there is the presumption that both nature and human knowledge about nature is a resource that can be translated and made interoperable across different linguistic, scientific, and political-legal environments. Towards these ends, the projects described above utilize hierarchical information classificatory systems that articulate seamlessly with one another—such as biological taxonomies and the International Patent Classification system.

Secondly, these systems are increasingly imagined as platforms for innovation and commercialization that might benefit the Indian nation as a whole. Towards these ends, the India techno-legal system that has emerged over time in an effort to rein in the excesses of intellectual property and fill the gaps in patent law, appears to also replicate some problematics associated with bio-piracy. These logics include positioning nature as an informational resource and property of the state that can be developed through scientific interventions and labour. In the case of India, a developmental state whose primary purpose is to ensure the economic uplift of its people, this presumes that public resources, such as nature and the associated knowledge, can be leveraged for improved economic security. This position is further re-ified through informational representations of nature and translations of its values via the three projects described above—all of which are attached to imaginaries of future economic returns. Finally, critics might well wonder whether the Indian central government, given the heterogenous and conflicted nature of the state, is best suited to, or even capable of, representing the interests of local communities in this scenario.

These tensions are exacerbated when considering the literature on information infrastructures which notes that the logics and structures of technological systems, once set, are difficult to undo. Instead, information infrastructures, such as the techno-legal system described above tend to accrete and solidify over time, particularly those systems that articulate seamlessly with other classificatory devices, such as Linnaen taxonomy, that are so deeply embedded as to appear as naturalized orderings of our worlds. Thus, the Indian techno-legal systems described above are most powerful not because they achieve their stated aim of identifying and resolving acts of biopiracy. Instead, these systems are powerful because they articulate with other naturalized orderings of our scientific, linguistic, and political–legal worlds.

Index

For the benefit of digital users, indexed terms that span two pages (e.g., 52–53) may, on occasion, appear on only one of those pages.